THE IRON TRIANGLE

Business, Government, and Colonial Settlers' Dispossession of Indian Timberlands and Timber

THE IRON TRIANGLE

*Business, Government, and Colonial Settlers' Dispossession
of Indian Timberlands and Timber*

Roberta Carol Harvey

SUNSTONE
PRESS
SANTA FE

Sunstone Press does not have any control over, or responsibility for, any third-party websites referred to or in this book. All internet addresses given in this book were correct at the time of publication. The author and publisher regret any inconvenience caused if addresses have changed or sites have ceased to exist, but can accept no responsibility for any such changes.

© 2022 by Roberta Carol Harvey
All Rights Reserved
No part of this book may be reproduced in any form or by any electronic or mechanical means including information storage and retrieval systems without permission in writing from the publisher, except by a reviewer who may quote brief passages in a review.

Sunstone books may be purchased for educational, business, or sales promotional use. For information please write: Special Markets Department, Sunstone Press, P.O. Box 2321, Santa Fe, New Mexico 87504-2321.
Printed on acid-free paper
∞
eBook 978-1-61139-691-1

Library of Congress Cataloging-in-Publication Data

Names: Harvey, Roberta Carol, 1950- author.
Title: The Iron Triangle : business, government, and colonial settlers' dispossession of Indian timberlands and timber / Roberta Carol Harvey.
Description: Santa Fe : Sunstone Press, [2022] | Includes bibliographical references. | Summary: "A book on how American Indians were cheated out of the inherent wealth of their land and timber, at times exterminated for it, by greedy settlers, bribed federal agents, land sharks, lumber barons and a derelict federal trustee who failed to protect its guardians' rights"-- Provided by publisher.
Identifiers: LCCN 2022050984 | ISBN 9781632934420 (paperback) | ISBN 9781611396911 (epub)
Subjects: LCSH: Indians of North America--Land tenure--Law and legislation--History--19th century. | Indians of North America--Legal status, laws, etc. | Indians of North America--Government relations. | Settler colonialism--United States--History--19th century. | Indian Removal, 1813-1903. | United States--Race relations--History--19th century.
Classification: LCC E98.L3 H37 2023 | DDC 333.208997--dc23/eng/2022125
LC record available at https://lccn.loc.gov/2022050984

WWW.SUNSTONEPRESS.COM
SUNSTONE PRESS / POST OFFICE BOX 2321 / SANTA FE, NM 87504-2321 /USA
(505) 988-4418

DEDICATION

This book is to honor the courageous Indians who endured the policies of extermination, starvation, disease, eradication of everything Indian and the annihilation of Indian nations.

Acknowledgments

Family

Nobody has been more helpful to me in the pursuit of this project than the members of my family. They encouraged me and made sure that whatever resources I needed for this project were available. Thank you to my most beloved husband (who made breakfast, lunch and dinner and took over all daily family responsibilities so I could focus on this project) whose love provides such joy and stability in my life.

Educators

For Mr. Scott, Tillie Walker, Santa Fe Preparatory School, Vice Chancellor John Rice, Professors Grant, Holland, Dorn, Carver, Romero and Assistant Dean Jesse Manzanares at the University of Denver. Every time I pass DU, I pray that I am able to use the education and professional employment they made possible to the best of my ability for the good of Indigenous peoples and Indian Nations.

For the Truth Tellers

My dear friends at DIHFS and Bill and Wanda and Tash and Elena and Cherry Steinwender, Executive Director, Center for the Healing of Racism, and Tom and Valarie and Jenny inspire me with their dedication and they live every day honoring Representative Evans' Mission below:

Representative Evans' motivation in The Debates and Proceedings in the Congress of the United States on the Indian Removal Act:

> If I could stand up between the weak, the friendless, the deserted, and the strong arm of oppression, and successfully vindicate their rights, and shield them in their hour of adversity, I should have achieved honor enough to satisfy even an exorbitant ambition; and I should leave it as a legacy to my children, more valuable than uncounted gold — more honorable than imperial power.

Representative Evans, speaking on S. 102, on May 18, 1830, 21st Cong., 1st sess., Register of Debates in Congress 1049.

CONTENTS

Preface ~ 31
    Series of Books
    Natural Resources
    Wealth Inherent in Natural Resources
    Valuing Natural Resources
    Metals Are Sole Reliance to Liquidate Interest on National Debt
    Natural Resource Exploitation and Depletion
    Indian Nations Not Parties to Disposal of Their Resources
    Corruption
    Human Capital

Chapter 1: Imperial Colonialism ~ 39

    Part 1: Path to U.S. 'Discovery' Claim ~ 39
    Continental Congress, 1773
    American Revolutionary War, 1775
    Declaration of Independence, 1776
    Articles of Confederation, 1777
    Treaty of Peace between the United States and Great Britain
    Constitutional Convention, 1787
    Title to 'Western' Lands (aka 'Back Lands')
    Fletcher v. Peck Is Fraudulent
    Additional Successions to U.S.

Part 2: U.S. Determines Property Law Applicable to Indian Lands, 1823 ~ 44

    Johnson Case Is Fraudulent
    'Doctrine of Discovery' Dogmatically Adopted by Marshall into Federal Law
    Censoring Chief Justice Marshall
    Marshall Disavows 'Discovery Doctrine'
    Jacksonian Supreme Court Ignores *Worcester,* Cites to *Johnson*
    Indians Not Parties to Carving Up Continent
    Twenty First Century Scholars' Analyses of *Johnson*

Chapter 2: Primacy of Opening U.S. to "Settlement and Civilized Habitation" ~ 51

    Part 4: Northwest Ordinances ~ 52

      The Ordinance of 1784
      The Ordinance of 1785
      The Ordinance of 1787

    Part 5: Congressional Legislation ~ 54

      1824, Office of Indian Affairs
      U.S. Land Acts
      Indian Removal Act
      Tenor of Times – They May Begin to Dig Their Graves and Prepare to Die
      Indian Territory Created
      Distribution–Preemption Act of 1841
      Act of June 5, 1850 (9 Stat. 437)
      Donation Land Claim Act of 1850
      Swamp Land Act of 1850
      Indian Appropriations Act
      Homestead Act of 1862
      Pacific Railway Act of 1862
      Indian Appropriations Act of 1871
      General Mining Act of 1872
      Indemnity Act – Lieu Lands
      Timber and Stone Act of 1878
          DOI Warns of Destructive Impact of Timber and Stone Act
          Don't Deprive Citizens of Timber for Cradles!
          Committing Fraud under Timber and Stone Act
          Prosecuting Violations of Timber and Stone Act Impossible
      Major Crimes Act of 1885
      General Allotment Act
      1888 Legislation Prohibiting Trespass upon Indian Reservations to Steal Timber
      Indian Appropriations Act of 1889
      1891 Timber Act, 26 Stat. 1093, Free Use of Timber on Mineral and Nonmineral Public Lands

Chapter 3: Converting Forests into Dollars – Green Gold ~ 71

    Business Start-Up
    Timber Scouts and Surveys
    Timber Appraisals
    Purchases or Leases of Timberlands
    Jerry-Building Transitory Logging Camps
    Toting Roads and Logging Roads
    Lumbering
    Introduction of Steam Engine
    Sawmills – Transforming Logs into Merchantable Lumber
    Water Transportation's Huge Role in Logging Industry
    Waterways Boost Production of Timber
    Railroads
    Clearing Large Areas – Slash and Burn
    Technological Advances
    High Lead Logging
    Highball Logging

Chapter 4: Timber Monopoly ~ 83

    Business Formation
    Corporate Strategies for Land Acquisition
    Company Growth Strategies—Vertical Integration vs. Horizontal Integration
    Upstream and Midstream Timber Businesses
    Acquiring Interests in Transportation Networks
    Downstream Timber Businesses
    Timber Industry Associations
    Increasing Scale of Timber Production
    Lumber Barons
    Scratching Each Other's Backs
    Timber Monopoly
    Tripartite Timber Concentration
    Timber Depletion, Lumber Prices, Lumber Exports, and Concentration of Timber Ownership
    Titans of Industry
    Stock Market Crash and Great Depression

Chapter 5: Theft of Indian Timberlands and Timber ~ 97

"Manifest Destiny" Is Paramount
Transcontinental Railroad Links East and West
Railroads Increase Timber Consumption
Railroads – Catalyst for Industrial Age
Population Growth
"The Great Barbecue"
Gilded Age
U.S. Navajo War from 1860–1868
U.S. Dakota War of 1862 in Minnesota
States Maneuver for Removal of Indians
DOI Schemes to Remove Indians
Industrial Landscape Transforms American Indian People and Lands

Chapter 6: Carving Up Michigan ~ 119

Part 1: Indian Land in Michigan ~ 119

Part 2: Cession and Removal Treaties ~ 119

1807 Cession Treaty, Detroit Area
1815 Peace Treaty with the Wyandots
1817 Cession Treaty, South Central Michigan and Northwestern Ohio
Saginaw Cession Treaty of 1819, Removal of Chippewas
1820 Cession Treaty of Sault Ste. Marie
1821 Chicago Cession Treaty, 4 Million Acres of Land Ceded in Southwest Michigan and Northern Indiana
1828 Potawatomi Nation Cession Treaty, 200,000 Acres, Southwest Michigan and Northeast Indiana
1833 Potawatomi Cession (5 Million Acres) and Removal Treaty
1836 Ottawa Indian Nation in Michigan Forced to Cede 16 Million Acres of Land
1837 Saginaw Band Cede 102,400 Acres
1841 Ottawa Petition to Michigan Legislature for U.S. Citizenship Support
1842 Chippewa Cession of Western Upper Peninsula
1837 and 1842 Chippewa Treaties DOI Summary – Valuable Mineral District and Pine Forests Ceded
1844 Ottawa and Chippewa Petition to President for U.S. Citizenship
1847 Resolution of Michigan to U.S. Congress in Support of Indians' Petition to Remain in Michigan
Chippewa Reservation to Be Allotted

Part 3: Experimental Allotment Policy ~ 134

    1854 and 1855 Chippewa Treaties, Experimental Allotment Policy
    1855 Detroit Treaty Allotment Provisions Applicable to Ottawa
    1855 Detroit Treaty Allotment Provisions Applicable to Chippewa
    Dissolution of Tribal Status

Part 4: Massive Loss of Indian Land due to Fraud ~ 136

    1866, Indians Are Prey to Unscrupulous Whites
    1871, Massive Sale of Indian Allotments by Grand River Ottawa and Chippewa
    1871, Saginaw Sale of Allotments with Timber on Isabella Reservation
    Commissioner Advocates for State Taking Over Responsibility for Indians
    Loss of Land due to Fraud and Otherwise
    "Outrageous Frauds" Committed at Isabella Reservation
    1886, Saginaw Timber Cut and Sold for Fraction of Value
    1887, Isabella Reservation Scheme to Dispossess Indians of Land Consummated
    Department Had Complete Knowledge of Frauds at Isabella Reservation between 1865 and 1884
    1889, Mackinac Indian Agency Abolished Without Regard to Numerous Frauds
    1905, No Fair Market Value in 200 Sales at L'Anse and Ontonagon Reservations
    1906, Theft of Large Amount of Timber Discovered at L'Anse Reservation
    1907, 200 Land Sales at L'Anse and Ontonagon Reservations Rejected due to Fraud

Part 5: Tribal Status Denied ~ 149

Part 6: Settlement of Michigan by Colonial Settlers ~ 149

    Land Act of 1820

Part 7: Logging Underway ~ 150

    New England and Maine Supplied Experienced Work Force
    Logging Underway in 1830's
    Michigan Statehood in 1837
    1850s, Logging in Lower Peninsula
    1860s, Saginaw Valley Maximum Production
    1870s, Timber Pirating on Federal Lands

    Lumber Production by Mill Town in Michigan, 1874
    Lumber Production by Mill Town in Michigan, 1883
    Lumber Production in 1889, m.b.f.
    1900s, Decline in Logging
    Lumber Barons

Part 8: Federal Land Disposal in Michigan 1800–1900 ~ 156

Part 9: Federally Recognized Indian Nations in Michigan ~ 157

Chapter 7: Minnesota: Fraudulent Legislation Enabling
                              Acquisition of Indian Land ~ 163

Part 1: Chippewas Are All the Same ~ 163

Part 2: Twin Cities Belong to Sioux ~ 164

    Pike's Expedition to Headwaters of Mississippi
    Pike's 1805 Meeting at Bdote
    Validity of Purported "Purchase" Questioned
    Purchase Document Defective
    Land Description Flawed
    No Consideration Stated
    Omitted Signatures and Witnesses
    No Presidential Proclamation of Pike's Document
    Major Long's Expedition
    After Fourteen Years, Secretary of War Orders Consideration Paid
    Fort Snelling Construction Completed
    Squatting Settlers Petition President for Protection of Their Rights
    Pike's Congressional Petition for Payment for Services Denied
    Sale of Fort Snelling

Part 3: The Shell Game ~ 173

    Settler Emigration to Minnesota Increasing
    Minnesota Indian Land Title Not Extinguished
    Treaty Establishing Boundaries of Minnesota Tribes
    U.S. Fraudulently Encourages Indian Tribes to Move West
    Timber Mining on "Alleged" Worthless Land of Indians
    Commission Appointed to Negotiate with Tribes to Reduce Their Land Base
    Indians' Trustee Kept Value of Indian Land Concealed
    U.S. Failed to Protect Indians

Part 4: The Flimflam Man ~ 177

    Cheated Out of Fourteen Million Acres
    Ojibwe Cede Land for Buffer Zone
    Minnesota Becomes Territory in 1849

Part 5: The Cruel Hoax ~ 180

    U.S. Uses Shock and Awe to Paralyze Dakotas
    Sioux Indians Starved into Ceding Lands in Minnesota
    Pushing Indians into Debt to Get Land Ceded
    Genocidal Sioux Treaties in Minnesota
    Sioux Treaties Open 35 Million Acres for White Settlement
    DOI Champions Ratification of Sioux Treaties
    Governor and Superintendent of Indian Affairs Ramsey's Breach of Faith
    Dakotas in Minnesota Cede More Lands

Part 6: Treaty Chicanery ~ 188

    Treaties to Move Indians to Reservations
    Concentrating Indians on Reservations
    Theft of Two Million Acres
    Settlers Pressure Chippewa to Cede Timbered Land
    Bring All Indians under My Charge
    Indians Able to Conduct Logging Operations

Part 7: War Crimes ~ 194

    U.S.-Dakota War
    Governor's Message to State Legislature
    Mass Hanging at Mankato
    Dakota Exiled from Minnesota
    U.S. Deports Dakota to Crow Creek

Part 8: Winnebagoes – Crimes against Humanity ~ 200

    President, Congress and DOI Failed to Save Winnebagoes

Part 9: Waterboarding ~ 203

    Subsistence Lakes Damned
    Damming Headwaters of Mississippi
    Payment for Damages to Ojibwes Delayed for Century

Part 10: The Swindle – Cession of 2 Million Acres at Red Lake ~ 207

    Con-Artists at Work
    Opposition to Cession of 2 Million Acres at Red Lake Defeated
    Voice of Deceit

Part 11: Beware the Grim Reaper ~ 209

    Northwest Commission's Gruesome Tasks

Part 12: Allotment ~ 209

    Nelson Act (Minnesota's Version of General Allotment Act)
    Nelson Act Synopsis

Part 13: Rice Commission Bullies Indians ~ 211

    Rice Commission Census
    Complaints by Various Chippewa Bands
    Removal Numbers to White Earth Reservation

Part 14: Tapping Sap ~ 214

    Sugar Point Uprising

Part 15: "Dead and Down" Timber ~ 215

    Logging Green Timber as "Dead and Down"

Part 16: The Cover Up ~ 216

    GLO Appointment of Timber Appraisers
    Crooked Sale of Ceded Lands from Red Lake
    Red Lake Fraud Investigation
    Massive Fraud in Timber Operations at Red Lake
    Inspector's Summary of Timber Appraisal Deficiencies
        I. Overcharge for Services – $99,290
        II. Incompetence
        III. Neglect of Duty
        IV. Method of Computing Quantity of Timber
        V. Questionable Behavior
        VI. Bribe

      VII. Insider Trading
      VIII. Conflict of Interest
Ceded Land Sales Ceased
Iron Triangle Cover-Up: DOI, Congressional Representatives and Timber Company Meet
GLO Commissioner Denies any Mismanagement of Timber Operations

Part 17: More Will Be Revealed ~ 220

GLO Forced to Investigate Timber Operations at White Earth
GLO Reports Fraud at White Earth
Office of Indian Affairs Confirms Fraud at White Earth
Sticky Eight-Year Fraud Problem
Keep Chippewa Lands Off Market until Demand Justified
Collusion and Conspiracy at White Earth

Part 18: King's X ~ 223

Secretary Reports Failed Timber Sales
Who's Watching the Hen House
Advantage of Institutional Expertise
White Pine Was King

Part 19: The Trojan Horse ~ 229

The Trojan Horse – Clapp Act and Steenerson Act
Adult Mixed-Bloods Free to Sell Their Land
Double or Nothing
Further Congressional Impetus to Assimilation

Part 20: The Iron Triangle ~ 231

The Grifter Heads to White Earth
How to Steal Indian Lands
Cast of Characters
Stage Was Set to 'Get Rich Quick' Off of Indian Land
Cat's Out of the Bag
Commissioner Valentine – Get to Bottom of Thieving
Iron Triangle and Artful Attorney Ransom Powell
U.S. Proves Criminal Conspiracy in Full-Blood Quantum Case
Quantum of Blood
Judicial Definition of Mixed-Blood Chippewa Indian
Cronies Lobby for Blood Quantum Congressional Legislation

    Hierarchical Skull Studies
    Allottees Can Bring Fraud Cases in State Court
    Government's Cases Weakened by Powell's Advocacy
    Out-of-Court Settlement Formula
    Iron Triangle Prevails
    White Earth Epilogue
    Minnesota's Timber Harvest

Part 21: Ecological Destruction ~ 239

    Collapse of Lake Superior Fishery
    Extinction of Passenger Pigeon due to Overhunting
    Ritual – Knights of the Forest
    Chart Minnesota Ojibwe (Chippewa) Treaties
    Chart Sioux Indian Treaties in Minnesota

Chapter 8: Wisconsin's Forced Indian Removal ~ 255

Part 1: Wisconsin's Indian Holocaust ~ 255

Part 2: Mining in Wisconsin ~ 255

    Upper Mississippi Valley: Illinois, Wisconsin and Iowa
    Copper Mining in Northern Wisconsin

Part 3: Logging Industry ~ 257

Part 4: Connecting Wisconsin's Waterways ~ 258

    Great Lakes Steamships and Canals

Part 5: Eliminating Indians' Land Base ~ 258

    Resolution of Legislature of Wisconsin for Removing Wisconsin Indians

Part 6: Indigenous Tribes in Wisconsin Territory ~ 260

    1. The Potawatomi of Wisconsin and Illinois River
    2. The Ho-Chunk (aka Winnebago)
       Threat to Exterminate Winnebago Indians
       Nature of Winnebagoes
    3. The Menominees

    4. The Ojibwe (aka Chippewa)

Part 7. Tribes Removed to Wisconsin from Northeastern U.S. ~ 275

    1. The Oneida
    2. The Stockbridge
    3. The Brothertown

Part 8: U.S. Treaty Obligations Ignored ~ 276

Part 9: Sandy Lake Tragedy and Wisconsin Death March ~ 276

    Annuities Used as Economic Sanctions
    Policy of Withholding Annuities to Secure Cession of Lands
    Chippewa Indians Request Homeland in Wisconsin
    Chippewa Indians Submit Petition to Congress
    President Taylor's Executive Order to Remove Ojibwe from Wisconsin and Michigan
    Minnesota Clamoring to Have Tribes
    Minnesota's Plan for Indian Removal
    Ojibwe Refuse to Move to Minnesota
    Governor Ramsey's Secret Plan
    Ojibwes' Opposition to Removal Stiffens
    Governor Ramsey Defends His Actions
    Battle of the Wills
    Lake Superior Ojibwe Sign New Treaty at La Pointe

Part 10: Theft, Theft and More Theft of Indian Timber ~ 282

    Ongoing Theft of Timber on Menominee Reservation
    Theft of Timber Predicted to Continue
    Mill Owners' Conspiracy to Keep Menominee Timber Price Low
    Agent's Wholesale Permission for Fraudulent Logging
    Fraudulent Timber Contracts
    Menominees' Unrealized Timber Industry Potential
    Green Bay Agency – 300,000,000 Feet of Pine Logged
    Timber Trespasses on Stockbridge and Munsee Reservation
    Menominees Get to Conduct Lumber Operations
    Cornell University's Investment in Wisconsin's 'Virgin White Pine Lands'
    Lumber Barons

Chapter 9: Montana: Big Business' Corrupt Political Clout ~ 294

Introduction

Part 1: Lady Liberty Heads West ~ 295

    Indian Land Title Questionable
    "Manifest Destiny"

Part 2: Boots on Ground ~ 297

    Fifty-Four Forty or Fight
    Oregon Trail
    Frontier Trading Posts

Part 3: Coming of Railroads ~ 300

    Railroad Surveys
    Railroads' Advantages
    Railroads Cut through Indian Lands

Part 4: Strategies to Divest Indians of Their Lands ~ 301
    Pacify the Indians
    Enter into Peace Treaties
    Extinguish Indian Title
    DOI Rallies for Extinguishing Indian Title in Montana

Part 5: "There's Gold in Them Thar Hills" ~ 304

    Grasshopper Creek
    Alder Creek
    Last Chance Gulch
    Bozeman Trail Cuts through Indian Country
    Renegades and Thieves
    Montana Territory Created
    Governor's Conflict of Interest
    Montana Militia
    Frontier Forts
    Miners' Demand for Timber
    Clamor for Railroads
    Montana's Railroads, A Greater Good

Part 6: The Iron Horse ~ 308

Northern Pacific Railroad Land Grant
   Subjugate Lawless Indians
   Northern Pacific Railroad Cuts through Indian Lands
   MHA Reservation Established by Executive Order
   MHA Forced Cession for Northern Pacific Right-of-Way (ROW)
   Crow Tribe Forced Cession for Northern Pacific ROW
   Asst. AG McCammon to Negotiate Northern Pacific ROW
   Tribes Bullied by Asst. AG McCammon
   Congress Starves Montana Indians
   Striking Spike

Part 7: Indians Fight Invasion ~ 314

   Settlers Killing Bison, Squatting on Indian Lands
   Massacre of Piegan Indians
   Indians Wage War against Railroads

Part 8: Railroad Spurs ~ 316

   Utah Northern Railroad from Salt Lake to Idaho
   Utah & Northern Railway to Butte, Copper Polestar

Part 9: Montana Gets Third Railway ~ 316

   Great Northern Railway from St. Paul to Washington State
   The Minnesota Club
   Hill's Team
   More Political Contacts

Part 10: Hill's Plan to Get Across Indian Reservations ~ 319

   Subpart A: Remove, Cede, ROW Three-Prong Strategy
   Subpart B: Urge MHA Indian Nations to Move to Indian Territory
     Remove Tribes Due to Depredations
     Blackfeet Will Be Tough to Move
   Subpart C: Private Meeting with DOI and Congress
   Subpart D: Hill Lobbies for Indian Land Cessions
   Subpart E: Hill Piggybacks on Northwest Commission's Land Cessions
     MHA Agree to Cede 1,600,000 Acres
     Blackfeet Agree to Cede 17,500,000 Acres
     Northwest Tribes Agree to Cede Land
     ROW Provision
     MHA Cession Still on Table in 1888, Not Enacted until 1890

Subpart F: Hill Lobbies for ROW Legislation
    President Cleveland Vetoes Generic ROW Bill
    Hill's Forces Waste No Time to Get Tailored ROW Bill
  Subpart G: Hill Strikes Spike
    Hill Recruits Emigrants to Northwest
    Glacier National Park Tourism

Part 11: Chicago, Milwaukee, St. Paul & Pacific Railroad ~ 332

Part 12: King Copper ~ 332

  Anaconda Company
  Copper and Timber Team Up

Part 13. Timber Operations in Montana ~ 334
  Lumber Baron Andrew Hammond
  Logging Partners: Northern Pacific Railroad, Copper Magnate Daly and Hammond
  Hammond's Vertical and Horizontal Integration Strategies Pay Off
  Scratching Each Other's Backs
  MIC and Northern Pacific Indicted
  Hammond's Navy

Part 14. Post-War Depression ~ 337

Chapter 10: Oregon: Governor Curry's Private Wars of Extermination ~ 345

Part 1: Introduction ~ 345

  Preemption Act of 1841
  Great Migration of 1843
  Provisional Government of Oregon (1843)
  Presidential Charge: Settle Oregon
  President Polk: Trifling Amount Will Avoid War
  Donating Oregon to Colonial Settlers
  Extinguish Indian Title West of Cascade Mountains
  Manifest Destiny
  Shock and Awe

Part 2: Starvation or Plunder ~ 354

  President Fillmore: Indians in Oregon Are Tenants at Sufferance

Part 3: Substituting Robbery for Purchase ~ 354

    Let Colonial Settlers Exterminate Indians

Part 4: Cayuse Indians Fight Invasion of Their Lands ~ 356

    Volunteer Regiment of Riflemen
    Volunteers Hunt Indians as Beasts of Prey
    Cayuse Indian Lands Forfeited
    Causes of Cayuse War

Part 5: Clamor to Remove Indians ~ 359

    Petition for Rogue River Military Force June 5, 1851
    Oregon Governor's Death Squads
    No Judicial Remedy for Indians

Part 6: True Purpose of Indian Removal ~ 362

    Inexhaustible Mineral and Agricultural Wealth

Part 7: President Orders Military Protection of Settlers ~ 363

    Quieting Indian Hostilities in Oregon
    Rogue River Indians – Remove Whites, Not Us
    Twenty Percent Mortality Blanketed Rogue River Indians

Part 8: Rogue River War Precipitated by Lupton Massacre ~ 364

    Unfriendly Indians Are Our Enemies

Part 9: Rogue River War Chronology ~ 366

Part 10: "Oregon's Trail of Tears" ~ 368

    Rogue River Indians Threatened with Slaughter
    Grande Ronde Indians Sick and Dying

Part 11: 'Off the Reservation' ~ 372

Part 12: Congressional and Executive Branches
                  Countenance Massacre of Indians ~ 373

President Pierce: Remove Indian Obstacle

Part 13: King Midas Touches Blood ~ 374

    Demonizing Indians

Part 14: "Private War" ~ 376

Part 15: Dividing Up Oregon: Casting Lots ~ 378

Part 16: Oregon Admitted as State in 1859 ~ 379

Part 17: Rogue-Umpqua Rivers Glittering Sands ~ 380

Part 18: Terror Tactics Used to Force Tribes to Cede Lands ~ 382

    Delay in Delivery and Insufficiency of Goods and Monies
    Appropriations Weapon
    Pitting Indian against Indian

Part 19: Umatilla Reservation's Wealth Mandates
                    Removal or Reservation Reduction ~ 385

Part 20: Treaty Chaos ~ 387

    I Can't Spend It in Grave
    Unratified and Ratified Treaties in Oregon

Part 21: Concentration Camps ~ 391

    Fort Hall Reservation
    Klamath Reservation
    Siletz Indian's Diet of Frozen, Rotten Potatoes
    Alsea Indian Sub-Agency: Death by Exposure

Part 22: No More Promises ~ 396

    Reduce the Size of Siletz Reservation

Part 23: Snake Indians Hunted like Wolves ~ 397
Part 24: Butcher Indians ~ 398

Part 25: Modoc War (1872–1873) ~ 399

    Return to Lost River
    Peace Commission Doomed to Fail
    Modocs to Be Punished
    U.S. Holds Grudge

Part 26: High and Frequent Turnover of Agents Cause of Modoc War ~ 407

    Cost of Modoc War

Part 27: Nez Perce 'Thief' War (1877) ~ 409

    Gold Discovered
    No Spirit Will Hinder Me
    Raging Torrent Unstoppable
    Polishing a Diamond
    Refuge in Canada
    Surrendering His Rifle
    1877 Nez Perce Treaty
    Good Words Do Not Last Long

Part 28: Bannock War (1878) ~ 419

    President Hayes: Lack of Food
    Cost of Bannock War
    Second Bannock War 1895

Part 29: President Hayes: Moral Duty ~ 421

Part 30: President Garfield: Treaties with Savages Mockery ~ 421

Part 31: President Arthur: No Sovereigns ~ 422

Part 32: President Cleveland: Allotment ~ 422

    Allotments
    Warm Springs Debacle
    U.S.' Genocidal Indian War (1887)

Part 33: President Harrison: Eradicating Tribal Relations ~ 424
Part 34: Death Squads' Atrocities ~ 424

        Coose County Death Squad's Coquille Massacre
        Massacre at Miller's Ferry
        A 'Personal' Hanging

Part 35: Liabilities ~ 431

        Outstanding Debts
        Spoliation Claims
        War Costs

Part 36: Back-Biting ~ 432

        DOI: "Damnedest Humbug"
        You're Fired
        Whose Side Are You On Anyway?

Part 37: Shout of 'Timber' – Green Gold ~ 435

        Oregon's Railroads (1866 Grant to State, 1870–1880 Completed)
        Corporate Logging Empires
        Midstream Businesses – Sawmills
        Downstream Businesses – Lumber Yards
        Scratching Each Other's Backs
        Denuding Lands in which Indians Have Beneficial Interest
        Indians' Lost Opportunities

Chapter 11: Washington: Governor Stevens' Private Wars of Extermination ~ 453

Part 1: Washington Territory Governor's Private Wars ~ 453

Part 2: Prized Indian Forests ~ 453

        Lewis and Clark Reported "Great Quantities of Excellent Timber"
        Hudson's Bay Company Proclaim Fortuitous Large Timber Profits
        British Captain Vancouver Described Entry to Puget Sound as "Continuous Forest"
        U.S. Naval Officer Wilkes Astonished at Magnificent Forests

Part 3: Promoting Washington's Lumber Industry ~ 456

Part 4: Puget Sound Mills ~ 458

Part 5: Lumber Kings of Pacific Coast ~ 459

    Trading Land for Christmas Presents
    Treaty of Point No Point Ceded Land around Port Gamble
    Pope and Talbot

Part 6: Extinguish Indian Title West of Missouri ~ 463

Part 7: Washington Territory Established (1853) ~ 464

    Isaac Stevens, Surveyor of Northern Transcontinental Railroad Route, Governor and ex officio Superintendent of Indian Affairs for the Washington Territory
    Surveillance of Indians in Washington Territory
    Indian Land Title Obstructing State's Growth

Part 8: Secretary of Interior Authorizes Treaty Negotiations with Tribes ~ 466

    Stevens to Conduct Treaty Negotiations
    Consolidation and Concentration of Indian Tribes

Part 9: Stevens' Treaties ~ 469

    Neah Bay Treaty
    Medicine Creek Treaty, Stevens' Treaty with Nisqually Indian Nation
    White Men Beat and Abuse Indians – Indians Need to Move
    Stevens' Treaty Statistics

Part 10: Reservations in Washington ~ 476

Part 11: Rumblings of War ~ 477

    Military Records Short on Substance
    1st Washington Territory Volunteers
    Reason for Indian Hostilities
    Gold Discovered
    Routing of Major Haller's Volunteer Forces
    Fragmented State Leadership
    Volunteer Citizen Group
    White River Assault

Part 12: War ~ 482

    Military Rendezvous Fails

Volunteers Mustered into Service
Washington and Oregon Volunteers' Yakama Stalemate
Death of Volunteer Moses in Aborted Action
Ruin of Industrial Community

Part 13: Puget Sound War ~ 484

Battle of Brennan's Prairie, Dec. 4, 1855
Battle of Seattle, Jan. 26, 1856
Battle of Muckleshoot Prairie, March 1, 1856
Battle at Connell's Prairie, March 10, 1856
Mashel Massacre, March 31, 1856

Part 14: Indian War on Plateau ~ 487

Battle of Union Gap, Nov. 7, 1855
Cascades Rapids Battle, March 26, 1856
Battle of Second Walla Walla Council, Sep. 1856

Part 15: Deadly Miscalculations ~ 488

Gov. Stevens: Strike Indians Now (Dec. 22, 1855)
Underestimating Your Opponent
Lack of Coordination between U.S. Army and Volunteers
Lack of Preparation
Lack of Discipline and Command: Scalping Redskins
Military Force "Totally Inadequate"
Command Center Six Thousand Miles Distant

Part 16: Nisquallies Seek Peace ~ 491

Part 17: Nothing but Death Is Mete Punishment (Jan. 25, 1856) ~ 492

War Chief Tenaskut Murdered in Cold Blood
Stevens Orders Chief Leschi's Hanging by Executioner

Part 18: Political Infighting ~ 494

Dissension Between Governor Stevens and Major General John Wool
Major General John Wool Pronounces Stevens' Barbarous Determination to Exterminate Indians a Deterrent to Peace
Governor Stevens Rudely Complains to Major Gen. Wool and Appeals to Secretary of War

Dissension between Gov. Stevens and Commissioner of Indian Affairs
All Indians Are Enemies to Governor Stevens
Dissension between Gov. Stevens and Settlers: Compulsory Military Service
Dissension between Gov. Stevens and Judiciary: Stevens Declares Martial Law
Dissension between Gov. Stevens and President Pierce: No Justification for Martial Law

Part 19: Post-War ~ 499

    Indian Internment Camps
    Stevens Elected to Congress
    Seattle Removes Indians

Part 20: Puget Sound – Business as Usual ~ 501

    Pope & Talbot Partner Advocated Indiscriminately Hanging Indians

Part 21: Coeur d'Alene/Spokane War ~ 501

    Battle of Pine Creek (May 15, 1858)
    Battle of Four Lakes (Sep. 1, 1858)
    Battle of Spokane Plains (Sep. 5, 1858)

Part 22: Pacific Northwest Ruled by Timber Speculation ~ 503

Part 23: Timber Companies Grow by Violating/Evading Laws ~ 503

    Pope & Talbot Partner Indicted and Found Guilty of Theft of Timber
    Fraud under Timber and Stone Act of 1878
    Bribery of Indian Agents
    Improper Influence of Secretary of Interior Planned
    Talbot Circumvents State Land Limits

Part 24: Washington Admitted as State in 1889 ~ 506

    Further Reconnaissance of Pacific Northwest: 1890 Gilman and O'Neil Expeditions

Part 25: Timber Industry Surges ~ 506

    Weyerhaeuser's Bold Arrival on Scene (1900)
    Washington 1st in Timber Production in 1905

Part 26: Forest Conservation ~ 508

    Olympic National Park (1897, 1909, 1938)
    USGS Timber Survey of Olympic Forest Reserve (1897–1900)
    Clear-Cutting – "I Hope The Son-Of-A-Bitch Who Logged That Is Roasting In Hell"

Chapter 12: Timber Is The Cry ~ 521

Part 1: Arizona Papago Reservation ~ 521

Part 2: Colorado Utes ~ 522

Part 3: Dakota Territory ~ 522

    Black Hills
    Fort Berthold Reservation
    South Dakota Lower Brule Reservation

Part 4: Indian Territory ~ 524

    Shawnee and Wyandot Reserve
    Osage and Miami Reserves
    Delaware and Osage Agencies

Part 5: Kansas Territory ~ 527

    Commissioner Dooley Warns Secretary of Timber Theft
    Osage River Agency
    Sac and Foxes of Missouri in Kansas
    Prairie Band of Pottawatomie Reserve

Part 6: Nebraska ~ 530

    Otoes and Missourias
    Iowa Reserve

Part 7: Nevada Truckee Reservation ~ 531

Part 8: North Carolina Eastern Cherokees ~ 532

Part 9: Oklahoma Muskogee Reserve ~ 532

Chapter 13: Patterns of Dispossessing Indians
of Their Land and Resources ~ 537

Part 1: Common Trajectory ~ 537

Executive Conflict of Interest

> President John Adams: Indian Trust Responsibilities Are Subordinate to Obligations to U.S. Citizenry
> President Thomas Jefferson (1801–1805)
> President James Madison (1809–1817), Policy Is Precursor to Allotment
> President James Monroe: Extinguishment of Indian Title Inevitable; Removal of Indians Paramount; Assimilation Policy Defunct

Stereotypical View of the Indian Expressed at Highest Levels of Government

> Congress
> U.S. Supreme Court Chief Justice Epithet of Indians Savagery, 1823
> Commissioner of Indian Affairs Stereotypical View
> DOI Labeled Indians as Colonizers of Reservations

States Maneuver for Removal of Indians

States with Timber Resources Pursued Removal or Extermination

Indians Left Destitute

> Washington, Tulalip Reservation, Destitute
> On Grand Ronde Reservation in Oregon, Income Below Poverty Line and Employment Menial
> New York – Common Laborers
> Crow Indians in Montana – Scant Opportunity for Employment

Failure to Protect Indians

Chapter 14: Epilogue ~ 551

Michigan
Minnesota
Wisconsin
Timber of No Value to Chippewas of Wisconsin
Pacific Northwest
Montana
Oregon
Washington
Forestry Management on Indian Lands

PREFACE

Series of Books

This book on timberland and timber resources is part of a series on the dispossession of Indian natural resources by the iron triangle of the federal government, big business and colonial settlers. The primary period covered in this book is 1840–1900. The areas focused on include the Great Lakes and the Pacific Northwest.

Natural Resources

Natural resources can be categorized as renewable and non-renewable. Renewable natural resources, when sustainably used, can be regenerated by natural processes of growth. Non-renewable natural resources are exhaustible and can't be regenerated after exploitation, e.g., gold and silver. The other aspect of renewable and non-renewable natural resources includes the environmental functions of ecosystems when not degraded, e.g., water purification and nutrient cycling and the capacity to assimilate wastes.

Indians possessed an abundant natural resource environment which included (1) renewable natural resources such as timber, water and arable land, along with wildlife resources such as fish and game; and (2) non-renewable natural resources, such as gold, silver, copper, iron ore, coal and oil

Wealth Inherent in Natural Resources

The wealth embodied in natural resources was the key component in Indian lands that aggravated the greed of colonial settlers and businesses. The immediacy of revenues that could be derived from natural resources was undeniable. The goal of colonial businesses and settlers was to harvest the maximum amount of the resources to make the most money.

As stated, in 1867, by the Acting Commissioner of Indian Affairs, Charles E. Mix, if it was a region of "fertility" or "abounding in mineral ores," it was the Indian who would be forced to relinquish the land or his life. Com'r Mix's warning was on page one of his Annual Report to Secretary of the Interior Orville H. Browning.[1]

The Department of the Interior, the trustee for Indian Nations, knew his wards were being robbed, defrauded and even, killed, for their natural resource wealth. It was a wealth that would not be invested in the Indian Nations' economic well-being, development and sustainability. The DOI said it could not "prevent crime."

James Steele, one of the Treaty Commissioners appointed to negotiate with the Arapahoes after Sand Creek for the cession of their lands in Colorado, stated as follows:

> We all fully realize that it is hard for any people to leave their homes and graves of their ancestors; but, **unfortunately for you, gold has been discovered in your country**, and a crowd of white people have gone there to live, and a great many of these people are the worst enemies of the Indians—men who do not care for their interests, and who would not stop at any crime to enrich themselves.
>
> *We want to give you a country that is full of game and good for agricultural purposes, and where the hills and mountains are not full of gold and silver.*
>
> We are sorry that we have bad people among us, as you are sorry that you have bad people among you; but this is unfortunately the case with all people, and however severe we make laws; it is impossible to prevent crime.
>
> You may accede to our wishes, and be happy and prosperous, or you may refuse to make a treaty, and be ruined in health and happiness. (Emphasis added).[2]

Valuing Natural Resources

The easiest way to quantify the value of a natural resource, such as fish or timber, is its market price. The option value is the ability to choose between use and non-use. The non-use value is the value of the raw resource in-hand and the value it will afford to an estate of a family-owned business or to a corporation which will continue beyond the life of the shareholders.

By dispossessing Indians of their natural resources, they lost this total value. Many times in compensating Indians for this loss, either due to legislation or lawsuits, the only determinable value was the direct use value, the commodity price, not the non-use value which is difficult to quantify. The boom and bust cycles make valuing the non-use of resources problematic. Yet corporations in their Securities and Exchange Commission (SEC) filings and their reports to shareholders are required to report the use values and non-use reserves. Reserves being held for future extraction are included as assets on their balance sheets and are the most important aspect in assaying the company's overall financial health, the company's attractiveness to shareholders and investors, and its ability to borrow on favorable terms. Investors are concerned with what a company is holding for future development to insure its vitality over time. For publicly traded companies in the U. S., the SEC is the primary regulatory body that provides companies with guidelines on how to report reserves.

Metals Are Sole Reliance to Liquidate Interest on National Debt

Given the federal government's need for money, Indians were seen as an obstacle whenever their interests collided with the U.S.' support for mining.

> The precious metals, our sole reliance to liquidate the accruing interest upon the national debt, are derived chiefly from the mining districts of Colorado, Oregon, California, Nevada, Idaho, and Montana, and any barrier which obstructs emigration to these mines, and retards their development, must prove highly prejudicial to the financial prosperity of the country.[3]

Natural Resource Exploitation and Depletion

The exploitation and depletion of Indian natural resources was a direct result of mismanagement by the federal government. Not only did the dispossession of valuable lands occur, but if they were not dispossessed the proper valuation did not occur.

The Central Superintendency reported Com'r D.N. Cooley's instructions to the Ute Treaty Commissioners as follows:

Colorado Territory. Last summer gold, silver, and coal were discovered in this section, which is reported to have many fertile valleys, abundance of timber and water powers, a fine climate, and all the requirements for profitable occupation. Many parties are preparing to invade this new land early in the spring ... It is important that a treaty be made with the Grand River and Uintah bands at as early a day as possible. *I need scarcely allude to the necessity of limiting, as far as possible, the amount which the government will be called upon to pay for a cession of the right of occupancy of the land by the Indians*, but deem it of importance that, so far as possible, no promises of money annuities shall be made, but that all payments shall be made in stock animals, implements, goods adapted to their wants, and for other beneficial objects. (Emphasis added).[4]

Indian Nations Not Parties to Disposal of Their Resources

Indian Nations were not permitted to participate in determining the disposal of their resources.

If they stand up against the progress of civilization and industry, they must be relentlessly crushed. The westward course of population is neither to be denied nor delayed for the sake of all the Indians that ever called this country their home. They must yield or perish; and there is something that savors of providential mercy in the rapidity with which their fate advances upon them, leaving them scarcely the chance to resist before they shall be surrounded and disarmed.[5]

Corruption

Gold, Silver, Copper, Iron Ore, Green Gold, Black Gold, Agricultural Land, Water, Game

Natural resource abundance lends itself easily to corruption by governments and businesses which have significant cumulative effects throughout the economy, impeding growth and development. The necessarily large size of firms operating reduce or eliminate competition, and firms often end up in monopolistic or cartel positions. Once installed in these positions, firms seek to protect their positions, which may involve bribery of governmental officials. The concentration of control over resources and resource revenues among a small group of firms and governmental officials thus sets up a situation in which corruption is more likely.

Outright bribery, though, was the principal weapon wielded by lumbermen in the Puget Sound. In the summer of 1883, for example, Interior Department agent T. H. Cavanaugh was sent to Puget Sound to investigate fraudulent land claim entries. William Renton, partner in the Port Blakely Mill Company, informed Cyrus Walker, Manager of the Puget Mill Company and the leading lumberman in Washington, that the Interior Department agent was a close friend of Seattle attorney H. G. Struve. Renton stated that several of the sawmills had paid Struve "to have him use his influence to present the matter in as favorable a light as possible to the Agent whom he (Struve) thinks can be fixed." Subsequently, a Renton assistant wrote that Interior Department agent Cavanaugh had "been entertained by Gamble and us and we know him to be all right."[6]

Will Talbot, for one, wished to "forever put to rest the thieving of Government agents in blackmailing large timber claim owners."[7]

Another instance of corruption involved federal Agent George Betts on the Chippewa Isabella Reservation in Michigan: five-sixths of the valuable pine timber land he had allotted to Saginaw-Chippewa Tribal members had been sold for very low or no consideration at all by alleged competent mixed-bloods to "land sharks." An investigation by Special Agent Edwin Brooks in 1878 found:

> *These facts, if no others existed, are sufficient to show fraud and collusion of the darkest character on one side, and on the part of the Indians, a degree of ignorance and incompetency alone sufficient to warrant the office in cancelling the whole list.* [p. 25].
> *The facts discovered by the brief investigation made, in my opinion, conclusively show that the schedule ... is in the main fraudulent, that it was prepared by an Agent in collusion with, and in the interest of a pack of unscrupulous land sharks seeking and conspiring to defraud the Government and the Indians of a large tract of valuable land* ...(Emphasis added). [pp. 34-35].
>
> The parties ... are wealthy and more than ordinarily influential in civil, religious and political circles, and will doubtless suppress an investigation ... (Emphasis added).[8]

Human Capital

While the federal government failed to act to defer the spoliation of timber and other natural resources, Indians starved to death, froze to death, died from imported European diseases and were wantonly exterminated.

Blackfeet Nation Their supplies had been limited and many of them were gradually dying of starvation. I visited a large number of their tents and cabins. All bore marks of suffering from lack of food, but the little children seemed to have suffered most; they were so emaciated that it did not seem possible for them to live long, and many of them have since passed away. *To feed these Indians, I was reduced to such a strait that I was compelled to issue over 2,000 pounds of bacon which had been condemned.* Indians stripped the bark from saplings to eat. The buffalo, on which these people formerly subsisted, is now extinct. (Emphasis added).[9]

It is a notorious fact that the Indians throughout this country are fast being swept by disease from the face of the earth.[10]

Notes

1. Report of the Commissioner of Indian Affairs to the Secretary of the Interior, United States. Office of Indian Affairs, U.S. Government Printing Office, 1868, p. 1.
2. Report of the Commissioner of Indian Affairs to the Secretary of the Interior, United States. Office of Indian Affairs, U.S. Government Printing Office, 1865, pp. 522-523.
3. Report of the Commissioner of Indian Affairs to the Secretary of the Interior, Office of Indian Affairs, Northern Superintendency, Omaha, Nebraska Territory, Upper Platte Agency, United States. U.S. Government Printing Office, 1865, p. 400.
4. Report of the Commissioner of Indian Affairs to the Secretary of the Interior, United States. Office of Indian Affairs, U.S. Government Printing Office, 1866, p. 160.
5. Report of the Commissioner of Indian Affairs to the Secretary of the Interior, United States. Office of Indian Affairs, U.S. Government Printing Office, 1899, p. 3.
6. Ficken, Robert E. The Forested Land: A History of Lumbering in Western Washington. University of Washington Press, 2012, pp. 42-43.
7. Id.
8. Report of Special Agent Edwin Brooks to Commissioner of Indian Affairs E.A. Hayt, dated January 18, 1878. https://search.library.wisc.edu/catalog/9910707404302121 (accessed June 21, 2022).
9. Report of the Commissioner of Indian Affairs to the Secretary of the Interior, United States. Office of Indian Affairs, U.S. Government Printing Office, 1884, pp. 106-107.

10. Report of the Commissioner of Indian Affairs to the Secretary of the Interior, United States, Reports of Agents in California, Office of Indian Affairs, U.S. Government Printing Office, 1879, p. 9.

CHAPTER 1: IMPERIAL COLONIALISM

Part 1: Path to U.S. 'Discovery' Claim

Continental Congress, 1773

Briefly, in 1773 the Continental Congress was created, comprised of delegates from the colonies. They met in 1774 in reaction to the Coercive Acts, a series of measures imposed by the British government on the colonies in response to the colonies' resistance to new taxes. In 1775, the Second Continental Congress met even though the Revolutionary War was underway. In 1776, it took the significant step of declaring America's independence from Great Britain.

American Revolutionary War, 1775

The first shots in the American Revolutionary War were fired at Lexington and Concord in Massachusetts on April 19, 1775. Realizing reconciliation with Great Britain was impossible, on May 15, 1776, the Continental Congress advised all of the colonies to form governments for themselves.

Declaration of Independence, 1776

On July 4, 1776, the Continental Congress approved the Declaration of Independence, written by a committee of five men. The Declaration listed the colonies grievances with Great Britain and then proclaimed their independence.

> We, therefore, the representatives of the United States of America, in General Congress, assembled, solemnly publish and declare, that *these united colonies are, and of right ought to be free and independent states*; that they are absolved from all allegiance to the British Crown, and that all political connection between them and the state of Great Britain, is and ought to be totally dissolved; and that as free and independent states, they have full power to levy war, conclude peace, contract alliances, establish commerce, and to do all other acts and things which independent states may of right do. (Emphasis added).[1]

Articles of Confederation, 1777

The Articles of Confederation to govern the thirteen states were adopted by the Continental Congress on November 15, 1777. Article II clearly stated that:

> Each state retains its sovereignty, freedom, and independence, and every power, jurisdiction, and right, which is not by this Confederation expressly delegated to the United States, in Congress assembled.[2]

Treaty of Peace between the United States and Great Britain

The Definitive Treaty of Peace between the United States and Great Britain of September 3, 1783, ending the Revolutionary War (aka War of Independence) was between the free and sovereign thirteen states and Great Britain.

ARTICLE 1ST.

> HIS BRITANNIC MAJESTY acknowledges the said UNITED STATES, viz. New Hampshire, Massachusetts Bay, Rhode Island & Providence Plantations, Connecticut, New York, New Jersey, Pennsylvania, Delaware, Maryland, Virginia, North Carolina, South Carolina & Georgia, to be free sovereign & Independent States; that he Treats with them as such, and for himself his Heirs & Successors relinquishes all Claims to the Government Propriety and Territorial Rights of the same & every Part thereof.[3]

According to the Thirteen States, as the Revolution was fought by the 'Thirteen Colonies,' the right and royal prerogatives of the defeated Crown devolved upon the victorious 'Thirteen States.'

Constitutional Convention, 1787

Under the Articles of Confederation governing the confederacy of the Thirteen States from March 1, 1781, until 1789, there was no authority to tax the individual states, leaving the confederacy without a revenue base. Disputes over territory, war pensions and trade threatened its unity. A movement for constitutional reform developed, culminating in the formation of the Constitutional Convention to revise the Articles of Confederation. A new Constitution was drafted and signed, requiring the ratification by nine of the thirteen sovereign states. It wasn't until 1789, that the thirteen independent states, were joined by a new federal constitution into a single nation. The states still retained their sovereignty, except as to those powers delegated to the federal government by the Constitution.

Title to 'Western' Lands (aka 'Back Lands')

At the time the Constitution was signed, the boundaries of the states, based on their colonial charters, were unclear and at times overlapped one another. The western boundaries were set at the Mississippi River, given France's claim to the Louisiana Territory. The map below sets forth the alleged boundaries which were a matter of contention between the thirteen states.

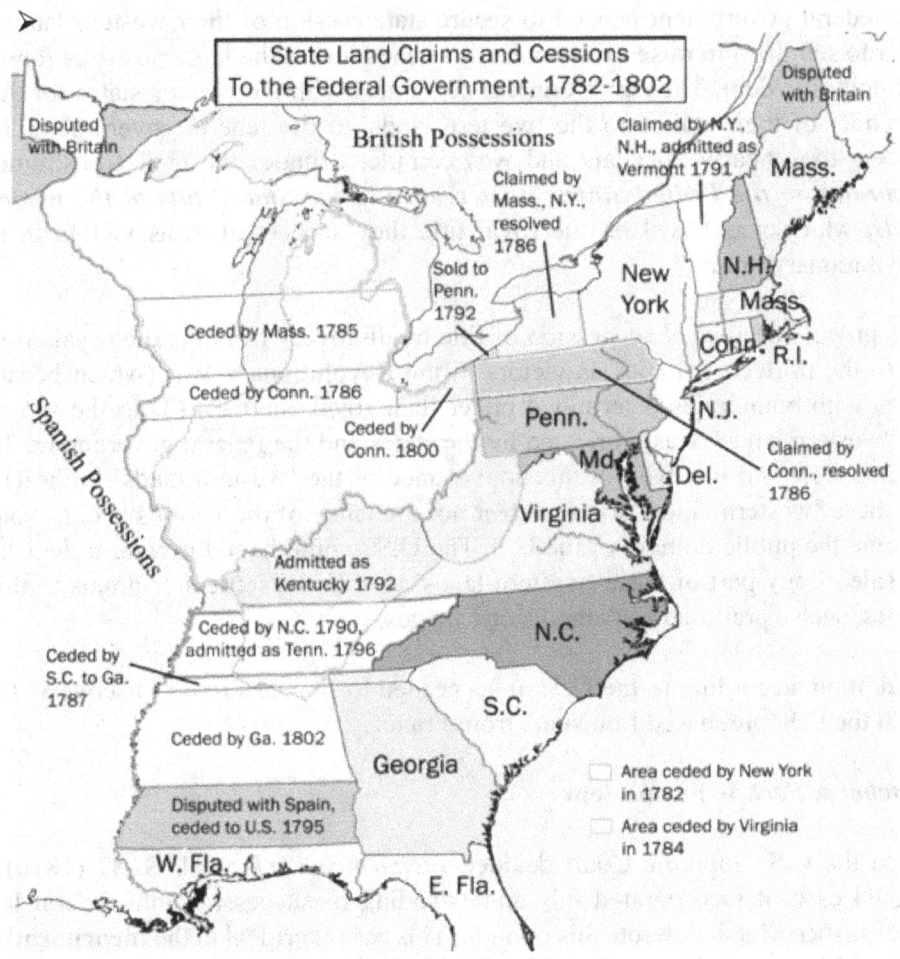

If the states bounded by the Mississippi River claimed all the land to the Mississippi River, their size and resources posed a threat to the 'landed' states on the Atlantic seaboard. Maryland posed the issue well in its Convention in November 1776.

"The back Lands [sic] claimed by the *British Crown*," contended Maryland legislators in November 1776, "if secured by the blood and treasure of all, ought in reason, justice, and policy...be considered as a common stock."[4]

With that declaration, Maryland voiced the opinion of the landed states as to what should become of the territory between the Appalachian Mountains and the Mississippi River, referred to as the "back lands" or the "western lands."

The federal government needed to secure state cession of their western lands in order to sell them to raise revenue, badly needed due to the large post-war foreign and domestic debt. The new Congress negotiated with the various states for their surrender of their claims to the 'western lands' to the federal government. The process took nearly 20 years and was completed under the U.S. Constitution. *According to the United States, it succeeded to the States' title to the western lands,* which was based on the royal title they succeeded to as victors in the Revolutionary War.

This process of alleged succession of title by discovery from (1) the royal crown (2) to the thirteen colonies as victors in the Revolutionary War (which became states with boundaries determined under their royal charters) (3) to the U.S. of the "western lands" was fabricated by the states and the federal government. The Indians were not involved in this conveyance of the 'western lands' to the U.S. Yet these 'western lands,' to the extent not the lands of the various tribes, would become the public domain of the U.S. The U.S. would have the right to legislate the sale of any part of these 'western lands' to colonial settlers or grants to third parties, such as railroads or schools or colleges.

In addition, according to the U.S., it succeeded to France's royal 'discovery' title when the U.S. purchased Louisiana from France.

Fletcher v. Peck **Is Fraudulent**

When the U.S. Supreme Court decided *Fletcher v. Peck*, 10 U.S. 87 (1810), a feigned case, it incorporated this understanding of succession into federal law. Chief Justice Marshall wrote this opinion. This case is critical in the **incorporation** of the 'doctrine of discovery' as the foundation of real property law in the U.S. The U.S. needed to *establish, as law*, its *succession to the States' title to the western lands,* which was based on the royal title they succeeded to as victors in the Revolutionary War. This case established the first two prongs of the U.S. 'discovery' claim. First, it validated Great Britain's alleged 'discovery' claim to 'Carolina, a colony in the New World.' *Second, it credited the states with the succession of Great Britain's discovery claim.*

Chief Justice Marshall seemed to step in at just the right time to establish a legal basis for the U.S. to take a 'valid title' to land for which no precedence existed. In a contrived case, Marshall would establish fundamental property law in a 'contract' case. In dicta, a mere aside, he granted the states fee title to Indian land within the state's boundaries. The state had a 'fee simple absolute' estate, notwithstanding that the Indian title had not been extinguished. It was the "majority opinion" of the court, though no analysis supported it.

The Supreme Court, prior to establishing the protocol binding on the court, was unregulated. It simply had no precedence, customs, regulations, formality, or etiquette limiting its dictatorial assertion of power to proclaim the law. The new government had not formulated effective constitutional limitations to assure that the checks and balances to protect against any branch of government—executive, legislative or judicial—exceeding its authority were operable. Impeachment of members of the Supreme Court or enacting legislation to counter decisions of the Supreme Court could not effectively challenge the authority of the Supreme Court in a fledging government focused on survival.

In *Fletcher*, Marshall first confirmed the validity of the "grant of Carolina by Charles second to the Earl of Clarondon and others," as varied thereafter.[5]

Second, he verified that:

> By the revolution, all the right and royal prerogatives devolved upon the people of the several states, to be exercised in such manner as they should prescribe, and by such governments as they should erect.[6]

Third, he validated that:

> the legislature of Georgia, unless restrained by its own constitution, possesses the power of disposing of the unappropriated lands within its own limits, in such manner as its own judgment shall dictate, is a proposition not to be controverted.[7]

Fourth, he clarified the doubt "whether a state can be seised in fee of lands, subject to the Indian title:"

> The majority of the court is of opinion that the nature of the Indian title, which is certainly to be respected by all courts, until it be legitimately extinguished, is not such as to be absolutely repugnant to seisin in fee on the part of the state.[8]

The state held fee title to all of the lands within its borders, including Indian lands.

Additional Successions to U.S.

Thereafter, the U.S. succeeded to the royal discovery title of Spain (which had devolved upon Mexico) when the U.S. defeated Mexico in 1848 in the Mexican American War. The U.S. succeeded to the discovery title of Spain and Russia when it purchased any title they had in what would become the Oregon territory. As between the U.S. and England, the U.S. would claim title to the Oregon Territory based on the 'discovery' of the mouth of the Columbia River by Captain Gray, an American citizen, in May 1792. The 'discovery' of the mouth of the Columbia River included all of the drainage basin of the Columbia River, under an axiom of the Law of Nations, which encompassed the present-day states of Oregon, Washington, and parts of Idaho and Montana. Since England capitulated to the U.S. assertion of its right to this territory, the U.S. had its own unique 'discovery' claim under the Law of Nations. With the 1854 Gadsden Purchase, the U.S. purchased the 'discovery' title of Mexico to lands in Arizona and New Mexico, acquired by Mexico in its defeat of Spain in the Mexican War of Independence.

Part 2: U.S. Determines Property Law Applicable to Indian Lands, 1823

United States Supreme Court Chief Justice John Marshall, based on his analysis of custom, broadly proclaimed the 'doctrine of discovery' as the supreme law of the land in 1823 in *Johnson v. M'Intosh*, 21 U.S. 543 (1823) (hereinafter "*Johnson*"). The 'doctrine of discovery' incorporated the axiom that whichever European nation first 'discovered' land, then not ruled by a Christian prince or people, could claim ownership of the land as against other European nations, even if it was inhabited. The discovering Christian country acquired the 'fee simple absolute' title to the land, which is a term meaning the unlimited ownership interest in the land. As the fee simple absolute title is an estate of total ownership of land, two parties cannot claim it as to a parcel of land. One party would own the fee simple absolute unlimited estate and the other party would have a lesser interest – such as a right to lease or occupy.

The second component concerned the method which would be used to address the presence of inhabitants. The discovering country had to be given land by the Indians, purchase it or conquer them to acquire it. As to purchasing the inhabitants' interest in their land, the 'discovering country' secured the right of preemption over any land it discovered, occupied by non-Christians – the exclusive first right of refusal if they should choose to sell their right to the land, what Chief Justice Marshall construed as a right of 'occupancy'. If the inhabitants did not want to sell their 'occupancy' interest and the discovering country still wanted the land, it would have to be taken by force.

The third component of Marshall's unanimous decision in *Johnson* was a new 'term of art,' a 'legal fiction,' a definition of 'conquest.' A legal fiction is a fact assumed or created by courts, which is then used in order to help reach a decision or to apply a legal rule. Since conquest earned a conquering country dominion over land, 'discovery' was equated with conquest, even though no actual warfare occurred. Conquest could either be the generally understood term of the subjugation and assumption of control of a people by the use of military force or under this new legal fiction, by being the first 'discoverer.' Walter Echohawk, renowned federal Indian law expert, argues that 'discovery' cannot logically be equated with conquest.[9]

The ruling in *Johnson* is still the law today. Unless a treaty granted an Indian Nation its land in fee simple, which a few did, the Indians were only granted the right to occupy certain land, with the underlying fee simple absolute estate in the federal government. Thus, most Indian Nations only have the right to occupy their land, without the ability to sell, lease or develop the natural resources, without approval by the federal government.

This decision is critical to understanding the rights of Indians today. It eliminated their ownership of their land. Ownership is a key facet in developing and improving land. If one is only a 'tenant,' there is no incentive to invest in the land. Also, it is uncertain as to if and when their tenancy might be extinguished, with or without compensation or credit for any improvements.

This 'Indian land title of occupancy' facilitated the dispossession of Indian lands by European colonizing countries. It approved the use of conquest to expropriate Indian lands. It also reduced the sovereign rights of Indian Nations. They could not sell or alienate their land to anyone other than the purported 'discovering' country. Their inherent sovereign right to the supreme, absolute ability to govern themselves and their land was diminished. They lost the political right to deal commercially and diplomatically in the international arena with any country other than their 'discoverer,' and the right to the absolute ownership of their lands, along with the right to dispose of them as they decided.

Johnson Case Is Fraudulent

Johnson resulted from a feigned land dispute. Even though Johnson and M'Intosh stipulated their land claims overlapped, Eric Kades, determined that there was no overlapping land dispute. His research found that the United Land Company's acreage was at least fifty miles from the closest M'Intosh holding.[10] There was no conflicting land claim to present to the U.S. Supreme Court. There was no actual case or controversy.

It was also collusive. In 1991, University of Oklahoma Law Professor Lindsay G. Robertson found fifty years of corporate records of the United Land Company documenting the collusive effort to confirm title to the purchased Indian lands through the *Johnson* case. He published his findings in 2005 in *Conquest by Law, How the Discovery of America Dispossessed Indigenous Peoples of Their Lands*. These records are now in the University of Oklahoma's Law Digital Collection. He summarizes his research as follows:

> This...is a story of how **a spurious claim gave rise to a doctrine**—intended to be of limited application—**that itself gave rise to a massive displacement of persons and the creation of a law that governs indigenous people and their lands to this day.**[11]

'Doctrine of Discovery' Dogmatically Adopted by Marshall into Federal Law

Without citing any statutes or legal cases or other authority for his decision, Chief Justice Marshall's decision held that, under the European 'doctrine of discovery,' the land discovered in the 'New World' belonged to the 'discovering' sovereign, so long as there was no Christian sovereign or Christian inhabitants.

The 'doctrine of discovery' promulgated for the United States by Chief Justice Marshall was as follows:

> They (Indians) were admitted to be the rightful occupants of the soil, with a legal as well as just claim to retain possession of it, and to use it according to their own discretion; but their rights to complete sovereignty as independent nations were necessarily diminished, and their power to dispose of the soil at their own will to whomsoever they pleased was denied by the original fundamental principle that *discovery gave exclusive title to those who made it*. (Emphasis added).[12]

Censoring Chief Justice Marshall

In 1823, Thomas Jefferson complained in a letter to Justice William Johnson regarding Chief Justice Marshall: "This practice of Judge Marshall, of travelling out of his case to prescribe what the law would be in a moot case not before the court, is very irregular and very censurable."[13] Without judicial rules regarding recusal due to conflicts of interest or basing a decision on the narrowest legal issue presented or anyone empowered to check the Chief Justice's behavior, he was free to range as arbitrarily and as dogmatically as he chose.

Marshall Disavows 'Discovery Doctrine'

Nine years later in a subsequent case authored by him, *Worcester v. Georgia*, 31 U.S. 515 (1832), U.S. Chief Justice Marshall definitively recanted his prior promulgation of the 'discovery doctrine' and instead stated:

> The extravagant and absurd idea that the feeble settlements made on the sea coast, or the companies under whom they were made, acquired legitimate power by them to govern the people, or occupy the lands from sea to sea did not enter the mind of any man.[14]

This recantation of the 'Doctrine of Discovery,' by none other than Marshall himself, is the best evidence of its falsity.

Jacksonian Supreme Court Ignores *Worcester,* Cites to *Johnson*

Marshall's change in the 'doctrine of discovery' in *Worcester* was rejected in the 1835 Supreme Court Term in *Mitchel v. United States*, 34 U.S. 711 (1835), followed by other cases. **The majority of Supreme Court Justices were President Jackson supporters/appointees**. In *Mitchel*, there is no reference to *Worcester* and *Johnson* is cited as having received 'universal assent.' **The Jacksonian partisan Supreme Court ignored the precedence of a prior Supreme Court decision without regard to what is known as 'stare decisis.'**

'Stare decisis' is Latin for "to stand by things decided." Courts defer to 'stare decisis' when a ruling has already been issued on the subject, even if the soundness of the decision is in doubt. Its purpose is to promote the evenhanded, predictable and consistent development of legal principles, to foster reliance on judicial decisions and contribute to the actual and perceived integrity of justice.

Indians Not Parties to Carving Up Continent

Indians were not parties to any of the Congressional legislation or legal cases establishing the adoption of the 'doctrine of discovery' by the United States. Nor were they parties to the negotiations between the states and the federal government as to title to the 'western lands.' The U.S. was willing to uphold its claims against any challenges by Indians through purchase of contested lands, if expedient, or war.

Lieutenant General John M. Schofield stated in his memoirs: "With my cavalry and combined artillery encamped in front, I wanted no other occupation in life than to ward off the savage and kill off his food until there should no longer be an Indian Frontier in our beautiful country."[15]

Twenty First Century Scholars' Analyses of *Johnson*

Numerous twenty first century scholars have pointed out how the 'doctrine of discovery' adopted into federal law by the United States Supreme Court in *Johnson* is unfounded.[16]

Notes

1. Declaration of Independence Transcription, https://www.archives.gov/founding-docs/declaration-transcript (accessed online July 22, 2022). On **July 19, 1776, the formal title was changed from** "A Declaration by the Representatives of the United States of America in General Congress Assembled" to "The Unanimous Declaration of the Thirteen United States of America."

2. Articles of Confederation, https://constitutioncenter.org/learn/educational-resources/historical-documents/articles-of-confederation (accessed online July 22, 2022).

3. "Definitive Treaty of Peace between the United States and Great Britain, 3 September 1783," *Founders Online,* National Archives, https://founders.archives.gov/documents/Franklin/01-40-02-0356. [Original source: *The Papers of Benjamin Franklin*, vol. 40, *May 16 through September 15, 1783*, ed. Ellen R. Cohn. New Haven and London: Yale University Press, 2011, pp. 566–575.] (accessed online July 22, 2022).

4. Opportunity and Challenge, The BLM Story, https://www.nps.gov/parkhistory/online_books/blm/history/chap1.htm (accessed online July 22, 2022).

5. *Fletcher v. Peck*, 10 U.S. 87, 91 (1810).

6. Ibid., p. 61.

7. Ibid., p. 72.

8. Ibid., pp. 95-96.

9. Echo-Hawk, Walter. *In the Courts of the Conqueror: The 10 Worst Indian Law Cases Ever Decided*. Fulcrum Publishing, 2018: 79.

10. Kades, Eric. "The Dark Side of Efficiency: *Johnson v. M'Intosh* and the Expropriation of American Indian Lands." U of Pa. Law Review 148 (Apr. 2000): 1065–1190.

11. Robertson, Lindsay G. *Conquest by law: How the discovery of America dispossessed indigenous peoples of their lands*. Oxford University Press, 2005.

12. *Johnson v. M'Intosh*, 21 U.S. 543, 574 (1823).

13. "From Thomas Jefferson to William Johnson, 12 June 1823," *Founders Online,* National Archives, https://founders.archives.gov/documents/Jefferson/98-01-02-3562 (accessed online November 12, 2020).
14. *Worcester v. Georgia,* 31 U.S. 515 (1832).
15. Schofield, John M. Forty-six Years in the Army. BoD–Books on Demand, 2020, p. 428.
16. Twenty First Century Scholars' Analyses of *Johnson*

Howard Berman, a lawyer concludes:

Marshall seized upon this controversy to establish a judicial mythology that would rationalize the origin of land titles in the United States. ... Marshall provided no historical context for the derivation of the conquest theory. He simply characterized the status quo, without analysis. Berman, Howard J. *The Concept of Aboriginal Rights in the Early Legal History of the United States,* 27 Buff. L. Rev. 643, 648 (1978).

Kent McNeil debunked Marshall's theory about Indian land title:

The Marshall Court created "an Indian interest unknown to the common law, the definition of which has understandably eluded judges ever since." McNeil, Kent. *Common law aboriginal title.* Clarendon Press, 1989: 236-237.

David Wilkins and Tsianina Lomawaima **assert that the 'doctrine of discovery' when defined . . . to mean that the federal government holds the fee-simple title to all the Indian lands in the United States, is a clear legal fiction that needs to be explicitly stricken from the federal government's political and legal vocabulary. Wilkins, David Eugene, and K. Tsianina Lomawaima. Uneven ground: American Indian sovereignty and federal law. University of Oklahoma Press, 2001:63.**

Others have described the 1823 Supreme Court decision as:

"conquest by judicial fiat," **Berman, Howard R.** "The concept of aboriginal rights in the early legal history of the United States." *Buff. L. Rev.* 27 (1977): 637, 648.

"a tortured rationale," **Frazier, Terry W**. "Protecting ecological integrity within the balancing function of property law." 28 *Envtl. L.* (1998): 53, 79 n.94.

"a tool of efficient expropriation of Indian lands," **Kades, Eric**. "The Dark Side of Efficiency: *Johnson v. M'Intosh* and the Expropriation of American Indian Lands." *University of Pennsylvania Law Review* 148.4 (2000): 1065, 1080.

"corrupt," **Norgren, Jill**. "Protection of What Rights They Have: Original Principles of Federal Indian Law." *NDL Rev.* 64 (1988): 73, 94.

"an extra-constitutional fiction ... developed ... to rationalize the subjugation of the Indian nations as a matter of law," **Skibine, Alex Tallchief**. "Braid of Feathers: Pluralism, Legitimacy, Sovereignty, and the Importance of Tribal Court Jurisprudence." (1996): 557, 565.

"fraught with incoherence and ad hoc rationalizations". **Green, Shelby D**. "Specific Relief for Ancient Deprivations of Property." Akron Law Review, Vol. 36: 264 (2003).

and a

"cruel joke." **Miller, Robert J.**, Presentation at the Indigenous Peoples Forum on the Doctrine of Discovery, March 23, 2012, Arizona State Capitol House of Representatives.

Robert Miller queries what to do about the 'discovery doctrine:'

the Doctrine of Discovery ... should have no place in the modern-day relationship between tribal nations, Indian people, and the United States. Miller, R. J. (2005). The doctrine of discovery in American Indian law. Idaho Law Review, 42:96.

CHAPTER 2: PRIMACY OF OPENING U.S. TO "SETTLEMENT AND CIVILIZED HABITATION"

The primacy of opening up the U.S. to settlement trumped Indian rights. To assure the U.S.'s uncontested ownership of the continent, settlement was crucial. "Settlement and civilized habitation"[1] were deemed national priorities. The colonial settlers, supported by the federal government, relied on Lord Mansfield's axiom: "Possession is very strong, rather more than nine points of the law."[2] Under English law, possession of real property was a matter of physical fact, not a right. As stated in Black's Law Dictionary, it is " ... the fact of having or holding property in one's power."[3]

To induce settlement west of the Mississippi River, favorable land laws with generous financial terms were enacted. In the 1800s, the going rate was $1.25 per acre. In many cases, ceded Indian lands would be similarly valued. The revenue derived from the sale of these ceded lands would be held in trust by the U.S. for the applicable Indian Nation. While Indians might voice their disagreement over the price for their ceded lands, which would inure to their benefit, the federal government had the final say.

What was even worse were the deductions made from the sales revenue, including (1) the cost of surveying; (2) the administrative costs of sales incurred by the General Land Office (GLO) and/or the Bureau of Indian Affairs; (3) any claims for credit advances incurred by a tribe or its members to traders or businesses; (4) any claims for damages to white settlers by Indians—depredation claims; (5) the costs of removal of the Indians, if any, to their new land; and (6) any other expenditures or payments due to the government. In the majority of cases, the credit and depredation claims were not specified, other than as to the amount by the claimant, nor verified by the government.

These charges to the Indians resulted in a positive benefit to the settler purchasers who were freed from these expenses and could apply the savings to their development of the land as "positive externalities." They also benefitted the federal government now freed from expenses paid for out of the gross proceeds due the Indians. The net proceeds of these sales to different tribes would have a long-lasting effect. The sale of their ceded lands, at government-set prices and financial terms, was final. The purchasers were protected by the real property law announced in the 1823 U.S. Supreme Court case, *Johnson v. M'Intosh*, 21 U.S. 543 (1823):

> The right of society to prescribe those rules by which property may be acquired and preserved is not and cannot be drawn into question, as the title to lands especially is and must be admitted to depend entirely on the law of the nation in which they lie.[4]

Part 4: Northwest Ordinances

At the beginning of the Confederation, the decision was made not to hold the public lands as a capital asset, but to dispose of them for revenue and to encourage settlement. The ceding of western lands by the states was accompanied by a series of ordinances passed by Congress to organize the areas and prepare them for statehood. Most significantly, it facilitated the disposal of the federal territorial lands. These measures included the Ordinances of 1784, 1785 and 1787 enacted under the Articles of Confederation.

The Ordinance of 1784

The Ordinance of 1784, drafted by Thomas Jefferson and passed by Congress (April 23, 1784), created a framework for the establishment of territorial governments in the area north of the Ohio River. It divided the territory into a handful of self-governing districts. Each district could send one representative to Congress upon its attaining a population of 20,000, and it would become eligible for statehood when its population equaled that of the least-populous existing state. (This Ordinance was superseded by the Ordinance of 1787.)

The Ordinance of 1785

In the Ordinance of 1785, Thomas Jefferson proposed that the vast new territories acquired by the cession of the states 'western' lands should be incorporated into the new union as separate (rather than expanded) states. This was important to states without 'western lands', the landed states, as they were concerned about the power these states might have based on an expanded land base.

Under the direction of the Surveyor General new land would be divided into townships 6 miles square, forming 36 plots of a square mile each, of which the revenues from the 16th square would be reserved for funding public education. An appointed Governor and three judges would rule a Territory until the population reached 5,000. At that time, the citizens could elect a legislature, and, when the population numbered 60,000, the Territory could apply for admission to the Union as a State on a basis of full equality with the original thirteen states. The Ordinance would govern settlement of millions of square miles of the American continent.

The Ordinance of 1787

The Northwest Ordinance of 1787[5] was adopted on July 13, 1787, by the Confederation Congress, the one-house legislature operating under the Articles of Confederation. It laid the basis for the government of the Northwest Territory and for the admission of its constituent parts as states into the union. The Ordinance divided the Northwest Territory into "not less than three nor more than five States." Under this Ordinance, each district was to be governed by a governor and judges appointed by Congress until it attained a population of 5,000 adult free males, at which time it would become a territory and could form its own representative legislature. An individual territory could be admitted to statehood after having attained a population of 60,000. A bill of rights protecting religious freedom, the right to a writ of habeas corpus, the benefit of trial by jury, and other individual rights; in addition the ordinance encouraged education and forbade slavery. New states were granted equal status to existing ones. The Northwest Ordinance of 1787 superseded the Ordinance of 1784.

As to Indians and their property rights it provided as follows under Art. 3:

> The utmost good faith shall always be observed towards the Indians; their lands and property shall never be taken from them without their consent; and, in their property, rights, and liberty, they shall never be invaded or disturbed, unless in just and lawful wars authorized by Congress; but laws founded in justice and humanity, shall from time to time be made for preventing wrongs being done to them, and for preserving peace and friendship.[6]

A determination of Indian lands in the 'western lands ceded by the states' to the U.S. government would have to be determined. If the U.S. wanted any of those lands, they would have to be acquired by purchase or war. Eventually, the Northwest Territory was organized into six states: Ohio, Indiana, Illinois, Michigan, Minnesota, and Wisconsin. In short, the Northwest Ordinances established the basis for United States expansion into the region.

Part 5: Congressional Legislation

Congress passed incremental legislation pertaining to Indians for removal, massive cession of tribal lands, concentration and consolidation of Indian Nations on reservations, allotment of tribal land to individuals, alienability of allotments and denial of sovereign treaty-making status. It also passed legislation for the sale of public domain lands and exploitation of the country's natural resources within the public domain.

1824, Office of Indian Affairs

In March of 1824, President James Monroe established the Office of Indian Affairs in the Department of War to oversee and carry out the federal government's trade and treaty relations with the tribes. In 1849, the Office of Indian Affairs ("OIA") was transferred to the newly created U.S. Department of the Interior to implement policies designed to *"subjugate and assimilate American Indians."* ... (Emphasis added). [7] The Interior Department formally adopted the name "Bureau of Indian Affairs" for the agency on September 17, 1947.

The Commissioner of Indian Affairs was the head of the Indian Bureau and reported to the Secretary of the Interior who was a member of the President's Cabinet.

U.S. Land Acts

The terms of sale under various U.S. land acts were many times applied to the lands (1) ceded by tribes or (2) taken from tribes after the allotment of lands, representing to the U.S. "surplus lands."

TERMS OF SALE UNDER VARIOUS U.S. LAND ACTS 1785-1862
1800-1862 Initial Sale by Public Auction

Year	Minimum Price	Terms	Minimum Purchase
1785	$1.00 per acre	Specie, loan-office or debt certificates	640 Acres
1796	$2.00 per acre	One-half down, one half due in one year	640 Acres
1800	$2.00 per acre	One-quarter cash, remainder to be paid in three annual installments	320 Acres
1804	$2.00 per acre	One-quarter cash, remainder to be paid in three annual installments	160 Acres
1820	$1.25 per acre	Cash	80 Acres
1830	$1.25 per acre	Land Scrip acceptable in lieu of cash	
1832	$1.25 per acre	Cash, Land Scrip	40 Acres
1841	$1.25 per acre	Squatters who built homes and improved land could purchase one-quarter section before it was offered for public sale	160 Acres
1855	$1.00 per acre	Land not sold for 10 years to be offered at $1.00 per acre; if not sold for 30 years, land could be disposed of at 12.5¢ per acre	40-320 Acres
1862	$10 (filing fee)	Title could be obtained after 5 years residence under Homestead Act	160 Acres

Terms of Sale under Various U.S. Land Acts 1785-1862, Ohio Lands Book

Roberta Carol Harvey 55

Indian Removal Act

Andrew Jackson's 1828 Presidential Campaign made American Indian Removal his goal - relocating eastern Indians west of Mississippi. Thomas Jefferson presaged Jackson's policy.

In his 1830 State of the Union Address, Jackson bragged about the Republic:

> What good man would prefer a country covered with forests and ranged by a few thousand savages to our extensive Republic, studded with cities, towns, and prosperous farms, embellished with all the improvements which art can devise or industry execute, occupied by more than 12,000,000 happy people, and filled with all the blessings of liberty, civilization, and religion?[8]

He refused to recognize Indian Nations as sovereigns. Jackson declared, "I have long viewed treaties with the Indians an absurdity not to be reconciled to the principles of our Government." The Indians, said Jackson, were subjects of the United States, pure and simple, "inhabiting its territory and acknowledging its sovereignty." It was a fiction that the tribes were in fact separate and independent entities, and it was absurd to negotiate with them as such.[9]

Tenor of Times – They May Begin to Dig Their Graves and Prepare to Die

Alfred Balch, Jackson's Commissioner of Indian Treaties, echoed the tenor of the times: "…removal of Indians would be an act of seeming violence — But it will prove in the end an act of enlarged philanthropy. These untutored sons of the Forest, cannot exist in a state of Independence, in the vicinity of the white man. If they will persist in remaining where they are, they may begin to dig their graves and prepare to die."[10]

The Removal Act states that:

> it shall and may be lawful for the President to exchange any or all of such districts [west of the river Mississippi], so to be laid off and described, with any tribe or nation of Indians now residing within the limits of any of the states or territories, and with which the United States have existing treaties, for the whole or any part or portion of the territory claimed and occupied by such tribe or nation, within the bounds of any one or more of the states or territories, where the land claimed and occupied by the Indians, is owned by the United States, or the United States are bound to the state within which it lies to extinguish the Indian claim thereto.[11] "An Act to provide for an exchange of lands with the Indians residing in any of the states or territories, and for their removal west of the river Mississippi," 4 Stat. 411.

Indian Territory Created

In 1834, Congress created the Indian Territory in present day Oklahoma for the removal of eastern Indians.

Distribution-Preemption Act of 1841

To encourage settlement, Congress passed the Distribution-Preemption Act of 1841 (5 Stat. 453), which recognized squatters' rights and allowed settlers to claim 160 acres of land. After residing on the property for 14 months, a claimant could purchase the property at $1.25 an acre. There was no stigma attached to being a squatter on the public domain. *The popular belief was that squatters were doing a national service by clearing the land and extending the area of civilization*.

Thomas Worthington, a leader in the squatter movement, leveraged his appointment as the register of the Chillicothe land office, a position that gave him immense influence over the interpretation of the law. Worthington negotiated with squatters and would-be speculators alike, determining what lands to sell and to whom. These negotiations allowed Worthington to build his own network of patronage made up of former squatters. He connected his local constituency to national politics, particularly the administration of Thomas Jefferson. He held several state offices, including that of Governor.

Act of June 5, 1850 (9 Stat. 437)

In 1850, Congress authorized the appointment of commissioners "to negotiate treaties with the several Indian tribes in the Territory of Oregon, for the extinguishment of their claims to lands lying west of the Cascade Mountains." Numerous other statutes were enacted for such commissions for various negotiation of cessions of tribal land or removal of tribes. Allegedly made up of distinguished men, they wanted distinction for themselves and to secure treaties they engaged in bullying, threatening, coercing, forcing, bribing or punishing Indians into ceding lands.

Donation Land Claim Act of 1850

On September 27, 1850, Congress passed the Donation Land Claim Act of 1850 (9 Stat. 496) which offered 320 federal acres at no charge to qualifying adult U.S. citizens, subject to the claimant residing on the property on or before December 1, 1850, and occupying it for four consecutive years, which could be counted retroactively. If married before December 1, 1851, a couple received an additional 320 acres in the wife's name. A certificate was issued to the claimant, granting immediate ownership once the land was occupied. Under an extension of the act in 1854, land could be purchased for $1.25 an acre. Indians were not U.S. citizens and therefore could not own land under the law, although Section 4 of the Act allowed "American half-breed Indians" of legal age, who were citizens of the United States (or declared to be), to participate.

Swamp Land Act of 1850

The Swamp Land Act of 1850 (9 Stat. 519) granted swamp lands to the various states on condition that they would drain and reclaim them. Over 63,000,000 acres of land, much of it timberland, was divested from the U.S. Much of the land was not really swamp land and never needed drainage. Disputes arose between Indian Nations and states over this issue when swamp lands existed on Indian lands.

Indian Appropriations Act

Indian Appropriations Acts provided government money to pay for goods or for removal onto reservations. Contemporary legislators and policymakers described reservations as a means to protect the Indian Tribes from encroachment by white settlers moving westward. Indian Tribes were strongly opposed to this federal policy as it sought to impose an agrarian, geographically restricted way of life on Indian populations.

Riders attached to appropriation bills were a favored way to secure Indian legislation, such as permitting mixed-blood or alleged competent full-bloods to sell their lands. While allotments were supposed to provide land for farming or grazing, riders might be attached to an appropriations bill to allow for timber lands to be allotted and thereafter alienated. A considerable number of acts were passed under the same name throughout the 19th and early 20th centuries.

Homestead Act of 1862

The Homestead Act of 1862 (12 Stat. 392) authorized outright grants of 160 acres to homesteaders after five years residence and cultivation. It permitted and encouraged the clearing of land, including timber for construction and domestic purposes on their sites. The Homestead Act of 1862 granted land claims in thirty states. These areas were the traditional or treaty lands of many tribes.

Pacific Railway Act of 1862

The Pacific Railway Act of 1862 (12 Stat. 489) provided federal subsidies in land and loans for the construction of a transcontinental railroad across the United States. The legislation authorized two railroad companies, the Union Pacific and the Central Pacific, to construct the lines. Congress eventually authorized four transcontinental railroads and granted 174 million acres of public lands for rights-of-way.

General Sherman is responsible for developing the strategy for conquering Plains Indians and to clear the plains for the Union Pacific and Kansas Pacific railroads by annihilating the buffalo population of the plains. On May 10, 1868, Sherman contacted General Sheridan and said, "as long as Buffalo are up on the Republican the Indians will go there. I think it would be wise to invite all the sportsmen ... there this fall for a Grand Buffalo hunt, and make one grand sweep of them all. Until the Buffalo and consequent Indians are out [from between] the Roads we will have collisions and trouble."[12]

Sherman believed military protection of the railroad construction parties was a task for the Army.

> These roads, although in the hands of private corporations have more than the usual claim on us for military protection, because the general government is largely interested pecuniary. They aid us materially in our military operations by transporting troops and stores rapidly across a belt of land hitherto only passed in the summer by slow trains drawn by oxen, dependent on the grass for food.[13]

Sherman supported railroad construction on the frontier and clearly envisioned its positive effects when he told the Secretary of War in 1880:

These railroads have completely revolutionized our country in the past few years, and impose on the military an entire change of policy. Hitherto we have been compelled to maintain small post along wagon and stage routes of travel. These are no longer needed, because no longer used, and the settlements which grew up speedily along the new railroads afford all the security necessary.[14]

Indian Appropriations Act of 1871

The Indian Appropriations Act of 1871, 102 Stat. 3641, ended treaty making with Indian tribes.

> "That hereafter no Indian nation or tribe within the territory of the United States shall be acknowledged or recognized as an independent nation, tribe, or power with whom the United States may contract by treaty: Provided, further, that nothing herein contained shall be construed to invalidate or impair the obligation of any treaty heretofore lawfully made and ratified with any such Indian nation or tribe."

Congress stipulated that rather than making treaties with tribes, the relationship should be governed by statutes passed by Congress or by executive orders.

General Mining Act of 1872

Prospecting and mining for minerals on public lands were authorized under the General Mining Act of 1872, 17 Stat. 91–96, signed by President Grant.

Indemnity Act – Lieu Lands

The Indemnity Act of 1874 (Act of Congress of June 24, 1874, entitled "An Act for Relief of Settlers on Railroad Lands," 18 Stat. 194), provided that if land included in a railroad grant was found in the possession of settlers, the railroad might select other lands in lieu of it. While this seemed equitable, it enabled railroads to acquire more valuable lands than their grants really entitled them to receive.

Timber and Stone Act of 1878

The Timber and Stone Act of 1878, 20 Stat. 89, entitled "An Act for the sale of timberlands in the States of California, Oregon, Nevada, and in Washington Territory," took two forms. (1) The Free Timber Act allowed residents to cut timber for building, agricultural, mining, or other domestic use in western states and territories. (2) It further provided for the actual sale of timberlands in California, Nevada, Oregon, and Washington Territory. In 1892, Congress extended this allowance to all public-land states.

The land was supposed to be chiefly valuable for timber or stone. The sale of this land, at not less than $2.50 an acre, was to citizens of the United States or persons who had declared their intention to become citizens. Not more than 160 acres was to be sold to any one person or association of persons. Each applicant was required to file a statement, verified under oath, that he was not applying for the land for speculation and that he wanted to appropriate it for his own exclusive use and benefit. The applicant also had to swear that he had not made a contract or agreement of any kind so the title to the land would not benefit anyone except the applicant. In addition, a penalty of $2.50 per acre was set for individuals caught illegally removing the timber.

DOI Warns of Destructive Impact of Timber and Stone Act

Even before the Timber and Stone Act of 1878 was passed, Commissioner Williamson of the General Land Office warned Secretary of the Interior Schurz that the give-away scheme was readily transparent:

> This bill is equivalent to a donation of all the timberlands to the inhabitants of those states and territories. The machinery of the Land Office is wholly inadequate to prevent the depredations which will be committed.[15]

Secretary Schurz also cautioned President Garfield of the deleterious ecological impact:

> "It will stimulate a wasteful consumption beyond actual needs and add to wanton destruction," he said, "for the machinery left to this department to prevent or repress such waste and destruction through enforcement of the regulations, will prove entirely inadequate, and as final result, in a few years, the mountain sides in those states and territories will be stripped bare."[16]

Even while expressing concern over the destruction of the nation's forests, President Chester A. Arthur still appointed Senator Henry Teller, a Colorado mine owner and railroad lawyer, as Secretary of the Interior in 1882. Teller favored western development and the privatization of the timber industry.

The complaints of fraud wouldn't go away. In 1883, Commissioner Sparks of the GLO pronounced his concern that the act operated "simply to promote the premature destruction of forests." He prudently exerted his influence as GLO Commissioner to establish a firmer control over the administration of the public domain:

> "I found that the magnificent estate of the nation in its public lands had been to a wide extent wasted under defective and improvident laws, and through a laxity of public administration astonishing in business sense if not culpable in recklessness of official responsibility."[17]

The Butte Miner newspaper typified Commissioner Sparks as "the kind of a man who could tear down Solomon's temple in twelve hours, and who could not build a decent pigpen in twelve years."[18] Nonetheless, he continued to rail about the vicious effects of the Timber and Stone Act in his Annual Reports, seeking its repeal.

In 1884, GLO Commissioner N. C. McFarland reported to Secretary Schurz's successor, Secretary Kirkwood, that:

> ... the result ... is the transfer ... in bulk, to a few large operators. The preventive measure's at the command of this office have proven wholly inadequate to counteract this result. The requirements of the law are slight and easily evaded, and evidence of fraudulent proceedings rest so much within the knowledge of interested parties that specific testimony can rarely be obtained.[19]

Don't Deprive Citizens of Timber for Cradles!

In 1890, Senator W. F. Sanders of Montana, countering the claims of concentration of timberlands in a few large operators, described the needs of the settlers in his region for wood to:

> ... make in to cradles to rock the children, shingles and roofs to cover the heads of the citizens, coffins in which to bury the dead and lumber in various forms which ... civilized man designated as wise and useful.[20]

In 1897, Representative Hartman from Montana angrily supported his constituents' rights to take timber:

> I defy the gentleman/Representative Bartlett of New York to name any timber ring that is in any way back of the effort which is being put forth by our people to prevent the settlers from being deprived of the right to take timber ... and to enable miners to run their tunnels ...[21]

In 1909, Special Agent of the GLO, H.H. Schwartz, under Secretary Bliss, stated officially that the Timber and Stone Act:

> ***Has resulted in the sale of over 12,000,000 acres of valuable timberlands, of which fully 10,000,000 were transferred to corporate or individual timberland investors by the entrymen.*** The lands brought to the people or general government a gross sum of $30,000,000. At the date of sale they were reasonably worth $240,000,000. The profit of over $200,000,000 went not to the needy settler engaged in subduing the wilderness, but to the wealthy investors. Not over a fractional part of 1 per cent of the timber purchased from the United States under this act is held, consumed, or even cut by the men and women who made the entries. (Emphasis added).[22]

Committing Fraud under Timber and Stone Act

Congress had not enacted legislation for the lumber industry to directly acquire forest tracts extensive enough for large-scale, longtime production of lumber for the general market. So, lumber companies would hire "dummy" entrymen to file an application for land under the Timber and Stone Act with the applicable field office of the General Land Office which was responsible for receiving and processing applications for title to public land. The lumber companies would pay all the entrymen's fees and expenses, plus add compensation for the assignment of their patents to them.

Land that was deemed "unfit for farming" was sold to those who might want to log timber and mine stone. Speculators used the Timber and Stone Act to get great expanses declared "unfit for farming," allowing them to increase their land holdings at minimal expense. Assignments could be made without regulatory oversight.

Prosecuting Violations of Timber and Stone Act Impossible

Herbert Knox Smith, the Commissioner of Corporations, noted the difficulty of prosecuting violations of the Timber and Stone Act—a law with "evil" effect:[23]

> The criminal prosecution of timber frauds under this law, and of other public-land frauds as well, has been greatly hindered and in many cases prevented by the statute of limitations (U. S. Comp. Stat. ch. 19), which provides that a prosecution for criminal offenses against the United States (other than certain excepted crimes) is barred after a lapse of three years. As to recovery of the lands themselves, fraudulent entries may be canceled by the Interior Department at any time prior to patent. After patent has issued, any suit by the United States to annul or cancel it and recover the lands must be brought within six years of the date of the patent. (Act of Mar. 3, 1891, 26 Stat. 1099.)[24]

For lawsuits, violations were almost impossible to prove, given the lack of written evidence. In *United States v. Clark*, 129 F. 241 (D. Mont. 1904), 138 F. 294 (9th Cir. 1905), aff'd, 200 U.S. 601 (1906), the Department of Justice (DOJ) tried to prosecute Montana violations supported by circumstantial evidence, the pattern of behavior by certain individuals and companies, and the "concert of action engineered by R.W. Cobban." The government charged that R. W. Cobban, subsequent to January 1, 1898, began procuring titles to lands obtained under the provisions of the Timber and Stone Act.

To rapidly accumulate the land, Cobban signed an agreement with C. L. Griswold on May 22, 1899, to secure land according to the provisions of the Timber and Stone Act. John B. Gatlin, a former official of the Missoula Land Office, also joined the enterprise. The government charged that these three individuals selected the timberland to be filed upon and secured 50 men and women to file upon the land. Cobban and his associates paid all the filing fees and paid the individuals who filed on the land $100 each. Cobban then sold the patents to W.A. Clark for $217,571.25.

The U.S. General Land Office was required to determine the validity of claims filed under the Stone and Timber Act prior to issuing a patent to the land. To avoid uncertainty, after issuing the patent and selling the land to an innocent purchaser, a court of equity would not set it aside. Clark's warranty deeds from Cobban were dated before the issuance of the actual patents to Cobban. Thereafter, the GLO did issue patents.

Clark was an industrial magnate in Montana. He established the Western Land Company and secured a monopoly on area electricity. He had an interest in the dam, the electric company, the streetcar, the sawmill, and the flour mill in the Bonner area of Montana. The electric mill could produce 130,000 board feet daily. Lumber was shipped to Chicago, Kansas City, St. Louis, New York, and Boston.

In 1882, Clark joined forces with Andrew Hammond and others to form the Montana Improvement Company to exploit the timber resources of western Montana. He testified "that he had no information or knowledge of any fact or facts which would lead him to believe that the title to any of the lands was in question, and that he had no notice, either actual or constructive, of any fraud on the part of his grantor, or of any other person whomsoever." 138 F. 294, 297 (9th Cir. 1905). Cobban's fraud in obtaining the 82 patents he sold to Clark for consideration could not be attributed to Clark, absent actual notice of the fraud.

The Ninth Circuit upheld Clark's position that he was "at the time of the respective purchases, an innocent purchaser of the said respective parcels of land, and for a valuable consideration." 138 F. 294, 297 (9th Cir. 1905).

In reviewing the case, which the government appealed to the U.S. Supreme Court, the Court first considered that "except in a very clear case where both courts have concurred, we do not disturb their findings of fact." 200 U.S. 601, 608 (1906). The Supreme Court stated that Clark "was not bound to hunt for grounds of doubt." 200 U.S. 601, 609 (1906). It affirmed the previous rulings that Clark was an innocent purchaser.

In other cases, the government was unable to give specific details concerning individual depredations or the persons involved because the operations were concealed within the various corporations formed to supervise the enterprises.

Nationally, the federal land fraud investigations they initiated indicted 1,021 people in 22 states resulting in 126 convictions. Some small fish were caught but the big fish eluded capture. The focus was not on preventing illegal timber harvests, but rather merely on ensuring the government received the value of the trees illegally cut.

Major Crimes Act of 1885

Under the Major Crimes Act of 1885, the federal government assumed jurisdiction over serious crimes committed by Indians on their own land. The Major Crimes Act was a part of the Indian Appropriations Act of 1885, 23 Stat. 385 (1885).

General Allotment Act

The General Allotment Act or Dawes Act of 1887, 24 Stat. 388-91, divided Indian tribal land into individual allotments, forcing Indians into private property ownership. Up until this time the reservations had been held communally by all members of the tribe(s) living on the reservation. The alleged rationale for the GAA was that it would assimilate Indians into the mainstream of U.S. society by encouraging farming and agriculture.

A transition to farming would lessen the amount of land needed by Indians such that it would justify reducing their land base. Alternatively, there was no need for a separate land base for Indians assimilated into the general society.

In October 1868, General Sheridan wrote to General Sherman that their best hope to control the Indians is to "make them poor by the destruction of their stock, and then settle them on the lands allotted to them."[25]

Commissioner Cato Sells in 1915 stated the truth about the majority of allotments:

> *I know of many allotments depending entirely upon which an Indian family would starve to death* and where no white family could be induced to attempt to make a living, and yet under these circumstances *an unsuccessful Indian farm is apt to be declared a failure*. There are thousands of acres of land on Indian reservations where 100 hundred acres would not feed a rabbit. (Emphasis added).[26]

The GAA resulted in a loss of more than 90 million acres, or nearly two thirds of tribal land across the U.S. To this day, large portions of many reservations are owned by non-tribal members.

1888 Legislation Prohibiting Trespass Upon Indian Reservations To Steal Timber

The laws the DOI urged for amendment to include tribal lands were the General Trespass Law of March 3, 1875 (18 Stat. 481) and Section 5388 of the Revised Statutes (1878), which only applied to timber on military reserves or other branches of the government. In 1888, Congress finally amended Section 5388 to cover timber trespass "Upon Any Indian Reservation, Or Lands Belonging To Or Occupied By Any Tribe Of Indians Under Authority Of The United States."

Indian Appropriations Act Of 1889

The Indian Appropriations Act of 1889, 25 Stat. 980, opened "unassigned" lands in Oklahoma to white settlers. Entering upon or occupying said lands before 12 o'clock noon on April 22, 1889, was prohibited. Any person violating this provision would be precluded from entering any of said lands or acquiring any rights thereto.[27] President Harrison's Proclamation 288 – Opening To Settlement Certain Lands In The Indian Territory, March 23, 1889, resulted in the "Land Rush" in Oklahoma Territory.

1891 Timber Act, 26 Stat. 1093, Free Use of Timber on Mineral and Nonmineral Public Lands

On March 3, 1891, the lumber interests finally secured Congressional passage of what they considered the first realistic timber cutting legislation. This was the 1891 Timber Act, allowing the free use of timber on mineral and nonmineral public lands.

The Act for the Protection of the People of Indian Territory, 30 Stat. 495 (1898) (aka Curtis Act) mandated the allotment of land in severalty of the Five Civilized Tribes and expanded federal authority over the tribes in Indian Territory.

Notes
Primacy of Opening U.S. to "Settlement and Civilized Habitation"

1. Report of the Commissioner of the General Land Office to the Secretary of the Interior. United States. U.S. Government Printing Office, 1878, p. 71.
2. Gerhart, Eugene C. Quote It! Memorable Legal Quotations: Data, Epigrams, Wit and Wisdom from Legal and Literary Sources. William S. Hein & Company, 1987: 499.
3. Black, Henry Campbell, et al. Black's Law Dictionary. Vol. 196. St. Paul, MN: West Group, 1999.
4. *Johnson v. M'Intosh*, 21 U.S. 543 (1823).
5. Northwest Ordinance of 1787, Officially titled "An Ordinance for the Government of the Territory of the United States North-West of the River Ohio."
6. Id.
7. Bureau of Indian Affairs, Mission Statement, BIA, https://www.bia.gov/bia (accessed online July 22, 2022).

8. President Andrew Jackson's Message to Congress "On Indian Removal," December 6, 1830; Records of the United States Senate, 1789–1990; Record Group 46; National Archives.
9. Andrew Jackson to James Monroe, March 4, 1817, Jackson Papers, 4: 93-98.
10. Alfred Balch to Andrew Jackson, January 8, 1830; Andrew Jackson Papers: Series 1, General Correspondence and Related Items, 1775–1885 (15,697).
11. "An Act to provide for an exchange of lands with the Indians residing in any of the states or territories, and for their removal west of the river Mississippi," 4 Stat. 411.
12. Sheridan Papers, 1868.
13. Secretary of War, Annual Report for 1867, 36.
14. Secretary of War, Annual Report for 1880, 4.
15. Annual Report of the Department of the Interior. U.S. Government Printing Office, 1878, p. XIII.
16. Ibid., p. XIV.
17. United States. Report of the Commissioner of the General Land Office to the Secretary of the Interior. United States. U.S. Government Printing Office, 1885, p. 3.
18. The Butte Miner, Dec. 2, 1885.
19. Bulletin, Issue 2, United States Forest Service. U.S. Government Printing Office, 1884, pp. 17-21; U.S., Interior Department, Annual Report of the Secretary of the Interior, 1884, Vol. I, p. 8.
20. Sanders United States Congressional Record, 51st Congress, 1st session, 1890, XVI, Part V, 10087.
21. Hartman United States Congressional Record, 54th Congress, 2nd session, 1897, XIII, Part 3, 970.
22. Van Hise, Charles Richard. The Conservation of Natural Resources in the United States. Macmillan, 1910, pp. 285-286.
23. United States. Bureau of Corporations. Letter to Department of Commerce and Labor from Herbert Knox Smith, Commissioner of Corporations, February 13, 1911.
24. United States. Bureau of Corporations. The Lumber Industry: Standing Timber, Volume 1 of The Lumber Industry, United States. US Government Printing Office, 1913, p. 263.
25. Secretary of War, Annual Report for 1878, VI. "W.T. Sherman to P.H. Sheridan, October 15th 1868," October 15, 1868, Container 75, Reel 80, Philip Henry Sheridan Papers, Library of Congress.
26. Report of the Commissioner of Indian Affairs, Office of Indian Affairs, United States. U.S. Government Printing Office, 1915, p. 62.

27. President Harrison's Proclamation 288 – Opening to Settlement Certain Lands in the Indian Territory, March 23, 1889, resulted in the "land rush" in Oklahoma Territory. https://www.presidency.ucsb.edu/documents/proclamation-288-opening-settlement-certain-lands-the-indian-territory (accessed online July 21, 2022).

CHAPTER 3: CONVERTING FORESTS INTO DOLLARS – GREEN GOLD

Resource extraction in the U. S. was fundamentally about rapid exploitation. "Taking the best and leaving the rest" is known as high grading. It is the selective extraction of only the most valuable part of the resource. It ignores the optimal production of the resource, often destroying its longevity. It also dismisses any concern for the surrounding environment, which could lead to the endangerment and destruction of species and ecosystems. The government refused to renounce the huge economic payoff by regulating the industry. After massive deforestation in the Great Lakes region and threatened in the Pacific Northwest, the federal government initiated forest management practices and procedures.

Business Start-Up

As a logging primer, this is a very brief summary of logging processes and business terminology.

Planning, organizing, developing procedures, budgeting, staffing, acquiring necessary resources, managing and critiquing governed the management process.

Timber Scouts and Surveys

Logging companies used timber scouts (aka timber cruisers) to locate areas for logging and to estimate the lumber available in board feet and water access for transportation. Timber scouts weren't employees of the company, but independent contractors with no loyalty to any one company. Their job was only to scout for timber, surveil a region, and then sell their intelligence, their knowledge to the highest bidder. Well-aware of going rates for timber and timberlands, they knew which mills were buying timber and at what prices. Scouts still exist today in every natural resource extractive industry. For example, Minnesota historian William Folwell reports:

Cruisers of lumber companies also made their examinations and notes. "As there were still standing on White Earth reservation some three hundred million feet of pine, as roughly estimated, it was worth their while."[1]

These lumber companies could then pay for the survey of these specific tracts of land. This reduced costs by narrowing the focus to a more limited area.

Timber Appraisals

Companies independently appraised the amount and value of timber on their own, without relying on government examinations.

They retained experienced, conscientious examiners (1) familiar with the value of various species of timber, such as white pine, Norway pine, red cedar, and birch; (2) capable of estimating the amount of timber by acreage and board feet; (3) knowledgeable about stand composition and value, and the terrain and difficulties associated with timbering in various environments; (4) guaranteeing independent, thorough, on-the-ground review of each tract in its entirety; (5) willing to work independently, fully examining each tract regardless of difficulty of terrain, accurately reporting on species, size, volume, and quality of timber with actual examination versus guessing, avoiding extrapolation of the amount and quality of timber on a tract by examining a portion without independent on-the-ground review of the full tract; and (6) avoiding lax behavior reflecting negatively on the company.

These independent appraisals allowed companies to review government examinations and determine where they may have under-or-over-estimated the amount of timber or failed to accurately report whether land was agricultural or timber.

Purchases or Leases of Timberlands

Many businesses used special employees called landmen to interact and negotiate with landowners to lease or purchase lands for timber extraction. This included public domain lands, Indian lands, and private lands. After determining ownership, surface accessibility, and the threshold amount of acreage required for acquisition and procuring the land's appraisal information, landmen negotiated for timberland ownership or lease on behalf of their employers.

A company bought or leased acreage based on financial analysis. Some important considerations were the market sales price of the timber, the taxation rates for land, whether the land was acquired for speculation or lumbering, and the long-term profitability of the operation.

For a purchase of timberland, the method of sales was important. For Indian lands, the government used auctions, sealed bids, or private negotiated sales. Private negotiated sales were favored.

> "Everybody ... knows," said one member, "that *wherever great bodies of these lands are thus offered at public sale at a fixed minimum price not one acre in a thousand is ever sold at public sale if thereafter the lands are to be subject to private entry... Gentlemen living in public land States know what this means."* (Emphasis added).[2]

The negotiations for leasing timber rights, surface use, and/or rights-of-way include (1) amounts for bonus, rentals, and royalties; and (2) logging obligations, timing, and severability of acreage logged if operations are not conducted across the leased acreage, etc. Ongoing lease maintenance is key.

When considering lumber sales, take-or-pay contracts were used to require a lessee to log a certain quantity of timber within a set time or pay as if logged. Railroad contracts might include a lower price for timber for laying track, or connecting to remote sites; and/or (2) access to a set amount of timber. They could also include a lower transport price.

Knowledge of lender and banking opportunities, competitors, and the possibility of entering into trades or joint ventures or operating agreements was important to minimize costs. Contracts stipulated that parties resolve disputes early on.

A company's appraisal information was key in determining what to bid on in advance of any auctions or sealed bids or private sales. As antitrust regulation was not in effect during this era and criminal investigation for fraud limited and difficult to prove, companies could risk collusion on bidding or risk conspiring on limiting competition by reducing the number of bidders or bribing key players.

Companies could decide how to use straw bids and straw buyers. A straw bid is a worthless bid—a bid for a contract the bidder does not plan to fulfill. It is used to distract from the real acreage the buyer is interested in buying, creates a feigned interest, and may result in higher bidding for that tract by other parties. A straw buyer is a person who purchases on behalf of another person so the real buyer is not disclosed. This may help to lower a price because the real buyer's financial backing is unknown. Companies took advantage of this practice:

Formerly there was nothing to prevent contractors putting in straw bids, or withdrawing after a contract had been awarded to them, in order that a bidder at a higher price (oftentimes the same party under another name) might receive the award.[3]

On the other hand, the Indian Agent overseeing logging was merely a passive recipient of payments due Indians. The payments were then allocated to Indian timber owners. His Agency lacked the personnel, acumen, or time to engage in the timber analysis that timber companies routinely performed. After allotment, the control of many agencies were assigned to School Superintendents. A single company might buy or lease massive acreage amounts. Internal controls for verifying data, auditing, inspections, and recordkeeping were nonexistent. Due to the lack of funding and personnel, Congressional action was required to conduct investigations. These investigations were well after the fact of the transgressions and, many times, resulted in no remedial action at all.

Jerry-Building Transitory Logging Camps

Logging camps housed hundreds of men needed to perform the seasonal tasks that turned trees into dollars. After clearing the area, felled logs provided construction material.

Toting Roads and Logging Roads

Companies built toting roads to haul equipment and supplies to the logging camps. Laborers hauled in lumber, tarpaper, building supplies, equipment, and food for the crew and horses across roads laid out on high ground, avoiding swampy and low areas. The cost of these circuitous routes was justified to prevent the tote wagons with heavy loads from getting stuck in the muck of low-lying areas.

They built logging roads with sled ruts. Filling the ruts with water was next so the ruts could freeze over and create ice roads for hauling the logs. Men woke up before sunrise to go the river to load barrels of water to pour in the sled ruts. They loaded logs onto sleighs pulled by oxen, or preferably by horses, over the frozen rutted roads to an area near a water transportation source. The logs were stored there until spring rivers thawed.

Lumbering

Logging was seasonal. In winter, sap dropped down to the tree roots, leaving less sap to gum up saws. Historian Walter O'Meara provides an eloquent and fitting description of felling a tree:

Comes the undercutter with his beautiful, double-bitted ax. His calculating eye runs to the upper branches of a century-old pine; he notes its lean, its field of clearance; he checks the wind's direction. Then, at precisely the proper point, his ax sinks into the rough, clean, cork-like bark. The undercutter's strokes have a deadly, professional accuracy; the kerf left by his blade is as smooth as paint; the chips that fly out upon the snow are as large as a man's hand, and cleanly curved. The pine is quickly and deeply notched on the side toward which it is to fall, and the undercutter, pausing for a chew of tobacco, gives over to the sawyers.

The big crosscut saw, six feet long, goes to work on the opposite side of the trunk, at a point several inches above the lowest part of the undercut. It clangs rhythmically as the mittened hands of the sawyers draw it back and forth. At each pull of the saw the teeth bite through half a dozen annual rings-half a dozen years of growing ... Presently the great hand of steel is buried in the tree; when it is completely out of sight, the sawyers drive steel wedges into the kerf. One of them takes from his hip pocket a whiskey flask encased in sheet metal; it contains kerosene which the sawyer pours on the saw to dissolve the pitch, the oozing life-blood of the pine. They resume their sawing, and at the end of each long, steady stroke their breath rises in a little white cloud on the frosty air ...

Suddenly comes the warning cr-r-ack!—sharp and crisp, like the report of a rifle. A few more strokes of the saw, and then a rending, tearing sound; the death rattle of the great tree. "Timber-r-r-r!" The traditional cry, half in warning, half in triumph, rings thinly through the woods; and the sawyers, looking to their footing, step away from danger, while all in the direction of the tree's fall scurry for safety. The pine, however, does not come down at once; it hesitates, trembles, seems to resist the wordless indignity it is about to suffer.

Slowly, very slowly at first, the great trunk begins to totter, to lean a little in the direction that the under-cutter, with the first stroke of his ax, determined it should fall. Then faster, as fibers snap and rend. The branches moan their protest as they sweep downward through the high air; the moan grows now to a whistle-to a shriek-as the big green-top gathers speed. The crash, of course, is tremendous, as the great pine comes to earth in clouds of snow and showers of broken twigs and branches. But the litter settles down, the branches of the fallen tree wave up and down for a little while, from the impact of the fall; then everything is still again, and the swamper comes to do his work.[4]

The swamper removes the brush from the fallen pine and then the undercutter returns, this time to mark the cuts for logs. The marking norm for white pine is 16-foot lengths. Branding the logs with the owner's mark (similar to a cattle brand) establishes ownership of each of the thousands of logs transported to sawmills.

Buckers cut the logs to size (18 feet long) for transport. Cut logs then go to the skidders. Skidders remove the bark from one side of a log making it easier to skid the log over the ice with the smooth side down. Large diameter wagon wheels, called Big Wheels (11 feet in diameter), made skidding logs from the woods on mud roads easier. Horse-drawn wagons haul the logs to a landing site.

During all the rugged stages of the logging process, loss of timber during logging was common. The shrinkage could easily be up to 50%.

After the logs arrived at the landing site, laborers gathered the cut logs in an area ready for spring transport. Sometimes floods or high rivers simply lifted the logs and carried them downstream. Other times log handlers, also called river hogs, pushed the logs or rode them into and down the river.

The glamour of the river hog job was due to the brutal and dangerous work in guiding logs. Greasing their legs up to the waistline with lard as protection against the icy rivers helped, but enduring wet and cold was the norm. Log handling was a killer job. If a man fell from a log and was caught beneath a floating wooden mass, he could easily die. Injuries were common and went with the job. The river hog's mission—avoid a log jam.

Unfortunately, on June 13, 1886, a log jam developed in the St. Croix River close to Taylor Falls, Minnesota and St. Croix Falls, Wisconsin. It took hundreds of men six weeks to clear the jam, eventually using steamboats and dynamite.

Introduction of Steam Engine

Up to the 1880s, the timber industry was homogenous in production—the same processes used in the Northeast had been transferred to the Great Lakes Region and would settle into the Pacific Northwest. For example, Minnesota imported Northeastern capital along with experienced loggers to train its work force. Science and invention lagged in making the backbreaking, dangerous work safer and easier. Injuries, maiming, and deaths continued. This was about to change.

John Dolbeer's invention had an enormous impact. In 1881, he developed a small, high-pressure steam engine to turn a rope spool that could reel in even the largest trees with ease. The steam engine was called a steam donkey and the operator a donkeyman. Dolbeer's steam engines significantly reduced manual labor.

In order to operate the donkey, three men, a horse and a boy were needed. The line was first attached to a horse and pulled through the forest to the site of a freshly fallen log. A choker setter was responsible for attaching the line to the fallen tree, a spool tender would use a short stick to guide the line back on the spool, and the donkey puncher operated the steam engine throughout the process. The boy, referred to as a "whistle punk," operated a communication wire which would sound a steam whistle when the choker was properly set on the log, signaling the donkey puncher and spool tender to begin pulling it in.[5]

In 1900, Oregon camps contained 35 steam donkeys. Washington led the way with 293 donkeys and California had 61, mostly in the redwood belt. Because of the size of the trees, the well-capitalized redwood industry had largely shifted to steam logging, employing both donkeys and locomotives.

Another invention, a Walking Dudley, was a steam engine mounted on a flat car to move logs—a power car on rails. It straddled a log flume, pushing the logs to start their journey (aiding the force of gravity) as they shot down the long chute into a river to begin their float to a sawmill.

River rafting was another way to move logs where schooners towed rafts laden with logs. Congress unsuccessfully tried to ban rafting due to safety concerns when the rafts broke free.

Sawmills – Transforming Logs into Merchantable Lumber

The business of sawmills alongside rivers or lakes depended on transforming the logs into merchantable lumber.

Logging technological improvements brought circular saws and steam power to mills. Steam power now made it possible to build sawmills wherever needed, not just on a river or stream that required hydropower.

Water Transportation's Huge Role in Logging Industry

Steamboats on the Mississippi River carried lumber and agricultural products to St. Paul, Minneapolis, and Duluth sawmills for manufacturing. Products manufactured included pulp, paper, lumber, paperboard, window and door components, cabinets and cabinet parts, wood furniture, pallets, and crating.

Sailing schooners carried the products on the Pacific coast. By 1900, oil burning steam schooners came into play. Steam schooners had a lumber capacity of 325,000 board feet. Soon large lumber vessels followed with a capacity of 1.5 million board feet. Ocean rafting was another dangerous rafting practice similar to river rafting. Yet Congress failed in its attempts to ban rafting.

The increasing number of settlements pushed the demand for improved transportation and connection between cities and waterways. Behind each plan for a canal or a harbor was a town and its promoters. Shipping timber and agricultural products from lake ports and receiving goods in return offered big financial rewards to settlers, businessmen, and promoters.

Waterways Boost Production of Timber

Connecting waterways allowed the logging industry to transport lumber to expanded markets. The next table shows the purpose of different waterways and the problems resulting from some efforts.

Waterways Support Expansion of Logging Industry			
Year	Waterway	Purpose	Problems
1825	Erie Canal	Linking Lake Erie with Hudson River & Atlantic Ocean	
1829	Welland Canal	Bypass Niagara Falls between Lake Erie and Lake Ontario	
1853	Sault Ste. Marie Locks	Bypass rapids between Lake Superior and Lake Huron	
1882	Recommended Dams at Lake Wiinibiigoshish, Leech Lake and Pokegama Falls	Control Mississippi River	Dams destroy sustenance - rice fields, cranberry marshes, meadows, and sugar bushes
1885	Dams at Lake Wiinibiigoshish, Leech Lake and Pokegama Falls to control Mississippi River completed.	Control Mississippi River	Damages Owed; Proposed Amounts: $15,466.90; $10,000 for property destroyed, annual appropriation of $26,800; Rice Commission $150,000 plus 5% interest plus $1.25/acre taken; DOI $150,000; 1972 Lawsuit filed; 1985 - out of court settlement $3,390,288
1887	Dam on Pine River completed.	Control Mississippi River	
1900	Chicago Ship Canal	Connect Lake Michigan to Illinois R., Mississippi R., and Gulf of Mexico	
1919	Welland Canal deepened	Better access to Great Lakes	
1959	St. Lawrence Seaway	Ships enter Great Lakes from Atlantic	

Railroads

Railroads made it easier to transport logs. Railroads could reach areas that rivers and streams couldn't. Logging companies laid tracks for customized trains to carry logs to their destinations. These logging railroads had to bridge steep gullies, cross tidal flats, or snake up steep mountainsides. Consequently, these logging railroads required substantial capital investments in bridges, trestles, and pilings. Lumber companies no longer had to rely on the unpredictable flow of rivers for transporting logs. Industrialization made logging easier and faster and cheaper.

Clearing Large Areas – Slash and Burn

After the Civil War, the logging industry used slash and burn techniques to facilitate clearing large areas. Trees were cut and raked into an area and burned. While slash burning reduced the immediate fire danger, it hindered regeneration. Because these fires burned so hot—up to 1,841 degrees Farenheit (°F)—they eliminated the protective duff layer and future sources of organic matter. The blackened soil absorbed sunlight and produced surface temperatures of 140°F when the air temperature reached 85°F, killing off 45 percent of Douglas fir seedlings that had managed to find their way into the clear cut.

Not only did these extremely hot slash fires eliminate 89 percent of the soil's organic matter, they also changed the soil pH from acidic to alkaline, and increased nitrogen and other plant nutrients. The excess nutrients favored rapid colonization by pioneer species, such as alder, and caused Douglas fir seedlings to develop large crowns and shallow root systems, making them susceptible to drought.

Technological Advances

Starting in 1900, logging became mechanized, machinery-dependent, and faster. The steam engine resulted in radical innovations rather than incremental changes. It transformed every phase of the industry. The most difficult, time-consuming, physically intensive, manpower-dominated stages were streamlined. Logging became possible year-round instead of dependent on nature's variable seasonal changes. Sawmills could operate 24/7.

High Lead Logging

High lead logging was one of the dangerous advances. The ropes, manpower, and oxen used in the backbreaking task of gathering and lifting felled trees from the ground up onto a sleigh were replaced with steel cables and engines. Imagine replacing the former method of logs secured by ropes and hauled by oxen-or horse-drawn wagons with 100-ton logs on cables flying at breakneck speed through the air.

One observer described a high lead operation as:

> [A] somewhat disconcerting maze of large and small cables running through the air in every direction, and the ground covered with stationary engines, pumps, wood-bucking power saws, steel rails, switches, locomotives, cars, telephones, humidity gauges, movable power plants, and traveling machine shops. It is, in short, a gigantic factory without a roof.[6]

Cables secured to the trees allowed lumbermen to haul logs out of the forest, free of obstructions on the ground. High lead logging required total clear-cutting to give room to yank logs into the air and move them across the landscape unimpeded. Dragging logs to a central point prevented natural regeneration as saplings were uprooted and the soil scrapped clean. Large clear-cuts with no trees remaining produced the infamous logging deserts, a seemingly endless landscape of stumps where nothing could grow.

Highball Logging

In the 1950s, S.L. Wixson and John H. Trisdale of Redding, California, developed highball logging to clear areas.

The big 4-to-5-foot tall stumps the loggers left when they cleared all the old growth trees out of the forest were deeply rooted and blocked the cables' path. The solution was simple and awesome. Wixson and Trisdale built an eight-foot diameter steel ball. A strong axle went straight through the ball and on either end connected it to the tractors pulling it through the forest. The ball itself was no flyweight. All that steel added up to a 10,000-pound curb weight. If the ball hit an object it couldn't roll over, the bulldozer drivers could use the winches on their machines to shift the ball left or right. "There were days on relatively flat ground where a single team of two tractors and one ball could clear over 200 acres before the sun went down."[7]

Two other technological advances were coming up. As timber became scarce, underwater recovery of trees became more advanced. Much later, around the middle of the 20th century, using helicopters to haul felled trees was another cost-saver, allowing access to difficult areas to reach.

Notes

1. Folwell, William Watts. *A History of Minnesota*. St. Paul: Minnesota Historical Society Press, revised edition 1961, p. 267.

2. United States Congressional Record, 50th Congress. 2nd Session (1888), p. 397.

3. United States. Office of Indian Affairs. *Annual Report of the Commissioner of Indian Affairs, The Work of the Purchasing Committee of the Board of Indian Commissioners, Methods of Conducting Business in Indian Office*. US Government Printing Office, 1878, p. LXV.

4. O'Meara, Walter. *The Trees Went Forth*. NY: Little and Ives, 1947, pp. 121-123.

5. http://www.clarkemuseum.org/qr-steam-donkey.html (accessed March 31, 2022).

6. Gordon, Gregory Llewellyn, "Money Does Grow on Trees: A. B. Hammond and the Age of the Lumber Baron" (2010), p. 128. Graduate Student Theses, Dissertations, & Professional Papers. 292. https://scholarworks.umt.edu/etd/676 (accessed March 24, 2022).

7. https://bangshift.com/general-news/bulldozers-and-steel-balls-bangshift-greatness-circa-1950 (accessed March 31, 2022).

CHAPTER 4: TIMBER MONOPOLY

Business Formation

The late 19th century marked the beginning of the rise of corporations as a new economic order. Businesses could incorporate and sell shares to investors to raise capital, with the payback to investors of dividends or not. This filtered into the logging and railroad industries. Northern Pacific Railroad Company was the first limited liability company in the U.S. The liability of the investors was limited to the amount of their investment. In the Great Merger Movement from 1895 to 1904, consolidations absorbed 1,800 firms. More and more people worked for wages, supervised by a managerial class, in a hierarchically structured business organization. Risk-taking was the key to success.

Corporate Strategies for Land Acquisition

Corporations had many ways to acquire public domain lands. Fur trade companies that had collapsed could now purchase choice land for resale to settlers using funds from debt payments secured through Indian treaties. Railroads sold land in the towns at their stations. Land speculation companies formed to secure land from the government and from failed homesteaders.

Company Growth Strategies—Vertical Integration vs. Horizontal Integration

As a deliberate, competitive business strategy, vertical integration allowed a company to streamline its operations based on its ownership of the various stages of the production process, rather than relying on external contractors or suppliers. In a survival of the fittest mode, horizontal integration allowed a company to acquire other companies in the same business sector. Small or underperforming companies were forced to sell to a larger company consolidating its competitive position.

Upstream and Midstream Timber Businesses

Upstream businesses engaged in the production of timber alone. Midstream timber businesses engaged in timber and in the next stage of production—milling and the ownership of sawmills. Their ownership of the feeder stock, the timber, allowed them to reduce their input costs. Milling had a thin profit margin, so companies pushed for industry consolidation. To capture part of the growing local housing construction market, a company would often build a sash and door factory next to its mill.

Acquiring Interests in Transportation Networks

To avoid being held hostage to transportation access or rates, businesses would invest in railroad branches and river transport for cargo. Recognizing the need for access to the Atlantic and Pacific, the timber industry lobbied for and invested in canals, harbors, reservoirs, and lock sections on rivers.

Downstream Timber Businesses

Moving even further downstream in the business, companies built lumber yards in major cities. A business controlling several lumber yards was known as a line yard, because their size usually allowed them to offer a diversified product line. Manufacturing businesses, such as the mass production of furniture, flourished in the Great Lakes region. Grand Rapids and Duluth, with water transportation access, were hubs for furniture and other wood manufacturing. Grand Rapids bore the iconic "Furniture City" nickname. Selling and distributing products are part of the downstream activities of the timber and other industries.

Timber Industry Associations

Timber companies formed an association of member companies to represent them and to lobby for their interests. Without any limiting anti-trust laws at the time, they shared information, determined when to restrict sales to keep prices high, and divided output among each producer.

Increasing Scale of Timber Production

The individual or family ownership of single sawmills, with sales to wholesalers, changed towards the end of the nineteenth century. As timber cutting reduced the accessible trees near settlements, the scale of operations increased, requiring larger logging crews to travel to more remote regions for six months or longer. Thus began the shift from independent owners toward heavily capitalized producers with men working for wages rather than for a share in the family business. Large industrialists purchased their own timberlands and owned multiple mills. Money flowed and the disparity of wealth grew.

Lumber Barons

Lumber barons flourished as a result of their access to capital. Conglomerates of companies were common to minimize business risk. Each business in the conglomerate performed in a different sector of the business, diversifying the participation of member companies.

The low price for the acquisition of timberland in the public domain or by lease from Indian tribes made it possible to procure enough timber acreage for logging, the foundation for growing a business (raw material). Ownership of the extractive resource could lead to owning sawmills (the means of production). Loggers and mill workers (the labor force), requiring limited expertise, were readily available for seasonal employment. Building localized railroads into internal forest areas made it possible to increase production and ease transportation. Moving to urban areas where manufacturing, wholesale, and retail lumber opportunities were possible was part of the downstream growth of a company with market power (the means of distribution).

Through joint ventures, partnerships, mergers, interlocking directorates, and subsidiaries, many conglomerates engaged in nearly every possible industry, including banking, railroads, shipping lines, lumbering, fishing and canning, livestock, mining, real estate, merchandising, and land speculation. Family income was distributed between members and invested. For example, the holdings of the Weyerhaeuser Timber Company included (but not limited to) not only its timber, but the timber of its direct subsidiaries—the Clarke County Timber Company, the Weyerhaeuser Land Company, the Pohegama Sugar Pine Lumber Company and the Pelton-Reid Sugar Pine Company.

Only the well-capitalized could survive in a boom-and-bust extractive, resource-based economy. Companies had to withstand the expansion, contraction, peaks, and troughs. A downturn was measured by the depth, the diffusion (spread across industries), and the duration. An upturn was measured by how pronounced, pervasive, and persistent it was expected to be.

In Minnesota, lumber barons invested millions in timber claims between 1874 and 1897. By investing in large acreage purchases, they could use economies of scale to minimize their operational costs. These lumber barons included James J. Hill, Thomas Barlow Walker, John S. and Charles Pillsbury, Charles Ruggles, Isaac Staples, Charles Hackley, and Friedrich Weyerhaeuser.

Michigan's lumber barons, Charles Hackley, William Montague Ferry, Wellington R. Burt and Charles Mears, were relatively obscure from a national perspective.

A few companies dominated the Wisconsin lumber industry. By 1890, Frank Stout, co-founder of the Knapp-Stout Lumber Company, of Menomonie, Wisconsin, was cutting more than 90,000,000 feet of lumber a year. Friedrich Weyerhaeuser's offer to buy-out Knapp-Stout for $7.5 million in the 1880s was rejected. Reflecting the rapid deforestation of Wisconsin, the company was dissolved in 1904.

Orrin H. Ingram of Massachusetts, founder of The Empire Lumber Company of Eau Claire, Wisconsin, reflected the common industry's interlocking business interests. Ingram was at one time director of the Chippewa Lumber and Boom Company, president of the Rice Lake Lumber Company, president of the Empire Lumber Company, a heavy stockholder in the Weyerhaeuser Timber Company, and president of the Eau Claire National Bank and Eau Claire Water Works Company.[1]

Weyerhaeuser bought extensively in the Chippewa River Valley of Wisconsin. He consolidated his business, the Mississippi River Logging Company, by merging with O. H. Ingram's firm in 1881 to form the Chippewa Logging Company. He witnessed first-hand how a seemingly inexhaustible resource could quickly be depleted.

With the high-grade lumbering of Wisconsin's white pine forests completed, they moved on. Significantly, Weyerhaeuser moved operations to Washington and Oregon, with a new business plan – timber speculation. Acquiring massive timber acreage, he realized if he held onto timberland, its price would go up. Then, he could sell part of their acreage or produce the timber to ultimately control the production and price of timber.

Andrew Jackson Pope and Frederic and William Talbot started with a steam sawmill, incorporated as the Puget Mill Company. They brought workers and supplies from their hometown, East Machias, Maine. This was a tactic used by other barons to assure a hard-working group who wanted a paycheck. They were less likely to join in the burgeoning labor unrest. By 1881, Pope and Talbot owned four sawmills, 19 cargo and lumber ships, and thousands of acres of timberlands in Maine, Oregon, California, and Washington.

George H. Emerson and A. M. Simpson owned the Northwestern Lumber Company and the Simpson Lumber Company. They operated a string of mills in Oregon and Washington. When Weyerhaeuser bought the 900,000 acres of Northern Pacific's grant land in western Washington, they hoped it was their ticket out of the sawmill business. Weyerhaeuser wanted timberland, not mills. In 1901, C. H. Jones of Tacoma, Washington, purchased a controlling interest in the Northwestern Lumber Company from the Simpson Lumber Company.

Captain William Renton, Charles S. Holmes, and John and James Campbell founded the Port Blakely Mill Company. It was known as "the largest sawmill on earth," capable of producing 1,000,000 board feet of lumber per day. The founders also invested in forest lands and sailing ships and built custom railroads to assure an adequate supply of logs for the mill. Egbert Oliver's description of the mills is incredible but insightful:

What made the mills so perturbing was the speed of the saws. When the large circular saws hit the timbers, they're "traveling at a speed of about one hundred miles an hour or near a thousand feet a second," Oliver explained, "it is of course invisible except as a motion like the wind, and as it strikes the log in a hurricane of roar and whirr and the mill shakes and the floor vibrates until as you stand there your teeth chatter."[2]

Andrew Hammond's dream of a Montana lumber empire morphed into an Oregon Territory lumber empire which crystallized into a Pacific Coast empire. Relying on his New Brunswick family who he trusted to run his businesses with him, he never left the family business structure behind.

Pacific Northwest timber investors included English syndicates as well as U.S. investors - William E. Boeing, Congressman Joseph Fordney of Michigan, R. D. Merrill, William S. Brackett, John D. Rockefeller, H. Harriman, David E. Skinner, and John W. Eddy. Behind the successful companies were trusted men such as Weyerhaeuser's George S. Long, Manager of the Coast Lumber Company, and Pope & Talbot's Cyrus Walker, Manager of the Puget Mill Company and one of Washington's leading lumbermen.

Franz Rickaby, an English professor who traveled 917 miles mostly by foot from Charlevoix, Michigan to North Dakota, collected songs of the "quickly disappearing" lumberjacks. A song from his 1926 book is fitting:

> But here's a proposition, boys; when next we meet in town,
> We'll form a combination and mow the forest down.
> We then will cash our handsome checks, we'll neither eat nor sleep,
> Nor will we buy a stitch o' clothes.[3]

Scratching Each Other's Backs

Political, social, and financial elements were intertwined. Lumber and railroad tycoons, financiers, industrialists, and politicians not only shared office buildings, but lived in the same neighborhoods. For example, the California lumber barons—the Popes, Talbots, Hoopers, and Hammonds—all lived within a six-block radius of each other. Their offices, too, were all clustered along lower California Street. San Francisco's particularly tight geography fostered formation of a close social, political, and financial network.

The synthesis between railroads and the lumber industry was manifest in the contract between Michael Foley and the Great Northern Railroad to cut white oak into lumber in Fenton County, Minnesota. Foley was catapulted into the lumber industry through his business contacts with James J. Hill, "the empire builder." When Foley's brothers Thomas, Timothy, and John moved to Minnesota, they expanded into the sawmill business and produced high-grade lumber for bridge timbers and frames for railway cars. Second-grade oak was made into railway ties and the railroad was operational by 1882. The brothers further expanded into other mill businesses.[4]

Chauncey W. Griggs bought 80,000 acres of Washington timber from the Northern Pacific Railway in 1888 and started the St. Paul and Tacoma Lumber Company. Northern Pacific agreed to build a subsidiary logging railroad into the forests below Mount Rainier to extract the timber.

In 1891, Friedrich Weyerhaeuser moved next door to railroad magnate James J. Hill in St. Paul. The two men soon became close friends. By the turn of the century, Hill needed cash to pay off bonds following his takeover of the Northern Pacific Railroad. Weyerhaeuser needed timberlands, which the Northern Pacific had in abundance as result of its federal land grant. The two tycoons struck a deal. On January 3, 1900, the Weyerhaeuser group bought 900,000 acres of Northern Pacific's grant land in western Washington for $5.4 million.

Family businesses intertwined—Charles A. Weyerhaeuser and Richard "Drew" Musser were bachelor owners of the Pine Tree Lumber Company in Little Falls, Minnesota, in 1898. Their fathers, Friedrich Weyerhaeuser and Peter Musser, along with seven other lumbermen, had organized the company in 1890. By 1893, The Little Falls Daily Transcript would write:

Weyerhauser's Pine Tree Lumber company ... is eating a big hole in the forests of northern Minnesota, as it runs steadily, rarely meeting an accident ... The Weyerhausers have secured a monopoly of the Mississippi River so far as the driving of logs is concerned.[5]

Timber Monopoly

In 1910, in response to rising lumber prices and a short supply, Congress demanded an investigation. The Bureau of Corporations, U. S. Department of Commerce and Labor, conducted a canvass of the industry and Commissioner Knox Smith reported accordingly in "The Lumber Industry, Part 1, Standing Timber." His report determined the magnitude of the problem was incredible, as revealed in these points:

> *The concentration of a dominating control of the country's standing timber was in a comparatively few enormous holdings, steadily tending towards a central control of the lumber industry.*
>
> There were vast speculative purchases and holding of timberlands far in advance of any use thereof.
>
> The commercial value of the privately owned standing timber in the United States at that time was estimated as at least six billion dollars...
>
> There was an enormous increase in the value of standing timber, with great profits to its owners. This value, by the very nature of standing timber, the holder neither created nor substantially enhances. (Emphasis added).[6]

Commissioner Knox Smith further found that the power of large timber owners was greatly augmented by a close interweaving of interests, by interlocking directorates, by ownership of subsidiary companies or of stock in other companies, and by close affiliation with other kinds of businesses, particularly those with close affiliation to transportation businesses.

Sole proprietors and small businesses were left behind by huge, capitalized corporations. Corporations often blocked in small businesses, charging exorbitant rates to cross their properties to access roadways and train stations. Pinched by the economic power wielded by these companies, small businesses sold out. The next table shows the concentration of lumber industry ownership in the primary timber states, with the bottom four lines showing the acreage covered by specific items in all regions.

Lumber Industry: Standing Timber, U.S. Bureau of Corporations, 1911	
Region	Concentration of Ownership
Pacific Northwest (CA, WA, ID, MT)	1,013 billion feet, owned by 37 holders; 3 holders have 25%
WI	96 holders have 75% of all timber; 10 holders have 24%
MN	6 holders have 54% of white and Norway pine; 75% owned by 32 holders
MI	110 holders have 66% of all timber; 12 holders have 28%
Specific Items in All Regions	Acreage Covered
Railroads	155,000,000 acres
Wagon Roads	2,987,000 acres
Canals	4,598,000 acres
River Improvements	1,405,000 acres

Tripartite Timber Concentration

In 1911, three companies—Southern Pacific Company, Weyerhaeuser Timber Company, and Northern Pacific Railway Company—and their subsidiary companies owned 238 billion feet, or nearly 11% of all privately owned timber. Another 195 holders held 48%. The Northern Pacific Railway had interests in Wisconsin, Minnesota, North Dakota, Montana, Wyoming, Idaho, Oregon, and Washington.

Timber Depletion, Lumber Prices, Lumber Exports, and Concentration of Timber Ownership

In 1920, the Forest Service issued its report, "Timber Depletion, Lumber Prices, Lumber Exports, and Concentration of Timber Ownership." Although the solution to the U.S. timber problem advocated in this 1920 report was reforestation, sufficient reforestation hasn't happened yet. Congress has lacked the will to fund and provide governmental oversight to combat the deforestation resulting from the private sector's clear-cutting practices. These are outstanding facts in the Forest Service report:[6]

> (1) That three-fifths of the original timber of the United States is gone and that we are using timber four times as fast as we are growing it. The forests remaining are so localized as greatly to reduce their national utility. The bulk of the population and manufacturing industries of the U. S. are dependent upon distant supplies of timber, as the result of the depletion of the principal forest areas east of the Great Plains.
>
> (2) That the depletion of timber is not the sole cause of the recent high prices of forest products, but is an important contributing cause whose effects will increase steadily as depletion continues.
>
> (3) That the fundamental problem is to increase the production of timber by stopping forest devastation.[7]

Titans of Industry

The titans of industry gathered to wine and dine Prince Henry of Prussia at the Waldorf Astoria in New York City on February 26, 1902. The banquet was attended by more than twelve hundred statesmen, financiers, railroad industry, miners, steel, iron industry, petroleum, timber executives, transportation executives, scientists, inventors, American Society of Mechanical Engineers laureates, telegraphic communications, ship building, tobacco, sugar refining, brewing industry, academics, military officers, and other public men.[8]

President Roosevelt, Kaiser Wilhelm and Whitelaw Reid sat beside the Prince, and on the toastmaster's left was Ambassador von Holleben. Among others at the Prince's table were Bishop Potter, Assistant Secretary Hill, Mayor Seth Low, Rear Admiral Evans, General von Plessen, Admiral von Seckendorff, Adjutant-General Corbin, Lieutenant-Governor Woodruff, Consul-General Buenz, Senators Lodge and Depew, Admiral von Tirpitz, Edward Uhl, and Admiral Count von Baudissin.

Invitees included Vanderbilt's son William, Rockefeller (and son), Morgan, Nikola Tesla with Thomas A. Edison, Adolphus Busch and Frederick Pabst, Marshall Field, James B. Duke and Ex-Postmaster-General Charles E. Smith. Newspaper media included Herman Ritter, Melville E. Stone and Whitelaw Reid.

Stock Market Crash and Great Depression

The Stock Market Crash and Great Depression affected the business world much the way an understory fire acts upon a forest, leaving the big trees unscathed while clearing out smaller ones. Those undercapitalized and carrying debt—for example, Henry Villard, a president of the Northern Pacific Railroad Company—toppled over, while men like John D. Rockefeller, Jay Gould, E.H. Harriman, and Andrew Carnegie profited from the reduced competition.

Notes

    1. Runge, C. Ford. Wisconsin's Northern Pineries: A Narrative Economic History. No. 1687-2016-137215. 2002.

    2. Beda, Steven Christopher. *Landscapes of Solidarity: Timber Workers and the Making of Place in the Pacific Northwest*, 1900–1964. Diss. 2014, p. 65.

    3. Minnesota: A History of the Land, Episode 1, https://www.youtube.com/ watch?v=Xec_3DOPY6Q (accessed February 9, 2022).

    4. https://ci.foley.mn.us/about-foley/history (accessed April 1, 2022).

    5. Cited in Cumulative Impacts: Past, Present, and Future. https://www.mnchippewatribe. org/pdf/Chapter%205_Cumulative%20Impacts_DRAFT.pdf, p. 4 (accessed March 24, 2022).

    6. United States. Bureau of Corporations. Letter to Department of Commerce and Labor from Herbert Knox Smith, Commissioner of Corpora-

tions, February 13, 1911. *The Lumber Industry: Standing Timber, Volume 1 of The Lumber Industry, United States*. US Government Printing Office, 1913, p. 263.

7. United States. Forest Service. *Timber Depletion, Lumber Prices, Lumber Exports, and Concentration of Timber Ownership: Report on Senate Resolution 311*. US Government Printing Office (1920), p. 3.

8. Partial List of Titans of Industry

The 19th century witnessed the rise of several industries that became the engines of the U.S. economy—steel, railroads, maritime, defense, powered flight, lumbering, fibers, medical, tobacco, liquor, manufacturing, oil, coal, banking, insurance, and retail department stores. Inventors (Edison, Tesla, Eilers, Hall, Kennedy, Langley, Remsen, Newcomb, Ward, etc.) and academicians, added to these engines and are included in the Titans of Industry. This is not a complete list, but it gives an idea of the incredible banquet hosted for Prince Henry of Prussia in 1902 at the Waldorf Astoria in New York City, with a vast number of premier industrialists in attendance.

Bingham, U. S. A., Military Aide
Bourne, Frederick, Singer Manufacturing Company, International Yachting
Bowditch, Henry Pickering, Dean Harvard Medical Sch.
Busch, Adolphus, Brewery
Cheney, Frank Woodbridge, Silk Manufacturing Company, Technology
Clark, Charles, Mississippi Valley Trust Company
Cogswell, William, Rensselaer Polytechnic, Mining Engineer, Entrepreneur
Converse, John H., Baldwin Locomotive Works
Corbin, Adjutant-General
Cowles, W. S., Navy
Cramp, Charles, Shipbuilding Company of Philadelphia
Crocker, Charles, Central Pacific Railroad
Duke, James B., Tobacco, Duke Univ.
Edison, Thomas A.
Eilers, Anton, Father of Smelting and Refining
Evans, Rear Admiral
Field, Marshall, Retail
Fish, Stuyvesant
Fisk, James, Wall Street Broker, Erie Railroad
Francis, David Rowland, Mayor of St. Louis, Governor of Missouri, Secretary of the Interior, Ambassador to Russia
Frick, Henry Clay, Steel Industry, Art Collector

Gary, Elbert, Founder U.S. Steel Allied with J. P. Morgan, Andrew Carnegie, and Charles M. Schwab. Gary, Indiana.
Goldberg, Ludwig Max, Berlin Exposition (World Fair), Businessman
Gould, George Jay, Son of Jason Gould, Railroad Magnate and Speculator
Hall, Charles Martin, Discovered Electrolytic Method of Producing Aluminum
Havemeyer, Henry, Industrialist, Entrepreneur, Sugar Refiner
Herriman, Edward, Railroad
Hewitt, Abram, Iron Manufacturer, Congressman, Mayor, Philanthropist
Hill, David, Assistant Secretary of State
Jesup, Morris, Banker, Am. Museum of Natural History
Kennedy, Julian, American Engineer and Inventor, Steel Industry
Langley, Samuel Pierpont, Aerodome, Powered Flight
Lincoln, Robert, Pullman Car Company
Livingston, Johnston, Wells, Fargo & Company
Macveagh, Franklin, Commercial National Bank of Chicago, Secretary of the Treasury in 1909
Markle, John Coal, Jeddo Drainage Tunnel, Pennsylvania Coal
Mather, Samuel, Cleveland's Millionaires' Row
Maxwell, John Rogers, Sr., Central Railroad of New Jersey, Atlas Portland Cement Company
Mayor Seth Low, Mayor
McCall, John, President of the New York Life Insurance Company
Mellen, Charles, Railroads
Melville, George W., Chief Bureau Steam Engineering
Michelson, President of the American Physical Society, Nobel Prize Physics
Mills, Ogden, Seabiscuit Horse Racer, Lawyer, Sec. of Treasury
Mitchell, S. Weir, Medicine
Moore, Charles, Maritime Shipbuilding Industry
Morgan, J. Pierpont
Morton, Henry
Morton, Levi Parsons
Nathan, Max, Manufacturer Railroad Equipment
Newcomb, Simon, Astronomer and Mathematician
Orr, Alexander, US VP, Ambassador to France, NY Rep. Gov NY Financier Headed the New York Produce Exchange, President New York Chamber of Commerce (1894), Equitable Insurance Company, Financing and Construction of New York's Subway System
Osgood, John C., Fuel and Iron Company
Pabst, Frederick, Brewery Industry
Parsons, William Barclay, Chief Engineer Rapid Transit Commission
Pickering, Edward Charles, Director of the Harvard Observatory
Pope, Albert, Bicycles
Prince Henry

Pritchett, Henry Smith, Astronomer, Educator 5th Pres MIT, US Coast and Geodetic Survey
Remsen, Ira, Chemist Who Discovered Saccharin
Reynolds, Edwin, President American Society of Mechanical Engineers
Rockefeller, John D.
Rockefeller, Morgan
Roebling, Washington, Construction Brooklyn Bridge
Rogers, Henry Huttleston, Oil Refining
Schwab, Charles M.
Scott, Irving M. Union Iron Works
Sellers, Coleman, 30 Patents Mechanics Niagara Falls Hydro-Power Dynamos
Smith, Charles E., Ex-Postmaster-General
Spencer, Samuel, President Six Railroads, Banks, Other Companies
Sprague, Frank, Electric Motor, Railways, Elevators
Stillman, James, Land, Banking, and Railroads in New York, Texas, and Mexico. Pres. National City Bank
Tesla, Nikola
Thurston, Robert, Steam Engine Technologies, ASME
Uhl, Edward, Fairchild Industries
Vanderbilt, William
von Baudissin, Admiral Count
von Holleben, Ambassador
Vreeland, Herbert H., Pres. NY Metro Steet Railway
Walcott, Charles Doolittle, Paleontologist and Fourth Secretary of the Smithsonian Institution
Walker, John C., Rear Admiral
Ward, George Gray, Telegraphic Communications, Submarine Cables, Commercial Cable and Postal Telegraph Companies
Weston, Edward, Weston Cell, Chemist, Inventor, Lighting Brooklyn Bridge
Westinghouse, George
Weyerhaeuser, Frederick
White, John, Montana Gold, Discovered Grasshopper Creek
Henry Pritchett, Astronomer, Educator 5th Pres MIT, US Coast and Geodetic Survey
Whitelaw Reid, New York Tribune
Herman Ridder, Mass Media, Knight-Ridder
Stone, Melville E., News Editor, Chicago Daily News, AP

CHAPTER 5: THEFT OF INDIAN TIMBERLANDS AND TIMBER

A historical overview of relevant historical documents over the course of more than a century evidences the lack of protection for Indian timberlands and timber by the federal government. In the westward onslaught of colonial settlers, many of them willfully ignored Indian rights to their land and resources. The federal government assisted them, by omission or commission, in their outright theft.

Commissioner of Indian Affairs Manypenny catalogued these abuses in his 1856 Annual Report:

> The existing laws for the protection of the persons and property of the Indian wards of the government are sadly defective. New and more stringent statutes are required. The relation which the federal government sustains towards the Indians, and the duties and obligations flowing from it, cannot be faithfully met and discharged without ample legal provisions, and the necessary power and means to enforce them. The rage for speculation and the wonderful desire to obtain choice lands, which seems to possess so many of those who go into our new territories, causes them to lose sight of and entirely overlook the rights of the aboriginal inhabitants. The most dishonorable expedients have, in many cases, been made use of to dispossess the Indian; demoralizing means employed to obtain his property; and, for the want of adequate laws, the department is now often perplexed and embarrassed, because of inability to afford prompt relief and apply the remedy in cases obviously requiring them.

Also, Commissioner Manypenny implored Secretary of the Interior McClelland to protect Indians from being despoiled of their lands and annuities:

> To preserve the small reservations already made, and hereafter to be made, by tribes who have or may resolve to settle down and till the land, and to preserve to all Indians their annuities, I again urgently recommend such penal and other legislation as may be required to effect these objects. But any measure of protection short of this will fail to guard the Indians against the artful schemes of those bad men, who, under more or less specious pretences, desire to obtain either their lands or their money, or both. Upon such protection depends the question of their future existence, for when stripped of their property, alms would only rapidly sink, not permanently elevate and preserve them. Humanity, Christianity, national honor, unite in demanding the enactment of such laws as will not only protect the Indians, but as shall effectually put it out of the power of any public officer to allow these poor creatures to be despoiled of their lands and annuities by a swarm of hungry and audacious speculators, attorneys, and others, their instruments and coadjutors. ... The security of their rights should be made as little dependent upon the virtue of a public officer as possible.[1]

In 1863, H. B. Whipple (Bishop of Minnesota), Thomas L. Grace (Bishop of St. Paul), and Thomas S. Williamson (Missionary to the Dakota) reported on the Chippewas of Minnesota as follows:

> The history of the past has demonstrated that our people are unwilling to permit the Indians to live peaceably in the more densely populated portions of country. Upon one pretext or another they are compelled to give up their homes whenever the cupidity of others covet them. No plea of justice or humanity has ever been able to save them from their fate.[3]

In 1876, when lumber was adding a significant value to the economy, Commissioner of Indian Affairs J. G. Smith reported on the constant effort of white settlers to dispossess Indians of their valuable land. He articulated the greed underlying the struggle for the dispossession of Indian lands by colonial settlers:

> Wherever an Indian reservation has on it good land, or timber, or minerals, the cupidity of the white man is excited, and a ***constant struggle is inaugurated to dispossess the Indian, in which the avarice and determination of the white man usually prevails***. (Emphasis added).[4]

Local lawsuits were only a waste of time and money because juries were simply unwilling to convict white offenders.

In 1880, Commissioner Marble pronounced the absolute need for legislation prohibiting the theft of Indian timber. This refrain was repeated year after year.

It is absolutely necessary that some stringent law should be enacted to prevent the continually-recurring depredations upon timber.[5]

Commissioner Marble continued to denounce the theft of Indian timber and the fraud by the military:

> Under this heading I desire to call your attention to a subject which occasions serious embarrassment to this office—the continued occupation of Indian reservations and destruction of timber thereon by the military, where the necessity for their presence in large numbers no longer exists. ... [and the] inordinate consumption of wood and timber cut upon the reservation and used under the direction and authority of the military, not only in the erection of barracks, &c., but also in the filling of contracts awarded by military officers to post traders, and other persons, for supplying steamers with wood-contracts made without consulting the agent or this office in the matter.[6]

In 1882, Commissioner Price reiterated the continuing occurrence of the wanton theft of Indian timber.

Timber depredations on Indian lands.

The necessity for legislation to protect the timber on Indian lands has been repeatedly and forcibly urged in prior annual reports.[7]

The impotency of the U.S. Department of the Interior (DOI) in its ability to secure legislation to protect Indian timber rights is evident in Commissioner Price's censure of the House of Representatives in 1884 for not acting on this need when "depredations are constant" as documented here:

> **TIMBER AND OTHER DEPREDATIONS ON INDIAN LANDS.** At the first session of the present Congress a bill (S. 1545) to amend section 5388 of the Revised Statutes in relation to timber depredations so as to apply to all classes of Indian lands, passed the Senate, but was not reached in the House. This legislation is much required, especially in the Indian Territory, where depredations are constant, and I would respectfully recommend that the bill be still further amended, so as to include coal and other minerals upon Indian lands.[8]

One year later, Commissioner Atkins alerted the Secretary of the Interior to the "incessant spoliation of timber on Indian lands" due to Congress' repeated failure to act on preventive legislation:

Timber Spoliation and Other Depredations on Indian Lands. The attention of the Department is called to the urgent necessity of legislation to prevent the incessant spoliation of timber on Indian lands, particularly those of the civilized tribes in the Indian Territory where the domain is so large that it cannot be effectively policed. Measures looking to a suppression of this traffic have been presented to Congress for some years past, but invariably have failed to receive the concurrent action of both houses; the last, being Senate bill No. 1544, Forty-eighth Congress in the House. I find the subject has been exhaustively treated in former annual reports of this office, and its importance cannot be overestimated. At present, according to the ruling of the United States court for the western district of Arkansas, there is no law in existence under which timber depredations on the lands of the civilized tribes can be punished (*U. S. v. Ben Reese*, 5 Dill., 405). Prohibitory legislation should also be made to include coal and mineral deposits on Indian lands, which offer equal temptations to unprincipled persons.[9]

The laws the DOI urged for amendment to include tribal lands were the General Trespass Law of March 3, 1875 (18 Stat. 481) and section 5388 of the Revised Statutes (1878), which only applied to timber on military reserves or other branches of the Government. In 1888, Congress finally amended section 5388 to cover timber trespass "upon any Indian reservation, or lands belonging to or occupied by any tribe of Indians under authority of the United States."[10]

This revision of the law to include Indian reservations, however, was not without fault. In 1887, Congress had approved the General Allotment Act, which provided for the allotment of tribal land in severalty to individual tribal members. Past treaties contained similar allotment provisions. The question raised shortly after the 1888 trespass revision was whether or not the recent law covered trespass that occurred on individual allotments. The question was submitted to the Attorney General's office for an opinion in 1888. In September of that year, G.A. Jenks, Acting Attorney General, wrote an opinion stating that the 1888 revision did not cover timber trespass on individual Indian allotments: "lands held ... by Indian allottees, can not be called properly Indian reservations."[11] This oversight was not corrected until 1909, when section 5388 became part of the Nation's penal code and the phrase "or any allotment while title to the same shall be held in trust by the Government" was added.[12]

In 1909, the Commissioner's appraisal of the value of Indian timber at $73,000,000 was used to the detriment of Indians by President Theodore Roosevelt who issued eight proclamations,[13] transferring to adjacent national forests, 15 million acres of Indian timber on reservations that had been established by Executive Order. The reservations included Fort Apache, Mescalero, Jicarilla, San Carlos, Zuni, Hoopa Valley, Tule River, and Navajo.[14]

When a proposal was made in 1914 to give individual tribal councils authority to approve the sale of their own resources, Commissioner Valentine Sells offered what had become a standard response: "I am confident that a successful administration of Indian affairs is dependent upon a maintenance of the principle that the United States has jurisdiction over tribal property."[15]

Only $247,000 was realized from timber sales in Wisconsin and Minnesota in 1906.

Timber Sales Proceeds in 1906	
Lac du Flambeau	6,685.86
Red River	317,838.14
Red Cliff	5,272.78
Lac Courte Oreille	19,823.64
Menominee	Unk.
Total	349,620.42

The private lumber industry in comparison held a dominant position as the second and fourth largest U.S. industry, with a growing value-added economic sector. The value added component dealing with revenues from limber products in 1860 was $54 million; in 1880 it was $87 million.

U.S. Industries by Value Added (Millions of 1914 $'s)			
1860		1880	
Industry	Value added	Industry	Value added
#2 Lumber	54	#4 Lumber	87

> Economics 323-2: Economic History of the United States Since 1865. http://faculty.wcas.northwestern.edu/~jmokyr/Graphs-and-Tables.PDF. (accessed online February 9, 2022).

As noted by the DOI:

> Before 1906 there was no widespread protection against forest fires, nor were there plans for broad development and utilization of forest resources; operations were confined almost exclusively to Wisconsin and Minnesota, where timber was cut by contractors, in 1906 realizing $247,000. Indian agents and superintendents were in charge of the work, having technical assistance only from a superintendent of logging. Forest resources outside of Wisconsin and Minnesota were given little attention, although the timber on Indian reservations in Arizona is valued at $11,000,000, in Washington at $13,000,000, and in Oregon at $27,000,000.[16]

While Congress' inaction permitted the continued deforestation of Indian lands, Indians were repeatedly reported as serving as menial labor for white logging companies:

> Many of them find employment in the lumber woods, cutting timber and pealing bark. Others are track hands on the various railroads which run through the reservation. They are good workers usually, and are growing in favor among the whites as common laborers.[17]

As late as 1916, the problem still persisted. Commissioner of Indian Affairs Cato Sells graphically described the greed and the unparalleled ruthlessness of the white man:

> While corruption and inefficiency may find its way into the rank and file of Government employees, the greatest danger to the Indian lies in the greed of the white man for his land and money. Where a tribe has these the grafter is sure to be in evidence. He comes from every breed known to mankind, and in the past has despoiled the Indian with a ruthlessness unparalleled.[18]

Manifest Destiny Is Paramount

Debasing Indians to the category of an animal permitted horrific treatment by others, even to the point of wantonly killing them. This wasn't a localized problem. Acting Commissioner Mix stated the following in 1867 regarding the "vicious, unscrupulous whites" on page one of his Report to Secretary Browning:

> No doubt the greatest obstacle to the consummation [progress of Indians] is to be found mainly in his almost constant contact with the vicious, unscrupulous whites, who not only teach him their base ways, but *defraud and rob him, and, often without cause, with as little compunction as they would experience in killing a dog, take even his life*. Another cause or hindrance is the fact that the Indian has no certainty as to the permanent possession of the land he occupies and which he is urged to improve, for he knows not how long he may be permitted to enjoy it. Should it be in a region of remarkable fertility, or in a country abounding in rich mineral ores, it may be wanted for the white man's occupancy or use. The plea of *"manifest destiny" is paramount and the Indian must give way, though it be at the sacrifice of what may be as dear as life*. (Emphasis added).[19]

Commissioner Walker, the guardian (trustee) for the Indians, bluntly stated in 1872 his support for fulfilling the U.S.'s Manifest Destiny:

> *The westward course of population is neither to be denied nor delayed for the sake of all the Indians that ever called this country their home. They must yield or perish...* (Emphasis added).[20]

Transcontinental Railroad Links East and West

As early as 1832, advocates for a transcontinental railroad began lobbying Congress. In 1845, dry-goods merchant Asa Whitney presented the first definitive plan to Congress. Southerners wanted a southern route. Not surprisingly, northerners wanted a northern route. This dispute left Congress at a stalemate.

In the meantime, California engineer Theodore Judah was mapping a western route for a railway. His famous quote revealed his determination: "The railroad will be built, and I will have something to do with it."[21]

Confronting Judah was the primeval, granite Sierra Nevada mountain range, with precipices 12,000 feet high. Obsessed with finding a railroad route to cross it, he made 23 trips into the Sierra Nevada. Later, he planned a route based on the infamous Donner Party that must have seemed impossible. It was the snow that conquered the Donner Party en route to California.

With the same grit he put into planning a route, Judah went after funding. He secured it from seven men who agreed to pay for an exhaustive survey of his proposed route. Principal among the seven were four Sacramento merchants—Charles Crocker, Mark Hopkins, Collis Huntington, and Leland Stanford. They had made their limited fortunes, not from mining for gold, but from outfitting and equipping those who did. Besides this private funding, Judah would need federal funding.

At the same time Judah was working on his survey, another engineer was completing his survey of the area between the Mississippi and the Rockies. Grenville Dodge, employed by the Rock Island Railroad (R.I.R.R.), spent five years completing his study. This was a harbinger of the transcontinental railroad.

In late 1861, Judah headed for Washington to lobby Congress for his route. By the time he arrived, all the pieces were in place for the transcontinental railroad to become a reality. Politicians in Washington were aware of Dodge's route and survey. Judah presented his survey, accompanied by watercolors painted by his wife Anna.[22]

With a viable transcontinental route mapped out and no substantial opposition since southerners left Congress at the outset of the Civil War, Congress felt no need to delay. They passed the Pacific Railway Act (12 Stat. 489). President Lincoln signed it into law on July 1, 1862. It granted two charters—one to Grenville Dodge's employer, the Union Pacific Railroad Company, and one to Theodore Judah's employer, the Central Pacific Railroad Company.

The charters granted 10 miles of land for each mile of track laid, plus loans of $16,000 per mile for rail laid on plains; $32,000 per mile for land in the Great Basin; and $48,000 per mile for land in the mountains. Its eastern terminus was Omaha and its western one was Sacramento. The two routes were to meet, though the location where they would do so was not specified. Telegraph lines laid along the railroad right-of-way created cross-country communication equivalent to today's Internet. Thousands of jobs would be created to produce tracks and tools in factories and to lay the tracks across rough terrain.

When the railroad was completed on May 10, 1869, a ceremonial spike was driven at Promontory Summit, Utah. It was celebrated and recorded for history by Andrew J. Russell's iconic photo, "East and West Shaking Hands at Laying of Last Rail," popularly known as "The Champagne Photo." Fittingly, the handshake was between Samuel S. Montague, Chief Engineer for the Central Pacific, and Grenville M. Dodge, Chief Engineer for the Union Pacific.

The transcontinental railroad and its many branches, many of them on rights-of-way through Indian lands, led to the decline and end of the emigrant trails, wagon trains, and stagecoach lines. Travel times for passengers and goods cross-country decreased from six months to six days. Towns sprung up at the train stations planned at each eight miles of track.

Congressional investigations of fraud pertaining to the transcontinental railroad didn't go far. The Civil War had ended, the railroad was complete, evidence was difficult to get, and it was more expedient to let it go. In simplified terms, the scandal was simple. The Union Pacific contracted with its financier, Crédit Mobilier, which it owned, to build the railway at rates greatly above cost. These construction contracts generated large profits for Crédit Mobilier, which were divided among the Union Pacific stockholders. It was reported that Crédit Mobilier received $72 million in contracts for building a railroad worth only $53 million.

Congress investigated 13 of its members in a probe that led to the censure of Oakes Ames and James Brooks. During the investigation, the government found that Union Pacific had given shares to more than 30 politicians.

Railroads Increase Timber Consumption

Railroads stepped up timber production in myriad ways. First, they were enormous consumers of wood products themselves, using 20-25 percent of the annual timber production between the 1870s and 1900 for railroad ties, bridges, trestles, stations, fences, and fuel. Second, railways enabled loggers to penetrate deeper into the forests by providing access to many more trees than before. Third, they lowered the cost of transporting logs out of the forests to mills and from mills to urban areas for manufacturing. In short, railroads revolutionized the timber industry.

This increase in timber consumption is shown in the private lumber industry's dominant position as a value-adding economic sector. The next table builds on the table earlier in this chapter to include 1900 and 1920. The lumber industry's gross domestic product remained among the top four industries through 1920, with increasing value added through 1900 and 1920:

U.S. Industries by Value Added (Millions of 1914 $'s)							
1860		1880		1900		1920	
Industry	Value added	Industry	Value added	Industry	Value added	Industry	Value added
#2 Lumber	54	#4 Lumber	87	#4 Lumber	300	#3 Lumber	393

> Economics 323-2: Economic History of the United States Since 1865. http://faculty.wcas.northwestern.edu/~jmokyr/Graphs-and-Tables.PDF. (accessed online February 9, 2022).

Railroads – Catalyst for Industrial Age

The railroads changed everything as the catalyst for a profound transformation from a regional agrarian society to an industrial one. Railroads created a national market for industrial products such as steel, copper, and lumber. They transported agricultural products and goods connecting rural areas to the cities. Railroad employee Richard Sears, realizing the consumer market at hand, started the first mail-order catalog business. The vast network of railroads fostered the rise of urbanization and urban markets. Time zones across the country were established and standardized to meet railroad schedules.

Population Growth

From 1780 to 1850, the population of the United States grew nearly eightfold, from nearly 3 million to about 23 million. For a while, the trees that farmers cleared for fields met the nation's demand for timber. But in the second half of the nineteenth century, lumber consumption rose from 5.4 billion to 44.5 billion board feet annually. To stimulate lumber production, the nation needed a more reliable transport system than seasonal and inconsistent river drives.

"The Great Barbecue"

In 1871, Henry George, in prose difficult to surpass, impugned the giveaway of millions of acres as follows:

> "Here are thousands of square miles of fertile land," cries an eloquent Senator, "the haunt of the bear, the buffalo and the wandering savage, but of no use whatever to civilized man, for there is no railroad to furnish cheap and quick communication with the rest of the world. Give away a few millions of these acres for the building of a railroad and all this land may be used. People will go there to settle, farms will be tilled and towns will arise, and these square miles, now worth nothing, will have a market and a taxable value, while their productions will stream across the continent, making your existing cities still greater and their people still richer; giving freight to your ships and work to your mills."[23]

This massive giveaway of land, with its natural resources, to corporations from 1850 to 1900 was part of the reason American historian Vernon L. Parrington famously described the era as "The Great Barbecue." Railroad officials and other plutocrats got fat, it seemed, while farmers and laborers went hungry.[24]

The next chart estimates the massive amounts of acreage granted to Union Pacific and Central Pacific for their east-west transcontinental route. More grants were given to other railroad companies to connect the north with the south.

Estimated Quantity of Lands Granted and Vested

Company	Acres Granted	Acres Vested	States	Agriculture	Grazing	Desert or Waste
Union Pacific	22,824,396	19,100,000	4,800,000 acres in Nebraska, 4,600,000 acres in Wyoming, 700,000 acres in Colorado, and 1,100,000 acres in Utah	3,500,000	4,000,000	3,700,000
Central Pacific	14,214,800	110,367,895				7,700,000 between Salt Lake and Sierra Nevada Mountains

Land grants to railroads. Letter from the auditor of railroad accounts, relative to land grants made by the United States to aid in the construction of the Pacific railroads, H.R. Misc. Doc. No. 10, 46th Cong., 3rd Sess. (1881).

Gilded Age

Mark Twain dubbed the late 19th century "the Gilded Age."[25] By this, he meant that the period was glittering on the surface but corrupt underneath. "In the popular view, the late 19th century was a period of greed and guile: of rapacious Robber Barons, unscrupulous speculators, and corporate buccaneers, of shady business practices, scandal-plagued politics, and vulgar display. It was an era of corruption, conspicuous consumption, and unfettered capitalism."[26]

During this time, Indians were confined onto reservations through renegotiation of treaties and 30 years of war. Their status as nations was demoted to mere wards of the government. The Navajo and Sioux Wars raged in the west.

U.S. Navajo War from 1860–1868

One such war was the U.S. Navajo War in Arizona, New Mexico, and Utah. A very long war, it continued from 1860 to 1868.

But first, let's take a quick look at the precursor history. After the Mexican-American War (1846–1848), the U.S. received the New Mexico territory, Texas, and California. This added the Southwest to the U.S. and the people living in these areas became American citizens under the Treaty of Guadalupe-Hidalgo.

Because the former Mexicans in Santa Fe were now American citizens, the U.S. protected them against Navajo raiding. This was a puzzle to the Navajos because no U.S. soldiers ever came to their aid when the Mexicans raided the Navajos and stole their children. The raiding back and forth between Mexicans and Navajos had been ongoing for centuries.

On August 31, 1849, the Americans met with the Navajo headmen to explain that they were going to build forts on the Navajo's land. The first fort the Americans built in Navajo country was Fort Defiance. The Americans ordered the Navajos to keep their livestock away, but because their land had no fencing that was impossible. One morning, the soldiers came out and shot all the Navajo livestock on the Fort premises.

In February 1860, Manuelito, a renowned leader, led 500 warriors against the Army's horse herd, which was grazing a few miles north of Fort Defiance, in retaliation for the American soldiers killing their livestock. The Navajos suffered more than 30 casualties but captured only a few horses. During the following weeks, the Navajos built up a force of more than 1,000 Navajos and in the darkness of the early hours of April 30, 1860, they attacked Fort Defiance. They were determined to wipe it off the face of the land. When daylight came, the Navajos retreated thinking they had taught the Americans a good lesson.

The Americans considered it an act of war. A few weeks later, Colonel Edward Richard Sprigg Canby led six companies of cavalry and nine of infantry into the Chuska Mountains to attack the Navajos. A year of cat and mouse followed, with small skirmishes but no success on the part of the Americans.

After the Confederates' defeat at Glorieta Pass in New Mexico, Brigadier General Carleton, Commander of the U.S. Army of New Mexico Territory, turned his attention to the Navajos. He considered them wolves that run through the mountains that he must subdue. General Carleton set a deadline for the Navajos' removal to Fort Sumner in New Mexico, 300 miles from the Navajos' homeland. He gave them until July 20 to turn themselves in. "After that day every Navajo that is seen will be considered as hostile and treated accordingly."[27] No Navajos surrendered.

The fighting continued and after Colonel Kit Carson's scorched-earth policy, Navajos began to surrender. They were forcibly marched from Ft. Canby to Fort Sumner. The detail here is only on three of the marches:

During March [1864] the Long Walk of the Navajos to Fort Sumner and the Bosque Redondo was set in motion. The first contingent of 1,430 reached Fort Sumner on March 13; ten died en route; three children were kidnapped, probably by Mexicans among the soldier escort.

Meanwhile a second group of 2,400 had left Fort Canby, their numbers already reduced by 126 who had died at the fort. The long caravan included 30 wagons, 3,000 sheep, and 473 horses. The Navajos had the fortitude to bear freezing weather, hunger, dysentery, jeers of the soldiers, and the hard threehundred-mile journey, but they could not bear the homesickness, the loss of their land. They wept, and 197 of them died before they reached their cruel destination.

On March 20 [1864] eight hundred more Navajos left Fort Canby [on the 300-mile march to Fort Sumner], most of them women, children, and old men. The Army supplied them only twenty-three wagons. On the second day's march, the officer in command reported, "a very severe snowstorm set in which lasted for four days with unusual severity, and occasioned great suffering amongst the Indians, many of whom were nearly naked and of course unable to withstand such a storm." When they reached Los Pinos, below Albuquerque, the Army commandeered the wagons for other use, and the Navajos had to camp in the open. By the time the journey could be resumed, several children had vanished. "At this place," a lieutenant commented, "officers who have Indians in charge will have to exercise extreme vigilance, or the Indians' children will be stolen from them and sold." This contingent reached the Bosque on May 11, 1864. "I left Fort Canby with 800 and received 146 en route to Fort Sumner, making about 946 in all. *Of this number about 110 died*." (Emphasis added).[28]

While imprisoned at Fort Sumner, more than 2,500 Navajos died out of the 10,000 imprisoned. For their families to survive, many of the women were forced into prostitution with the Army soldiers and became diseased with syphilis. To shelter themselves from rain and sun they had to dig holes in the sandy ground, and cover and line them with mats of woven grass. They lived like prairie dogs in burrows.[29]

The reports of syphilis by Commissioner N. G. Taylor to Secretary Browning and on to President Lincoln can only be described as a horror:

> The most loathsome, lingering, and fatal diseases [syphilis], which reach many generations in their ruinous effects, are spread broadcast, and the seeds of moral and physical death are planted among the miserable creatures.
>
> If you wish to see some of the results of establishing military posts in the Indian country, I call your attention to ... Fort Sumner in New Mexico, before the Navajo exodus, and to all our military posts in the Indian country, with no known exception. *If you wish to exterminate the race, pursue them with the ball and blade; if you please, massacre them wholesale, as we sometimes have done; or, to make it cheap, call them to a peaceful feast, and feed them on beef salted with wolf bane; but, for humanity's sake save them from the lingering syphilitic poisons, so sure to be contracted about military posts*. (Emphasis added).[30]

Major General James H. "Star Chief" Carleton reported to Washington on the surrender of the Navajos' "magnificent pastoral and mineral country," again recognizing the dispossession of valuable land and resources:

These six thousand mouths must eat and these six thousand bodies must be clothed. *When it is considered what a magnificent pastoral and mineral country they have surrendered to us, a country whose value can hardly be estimated, the mere pittance, in comparison, which must at once be given to support them sinks into insignificance as a price for their natural heritage.* (Emphasis added).[31]

In his vision of Manifest Destiny, Carleton reported on the "insatiable progress of our race," from the P.O.W. Camp at Fort Sumner:

The exodus of this whole people from the land of their fathers is not only an interesting but a touching sight. They have fought us gallantly for years on years; they have defended their mountains and their stupendous canyons with a heroism which any people might be proud to emulate; but when, at length, they found it was their destiny, too, as it had been that of their brethren, tribe after tribe, away back toward the rising of the sun, to give way to the insatiable progress of our race, they threw down their arms, and, are brave men entitled to our admiration and respect, have come to us with confidence in our magnanimity, and feeling that we are too powerful and too just a people to repay that confidence with meanness and neglect, feeling that having sacrificed to us their beautiful country, their homes, the associations of their lives, the scenes rendered classic in their traditions, we will not dole out to them a miser's pittance in return for what they know to be and what we know to be a princely realm.[32]

As Manuelito said:

We fought for that country because we did not want to lose it. We lost nearly everything. The American nation is too powerful for us to fight. When we had to fight for a few days we felt fresh, but in a short time we were worn out and the soldiers starved us out.[33]

On September 1, 1866, six years after the War's start, Manuelito surrendered with 23 warriors:

They were all in rags, their bodies emaciated. They still wore leather bands on their wrists for protection from the slaps of the bowstrings but they had no bows or arrows. One of Manuelito's arms hung useless at his side from a wound. Now there were no more war chiefs. (Emphasis added).[34]

The new superintendent of Fort Sumner, A. B. Norton, pronounced the soil unfit to cultivate grain because alkali was present. Further,

> The water is black and brackish, scarcely bearable to the taste, and said by the Indians to be unhealthy, because one-fourth of their population have been swept off by disease.[35]

General William Tecumseh Sherman was sent from Washington to conclude a treaty with the Navajos, which was signed on June 1, 1868, allowing the Navajos to return to their homeland. Not all of their land was restored, but at least the Navajos would not go to the Indian Territory in Oklahoma. They received one-quarter of their original homeland.

U.S.-Dakota War of 1862 in Minnesota

In 1862, in the middle of the U.S. Civil War, the U.S. government failed to provide treaty-promised food and funds to the Dakota people in Minnesota. *Without a large enough land base to support themselves through hunting and gathering, the Dakota were starving*. Their desperation and humiliation sparked the U.S.-Dakota War in the late summer of 1862. At the War's outset, Governor Alexander Ramsey told the legislature: *"The Sioux Indians of Minnesota must be exterminated or driven forever beyond the borders of Minnesota."* (Emphasis added).[36]

Governor Ramsey appointed Henry Sibley, a colonel in the state's military forces, to lead the four volunteer state armed companies of the Sixth Infantry Regiment. The state's military forces came under federal control on September 16, when Major General John Pope assumed command of the newly created Military Department of the Northwest. Sibley, promoted to a Brigadier General of U.S. Army volunteers, directed the forces in the Battle of Wood Lake on September 23. It was the final battle of the war. The Dakota were defeated.

On September 28, 1862, a commission of military officers established by Sibley began trying Dakota men accused of participating in the war. On November 5, the commission completed its work. Of the 392 prisoners tried, the commission sentenced 303 Dakota men to death and gave 16 men prison terms.

President Lincoln's original criteria for the death penalty was for those guilty of rape. Because the commission charged only two Dakota men of rape, President Lincoln expanded the criteria to include those who had participated in massacres of civilians rather than just in battles. Lincoln then made his final decision and forwarded to Sibley a list of 39 names from the 303 sentenced to death. On December 26, 1862, 38 Dakota men were hanged en masse at Mankato on a scaffold constructed to hang them simultaneously. An estimated 4,000 spectators crammed the streets to watch.

The remaining convicted Dakota warriors were imprisoned from 1863 to 1866. One-third of them died during imprisonment. More than 1,600 Dakota noncombatants, including women, children, and the elderly who opposed the war, were imprisoned in a stockaded trench constructed for them at Pike Island near Fort Snelling. In May 1863, the surviving 1,300 Dakota were forcibly moved to Crow Creek Reservation in South Dakota. In addition to those who died during the journey, more than 200 Dakota died within six months of arriving, many of them children.

States Maneuver for Removal of Indians

Indian Nations faced numerous states thirsting for their removal, including the following States/Territories that went as far as passing state legislation petitioning for Presidential extinguishment of Indian title in their States/Territories: Georgia, Illinois, Indiana, Kentucky, Michigan Territory, Mississippi, Missouri, New York, North Carolina, Ohio, South Carolina, Tennessee and Wisconsin.

DOI Schemes to Remove Indians

In 1877, Commissioner of Indian Affairs Smith recommended the removal of all Indians in Colorado, Arizona, and New Mexico to the Indian Territory. Southern Indians, however, who are in Colorado, Arizona, and New Mexico, should be settled in the Indian Territory, the climate being favorable to them, and there being sufficient arable land for their maintenance.[37]

> ... I recommend the removal of all the Indians in Colorado and Arizona to the Indian Territory ... all the arable land in the State is required for its white settlers. A mining population needs in its immediate vicinity abundant facilities for agriculture to feed it. *The question of feeding the white population of the State is one of paramount importance*, and will certainly force itself on the attention of the government. (Emphasis added).[38]

In 1890, the State of Colorado petitioned the Secretary of the Interior for the removal of the Southern Utes, the last tribe in the State. Commissioner of Indian Affairs Morgan responded that Colorado was much more fortunate than many of her sister States, having only one tribe with a population of 2,000:

This little band constitutes the last remnant of Indians in the great State of Colorado, and in comparison with the number of Indians in other States—South Dakota, Montana, Nebraska, California, etc.—is very small indeed [number less than 2,000]. Minnesota, Michigan, and Wisconsin each have over three times as many, Montana five, and California six times as many, North Dakota and South Dakota four and ten times as many, respectively, and the State of Washington five times as many; so that in the distribution of our Indian population, to those who regard their presence as a detriment, Colorado seems to have been much more fortunate than many of her sister States.[39]

While removal and confinement on reservations continued, with allotment, the overall goal of weakening tribal relations and destroying tribes continued as lumber companies amassed fortunes.

Industrial Landscape Transforms American Indian People and Lands

The arrival of the railroad, the conversion of forests into lumber, increased agricultural production, and pervasive mining activity transformed the landscape and marginalized the people who had inhabited it for thousands of years. Despite their resistance, Indians were caught in the cogs of an industrial juggernaut that was steamrolling across the country. The federal government was trying to make farmers out of Indians when the profitability of the agricultural sector had already switched to the mechanized mass production of the Industrial Age.

Notes

1. United States. Office of Indian Affairs. *Report of the Commissioner of Indian Affairs to the Secretary of the Interior*. US Government Printing Office, 1856, pp. 21, 22.

2. United States. Office of Indian Affairs, Northern Superintendency. *Report of the Commissioner of Indian Affairs to the Secretary of the Interior*. US Government Printing Office, 1864, p. 345.

3. United States. Office of Indian Affairs, Northern Superintendency. *Report of the Commissioner of Indian Affairs to the Secretary of the Interior*. US Government Printing Office, 1876, pp. VIII-IX.

4. United States. Office of Indian Affairs. *Report of the Commissioner of Indian Affairs to the Secretary of the Interior*. US Government Printing Office, 1880, p. XX.

5. Ibid., p. XXIX.

6. United States. Office of Indian Affairs. *Report of the Commissioner of Indian Affairs to the Secretary of the Interior*. US Government Printing Office, 1882, p. 14.

7. United States. Office of Indian Affairs. *Report of the Commissioner of Indian Affairs to the Secretary of the Interior*. US Government Printing Office, 1884, p. XVI.

8. United States. Office of Indian Affairs. *Report of the Commissioner of Indian Affairs to the Secretary of the Interior*. US Government Printing Office, 1885, pp. XXXII-XXXIII.

9. United States. Office of Indian Affairs. *Report of the Commissioner of Indian Affairs to the Secretary of the Interior*. US Government Printing Office, 1890, p. XXXIV.

10. Id.

11. Felix S. Cohen, Handbook of Federal Indian Law (Albuquerque: University of New Mexico Press, 1968), p. 316.

12. United States. Office of Indian Affairs. *Report of the Commissioner of Indian Affairs to the Secretary of the Interior*. US Government Printing Office, 1909, pp. 24-25.

13. Aune, Keith and Glenn Plumb. *Theodore Roosevelt & Bison Restoration on the Great Plains*. Arcadia Publishing, 2019, p. 61.

14. Frederick E. Hoxie, A Final Promise: The Campaign to Assimilate the Indians, 1880–1920, Bison Books, U of Nebraska Press, 2001, p. 185.

15. United States. Office of Indian Affairs. *Report of the Commissioner of Indian Affairs to the Secretary of the Interior*. US Government Printing Office, 1912, p. 6.

16. United States. Office of Indian Affairs. *Report of the Commissioner of Indian Affairs to the Secretary of the Interior*. US Government Printing Office, 1902, p. 285.

17. United States. Office of Indian Affairs. *Annual Report of the Secretary of the Interior, Vol. II, Report of the Commissioner of Indian Affairs*. US Government Printing Office, 1917, p. 71.

18. United States. Office of Indian Affairs. *Report of the Commissioner of Indian Affairs to the Secretary of the Interior*. US Government Printing Office, 1868, p. 1.

19. United States. Office of Indian Affairs. *Report of the Commissioner of Indian Affairs to the Secretary of the Interior*. US Government Printing Office, 1872, p. 9.

20. https://merehistory.weebly.com/uploads/1/5/1/5/15155754/ccr--heartland_ transcript. pdf (accessed April 17, 2022).

21. Christopher Bates, for the History 139B website, http://www.sscnet.ucla.edu/ history/ waughj/classes/gildedage/private/pacific_railroad/history/railroad_part_1.html (accessed April 9, 2022).

22. George, Henry. *Our Land and Land Policy, National and State*. White & Bauer, 1871, p. 9.

23. Parrington, Vernon Louis. *Main Currents in American Thought, Volume 3*. Harcourt, Brace, 1954, p. 23.

24. Twain, Mark, and Charles Dudley Warner. *The Gilded Age: a tale of today*. Penguin, 2001.

25. https://www.digitalhistory.uh.edu/era.cfm?eraid=9 (accessed March 30, 2022).

26. Brown, Dee. *Bury My Heart at Wounded Knee: An Indian History of the American West*. Macmillan, 2007.

27. Id.

28. Id.

29. United States. Office of Indian Affairs. *Report of the Commissioner of Indian Affairs to the Secretary of the Interior*. US Government Printing Office, 1868, pp. 7-15.

30. Brown, Dee. *Bury My Heart at Wounded Knee: An Indian History of the American West*. Macmillan, 2007.

31. Id.

32. Id.
33. Id.
34. Id.
35. Message of Governor Ramsey to the Legislature of Minnesota, delivered at the extra session, September 9, 1862.
36. United States. Office of Indian Affairs. *Report of the Commissioner of Indian Affairs to the Secretary of the Interior*. US Government Printing Office, 1877, p. 2.
37. Ibid., p. 6.
38. United States. Office of Indian Affairs. *Report of the Commissioner of Indian Affairs to the Secretary of the Interior*. US Government Printing Office, 1890, p. XLIV.

CHAPTER 6: CARVING UP MICHIGAN

Part 1: Indian Land in Michigan

Indian Tribes of Michigan

Michigan's Indian Nations lived along the coastline and the Upper Peninsula.[1] Michigan's story is about the massive cession of Indian lands and the establishment of small reserves.[2]

The general name "Chippewa" is used to refer to a large group of American Indians who historically lived near the great lakes. The names "Anishinaabeg," "Annishinaabe," "Ojibwe," and similarly, the terms "Indian" or "American Indian" will be used to refer more generally to the large group of Americans whose ancestors lived in the United States prior to the arrival of Europeans.

Part 2: Cession and Removal Treaties

The gordian knot of treaties, including Ottawa, Chippewas, Pottawatomies and other Indian Nations across-states and within states by different Bands, including overlapping land, is almost impossible to decipher. Stipulations went unenforced that had to be corrected by subsequent treaties or treaties were superseded. Annuities went unpaid for many years. Educational funds were misspent.

The treaties included 'peace' treaties after the War of 1812, cession treaties of multi-million acres of land, removal treaties and 'grants' of reservations, including 'experimental allotment.' Tribes experienced the most unbelievable loss of land and resources and monies. Cultural heritages were ignored in the drive to concentrate, consolidate and eradicate Indian peoples, Nations and lands.

Prominent and wealthy businessmen wantonly engaged in fraud, evading investigations and prosecution. Indians were placed on lands which the government expected them to farm but which were, in reality, incapable of agriculture due to extreme climatic conditions. Then, the Indians were labeled and treated as lazy and indolent. The Indians' trustee, the Department of the Interior, confirmed its knowledge of all of this, yet utterly failed to fulfill its guardianship role. It is only the strength of Indian peoples that allowed them to survive versus facing the extermination desired by many in prominent positions of authority and business.

1807 Cession Treaty, Detroit Area

The 1807 Treaty with the Ottoway, Chippeway, Wyandotte, and Pottawatami Nations of Indians ceded the southeastern portion of what is today Michigan, a cession consisting of just *over five and a half million acres*.[3] The ceded area included what are today the cities of Detroit and Ann Arbor. Under Article II, in exchange for the cession, the Indian Nations received ten thousand dollars, in money, goods, implements of husbandry, or domestic animals, split between the Nations. Under Art. V, they reserved the right to hunt and fish on the ceded lands, as long as they remained the property of the U. S. Under Art. V, reservations were specified.

1815 Peace Treaty with the Wyandots

The September 8, 1815, Treaty at Spring Wells, near Detroit, restored the relations of peace and amity with the U.S. after the War of 1812. It renewed and confirmed the Treaty of Greenville, made in 1795.

1817 Cession Treaty, South Central Michigan and Northwestern Ohio

In the 1817 Treaty with the Wyandot, Seneca, Delaware, Shawanese, Potawatomees, Ottawas, and Chippeway of September 29, 1817, the Indian Nations ceded land in what is now south-central Michigan and in northwestern Ohio. There were several grants of land to individuals. The U.S. agreed to pay the Potawatomi Nation $1300 annually in specie for 15 years; the Ottawa Nation $1000 annually in specie for 15 years; and the Chippewa Nation $1000 annually in specie for 15 years; along with consideration to other Indian Nations signatory to the Treaty.

Under Art. 11, they retained the stipulations in the Treaty of Greenville, relative to the right of the Indians to hunt upon the land hereby ceded, while it continues the property of the United States; and the Indians, for the same term, reserved the privilege of making sugar upon the same land, committing no unnecessary waste upon the trees.

Saginaw Cession Treaty of 1819, Removal of Chippewas

General Cass, then Governor of the Northwest Territories and Superintendent of Indian Affairs, was authorized to enter into negotiations for the removal of the Chippewas to lands west of the Mississippi, in addition to the cession of the valuable body of land lying upon the Saginaw and its tributaries. He got off to an inauspicious start. General Cass wrote to the Secretary of War, James Calhoun, in September 1819, as follows:

> I shall leave here on Monday next to meet the Indians at Saginaw, and endeavor, agreeable to your instructions, to procure a cession of that valuable territory. It would be hopeless to expect a favorable result to the proposed treaty, unless the annuities previously due are discharged. Under these circumstances I have felt myself embarrassed and no course has been left me but to procure the amount of the Chippewa annuity upon my private responsibility. I trust the receipt of a draft will soon relieve me from the situation in which I am placed, and enable me to perform my promise to the bank.[4]

In mid-September 1819, several thousand Chippewas gathered at Saginaw City for a treaty council to listen to what the federal treaty commissioner, Gov. Cass, had to tell them. The Chief O-Ge-maw-ke-to addressed Cass' proposal of cession as follows:

> You do not know our wishes. Our people wonder what has brought you so far from your homes. Your young men have invited us to come and light the council fire. We are here to smoke the pipe of peace, but not to sell our lands. Our American Father Wants them. Our English Father treats us better. He has never asked for them. Your people trespass upon our hunting grounds. You flock to our shores. Our waters grow warm; our land melts like a cake of ice. Our possessions grow smaller and smaller. The warm wave of the white man rolls in upon us and melts us away. Our women reproach us. Our children want homes. Shall we sell from under them the spot where they spread their blankets? We have not called you here. We smoke with you the pipe of peace.

The account of Gov. Cass' response reads as follows:

To this the Commissioner replied ... that *their Great Father at Washington had just closed a war in which he had whipped their Father, the English king, and the Indians too; that their lands were forfeited in fact by the rules of war*, but that he did not propose to take them without rendering back an equivalent, notwithstanding their late acts of hostility; that their women and children should have secured to them ample tribal reserves on which they could live, unmolested by their white neighbors, where they could spread their blankets and be aided and instructed in agriculture. (Emphasis added).[5]

While General Cass could not get the Chippewas to leave Michigan, they were at least removed west of Lake Michigan. In exchange for the cession of the Saginaw country, lands were reserved for them and they received $1,000 in silver. Under Article 5, they reserved the right to hunt upon the land ceded, while it continued the property of the United States.

With the Treaty of Saginaw, Governor Cass obtained for the United States about 6,000,000 acres of land, including the heavily-timbered area of Saginaw and central Michigan. To give an idea of the vast amount of timber in the area ceded, the timber of the Saginaw River logged by colonial settler businesses' was accounted for as follows:

Lumber Production of Saginaw River[6]		
Year	Lumber Feet	Shingles
1851	92,000,000	
1860	125,000,000	
1870	576,726,60	178,570,000
1880	873,047,731	241,075,160
1890	815,054,465	221,839,000
1897	339, 991,000	48,276,000

1820 Cession Treaty of Sault Ste. Marie

In 1820, the Treaty of Sault Ste. Marie[7] was negotiated by Cass. The Indians ceded a 16-square-mile tract on the western shore of St. Mary's River, 1,395 acres, for a fort site for a "quantity of goods."

Under Article 3, the Indians reserved a perpetual right of fishing as follows:

The United States will secure to the Indians a perpetual right of fishing at the falls of St. Mary's, and also a place of encampment upon the tract hereby ceded, convenient to the fishing ground, which place shall not interfere with the defences of any military work which may be erected, nor with any private rights.

During the negotiations,

While some of them indicated a consent that Americans might settle there, they gave the governor to understand that a military post was not wanted, and that if one was established it might be subject to attack by the young men who were still determined to hold the country as a heritage of their own.

The governor was not to be trifled with, or driven away through fear, and he made response that a fort would be built whether they liked it or not.

In this council was a certain chief called the "count" dressed in the costume of an English brigadier and he, during a speech, as if to emphasize his displeasure and his determination, with a vigorous flourish of his war-lance thrust it and planted it in the ground as a symbol of Indian possession of the soil. On leaving the governor's tent the Indians went to their own village on a hill near where the old French fort had previously stood, and there in front of the wigwam of the "count" they hoisted the English flag.

Immediately on learning of this, Governor Cass, with only his interpreter to accompany him, walked to the Indian village, took down the flag, and, after telling them that none but an American flag could be used there, boldly carried away the British colors.

This boldness of the governor overawed them, but, nevertheless, they dispatched their women and children to more remote parts, and the men of the village made preparations to attack the governor's party; the Americans, at the same time, numbering in all sixty-six persons and all well armed, prepared to defend themselves.

Shingobawassin was the head chief and had been absent from the council, but now, under pacifying influences to be noted later, put in appearance, prevented the attack, and renewed the council with the governor, with the result that a treaty was signed by which the Indians released to the Americans a tract of sixteen square miles, though the "count" maintained his opposition and refused to sign the treaty.[8]

The importance and value of the ceded area is best expressed by the Michigan State Legislature in House Resolution No. 110 to the Sec. of War and the U.S. Congress, dated April 4, 1913:

Whereas, The great highway of commerce on the Great Lakes and the highway of commerce between the United States and Canada converge at Sault Ste. Marie, and the commerce passing through this great gateway is of such magnitude that it is of vital interest to our whole country that these highways of commerce be protected, the *commerce on the lakes passing this place having grown from nothing fifty years ago to seventy-two million tons in the year 1912, and valued in round numbers at seven hundred ninety millions of dollars*, while the commerce by land has also reached an enormous sum; and ...

> Whereas, Fort Brady is situated at the border of our country, and on the great highways of commerce, both foreign and inland, by land and by water, a commerce which in its magnitude affects nearly every state in the Union, and the post is, therefore, *strategically located for the protection of this great volume of commerce and vast public works from strikes and riots and the country's possible future invasions...*[9] (Emphasis added).

Control of the straits, which connected Lake Superior with the lower Lakes, meant control of the U.S.' interests in the entire northwest. In 1822, Fort Brady was built and in 1823 an Indian Agency, with jurisdiction over the entire Northwest, was opened near the Fort. Colonel Hugh Brady's success at this post earned him a promotion to brigadier general.

1821 Chicago Cession Treaty, 4 Million Acres of Land Ceded in Southwest Michigan and Northern Indiana

Cass negotiated a treaty at Chicago on August 29, 1821, gaining from the Potawatomi the cession of almost 4 million acres of their land in southwestern Michigan and a swath of land across northern Indiana.[10] The U.S. agreed to pay the Potawatomi Nation $5000 annually for 20 years and $1,000 for fifteen years in the support of a blacksmith and teacher.

1828 Potawatomi Nation Cession Treaty, 200,000 Acres, Southwest Michigan and Northeast Indiana

The Treaty with the Potawatomi, on September 20, 1828, at St. Joseph,[11] ceded land in present-day northeast Indiana and southwest Michigan.

The consideration for the 200,000 acre cession under the Treaty was as follows and gives an idea of how difficult it was for a U.S. Agent to assure compliance with the varied stipulations, given the number, timing and variety of amounts due:

> Permanent annuity of $2,000;
> Annuity of $1,000 for the term of twenty years;

Goods of $30,000;
Goods of $10,000;
$5,000 in specie, in 1829;
$7,500 in clearing and fencing land, erecting houses, purchasing domestic animals and farming utensils, and in the support of labourers to work for them;
2000 pounds of tobacco, 1,500 weight of iron and 350 pounds of steel, shall be annually delivered to them;
$1,000 for the purposes of education, as long as Congress may think the appropriation may be useful;
$100 in goods, shall be annually paid to To-pen-i-be-the, principal chief of the said Tribe, during his natural life;
The blacksmith, stipulated by the treaty of Chicago to be provided for the term of fifteen years, shall be permanently supported by the U.S.;
Three labourers shall be provided, during four months of the year, for ten years, to work for the band living upon the reservation South of the St. Joseph; and
Certain individuals received grants of land.

A supplementary article gave a minority of the Michigan Potawatomi the right to remain in Michigan if they relocated to the Ottawa community of L'Arbre Croche. Four scattered Michigan Potawatomi communities were covered by this provision. Collectively these four communities became known as the Pokagon Band, after one of the leaders. The common link between the four was that each community had adopted the Catholic faith.

At the same time that Pokagon and his band were embracing Catholicism, Pokagon was also moving to obtain fee simple title to the land on which his people lived. Rather than trust in treaty reserves, the Pokagon used money received at the 1833 Treaty signing, as well as federal annuity funds saved from earlier years, to purchase land. By 1838, the Pokagon owned 874 acres in fee simple on Silver Creek and had resettled on this property.

1833 Potawatomi Cession (5 Million Acres) and Removal Treaty

In 1833, approximately 6,000 to 7,000 Potawatomi lived in Michigan. Under the Treaty of 1833, they ceded about five million acres. In return, five million acres of land for removal of the Indians west of the Mississippi were designated.[12] They would be removed first to Iowa and then Kansas and Oklahoma. About 1,500 to 2,500 of them fled to Canada.

Again, to illustrate the varied stipulations, the consideration was as follows:

One hundred thousand dollars to satisfy sundry individuals, in behalf of whom reservations were asked, which the Commissioners refused to grant: and also to indemnify the Chippewa tribe who are parties to this treaty for certain lands along the shore of Lake Michigan, to which they make claim, which have been ceded to the United States by the Menominee Indians.

One hundred and fifty thousand dollars to satisfy the claims made against the said United Nation which they have here admitted to be justly due.

One hundred thousand dollars to be paid in goods and provisions, a part to be delivered on the signing of this treaty and the residue during the ensuing year.

Two hundred and eighty thousand dollars to be paid in annuities of fourteen thousand dollars a year, for twenty years.

One hundred and fifty thousand dollars to be applied to the erection of mills, farm houses, Indian houses and blacksmith shops, to agricultural improvements, to the purchase of agricultural implements and stock, and for the support of such physicians, millers, farmers, blacksmiths and other mechanics, as the President of the United States shall think proper to appoint.

Fund for the purposes of education, etc.

Seventy thousand dollars for purposes of education and the encouragement of the domestic arts.

Minor additional amounts for cessions of lands described.

It is difficult to ascertain if this consideration was fully tendered.

The Potawatomi bands that resisted removal under the 1833 Treaty of Chicago were denied governmental status under the argument that they severed their connection with the united nation, and thereby lost their identity with the Pottawatomies as a tribe, in order that they might avail themselves of the privilege of remaining in the Territory of Michigan. In ceasing to be a part of the united nation, they did not retain any part of the political or corporate power of the tribe, that was undivided and still inherent in the body which emigrated beyond the Mississippi. In 1994, their tribal status was restored.

1836 Ottawa Indian Nation in Michigan Forced to Cede 16 Million Acres of Land

With the pressure on tribes for forcible removal from Michigan, the Ottawa realized they had to enter into a treaty to retain land in Michigan or they would be removed to Kansas or Oklahoma. Settlers were trespassing on Ottawa land in southern Michigan. The Territory of Michigan, about to become a state, wanted title to Ottawa land so that settlement could continue.

The Ottawa appealed to the federal government to council with them regarding remaining in Michigan. Without any response, in 1835, the Tribe went so far as to send a delegation of Ottawa leaders to Washington D.C. to petition against removal. They were willing to relinquish their title to Drummond Island and certain upper peninsula land they claimed jointly with the Chippewa, in return for needed annuities.

On December 5, 1835, Ottawa head man and interpreter for treaty negotiations Augustin Hamlin wrote this powerful letter to Lewis Cass, then Secretary of War under President Jackson:

> The principal objects of our visit here, are these: we would make some arrangements with the government remaining in the Territory of Michigan in the quiet possession of our lands, and to transmit the same safely to our posterity. We do not wish to sell all the lands claimed by us and consequently not to remove to the west of the Mississippi...
>
> It is a heart-rending thought to our simple feelings to think of leaving our native country forever, and which has been bought with the price of, their native blood, and which has been thus safely transmitted to us. It is, we say, a heart-rending thought to us to think so; there are many local endearments which make the soul shrink with horror at the idea of rejecting our country forever—the mortal remains of our deceased parents, relations and friends, cry out to us as it were, for our compassion, our sympathy and our love.[13]

The trip had no effect and the Ottawa were forced to cede 16 million acres of land in the Upper and Lower Peninsula. Lands north of the Grand River and along the Manistee River and Little Traverse Bay were set aside as Indian reservations, and the Ottawa reserved the right to hunt and fish on the ceded land. Land west of the Mississippi River was promised when the tribes decided to move, as preferred and urged by the U.S. To the dismay of the Indians, *the Senate unilaterally added a stipulation that the Ottawa and Chippewa could remain on their reservations for only five years*, unless extended. When they surrendered their reservations, they would receive the sum of $200,000, and, until that time, the annual interest on that amount, would be paid. The five years expired in 1841.

After the expiration of the five years, the tribes continued to reside on the ceded lands.

> Superintendent Murray was instructed to visit these Indians, and, with a view to the future policy of the Government in reference to them, to report their general condition, the contiguity of their settlements to the whites: and the necessity, if any, for their removal ... From the flattering account given by him and Agent Sprague of the present condition of these Indians ... I would therefore recommend ... their permanent settlement in the country where they now reside.[14]

1837 Saginaw Band Cede 102,400 Acres

Under the 1837 Treaty between the Chippewa Nation and the U. S.,[15] the Saginaw Band ceded 102,400 acres and in return were to receive the net proceeds of the sale of the lands. They agreed to "remove from the State of Michigan, as soon as a proper location can be obtained."

> Commissioner Harris alerted the President regarding the Saginaw Indians, of about 1000, living on choice lands in Michigan and who without federal assistance would "very rapidly depopulate and perish." Their treaty for removal was awaiting Senate approval.[16]

The U.S. advanced $70,000 and only received $68,094.26 from the sale of the lands, so there was no credit to the Saginaw Band.

1841 Ottawa Petition to Michigan Legislature for U.S. Citizenship Support

In 1841, the Ottawa petitioned the Michigan legislature to support their request to remain in the state and be granted U.S. citizenship. They thought citizenship would aid in their supplication to remain on the lands they had improved and were farming.

> To the Honorable the Legislature of the State of Michigan, now convened at Detroit:
>
> This petition of the Ottawa Indians, residing at L'arbre Croche, on the Northwest extremity of the Southern Peninsula, humbly showeth, That your petitioners are most anxious to enjoy the rights and privileges of American citizenship. That such should be our wish-our prayer-the object of our constant solicitude, and of trembling, yet enduring hopefulness, is a natural and becoming tribute to the common feeling of humanity-to the love of home, and the love of country, which we share in common with our brethren. *The red men are strangers—not in a strange land, where the bright streams of memory might mingle with the dark waters of their sorrows—but strangers in their own land, the homes of their childhood, the burial-ground of their race.*
>
> Your petitioners are few in number—the small remnant of a once-powerful nation, occupying a sequestered bay, that opens, into Lake Michigan on the east. Their manners, informed by civilisation and ameliorated by the influence of Christianity, disqualify them for the rude and unskilled habits of their natural condition. *They have erected comfortable dwellings, in imitation of the white men*, and are maintaining their families by cultivating the soil. The spell of home is strong upon them. They love their forests and the streams where they were born, the earth which sleeps upon the bodies of their sires, and the music of the great Lake upon their shores.
>
> In the strong spirit of their hopes, they pray their brethren to join with them in supplicating their common Father to extend his wings over the little band, and gather them among his children.
>
> *They ask it of your justice; for you have the homes which once were theirs, and have grown rich with the heritage of their fathers*. (Emphasis added).[17]

The Ottawa petitioned again for U.S. citizenship in 1843 and 1844. Many Ottawa were cultivating their land and others were becoming wage laborers in commercial fishing enterprises. Also, the Chippewa petitioned the Michigan Legislature for citizenship support.

1842 Chippewa Cession of Western Upper Peninsula

In 1841, Congress appropriated money for the expenses of treaty negotiations with Indian tribes in Michigan for the purpose of extinguishing all of their land titles.[18] In 1842, Robert Stuart was appointed to negotiate a treaty with the Chippewa, the only Indians still holding lands in Michigan. Commissioner of Indian Affairs T. Hartley Crawford told Stuart to purchase the land in the upper peninsula of Michigan and to expand the purchase to lands south of Lake Superior in present day Wisconsin. Crawford also told Stuart that the treaty should contain a provision for the eventual removal of the Chippewa from the territory, but stated that it "is not likely that it will be necessary for them to remove for a considerable time:"

> I have also learned, unofficially, from the commissioner authorized to treat with the Chippewas, in the northwest of Michigan ... that he has succeeded in obtaining a cession of their land in Michigan... This acquisition, covers a valuable mineral region in Michigan ...[19]

The Treaty of 1842 provided that "The Indians residing on the Mineral district, shall be subject to removal therefrom at the pleasure of the President of the United States." Article 2 provided that the Indians "stipulate for the right of hunting on the ceded territory, with the other usual privileges of occupancy, until required to remove by the President of the United States..." The term provisions were ambiguous and, of course, resulted in varied interpretation and conflict.

1837 and 1842 Chippewa Treaties DOI Summary – Valuable Mineral District and Pine Forests Ceded

In 1852, Commissioner Lea summarized the status of the 1837 and 1842 Chippewa Treaties as they pertained to Michigan as follows:

> The most important treaties to which the Chippewas have at any time been parties, are the treaties of 1837 and of 1842. In these, *they ceded to this government all their possessions in Michigan and Wisconsin, comprising the rich mineral district which extends along the south coast of Lake Superior and the valuable pine forests* which skirt Black, Chippewa, St. Croix, Rum, and Wisconsin rivers, and tributaries. For these cessions, the United States agreed to pay them in money, goods, &c., the sum of $1,865,000 in manner and form as prescribed in the treaties. Article five of the treaty of 1837, and articles two and six of the treaty of 1842, provided for their continuance upon the ceded territory, with the usual privileges of occupancy, until required to remove by the President of the United States. (Emphasis added).[20]

While an order for removal, in accordance with treaty stipulations, was issued by President Taylor on February 6, 1850, it was never implemented.[21]

1844 Ottawa and Chippewa Petition to President for U.S. Citizenship

The Ottawas and Chippewas, still fearful of removal, submitted a joint petition to the President for U.S. citizenship.

> FATHER: At the last session of the Legislature of the State of Michigan, the chiefs and headmen of our brethren the Ottowas of Arbre Croche presented a petition praying our brothers of the Legislature to take such steps as to them might seem proper, to secure to those Ottowas a permanent location in the land of their birth, and ultimately the rights and privileges of American citizens. To the prayer of that petition the Legislature responded by unanimously instructing their Senators and requesting their representatives in Congress to exert their influence in obtaining for the Ottowas the rights and privileges for which they prayed…
>
> We have been informed by our father, the superintendent of our affairs, that our brethren in Congress were prevented, by the exigency of other and previous applications, from attending to our wishes at the last session. …
>
> *We desire earnestly to become good citizens, and to live in friendship with our brethren the white men, to die on the soil where we have always lived, and to leave it as an inheritance to our children.* … [Signed by sixty-one Indians.] (Emphasis added).[22]

1847 Resolution of Michigan to U.S. Congress in Support of Indians' Petition to Remain in Michigan

In 1847, Michigan submitted a resolution to allow the Indians in Michigan to remain, subject to their purchasing at the minimum price, the lands occupied and cultivated by them.

> JOINT RESOLUTION relative to a Petition of the Chippewa Indians. Whereas, Certain of the Chippewa Indians, residing in a portion of the Upper Peninsula, and employed in the cultivation of the soil, have petitioned the legislature of this state to aid them in procuring from Congress the passage of a law granting to them the right "of purchasing the lands on which they have made improvements, and holding them the same as American citizens;" …

> *Resolved*, That the consent of this state is hereby given to the passage of a law by congress granting the prayer of the petitioners, so far as to allow them and other Indians within this state, occupying and cultivating the soil, pre-emption rights in, and the ***privilege of purchasing at the minimum price, the lands so occupied and cultivated by them***, on the same footing as other inhabitants of this state. ...
> Approved March 17, 1847. (Emphasis added).²³

Chippewa Reservation to Be Allotted

By 1853, Commissioner of Indian Affairs Moneypenny was in support of the Chippewas being allowed to stay in Michigan on reservations, rather than being removed west.

> ***Most of them have comfortable homes, and, under the influence of the devoted efforts of several Christian denominations, are gradually improving and acquiring the habits and tastes of civilized life.*** By a provision of the State constitution, they are entitled to citizenship on becoming qualified therefor by intelligence and good character, and abandoning their tribal connection; and numbers have manifested a proper appreciation of this high privilege, and a laudable ambition to fit themselves for it. ***By treaty, these Indians have the right to a home west of the Mississippi should they desire to emigrate; but there is no prospect of their ever being willing to do so***, and the citizens of Michigan, it is understood, entertain no desire to have them expelled from the country and home of their forefathers. ***Suitable locations, it is understood, can be found for them in the State, where they can be concentrated*** under circumstances favorable to their comfort and improvement, without detriment to State or individual interests, and early measures for that purpose should be adopted. (Emphasis added).²⁴

The State of Michigan, in 1850, recognized Indians as citizens, so long as they became "civilized" and renounced their tribal membership: "... every civilized male inhabitant of Indian descent, a native of the United States and not a member of any tribe, shall be an elector and entitled to vote..."²⁵

Manypenny's reservation policy included "allotment," in which tribal lands would be divided among individual members. The new arrangements were revolutionary—along with allotment, a ten year period on restriction of convenance of land was imposed, and state citizenship, with a relinquishment of tribal affiliation was urged. He alerted the Department and the State in his Annual Message:

> The peculiar and unfortunate situation of the Indians in the State of Michigan, consisting, mainly, of the confederated bands of Ottowas and Chippewas, was fully stated last year, and the measure deemed best for their preservation and welfare suggested. It is requisite that there be new conventional arrangements with them, providing for material changes in their affairs, and in their relations with the United States and the State of Michigan.[26]

As the DOI prepared to make Moneypenny's changes, Henry Gilbert, the Indian Agent reported that not all Indians had received annuities due. This would have to be taken into account in the upcoming Treaty.

> The Interior Indians have received no annuities, until this year, under the treaties of 1837 and 1842, since the payment of 1851. ... I think justice requires that the United States should in some manner compensate them for the loss. The government has been in fault, and the Indians have suffered by it.[27]

Agent Gilbert also reported on the failure to judiciously expend educational funds:

> None of these funds have ever been disbursed through the medium of the agency and the agents, and consequently the government has never taken much interest in, or bestowed much attention on educational matters. The Indians are never informed how their money is expended, and they will now be very slow to believe that all the money due them from the United States under this head has ever been appropriated. I have myself but very recently been informed as to the disposition of this fund, and regret to say that, in my judgment, much of it has been very injudiciously expended. One school has received, for twenty years, from $1,600 to $1,800 per annum, at a point and under circumstances where $600 would have been a liberal allowance. Another school has been sustained by an appropriation of $1,200 per annum, when $400, judiciously expended, would have secured more beneficial results. The Indians have now been so far civilized that they will no longer acquiesce in any such [injudicious] policy...[28]

Part 3: Experimental Allotment Policy

1854 and 1855 Chippewa Treaties, Experimental Allotment Policy

In treaties signed in 1854 and 1855, the L'Anse and Lake Vieux Michigan Bands, the Ottawa and Chippewa and the Saginaw, Swan Creek, and Black River Bands became part of the federal experimental "allotment," policy, in which tribal lands were divided among individual members.[29] The treaties legally ended the threat of removal and made provisions for the allotment of reservations:

> The cornerstone of this ideology demanded that Indians everywhere abandon their traditional economic behaviors and become settled agriculturalists. But the climate and soils of northern Michigan presented significant barriers to developing a society dependent on agriculture. The Anishnabeg were neither more nor less successful than non-Indians in pursuing agriculture in the region, but that did not prevent the Indian Office from doggedly pursuing its goal of fostering agricultural dependence among them into the twentieth century.[30]

1855 Detroit Treaty Allotment Provisions Applicable to Ottawa

The Treaty of July 31, 1855,[31] made at Detroit, with the Ottawa and Chippewa Indians of Michigan, established reservations in Mason and Oceana counties and on Grand Traverse and Little Traverse bays. The reserved land was to be divided among individual Ottawa. Each head of a family was entitled to receive eighty acres; each person over the age of twenty-one but not the head of a family received forty acres; and each family of orphaned children under the age of twenty-one also received forty acres. The Indians had five years in which to select individual parcels and file their claims. The land would then be held in trust by the U.S. for ten years. During that time, it could not be taxed nor could it be sold. The U.S. was, also, released and discharged from all liability on account of former treaty stipulations.

Allotments were limited to the generation in 1855, even though more land existed. In the 1860s and 1870s, the Ottawa petitioned to allow the next generation to also claim allotments. In 1872, Congress enacted legislation permitting Ottawa who came of age after the 1855 treaty to claim 160 acres each within either the Oceana County reserve or ones at Grand Traverse Bay or Little Traverse Bay, under *the Homestead Act.* This meant, the lands would not have the protection afforded allotments. The claimants had to dwell on and improve their property for five years before they could be awarded a fee-simple patent. *Failure to improve the property or to dwell there could result in a loss of the claim.* It was common for colonial settlers and timber businesses to file suit for the invalidation of claims on land that would then be open for their settlement. These claims could be based on failure to *improve the property or dwell thereon or failure to comply with a technicality in applying for the land or challenging the status of the land as open for Indian settlement.*

After, the ten years were up, individual Ottawa landholders received patents and their land became freely alienable. Less than one year after four-hundred patents had been issued, one timber land speculator had already bought up more than six-thousand acres of land.

In 1872, surplus lands under the Detroit Treaty of 1855 were opened for non-Indian settlement. A railroad connecting Little Traverse Bay with the national rail network had opened for service, making transport possible, more reliable, available year-round, and not dependent on water access; thus, enhancing the demand for and value of the land and its resources.[32]

1855 Detroit Treaty Allotment Provisions Applicable to Chippewa

The 1855 Detroit Treaty provisions applicable to the Chippewa mirrored those of the Ottawa.

Dissolution of Tribal Status

The Treaty of 1855 had a unique provision regarding tribal status that would be the subject of legal controversy well into the twenty-first century. Article 5 simply provided that:

The ***tribal organization of said Ottawa and Chippewa Indians***, except so far as may be necessary for the purpose of carrying into effect the provisions of this agreement, ***is hereby dissolved***; and if at any time hereafter, further negotiations with the United States, in reference to any matters contained herein, should become necessary, no general convention of the Indians shall be called; but such as reside in the vicinity of any usual place of payment, or those only who are immediately interested in the questions involved, may arrange all matters between themselves and the United States, without the concurrence of other portions of their people, and as fully and conclusively, and with the same effect in every respect, as if all were represented. (Emphasis added).

Part 4: Massive Loss of Indian Land due to Fraud

1866, Indians Are Prey to Unscrupulous Whites

In 1866, Agent Richard M. Smith, Mackinac Indian Agency, reported on the plunder of Indian property by unscrupulous whites:

> Watched and pursued, and preyed upon as they have been by large numbers of unscrupulous white men, more powerful because more intelligent, it appears to me somewhat remarkable that their conduct and lives are as good and creditable as they are.
>
> Nor is the poor Indian wronged more by bad white men, but it is a fact which is made more apparent to me every year of my connection with this branch of public service, and I mention it more in sorrow than in anger, that many of the better class of society seem to regard him as an evil and forlorn bird of prey, to be plucked at will, and who do not hesitate to lend a helping hand in the foul and nefarious work, whenever an opportunity offers itself.
>
> And especially is this the case whenever the cash and goods annuities are paid to them in fulfilment of treaty stipulations. These, together with ***the lands reserved*** and set apart by the government for their use and benefit in their destitute and almost homeless condition, ***are very generally regarded as legitimate plunder***. Often their annuities obtained without a just equivalent, and their lands trespassed upon with impunity and without redress. ...

Trespasses are constantly increasing in number upon their reservations, and will undoubtedly continue to do so from year to year, as the tide of population sweeps over the northern portion of the State. It is constantly in motion, and *the restless and grasping white man looks upon, covets, and then appropriates the land designed and set apart by the government as the permanent and perhaps the last home of the Indian, who seems to have no efficient means of resistance or redress.* ...

The Indians in Michigan having heretofore ceded to the government large tracts of agricultural, timber, and mineral lands for an exceedingly small consideration, which are yielding immense wealth to the country, it can well afford to be not only just but generous towards them in the fulfilment of existing, and in the making and executing new treaties with them, and in which the rights of the Indians should be clearly defined, fully protected and faithfully enforced. (Emphasis added).[33]

1871, Massive Sale of Indian Allotments by Grand River Ottawa and Chippewa

In 1871, Agent Richard M. Smith, Mackinac Indian Agency, reported that about 400 patents were transmitted to the Grand River Ottawa and Chippewa by his immediate predecessor with the following consequences:

[T]he keen-scented and grasping white man, with his artful cunning, had already been there, and that by deed and other expedients he had actually possessed himself of more than 6,000 acres of the land so patented to them as their future homes. I consider that reserve in a fair way to be broken up, and that at no distant day; for I understand that the work of dispossessing those Indians of the title of these lands is still going on without let or hinderance.

And what is and will be true of this reserve will, in all probability, sooner or later be true of the other reserves of the agency, provided the like patents shall be issued to the Indians located thereon. And most assuredly this will be the case if the greed of gain, whisky, the general taxation of the Indians, and other pernicious influences, can accomplish it. *In my opinion, the general result of all this will be an unnecessary amount of poverty and wretchedness to the Indian and the hastening him to utter extinction as a race, and to the State of Michigan an increased amount of pauperism and crime within its borders*. (Emphasis added).[34]

1871, Saginaw Sale of Allotments with Timber on Isabella Reservation

The 1864 Treaty with the Saginaw, Black River, and Swan Creek Chippewa established the Isabella Reservation in Isabella County, Michigan, providing that the land was set aside for the "exclusive use, ownership, and occupancy of the Saginaw Chippewa." Even before patents to the land had been delivered to the Ottawa and Chippewa in Isabella County,

> *"more than 500 contracts, large and small, written and otherwise, have been made with those Indians, chiefly for their pine timber* ... under which 50 to 100 million feet of their pine timber had already been cut and removed. ... And furthermore, information has reached this office, which is regarded as reliable, that it is in contemplation by the parties in interest in those contracts to cut and remove millions upon millions of feet more of the timber now standing... *nearly all of the above contracts ... have been in fraud of the treaty and other rights of those Indians.* Report of Richard M. Smith, Mackinac Indian Agency (Sept. 18, 1871) (Emphasis added).[35]

The Saginaw Chippewa Indian Tribe of Michigan describes this period as follows:

> When our people moved to the Isabella Indian Reservation the conditions were extremely grim and our annuity payments were delayed, causing many of our people to succumb to hunger and sickness. During this time, Isabella County had some of the best stands of white pine in the whole state of Michigan and lumbermen were eager to swindle us out of our lands. *Many of our people sold their allotments to lumber sharks for a small fraction of their value. For many, selling their allotment was the only way to feed their families. This, coupled with numerous shoddy deals between Indian Agents and timber barons, led to a rapid dispossession of our land base. Of the more than 1,500 allotments issued to our ancestors in the late 1800s, only a handful of these were owned by tribal members by 1934.* (Emphasis added).[36]

Commissioner Advocates for State Taking Over Responsibility for Indians

Commissioner Edw. P. Smith advocated for the State to assume responsibility for the Indians in Michigan:

Four-fifths of the Indians within her borders are prepared for full citizenship, living in their own homes and farms; and the others are in such a condition of advancement as to be quite unlikely to receive any further Government aid than is provided in their treaty stipulations. It is, therefore, largely for the interests of Michigan as well as for her Indians, that she should take charge of this people; and that the treaty-funds still due them should be so expended through her local officers that the most benefit shall be derived therefrom in the direction of the civilization and preparation for citizenship of a people who are a part of her body politic.[37]

Loss of Land due to Fraud and Otherwise

When owners of the lands had to leave to work in the timber or fishing industries, non-Indians that desired the lands reported that they were abandoned; the Indians would return from their labors to find the complainant had received a certificate to the land in their stead. Report of George Lee, Michigan Agency (August 28, 1877).

In 1878, Agent Geo. W. Lee reported that when he tried to stop the illegal taking of land, he found himself victim to "the most vindictive assaults from these individuals, as they seem to think the Indians and their property are their lawful prey." He reported that the lands of the Grand Traverse Ottawa were fast passing from their hands, while among the Saginaw, Swan Creek, and Black River Chippewa, "not one in ten ... who have had these lands owns an acre, and they are as poor as if they never owned them."

> The Chippewas of Saginaw, Swan Creek, and Black River were in 1855 granted by treaty made at that time certain unsold lands in six townships selected in Isabella County, upon which the most part of the tribe located.
>
> All who were of the age of 21 years or over received lands in severalty, but through the shameful neglect of the agents then and since in charge, they have frittered a large proportion of them away, and today, I am of the opinion, not one in ten who have had these lands owns an acre, and they are as poor as if they had never owned them. More than two-thirds of the tribe are now living in scattered groups along the Saginaw River or Bay, near the homes of their childhood, living as best they can; those who remain on the reservation are in far the most favorable circumstances.

There are many of the younger people who are coming of age who are now receiving allotments of land, upon which I most earnestly recommend in all cases that an inalienable clause be inserted, which, if insisted upon and adhered to, would have added more than a million of dollars to the wealth of former allottees of these lands. This squandering of their patrimony in the past cannot now be remedied, but enough remains for the future to help very materially the generation now coming into possession of their heritage.

Large trespasses have been committed from year to year upon these lands, to which the attention of the proper officers has been called, but still the work of robbery and destruction goes on unchecked. (Emphasis added).[38]

Other lands were lost due to barriers created by the non-Indian legal system. Under the 1872 Act, for example, Indians were required to pay $14 for a certificate to remain on their lands and needed that much more to finance the trip to the Land Office to obtain it. The many that could not afford this were evicted when non-Indians obtained certificates for these "unclaimed" lands.

Much other land was sold for failure to pay taxes on the lands, although in some cases the taxes were imposed before the period of tax immunity had expired.

"Outrageous Frauds" Committed at Isabella Reservation

An investigation by Special Agent Edwin Brooks in 1878 at the Isabella Reservation uncovered "outrageous frauds." He was called back to Washington on his arrival at the Reservation but stayed an extra day to complete his brief investigation due to the extent of the frauds he uncovered. His handwritten Report is 38 pages long (names are redacted herein). He urged that the DOI consider criminal prosecution, finding in particular that in issuing 1,735 patents at Isabella, Indian Agent George Betts had deemed a mere 24 allottees as "not so competent" to receive their patents in fee.[39]

Competency was described as follows: "Those who are intelligent and have sufficient education and are qualified by business habits to prudently manage their own affairs." [p. 10].

Agent Brooks described the land as follows: "large quantities of it was very valuable pine, and the remainder among the finest agricultural land in the State" [p. 12].

"At the time the selections were made, there was a great struggle on the part of various speculators and lumbermen to obtain title to the lands selected. Prior to the making of the lists, these parties had, by competent agents, been over the whole reservation and estimated the timber on the tracts. When the lands were selected and before the lists were approved or patents issued deeds to the timber on large quantities of the pine lands were taken by various parties among them ___ ..." and for a large portion of which but a *mere tithe of the actual value of the timber was paid*. [pp. 12-13] ...

[O]f the records of Isabella County ___ have 822 deeds for timber purchased from Indians on record and up to the present time they have recorded in said records 855 deeds... [pp. 14-15]. ___ has title to, I think, at least one hundred selections ... and a pretended receipt taken which was in fact a Warranty Deed. [p. 16].

I saw at least a hundred Indians ... listed as competent, not one of whom was, in my judgment, in any way capable of transacting any kind of business. (Emphasis in original). [p. 18].

... such wholesale frauds could not have been conceived and executed without the connivance of the agents. [p. 20].

These facts, if no others existed, are sufficient to show fraud and collusion of the darkest character on one side, and on the part of the Indians, a degree of ignorance and incompetency alone sufficient to warrant the office in cancelling the whole list. [p. 25].

The facts discovered by the brief investigation made, in my opinion, conclusively show that the schedule ... is in the main fraudulent, that it was prepared by an Agent in collusion with, and in the interest of a pack of unscrupulous land sharks seeking and conspiring to defraud the Government and the Indians of a large tract of valuable land ...(Emphasis added). [pp. 34-35].

The parties ... are wealthy and more than ordinarily influential in civil, religious and political circles, and will doubtless suppress an investigation ... [p. 37].

Eventually a government investigation forced Agent Betts to *resign*, but not before five-sixths of the land he had allocated to Saginaw-Chippewa Tribal members had been sold.[p.19] In all, about 75,000 acres were sold, of which the federal government eventually returned 6,500 acres to reserve land status.

1886, Saginaw Timber Cut and Sold for Fraction of Value

In 1886, Mark W. Stevens, Mackinac Indian Agency, reported that Saginaw timber was being cut and sold for a fraction of its value:

> Of the amount patented in fee simple not over 2,000 acres are owned by the Indians. *They have parted with the land and have not received in compensation the merest fraction of its value*. A portion of these lands were valuable for their pine timber, and the balance of it was valuable for hardwood timber and farming purposes. Of the amount granted by restricted patents, it has been sold. *The valuable timber on the remaining 5,920 acres has nearly all been cut and taken away*. (Emphasis added).[40]
>
> The prosperity of the Indians upon the *Isabella Reservation has not been all that could be desired; indeed, it has not been what it might have been and what it would have been had their rights and their interests been protected and properly guarded by the Government*. To illustrate: Take the Isabella Reservation, as above stated; the amount of land ceded to them under the treaty and subject to allotment was 98,760 acres. The amount patented to them in fee simple, which they had a right to dispose of, experience has shown was a gross and wanton outrage. These lands in Isabella County, a large portion of them at least, were valuable for their pine timber. *The timber upon the lands has been cut and taken away from the lands, and neither, the Indians nor the Government have ever received the smallest pittance therefor*. The 6,640 acres which was given to them by restricted patents they are now possessed of; and the 886 acres of improved and tillable land is a portion of the land that was granted to them by restricted patents. This fact alone shows that for the best interest of the Indians not an acre of land ought ever to have been given to them in fee simple. (Emphasis added).

A few years ago the Indians on the Isabella Reservation numbered in the neighborhood of 2,000; but because of the frauds, the intimidations, and the threats that have been brought to bear upon them by the whites in the vicinity, they have been compelled for their own safety and welfare to seek other places of abode. Thus, the Indians of this band are scattered all over Northern Michigan, mingled with other bands. Large numbers of them have gone West and many of them have gone to Canada. Had their interests been properly guarded, today they might be living upon the reservation with a large area of improved land, prosperous and happy.

Another cause preventing their prosperity is that certain land speculators claim title to very much of the lands that were never patented, also claim to have titles to the lands that have been patented by restricted patents. The Indians are aware of their claim of title, consequently, cannot be induced to go upon the land and work and improve it, for the reason they believe at some time they would be ejected from the land and thereby lose their labor and the land. A large amount of land on the reservation, some of which are vacant lands and some of which have been patented by restricted patents, are covered by tax titles, thus intimidating and preventing the Indians from improving the land, although as a matter of fact and law these claims of title are not valid; but the effect upon the Indian is the same as though they were. *In short, the Indians on the Isabella Reservation have been the victims of long and continuous frauds and outrages, without interruption and without measures of prevention being instituted, until they are entirely discouraged and disorganized and their identity nearly destroyed.* ...

I desire to urge upon the Department that no more patents in fee-simple be issued to the Indian, in Michigan. In case frauds and trespasses in reference to lands and timber have been perpetrated upon lands where patents have been issued in simple, redress can be had for the Indians only in the State courts, which substantially means no redress at all, for the reason that the Indian has not the money nor the ability to conduct a suit. (Emphasis added).[41]

1887, Isabella Reservation Scheme to Dispossess Indians of Land Consummated

In 1887, Agent Mark W. Stevens, Mackinac Indian Agency, reported that Isabella Reservation had been the subject of conspiracy and fraud:

> The Indians on the Isabella reservation have not been and are not prosperous; they are more or less discontented, unsettled, and indolent. It can be attributed to no other cause than the fact that the largest part of their lands were patented to them in fee simple without any restrictions as to the sale of them, resulting in the almost entire dispossession of their land by bartering them away without scarcely any equivalent therefor. They are fast disappearing from the reservation, some going to Canada, others farther north and west.
> ... *Their present condition is the result of a well laid scheme contemplated many years ago, ripened and consummated openly and publicly without the intervention of the Government*, whose duty it was to bring the strong arm of the law to bear upon the men who have grown wealthy by their ill gotten gains, taken from the people whom they now despise. However satisfactory may be the result of the efforts now pending, but little will be accomplished in restoring that of which they have been despoiled. (Emphasis added).[42]

Department Had Complete Knowledge of Frauds at Isabella Reservation between 1865 and 1884

If there is any doubt that the DOI had complete knowledge of the frauds committed at the Isabella Reservation, one need only read the written statement by *Com'r Ezra A. Hayt* detailing the frauds. **This statement documents the absolute and total failure of the DOI to protect Indian lands at the Isabella Reservation and elsewhere.**

> **A Permanent Land Title** But after the issue of patents, the difficulties surrounding them do not cease. A few, it is true, hold to their land and make rapid and encouraging progress in agricultural pursuits. The major portion of them, however, yielding to the pressure surrounding them, *fall victims to the greed of unscrupulous white men, and, one by one, part with or are defrauded of their lands. Every means that human ingenuity can devise, legal or illegal, has been resorted to for the purpose of obtaining possession of Indian lands.*
>
> In some cases title in severalty in fee simple has been given to the individual members of the tribes for a certain quantity of the land embraced in the reservation.

Experience has shown that even the most advanced and civilized of our Indians are not capable of defending their lands when title in fee is once vested in them. The reservations in such cases are at once infested by a class of land-sharks who do not hesitate to resort to any measure, however iniquitous, to defraud the Indians of their lands. *Whiskey is given them, and while they are under its influence they are made to sign deeds of conveyance, without consideration. They are often induced to sign what they are informed is a contract of sale for a few trees growing on their land, with a receipt for the consideration paid; or some party goes to them claiming to be an agent of the State or county, distributing funds to the poor. This party will pay the Indian five or ten dollars, and procure his signature to a pretended receipt for the same, when in reality the paper signed is a warranty deed, which is recorded, and generally the land is sold to a third and innocent party before the Indian discovers the fraud which has been practiced upon him.*

In other cases the Indians complain, and, as it appears, not without cause, that *they are subjected to unequal and unjust taxation which they are unable to meet, and are thus divested of the title to their lands.*

Again they are induced to mortgage their lands for small sums which they are told will enable them to make money and improve their farms as their white neighbors have done. These mortgages are small payable generally at a time when the Indians are likely to have no money; an attorney fee of seventy-five or one hundred dollars is inserted. At maturity if the mortgage is not satisfied, which generally happens, foreclosure is had, the land is sold, and the Indian is left homeless and hopeless, a pauper for the community to support.

Out of 1,735 Indians to whom patents were issued about the year 1871 on the Chippewa Reservation of Isabella County, Michigan, fully fivesixths have sold, or in some manner have been cheated out of, their lands. A few of them have sold at something near a fair consideration. *Many have been defrauded of their lands by some of the measures above named or other equally nefarious practices, while others, in large numbers, sold their lands before the selections were approved or patents issued, receiving only a nominal price (about twenty-five cents per acre) for lands worth from $3 to $25 per acre. One of these selections was purchased for $15, and the party who purchased the same has been offered $4,000 for it but refused to sell.*

> *All the circumstances connected with these sales point directly to collusion between the agent and the parties purchasing in the execution of these unmitigated frauds.*
> ...
> [T]he reports of this office, and of each and every officer who has intelligently investigated this question, all go to show the necessity for a permanent home for the Indians with an indefeasible title to the same. (Emphasis added).[43]

Agent Stevens similarly reported:

> When I first assumed charge of this agency, it was brought to my notice that for many years, more particularly since 1870, trespassers had been despoiling the Indian lands on the Isabella Reservation of the timber, much of which was very valuable pine. I made a sufficient investigation to convince me beyond a doubt that the charges against trespassers were well founded. I reported the same to the honorable Commissioner of Indian Affairs, who at once directed me to use all diligence in an effort to recover the value of the timber and to bring the trespassers to justice; since which time six suits were commenced in the United States court for the recovery of the timber, against prominent lumber-men in Saginaw and Mount Pleasant, in four of which judgments were obtained in favor of the United States. Four criminal suits were commenced, in three of which convictions were obtained, and in one the jury stood eight for conviction and four for acquittal. ...
>
> There is now but little green pine timber on the Isabella Reservation ... I will not, in this report, attempt, to go into the question of the frauds and timber steals on the Isabella Reservation, for at best I could only convey a faint idea of them; but *had the United States, by its officers, used the means within their power, (for the Interior Department had full and complete knowledge, which was unmistakable, of the extent of the frauds between the years 1865 and 1884), thousands of dollars could, and would, have been saved to the Government and Indians.* (Emphasis added).[44]

1889, Mackinac Indian Agency Abolished Without Regard to Numerous Frauds

It is not surprising that the Mackinac Indian Agency would be abolished, without regard to the numerous frauds occurring there. Agents Smith and Stevens had been justifiably outspoken about the frauds occurring at their agency. While the Department stated it did not think the Indians would suffer materially without an Agent assigned to this area, it was extremely wrong in not fighting to keep this agency open. Ongoing frauds continued in the absence of any Departmental oversight.

The abolishing of this agency was not recommended by the Department, nor was this office consulted in the matter. The wisdom of such summary action may be questionable but it is not probable that any serious embarrassment to the service will result, or that the Indians now left to their own resources will suffer materially. They are fairly advanced in civilization, and should be allowed all the privileges of citizenship and the protection of State law; and the State should also make provision for the education of their children. At present they have no educational facilities, but they have been induced to send some of their children to Indian training schools, especially the school located at Carlisle, Pa.[45]

1905, No Fair Market Value in 200 Sales at L'Anse and Ontonagon Reservations

In 1905, in 200 land sales at L'Anse and Ontonagon Reservations, the consideration was *far below* market value and in some cases, no payment evidenced. Once again, the Department would have to conduct an investigation.

... Joseph R. Farr, superintendent of logging, was directed on April 8, 1905, to proceed at once to Baraga, Mich., and ascertain the value of timber and land sold on the L'Anse and Ontonagon reservations. His reports of May 26 and July 15, transmitted to the Department on August 7, showed that the consideration named in the deeds was far below the valuation placed by him upon the land and timber, and that, except in a few cases, no evidence of payment of the consideration accompanied the deeds.

On August 10 the Department directed that future sales must be made by petition and on sealed bids, all sales of the timber and lands of the L'Anse allottees to be, as far as practicable, under the general supervision of Superintendent Farr. On September 8 the Department, concurring in Office recommendation of the same date, directed the submission to the Department, for disapproval, of all the deeds where the consideration was less than the value ascertained by Superintendent Farr, the vendee to be allowed to present new deeds which should show the consideration named by him and be accompanied by proper certificates of deposit or other exchange.[46]

1906, Theft of Large Amount of Timber Discovered at L'Anse Reservation

Special Disbursing Agent Romulus S. Buckland's Report speaks for itself:

The local superintendent of logging at this agency has examined about all the lands on the L'Anse and Ontonagon reservations and has been assisted by a compass man when necessary. *A large amount of timber was removed from the L'Anse Reservation some years ago by unknown persons*, but the past year no timber has been removed or cut from this reservation without the approval of the Department. Romulus S. Buckland, Special Disbursing Agent (Emphasis added).[47]

1907, 200 Land Sales at L'Anse and Ontonagon Reservations Rejected due to Fraud

In 1907, Commissioner Francis E. Leupp reported on the land sales fraud at L'Anse and Ontonagon Reservations and the remedial action instituted:

Two years ago I referred in my report to the suspension of action, at my instance, on nearly 200 deeds executed by members of the L'Anse and Ontonagon bands of Chippewa Indians, in Michigan, covering timber lands. An appraisement of these lands during the summer of 1905, by J. R. Farr, superintendent of logging in the Indian Service, showed that the *lands were worth from three to four times the amounts for which the deeds were executed*; and on this representation of the facts the President, on November 7, 1905, disapproved all the conveyances. The grantees in the deeds then offered to pay the difference between the sums named in the deeds and the appraisal and asked for an opportunity to submit proof of goods furnished and money paid on account of the original purchase prices. This was granted. After a delay of several months they submitted sundry receipts for money and unitemized bills purporting to be for goods delivered; but since the Indians denied that goods in the quantities indicated by the bills had been delivered to them, and declared that many of the money receipts did not represent actual payments or were greatly in excess of the amounts paid, I insisted upon more satisfactory proof from the grantees. It was not furnished; and the Department being convinced that none of the evidence submitted constituted satisfactory proof of payment, all was rejected.

The purchasers under the disapproved deeds were notified that unless they deposited, within thirty days, the amount of the appraisement made by Mr. Farr, the lands would immediately thereafter be offered for sale to the highest bidder. In every instance the deposit was made within the time fixed.[48]

Part 5: Tribal Status Denied

Although Michigan today is home to twelve federally recognized Indian tribes, each of them has experienced long periods during which the federal government denied their tribal status. Starting in 1872, the federal government began to use Article 5 of the Detroit Treaty and the fact that the federal government no longer held lands in trust for the tribes to deny that these tribes retained any sovereign status. Secretary of the Interior Columbus Delano was apparently the first to make this mistake, declaring in a March 27, 1872, letter to the Commissioner of Indian affairs that once the annuity payments called for in the 1855 treaty were completed later that year "tribal relations will be terminated."[49]

Tribal representatives going to Washington to press their treaty claims were told that the United States no longer maintained a governmental relationship with them.[50]

Part 6: Settlement of Michigan by Colonial Settlers

On Jan. 11, 1805, Congress passed an act for the organization of Michigan Territory. Governor William Hull was appointed and he arrived at his post in Detroit in July of 1805.

The pioneer settlers of the 1820s found a land covered by dense stands of virgin timber. It grew on the eastern side of Michigan and all over northern Michigan. Michigan's watershed divide in the middle regions resulted in surface stream and river water flowing both east and west. The eastern flowing rivers benefitted the Saginaw country, and the westerly flowing waters made Muskegon a commercial timber leader.

The most valuable forests were in the central part of the Lower Peninsula of Michigan, where Isabella County is located. By 1853, there were twenty-three sawmills operating on the Saginaw River, with twenty-one more under construction. "Timber cruisers," in their reconnaissance of the area for standing timber to feed the mills, recommended buying thousands of acres of land.

The lumber industry's heavy, unwieldy product was of commercial value only in large volume. Acquiring sufficient timber, removing it from the forest, transporting to where it could be milled and getting it to market, in bulk, was made profitable by cheap land prices.

Land Act of 1820

Previous to 1820 the price of public lands was $2.00 per acre, on the installment plan, 50 cents down and 50 cents per year. The option to pay in installments encouraged buying land, not for settlement, but to hold it, waiting for prices to increase. To reduce this speculation, the policy was changed in 1820 to the sale of ***80 acre plots at $1.25 per acre***, for cash in full at the time of purchase. (Emphasis added).[51]

While this new Act was intended to cut down speculation, it may have worked in states other than Michigan. "The average yield of timber from the Michigan pine lands was 5,000 board feet at an average stumpage value of $3.00 per thousand. In addition, these early lands were not average, some of those on the western side of the High Plains yielded almost 30,000 board feet per acre." So for a mere $1.25 per acre, it was worth buying as much land as possible for future logging or sale.

Among the more prevalent business practices employed by the early lumbermen were such questionable tactics as the use of dummy entrymen, cutting "around forty, and the denial of access or right-of-way to a competitor.

Part 7: Logging Underway

New England and Maine Supplied Experienced Work Force

New England, especially Maine and New York, provided an experienced business model and work force for Michigan. The eastern forests had been clear-cut and the labor force was eager to move westward. The elementary skill set was the same, so the logging expertise was readily transferable. Logging camps sprung up in the dense Michigan pine forests. Eastern money readily flowed west to support the logging and mill industry.

Logging Underway in 1830s

Between 1830 and 1840, Lakes Huron, Michigan and Superior, and Michigan's many streams and rivers, served as natural transportation conduits for logging. The map below depicts the markets eager for lumber. Michigan could readily serve the huge markets of Chicago and Milwaukee just across Lake Michigan. The Saginaw, Au Sable, Manistee, Escanaba, Muskegon, Thunder Bay and Menominee Rivers (and their tributaries) provided transportation for many of the harvested logs to mills and markets, and, most importantly, provided hydro-power for the mills. Numerous sloughs, oxbows, and bays provided ideal holdings areas for cut timber waiting to be milled. They reduced logging costs by providing "log booms" for sorting and storage.

With the completion of the Erie Canal in 1825 and the Welland Canal in 1829, Michigan was primed to serve markets in New York and Pennsylvania which had been deforested, yet were still in need of lumber. It could serve Ohio, Indiana, Illinois and the upcoming agricultural settlements in Iowa, Kansas, and Nebraska.

Any investor could see the pristine and prime environment Michigan provided for logging. In 1832, a two thousand foot capacity mill was placed in operation in eastern Michigan's Lower Peninsula at the Saginaws, with a natural Bay and ready access to Lake Huron. Muskegon, on the Muskegon River, and Lake Michigan, along with South Haven. It would serve the huge markets of Chicago and Milwaukee, just across Lake Michigan.

In general, the pine lands in the northern part of the Upper Peninsula and the central and southern, and eastern areas were logged first and most completely. Pine was the ideal wood for home construction that the exploding influx of settlers demanded. Pine floated; it was easily worked and straight-grained. Michigan's pine belt was accessible by water for shipping.

While the Saginaw region prospered in the eastern Lower Peninsula, the founding of Muskegon in 1837 marked the west coast's entrance into the lumber business. Once under way, logging progressed rapidly.

Throughout the 1840s, Michigan pine was in high demand in the Albany, Chicago and prairie states. The rush was on and most of the land sold for a modicum of $1.25 an acre. Profitably was assured and fortunes would be made.

> "The first cargo shipped from the Saginaws was from the Emerson mill in 1847. It was consigned to C. P. Williams & Company, of Albany, New York."[52] This shipment to a distant market proved up the lumber business of the Saginaw valley. Emerson became a thriving hub of lumbering.

Michigan Statehood in 1837

Michigan became a state in 1837 and its legislature immediately began petitioning Congress to remove the tribes.

1850s, Logging in Lower Peninsula

Logging companies soon dominated the area known as the "High Plains," in the northern, central Lower Peninsula, with the largest and best pine stands. The AuSable and Manistee Rivers provided transport. There were no settlements in the pine country, except along the lake shore. The region, though, had been officially surveyed with marked township and section lines. A Land Office was opened at Ionia. By 1850, there were mills in western Michigan, along the coast line of Lake Michigan, at Muskegon and at Manistee, the mouth of the Manistee River.

By 1854 there were, upon the authority of John S. Estabrook, twenty-nine mills on the river, and nine others in process of building, with an estimated cutting capacity of one hundred million feet a year. At Saginaw there were fourteen sawmills in 1857, and nine on the tributary streams, which in that year cut sixty million feet of lumber.[53]

The map below gives an idea of the production that could be expected in the three areas of the Muskegon River, AuSable and Saginaw.

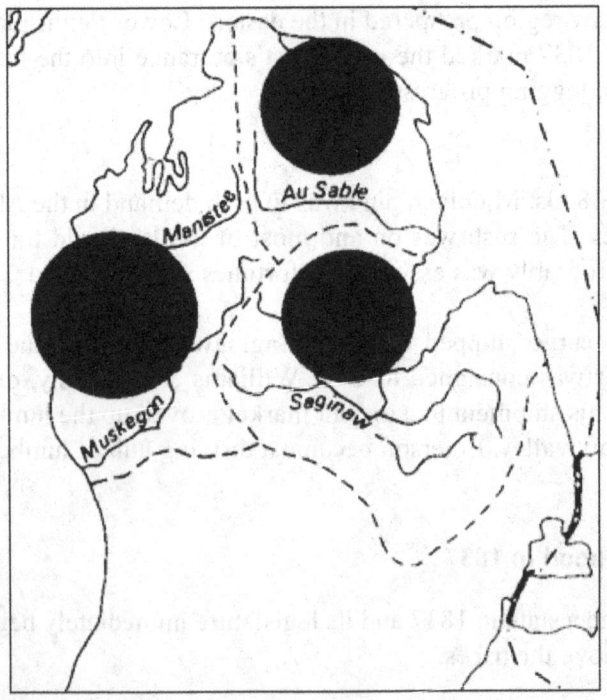

Estimates of the Number of Standing White Pine in Major Watersheds 1880, Michigan, The Lumber Industry https://slideplayer.com/slide/4048916/ (accessed online June 29, 2022).

The huge population increases in the Great Lakes area accounted for the growth of the timber industry in Michigan.

Population Increase			
State	1850	1900	%age Increase
Minnesota	6,077	1,750,394	2,920%
Wisconsin	305,391	2,069,042	680%
Illinois	851,470	4,821,550	570%
Iowa	192,211	2,231,853	1,160%

1860s, Saginaw Valley Maximum Production

The Saginaw Valley was the leading lumbering area between 1840 and 1860. By 1860, lumbering was second only to agriculture as the state's principal means of livelihood.

By 1869, Michigan was producing more lumber than any other state, a distinction it continued to hold for 30 years. This was possible due to (1) the fraudulent dispossession of Indian lands; (2) the abundance of timber; (3) easy access to water or rail transport; (4) continually escalating demand due to the increase in population and settlement of not only the Great Lakes but the central U.S.; (5) investment from eastern capitalists who knew, based on resource analyses, that a hefty return on their investment was guaranteed; and, (6) a skilled labor force from the denuded eastern forests. *The peak of Michigan's great timber harvest was reached in 1889–1890 when mills cut a total of 5.5 billion board feet of lumber, mostly pine. By 1900, most of the pine in the Lower Peninsula was gone.*

1870s, Timber Pirating on Federal Lands

By the 1870s there were over 400 sawmills and 800 logging camps in the Lower Peninsula. There was also a tremendous increase in lumber orders from railroads. This demand resulted in timber pirating on federal lands.

In 1879, President Rutherford B. Hayes highlighted the problem in his State of the Union message:

The efforts made by the Department of the Interior to arrest the depredations on the timber lands of the United States have been continued, and have met with considerable success. A large number of cases of trespass have been prosecuted in the courts of the United States; others have been settled, the trespassers offering to make payment to the Government for the value of the timber taken by them.

I therefore earnestly invite the attention of Congress to the recommendation made by the Secretary of the Interior, that a law be enacted enabling the Government to sell timber from the public lands without conveying the fee, where such lands are principally valuable for the timber thereon.[54]

Lumber Production in 1889, m.b.f.

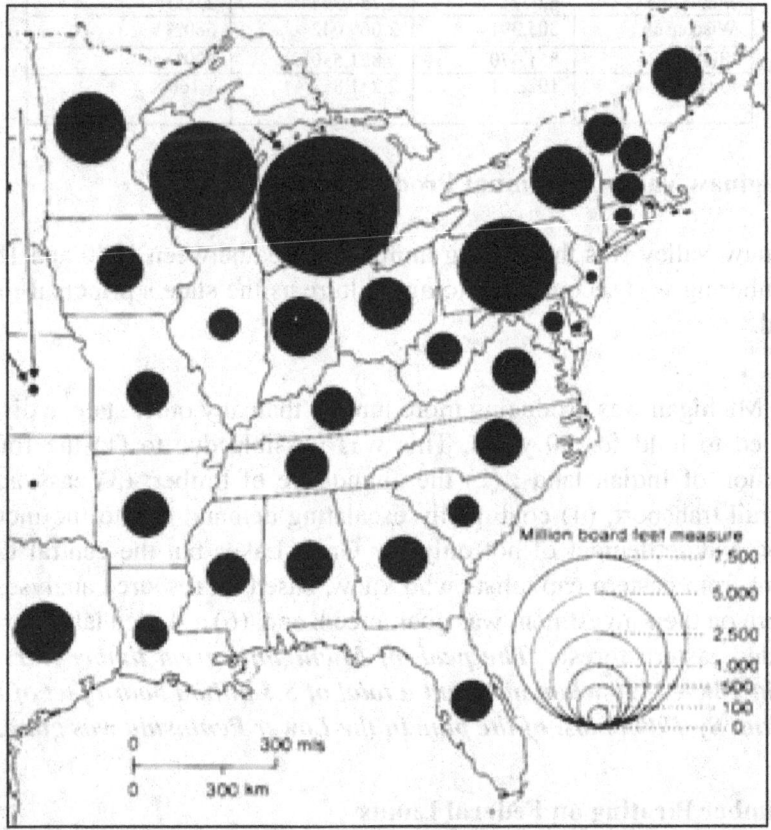

Lumber production in 1889, in m.b.f. Michigan, The Lumber Industry https://slideplayer.com/slide/4048916/ (accessed online June 29, 2022).

1900s, Decline in Logging

The industry grew rapidly from the 1850s through the 1890s, encouraging the settlement of the state's northern regions and development of a wood products industry. Many felt that the huge forests of Michigan would last for many, many years, yet within a 20 year period, 1870 to 1890, most of the trees were cut. The peak of Michigan's great timber harvest was reached in 1889–1890 when mills cut a total of 5.5 billion board feet of lumber, mostly pine. By 1900, most of the pine in the Lower Peninsula was gone.

Lumber Barons

The production numbers below resulted in lumber barons acquiring large holdings. Investment capital came from the east and from the Chicago area. The window of opportunity was narrow. By 1911, logging moved west. By 1926, 92% of Michigan's forest was gone.

Michigan Lumber Production (By Species – Millions of Board Feet)						
Species	1889	1899	1905	1910	1915
White Pine	3489	1285	463	128	64
Hemlock	600	842	570	637	373
Maple	400	400	358	508	340
Total (All Species)	5478	3018	1720	1681	1032

Source: Reynolds and Pierson, Forest Product Statistics of the Lake States, pp. 5-6.

The Michigan Lumber Industry 1860-1870			
	1860	1870	Increase
Production (Millions of Feet)	796	2121	267%
Value of Product (Thousands of Dollars)	9,303	31,946	343%
Capital in Sawmills (Thousands of Dollars)	7,736	26,990	351%
No. of Sawmills	986	1,571	159%
No. of Employees	7,491	21,881	292%

Source: Benson, "Logs and Lumber," p. 213. Neithercut, Mark Edward. *THE WHITE PINE INDUSTRY AND THE TRANSFORMATION OF NINETEENTH CENTURY MICHIGAN*. Diss. University of British Columbia, 1984, p.140

David Whitney, Jr., made his millions in Massachusetts as a lumber baron, then moved to Detroit in 1857. Known as "the man who could out-lumber Paul Bunyan," Whitney was a multi- millionaire lumberman, vessel owner, and banker who built a fortune from the pine forests of Michigan and Wisconsin. When he died in 1900, Whitney was the wealthiest man in Detroit, with a fortune estimated at $15 million.

Henry Crapo was another easterner. He was a successful businessman from Massachusetts before migrating with his family to Flint in 1856. He became mayor of Flint in 1860, a member of the state senate in 1862, and was elected governor in 1864.

Charles Hackley was another famous lumber baron, making up to $6,000,000. His philanthropy built the city of Muskegon, along with, hospitals, schools, parks and libraries.

Charles Mears purchased about 40,000 acres of land, constructed and operated 15 mills, and built five harbors along the western coast of Michigan to transport his lumber.[55]

Part 8: Federal Land Disposal in Michigan 1800-1900

Michigan

    1800 Land Held by Federal Government
    Total Acreage: 36,357,760
    1850 25.4 Million Acres
    1870 8.1.Million Acres

Homestead Act

    19,861 Homesteads:
    Total Homestead Acreage: 2,321,937
    Total Percentage: 6%

Land Grants (Railroads, Universities (Morrill Act)

    1870 About 12 Million Acres

Land Grant College 240,000 Acres

Railroads 3.1 Million Acres

Canals (Other Improvements) 750,000 Acres

Swamp Lands 5.8 Million Acres

Military Warrants 3.6 Million Acres

Part 9: Federally Recognized Indian Nations in Michigan

The dispossession of Indian Nations' timberland resources dramatically affected their well-being and economic development. The DOI could have encouraged tribes to hold on to their valuable lands, ceded by the millions of acres at the urging of the Treaty Commissioners. Instead, with the massive cession of lands, removal, concentration and consolidation of tribes on small tracts of non-arable land, establishment of reservations akin to concentration camps, and allotment, that Indian Nations once self-sufficient became destitute paupers. It is only through the courage of the Indians that lived through the era of 1850–1900 that there are currently twelve (12) federally recognized Indian Nations in Michigan who will be able to exercise their sovereignty and self-determination to thrive.

    Bay Mills Chippewa Indian Community
    Grand Traverse Bay Band of Ottawa and Chippewa Indians
    Hannahville Indian Community Band of Potawatomi
    Keweenaw Bay Indian Community, Lake Superior Band of Chippewa Indians
    Lac Vieux Desert Band of Lake Superior Chippewa Indians
    Little River Band of Ottawa Indians
    Little Traverse Bay Bands of Ottawa Indians
    Match-e-be-nash-she-wish Band of Potawatomi Indians of Michigan (Also known as Gunn Lake Tribe)
    Nottawaseppi Huron Band of Potawatomi
    Pokagon Band of Potawatomi Indians
    Saginaw Chippewa Indian Tribe (Mt. Pleasant)
    Sault Ste. Marie Tribe of Chippewa Indians (Sault Ste. Marie)

Notes: Carving Up Michigan

1. http://uptreeid.com/History/PreSett.htm (accessed online June 20, 2022).
2. Atlas of Michigan, ed. Lawrence M. Sommers, 1977. https://project.geo.msu.edu/geogmich/Indian_cessions.html (accessed online June 18, 2022).
3. Treaty with the Ottawa, Etc., 1807. November 17, 1807, 7 Stat. 105.
4. Historical Collections, Volume 7, Michigan State Historical Society, Michigan Historical Commission, 1886; https://project.geo.msu.edu/geogmich/saginaw-cession.html (accessed online June 18, 2022).
5. History of Saginaw County, Michigan: Historical, Commercial, Biographical. No. 223. Seemann & Peters, 1918, p. 403.
6. Id.
7. Articles of a Treaty (1820), 7 Stat. 206.
8. Sawyer, Alvah Littlefield. A History of the Northern Peninsula of Michigan and Its People: Its Mining, Lumber and Agricultural Industries. Vol. 1. Lewis Publishing Company, 1911, p. 178.
9. Journal, Volume 2, Michigan Legislature, Senate, Publisher John S. Bagg, printer to the Legislature, 1913, p. 1291.
10. Treaty between the Ottawa, Chippewa, and Pottawatamie Nations and the United States, Aug. 29, 1821, art. 4, 7 Stat. 218, 220.
11. Sept. 20, 1828, 7 Stat. 317; Edmunds, R. David. The Potawatomis, Keepers of the Fire, University of Oklahoma Press, 1978.
12. See Treaty with the United Chippewa, Ottawa & Potawatomi, 7 Stat. 431 (1833).
13. https://www.nps.gov/articles/leaving-our-native-country-forever.htm (accessed online June 19, 2022).
14. Report of the Commissioner of Indian Affairs to the Secretary of the Interior, United States. Office of Indian Affairs, U.S. Government Printing Office, 1851, Gideon and Co. Printers, pp. 5-6.
15. Treaty between the Chippewa Nation and the United States, Jan. 14, 1837, art. 3, 7 Stat. 528, 529.
16. C. A. Harris, Commissioner of Indian Affairs. Hon. B. F. Butler, Secretary of War, Report of the Commissioner of Indian Affairs to the Secretary of the Interior, United States. Office of Indian Affairs, Printer: Thomas Allen, 1837, p. 571.
17. https://digital.history.pcusa.org/islandora/search?type=dismax&f%5B0%5D=mods_titleInfo_title_ms%3APetition%5C%20from%5C%20Chippewa%5C%20Indians%5C%20for%5C%20American%5C%20citizenship%5C%20to%5C%20the%5C%20legislature%5C%20of%5C%20the%5C%20state%5C%20of%5C%20Michigan%2C%5C%20March%5C%2011%2C%5C%201844 (accessed online June 19, 2022).
18. Act of March 3, 1841, sec. 2, 5 Stat. 417, 419.

19. Report of the Commissioner of Indian Affairs to the Secretary of the Interior, United States. Office of Indian Affairs, U.S. Government Printing Office, 1843, p. 372.
20. Report of the Commissioner of Indian Affairs to the Secretary of the Interior, United States. Office of Indian Affairs, Robert Armstrong, Printer, 1852, p. 39.
21. Report of the Commissioner of Indian Affairs to the Secretary of the Interior, United States. Office of Indian Affairs, Gideon & Co., Printer, 1851, p. 268.
22. United States Congressional Serial Set, Volume 463, United States. Congress. U.S. Government Printing Office, pp. 476-477.
23. Acts of the Legislature of the State of Michigan, W.S. George, 1847, p. 207.
24. Report of the Commissioner of Indian Affairs to the Secretary of the Interior, United States. Office of Indian Affairs, Printer: Robert Armstrong, 1853, p. 4.
25. Michigan Const. art. 7 § 1 (1850).
26. Report of the Commissioner of Indian Affairs to the Secretary of the Interior, United States. Office of Indian Affairs, Printer: A.O.P. Nicholson, 1856, p. 3.
27. Ibid., p. 30.
28. Ibid., p. 33.
29. Treaty with the Chippewa, 10 Stat. 1109 (1854) (concerning L'Anse and Lake Vieux Michigan bands); Treaty with the Ottawa and Chippewa, 11 Stat. 621 (July 31, 1855); Treaty with the Saginaw, Swan Creek, and Black River Chippewa, 11 Stat. 633 (August 2, 1855). https://treatiesmatter.org/relationships/business/timber-and-milling (accessed online June 11, 2022).
30. Gills, Bradley J. "Navigating the landscape of assimilation: the Anishnabeg, the lumber industry, and the failure of federal Indian policy in Michigan." *Michigan Historical Review*, vol. 34, no. 2, fall 2008, pp. 57+. *Gale Academic OneFile*, link.gale.com/apps/doc/A194330826/AONE?u=googlescholar&sid=bookmark-AONE&xid=136ff711 (accessed online June 11, 2022).
31. The Treaty of July 31, 1855 (11 Stat. 621).
32. Senate Bill 1035, A Bill for the Restoration to Market of Certain Lands in Michigan, 42nd Forty-second Congress, 2nd Session second session, June 10, 1872.
33. Report of Richard M. Smith, Mackinac Indian Agency, Oct. 8, 1866. Report of the Commissioner of Indian Affairs to the Secretary of the Interior, United States. Office of Indian Affairs, U.S. Government Printing Office, 1866, pp. 300-301.
34. Report of the Commissioner of Indian Affairs to the Secretary of the Interior, United States. Office of Indian Affairs, U.S. Government Printing Office, 1872, pp. 509-510.

35. Report of Richard M. Smith, Mackinac Indian Agency (Sept. 18, 1871). Report of the Commissioner of Indian Affairs to the Secretary of the Interior, United States. Office of Indian Affairs, U.S. Government Printing Office, 1872, pp. 510-511.
36. http://www.sagchip.org/ziibiwing/aboutus/history.htm (accessed online June 19, 2022).
37. Report of the Commissioner of Indian Affairs to the Secretary of the Interior, United States. Office of Indian Affairs, U.S. Government Printing Office, 1875, p. 17.
38. Report of George Lee, Michigan Agency (August 28, 1877). Report of the Commissioner of Indian Affairs to the Secretary of the Interior, United States. Office of Indian Affairs, U.S. Government Printing Office, 1877, p. 121.
39. Report of Special Agent Edwin Brooks to Commissioner of Indian Affairs E.A. Hayt, dated January 18, 1878. https://search.library.wisc.edu/catalog/9910707404302121 (accessed June 21, 2022).
40. Report of the Commissioner of Indian Affairs to the Secretary of the Interior, United States. Office of Indian Affairs, U.S. Government Printing Office, 1886, p. 164.
41. Ibid., pp. 167-168.
42. Report of the Commissioner of Indian Affairs to the Secretary of the Interior, United States. Office of Indian Affairs, U.S. Government Printing Office, 1887, p. 126.
43. Report of the Commissioner of Indian Affairs to the Secretary of the Interior, United States. Office of Indian Affairs, U.S. Government Printing Office, 1878, pp. VIII-X.
44. Report of the Commissioner of Indian Affairs to the Secretary of the Interior, United States. Office of Indian Affairs, U.S. Government Printing Office, 1888, pp. 143-144.
45. Report of the Commissioner of Indian Affairs to the Secretary of the Interior, United States. Office of Indian Affairs, U.S. Government Printing Office, 1890, p. 49.
46. Report of the Commissioner of Indian Affairs to the Secretary of the Interior, United States. Office of Indian Affairs, U.S. Government Printing Office, 1906, p. 63.
47. Ibid., p. 243.
48. Report of the Commissioner of Indian Affairs to the Secretary of the Interior, United States. Office of Indian Affairs, U.S. Government Printing Office, 1907, p. 110.
49. *Grand Traverse Bands of Ottawa & Chippewa Indians v. U.S. Atty. for the W. Dist. of Mich.*, 369 F.3d 960, 961 n.2 (6th Cir. 2004).

50. Status of the Beaver Island and Nahma Indians, Frederic L. Kirgis, Acting Solicitor, U.S. D.O.I. (May 1, 1937) (discussing proposed 1917 trip of tribal representatives to Washington). https://thorpe.law.ou.edu/sol_opinions/p726-750.html (accessed online June 20, 2022).
51. "1820, April 24, 03 Stat. 566, Act Making Further Provision for Sale of Public Land" (2016). US Government Legislation and Statutes. https://digitalcommons.csumb.edu/hornbeck_usa_2_d/1 (accessed online June 20, 2022).
52. History of Saginaw County, Michigan: Historical, Commercial, Biographical. No. 223. Seemann & Peters, 1918.
53. Id.
54. http://www.let.rug.nl/usa/presidents/rutherford-birchard-hayes/state-of-the-union-1879.php (accessed online June 15, 2022).
55. https://www.connerindustries.com/5-important-lumbermen-you-should-know/ (accessed online June 15, 2022).

CHAPTER 7: MINNESOTA – FRAUDULENT LEGISLATION ENABLING ACQUISITION OF INDIAN LAND

Part 1: Chippewas Are All the Same

The stories of the Ojibwe of Minnesota, Wisconsin, and Michigan are inextricably linked. The Department of the Interior realized that if they had to deal with the various Ojibwe Bands it would be more difficult. Also, the claim of each Band strengthened its relationship to its lands. It would be easier for the DOI to remove them from their lands and concentrate them on two reservations if it treated them as one group, and not separate political entities.

In 1847, specific reference to treating with them as one group is found in these communications between Commissioner Medill and Treaty Commissioner Isaac Verplank:

> ... so far as I am aware, it has been the impression that all the unceded lands of the Chippewa of Lake Superior and the Upper Mississippi as well as those east as those west of that river were the common property of the whole, but as you are aware, it has recently been represented that this is not the case, and that ***different bands claim the exclusive title to different portions of it***. (Emphasis added).[1]

He instructed Treaty Commissioner Verplank that he should avoid this issue if possible:

> ... it is very desirable, however that no question of this kind be raised as it is a leading object with the department to consider the Chippewas and to ***have them think themselves one united people***, with possessions and interest in common, especially for the future. And should you succeed in effecting a treaty with them, it should as far as possible be made clearly and unequivocally to express this meaning and intention. (Emphasis added).[2]

Surveillance of Indian lands for acquisition can be seen in Lt. Zebulon Pike's 1805 Expedition up the Mississippi River.

Part 2: Twin Cities Belong to Sioux
Pike's Expedition to Headwaters of Mississippi

General James Wilkinson, Governor of Louisiana Territory, ordered his protégé's, Lt. Pike's, expedition to explore the upper Mississippi River. His July 30th, 1805, order specifically provided:

> Having completed your equipments, you are to proceed up the Mississippi with all possible diligence, taking the following instructions for your general government, which are to yield to your discretion in all cases of exigency.
>
> You will please to take the course of the river, and calculate distances by time, noting rivers, creeks, highlands, prairies, islands, rapids, shoals, mines, quarries, timber, water, soil, Indian villages and settlements, in a diary, to comprehend reflections on the winds and weather.
>
> It is interesting to government to be informed of the population and residence of the several Indian nations, of the quantity and species of skins and furs they barter per annum, and their relative price to goods; of the tracts of country on which they generally make their hunts, and the people with whom they trade.
>
> *You will be pleased to examine strictly for an intermediate point, between this place and the Prairie des Chiens, suitable for a military post, and also on the Ouiscousing, near its mouth, for a similar establishment; and will obtain the consent of the Indians for their erection, informing them that they are intended to increase their trade and ameliorate their condition.*
>
> You will proceed to ascend the main branch of the river until you reach the source of it, or the season may forbid your further progress without endangering your return before the waters are frozen up.

You will endeavor to ascertain the latitude of the most remarkable places in your route, with the extent of the navigation and the direction of the different rivers which fall into the Mississippi, and you will not fail to procure specimens of whatever you may find curious, in the mineral, vegetable, or animal kingdoms, to be rendered at this place.

In your course you are to spare no pains to conciliate the Indians and to attach them to the United States, and you may invite the great chiefs of such distant nations as have not been at this place, to pay me a visit.

Your own good sense will regulate the consumption of your provisions, and direct the distribution of the trifling presents which you may carry with you, particularly your flags.

P. S. In addition to the preceding orders, you will be pleased to obtain permission from the Indians who claim the ground, for the erection of military posts and trading-houses at the mouth of the river St. Pierre, the falls of St. Anthony, and every other critical point which may fall under your observation; these permissions to be granted in formal conferences, regularly recorded, and the ground marked off. (Emphasis added).[3]

Pike's 1805 Meeting at Bdote

In September, Pike and his party arrived at Bdote (the confluence of the Mississippi and Missouri Rivers). There they met with a group of about 150 Dakota people, including the leaders Cetaŋ Wakuwa Mani and Waŋyaga Inaźiŋ of two local villages. Pike presented the Dakota with a document he had drawn up. His proposal asked the Dakota to grant to the United States the land on which they stood at Bdote as part of a broader tract of about 100,000 acres along Ḣaḣa Wakpa. There, the document stated, the United States would build a military fort and the Dakota would retain the right to travel and hunt on the land as they had always done.

Sept. 23d. I then addressed them in a speech, which ... had for its principal object the granting of land at this place, falls of St. Anthony, and St. Croix [river], and making peace with the Chipeways. I was replied to by Le Fils de Pinchow, Le Petit Corbeau, and l'Original Leve. They gave me the land required, about 100,000 acres, equal to $200,000, and promised me a safe passport for myself and any [Chippewa] chiefs I might bring down; but spoke doubtfully with respect to the peace. I gave them presents to the amount of about $200, and as soon as the council was over, I allowed the traders to present them with some liquor, which, with what I myself gave, was equal to 60 gallons. ... It was somewhat difficult to get them to sign the grant, as they conceived their word of honor should be taken for the grant without any mark; but I convinced them it was not on their account, but my own, that I wished them to sign it.[4]

"ARTICLE 1. That the Sioux Nation grants unto the United States for the purpose of the establishment of military posts, nine miles square at the mouth of the river St. Croix, also from below the confluence of the Mississippi and St. Peters, up the Mississippi, to include the falls of St. Anthony, extending nine miles on each side of the river. That the Sioux Nation grants to the United States, the full sovereignty and power over said districts forever, without any let or hindrance whatsoever."[5]

Pike's document was inconsistent. It appeared to be a license for the United States to build forts on land that the Sioux could continue to use for subsistence purposes. Yet, the second sentence is unclear as to whether the document is intended as a bill of sale for the land. The consideration was left blank in Article 2. Pike expected the federal government to fill in an appropriate amount later.[6]

Validity of Purported "Purchase" Questioned

In an 1856 Report to the Senate, T. Hartley Crawford, Commissioner of Indian Affairs, proclaimed to the Senate that there was no evidence that Pike's purchase was ever binding on the Indians:

It does appear that General Pike made an arrangement, in 1805, with two Sioux Indians, for the purchase of the lands of that tribe, including the Faribault island, but there is no evidence that this agreement, to which there is not even a witness, and in which no consideration was named, was ever considered binding upon the Indians, or that they ever yielded up the possession of their lands under it.[7]

In the same Report Commissioner Crawford included the prominent officials in the Department of War also opining that they did not consider Pike's purchase binding:

> ***Governor Doty*** states that ***General Leavenworth*** did not consider Pike's treaty as binding upon either the government or upon the Indians, and that such was the opinion of ***General Cass***. (Emphasis added).[8]

General Cass' Career	
Year	Position
1806	Elected to Ohio House of Representatives
1807	U.S. Marshal for Ohio (appointed by President Jefferson)
War of 1812	Promoted to rank of General
1813-1831	Governor of Michigan Territory
1831	Secretary of War (appointed by President Jackson)
1836-1842	U.S. Minister to France
1845–48, 1849–57	U.S. Senator from Michigan
1848	Democratic Presidential Nomination (Lost)
1857	Secretary of State (appointed by President Buchanan)

Governor Doty's Career	
Year	Position
1863-1865	Governor of the Utah Territory
1849–1853; 1839–1841	U.S. House of Representatives from Wisconsin
1841–1844	Governor of the Wisconsin Territory

Confirming General Leavenworth's position that he did not consider Pike's treaty as binding, he sought to purchase the same land in 1821. "In the year 1821, Col. Leavenworth called together the chiefs and head men of the Sioux Bands, and procured from them a grant of land nine miles square at the junction of the Mississippi and Minnesota rivers." He included an unauthorized donation of "Pike's Island" to the wife and children of Mr. Faribault to thank them for acting as a go-between with the Indians.[9]

In 1839, to avoid a cloud on title based on Colonel Leavenworth's unauthorized grant to the Faribault's, a Congressional committee recommended buying them out. Commissioner of Indian Affairs Crawford, in a letter to the Secretary of War, dated February 28, 1839, approved paying the Faribaults' for Pike's Island as a matter of expediency, even though their title was questionable.

> As a principle of general observance, the United States, in my judgment, cannot recognize such grants. This case, however, occupies a position of its own. The island is wanted for the purposes of the government, and to avoid delay, difficulty, and controversy, it may be judicious to purchase it.[10]

The committee authorized payment of $12,000, with interest from the date of the contract, but it is uncertain whether Congress approved it, given a later petition for payment by Faribault's heirs.

Purchase Document Defective

While Pike may have considered the document he prepared and presented to Le Fils de Pinchow, Le Petit Corbeau, and l'Original Leve as a purchase of 100,000 acres of Dakota land, its legality was questionable. Elliott Couse, in his 1895 annotation to The Expeditions of Zebulon Montgomery Pike, comprehensively communicates the fatal defects of the Bill of Sale. Elliott Couse was a renowned scholar in his era. He served as the Late Captain and Assistant Surgeon, United States Army; Late Secretary and Naturalist, United States Geological Survey; Member of the National Academy of Sciences; Editor of Lewis and Clark Journals, and numerous other prestigious roles. The understanding of the Department of the Interior, the Department of War, Congress and other parties is presented as well, questioning the validity and legitimacy of the purported purchase.

Couse declares as follows:

> As originally drafted by Pike, and by him communicated to General Wilkinson ... it appears to have been *scarcely legible* ... I doubt that this extraordinary document ever existed in a form which might not be set aside as *fatally defective* and I do not doubt that we acquired legal title to the lands by some means subsequent to this invalid instrument. (Emphasis added).[11]

Land Description Flawed

Elliott Couse opined that Pike's land description constituted a "fatal flaw in the title, if contested:"

> ARTICLE 1. That the Sioux Nation grants unto the United States *for the purpose of the establishment of military posts*, nine miles square at the mouth of the river St. Croix, also from below the confluence of the Mississippi and St. Peters, up the Mississippi, to include the falls of St. Anthony, extending nine miles on each side of the river.

According to Couse, *"Nine miles square at the mouth of the St. Croix, is in the first place an impossibility, because the mouth of the St. Croix has no such dimensions ..."* (Emphasis added).[12]

No Consideration Stated

There is no amount for consideration in Article 2. Pike wrote in his journal he thought the land was worth US$200,000. Coues examined two manuscript copies of the "treaty," on file in the War Department. *His examination found three different versions of Article II, none of which include an amount for the consideration*:

> "Article 2nd.–That in consideration of the above Grants, the United States"
>
> The second manuscript reads: "Art. 2ᵈ That in consideration of the above grants the U.S."
>
> A third version of Article 2, in an official imprint of the treaty, published by the Indian Bureau is: "ARTICLE 2. That in consideration of the above grants the United States ******."[13]

Having no Presidential or Congressional authority, Pike could not bind the United States to do anything, including paying any consideration to the Indians. Knowing this defect existed, Pike recommended to General Wilkinson that he fill in the blank amount for consideration with the $250 Pike had expended from his personal funds to entertain the chiefs.

> Pike informs Wilkinson by letter of equal date that lands to the extent of about 100,000 acres had been obtained *"for a song"*; calls the general's attention pointedly to the fact "that the 2d article, relative to consideration, is blank"; that the "song" in mention was worth about $250, being the value of certain presents with which he had personally and privately feed [sic] the two chiefs who signed the treaty, these presents being partly from articles of his personal property; and suggests to the general "to insert the amount of those articles as the considerations." (Emphasis added).[14]

General Wilkinson was smart enough to ignore Pike's request to remedy his defect, and left Article 2 blank as to consideration.

Omitted Signatures and Witnesses

Couse further questions the omission of any signatures and that *only one version* of the three copies of Pike's purported purchase, at the War Department, contains names of witnesses.

> In the present case, no signatures of witnesses appear on the face of the instrument... But one of the manuscript copies before me has the names of four persons as witnesses, all whites. ...[15]

No Presidential Proclamation of Pike's Document

When Pike sought compensation for his Expedition after-the-fact, Secretary of War Dearborn, unequivocally stated in a letter, dated December 7, 1808, "the two exploring expeditions you [Pike] have performed were not previously ordered by the president of the United States..." Thus, Pike was acting on his own accord for General Wilkinson, a suspect party. He was not acting in a legal capacity for the United States. General Wilkinson was accused of being a paid spy for Spain for 15 years, reporting to them on the Lewis and Clark U.S. Army Expedition, and was involved in the suspect Aaron Burr conspiracy to form an independent empire west of the Mississippi.

Congress, more tactfully stated "... no special encouragement was given to the individuals who performed these laborious and dangerous expeditions..." No compensation was awarded to Pike.[16]

Couse further writes that he made a diligent search but was ***unable to locate any proof*** that it was ever included in the U.S. Statutes as Large, which is customary. Based on his research, a version of the purchase was submitted by the President to the Senate on March 29, 1808, more than three years after Pike's draft of the instrument. The Senate reported favorably upon it on April 13, 1808, and filled in the consideration blank with $2,000.[17]

Major Long's Expedition

In the summer of 1817, Major Stephen H. Long, inspected the sites that Pike allegedly purchased from the Sioux and recommended the Bluff overlooking the two rivers for a "military work of considerable magnitude."[18]

After Fourteen Years, Secretary of War Orders Consideration Paid

Given the urgent need for this prime strategic location for a fort, in 1819, *fourteen years after the purported purchase*, the Secretary of War Orders Governor Clark to send Major Thomas Forsyth, Indian Agent at St. Louis, to deliver "a certain quantity of goods, say $2,000 worth,"... "in payment of lands ceded by the Sioux Indians to the late Gen. Pike for the United States."[19]

In Major Thomas Forsyth's lengthy Letter to Governor Wm. Clark, of September 23, 1819, he details his trip to the St. Peter's area, yet there is *no proof whatsoever of the proper payment* "to the Sioux [of] two thousand dollars, or deliver[ing] the value thereof in such goods and merchandise as they shall choose." *According to Major Forsyth*, he met with Little Crow who...

> ...acknowledged the sale of the land at the mouth of the St. Peter's river to the United States, and said he had been looking every year since the sale for the troops to build a fort ... I [Forsyth] gave him a better present than to any one at the villages below, as he lived immediately in the vicinity of the troops ... He also met with Pinichon and was equally as liberal as I was to Little Crow, and for the same reason, and they returned home contented.[20]

Fort Snelling Construction Completed

The construction of a fort at the confluence of the Mississippi and Missouri (Bdote) was completed in 1825. It was eventually named Fort Snelling. The Mississippi and its tributaries afforded a transportation route for people and goods and the U.S. could monitor and control the river traffic and trade in the Upper Mississippi River Watershed.

Along with the construction of the fort an Indian Agency was constructed on the military Reservation opposite the fort at Mendota. It was operated from 1820 to 1853. Major Lawrence Taliaferro was to serve as the Indian Agent. The U.S. never treated with the Sioux Nation for this land; they simply confiscated it.

Squatting Settlers Petition President for Protection of Their Rights

Certain settlers in 1837 hearing that Pike's purchase of 1805 was under question, jeopardizing their settlements contiguous to Fort Snelling, petitioned President van Buren for protection of their rights or recompense for their improvements if they were removed.

In 1804 a treaty was made by General Pike with the Sioux Indians, under which he purchased a certain portion of their country, extending from the falls of St. Anthony to the mouth of St. Peter's river, and the *prevailing opinion has been, until very recently, that this treaty had received the sanction of government*. It was under this impression that the undersigned settled upon the lands they now occupy as part of the public domain. They were permitted to make improvements and retain unmolested possession of them for many years by the commanding officer of the post and the other officers of the government employed here, who believed the land belonged to the United States ... (Emphasis added).[21]

Pike's Congressional Petition for Payment for Services Denied

In 1808, Pike petitioned Congress for payment for his services, including his expedition to Bdote. In an effort to retroactively approve his expeditions, Congress justified his actions based on communication and approval of his expedition by the President and the value of the information "of the Mississippi and the natives in that quarter, and the country generally." His petition for compensation ended up denied, even though Secretary of War Dearborn supported it.

> ... although the two exploring expeditions you have performed *were not previously ordered by the president of the United States*, there were frequent communications on the subject of each between General Wilkinson and this department, of which the president of the United States was from time to time acquainted... (Emphasis added).

> *Although no special encouragement was given* to the individuals who performed these laborious and dangerous expeditions, yet it was but reasonable for them, should they fortunately succeed in their objects, to expect a liberal reward from the government... H. DEARBORN. [Secretary at War.] (Emphasis added).[22]

President Jefferson never Proclaimed it as a Treaty of the U.S.[23]

More than thirty years after Pike's death, his widow, Clara, petitioned Congress for compensation for Pike's services on his two expeditions. She received $3,000.[24]

Sale of Fort Snelling

In another snafu, Secretary of War Floyd, thinking Fort Snelling was no longer needed, assigned about 7,000 acres to a Mr. Steele on July 2, 1857. Secretary of War Floyd's sale was found to be fraudulent. In a letter from Lieutenant General Sherman to Brevet Major General E. D. Townsend, Assistant Adjutant General, March 10, 1868, Lieutenant General Sherman declared that the Fort was "eminently necessary for the military uses of the United States for all time to come." Mr. Steele played no part in the fraud. To repurchase Mr. Steele's title, he was paid $30,000 (and interest), and debited with moneys already received.[25]

Part 3: The Shell Game

Settler Emigration to Minnesota Increasing

In 1849, Commissioner of Indian Affairs Orlando Brown reported increasing white settler emigration to the Territory of Minnesota:

> Since the establishment of the new Territory of Minnesota, the attention of a large number of our enterprising citizens has been directed to that quarter, in consequence of the fine climate, and the richness and fertility of the lands on the Mississippi, and within a wide sweep on both sides of it; by the superabundant water-power afforded by that river and some of its tributaries, and by the superior advantages offered by the extensive forests of pine, convenient to water transportation, for a *large and lucrative trade in lumber*. There has consequently been considerable emigration there during the past year, and it will, no doubt, go on increasing annually, so that in a very few years the population will be sufficient to justify demand for admission into the Union as a state. (Emphasis added).[26]

Minnesota Indian Land Title Not Extinguished

At the same time, he reported that only a small part of the title to Indian lands had been extinguished. "*The Indian title has been extinguished to but a comparatively small portion of the country within the limits of the Territory* ..." (Emphasis added).[27]

Treaty Establishing Boundaries of Minnesota Tribes

In 1825, the Prairie du Chien Treaty between the U.S. and the tribes in Minnesota set the boundaries of tribal land for the following tribes: Dakota, Ojibwe, Menominee, Winnebago, Sac and Fox, Iowa, Potawatomi, and Ottawa. After that, it was simpler for the government to negotiate with the Indians for the purchase of their lands.

U.S. Fraudulently Encourages Indian Tribes to Move West

In what would become a common deceptive and fraudulent justification for taking Indian lands located in a natural resource area, the federal government would encourage westward removal to tribes:

> The game having become scarce in that portion of their country desired, many are leaving it and emigrating westward, where the toils of the chase are better rewarded. It is, therefore, comparatively *valueless to them*, though much of it on the Mississippi and Minnesota or St. Peter's rivers, is rich and fertile, and capable of sustaining a dense civilized population; and, when open to settlement, will soon be occupied. (Emphasis added).[28]

The population in Minnesota in the 1850's had not yet decimated the game. That would come as the population increased and a new breed of hunter arrived. Professional hunters sought game for its commercial value. Instead of a deer, they saw a hide representing cash, $4. Their rifles permitted an easy kill.[29]

STATE POPULATION	1850	1860	1870	1880	1890	1900
MINNESOTA	6,077	172,023	439,706	780,773	1,310,283	1,751,394

The Indians in the Great Lakes region did not desire to move west, they were being coerced to *relocate to government assigned lands*.

Timber Mining on "Alleged" Worthless Land of Indians

The following companies mined timber on the "alleged" worthless land of the Minnesota Indians:

> The Tower, Cook, and Ketcham, and Alger, Smith lumber companies cleared the Lake Vermillion area from 1891–1911; the G.W. Knox Lumber Company and Swallow and Hopkins Lumber (1898) cleared the region from Ely east to the present-day boundary waters into the 1920s; the Pigeon River Company, General Logging, and the Cloquet Logging companies (these companies were subsidies of the Weyerhaeuser's in the 1920s) and

Rainy River Lumber, International Lumber and Shevlin-Clark Lumber, cleared the vast forests throughout northeastern Minnesota.30

Commission Appointed to Negotiate with Tribes to Reduce Their Land Base

A Treaty Commission was appointed to negotiate with Minnesota tribes to reduce their land base. Anytime, you read of a Commission being appointed to negotiate with a Tribe for a cession of their lands, know that a great lie is about to be perpetuated – that what the U.S. desires is of no value or use to Indians. In fact, what will be stolen are lands valuable for their extractive resources – timber, minerals, arable land, etc.

> In view of the facts and circumstances … it was deemed advisable, as soon as possible … to make an effort to obtain a cession of the lands referred to; and two commissioners were accordingly appointed for that purpose … one of them, the excellent and efficient Governor of the territory, who is ex officio Superintendent of Indian Affairs of Minnesota, and the other a distinguished citizen…[31]

The distinguished citizen appointed to head the Treaty Commission was Luke Lea, the Commissioner of Indian Affairs. Commissioner Lea had a duty to represent Indian interests as their trustee, their guardian. He stood in a position of 'trust' in relation to Indians. As a representative of the federal government, in the highest-ranking position, appointed to protect the value of Indian assets, he failed to explain to the Indians the value of their land. He knew the Indians could hold title to their land and sell the massive amount of timber they possessed which was in high demand or simply hold the land as a highly valuable asset. In order to market the timber, they did not need to sell the land. Instead, the government would routinely wait until Indians faced hunger or disease or extermination by volunteer militias and then negotiate for a cession for a minimal amount.

Commissioner Lea recommended to the Secretary of the Interior, given the Indians destitute state, that they cede a major part of their lands so that they might be brought "nearer" to one another:

> Some of them are very destitute, having no annuities or other means to encourage or enable them to endeavor to effect a change in their condition as hunters and vagabonds; and as the diminution of game within their reach has rendered the avails of the chase – the only means of sustaining themselves – very uncertain and precarious, they are frequently subjected to great hardship and suffering … In view of this state of circumstances, I would respectfully recommend the adoption, at the earliest practicable period, of the proper measures for bringing them [Indian tribes in Minnesota] nearer together…[32]

Indians' Trustee Kept Value of Indian Land Concealed

Lumber would be needed for construction of homes and towns, as well as continuing to supply the shipbuilding industry. The abundant timber of the Great Lakes wouldn't only supply Wisconsin, Michigan and Minnesota, the Mississippi River would allow for downstream shipment to St. Louis and other commercial hubs. The chart below demonstrates the population increase and the huge profit for those owning timber, a valuable, extractive resource, which would diminish over time and thus increase in value. Indians weren't merely tricked into selling land, they were being conned out of the income from the land and the timber—the investment value, the collateral for credit and the inheritance value for their children. They weren't just losing money, they were losing opportunities—the economist's "opportunity costs," the foregone opportunity of wealth instead of poverty. Numerous times, the Commissioner of Indian Affairs refers to Indians as the "untutored wards of the government." It is these wards that were forever cheated.

Population Increase			
State	1850	1900	%age Increase
Minnesota	6,077	1,750,394	2,920%
Wisconsin	305,391	2,069,042	680%
Illinois	851,470	4,821,550	570%
Iowa	192,211	2,231,853	1,160%

The U.S. continually expounds on the need to protect Indians, by moving them to remote locations out of harm's way from lawless whites. Instead of being accountable for the duty to protect Indians in their homelands—*from being overrun or exterminated*—the federal government breached its most profound duty.

> Such an arrangement … would, as remarked by my predecessor, open a wide sweep of country between our northern and southern Indian colonies, for the expansion and egress of our white population westward, and thus *save our colonized tribes from being injuriously pressed upon, if not eventually overrun and exterminated*, before they are sufficiently advanced in civilization …. (Emphasis added).[33]

U.S. Failed to Protect Indians

Commissioner Lea's solution to the (1) colonial settlers' illegal encroachment on Indian lands, and (2) the even more unlawful extermination of the Indians themselves, was not to engage the U.S. military to remove squatters and to punish the murder of any Indians; rather it was to remove the Indians purportedly out of harm's way. Repeatedly, throughout the fulfillment of the U.S.' Manifest Destiny to build a continental empire, Indians would be forced off of their prime land and be relocated on 'government assigned lands,' which lacked the natural resources which would permit their survival. If they did not willingly move, they would be placed under military control and the U.S. Army would assure their eviction.

Part 4: The Flimflam Man

Cheated Out of Fourteen Million Acres

In 1837, the U.S. negotiated a treaty with the Chippewa to acquire 13,664,871 acres in present day Wisconsin and Minnesota. Funding and authorization were provided by an 1837 general appropriations act that provided $10,000 "for holding treaties with the various tribes of Indians east of the Mississippi river, for the cession of lands held by them respectively, and for their removal west of the Mississippi." Act of March 3, 1837, 5 Stat. 158 at 161.

On May 13, 1837, *Commissioner of Indian Affairs Carey A. Harris* stated that "*it is understood, that this tract is valuable for its pine woods which cover it, but is unfit for cultivation.*" He continued:.

> Its acquisition by the U.S. will be beneficial to both parties. *To the United States, by opening to its citizens an extensive wood land,* important especially from the rapidity with which settlements are multiplying: to the Indians, by giving them an ample consideration in money, provisions, agricultural and mechanical establishments, education, and other means of improvement. (Emphasis added).[34]

Henry Dodge, Governor of Wisconsin and *ex oficio*, Superintendent of Indian Affairs, conducted the Proceedings of a Council with the Chiefs and principal men, of the Chippewa Nation of Indians near Fort Snelling, at the confluence of the St. Peters and Missisippi (sic) Rivers, commencing on the 20th day of July 1837.

At the beginning of the negotiations, Governor Dodge, explained that the U.S. wanted to purchase the land to harvest its pine timber:

> This country, as I am informed, is not valuable to you for its game, and not suited to the culture of corn, and other Agricultural purposes. Your Great Father wishes to purchase your country on the Chippewa and St. Croix Rivers, for the advantage of its **Pine Timber,** with which it is said to abound. (Emphasis added).[35]

Sub-Agents Vineyard and Bushnell were available to assist the Indians, if necessary. Son-ga-ko-mik (The Strong Ground) stated: "We do not know the value or use of money, & don't want it." He preferred that goods be provided to them.[36]

Governor Dodge and representatives of twelve Chippewa Bands, including the Mille Lacs Band, signed the Treaty with the Chippewa of 1837 on July 29, 1837.[37] The Treaty stated in part:

> Article 1. The said Chippewa nation cede to the United States all that tract of country included within the following boundaries:
> Article 2. In consideration of the cession aforesaid, the United States agrees to make the Chippewa nation . . . the following payments:
>
>> Nine thousand five hundred dollars, to be paid in money.
>> Nineteen thousand dollars, to be delivered in goods.
>> Three thousand dollars for establishing three blacksmiths shops, supporting the blacksmiths, and furnishing them with iron and steel.
>> One thousand dollars for farmers, and for supplying them and the Indians, with implements of labor, with grain or seed; and whatever else may be necessary to enable them to carry on their agricultural pursuits.
>> Two thousand dollars in provisions.
>> Five hundred dollars in tobacco.
>
> Article 5. The privilege of hunting, fishing, and gathering the wild rice, upon the lands, the rivers and the lakes included in the territory ceded, is guaranteed to the Indians, during the pleasure of the President of the United States… (Emphasis added).[38]

On August 7, 1837, in a letter from Governor Dodge to Commissioner Harris he confirmed the following:

"The country purchased is of large extent containing from nine to ten million acres and abounding in **Pine Timber**." (Emphasis added).[39]

Ojibwe Cede Land for Buffer Zone

Due to the scarcity of game, the Ojibwe and Dakota found themselves engaged in frequent conflict in a specific area. It was thought that a buffer zone could be created by having the Chippewa of the Mississippi and Lake Superior cede part of the conflicted area to the United States, along with the Pillager Band of Chippewa Indians, also, ceding a particular tract. The lands thus ceded by the Chippewas would be given by the U.S. in two separate parcels to the Ho-Chunk and Menominee. The idea of creating a buffer zone was not new; it had been tried before in 1830, to separate the Dakota from the Sac and Fox. The Ho-Chunk Nation served as the buffer. It was a dismal failure because it just added another combatant to the mix.

Under the (1) Chippewa of the Mississippi and Lake Superior Treaty, 9. Stat. 904, August 2, 1847; and (2) The Pillager Band of Chippewa Indians Treaty, 9 Stat. 908, August 21, 1847, the Ojibwe Bands ceded land for the buffer zone that would separate them from the Dakota.

Under the Menominee Indian Tribe of Wisconsin, October 18, 1848 Treaty, the Menominee's *ceded all of their land in Wisconsin*, wherever situated, and in exchange were given, "for a home," the land, ceded by the Chippewas under the two 1847 Treaties, not given to the Winnebagoes (aka Ho-Chunk). The Menominee Tribe was allowed to remain in Wisconsin for two years, after with time they would move to Minnesota. In 1850, the Menominee refused to move to Wisconsin, arguing they were pressured into signing the 1848 Treaty. President Millard Fillmore, sympathized with the tribe, and, in 1852, granted the Menominee a temporary 250,000-acre reservation along the Wolf River.

Under the Menominee Indian Tribe of Wisconsin Treaty of May 12, 1854, the Menominee's ceded all the land assigned to them under the Treaty of 1848, including the buffer zone area, back to the United States, and the temporary reservation along the Wolf River was made permanent.

Neither the Menominees nor the Ho-Chunk ever resided on the buffer zone land.

Minnesota Becomes Territory in 1849

Minnesota became a Territory in 1849. It included parts of the present-day states of North and South Dakota.

Part 5: The Cruel Hoax

U.S. Uses Shock and Awe to Paralyze Dakotas

In 1837, a group of Dakota leaders was invited to Washington, D.C., having been told that they would be negotiating the settlement of their southern boundary. Instead, they were pressured into ceding all of their land east of the Mississippi. This tactic of demonstrating the power of the U.S. by isolating a small group of Indians in the capital city of Washington and then bullying them to relinquish land was common. While the land was valued at $1,600,000, the U.S. would pay $300,000 over time. They would receive the interest on $300,000, invested at 5 percent. This amounted to $15,000 per year. Another $200,000 was paid to friends and relatives of the tribe and to settle debts, and $16,000 was given to the Dakota leaders as an incentive to sign the treaty. Each year for 20 years, $23,750 was supposed to be allocated for annuity payments, food, education, equipment, supplies, and government services.

The military tactic to "awe the Indians" by exposing them to the U.S.' military capabilities was used to intimidate Indians into realizing there was no way they could defeat the U.S. Therefore, it was in their best interest to succumb to the will of the federal government.

This tactic was first stated by General George Washington:

> First. A regular and standing force, for Garrisoning West Point & such other Posts upon our Northern, Western, and Southern Frontiers, as shall be deemed *necessary to awe the Indians*…(Emphasis added).[40]

Negotiators with Indian tribes realized that their remoteness might obscure the potent power of the U.S., such that it would be helpful to make them aware of this by hosting tribal leaders in Washington, D.C.

Sioux Indians Starved into Ceding Lands in Minnesota

Scarcity of animals hunted for food, declining demand for peltry marketed in the fur trade, and escalating prices of trade goods engendered widespread indebtedness among Santee Sioux communities. Poverty weakened the Santees' bargaining leverage, and after two failed attempts in 1841 and 1849, federal authorities finally succeeded in persuading all four Bands to sign treaties in 1851. Threatened with military force, the Dakota were forced to cede nearly all their land in Minnesota and eastern Dakota Territory in the 1851 treaties of Traverse des Sioux and Mendota. Governor Ramsey and Commissioner Lea, enlisting the aid of Territorial Delegate and trader Henry Sibley, took advantage of the starvation the Dakota were experiencing. Martin McLeod, a U.S. licensed Indian Trader reported to Sibley that after a succession of bad winters, the Sioux had suffered from hunger, often bordering on starvation, and were desperate for relief. In fact, he was confident that "they would sign almost anything."[41]

Governor Ramsey shared this information with Commissioner Lea which was included in their Annual Report to the Secretary of the Interior as justification for entering into negotiations with the Sioux: "The only alternative which seemed to be left them, at the time of the pendency of the negotiations, was **starvation or a sale.**" (Emphasis added).[42]

The desperation of the Indians made it possible for the U.S. Commissioners to have the upper hand in the one-sided intervention to confiscate the Sioux lands. Their furtive plan to swindle their wards had to be covered by a fabricated largesse – it was as beneficial to the Sioux as to the U.S. Governor Ramsey would state the following:

In the mere light of a *bargain* the treaties are eminently advantageous to both parties. … To the United States the purchase is of immense value. (Emphasis in the original Letter to Commissioner Lea).[43]

Governor Ramsey declared the Sioux's nomadic occupancy a *"positive evil."* (Emphasis added).[44]

To the reader, allow Governor Ramsey, the Indians' trustee, to **eloquently** describe the **"valueless"** Indian land the white colonial settlers desired, **the cession of which he would facilitate**:

The region of country acquired lies in the great heart of the North American continent, is larger than the island of Cuba, and computed to contain over **thirty-five millions of acres**. It is so diversified in natural advantages, that **its productive powers may be considered almost inexhaustible**. Probably no tract upon the surface of the globe is equally **well watered**. Many of its valleys almost realize the beauties of that "happy valley" described in allegory. No ranges of mountains or arid deserts intersect its vast extent, and the whole is capable of yielding something for the use of man. A large part is **rich, arable land**; portions are of unsurpassed fertility, and eminently adapted to the production in incalculable quantities of the cereal grains. The boundless plains present inexhaustible **fields of pasturage**, and the river bottoms are richer than the banks of the Nile. In the bowels of the earth there is every indication of **extensive mineral fields**, which only await the energies of an American population to reveal **hidden treasures of uncounted wealth**. (Emphasis added).[45]

Pushing Indians into Debt to Get Land Ceded

Sibley's conflict of interest as a partner in the Northern Outfit which combined the Dakota, Winnebago and Ojibwe trade under a single business unit was ignored, as was his interest in steamboats and trade on the Mississippi. He should never have been invited to serve as an advisor to the Treaty Commission. Clearly, as a trader, he would want to be assured that he and other traders would receive payment for the alleged debts of the Indians out of any sums they received for the sale of their lands. Traders alleged, unverified, unaudited claims of $275,000 for debts owed by the Sisseton and Wahpeton Bands were at stake. Similarly, claims of $160,000 would be alleged against the Mdewakantons and Wahpekutes Bands. At a treaty negotiation, with the federal government's support, the collective amount of the debts would be used as an offset against the amount due to the Indian Nations. As Indian Nations were held liable for individual member debts, this could result in appalling circumstances. Sibley's lobbying assured that the debt he aggregated would not be forfeited.

The trading houses deliberately changed the consumption patterns of the Indians so they would adopt American consumerism lifestyles and be forced to cede lands when the debts, along with the usurious interest, became impossible of ever being paid. The debts assured and accelerated their impoverishment. To entice them into becoming consumers, we see the following excerpt on changing their tradition value systems:

The "Savages" aren't ashamed of their bodies and wear no clothes, and Carleill believes that this naïve worldview can easily be corrected: [The Savages] shall have wonderful great use of our said English clothes, after they shall come once to know the commodity thereof. The like will be also of many other things, over many to be reckoned, which are made here by our artificers and laboring people ...[46]

President Jefferson wrote in a private letter to William Henry Harrison on February 27, 1803, the following, which Harrison was not to disclose:

>...we shall push our trading houses, and be glad to see the good & influential individuals among them run in debt, because we observe that when these debts get beyond what the individuals can pay, they become willing to lop th[em off] (sic) by a cession of lands...*you will also percieve (sic) how sacredly it must be kept within [your] own breast, and especially how improper to be understood by the Indians* [for] their interests & their tranquility it is best they should see only the present age of their history. (Emphasis added).[47]

It is critical for the indigenous community to realize that President Jefferson's ideas were to be shrouded in secrecy lest Indians realize his intent to create a continental empire at their expense. Indian agents and the Commissioner would have been aware of accounting precepts such as debt to assets and to avoid Indians getting into the position where there land cession or other treaty assets would be overwhelmed by their debts to traders.

Politically, Sibley represented the Wisconsin Territory in Congress and thereafter the Minnesota Territory from 1849 to 1853. In his future Indian activities, he would be remembered for creating the military commission that sentenced 307 men to death, with 16 others given prison terms. Thereafter, he was elected Governor of the State of Minnesota.[48]

Genocidal Sioux Treaties in Minnesota

Treaty with the Sioux, Signed July 23, 1851, at Traverse des Sioux, MN (10 Stat. 949, July 23, 1851, Proclaimed February 24, 1853)

In the July 23, 1851, Treaty with the Sioux, Sisseton and Wahpeton Bands, they ceded all of their lands in the State of Iowa and the Territory of Minnesota, *21 million acres* for $1,665,000, or about **7.5 cents an acre**.

Of the $1,665,000, the following amounts totaling $648,000 were set aside:

        $275,000 to pay the chiefs;
        $275,000 to pay debts claimed by traders;
        $12,000 for a general agricultural improvement and civilization fund;
        $30,000 for establishing schools and for farming and other purposes;
        $6,000 for education;
        $10,000 for the purchase of goods and provisions; and
        $40,000 for cash annuity.

The U.S. government kept the remainder in trust, over a million dollars, with only the interest on the amount, at 5 percent for 50 years, payable to the Sioux. It is uncertain how much they actually received.

Once the Upper Sioux Bands signed a treaty, the U.S. reasoned, the Mdewakantons and Wahpekutes would follow suit. The terms of the Mendota Treaty were similar, except the payments were even smaller.

On August 5, 1851, Commissioner Lea threatened the Dakota during the Mendota Treaty negotiations to get his way: **"Suppose your Great Father wanted your lands and did not want a treaty for your good; he could come with 100,000 men and drive you off to the Rocky Mountains."** (Emphasis added).[49]

Under the Treaty of Mendota, the U.S. paid $1,410,000 over time. The Mdewakantons and Wahpekutes Bands were to receive the interest on $1,410,000 that was to be applied to agricultural implements, provisions, education, and annuities in return for relocating to the Lower Sioux Agency, near present-day Morton and ceding much of their remaining territory in southwestern Minnesota and Iowa. The Wahpekute agreed to pay traders $90,000. The Mdewakanton paid traders $70,000 and were given $20,000 which was shared between seven chiefs.

Sioux Treaties Open 35 Million Acres for White Settlement

Under the Treaties, reservations of land ten miles wide on each side of the Minnesota River were established, *until needed for white settlement*. According to the Minnesota Historical Society, thirty-five million acres of land were opened for white settlement, comprising a region fully equal in extent to the States of Pennsylvania and New Jersey today. The traders received a total of $475,000, almost half a million dollars which was far greater in value in 1852.[50]

DOI Champions Ratification of Sioux Treaties

Commissioner Lea described the difficulty with which the two westernmost Bands (Sissetons and Wahpetons) reconciled themselves to the surrender of land at the July 1851 Traverse de Sioux negotiations:

> It was soon perceived that although there was a vague and indefinite idea on the part of these people that it was necessary for them to sell at least a portion of their country, in order to secure them against the misery and almost starvation which the diminution in the number of the buffalo and other game for the last few years had inflicted upon them; yet, when they were brought to meet the proposition in a distinct and intelligible form, they appeared to shrink, with undisguised reluctance, from taking a step so important in its results. Annual Report of the Department of the Interior, Volume 2, United States, Department of the Interior, U.S. Government Printing Office, 1850, p. 279.

Commissioner Lea promptly championed the Sioux Treaties before the Secretary and provided the ammunition for the Secretary to seek Congressional approval. The theft of Indian Nations' financial resources is evidenced by the deliberate undervaluation of Indian resources. Lea himself provides us this premise as promulgating one basis for approval: the consideration is "merely nominal."

> The consideration agreed to be paid, though in view of the actual value of the lands **merely nominal**, was esteemed to be as large as would be for the real good of the Indians, and ample to supply their present wants and minister to their future comfort. *To the United States the purchase is of immense value*. (Emphasis added).[51]

Secondly, the Manifest Destiny of the U.S. can be seen in the Indians' trustee describing the wave of white settlement across the country:

> A review of the history of this nation presents no fact so striking as the noiseless, multitudinous movements of its people westward. This is not a local or transitory accident. **We see wave following wave in endless succession**. First, last, everywhere, and always, this mighty political fact strikes us. It is not the ripple of the rivulet that breaks along the margin of the wilderness; but "the long swell of the Atlantic," wafted from foreign realms, and augmented by contributions from every State. (Emphasis added).[52]

The federal government knew this inundation of Indian lands would be interminable, yet did nothing to shield the Indians from the incessant invasion and encroachment about to befall them. The U.S.' publicly proclaimed gross and cruel Indian negative stereotypes would allow the colonial settlers to treat Indians like animals, justifying the abuse of their human rights, the enjoyment of their lives, liberty and property. The U.S., a nation of laws, would utterly disregard the settlers' disavowal of the law. Indians, though, would be bound to comply with the myriad of laws protecting the property rights of the settlers or face punishment or death. There was no official government will, whatsoever, to prevent the settlers' usurpation of Indian lands and rights.

> Even now, the ceaseless, irresistible tide of migration, in its occidental development, is fast encroaching upon them, **reckless of the rights of the present possessors, and contemptuous of the authority of law.** (Emphasis added).[53]

Governor and Superintendent of Indian Affairs Ramsey's Breach of Faith

Governor and Superintendent Ramsey continued in his deft compromise of the Sioux Indians' trust and inability to comprehend the enormity of the breach of faith occurring. His deceitful diplomacy with the Secretary of the Interior and Congress was instrumental in inducing Congress to ratify the Treaties he negotiated: the Indians did not want the land, weren't using the land, didn't need it, were willing to move, and that it was worthless. This propaganda assured Congress that it was reasonable and even just to appropriate it.

Governor Ramsey preached an appealing message of national unity and a utopian future that resonated with settlers. They were imperiously "clamoring" to enter upon the Indians land and in anticipation of Congress' approval, encroachment was viable. Manipulating the truth, he even claims Indian lands are America's land.

> *Should the treaties which have been made receive the approbation of the Senate, an industrious population will, in a short time, cover the whole agricultural portion of the ceded regions*, as the waters cover the sea. The clamor for entrance upon the new purchase grows each day louder, more pressing, more imperious. Causes and agencies, already in actual operation, are rapidly conducting *our people to the occupancy and reclamation of its unharvested solitudes*. (Emphasis added).[54]

To embarrass Congress, he depicted the reality they faced: (1) ratify the Treaties; or (2) admit its inability to protect the Indians from the whites' encroachment; or (3) evict the trespasser settlers from the Indian lands.

> *I ... can solemnly declare my deep conviction "that the time has come when the extinguishment of the Indian title to this region should no longer be delayed, if Government would not have the mortification, on the one hand, of confessing its inability to protect the Indians from encroachment; or be subjected to the painful necessity, upon the other, of ejecting thousands of its citizens, by the strong arm, from a land which they ask only the opportunity of cultivating, and which, without their labor, will be comparatively useless and waste."* (Emphasis added).[55]

To avoid admitting its impotency, Governor Ramsey, instead, elicited Congress' passivity and acceptance of the impending debacle of cheating the Indians out of their lands by pointing out the apocalyptic result if they failed to act – evicting thousands of voting citizens from land they asked only to farm.

The actions of Governor Ramsey and Trader Sibley constitute fraud. Sibley's conflict of interest lay concealed to the Indians and Governor Ramsey misrepresented the value of their land. Governor Ramsey utterly failed in his trusteeship role to protect the rights of his wards, the Indians.

Of course, congressional legislation would follow for the appropriation of the most minimal amount possible as consideration for the cession of the Sioux Bands' lands. The treaties of 1851 also called for setting up reservations on both the north and south sides of the Minnesota River. But the U.S. Senate changed the treaties by eliminating the reservations and leaving the Dakota with no place to live. Congress required the Dakota to approve this change before appropriating desperately needed cash and goods. President Millard Fillmore agreed that the Dakota could live on the land previously set aside for reservations, but only until it was needed for white settlement.

A state propaganda apparatus headed by the Commissioner of Indian Affairs manipulated and deceived the U.S. citizenry, its executive, legislative, judicial bodies and the outside world that its policy was morally righteous and necessary. The policy of removal, the ever-westward movement of settlers without regard for Indian rights, the confiscation of Indian land at bargain basement prices and the trespass on Indian land for valuable minerals, timber and agricultural, arable land is reported year after year as part of our history.

Dakota in Minnesota Cede More Lands

In 1858, a month after Minnesota became a state, a group of Dakota traveled to Washington, D.C., to discuss their reservation. The Dakota were pressured to cede the lands on the north side of the Minnesota River. They received 30 cents per acre, estimated to be only about 5 percent of the land's value. When the funds were finally distributed in 1860, most of the $266,880 promised went to pay debts claimed by traders. By 1858, they had only a small strip of land in Minnesota. Without access to the land upon which they had hunted for generations, they had to rely on treaty payments for their survival. The inadequate money and goods often arrived late. By summer 1862, most of the Dakota were starving—one of the causes of the U.S.-Dakota War, which lasted six weeks.

Part 6: Treaty Chicanery

Treaties to Move Indians to Reservations

The U.S. decided to seek a treaty extinguishing the Ojibwe title to all lands in Minnesota and Wisconsin and to settle the Bands on reservations. An authorization act was debated in May of 1854, but it ***did not pass the Senate***.[56]

Nonetheless, Commissioner Manypenny initiated the treaty process. On August 11, 1854, he instructed Agent Gilbert to begin negotiations for the purchase of "all the country [the Chippewa] now own or claim in the territory of Minnesota, the State of Wisconsin or elsewhere" except for an amount of land that would be used for reservations.[57]

On December 17, 1854, Congress passed the bill that was debated in the House of Representatives in May of 1854, providing retroactive authority for the 1854 treaty and the treaty later negotiated in February of 1855.[58] It directed the President to include a provision in the new treaty to reserve lands for the Chippewa within the ceded territory, to pay annuities at villages in the ceded territory, to give the same privileges to mixed bloods living on ceded lands as to full blood Chippewa, and to extend federal and territorial law over the lands that would be ceded.

On January 10, 1855, the 1854 treaty was ratified, and it was proclaimed on January 29, 1855.

In 1855, several bands of Chippewa, including the Mille Lacs Band, signed a Treaty creating a single reservation in the territory of Minnesota, which stated: "And the said Indians do further fully and entirely relinquish and convey to the United States, any and all right, title, and interest, of whatsoever nature the same may be, which they may now have in, and to any other lands in the Territory of Minnesota or elsewhere."[59]

The Indians' trustee, Commissioner Manypenny, supported the Treaty:

> I have the honor to transmit, herewith, to be laid before the President, and, if deemed proper to be submitted to the Senate for its constitutional action, certain articles of agreement and convention, concluded on yesterday, with the Mississippi, Pillager, and Lake Winnibigoshish bands of Chippewa Indians, in Minnesota, by which they cede and convey to the United States all the lands owned and claimed by them in that Territory, and whatever right or interest they may have in other lands in common with other Indians there or elsewhere.
>
> The quantity of land ceded, according to the boundaries defined in the first article, is estimated at from ***eleven millions to fourteen millions of acres***, besides which, those Indians (and especially the Pillager and Lake Winnibigoshish bands) have some right [or] interest in a large extent of other lands in common with other Indians in Minnesota, and which right or interest, as above stated, is also ceded to the United States. (Emphasis added).[60]

	Chippewa 1855 Treaty	
Pillager Band	Cass Lake, Leech Lake and Lake Winnibigoshish Reservations to be created.	Three Reservations later consolidated to form Greater Leech Lake Indian Reservation.
Mississippi Chippewa	Gull Lake, Mille Lacs Lake, Pokegama Lake, Rabbit Lake, Rice Lake and Sandy Lake Reservations to be created.	Rice Lake Indian Reservation never established. Gull Lake, Pokegama Lake and Rabbit Lake Indian Reservations were extinguished.

The Treaty was supposed to create nine reservations. The Pillager Band was to get three reservations: Cass Lake, Leech Lake and Lake Winnibigoshish. The Mississippi Chippewa were to get six reservations: Gull Lake, Mille Lacs Lake, Pokegama Lake, Rabbit Lake, Rice Lake and Sandy Lake.

Of these reservations, Rice Lake Indian Reservation was never established. Gull Lake, Pokegama Lake and Rabbit Lake Indian Reservations were extinguished.

Later, the three Pillager Chippewa Reservations were consolidated to form the Greater Leech Lake Indian Reservation.

In years to come, various tracts of reservation land established in the Treaty of 1855 would be enlarged, ceded, stolen, restored, co-opted and vacated through treaties, acts of Congress, and the actions of corporations, Indian agents and others.

Concentrating Indians on Reservations

Commissioner Greenwood further lauded the Treaties of 1854–1855:

> The concentration of the Chippewas in Wisconsin and Minnesota upon the circumscribed reservations assigned to them by the treaties of 1854–5, besides *redeeming a large body of lands from the incubus of the Indian title and vagrant occupancy, and throwing them open for settlement by the whites*, must result in great advantage to the Indians themselves, in giving them fixed places of abode, in *bringing them under more easy and efficient control*, and in enabling the department to apply, with greater effect and advantage, the means and instrumentalities necessary for their improvement. (Emphasis added).[61]

In "Timber and Men: The Weyerhaeuser Story by Ralph W. Hidy, Frank Ernest Hill, and Allan Nevins," Evan Kek notes as to Indians:

> However, after 1837 various treaties opened the land. *The Sioux were pushed across the Missouri, the Chippewas and other tribes confined to reservations*. By 1855, general settlement became possible and went forwardly rapidly after the coming of the railroads in 1862. By 1890 the trunk lines of both the Northern Pacific and the Great Northern crossed the state, while in the southern areas numerous other roads had been built. The forest had melted to ax and flame as the settlers cleared the land for farms, and the prairie filled rapidly. The market for lumber grew comparably ... *When extensive tracts of white and red pine were sold by the government in the seventies and eighties, rich men like John S. Pillsbury and Thomas B. Walker increased their already notable holdings. ... By 1890, the Mussers, Laird-Nortons, Weyerhaeusers, and Denkmanns were ready to operate in farther Minnesota.* (Emphasis added).[62]

Theft of Two Million Acres

In 1859, Commissioner Greenwood recommended negotiating a treaty with the Red Lake Chippewa for the cession of two million "fertile and valuable" acres to bring them under the "necessary control and subjected to our modified reservation policy." Also, the DOI desired to protect the safe transit of our citizens between Canada and Minnesota engaged in commerce. "The negotiation of a treaty with them would, therefore, seem to be required, as well for their benefit and welfare as for the protection and advancement of the interests of our own citizens."[63]

Settlers Pressure Chippewa to Cede Timbered Land

Also, a Treaty was advised for the Lac Courte Oreille and Lac La Flambeau Bands whose lands "are heavily timbered with pine" and over which "the whites have trespassed ... cutting down and removing the most valuable they could reach, to the great annoyance and injury of the Indians."[64]

In 1863, a Treaty was entered into with the Chippewas of the Mississippi and the Pillager and Lake Winnibigoshish Bands for the cession of the Gull Lake, Mille Lac, Sandy Lake, Rabbit Lake, Pokagomin Lake, and Rice Lake Reservations, in return for the establishment of a reservation where they would be concentrated.[65] As long as the Mille Lac Indians did not interfere with or molest the persons or property of the whites, they would not be compelled to move. In record time, the Treaty was entered into March 11, 1863, ratified by Congress March 13, 1863, and proclaimed by President Lincoln on March 19, 1863.

From 1865 to 1889, speculators filed claims on lands on the Mille Lacs Reservation and illegally harvested most of the pine timber, while the Mille Lacs Band tried to preserve the Reservation and its right to live there by not interfering with the actions of the whites.[66]

Surprisingly, the Acting Commissioner characterized the Mille Lacs Band's lands as incapable of ever belonging to them, as title was limited to their good behavior, and it was "coveted and trespassed on by the whites."[67]

Bring All Indians under My Charge

As early as 1873, the Indian Agent in Minnesota begin lobbying for a consolidation of several of the Chippewa Indians onto the White Earth Reservation. In 1873, Indian Agent E. Douglass and in 1874 Special United States Indian Agent James Whitehead, advocated for this policy:

It is evident that the true policy of the Government should be one of concentration, to bring all the Indians under my charge, with the exception of the Leech Lake Pillagers, upon White Earth reservation.[68]

In 1879, Agent C. A. Ruffee continued the recommendation of removal of many Chippewa Bands to White Earth. He advised that the White Oak Point, Sandy Lake and Mille Lacs Chippewas could be removed and that Leech Lake and Red Lake Indians would "voluntarily" come to White Earth, since their land was "chiefly valuable for pine timber," and not agriculture. Removal made sense.

> Should the Indian title be extinguished, a ready sale could be made of the timber and a fund so created ample to meet the expenses incident to their removal and their establishment in comfortable houses upon this reservation.[69]

In 1880, Acting Commissioner E. M. Marble supported Senate Bill No. 1630, providing for the removal to and consolidation upon the White Earth Reservation of the several Bands of Chippewas, along with the "sale of the lands vacated, and investment of the proceeds for the benefit of said Indians, and for allotment to them of all lands in severalty upon the White Earth Reservation." With the continued advocacy of the DOI, at the highest levels, for the removal of the Chippewas, it became a foregone conclusion that Congress would act upon their judgment.[70]

Commissioner Hiram Price noted in his 1883 Secretarial report the "*proposed consolidation* of the various several bands of Chippewas in Minnesota upon the White Earth Reservation." (Emphasis added).[71]

Indians Able to Conduct Logging Operations

Indian Agent R. M. Pratt's report in 1875 recognized *the ability of the Red Lake Indians to successfully sustain logging operations.*

> The mill is now in good working condition, capable of turning out 10,000 feet of lumber in a day, having one run of burrs, which will grind corn and wheat, but will not bolt the flour or meal; also, having a good cut-off saw, an edging-saw, a planer, and a matcher. Logs were cut and placed in the pond last winter to the amount of 375,000 feet, and about 100,000 feet have been sawed.[72]

No sooner do the Indians demonstrate their logging expertise, then they are ordered to cease.

Similarly, Indian Agent Lewis Stowe reported on the logging by Indians at the White Earth Reservation: The Indians have cut and hauled to the river and run to the mill about 800,000 feet of dead pine, which was going to waste. This will be sawed into lumber for fencing and house-building.[73]

Part 7: War Crimes

U.S.-Dakota War

In 1862, in the middle of the U.S. Civil War, the U.S. government failed to provide treaty-promised food and funds to the Dakota people. Without a large enough land base to support themselves through hunting and gathering, the Dakota were starving. Their desperation and humiliation sparked the U.S.-Dakota War in the late summer of that year.

Governor's Message to State Legislature

At the war's outset, on September 9, 1862, Governor Alexander Ramsey addressed the State in an Extra Session. His message would mean tragedy for the Sioux.

Our course then is plain. *The Sioux Indians of Minnesota must be exterminated or driven forever beyond the borders of the State*. The public safety imperatively requires it. Justice calls for it. Humanity itself, outraged by their unutterable atrocities, demands it. The blood of the murdered cries to heaven for vengeance on these assassins of women and children. They have themselves made their annihilation an imperative social necessity. Faithless to solemn treaty obligations, to old friendships, to the ties of blood, regardless even of self interest when it conflicts with their savage passions, incapable of honor, of truth or of gratitude; amenable to no law; bound by no moral or social restraints, they have already destroyed in one monstrous act of perfidy, every pledge on which it was possible to found a hope of ultimate reconciliation. They must be regarded and treated as outlaws. If any shall escape extinction, the wretched remnant must be driven beyond our borders and our frontier garrisoned with a force sufficient to forever prevent their return. *So entirely have they destroyed all confidence among our people in the securities of life and property in the neighborhood of Indians, that much as many might regret it, it will doubtless be necessary sooner or later to remove the Winnebagoes, now dwelling in the heart of one of our most populous and beautiful agricultural districts, beyond the borders of the State*. (Emphasis added).[74]

Mass Hanging at Mankato

After the war, which lasted only a few months, troops imprisoned Sioux men of fighting age in Mankato, where they faced military trials, even though they had been military combatants. Nearly 400 men were tried by a military commission and 303 were sentenced to death.

> The summary haste of the trials (from twenty to forty-two cases being disposed of in a day), and the fact that no Indian was given an opportunity to make any defense or even to know what he was accused of, made the proceedings of this tribunal much of a farce. Our modern courts spend twice to five times as long trying one murderer than that court spent trying 425. ... Doubtless among the Indians convicted there were many who were guilty, but there is no question, but that there were many, also, who were innocent.[75]

An account of the mass hanging was reported by Thomas Hughes in 1901. It is lengthy but it is included here as a testament to the Sioux men who were unjustly murdered on December 26, 1862. It is incontrovertible evidence of the brutality of the whites. *A photograph of the Sioux men hanging from the gallows, which permitted their simultaneous death, should be posted at the Lincoln Memorial, lest we ever forget.*

It was General Sibley's intention to have the 303 sentenced to be hung executed at once, but the religious sentiment of the east was so shocked by the idea of hanging so many human beings at once, especially in view of the provocation they had for the outbreak, that President Lincoln was induced to interfere and ordered that none be executed until he had approved their sentence.

President Lincoln replied by requesting that all the evidence upon which the Indians had been condemned be forwarded to him by mail. On receipt of the evidence the President turned it over to Geo. C. Whiting and Francis H. Buggies, two of his clerks, with instructions to examine it and select forty of the worst ones. This they did, and on Dec. 6th, 1862, the President signed an order approving the sentence imposed on these forty and fixing Friday Dec. 19th, 1862, as the day for the execution.

On receipt of the order for execution preparations were made at once to carry it into effect. It was discovered soon that there was not enough rope in Mankato of suitable size and quality and that it could not be gotten by the 19th, so a request was telegraphed to the President for a postponement of the execution for one week, which was granted.

SPECIAL ORDER NO. 11.

HEADQUARTERS INDIAN POST, MANKATO, DEC. 17th, 1862. The President of the United States, having directed the execution of thirty-nine of the Sioux Indians and halfbreed prisoners in my charge, on Friday, the 26th instant, he having postponed the time from the 19th instant, said execution will be carried into effect in front of the Indian prison at this place on that day at 10 o'clock A.M. The executive also enjoins that no others of the prisoners be allowed to escape, and that they be protected for the future disposition of the Government; and these orders will be executed by the military force at my disposal with utmost fidelity.

The aid of all good citizens is invoked to maintain the law and constitutional authority of the land on that occasion. The State of Minnesota must not, in addition to the terrible wrongs and outrages inflicted upon her by the murderous savages, suffer, if possible, still more fatally, in her prosperity and reputation, at the hands of a few of our misguided, though deeply Injured fellow citizens.
STEPHEN MILLER, Col. 7th Minn. Regt. Vol. Commanding Post.

On the morning of the 26th, they sang their death song in Dakota, Tazoo leading, which was very exciting. At 7:30 A.M., all persons were excluded, except those needed to prepare them for execution. Maj. Brown and Capt. Redfield superintended the affair. Their irons were knocked off and their arms pinioned, elbows behind and wrists in front about six inches apart. This took until 9 o'clock. They went around shaking hands with the soldiers and bidding them good bye.

As soon as they caught sight of the gallows, they began singing their death dirge, keeping step to the music. Still following the lead of Capt. Redfield, they ascended the steps to the platform of the gallows and were ranged in their places by eight soldiers, two for each section of the gallows. After adjusting the nooses and pulling down the muslin caps, or sacks, over their faces, the soldiers walked down from the platform. In the meantime the Indians kept up continuously their singing and dancing and some managed to clasp each other's hands. Their chant mainly consisted of the simple repetition in Dakotah of "This is me." It was a wild, gruesome, impressive scene. Thirty human beings, all but three dressed in Indian costumes, ranged round the four squares of the gallows on an elevated platform, with ropes round their necks, dancing and chanting a weird, fantastic dirge.

In all 1419 soldiers were on the ground.

Beyond the military were the populace, a great and motly throng of men, women and children, who had gathered into Mankato from a radius of fifty miles in their lumber wagons drawn by oxen. Many had been on the road all night. The weather was remarkably fine. There was scarcely any snow and the day was so warm that people went about in their shirt sleeves. ... As the river was low there was a long sand bank in front of the levee. This was covered with spectators, and so was the opposite bank of the river ...

At 10:16 A.M., everything being ready, Capt. Burt waved his sword as a signal to Maj. Brown, who gave three distinct taps on his drum. At the last tap the props, which had been put under the platform as a precaution against accident, were knocked down and Captain Duly, then took his revenge. Through nervousness he failed on the first stroke, but a second blow of his ax severed the rope, and the platform fell with a crash. The doleful sound of the death dirge suddenly ceased and in its stead a great shout of exultation, rose from the spectators.

> In twenty minutes the doctors pronounced all dead, and the four teams detailed for the purpose, drove to the scaffold, and the bodies were cut down and conveyed to their burial. A long wide trench had been dug in the gravel bed at the upper end of the levee between Front street and the river. Here they were interred by Capt. Burke's company, who acted as a burial party. The interment, however, proved of little value as the bodies were all exhumed that night and carried off for dissection by various doctors of Southern Minnesota.[76]

Those not executed were imprisoned at Fort Snelling. The remaining Dakota were sent to prison in Iowa or to reservations at Crow Creek in what is now South Dakota, and at Santee in Nebraska Territory.

The Commission appointed by the government to pass on the claims for damages by reason of the massacre met at Mankato from the 16th to the 24th of July, 1863. In all 2,940 claims were filed, amounting to $2,600,000 and of these $1,350,000 were allowed. As the appropriation was only $200,000, and all expenses had to be paid out of this, including a salary of $2,500 to each Commissioner, the claimants got a de minimus amount.

On January 7, 1863, Governor Ramsey gave his Annual Message to the Legislature of Minnesota. For the imprisoned Sioux, he recommended their immediate expulsion from the State.

> The absolute and immediate removal of these savages beyond our borders has become an imperative social necessity. The moral and physical safety of the Indian urges it; the rising fortunes of our State require it; and the united voice of our people demand it. ***The recognition of these savages as independent nations, competent to declare war, to make laws for their own guidance and to hold and dispose of property, has always been a fraud upon the Indians.*** It is an attempt to raise these ignorant savages to a position, to which their wild and roving habits and their child-like ignorance necessarily unfits them, and while affording abundant opportunity for the frauds of the designing has taught the Indian only arrogance in his demands, a contempt for the authority, and a suspicion of the integrity of the Government. (Emphasis added).[77]

Dakota Exiled from Minnesota

On March 3, 1863, Congress passed a law exiling the Sioux Indians from the State of Minnesota. It is still in effect today.

U.S. Deports Dakota to Crow Creek

By May of 1863, there were 176 elderly men, 536 women, and 606 children that had to be removed. Governor Ramsey recommended their removal by steamship from St. Paul to Crow Creek, rather than a more direct overland route, to reduce their chance of escape. On May 4 and 5, steamships took more than 1,100 Dakota women, children, and elders from St. Paul to the newly created Crow Creek Reservation in the Dakota Territory. Elsewhere, U.S. troops force marched approximately 1,700 Dakota prisoners, mostly women and children, from western Minnesota to Fort Snelling. They walked 150 miles in bitter November conditions through hostile towns. They were held at a concentration camp below the Fort over the winter, where several hundred died due to exposure, hunger, and disease.

Governor Swift, in his Annual Message to the Legislature of Minnesota on January 11, 1864, was cruel and vindictive.

> Hunger and destitution have followed like avenging angels upon the track of the fugitive assassins to insure the punishment left incomplete by the forces sent out against them. In all probability many of them will perish this winter from cold and starvation, and it should not be forgotten that, under the circumstances, the distruction [sic] of large quantities of provisions and clothing, upon which they had relied for their winter's support and protection, by the troops under Generals Sibley and Sulley, must be regarded as scarcely less fatal to them, than the more sudden and sanguinary havoc of the sword.

He stated that the corps organized to track any remaining Sioux was still active:

> A corps of State scouts was organized to track these savages to their hiding places, and *in order to enlist the inhabitants of the menaced district in their extirpation, arms were issued to them, and a reward of twenty-five dollars, afterwards increased to $200, was offered for every hostile Sioux warrior killed.* (Emphasis added).[78]

Governor Miller, in his Inaugural Address to the Legislature of Minnesota on January 13, 1864, was no less heinous. It is tantamount to a confession of genocidal crimes.

The expeditions under Generals Sibley and Sulley, the command of the first named officer consisting entirely of Minnesota troops, who successfully performed one of the longest marches upon record, have slain, scattered or paralyzed these perpetrators of the inhuman butcheries of 1862, who unfortunately escaped the immediate punishment meted out to their associates in crime, together with the powerful western bands by whom they were harbored or assisted.[79]

Part 8: Winnebagoes – Crimes against Humanity

Ho-Chunk people are indigenous to Wisconsin and had lived on the land within its borders since time immemorial. Yet, they were forced to move to the Blue Earth region in Minnesota. The U.S. had attempted to move all of them to Iowa. Many Ho-Chunk were able to evade removal from Wisconsin. Others returned after removal. There were about 400 Ho-Chunks estimated in Wisconsin after the 1840 removal effort, a number that increased to around 1000 by 1871.[80]

The Knights of the Forest was an 1863 secret society that formed in Mankato, Minnesota, after the mass hanging of innocent Sioux. They targeted the Ho-Chunk Tribe based on its proximity to their headquarters, though they did have branches in other cities.

The citizens of Mankato placed a time capsule in a city building in 1869, amongst great fanfare. In 2004, a long-buried Knights of the Forest document was unearthed when the capsule's documents were first listed online. Why it wasn't made public when the capsule was opened in 1922 and in 1968 is unknown. Thomas Hughes in his 1901 History of Blue Earth had exposed them in a chapter of his book.[81]

Members took a solemn oath to do everything in their power to remove "all tribes of Indians from the State of Minnesota." Their terrifying Initiation is printed in full in the Notes section of this Chapter. They promised to be bound "together as brothers in common" so they could go forth "stronger and braver in the determination to banish forever from our beautiful State every Indian who now desecrates our soil." A candidate for membership took the following oath (quoted in part):

> I__ ... do most solemnly promise, without any mental reservation whatever, to use every exertion and influence in my power to cause the removal of all tribes of Indians from the State of Minnesota.[82]

New initiates were welcomed because they had "chosen the only path which will give security and safety to the future and prevent the blow of the glittering knife and merciless tomahawk." An article in a local newspaper reported the following:

One noteworthy act of the Mankato Lodge, however, merits particular attention. This was the employment of a certain number of men whose duty was to lie in ambush on the outskirts of the Winnebago Reservation, and shoot any Indian who might be observed outside the lines. It is not the province of this sketch to relate how many, if any, Indians were thus disposed of. It is sufficient to say that the designated parties went out on their scouting excursions, and in due time returned and reported. For obvious reasons their reports were not made a matter of record.[83]

At least three members of a secret hate group in Mankato, the Knights of the Forest, were eyewitnesses to the largest mass execution in U.S. history. "Asa Barney, Charles Chapman, and John Meagher all signed a letter swearing to their eyewitness of the hanging."[84]

In an effort to demonstrate to the whites that they were not friends of the Sioux and had not participated in the war, the Winnebagoes killed two Sioux.

A party of about twenty young bucks decked in paint and feathers, with wreaths of weeds and grass on their heads, brought the two Sioux scalps and the tongue, adorned with gay ribbons and fastened on poles, to Mankato with them and paraded along main and Front streets yelling and hooting to the accompaniment of half a dozen Indian drums. ***This was done to curry favor with the whites*** and make them think they were the enemies of the Sioux. (Emphasis added).[85]

President, Congress and DOI Failed to Save Winnebagoes

Commissioner Dole reported the demand for the removal of the Winnebagoes, even though they had played no role in the recent Sioux War. They lived on 200,000 acres along the Blue Earth River, which was prime farmland. They did not want to move and considered the State's demand unjust. Both the Commissioner and Agent Lieutenant A. D. Balcomb knew the Indians justifiably feared for their lives, given the hostility of the whites. The Knights of the Forest had joined the chorus in Washington for the Indians removal and the DOI did not doubt that they would kill any Winnebagoes off their reservation. The situation was a powder keg waiting to go off. In another genocidal move, the state and its citizens wanted the U.S. to 'clean' their state of any Indians.

> The condition of the Winnebagoes is peculiar ... the exasperation of the people of Minnesota appears to be nearly as great towards these Indians as towards the Sioux. They demand that the Winnebagoes as well as the Sioux shall be removed from the limits of the State. The Winnebagoes are unwilling to remove. So exasperated are the people that *they only leave their reservation at the imminent risk of their lives.* (Emphasis added).[86]
>
> ***The least depredation on the part of anyone of their number, it is feared, would expose the whole tribe to an assault from the whites***, which would be inevitably attended with deplorable results. Under these circumstances measures must be taken to provide for their subsistence, until some line of policy can be adopted which will be alike just to them and to the whites. (Emphasis added).[87]
>
> The hostile feelings of the white people are so intense that I am necessitated to use extra efforts to keep the Indians upon their own lands, for the reason that *I have been notified by the whites that the Indians will be massacred if they go out of their own country;* and it is but a few days since *a Winnebago was killed* while crossing the Mississippi river for no other reason than that he was an Indian, and such is the state of public opinion that the murderer goes unpunished. (Emphasis added).[88]
>
> The Indians have been informed that, notwithstanding, their fidelity to the government and the people, the people of this State are memorializing Congress to remove them out of the State, which they consider very unjust under the circumstances, for they have become attached to this location, and would not leave it willingly, and think their fidelity ought to entitle them to respect and kind treatment.[89]

William Windom, a Congressman representing southern Minnesota, introduced a bill in Congress to remove the Winnebago. Minnesota U.S. Sen. Morton Wilkinson, who lived in Mankato, carried the bill in the Senate. The Winnebago Removal provided both for relocating the Winnebago, and also for selling their reservation lands to settlers. It reads in part:

> And be it further enacted, That upon the removal of the said Indians from the reservation where they now reside, it shall be the duty of the Secretary of the Interior to cause each legal subdivision of the said lands to be appraised....
> And be it further enacted, That after the appraisal of the said reservation the same shall be opened to pre-emption, entry and settlement in the same manner as other public lands ...[90]

On April 10, 1663, the Secretary ordered the Commissioner to forward a copy of the act passed by Congress for the removal of the Winnebagos to Lieutenant Balcomb and to have the Indians' armaments confiscated. Enclosed was "AN ACT for the removal of the Winnebago Indians, and for the *sale of their reservation in Minnesota for their benefit.*" (Emphasis added).[91]

The Ho-Chunk were forced to leave Blue Earth County for the Crow Creek Reservation in South Dakota. More than 550 Ho-Chunk died in the hostile conditions of their relocation.

The Mankato Independent newspaper announced the "Departure of the Winnebagoes" on one page, and "Valuable Land For Sale," which were Winnebago Trust Lands on another page.[92]

Benjamin Thompson played an ugly role in the Dakota exile of 1863. It was Thompson who chose Crow Creek in the Dakota Territory as the Dakota people's home in exile. Crow Creek was a dry, unproductive, and isolated piece of land. *Thompson became the Indian agent there, and under his directions, "rations were given on Saturday, eaten up by Sunday and the Indians starved for the rest of the week."* (Emphasis added).[93] The Ho-Chunk were expected to settle on this death trap, as well.

By the fall of 1863, the Winnebagoes were still trying to find a place to settle. They had reached the Omaha Indian Agency in Nebraska, in a state of starvation. Indian Agent O. H. Irish wasn't happy with their arrival, as the Poncas had also settled with the Omahas, straining the resources of the underfunded Agency.

Winnebagoes are constantly arriving in canoes, locating on our reserve, and begging for food to keep them from starving. (Emphasis added).[94]

Part 9: Waterboarding

Subsistence Lakes Damned

Jane Lamb Carroll in her article "Dams and Damages The Ojibway, The United States, and the Mississippi Headwaters Reservoirs" describes the early history of the Ojibwe and their connection with the Lakes of the Headwaters of the Mississippi as follows:

In 1881 the Ojibway of Minnesota resided on reservations scattered across the northern half of the state. The major lakes that comprised the headwaters of the Mississippi—Winnibigoshish, Leech, Pokegama, Sandy, and Gull—had been the sites of Ojibway villages since the early 18th century. These waters had also provided the primary means of subsistence for the headwaters bands, whose culture was intimately bound to the lakes and their nearby resources. The bands' yearly cycle revolved around seasonal variations in the bounty provided by the lakes and surrounding woods.[95]

Damming Headwaters of Mississippi

Starting in 1850, the Corps of Engineers, as well as private commercial interests, weighed the feasibility of damming the Headwaters in order to regulate the flow of the river downstream. St. Anthony Falls was a prime sawmill site on the Mississippi and needed a secure and constant flow of water. Logs were driven on the River to the mill. A flourishing colonial settler community had developed around the mill.

Johannes Kohl, a German geographer and scientist, described the Falls as they appeared in 1856:

> Walls and dams have been built out onto the falls .... The water being so low, the Mississippi could not carry away the load of sawdust, chips, odds and end of board and plank, and logs dumped in upstream. This industrial waste was stuck everywhere in big jumbled heaps in the falls attractive little niches and in the rocky clefts intended by Nature for the joyous downward passage of crystalline waters.[96]

To supply their mills with water, millers had driven shafts through the limestone bedrock and excavated canals in the sandstone underneath. Dams built to divert water to the mills left large sections of the limestone dry, exposing the rock to more freezing and thawing, and causing cracking. Water flowed down through the cracks, eroding the underlying sandstone.

In 1869, St. Anthony Falls collapsed due to excessive tunneling. The Corps of Engineers commissioned a survey by engineer Franklin Cook to save the Falls.

In 1878, William D. Washburn, a leading Minneapolis flour miller and United States Senator, led the campaign for a federally funded reservoir project. Communities along the River hoped an increase in the river's flow would boost navigation. The railroads dominated the transportation sector and the businesses along the River had suffered as a result of their inability to compete for river traffic.[97]

Minneapolis saw itself as the center of revived river commerce. Lumber mills and yards dominated the Mississippi's east and, especially, west banks from St. Anthony Falls north to near the Minneapolis city limits. Lumber had become king in north Minneapolis.

In 1878, the Secretary of War was directed to examine the practicality and cost of a system of reservoirs. The survey was completed by Captain Charles J. Allen of the Corps of Engineers. He recommended dams at Lake Wiinibiigoshish, Leech Lake and Pokegama Falls.

Under the Act to Improve Rivers and Harbors of June 14, 1880[98] and Act to Improve Rivers and Harbors of March 3, 1881,[99] the U.S. Secretary of War authorized the construction of two dams at the Mississippi River headwaters and compensation to landowners who would be affected. Three dams were completed in 1885. The fourth dam on the Pine River was finished in 1887.

Payment for Damages to Ojibwes Delayed for Century

In his August 13, 1880, Opinion, U.S. Attorney General Devens concluded that the Ojibway's compensation for damaged land could not be limited to the aggregate of five thousand dollars as allowed under the Act to Improve Rivers and Harbors.[100]

The chart below summarizes the various proposals over a hundred years for Chippewa flooded lands as a result of the construction of the dams.[101]

Act of June 14, 1880	Damages paid shall not exceed $5,000.	
8/13/1880	AG - limiting amount of damages to $5,000 would amount to taking tribes' land without just compensation.	
1881	$15,466.90	Approved by DOI. Cong. Legis. Cap of $22,500. Lands flooded that belonged to Ojibwe Bands.
12/82 Second Commission	$10,038.18 + Annual Award of $26,800. Proposed by Sibley, William R. Marshall (former Minn. Gov.) and Joseph A. Gilfillan (Episcopal).	Not acceptable to Ojibwe. No annuity in Cong. Legislation.
8/1886	Northwest Indian Commission recommended $150,000.	Congress did not accept proposed damages compensation.
2/1889	Rice Commission $150,000 plus 5% interest plus $1.25/acre taken.	Congress did not accept proposed damages compensation.
1890		Congress approves $150,000 but never paid in full. Ojibwes did not agree.
1972	Federal suit filed.	
1985	Out of court settlement for $3,390,288.	178,000 acres of reservation land, plus loss of rice marshes and 5 percent accumulated interest since 1884.

206 THE IRON TRIANGLE

Part 10: The Swindle – Cession of 2 Million Acres at Red Lake

Con-Artists at Work

In 1884, Congress' Committee on Indian Affairs begin debating legislation for the cession of all 3,000,000 acres of the Red Lake Band lands to afford the people of Northwestern Minnesota an opportunity to avail themselves of the pine timber on the reservation and opening "up a large area to thrifty, energetic settlers all over the land." According to the Committee, the reservation "occupied by less than 1,200 semi-civilized Chippewa Indians … is of little use or benefit to the Indians, and of no use or value at all to their white neighbors." The white settlers were having to pay for scarce timber and its transportation from 250 to 400 miles by rail, while the timber on the reservation was within 50 to 75 miles by water.[102]

The congressional debate on the bill introduced for the cession of land vilified Indians in a most racist and degrading manner. Representative Joseph McCrum Belford of New York led the charge.

> According to him, [June 10, 1884, p. 4991], …no Indian territory shall be a barrier against the swelling tide of American commerce. … It would be a good thing if we could push them off into the ocean. [Laughter.] What good are they? What do they do to promote our civilization? … I believe God made this country for us, the dominant civilizing race of the world.[103]

Most offensive was his description of the Cherokee removal, which generated laughter in Congress:[104]

> Yes, my dear friend from Arkansas, do you recollect how they dragged those poor Indians out of the State of Georgia? Why, sir, they absolutely tied them to the tails of their horses. [Laughter.]

This was followed by an ignominious reply from Representative Poindexter Dunn of Arkansas:[105]

> I will give my friend the benefit of a story my father's servant, Dick, told him. He said that the first impression he had of the Indians was what he saw of them on their move from Georgia to the Territory, and that every Indian was part man and part horse for they were all tied together. [Laughter.]

Opposition to Cession of 2 Million Acres at Red Lake Defeated

In the same debate, Representative James H. Blount of Georgia denounced the state for pandering to the lumber lobby. He recognized that while the U.S. could sell public lands at the low value of $1.25 per acre "for the purpose of inducing settlement and occupation" it had no right to "take from these poor, ignorant savages" their valuable agricultural and timber lands and pay them the same discounted rate.

Here are the best lands, those fitted for cultivation, and they are to be taken from these Indians! I do not care whether you call it robbery or not. It is an outrage and a disgrace to the Government to take those valuable lands belonging to these Indians, not to the Government, and let settlers go in and occupy them at the same rate as which the public lands are sold. ... *there are gentlemen engaged in lumbering, and it is this great lumber interest in that state which is so anxious to get hold of these pine lands*. ... (Emphasis added).[106]

Further declaring the outcome for the Chippewas, he stated: "The end will be the poverty and the further degradation of the Indians."[107]

Representative James Buchanan of New Jersey, joining in the opposition, summarized Congress' proposal:

> The Indians surrender in the first instance all their title to these 3,000,000 acres. It all passes away from them, and not a solitary cent is obtained by the Indians as payment until this land is disposed of by the General Government. Then how much is obtained for this agricultural land? Only $1.25 per acre, after taking out the expenses of the survey and all other expenses and after giving the pitiful amount of one hundred and sixty acres to each head of a family.[108]

Voice of Deceit

Minnesota Representative Nelson, employing the artful disguise of deceit, stated, in his congenial and persuasive manner, the need to dispose of the Indian's land for the benefit of the white settlers:

> *Here is a body of timber lying on the borders of this Red River Valley, of no practical use to the Indians, that we feel ought to be made accessible, and the benefit of which the white settlers ought to have*. (Emphasis added).[109]

Part 11: Beware the Grim Reaper

In 1885, Commissioner J. D. C. Atkins reported the severity of timber theft occurring on the Red Lake Reservation:

> Unless some more effective means be adopted than have hitherto been employed to prevent timber depredations on the Red Lake Reservation in Minnesota, the *valuable timber forests of that reservation will soon disappear without the Indians deriving the benefit therefrom to which they are justly entitled.* (Emphasis added).[110]

Northwest Commission's Gruesome Tasks

Congress approved forming a commission to negotiate with Indians in Minnesota, and in the Dakota, Montana, Idaho, and Washington Territories. John V. Wright, Henry B. Whipple and Charles F. Larrabee were appointed as Commissioners. In Minnesota, the Northwest Indian Commission (as it was referred to) negotiated two agreements: (i) for the concentration of the Chippewa Indians at White Earth; and (2) reduction of the Red Lake Reservation by 2,000,000 acres. A Letter seeking approval of the two agreements was transmitted to Congress by the President on February 18, 1887.[111]

Commissioner Atkins announced that the ratification of the agreement would place about 2,000,000 acres of land on the market, embracing a vast timber zone of very great value.[112] In the following year, 1888, Secretary Wm. F. Vilas forwarded his recommendation for Congress' approval.[113] *Nonetheless, the agreements negotiated by the Northwest Indian Commission with Indians in Minnesota were not ratified by Congress.*

Part 12: Allotment

Nelson Act (Minnesota's Version of General Allotment Act)

Minnesota's logging companies backed an 1889 federal statute introduced by Representative Nelson—an act for the "relief and civilization of the Chippewa Indians in the State of Minnesota." Congress passed the Nelson Act on January 14, 1889.[114] It implemented, in Minnesota, the applicable provisions of the General Allotment Act.

It instructed the President to negotiate with all of the Chippewa Indians in the State of Minnesota for the complete cession of all of their title and interest to all of the reservations in the State, except the White Earth and Red Lake Reservations. It further opened the surplus land left after allotting White Earth and Red Lake to the Chippewas to white settlement.[115] Section 3 of the Act provided an exception to removal to White Earth for those Indians who took an allotment on their existing reservation.

Allotment in Minnesota meant sequestering Indians on an 80 acre (sometimes 160 acre) allotment of land from the largesse of the government. The idea was to make Indians into farmers by providing every tribal member with a plot of land carved out of the tribal reservation. Not so incidentally, the land not allotted would be declared "surplus" and opened for settlement by non-Indians. The ruse of making Indians into farmers was that they wouldn't need as much land for subsistence.

Nelson Act Synopsis

(1) The Chippewa of Minnesota were to cede to the United States all of the Indian reservations in the state, except land required for allotments to the Chippewas at White Earth and Red Lake Reservations.
(2) All of the Chippewa of Minnesota, except the Red Lake Bands, were to be concentrated on the White Earth Reservation and given allotments in severalty on agricultural lands. The Red Lake Indians were to take up their allotments on their own reserve.
(3) Consent of two thirds of all the male adults over the age of eighteen was required for cessions of land.
(4) Any Indian could take his allotment in severalty on the reservation where he lived, instead of being removed to the White Earth Reservation.
(5) Three commissioners, one of them to be a citizen of Minnesota, would be appointed to (a) to negotiate for the cession in writing; (b) take the census; (c) conduct the vote; (d) make the allotments and payments; and (e) supervise the removal of the Indians.
(6) The lands ceded by the Indians were to be surveyed by the General Land Office. The Secretary of the Interior was to appoint examiners to appraise the ceded lands. Lands classified as agricultural lands were to be disposed of at a $1.25/acre under the Homestead Act. The pine lands were to be appraised and auctioned off in forty-acre lots at public auction to the highest bidder for cash, but at not less than three dollars per thousand feet board measure of the pine timber thereon. The unsold residue was to be offered at private sale. Not more than one-tenth of the pine lands were to be auctioned in any year.

(7) All monies received from the sales, after deductions were made for the costs of the census, of the removals, and of the surveys and appraisals, were to be deposited to the credit of the Chippewa of Minnesota in the Treasury of the United States, to remain there for fifty years and to draw interest at five per cent annually. One-half of the interest was to be paid in equal shares in cash to heads of families and guardians of orphan minors; one-fourth was to be paid in equal shares to all other classes of Indians; and the remaining fourth was devoted exclusively to the establishment and maintenance of a system of free schools among said Indians. The permanent fund was to be divided and paid to all Chippewa Indians and their issue then living at the end of the said fifty-year period.

Indian Commissioner Atkins would expound from the bully pulpit:

> The advantages to the Indians of taking their lands in severalty are so important and far-reaching in their effects that I fear to dwell upon them in this report …Every step taken, every move made, every suggestion offered, everything done with reference to the Indians should be with a view of impressing upon them that this is the policy which has been permanently decided upon by the Government in reference to their management. ***They must abandon tribal relations; they must give up their superstitions; they must forsake their savage habits and learn the arts of civilization; they must learn to labor, and must learn to rear their families as white people do, and to know more of their obligations to the Government and to society. In a word, they must learn to work for a living, and they must understand that it is their interest and duty to send their children to school.*** (Emphasis added).[116]

Part 13: Rice Commission Bullies Indians

President Harrison implemented the Nelson Act on February 26, 1889, by appointing Former Senator Henry M. Rice of Minnesota, Catholic Bishop Martin Marty, and Joseph B. Whiting of Wisconsin to the Chippewa Commission to perform the responsibilities specified under the Act. Given the leadership of Former Senator Rice, it came to be referred to as the "Rice Commission."[117]

The Rice Commission's encouragement for the Chippewas' cession included:

> (1) Commissioner Whiting told the Chippewas at Red Lake, "Unless something is done for you now, *five years hence this vast body of timber will be destroyed.*"
> (2) Bishop Marty said: "*The rest of the land which is now being used up, stolen from you, or burnt off will be taken hold of by the Great Father for his children. He will sell your pine.*"

(3) Hon. Rice said to the Indians at White Earth, "The pines [at Red Lake] are burning rapidly;" and later he said to the same Indians, "You all know that your pines are burning. ... **Your trees are being stolen and burned.**" (Emphasis added).[118]

A spokesman of the Red Lake Indians said "We are never the cause of the destruction of any pine on this reservation. We are surrounded by whites; they keep thieving from us and setting fires."[119]

Rice Commission Census

The Rice Commission reported the following census:

Chippewa Bands	Total Population	Adult Males	Acres of Land
Red Lake and Pembina Bands	1,386	386	3,200,000
Mississippi Bands	3,002	734	857,686
Pillager and Lake Winnibigoshish Bands	2,208	600	423,440
Lake Superior Bands	1,708	458	275,815
Total	8,304	2,178	4,756,941

Complaints by Various Chippewa Bands

The Rice Commission also reported the following complaints by various Chippewa Bands:

Tribe	Complaint		
Red Lake	East boundary line wrong.		$573,630 recommended for all claims. Payment unknown.
Pillager and Mississippi Bands	Damages caused by reservoir dams on Lake Winnibigoshish, Leech Lake, and Pine River, 46,920 acres of land ruined.		
Pillagers	700,000 acres ceded for Menominee, paid $15,000.	Menominee refused removal; paid $242,686 for cession to US.	
Mille Lacs	Boundary line errors, squatting, theft of timber.		
Fond du Lac	Wrong survey.		
United Bands	$177,600 due under La Pointe Treaty.		

Roberta Carol Harvey

Removal Numbers to White Earth Reservation

On August 27, 1900, the Secretary of the Interior reported that out of 7,000 subject to removal, only 1,107 Indians moved.[120] The Nelson Act contained a 'discordant' provision allowing Indians to take their allotments on their existing reservations, thereby avoiding removal – a preeminent goal of the Act failing. The U.S. never succeeded in consolidating all of the Ojibwe onto Red Lake and White Earth; today there are six Ojibwe reservations in Minnesota.

After the passage of the Nelson Act, Indian land ownership dropped to 1.4 million acres. Today, Indian land ownership is less than 1 million acres, or 2% percent of the State. Red Lake avoided the allotment process through a strategic move by its chiefs at the time. It has 564,000 acres, or more than half of all lands in Indian ownership in Minnesota.

Part 14: Tapping Sap

Sugar Point Uprising

The Sugar Point Uprising in October 5, 1898, could have been avoided. Chippewa members of the Third Regiment of the United States infantry, commanded by Captain Wilkinson, Second Lieutenant Tenny Ross, and General Bacon were ordered to track down Bug-O-Nay-Ge-Shig, who was wanted as a witness in a bootlegging case. Unable to find Bug-O-Nay-Ge-Shig, they searched nearby villages for fugitive Ojibwes. In one encounter, after a rifle misfire by an Army soldier on October 5, 1898, the Ojibwe fired upon the soldiers. General Bacon and Captain Wilkinson took command. The battle lasted roughly three and a half hours. While shouting "Give it to them boys; give 'em hell! We've got 'em licked! Give 'em hell," Captain Wilkinson was wounded in the leg. Later in the battle, he was mortally wounded. He was one of six deaths on the U.S. side in this battle, along with 10 wounded. In addition, two civilians were killed, and 4 others wounded. Lieutenant Colonel Abram A. Harbach arrived with reinforcements on October 6, but the uprising was over.[121]

Part 15: "Dead and Down" Timber

It is extremely important to separate the parallel programs of fraud occurring in regard to timber operations pertaining to Chippewa Indians in Minnesota that prevailed for over a decade! The first timber operations were the logging and sales under the "Dead and Down Program" on the various Chippewa Indian Reservations, Allotted or Unallotted; and the second timber operations were the logging and sale of timber on ceded lands by the U.S. to white logging businesses.

In 1897, Congress authorized the Indians residing on any Indian reservation in the State of Minnesota, allotted or unallotted, to cut, remove, sell, or otherwise dispose of the dead timber standing or fallen. In 1899, it was amended to apply only to trust lands and reduce fraud resulting from burning timber or cutting green timber.

Since the Indians did not have the logging equipment to act on their own, the logging regulations allowed them to contract out to logging companies.[122]

> Ninth. Any logging Indian, on a proper showing of his inability to furnish his logging outfit, or to sustain himself or his family during the logging operations, may receive advances of goods or cash from any party with whom he may contract, which contract shall first be approved by the Indian agent to such limit as the Indian agent may fix, and such advances shall be paid by the Indian agent to the party making the same from the amount to which such Indian is entitled for his logging work. F. W. Mondell, Acting Commissioner.[123]

The enforcement of the regulations relative to the cutting and sale of "dead and down" timber on the diminished reserves of the Chippewa Indian Reservations lay with the Commissioner of Indian Affairs. The contractor companies that performed the logging on behalf of the Indians committed fraud in many ways under this 'down and dead' timber program. Most likely, those in the lumber industry can list many other ways that fraud and theft could be committed.

> Underestimate the amount of dead and down timber;
> Cut green timber;
> Start fires to burn green timber or damage it so that it would be dead and down;
> Damage trees;
> Under pay for the amount of timber cut;
> Overcharge for ancillary services, such as appraising, which were deducted from the Indian's share of payment;
> Overcharge Indians for goods supplied by contractors;
> Employ whites instead of Indians, avoiding the payment of wages to

Indians;
Failure to have contracts approved by the DOI;
Outright theft;
Collusion on timber sales; and
Conspiracies to limit competition and reduce timber prices.

Secretary Hitchcock remarked that the sale of dead and down timber was "the most convenient vehicle for fraud that had yet been furnished those who were seeking to despoil the Indians."[124]

Logging Green Timber as "Dead and Down"

In 1901, Commissioner Jones approved the resumption of the logging of 'dead and down' timber. Again, fraud occurred. The logging of dead and down timber was discontinued on April 24, 1901. One company was sued for cutting green timber and ended up paying $18,138.01.

Part 16: The Cover Up

GLO Appointment of Timber Appraisers

In August of 1891, examiners for the ceded pine lands by the Red Lake Chippewas were appointed by the General Land Office, under the authority of Secretary of the Interior John W. Noble. The Commissioner of the General Land Office, by the act of January 14, 1889 (25 Stat. 642), was specifically charged with the survey of and timber estimation on the lands ceded by the Chippewas, which would be sold for the benefit of the Chippewas.

In March 1893, Hoke Smith became Secretary of the Interior. He was informed that the previous examiners' work was wholly unreliable. They were discharged. In May of 1893, a *second* crew was appointed, thirteen from Minnesota and fourteen from other states, the latter not familiar with pine. David R. Francis, appointed Secretary on August 24, 1896, *discharged the second crew* of examiners based on reports of gross incompetence.

Crooked Sale of Ceded Lands from Red Lake

The first sale of ceded timber lands at Red Lake was held at Crookston on July 15, 1896. Prominent lumbermen selected, without contest, the tracts they desired. The Crookston Times, July 15, 1896, reported light sales at the auction and heavier purchases at private sale. Whole townships of 23,040 acres were taken at private sale. The Graham Report contains the following testimony: "The auctioneer read the descriptions.... He calls it and there was no bidders at all, only two men. Meehan ... and Tom Shevlin was there. On one side of the lake [Red Lake] Meehan was bidding and on the other side Shevlin was bidding. On one side Shevlin would say 'I will take it' and on the other side Meehan would say 'I will take it' and that was all there was to it. I was there for two days."[125]

Red Lake Fraud Investigation

Secretary Francis appointed Inspector J. George Wright to investigate the Red Lake land sales, examining the accounts of the timber operations and the cutting of the 'dead and down' timber on said Reservation. Wright submitted an incredibly, beyond belief, damaging report on December 31, 1896. Underestimation of pine, neglect of duties and massive overcharges ($99,000) were just the tip of the iceberg.

Massive Fraud in Timber Operations at Red Lake

In his December 31, 1896, report, Inspector Wright found that 12,000,000 feet of green timber had been unlawfully cut under 'dead and down' contracts, and over 8,000,000 feet cut without authority on individual allotments.[126]

Also, his 130 page report details the following significant deficiencies under the appraisal contracts for lands ceded by the Red Lake Chippewas: (1) overcharge for services of $99,290; (2) incompetence due to lack of managerial oversight and estimator inexperience; (3) gross fabrication of timber amount without examination, resulting in flagrant underreporting; (4) reporting land as agricultural which would be sold for $1.25/acre, when timber present; (5) absence from duty while receiving pay; (6) bribes; (7) allegedly sharing insider information with timber companies; and (8) a former employee purchasing significant land.[127]

Inspector's Summary of Timber Appraisal Deficiencies

I. Overcharge for Services: $99,290

$151,290 Charged When Charge Should Not Have Been in Excess of $52,000, Overcharge of $99,290

II. Incompetence

Lack of Oversight by Managers
Estimators with No Experience
Estimators with Lack of Significant Experience [13 Experienced v. 18 (None); 10 Experienced v. 25 (None)]
Estimators with Lack of Experience with Norway Pine Timber

III. Neglect of Duty
Fabricating Amounts of Timber w/o Examination
Agreeing Upon Certain Quantity and All Estimators Reporting Same Amount
All Three Estimators Examining Timber Stands Jointly, Not Separately
Coordinating Estimates of Timber, Using Average or Comprising Amount to Avoid Difference in Amount Reported Which Would Require Redoing That Part of Survey
Using Another Estimator's Numbers
Reporting Examination with Estimates when Absent from Site
Using Cook as Estimator (Patsy Needham)
Separating Tract, Report on Part, Adding Together Each Report as Total, w/o Independent Examination of 40 Acres

IV. Method of Computing Quantity of Timber
Reporting No Presence of Timber When Timber Present
Reporting Land as Agricultural When Timber Present (Agricultural Land Would Be Sold at $1.25 an Acre)
Tracts Difficult of Access Unsurveyed or Reported w/o Examination
All Pine Without Reference to Kind or Quality or Accessibility Offered at Same Price

V. Questionable Behavior
Liquor on Premises
Working while Intoxicated
Significant Time Spent at Local Hotels
Cannot Ascertain from Records Whether or Not Estimator Unnecessarily Absent from Duty While Receiving Pay
Absent for Significant Periods (Weeks and Months), with Pay
Work Reported as Performed When Estimator Absent

VI. Bribe
Payment (Bribes) to Woman for Child Born out of Wedlock to Estimator – She Threatened to Report It to Sec. of Interior

VII. Insider Trading
Large timber companies independently surveyed area on own to determine

amount of timber and when to bid, due to underreported government amounts.

Mr. Spears, a licensed trader at the Red Lake Agency, stated, that in the winter of 1893 and 1894, Mr. P. Meehan, owner of The Meehan Lumber Company in Thief River Falls, who made large purchases of timber land, quoted from a book in his possession the estimates as being then made by Government's examiners, and that they were too high and would not be sold. Mr. P. Meehan denied this conversation.

VIII. Conflict of Interest

It is also represented that a Mr. Staples, chief of former corps of examiners, purchased large tracts on the day of sale and has continued to do so at intervals since, both in his own and other names.

Mr. Wright's Audit: Eighty-Five 40-Acre Tracts Examined, Fraudulent Discrepancies in Amount of Timber			
40 Acre Tracts	Amt. Reported	Audit Amount	Difference
85	9,635,000 Feet	17,271,000 Feet	7,636 Feet
61	5,547,000	12,472,000	6,925 Feet
24	4,088,000	4,799,000	711 Feet
	No Pine Reported	Pine Present	
	Rept. as Agri. Land; Price at $1.25/acre	White Pine, Norway Pine Present	

Ceded Land Sales Ceased

On January 4, 1897, Secretary Bliss withdrew all of the unsold pine lands at Red Lake from sale. Reexaminations were ordered, which were to be made by an experienced board of examiners of three, selected in August 1897.

Iron Triangle Cover-Up: DOI, Congressional Representatives and Timber Company Meet

Secretary David R. Francis met with (1) Thomas H. Shevlin, Logging Company Owner, (2) Minn. Senator Cushman K. Davis, (3) Minn. Representative Loren Fletcher, and (4) Commissioner of Indian Affairs Lamoreux on February 5, 1897, to discuss how to address this fraud.

GLO Commissioner Denies any Mismanagement of Timber Operations

In an October 3, 1898, letter to Commissioner Hermann, Hon. Loren Fletcher, a Minnesota U.S. Representative from Minneapolis, complained to the GLO Commissioner that the cutting of down and dead timber is a "fraud and a steal from beginning to end." Commissioner Hermann responded:

> I have given the matter my careful attention and *can find no evidence of fraud, injustice, or carelessness in the management of the business*. Binger Hermann, GLO Commissioner. (Emphasis added).[128]

Part 17: More Will Be Revealed

GLO Forced to Investigate Timber Operations at White Earth

Continued attacks upon the GLO in Minnesota newspapers finally reached a crescendo in the Fall of 1898. Commissioner Hermann appointed Special Agents H.H. Schwartz and F.J. Parke to investigate the claim that the Chippewa Sugar Point Uprising was due to timber mismanagement. The Commissioner of Indian Affairs added Special Agent Jenkins. While they cleared the charges that the uprising itself was due to timber irregularities, they each determined and reported the occurrence of ongoing fraud in timber operations.

GLO Reports Fraud at White Earth

In a December 8, 1898, letter to the GLO Commissioner, H. H. Schwartz gave several examples of the massive, fraudulent downing of green timber for booms, without reason, and where roads were cleared unnecessarily in areas with green timber:

The logs taken from boom-stick trees and the logs cut from the boom sticks after the booms were across the lake were among the finest logs to go to Minneapolis last winter. It is no exaggeration to say that *80 per cent of the green cut* for booms were not required. (Emphasis added).[129]

He also reported that it was chimerical to expect many Indians to be employed:

There is and will be no competition for Indian labor, as you suggest. The Indian was employed because it was in the contract and to pacify him. He was paid $1 because he will not work for less. The hardy Norsemen have swept over this Northwest like an ice blast, and the labor market will remain glutted long after the last log leaves the reservation. H. H. Schwartz, Special Agent General Land Office. (Emphasis added).[130]

Office of Indian Affairs Confirms Fraud at White Earth

Special Agent Jenkins forwarded his Report to the Commissioner of Indian Affairs on December 12, 1898. He stated that (1) there is no merchantable 'dead and down' timber; (2) green timber is being cut and wasted; and (3) the Indians are being defrauded. He emphatically recommended the suspension of all logging of 'dead and down' timber. The Indians favored a system where they would do the logging and have mills to cut the timber.

On several tracts I found three or four thousand logs cut and skidded. Of these fully 60 per cent were cut from green trees. In one pile of 99 logs on skids, 86 were found to have been cut green, and 13 dry. In many places roads were cut through the best timber and scores of green trees sacrificed. Jas. E. Jenkins, Special Agent.[131]

Jenkins continued: Some of the oldest and most reliable woodmen and lumbermen in the Northwest will tell you that there is practically no dead and down merchantable timber on these reservations and that the *cutting of so-called "dead and down" is a farce*, and my observations and investigations bear out the statement. I would most emphatically recommend the suspension of all logging of dead and down timber, for the following reasons: First, that the present system is unsatisfactory and cumbersome; second, that under this system both the Government and Indians are losing thousands of dollars annually; third, that green timber is being cut and wasted under false pretenses; fourth, that the Indians are being so plainly defrauded that they are greatly dissatisfied, and their discontent is assuming serious proportions. The Indians are, however, desirous of having timber operations resumed on a basis of common sense and common honesty. They favor the selling outright of all their pine timber at not less than $2 per thousand for Norway and $3 for white, as it stands, or the putting in of mills by the Government under the Menomonee plan. Either, I think, would be practicable and result satisfactorily to both Indians and Government. (Emphasis added).[132]

Sticky Eight-Year Fraud Problem

The fraud allegations would not go away after **eight years** and when Ethan Allen Hitchcock was appointed as Secretary on February 20, 1899, he (1) suspended all appraising, examining, and cutting of timber and all land sales; (2) instituted an investigation of alleged illegal cutting of timber and of the methods being employed by the examiners; and (3) given pressure from lumber companies, he approved a sale, to be held on November 27, 1900, of 40,000 acres of appraised timber land from ceded lands at White Earth, again to be held at Crookston.

Keep Chippewa Lands Off Market until Demand Justified

In 1899, the Board of Indian Commissioners recommended that the Chippewas' lands not be put on the market until "the demand justifies a good price for the same." They expressed the same concern regarding their timber.[133]

Collusion and Conspiracy at White Earth

To be expected, there were well-founded allegations of collusion among bidders and a conspiracy to limit competition at the 1900 Crookston sale of 40,000 acres of timber land. Secretary Hitchcock refused to approve the sales and ordered that patents be withheld until his further orders. Due to legal complications in proving fraud, securing evidence and the passage of time, the Secretary instructed the GLO Commissioner to approve the sales, except for two, one of which was for the purchase of nearly one-fourth of all the lands. The two buyers whose sales were disapproved entered into a settlement with the DOI.

Part 18: King's X

Secretary Reports Failed Timber Sales

In his 1900 Annual Report Secretary of the Interior Ethan A. Hitchcock reported briefly on the *failure of the Nelson Act to implement a functioning program for timber sales in Minnesota*:

> The results obtained from the administration of the act of January 14, 1899 (Nelson Act), have not been satisfactory to the Department, as the system devised thereunder has *failed to secure to the Indians the largest benefit from the sale of the pine and agricultural lands*. (Emphasis added).[134]

Who's Watching the Hen House

In January 1901, Secretary Hitchcock met with (1) Representative Nelson of Minnesota, (2) Representative Frank M. Eddy of Minnesota, (3) Representative James T. McCleary of Minnesota, (4) Representative Page Morris of Minnesota, (6) the Commissioner of the GLO and (7) the Commissioner of Indian Affairs. It was decided Representatives Eddy and Morris would draw up a bill, which they did. The problem with this alliance was the DOI's abdication of its trust responsibility for the Ojibwe Indians to Congressional representatives from Minnesota who were subject to (1) their voting constituency and (2) the timber industry that wanted Indian timber and agricultural lands opened. Minnesota Representative Morris claimed credit for the resulting bill which was passed by Congress in 1902.

The Morris Act was a logging company's dream legislation:

> Opening 25,000 acres of Indian ceded agricultural land at $1.25/acre to settlement [Homestead Act rate may have been amount set by federal government to induce white settlement, but it was not amount determined by Indians or representative of fair market value for their lands];

Permitting the sale of 200,000 acres of green or dead pine timber, standing or fallen, on ceded Indian lands with proceeds to be paid "to the benefit of the Indians;"

Repealing the right of Indians to log and sell "dead and down timber" [thus reducing competition and supply on market];

Allowing for the sale of tracts, up to 100,000 acres, as soon as they were surveyed and examined, without having to wait for the entire area [getting tracts on market sooner, given depletion of timber];

Allowing bids for up to ten sections (6,400 acres) in any one bid;

Mandating for only twenty per cent of the cash for the tract with each bid [bidders could distribute cash over several tracts and later withdraw bid(s) if they lacked consideration for tract];

No limit set on the number of bids submitted by any entity or person (creating near monopoly opportunities – in one sale there were two bidders, who bid on each side of lake versus bidding against each other for a particular tract];

Requiring the prompt completion of allotments [opening up unceded Indian allotments for purchase];

Furnishing the minutes of the examiner to any person desiring the same [allowing bidders to strategize on where to place bids, based on inside government information];

When practicable, employing Indian labor [vague language impossible to enforce];

Permitting leasing up to three hundred acres of land for a mill in the vicinity of timber lands purchased [facilitates vertical integration for added profit with logging and milling concentration in a limited number of companies];

Building on the rivers and lakes on or within said ceded lands, dams, cofferdams, booms, and to make other river and lake improvements necessary to facilitate logging operations, subject to the payment of any damages [DOI had no manpower to assess damages, so waterway pollution was given with multiple layers of sunken logs, timber debris, dust debris from milling, waste dumping, etc., trout were killed off in Lake Superior];

Authorizing the charge to the Indians of all expenses incurred in carrying out the provisions of this Act, as to the examining and listing of said lands, and the selling, cutting, and scaling of said timber, out of the proceeds of the sale of said timber;

The Indians had no right to demand employment for wages or question the need and/or veracity of such production and post-production costs which were paid out of the Indian proceeds by the DOI [which, in some instances, wiped out any proceeds due Indians]; and

In a new twist, reserving 6,400 acres and areas of land and allotments from sale or settlement for reforestation and a forest reserve [Ojibwes weren't consulted on whether they wanted a forest reserve or which lands should be in reserve or whether they would receive compensation].

Under the Homestead Act, the federal government offered the Indians' agricultural lands for sale at $1.25 per acre. They sold timberlands for a price which would yield at least three dollars per 1,000 feet of lumber (board measure) for all the pine found in a given tract. The Indians received pay from the government *only* after the government sold the land and/or timber *and after the government deducted costs incurred in selling the lands, such as surveying, appraising, advertising for sale, and whatever other ingenious costs they might invent as well as the lumbering costs.*

Given the DOI's unfathomable recommendation over decades to concentrate Ojibwes on one or two reservations, rather than protecting their valuable and substantial timber and agricultural lands, the Morris Act acted in tandem with the DOI's Act of May 17, 1902, permitting adult Indians to sell inherited lands, conveying a fee simple title to the purchaser. There was no countervailing authority to stop the combined power elite of business and political entities from pauperizing Indians. The power of the presidency combined with the timber lobby and congressional representatives, subservient to their voting constituencies, constituted the iron triangle of its day. The Supreme Court considered Congressional Indian legislation a political question outside of judicial review. Furthermore, the judicial plenary power doctrine upheld Congress' expansive, virtually unlimited authority to regulate tribes. Tribes were left without any judicial recourse against pernicious breaches of the federal trust responsibility and private intrusions upon tribal interests and sovereignty. The scandal here was not what was illegal, but what was legal.

Advantage of Institutional Expertise

The logging industry possessed capabilities not within the realm of Indian tribes. *Yet, the DOI delegated the responsibility for timber sales to Indian Agents, who lacked the expertise, and many times, the willingness or even desire to assure Indian property rights were protected.* The dark back smoked rooms of deal making were held in the plain light of the DOI offices, their institutional incompetency on public display. Unapologetically, Indians weren't part of the equation. Spin cycles of how Indian's didn't need the land or the land held no value to Indians filled the tainted air.

On the other hand, logging companies retain experienced, reliable timber scouts/cruisers to examine and appraise the lands of interest. The company could compare the various tracts to determine whether they were under or over valued by the DOI, since its examiner notes were public information.

Landmen of various levels of expertise and abilities, set forth below, advise the company regarding acquisitions.

>Knowledge of timber and marketing terminology;

>Knowledge of basic logging processes and equipment;

>Awareness of industry competitors;

>Familiarity with existing rules and regulations concerning logging, rights-of-way, transportation, milling and manufacturing;

>Able to research and analyze title to ascertain legal ownership;

>Competent to review U.S. surveys and riparian and accretion rights pertinent to the land of interest;

>Adept at performing timber evaluation and appraisal (burnt over tracts, previously logged, type of timber – white pine, Norway pine, standing, down, green or dead, etc.) to determine value of tracts;

>Capable of determining the quality of timber, accessibility for logging; accessibility of transportation; access for milling; access for shipping to manufacturing sites;

>Proficient at recommending tracts for bidding;

>Qualified to recommend bid amounts;

Skilled in developing scheduling plan required for logging, transportation, milling, manufacturing;

Determine vendors of services needed, along with availability;

Perform on-site inspections;

Analyze any potential surface damages;

Analyze profitability of logging operation, size of tract needed, etc.;

Prepare map of tracts, timber types, especially high-value white pine; logging capacity; density, and information such as sections, townships, rivers, lakes, streams, villages, cities, and settlements;

Calculate payments due on acquisitions;

Calculate rental payments due on mill sites;

Knowledge of legal documents;

Recommend marketing programs that include marketing to affiliated third parties, reducing costs, exchange of timber for coal or other resources, hedging purchases and sales to maximize seasonal nature of business;

Awareness of trading strategies, financial lenders, taxes, partnership and joint-venture opportunities;

Supervise and coordinate work of other relevant employees; and

Know tricks of trade – cunning and calculated network with government officials and competitors; bidding on several tracks thus tying them up, knowing the intention is to drop certain bids; maneuvering tracts to private sales versus sealed bids; given lack of anti-trust laws at time, cooperation with other bidders.

White Pine Was King

White Pine was King. Businessman G. W. Allen, described the Big Woods of Minnesota: "As it now stood, covered with timber, it was not furnishing anyone with anything." Allen was one of the incorporators in 1882 of Curtis Bros. & Co., a manufacturer of sash, doors, blinds, mouldings, stair work and everything pertaining to that class of manufacturing. Curtis Bros. had a factory at Wausau, Wisconsin, in 1882, which was heavily dependent on lumber.[135]

Under the guise of saving Indian timber wealth from the destruction of fires and theft by white settlers, the timber companies, the DOI and their cronies in Congress spent years conspiring to steal Indian lands and timber. Playing the game of trusteeship, they pretended to be acting on behalf of the Indians—you are impoverished on these vast land bases, there is no way you can use this much land, it has no value to it—we're here to help and protect you by buying it and then selling it to white settlers and companies, holding the proceeds in trust for you.

In a room of high-powered politics and business, the bureaucrats stood by—cratering to greed, hoping to land a cushy job in the business it was charged with regulating. A few did slip through the wire nets. Beneath the game table lurked the hidden plot—the Manifest Destiny to build an empire where Indians once lived. Thomas Jefferson's instructions to George Rogers Clark to take Fort Detroit envisioned a future of commerce and expansion:

> We shall divert through our own Country a branch of commerce which the European States have thought worthy of the most important struggles and sacrifices and ... add to the Empire of Liberty an extensive and fertile Country ...[136]

This false narrative of spreading liberty across the continent was used to justify removing Indians who were seen as obstacles to progress.

Part 19: The Trojan Horse

The Trojan Horse – Clapp Act and Steenerson Act

The logging industry soon realized a huge profit could be gained if they could get access to the timber and land on the Minnesota Indian allotments. Thus, began the lobbying of Minnesota legislators to enact laws allowing loggers access to timber on tribal allotments. Coincidence and circumstance to get at Indian timber would be inexplicably intertwined, hidden within the Trojan Horse of Congressional action—the Clapp Rider combined with the Steenerson Act of 1904. It is best described in the article How Minnesota Politicians Helped Cheat White Earth Out [of Their] Timber.[137]

A Trojan Horse is defined as **"any kind of deception or trick that involves getting a target willingly to allow an enemy into a secure place."**

Adult Mixed-Bloods Free to Sell Their Land

Senator Moses Clapp's rider on the Indian Appropriations Act removed the restriction prohibiting adult "mixed-blood" Indians from selling their allotments prior to the expiration of the twenty-five year trust period. They did not have to wait before receiving a fee patent. They were free to sell their lands. The Clapp Rider further allowed full-bloods to apply for the removal of restrictions on the sale of their allotments, if the DOI determined he/she was competent of managing his/her affairs.

Double or Nothing

The Steenerson Act doubled the size of allotments from 80 to 160 acres, which could include timber lands.

The Steenerson Act furnished the timber lands and the Clapp Rider made it possible to buy them.

The Steenerson Act of 1904 was a Trojan Horse for Minnesota's Anishinaabe people. It looked like a gift and it ended up being a trap to get access to the tribe's valuable timber. The act was named for its author, Minnesota U.S. Rep. Halvor Steenerson of Crookston.[138]

The Indians were thrilled with the Steenerson legislation. He was adopted by the Indians and was gifted with a quarter section of land.

Was it not the unanimous wish of the Indians to have Mr. Steenerson adopted? —A. That was what they all seemed to say. They were all of the same mind—to adopt; Mr. Steenerson. Q. Did they urge Mr. Steenerson to take an allotment, or not?— A. Yes; that is what they said. Q. And what did Mr. Steenerson say?[139]

Now, therefore, be it Resolved by the Mississippi Bands of Chippewa Indians, through their chiefs and headmen, as in council assembled, That the said Halvor Steenerson; be, and is hereby, declared to be a member of the said Mississippi Bands residing on the White Earth Reservation, Minn., together with any and all rights to land, annuities, and other tribal interests, the same as any other member of the bands aforesaid.[140]

Mr. Steenerson did not want to do anything against the Indians, and he said if his adoption ever did go through the Secretary he would either give it back to the tribe as a tribe or would sell the pine and ... do something with the funds for the benefit of the tribe; that he wasn't taking it for his own piece of land.[141]

Further Congressional Impetus to Assimilation

The 1906 Clapp Act Amendment included several provisions aimed at further assimilation of the Indians. It did not apply to Indian Territory.

(1) Extended the laws of the United States and the Territories over the Indians at the expiration of the allotment trust period;
(2) Extended citizenship to Indians who had received a fee patent or who were living apart from the reservation;
(3) Permitted the Secretary to determine if an Indian allottee was competent thereby issuing such allottee a patent in fee simple, salable upon receipt; and

(4) Made the Secretary responsible for ascertaining the legal heirs of a deceased Indian and issuing a patent in fee simple for said land to them, or cause the land to be sold and issue a patent to the purchaser and pay the net proceeds to the heirs.

Part 20: The Iron Triangle

The Grifter Heads to White Earth

In 1905, the White Earth Reservation, comprising 750,000 acres in northwestern Minnesota, belonged to the Chippewa Indians residing there, either as individual allotees or as property held in trust for them by the federal government. The land was physically varied with good soil for farming; plentiful timber; and amidst the lakes and streams, hunting, fishing and wild rice for bountiful harvesting. Railroad lines ran near the Reservation's northern and southern boundaries and along its western edge.

The lumber industry had harvested the southern timber. It needed to move north in search of more pine to feed the state's mills—three out of four were the world's largest. More were springing up.

How to Steal Indian Lands

The influence of the DOI and big business resulted in incremental Congressional legislation over five years, from 1902–1907, dismantling the White Earth Reservation. The combination of logging companies, bankers, mortgage companies, wealthy investors and attorneys stood to make a bundle of cash. The timber industry had a business they knew, with powerful political connections, and they offered investors the chance to parley their money into sizable profits. They needed to stay under the radar long enough to get the pieces in place. The saga of White Earth's dismantling would serve as a microcosm for the further dispossession of Indian land and resources.

Cast of Characters

We know the cast at the top of the pyramid: President Theodore Roosevelt had served as Vice President under former President McKinley. The Congressmen and Senators of Minnesota had the full support of their voting constituency.

The major logging companies were:

> Nichols-Chisholm Lumber Co. and Lyman Lumber (controlled by Minneapolis businessman Thomas L. Shevlin, who also owned Crookston

    Mill and Lumber Yards);
    Park Rapids;
    Wild Rice; and
    Wisconsin lumber tycoon Fred Herrick, an unwelcome part of the group.

The major attorneys to advise on staying within the bounds of the law included: Attorneys W. B. Carman, P. S. Converse and Ransom J. Powell. In this case, it would be easy because of the blurred boundaries of the law. The logging companies, as an association, would jointly retain and pay for legal services to minimize costs, rather than each hiring their own legal counsel.

These attorneys stayed on top of industry affairs, so they were ready at the drop of a hat to start the clock running. They knew, not only the law, but the logging processes, as well. The attorney-client relationship assured their discretion. Their knowledge of their competitor law firms and the judges at every level and their penchants was key. Their contribution was their unquestionable dedication to winning – their seamless effort belying their indefatigable commitment. Their network with the key players relied on their wealth, power and political influence, conservatively and quietly applied. Their role was to be invisible to the public eye. Nothing was left to chance; the military precision understood and even relished.

The banks, local and statewide, included: M. J. Kolb of Ogema; I. S. Waller of Waubun; E.G. Holmes of Detroit; A. F. Anundsen of Detroit, and Park Rapids Bank. They provided capital and access to capital when needed, in the way that money breeds more money.

Public and governmental relations were an arena of their own. Prominent businesses don't want an unwanted light cast into their offices—no publicity, no inopportune press releases and no flying above the radar.

The mixed blood Indians that offered their services were part of the success of the operation. The murky, risky intelligence they offered had been part of the government and business strategy from the start. They reaped the benefit of the blurred boundaries in blood quantum built into the law, but their proprietary knowledge had a price.

The CEO's expected all of this to hum along, without any glitches. This was business – no quarter given.

Stage Was Set to 'Get Rich Quick' Off of Indian Land

Anthropologist Warren Moorehead's incredulous first-person account discloses the confederation behind the scenes to 'get rich quick' off of Indian timber and arable land:

> The effect of the allotment on the Whites near White Earth was immediate. Mushroom banks sprang up in the surrounding small towns. The Indians in their affidavits (of which Linnen and myself took 505) testified that lawyers, banks, county officials, and business men of prominence in Detroit, Ogema, Mahnomen, and other towns, joined in the scramble to secure their pine lands and farm tracts... in the majority of cases, as the Indian could neither write nor read, he did not know whether he was signing receipts, mortgages, deeds or releases.[142]

In tandem with Moorehead, contemporary historian William Folwell reported:

> Purchases from adult mixed-bloods might be strictly legal, even though they were not equitable; but fullbloods and minors were not legally competent to sell. In utter violation of law, land sharks from near and far bought allotments of full-bloods and took their deeds and had them recorded. Such deeds were accompanied by affidavits that the allottee was an adult mixed-blood Indian. Some operators did not scruple to obtain conveyances from minors, also reenforced by affidavits that the grantors were of full age. Ignorant Indians were fleeced, not merely in the amounts of money paid or promised them, but also in the kinds of money. Buyers of land gave them tokens of tin redeemable only in merchandise at certain stores. Lumber companies paid in due bills, which storekeepers and saloon-keepers cashed at a discount, the heavier because they were marked on their face "non-negotiable."[143]

Cat's Out of the Bag

On July 18, 1906, a leading newspaper in Minneapolis charged that disgraceful conditions existed in Detroit where land speculators were plying the Indians with liquor in order to secure deeds or mortgages to their lands for small amounts; that the town had been filled with drunken Indians since June 21, when the Clapp Amendment became effective, and that 250 allotment mortgages had been filed at Detroit and many more in Norman County.

Commissioner Leupp telegraphed its agent at White Earth to investigate the matter, and he answered by telegraph on July 19 that "many of the mixt bloods had taken advantage of the provisions of the act to sell or mortgage their lands; that some of them were squandering the proceeds for intoxicants; but that this was true of only a limited number, and that no case had come under his observation where an Indian had first been plied with liquor to secure his consent to dispose of his land."[144]

Commissioner Valentine – Get to Bottom of Thieving

Indian Commissioner R. G. Valentine ordered an investigation to get to the bottom of the thieving. In 1909, the U.S. Attorney General appointed prosecutor Marsden Burch to handle the case. Wanting to confirm the accuracy of Moorehead's Report, Edward B. Linnen, an experienced Indian inspector, along with Moorehead, conducted a further joint investigation. They issued a grim joint report on September 30, 1909:

> It disclosed that, according to the estimates of the inspectors, *fully ninety per cent of the allotments to fullbloods had been sold or mortgaged and that eighty per cent of the whole acreage of the reservation had passed into private hand*s. *Full-bloods had received not more than ten per cent of the value of their land and timber.* Mortgages had been placed to run as long as ten years, interest had been paid in advance out of the loans, and foreclosures had been prompt. In scarcely any case did the Indian know what he was doing. (Emphasis added).[145]

The reports of trickery, deception and fraud were substantiated by the DOI in its investigation in 1910.

> The allottees began to sell their lands as soon as the act was passed. The cupidity of the white purchasers led to flagrant violations of the law. They purchased lands of Indians who were unquestionably full-bloods and plainly not competent to sell their lands under the law. *Trickery and fraud of all kinds was resorted to, and finally about 95 per cent of the allotments, or the timber on the allotments, of White Earth allottees had been disposed of under the pretended authority of the law mentioned. Millions of dollars were involved in these illegal sales. DOI needs to get lands back.* (Emphasis added).[146]

In 1911, the Commissioner of Indian Affairs further reported:

It was early discovered that there existed hundreds of fraudulent conveyances of both land and timber of full-blood and minor Indians, and the question of protecting the interests of these Indians by actions in the courts was, as soon as the facts could be obtained, referred to the Department of Justice.[147]

White Earth's Indian Agent, Simon T. Michelet, allegedly used the alias 'C.M. Martin' to buy parcels.

Iron Triangle and Artful Attorney Ransom Powell

The timber industry turned to Ransom Powell for the litigation. It turned out to be the perfect fit. *First*, he used the easiest and strongest defense of all: delay. Documents get lost; memories fade; witnesses can't be located; government attorneys turn over frequently versus having an attorney handling one issue for the long run; and parties give up. *Second*, he needed to establish mixed blood status since (a) they had the right to sell their allotments; and (b) they presented the majority of the cases. *Third*, knowing most Indians didn't have the money to bring a case, he pursued a novel theory: the federal government didn't have the right to represent the Indian defendants since they had a state court forum for their fraud cases.

U.S. Proves Criminal Conspiracy in Full-Blood Quantum Case

In the meantime, an early prosecution of a full-blood case was successful for the government and the Indians. Powell's client, banker and developer M. J. Kolb, was found guilty of "criminal conspiracy and inducing federal officials to issue land patents to full blood Indians."[148]

Quantum of Blood

During the 1909 investigation into reservation fraud, anthropologist Warren Moorehead and Indian inspector Edward B. Linnen prepared an enrollment list that identified 591 full bloods. Since they didn't question all of the allottees, their report was incomplete. A second effort was undertaken in 1910 by White Earth Special Indian Agent John H. Hinton. His study was based on the hearsay testimony of allottees, family, relatives and elder community members. He identified 927 full-bloods. Rather than rely on either study, Ransom decided to produce his own ancestral roll in an effort to reduce the number of full-bloods. He paid Ojibwes to do the inquiries, coordinated by N. B. Hurr, a former Reservation boarding-school principal familiar with the community, and more importantly, the owner of a land-and-loan company in the reservation village of Ponsford.

Judicial Definition of Mixed-Blood Chippewa Indian

The DOI had considered anyone with less than 50% Ojibwe blood quantum a mixed-blood. The parties agreed to a test case to garner a judicial determination of blood quantum status. Federal District Court Judge Morris ruled that one-eighth or more non-Indian blood quantum constituted classification as a mixed-blood. The government and the timber companies appealed. The final ruling in *United States v. First National Bank,* 234 U.S. 245 (1914) gave the phrase an even broader meaning. ***The U.S. Supreme Court ruled that any non-Indian ancestry, no matter how small, made an individual a mixed-blood—and thereby capable of selling his or her allotment***. Powell couldn't have asked for a better decision.

Cronies Lobby for Blood Quantum Congressional Legislation

To avoid what was clearly controversial and conflicted, the timber industry and settler coalition lobbied their Congressional cronies to fund a study to determine the blood quantum of White Earth Indians. Congress passed a bill and, more importantly, funded it at $5,000 per year. The Justice Department appointed Gordon Cain and Judge Morris of the Minnesota Federal District Court appointed Powell. The bill charged the panel with determining the "fractional amount of Indian ancestry" of every White Earth allottee. Powell's appointment to the panel would be considered an absolute conflict of interest today. Again, with contacts being important, it is presumed that probably Judge Morris knew Powell since he was a Duluth businessman and Morris was city attorney. It was in Powell's clients' interests to get as many Indians as possible classified as mixed-bloods, since they had a legal right to sell their allotments. That is exactly what happened.

Hierarchical Skull Studies

In 1914 with timber-company funds, Powell hired two social science physical anthropologists to assist the Panel's identification of full-bloods and mixed-bloods. Questionable by today's standards, Dr. Albert E. Jenks, a professor at the University of Minnesota, and Dr. Ales Hrdlicka conducted studies using their theoretical studies.

> In 1915 and 1916, they examined 696 allottees who claimed to be full bloods, comparing their physical attributes to the Pima Indians of the southwestern United States, whom the anthropologists considered the most racially "pure" American Indians. They carefully measured and calibrated hair, eyes, nails, gums, head shapes, and teeth of White Earth Ojibwe and compared this data to measurements of the Pima.[149]

Their studies narrowed the pool of full-bloods. *Of the 5,173 White Earth allottees, only 408 were considered to be full bloods—and 306 of them died before the roll was finalized in 1920.* Based on the government studies, in 1920, there were *102 full-blood White Earth Chippewas*.

Allottees Can Bring Fraud Cases in State Court

In another tack, knowing most Indians didn't have the money to bring a case, Powell brought a case challenging the right of the federal government to represent the defendants. Federal District Court Judge Morris ruled that once a minor reached adulthood, the federal government could not bring actions alleging fraud since an adult could do so in state court. The case wasn't appealed. Again, Powell tallied a win.

Government's Cases Weakened by Powell's Advocacy

More than 2,000 suits had been filed by the federal government involving over 2,500 allotments and 142,000 acres of land, asserting that allotments had been wrongfully obtained from both full- bloods and minors. Powell's timber company clients had logged most of the contested parcels, while the cases were being pursued.

Due to Powell's *first defense* – the mere passage of time, he had won. DOJ prosecutor, Francis J. Kearful, determined that it would be difficult to successfully prevail at trial given the decade that had passed since starting the litigation.

Powell's *second defense* of eliminating mixed-blood cases was also successful. The more than 2,000 suits had paled given the Supreme Court's ruling on the definition of a mixed-blood, leaving only *102 full-blood White Earth Chippewas*.

Powell's novel *third defense* of the state court forum for the allottee fraud cases was also a win. It wasn't appealed and it was a barrier in the prosecution of any fraud cases.

Powell ensured that most of his clients' purchases were protected for a comparatively small cost. Nichols-Chisholm paid out only $48,497 and its sister firm, Park Rapids Lumber, only $23,015.

Out-of-Court Settlement Formula

Powell and Daniels agreed on a settlement basis:

Land would be restored to full bloods; the cases involving mixed bloods who were competent to sell would be dismissed; and others who were defrauded, such as minors, would receive the difference between their original payments and the fair value of the property at time of sale, plus six percent interest to the time of settlement [not their land]. Significantly, no remedy was established for mixed bloods who had been defrauded.[150]

In 1911, the Commissioner of Indian Affairs had reported that:

> Complete success means the recovery of 142,000 acres, valued at over $2,000,000, and for timber valued at $1,755,000, on behalf of more than 1,700 Indians, forming almost 34 per cent of the White Earth allottees.[151]

This never happened.

Iron Triangle Prevails

The triangle of a united coalition of opponents to the U.S. DOJ cases; strong, politically connected legal representation; and Congressional cronies prevailed. Powell had been a formidable opponent. His Memorial description described him as follows:

He enjoyed nothing more than living in lumber camps where, from day to day, he could see and come to understand the methods of operation and business hazards and difficulties of those whom he represented in the courts. This combination of practical and theoretical knowledge made him a difficult and respected opponent.[152]

White Earth Epilogue

The Nichols-Chisholm Company bought about one hundred and fifty million board feet of timber, the Park Rapids Company about thirty-eight million, and the Wild Rice Company about twenty million, all in eight townships in the southeastern part of the Reservation.

By 1909, "85 percent of White Earth's land had passed into private hands at minimal cost to the purchasers." (Emphasis added).[153]

White Earth members also lost an estimated 100,000 acres through tax foreclosures. Under the state's interpretation of the Clapp Rider of 1906, allotments were subject to property taxes which, if unpaid, resulted in foreclosure. This was reversed in 1978. *According to the court, "the removal of the U.S. government's trust responsibility under the 1889 Nelson Act should not have occurred unless the allottee applied for such removal."* (Emphasis added).[154]

Former DOJ prosecutor Cain joined Powell's law firm to handle Indian land title cases.[155]

Minnesota's Timber Harvest

Minnesota's timber harvest grew until 1899 with a cut of 2,341,619,000 board feet, surpassed only by Michigan and Wisconsin. By 1920, the annual cut had fallen to 576 million feet or 2/3 of the state's annual consumption. Minnesota had to import fir from the Pacific Coast and yellow pine from the South, paying astronomically due to the resource scarcity and freight charges. What had cost $6 to $10 for a thousand board feet now was $40 to $100 for a thousand board feet of poorer grade lumber.

From 1900 to 1910, Duluth sawmills alone produced more than 3 billion board feet of lumber. It left Minnesota with legacy pollution due to lumber mills in the late 1800s and early 1900s dumping waste wood right into the St. Louis River. In shallow bays that wood is up to 20 feet thick in some places, most of it hidden underwater. It impedes plant growth and has been destructive of the ecosystem.

Part 21: Ecological Destruction

The Morris Act commodified the Ojibwe lands, considering their value based on their natural resources – forests for the green gold of timber, prairies for farms, water for power and navigation, and land for single family homesteads. The segregation of agricultural and timber lands fragmented the ecological systems with adverse consequences. The Ojibwe had successfully stewarded this land for millennia. Yet, in fifty years, Minnesota's forests were gone, denuded by the logging companies who moved on. Congressional Hearings could not reach within the secret web of corporate cronyism and political favors. The long and sordid history of industry, congressional committees and the government's bureaucracy relationship resulting in the genocide of Indian peoples and their landscapes was incontrovertible, yet unstoppable.

Collapse of Lake Superior Fishery

The opening of the Welland Canal provided a means to economically transport commodity items in mass via giant Lake Freighters to the world. Prior to the Canal such shipments were impossible due to the Niagara Falls. Unfortunately, it opened up a navigable waterway for invasive species and resultant detriment to a healthy fishery. The worst of these alien attackers proved to be the Sea Lamprey. Their attack on the Big, Bold and Cold trout resulted in the Lake Superior trout fishery collapse. It is painful just to view a trout with a lamprey leeched on to it.

Extinction of Passenger Pigeon due to Overhunting

"The passenger pigeon, once one of the most abundant birds in the world, was pushed to extinction by overhunting and habitat destruction in 1914 when the world's last passenger pigeon died. Deforestation after the European colonization contributed to the bird's extinction."[156]

Ritual – Knights of the Forest

OPENING.

[When the hour arrives for opening the Lodge, the Worthy Chancellor (and in his absence the Worthy Vice Chancellor) will take the chair and call the Lodge to order by giving one rap.]

Worthy Chancellor. The Officers will take their stations. The Conductor will see that the Lodge is guarded in a proper manner. The Conductor will examine those present, that all may be worthy.
[If any are present without the pass word, they must leave the room.
C. [Reports to W.C.]
W.C. [The Chancellor gives three raps, all the members rise.]
Officers and members: The objects for which we are assembled, are worthy of our cause. It is no less than the preservation of our lives, our families, and our homes. Let us be ever watchful and keep constantly in mind the sacred obligation which binds us together as brothers in one common interest. I sincerely hope this meeting may be profitable to each one of us, and that we may go forth from this Lodge stronger and braver in the determination to banish forever from our beautiful State every Indian who now desecrates our soil.
W.C. The Worthy Chancellor will now open this Lodge.

W.V.C. By direction of our Worthy Chancellor, I declare this Lodge open for the transaction of business and for extending universal opposition to all tribes of Indians in the State of Minnesota.
[The W.C gives one rap and the members take their seats.]
W.C. The Financial secretary will call the roll of members.

INITIATION.

[When the Lodge is ready for initiation, the F.S. will retire with the Assistant Conductor, to collect the initiation fee, when the A.C. shall propound to the candidate the following questions:]
C. Before you can proceed any further, you must give your assent to the following questions.
Question. Do you promise upon your honor that you will keep all secrets and information which I may here reveal to you?
Answer. I do.
Question. Are you in favor of the removal of all tribes of Indians from the State of Minnesota?
Answer. I am.
Question. Will you sacrifice all political and other preferences to accomplish that object?
Answer. I will.
Question. Will you do all in your power to elect to office such men only as will favor such removal?
Answer. I will.
Question. Do you desire to become a member of an order having for its object the removal of all Indians from this State, called the Knights of the Forest?
Answer. I do
[The F.S. collects his fee, and the questions having been answered in the affirmative the officers return to the Lodge room and report.]
F.S. All correct, Worthy Chancellor.
C. The usual questions are answered in the affirmative, Worthy Chancellor.
W.C. The Conductor will introduce the candidate.
[The Conductor, taking the candidate by the arm and leading him to the door, gives three raps. The Conductor introduces the candidate to the Worthy Vice Chancellor]
C. Worthy Vice Chancellor, permit me to introduce our friend, who wishes to become a member of our order.

W.V.C. My friend: it is with the utmost gratification that we proceed to comply with your wishes. None but those whose honor and integrity are unquestioned, can enter our circle. We have full faith in your integrity. We place implicit confidence in you, that you will never betray the secrets of our order. The atrocious murders visited upon innocent, honest and industrious citizens has proved to us, that our only security is in mutual protection and united action. We have learned, at the cost of many lives, that the white man and the Indian cannot dwell together in peace and harmony. The chief object of this order is to prevent the permanent location of any tribe of Indians in this State. The field open before us is wide and our success will depend in a great measure upon our energy. You have chosen the only path which will give security and safety to the future, and prevent the blow of the glittering knife and merciless tomahawk. In becoming a member of this organization you will be required to bind yourself to its laws by a solemn obligation – an obligation which will in no way transcend that inherent right implanted in our natures by a wise Creator. "The right of self-preservation." With these assurances and this warning, we now proceed to inform you further in relation to the duties of our order.

W.V.C. Conductor, take charge of our friend and present him to the Worthy Chancellor for obligation and instruction.

C. Worthy Chancellor, I here present our friend for obligation.

W.C. My friend, before you can become a worthy member of our fraternity, you must give your free and cordial assent to a solemn and binding obligation. That obligation requires that you should use all your influence and power for the removal of all tribes of indians from the State of Minnesota. We deem it in accordance with the duty which every citizen owes to himself, his neighbors, and his country.

OBLIGATION.

I ____ ____, of my own free will and accord, in the full belief that every Indian should be removed from the State, by the memory of the inhuman cruelties perpetrated upon defenseless citizens, and in the presence of the members of this order here assembled, do most solemnly promise, without any mental reservation whatever, to use every exertion and influence in my power to cause the removal of all tribes of Indians from the State of Minnesota. I will sacrifice every political and other preference to accomplish that object. I will not aid or assist in any manner to elect to office in this State or the United States any person outside of this order, who will not publicly or privately pledge himself for the permanent removal of all Indians from the State of Minnesota. I will protect and defend, at every hazard, all members in carrying out the objects of this order. I will faithfully observe the constitution, rules and by-laws of this Lodge or any Grand or working Lodge of Knights of the Forest to which I may be attached. I will never in any manner reveal the name, existence, or secrets of this order to any person not entitled to know the same: and in case I should be expelled or voluntarily withdraw from this order, I will consider this obligation still binding. To all of which I pledge my sacred honor.

The candidate will now sign our constitution and obligation.
W.C. You will now sign our constitution, after which you will be further instructed.
W.C. I will now instruct you in the signs, pass words, grips and tokens of this order.
1st. I will first instruct you in the signs of recognition and the test word.
2d. The pass-word is to be given only by the Worthy Chancellor in the Lodge room.
3d. The Conductor will now instruct you in the grip.
4th. I will now inform you how to work your way into or out of this or any other Lodge.
I have some further instructions to give to you in reference to the acquiring of members to our order.
The P.W. will instruct the candidates upon the constitution in reference to admission of members.
C. Past Worthy Chancellor, I am directed by the Worthy Chancellor to present this friend to be further instructed in the duties of this order.

P.W.C. I extend to you our heartfelt congratulations on the progress you have made thus far in the order of Knights of the Forest. You are bound by every honorable motive to conduct yourself in such a manner as never to bring reproach upon our order. You will ever keep in mind your sacred obligation, and you will remember that one of the great duties of your life is not only to advocate the banishment of all Indians from this State, but to prevail on others to do so. Every influence in your power should be given to this one great object; and when this accursed race of infuriated demons shall be driven far away towards the setting sun – when these beautiful prairies which are now homeless and desolate shall again bloom into a paradise of industry and wealth – you will have cause to rejoice that you were ever a member of this order.

W.C. The Worthy Vice Chancellor will now make the proclamation

W.V.C. Worthy associates, our Chancellor is about to proclaim this person a worthy knight. Is such your will and pleasure?

All respond. It is.

W.C. Then in the name of the Grand Lodge of Knights of the Forest, I proclaim this person a worthy knight, and he is entitled to all the rights guaranteed by our Constitution and by-laws. Trusting you may become a worthy knight of our fraternity, I now welcome you to our circle.[157]

Chippewa Indian Treaties, Agreements, Legislation in Minnesota
[This list is not meant to be inclusive. This list does not infer any legality or validity of any of the Treaties listed.]

Year	Indians	Acreage	Terms	Term of Treaty Rights	Purpose (If Expressed)
1820 Saúlt de St. Marie, Michigan Territory. Ratified Indian Treaty #110	United States and Chippeway tribe of Indians	Sixteen square miles of land.	Goods	Perpetual right of fishing at falls of St. Mary's, and encampment upon tract ceded reserved, no interference with private rights.	Islands in Lake Huron contained deposits of gypsum. Effort to remove Indians from Old Northwest Terr.
1825 7 Stat. 272 (1825)	Chippewas and Sioux		Established boundary between them.		No land was ceded.
July 29, 1837 7 Stat. 536 (1837)	Treaty with Twelve Bands of Chippewa, including Mille Lacs Band	13,664,871 Acres of Land in Present-Day Wis. and Minn.	$1,865,000 Chippewa privilege of hunting, fishing, and gathering wild rice.	During pleasure of President.	For pine timber. Land located in (what is now) Crow Wing, Morrison, Benton, Mille Lacs, Aitkin, Kanabec, Isanti, Chisago, and Pine Counties.
1842	Chippewa	All lands in Mich. (Upper Peninsula) and lands south of Lake Superior in Wis.	Reserved right of hunting on ceded land.	Until required to remove; Mineral district, subject to removal at pleasure of President.	Mineral district along south coast of Lake Superior and pine forests (CIA 1849).
August 2, 1847 9 Stat. 904 (1847)	Chippewa of Mississippi and Lake Superior	Ceded lands in central Minn.			
August 21, 1847 9 Stat. 908 (1847)	Pillager Band of Chippewa	West of lands ceded in central Minn.			
February 6, 1850	President Zachary Taylor issued Executive Order.		Revocation of Chippewa's hunting and fishing rights; removal of Indians OFF CEDED LANDS TO unceded lands.		In 1999, the U.S. Supreme Court holds that Taylor's order is *invalid in its entirety*. *Mille Lakes Band of Chippewas v. Minnesota*, 861 F. Supp. 784, 794 (D. Minn. 1994), aff'd, 124 F. 3d 904 (8th Cir. 1997), 526 U.S. 172 (1999).
October 4, 1850	Mississippi and Lake Superior Ojibwe, La Pointe, WI	Ceded lands on southern shore of Lake Superior.	Reserve hunting and fishing rights.		
October 25 - Dec. 23, 1850	Thousands of Lake Superior Ojibwe Sandy Lake, MN Hard currency needed for businessmen in St. Paul			Gathered for annuity distribution, prev. at La Pointe, Wisconsin.	Delayed until Dec. 3, 1850; if they did not remove to Sandy Lake; no ann. paymt. Once they arrived at Sandy Lake, Ramsey would delay payment until late in year so that waterways would freeze over, preventing Ojibwe from returning to their homes.
Treaty of La Pointe Sep. 30, 1854 10 Stat. 1109 (1854)	Lake Superior and Mississippi Bands	11- 14 millions of acres and lands held in common with other Indians in Minnesota (esp. Pillager and Lake Winnibigoshish Bands).	Ojibwe assigned permanent reservations - Bad River, Red Cliff, Lac du Flambeau, and Lac Court Oreilles. Ceded all other land in Minn, Wis, or elsewhere.		US wants cession of tract east of Mississippi, with "great mineral resources." Copper discovery.
1855 10 Stat. 1165 (1855)	Mississippi Chippewa, Pillager and Winnibigoshish Bands	All Minn. and lands elsewhere (lands East of Miss.).	Mississippi Bands got Reservations on Mille Lacs, Rabbit Lake, Gull Lake, Sandy Lake, Rice Lake and Lake Pokagomin; Pillager		Obtain consent of Chippewa to move west. Rice Lake Indian Reservation never established. Gull Lake, Pokegama Lake and Rabbit Lake Indian Reservations

Notes: Minnesota – Fraudulent Legislation Enabling Acquisition of Indian Land

1. Medill to Verplank and Mix, June 4, 1847; Fish in the Lakes, Wild Rice, and Game in Abundance: Testimony on Behalf of Mille Lacs Ojibwe Hunting and Fishing Rights, Editor James M. McClurken, MSU Press, 2000, p. 52.
2. Fish in the Lakes, Wild Rice, and Game in Abundance: Testimony on Behalf of Mille Lacs Ojibwe Hunting and Fishing Rights, Editor James M. McClurken, MSU Press, 2000, p. 52.
3. Pike, Zebulon. Coues, Elliott (ed.). The Expeditions of Zebulon Montgomery Pike. Vol. II. New York: Francis P. Harper (1895), pp. 842-843.
4. Ibid., p. 83.
5. Government relations with the Dakota Sioux (1851–1876), University of Montana Dissertation, Kenneth Burton Moore, 1937.
6. Pike, Zebulon. Coues, Elliott (ed.). The Expeditions of Zebulon Montgomery Pike. Vol. III. New York: Francis P. Harper (1895), p. 83.
7. Report: Memorial of J. and P. Faribault, Rep. No. 193, 34th Cong., 1st Sess. (1856), p. 3.
8. Ibid., p. 4.
9. Ibid., p. 177.
10. Ibid., p. 4.
11. Pike, Zebulon. Coues, Elliott (ed.). The Expeditions of Zebulon Montgomery Pike. Vol. II. New York: Francis P. Harper (1895), p. 232.
12. Id.
13. Ibid., p. 237.
14. Id.
15. Ibid., p. 238.
16. Ibid., pp. 840-841.
17. Ibid., p. 239.
18. National Register of Historic Places Inventory – Nomination Form, Fort Snelling. https://npgallery.nps.gov/NRHP/GetAsset/NHLS/66000401_text, p. 8 (accessed online March 24, 2022).
19. Clarence Carter, "The Territorial Papers of The United States," Issue 51, Part 9, Department of State, National Archives and Records Service, U.S. Government Printing Office, 1951, p. 527.
20. Letter Maj. Thomas Forsyth to Gov. Wm. Clark, Sep. 23, 1819, Report and Collections of the State Historical Society of Wisconsin, Volume 6, State Historical Society of Wisconsin, The Society, 1872, pp. 215-219.
21. Sale of Fort Snelling Reservation, Letter from the Secretary of War, transmitting papers relative to the sale of the Fort Snelling Reservation. H.R. Rep. No. 9, 40th Cong., 3rd Sess. (1868), pp. 2, 14-15.

22. Pike, Zebulon. Coues, Elliott (ed.). The Expeditions of Zebulon Montgomery Pike. Vol. II. New York: Francis P. Harper (1895), pp. 844-845.
23. Id.
24. See U.S. Congress, Senate, Mr. Benton made the following Report [on petition of Mrs. General Pike), S. Rep. 66, 26th Cong., 1st sess., 1846, serial 473, 1-4.
25. Sale of Fort Snelling Reservation, Letter from the Secretary of War, transmitting papers relative to the sale of the Fort Snelling Reservation. H.R. Rep. No. 9, 40th Cong., 3rd Sess. (1868), pp. 9-10.
26. Report of the Commissioner of Indian Affairs to the Secretary of the Interior, United States. Office of Indian Affairs, U.S. Government Printing Office, 1850, p. 9.
27. Id.
28. Ibid., p. 10.
29. Minnesota: A History of the Land, Episode 1 https://www.youtube.com/watch?v=Xec_3DOPY6Q (accessed online February 9, 2022).
30. Searle, R. Newell. Saving Quetico-Superior: A land set apart. Minnesota Historical Society Press, 1979, pp.12-13.
31. Report of the Commissioner of Indian Affairs to the Secretary of the Interior, United States. Office of Indian Affairs, U.S. Government Printing Office, 1850, p. 10.
32. Ibid., p. 11.
33. Ibid., p. 12.
34. *Mille Lakes Band of Chippewas v. Minnesota*, 861 F. Supp. 784, 794 (D. Minn. 1994), *aff'd*, 124 F. 3d 904 (8th Cir. 1997), 526 U.S. 172 (1999).
35. Ratified treaty no. 223, documents relating to the negotiation of the treaty of July 29, 1837, with the Chippewa Indians. http://digital.library.wisc.edu/1711.dl/History.IT1837no223 (accessed online April 5, 2022).
36. Id.
37. 7 Stat. 536.
38. Ratified treaty no. 223, documents relating to the negotiation of the treaty of July 29, 1837, with the Chippewa Indians. http://digital.library.wisc.edu/1711.dl/History.IT1837no223 (accessed online April 5, 2022).
39. Id.
40. Washington, George. "Washington's sentiments on a peace establishment." Founders Online (1783) (accessed online April 20, 2022).
41. Wingerd, Mary Lethert (2010). North Country: The Making of Minnesota. Minneapolis: University of Minnesota Press. pp. 186–189.
42. Report of the Commissioner of Indian Affairs to the Secretary of the Interior, Minnesota Superintendency, United States. Office of Indian Affairs, U.S. Government Printing Office, 1851, p. 156.

43. Id.
44. Id.
45. Id.
46. Quinn, David B., ed. Voyages and Colonising Enterprises of Sir Humphrey Gilbert. London, Hakluyt Society, 1940: 358.
47. "From Thomas Jefferson to William Henry Harrison, 27 February 1803," Founders Online, National Archives, https://founders.archives.gov/documents/Jefferson/01-39-02-0500. [Original source: The Papers of Thomas Jefferson, vol. 39, 13 November 1802–3 March 1803, ed. Barbara B. Oberg. Princeton: Princeton University Press, 2012, pp. 589–593.] (accessed online November 6, 2020).
48. Gilman, Rhoda R. Henry Hastings Sibley: Divided Heart. St. Paul: Minnesota Historical Society Press. 2004, p. 122.
49. Meyer, Roy Willard. History of the Santee Sioux: United States Indian Policy on Trial. United States, University of Nebraska Press, 1993, p. 83.
50. https://www.mnhs.org/capitol/learn/art/8961 (accessed online February 9, 2022).
51. Report of the Commissioner of Indian Affairs to the Secretary of the Interior, Minnesota Superintendency, United States. Office of Indian Affairs, U.S. Government Printing Office, 1851, p. 156.
52. Ibid., p. 158.
53. Id.
54. Id.
55. Id.
56. Cong. Globe, 33rd Cong., 1st Sess. 1032 (1854).
57. Manypenny to Gilbert, Aug. 11, 1854. Fish in the Lakes, Wild Rice, and Game in Abundance: Testimony on Behalf of Mille Lacs Ojibwe Hunting and Fishing Rights, Editor James M. McClurken, MSU Press, 2000, FN 298.
58. Cong. Globe, 33rd Cong. 2d Sess. 53-54 (1854).
59. 10 Stat. 1165. Chippewas of Minnesota. Hearings Before the United States House Committee on Indian Affairs, Sixty-Sixth Congress, Second Session, 1920, p. 292; Fish in the Lakes, Wild Rice, and Game in Abundance: Testimony on Behalf of Mille Lacs Ojibwe Hunting and Fishing Rights, Editor James M. McClurken, MSU Press, 2000, p. 93.
60. Sen. Exec. Doc. No. 20, 33rd Cong., 2d Sess. (1855).
61. Report of the Commissioner of Indian Affairs to the Secretary of the Interior, United States. Office of Indian Affairs, U.S. Government Printing Office, 1860, p. 11.
62. Kek, Evan R. "Timber and Men: The Weyerhaeuser Story by Ralph W. Hidy, Frank Ernest Hill, and Allan Nevins." Indiana Magazine of History (1964), p. 105.

63. Report of the Commissioner of Indian Affairs to the Secretary of the Interior, United States. Office of Indian Affairs, U.S. Government Printing Office, 1860, p. 11.
64. Ibid., p. 73.
65. 12 Stat. 1249 (1863).
66. Fish in the Lakes, Wild Rice, and Game in Abundance: Testimony on Behalf of Mille Lacs Ojibwe Hunting and Fishing Rights, Editor James M. McClurken, MSU Press, 2000, pp. 46-118.
67. Report of the Commissioner of Indian Affairs to the Secretary of the Interior, United States. Office of Indian Affairs, U.S. Government Printing Office, 1880, p. XL.
68. Report of the Commissioner of Indian Affairs to the Secretary of the Interior, United States. Office of Indian Affairs, U.S. Government Printing Office, 1874, pp. 182, 196.
69. Report of the Commissioner of Indian Affairs to the Secretary of the Interior, United States. Office of Indian Affairs, U.S. Government Printing Office, 1879, p. 87.
70. Report of the Commissioner of Indian Affairs to the Secretary of the Interior, United States. Office of Indian Affairs, U.S. Government Printing Office, 1880, p. XVII.
71. Report of the Commissioner of Indian Affairs to the Secretary of the Interior, United States. Office of Indian Affairs, U.S. Government Printing Office, 1883, pp. LIX, 96.
72. Report of the Commissioner of Indian Affairs to the Secretary of the Interior, United States. Office of Indian Affairs, U.S. Government Printing Office, 1875, p. 297.
73. Report of the Commissioner of Indian Affairs to the Secretary of the Interior, United States. Office of Indian Affairs, U.S. Government Printing Office, 1877, p. 131.
74. EXTRA SESSION. MESSAGE OF GOVERNOR RAMSEY TO THE LEGISLATURE OF MINNESOTA, DELIVERED SEPTEMBER 9, 1862. SAINT PAUL: WM. R. MARSHALL, STATE PRINTER, 1862.
75. Hughes, Thomas. History of Blue Earth County and Biographies of its Leading Citizens. Marceline, Mo.: Walsworth Publishing Company, 1901, p. 126.
76. Ibid., pp. 133-134.
77. https://www.lrl.mn.gov/mngov/stateofstate (accessed online April 22, 2022).
78. Id.
79. http://discovery.civilwargovernors.org/document/KYR-0001-009-0013 (accessed online April 22, 2022)

80. Coats, Catherine M., "Extermination or Removal": The Knights of the Forest and Ethnic Cleansing in Early Minnesota" (2017). Culminating Projects in History, pp. 35-37. https://repository.stcloudstate.edu/hist_etds/11 (accessed online April 21, 2022).
81. Hughes, Thomas. History of Blue Earth County and Biographies of Its Leading Citizens. Middle West Publishing Company, 1901.
82. Initiation, Grand Lodge of the Knights of the Forest. Old Main Cornerstone. Collection. MSU Archives Collection 200. Mankato State University Library, Mankato, Minn., 1869–1969.
83. Mankato Review, April 27, 1886; Mankato Daily Review, April 18, 1916. Coats, Catherine M., "Extermination or Removal": The Knights of the Forest and Ethnic Cleansing in Early Minnesota" (2017). Culminating Projects in History, p 62. https://repository.stcloudstate.edu/hist_etds/11 (accessed online April 21, 2022).
84. United States Senate. Reports of Committees of the Senate of the United States for the First Session of the Fiftieth Congress, 1887–88. Committee on Pensions. Report no. 2282. (Washington, D.C.: GPO, 1888); Secret hate group bent on banishing Ho-Chunk Indians in 1863. Curt Brown. March 3, 2018. https://www.startribune.com/secret-hate-group-bent-on-banishing-ho-chunk-indians-in-1863/475744423/ (accessed online April 21, 2022).
85. Hughes, Thomas. History of Blue Earth County and Biographies of its Leading Citizens. Marceline, Mo.: Walsworth Publishing Company, 1901, p. 139.
86. Report of the Commissioner of Indian Affairs to the Secretary of the Interior, United States. Office of Indian Affairs, U.S. Government Printing Office, 1863, pp. 22, 58.
87. Ibid., p. 22.
88. Ibid., p. 92.
89. Ibid., p. 93.
90. https://healingmnstories.wordpress.com/2019/02/21/this-day-in-history-feb-21-1863-congress-expels-winnebago-nation-from-minnesota-more-than-550-die-during-forced-relocation/ (accessed online April 22, 2022).
91. Report of the Commissioner of Indian Affairs to the Secretary of the Interior, United States. Office of Indian Affairs, U.S. Government Printing Office, 1864, p. 305.
92. Mankato Independent, May 15, 1863. Coats, Catherine M., "Extermination or Removal": The Knights of the Forest and Ethnic Cleansing in Early Minnesota" (2017). Culminating Projects in History, pp. 35-37. https://repository.stcloudstate.edu/hist_etds/11 (accessed online April 21, 2022).

93. https://healingmnstories.wordpress.com/2020/04/07/this-day-in-history-april-7-1866-bois-forte-band-forced-into-treaty-to-open-land-for-minnesotas-gold-rush/; https://treatiesmatter.org/treaties/land/1866-ojibwe (accessed online April 22, 2022).
94. Report of the Commissioner of Indian Affairs to the Secretary of the Interior, United States. Office of Indian Affairs, U.S. Government Printing Office, 1864, pp. 322-325.
95. Carroll, Jane Lamm. "Dams and Damages: The Ojibway, the United States, and the Mississippi Headwaters Reservoirs." Minnesota History 52.1 (1990). p. 5.
96. Carroll, Jane L., and Tak M. Wong. Engineering the Falls: The Corps of Engineers' Role at St. Anthony Falls. CORPS OF ENGINEERS ST PAUL MN ST PAUL DISTRICT, 1993.
97. Billington, David P., Donald C. Jackson, and Martin V. Melosi. The history of large federal dams: Planning, design and construction. Government Printing Office, 2005. https://www.usbr.gov/history/HistoryofLargeDams/LargeFederalDams.pdf (accessed online February 25, 2022).
98. Act to Improve Rivers and Harbors of June 14, 1880 (21 Stat. 180).
99. Act to Improve Rivers and Harbors of March 3, 1881 (21 Stat. 468).
100. U.S. Army Corps of Engineers Upper Mississippi River Headwaters Bemidji to St. Paul, Final Integrated Reservoir Operating Plan Evaluation and Environmental Impact Statement 2009 at https://www.bestofdocument.com/pdf/upper-mississippi-river-headwaters-bemidji-to-stpaul-integrated-reservoir-operating-plan-evaluation/ (accessed online April 17, 2022).
101. 48th Cong., 1st sess., 1884, House Executive Document, no. 76, Damages to Chippewa Indians. Letter from the Secretary of the Interior, transmitting a copy of a communication from the Commissioner of Indian Affairs, together with papers and report of Messrs. Marshall, Gilfillan, and Sibley, appointed December 22, 1882, to re-examine and ascertain the damages accruing to the Chippewa Indians residing upon Lake Winibigoshish and Leech Lake Indian Reservations in the State of Minnesota, "Damages to Chippewa Indians," 29 H.R. Exec. Doc. No. 76, 48th Cong., 1st Sess. (1884). https://digitalcommons.law.ou.edu/cgi/viewcontent.cgi?article=4729&context=indianserialset (accessed online February 28, 2022).
102. Red Lake Indian Reservation, Minnesota, H.R. Rep. No. 183, 48th Cong., 1st Sess. (1884), pp. 1-2. Letter from the Secretary of the Interior, transmitting, in response to Senate Resolution of May 11, 1897 the report of Indian Inspector, J. George Wright, together with accompanying papers, relative to pine lands and pine timber on the Red Lake Reservation, in the State of Minnesota. (153 Pages of Testimony), S. Doc. No. 70, 55th Cong., 3rd Sess. (1899).

103. Letter from the Secretary of the Interior, transmitting, in response to Senate resolution of January 6, 1899, copies of letters and accompanying inclosures from the Commissioner of the General Land Office and the Commissioner of Indian Affairs, relating to the estimating of timber and the cutting of dead and fallen timber on the Chippewa Indian Reservations in the State of Minnesota. S. Doc. No. 70, 55th Cong., 3rd Sess. (1899), p. 25.
104. Ibid., p. 30.
105. Ibid., p. 32.
106. Ibid., p. 86.
107. Ibid., pp. 86-87.
108. 30th Annual Report of the Board of Indian Commissioners, United States. U.S. Government Printing Office, 1899, p. 1.
109. Searle, Newell. "Minnesota National Forest: The Politics of Compromise, 1898–1908." Minnesota History 42.7 (1971): 242, 247.
110. https://www.youtube.com/watch?v=tmGpv0oZaWA (accessed online March 30, 2022).
111. "From Thomas Jefferson to George Rogers Clark, 25 December 1780," Founders Online, National Archives, https://founders.archives.gov/documents/Jefferson/01-04-02-0295. [Original source: The Papers of Thomas Jefferson, vol. 4, 1 October 1780–24 February 1781, ed. Julian P. Boyd. Princeton: Princeton University Press, 1951, pp. 233–238.] (accessed online November 13, 2020).
112. How Minnesota Politicians Helped Cheat White Earth Out [of Their] Timber. https://healingmnstories.wordpress.com/2016/04/28/this-day-in-history-how-minnesota-politicians-helped-cheat-white-earth-out-timber/ (accessed online March 18, 2022).
113. Id.
114. Report in the Matter of the Investigation of the White Earth Reservation, 62 Cong., 3 sess., 1913, House Report 1336, p. 1519.
115. Ibid., p. 1794.
116. Ibid., p. 835.
117. Moorehead, Warren King. The American Indian in the United States, Period 1850–1914. Andover MA: Andover Press, 1914, pp. 73, 75.
118. William W. Folwell, History of Minnesota, rev. ed. (St. Paul: Minnesota Historical Society, 1969), 4: 278-279.
119. Report of the Commissioner of Indian Affairs to the Secretary of the Interior, United States. Office of Indian Affairs, U.S. Government Printing Office, 1906, p. 148.
120. United States. "White Earth Reservation: hearings before the Committee on Expenditures in the Interior Department of the House of Representatives on House resolution no. 103 to investigate the expenditures in the Interior Department." Washington: U. S. Govt. Print. Off., 1911–1912, p. 739.

121. Report of the Commissioner of Indian Affairs to the Secretary of the Interior, United States. Office of Indian Affairs, U.S. Government Printing Office, 1911, p. 53.
122. Report of the Commissioner of Indian Affairs to the Secretary of the Interior, United States. Office of Indian Affairs, U.S. Government Printing Office, 1912, p. 40.
123. Peterson, Ken. "Ransom Powell and the Tragedy of White Earth." Minnesota History 63.3 (2012): 96.
124. Ibid., p. 97.
125. Report of the Commissioner of Indian Affairs to the Secretary of the Interior, United States. Office of Indian Affairs, U.S. Government Printing Office, 1912, p. 43.
126. Peterson, Ken. "Ransom Powell and the Tragedy of White Earth." Minnesota History 63.3 (2012): 97.
127. Ibid., p. 91.
128. Ibid., p. 93.
129. *See State of Minnesota v. Zay Zah*, 259 N.W.2d 580, 1977, *cert denied*, 436 U.S. 917 (1978).
130. Peterson, Ken. "Ransom Powell and the Tragedy of White Earth." Minnesota History 63.3 (2012): 99.
131. Id.
132. https://www.environmentandsociety.org/tools/keywords/extinction-passenger-pigeon#:~:text=The%20passenger%20pigeon%2C%20once%20one,contributed%20to%20the%20bird's%20extinction (accessed online March 30, 2022).
133. Ritual/Initiation, Grand Lodge of the Knights of the Forest. Old Main Cornerstone. Collection. MSU Archives Collection 200. Mankato State University Library, Mankato, Minn., 1869–1969.

CHAPTER 8: WISCONSIN'S FORCED INDIAN REMOVAL

Part 1: Wisconsin's Indian Holocaust

James Washinawatok, a Menominee attorney, wrote an article about the General Allotment Act (GAA) equaling genocide as defined by the United Nations. It is appropriate that this section should begin with his analysis, since what happened in Wisconsin is a tragic repeat of the cycle of cession of Indian lands, removal, establishment of reservations, allotment and opening up "surplus lands" for white settlement. Ceded and surplus lands would be sold, allegedly for the benefit of the affected tribes.

> Eliminating one's land base, hence one's control and use of it, destroys all that land encompassed to the people who considered that land home. By physical destruction, a person's life is ended, but by destroying a person's culture, religion, and way of life, they cease to exist as they once did, and not by choice. Tribes physically exist today, but the damage of the GAA is currently experienced almost one-hundred fourteen years later, therefore, a broader definition of genocide is necessary to prevent the further destruction of the GAA.[1]

Wisconsin sought to pen Indians up early on "assigned lands," to negotiating treaties for the cession of large tracts of Indian land. In 1834, the federal government opened land offices in Mineral Point and Green Bay, speeding up the Euro-colonial settlement of Wisconsin.

The history of the Great Lakes Indians is intertwined since the Wisconsin Territory established in 1836 included all of the present-day states of Wisconsin, Minnesota, Iowa and parts of North and South Dakota. Many of the early Indian treaties crossed the boundaries of the current states. The first Territorial Governor and ex officio Superintendent of Indian Affairs was Henry Dodge.

Part 2: Mining in Wisconsin

Upper Mississippi Valley: Illinois, Wisconsin and Iowa

In his 1827 Report, Secretary of War Barbour confirmed the importance of purchasing the land encompassing the Upper Mississippi Valley Lead-Zinc area which included northwest Illinois, southwest Wisconsin, and northeast Iowa. The expected annual supply of lead was equal to 10,000,000 pounds. One critical use at the time was for the manufacturing of bullets.

> To obviate any ground of complaint, and to meet the wishes of our Western citizens, it is proposed to procure, by purchase, an enlargement of our boundaries in that quarter, so as to embrace the whole of the highly valuable lead mines, said to abound in that region, and for which an appropriation will be hereafter asked.[2]

Place names such as Mineral Point describe the focus of early settlement in Wisconsin. Lead mines produced much of the nation's lead which was used in the manufacture of pewter, pipes, weights, and, of course, ammunition for the U.S. military. *By 1829, more than 4,000 miners worked in southwestern Wisconsin, producing 13 million pounds of lead a year.* The cession of Chippewa lead lands in 1832 coincided with this strong demand for lead. Communities sprang up quickly around the mines, as other industries and businesses started up to serve the residents that mining attracted.

By the 1840's, Wisconsin lead mining peaked. High grading left the supply of easily obtainable ore exhausted. In 1844, a third of the region's residents left for copper and iron mines elsewhere and the California Gold rush in 1849 lured others away. Yet the lead boom and bust cycle changed the lives of the Chippewas in southern Wisconsin forever.[3]

> Recognizing the detrimental consequences of mining, the Wisconsin legislature passed important and comprehensive mining legislation in the early 1980s that recognized that all forms of metallic mining, whether iron, copper, lead, zinc, or precious metals, harm the environment (especially due to acid mine drainage) and have significant impacts to local communities due to its boom-and-bust nature. But before the Prove It First law (also known as the Mining Moratorium law) was approved, the state challenged the mining industry to give one example of a metallic sulfide mine that had been safely operated and closed without polluting the environment. Predictably, the industry has failed to identify a single example to this day.[4]

Unfortunately, the legislature repealed the Mining Moratorium law in 2017.

Copper Mining in Northern Wisconsin

Having depleted the easily accessible lead ore, the miners headed for northern Wisconsin for more lead and copper mining. The exploitation of the Ojibwe lands of Lake Superior for copper would be next. Writing in 1855, James Gregory declared, "Iron ore of unlimited extent and of great purity may be found at Lake Superior, in the Baraboo district, and at the Iron Ridge in Dodge and Washington counties." Mining in northern Wisconsin attracted eastern investment for those eager to make a quick fortune. The financial panic of 1857 and the high grading of the ore left northern Wisconsin abandoned. There would be another short-lived boom and bust resurgence in the 1870s.[5]

Part 3: Logging Industry

It did give a start, though, to the timber industry which would become a boon to the State's economy. The pine forests provided a seemingly endless supply of lumber. The Wisconsin River provided easy transport for pine logs from forests to mills. Cities such as Stevens Point and Wausau developed around mills. Dozens of small companies in the northeastern region around the Wolf River combined into a conglomerate led by Friedrich Weyerhaeuser. Governor Hoard's (1889–1891) testimonial to the logging in Wisconsin would unveil a painful truth:

> The opinion which formerly widely prevailed, that white pine did not reproduce itself on areas where it has been cut off, but gave way to poplar and other inferior species, has been proven erroneous by observations both in this state and elsewhere. While it is perfectly feasible to restock these lands with pine, it is quite as undeniably true that the bulk of them will not be so restocked as long as they are left to themselves. If no steps are taken towards a proper care these millions of acres will become wildernesses of scrub, covered according to circumstances with crippled aspen, runts of jack pine, dwarf oak, or even merely coarse grass and sweet fern. That condition they will remain in for an indefinite period. ... ***There is consequently no prospect that our denuded lands will be put to agricultural uses***. The only way, therefore, in which they can be made useful is to restock them with the timber which formerly covered them and for which they are peculiarly adapted. But we have already seen that it is improbable that any considerable number of private parties will find it profitable to take the steps which are necessary to reach this end. (Emphasis added).[6]

Part 4: Connecting Wisconsin's Waterways

Great Lakes Steamships and Canals

Steamboats on the Mississippi River connected Wisconsin to the Gulf of Mexico, while immigrants and goods from the East came into the Territory on Great Lakes steamships. Bordering these two great waterways, Wisconsin residents faced the problem of how to connect the two transportation systems. With the economic success of the Erie Canal, opened in 1825, the answer for many in Wisconsin seemed to be canals.

Part 5: Eliminating Indians' Land Base

Mining and logging created an insatiable need for land for white settlement. Numerous treaties were entered into with the various tribes in Wisconsin ceding large tracts of Indian lands to the U.S. The Ho-Chunk and the Pottawatomi were left without land at all, other than what they purchased. Others were left with a vastly diminished base and were confined to reservations. In a tragedy of vast dimension, the federal and state governments knowingly and deliberately dispossessed the Indians of "fertile tracts" and "mineral wealth" and "pineries," leaving them in a destitute and starving condition.

The Legislature of Wisconsin sent a Memorial to the President and Senate of the United States in 1838 supporting ratification of the Treaties entered into which would open the mineral and timber lands of the Winnebago, Sioux, and Chippewa Indians for white settlement:

> That, during the summer and fall of the year one thousand eight hundred and thirty-seven, treaties were concluded on the part of the United States, in conformity with appropriations made for that purpose, with the Winnebago, Sioux, and Chippewa Indians, for the purchase of a large and valuable tract of country lying north of the Wisconsin, and east of the Mississippi river. ***The land thus purchased of the Winnebagoes, from its geographical position, from the nature and quality of the soil, and from the mineral wealth*** which it is believed to contain, may be considered as a most valuable acquisition to the Territory of the United States: And the country purchased of the Sioux and Chippewas, ***embracing, as it does, all, or nearly all, the pineries on the head waters of the Mississippi***, is of great importance in affording supplies of pine lumber to the inhabitants residing on the borders of that river. (Emphasis added).[7]

A very large number of people have, upon the faith of the treaties made, taken up their residence on the land purchased: they are engaged in cutting and rafting the pine lumber, and in the construction of mills; and difficulties of a very serious character between the white and red men upon our borders must immediately ensue, upon the rejection of the treaties by your honorable body. The combined forces of the Winnebagoes, Sioux, and Chippewas, assisted as they naturally would be by the Sacs and Foxes, would form a powerful alliance, and it would cost the General Government much blood and treasure to protect her citizens from the aggressions of an enemy so strong and so evil minded.[8]

It is a fact well known that the country owned by the Winnebago Indians, north of the Wisconsin River, would be of great value to the United States as well as to the citizens of Wisconsin, and is not suited to the state and condition of the Indians who claim it. From the intemperate and reckless character of the Winnebago Indians, I have no hesitation in saying that unless they are removed from the country north of the Wisconsin River difficulties will ensue between them and the whites that will end in war.[9]

The Ho-Chunk, once possessed of a reservation of incalculable value due to its arable land and mineral wealth, would find themselves threatened with extermination. In three decades, the Governor of Wisconsin, in 1863, would warn the Secretary of the Interior that the Winnebago Indians in Juneau Country were subject to extermination by its citizens. Further, a Wisconsin Congressional Representative and member of the Committee on Indian Affairs wrote to Secretary Usher that Wisconsin citizens would *"adopt such measures as will protect ourselves, either by the removal of the Indians or other effective means." County officials petitioned the Governor for their removal, as well.* (Emphasis added).[10]

Annuities in monies and goods that were a federal obligation were used as economic sanctions to get Indians to cede lands and to move out of the State of Wisconsin. Governor Ramsey and John Watrous, an Indian Agent at La Pointe, conspired to lure the Ojibwe's to Minnesota and then extend the time for payment, making it impossible for them to return home in the dead of winter. They were forced to travel three to five hundred canoe and portage miles to Sandy Lake in Minnesota to receive their annuities. While waiting to receive their annuities at Sandy Lake, Agent Watrous wrote to Governor Ramsey that as many as 150 Ojibwe had died. With the waterways frozen over, the Ojibwe abandoned their canoes and returned home to Wisconsin on foot in what is referred to as the Wisconsin Death March. Chief Buffalo told Commissioner Luke Lea that another 230 died during the long, cold march home.

The disease and starvation the Ojibwe experienced strengthened their resolve to remain in Wisconsin. Governor Ramsey was allowed to engage in a battle of wills, requiring the Ojibwe to travel to Sandy Lake for their annuities, but he lost. In 1854, the Lake Superior Ojibwe signed a new treaty at La Pointe that promised permanent reservations and on-site annual payments in their homeland.

Resolution of Legislature of Wisconsin for Removing Wisconsin Indians

As with many other states, Wisconsin's state legislature would endorse the removal of all Indians from the state to Indian Territory or any other western location.

> 43D CONGRESS, 1st Session. HOUSE OF REPRESENTATIVES. MIS. DOC. NO.155. **REMOVING WISCONSIN INDIANS.** RESOLUTION OF THE LEGISLATURE OF WISCONSIN, INDORSING The action of the Secretary of the Interior in removing Indians from the State of Wisconsin, and asking that all tribes be removed from the borders thereof. FEBRUARY 24, 1874.-Referred to the Committee on Indian Affairs and ordered to be printed.
>
> *Resolved by the senate, the assembly concurring*, That it is the sense of this legislature that the policy of removing the Indians of this State to proper reservations in the Indian and other Western Territories and States be approved, and request that the removal may be continued until all the tribes are removed from the borders of the State. [11]

Part 6: Indigenous Tribes in Wisconsin Territory

For Indian tribes of Wisconsin, the federal approach created a century of wanton geographical upheaval and the massive loss of land. For some, outright ouster from the Territory was the State's response, facilitated by the federal government. While some tribes reserved hunting, fishing and gathering rights to preserve their former traditional lifestyles, those rights would be continually infringed upon by settlers and the State. Others thought they had done so only to find it wasn't put into the written treaties and there was no record of their claim.

1. The Potawatomi of Wisconsin and Illinois River

Potawatomi of Wisconsin and Illinois River Treaties

[Brief summary. This list is not meant to be inclusive. This list does not infer any legality or validity of any of the Treaties listed.]

Year	Cession	Compensation	Purpose
1816 Potawatomi of Wisconsin and Illinois River	Potawatomi of Wisconsin had no interest in land ceded by Illinois River Potawatomi.	Goods such as cloth, tobacco, and guns; 12-year annuity of $1,000 in goods. Strip of land from Prairie du Chien, WI to Moline, IL, which was part of Sauk and Fox land.	Potawatomi of Wisconsin shared in proceeds.
1825 Peace Treaty, Prairie du Chien			Establish boundaries between tribes.
1829 Potawatomi of Wisconsin and Illinois River		$12,000; 50 bb of salt every year indefinitely; $12,000 in goods; blacksmith shop in Chicago.	Ceded strip of land rec'd in 1816 Treaty. WI wanted valuable mineral land.
1833 Potawatomi of Wisconsin and Illinois River	Ceded land in northern Illinois and all land in SE Wisconsin. Claim Menominee had no right to lands along Lake Michigan's western shore. U.S. agreed. Compensated the Potawatomi.	5 million acres of land in Iowa; $100,000 in goods; $14,000 in cash every year for 20 years; $150,000 for grist mills and ag. implements; $70,000 for schools; paid off $250,000 of alleged debts to traders. Established reservation in Kan. Annuities only paid to Indians that moved to Kan.	Hoping to curry favor and avoid removal, allied with U.S. in Black Hawk War of 1832. Backfired. Potawatomi had to leave Wisconsin by 1838. Many did but some stayed in Forest County, WI.
1913		U.S. paid $447,339 to Potawatomi that stayed in WI; used $150,000 to purchase reservation in Forest County.	Annuities paid to rectify non-payment of annuities.

In an 1887 Report of Indian Agent J.T. Gregory, Pottawatomies still living in Wisconsin were found to be homeless. The Lac du Flambeau Indians took them in and they settled on their reservation.

> I was ordered last November to look into and report upon the condition of a small band of Pottawatomie Indians, **who were said to be trespassing in Lincoln County, Wis**. I found upon investigation that the band, numbering about 100, lived near Marshfield, Wis., and that **they had no settled home, having no reservation upon which to move**. They were, however, very friendly with the Lac du Flambeau Indians, with whom they had intermarried somewhat. I at once entered into negotiations with the Flambeaus to allow them to settle upon their reservation. After some delay these negotiations were brought to a successful termination, the **Flambeaus evincing their willingness to allow them to take up their residence upon their reservation**. (Emphasis added).[12]

2. The Ho-Chunk (aka Winnebago)

Governor Swift in his 1864 Annual Message to the State Legislature described the Winnebago Reservation as: "the fertile tracts [which have] long been justly regarded as one of the gardens of the State."

Ho-Chunk Treaties
[Brief summary. This list is not meant to be inclusive. This list does not infer any legality or validity of any of the Treaties listed.]

Year	Cession	Compensation	Purpose
1816 Peace Treaty			End hostilities post War of 1812.
1821 and 1822	Not ratified.		Land for Oneida, Stockbridge-Munsee, and Brothertown.
1825 Peace Treaty, Prairie du Chien			Establish boundaries between tribes.
1827 Little Lake Butte des Morts		$15,682 in goods and $3,000 to establish schools among three tribes.	Establish boundaries between Menominee, Ho-Chunk, and Ojibwe.
1829	Ceded lead ore lands.		30-year annuity of $18,000; 3,000 pounds of tobacco; 50 barrels of salt; one-time gift of $30,000 in gifts such as guns, metal cooking utensils, and cloth; establish three blacksmith shops and maintain them for 30 years; paid off $33,000 of the tribe's debts incurred with local traders. Leaders of Red Bird uprising received pardons, spared death penalty.
1832			Black Hawk War of 1832
1837	Ho-Chunk ceded last of their Wisconsin land.	Received land in Minnesota, then South Dakota, and finally Nebraska.	$1.1 million in trust, receiving interest as an annuity of about $55,000 a year. Used to pay for schools, ag. teachers, grist mill, and medical services. Remainder belonged to tribe, but only $20,000 could be paid in cash, with remainder paid in goods and food only, for a period of 22 years. $400,000 set aside to pay alleged debts tribe had incurred with traders.
1870s and 1880s	Many Ho-Chunk kept returning to homeland in Wisconsin.	Given 40-acre homesteads like white settlers.	
1963			Gain federal recognition for Wisconsin Ho-Chunk.

Threat to Exterminate Winnebago Indians

In the summer of 1863, one hundred and twenty-five Wisconsin citizens threatened *in self-defence, to exterminate the* Winnebago Indians in Juneau County, Wisconsin. The history of this genocidal peril is in the 1863 Report of the Commissioner of Indian Affairs to Secretary Usher, a member of President Lincoln's Cabinet.

WISCONSIN, 1863. We, the undersigned, citizens of Juneau county, would respectfully represent, that there are from one to two thousand Indians in this county and vicinity, who are murdering and constantly committing serious depredations upon our people, and in whose power it is, unarmed, unorganized, and unprotected as we are, to utterly destroy us at any hour. Many families have already left their homes, and others are leaving them. We are kept in perpetual excitement, fear and dread, and a stop is being put to all regular business. We cannot endure this state of things much longer. We have spent sleepless nights and anxious days enough already. We therefore most earnestly petition the government, through you, to remove these barbarians from among us; pledging you all assistance in our power, and assuring you that unless government does remove them, *we shall be compelled, in self-defence, to exterminate them*. Signed by G. W. Bailie, Robert Henry, and one hundred and twenty-four others. (Emphasis added).[13]

A notice by various officials from the area requested removal of the Indians:

Wm. M. Blanding, County Judge of Polk County and Others August 13, 1863. We take the liberty to call your attention to an unpleasant state of affairs in this and the adjoining towns. The Indians who are now and have for years been in the habit of spending more or less time about the settlements here have lately manifested an unusually lawless and malevolent spirit towards the settlers; and this has been manifested by killing hogs and cattle to such an extent that many of our most exposed settlers consider their stock to be very insecure, and we would respectfully ask you to take such steps as may be necessary to *secure their removal* ... (Emphasis added).[14]

Citizens also submitted Petitions requesting removal of Indians:

Petition of the inhabitants of Washington County praying for the removal of the Indians. Date 1841. Description: Petitioners request an act that would remove "the remaining Indians" from the county. They state that previous petitions requesting this have not been acted on, and they fear that citizens will act on their own, endangering the lives of both whites and Native Americans.

Petition of Wm. Amery and other citizens of the County of Polk for the removal of Indians from said vicinity, 1866 January 31 Scope and Content Note: Pass legislation to remove Native Americans from the northwest part of the state to make way for white settlement. City: St. Croix Falls County: Polk Petition Number: 360A

Petition of Barney P. Pitterman and other citizens of the County of Polk for Legislative action for the removal of vagabond Indians from said County, 1866 January Scope and Content Note: Pass legislation to remove Native Americans from the northwest part of the state to make way for white settlement. City: Oceola County: Polk Petition Number: 374A

Petition of E.J. Tyler and other citizens of Polk County, for the Removal of Indians from said county, 1867 January 14 Scope and Content Note: Remove American Indians from Polk and Burnett Counties to encourage further settlement of the area. County: Polk, Burnett Petition Number: 1A

Petition of Wm. H. Parks and others, citizens of Polk County for the removal of Indians therefrom, 1867 January 30 Scope and Content Note: Remove American Indians from Polk and Burnett County to encourage further settlement of the area. County: Polk Petition Number: 9A

Petition of James T. Cragin and other citizens of Polk County for the removal of Indians from said county, 1867 January 31 Scope and Content Note: Remove American Indians from Polk and Burnett County to encourage further settlement of the area. County: Polk Petition Number: 15A[15]

This threat of extermination of the Winnebago Indians by Wisconsin citizens continued into the fall of 1863 as evidenced by the Letter from Representative W. D. McIndoe, Member of Congress, Sixth District, Wisconsin and a member of the Committee on Indian Affairs, To The Hon. William P. Dole, Commissioner of Indian Affairs:

> Warsaw, Wisconsin, September 25, 1863. The inhabitants of Juneau and adjoining counties were much excited and exasperated, and on the 8th of August a mass convention was held in New Lisbon, when a resolution was passed, "That if the general government or the governor of the State shall fail to act in the matter for the safety and protection of the settlers, then, as a matter of self-protection, *we shall be compelled to adopt such measures as will protect ourselves, either by the removal of the Indians or other effective means.*" After the arrival of the troops the Indians left the vicinity of New Lisbon, and are now scattered through the four counties before mentioned. (Emphasis added).[16]

The Hon. J. P. Usher, Secretary of the Interior responded to the Governor of Wisconsin that the Indians would be rounded up and returned to their reservation.

To Edward Salomon, Governor of Wisconsin from Hon. J. P. Usher, Secretary of the Interior, Washington, D. C. Sir: ... "the Indians will be removed to the reservation of their tribe on the Upper Missouri river as soon as they can be gotten together."[17]

The Governor of Wisconsin was concerned that the *Secretary of the Interior was not aware of the gravity of the circumstances* and reminded him of the federal government's responsibility to protect its citizens:

By Letter from Governor Edward Salomon of Wisconsin to Hon. J. P. Usher, Secretary of the Interior, Washington, D. C., July 21, 1863, the Governor informed the Secretary that he had armed citizens for border defense:

> I deem it but justice to myself to say that, to the extent which the existing circumstances seemed to require last year, *I acted by distributing at convenient points and to proper parties, for border defence, some 2,000 stand of arms, which had the desired effect of assuring, the alarmed settlers* for a time. The case seems now to have assumed a more serious appearance, and I earnestly invoke the immediate attention of the government authorities. (Emphasis added).[18]

By Letter from Governor Edward Salomon of Wisconsin to Hon. J. P. Usher, Secretary of the Interior, Washington, D. C., July 24, 1863. Sir: I have the honor to acknowledge the receipt of your communication ... *the relations between the white people and the Indians are of a more serious character than is contemplated by you.* From the report made by a committee of the legislature of 1862, composed of gentlemen from the region interested, it would appear that the number of these Indians is greatly underestimated by your department—that report placing the number at seven or eight hundred. I am still of the opinion that the circumstances of the case call for the action of the government authorities, at least to the extent of sending a proper agent among these Indians to hold council with their controlling chiefs, and endeavor to quiet the present difficulty. Nothing appears to be clearer than the fact that *the government, having extinguished the Indian title to these lands, and offered them for sale, is bound, by every obligation of justice to those who purchase the land, to protect them in the enjoyment of their property, so far as any apprehension from the Indians is* concerned. I earnestly hope that some action may be taken by your department. (Emphasis added).[19]

By Letter from Governor Edward Salomon of Wisconsin to Hon. J. P. Usher, Secretary of the Interior, Washington, D. C., SIR: I beg leave to call the earnest attention of your department to sundry matters concerning the Indian tribes in this State, particularly to those which are roaming at will over the central and northwestern portions, comprised in the sixth congressional district. ... Mr. Mix is doubtless correct in stating that these Indians are "old residents of Wisconsin," but I can perceive nothing in that fact which can in any manner shift from the government the responsibility of controlling them. I have not been able to learn the precise circumstances under which these Indians remain in this State. *Certainly, it appears that their title to the lands is held by the government to have been extinguished, and passed over to the United States, since the lands are nearly all surveyed and open to purchase and settlement. This being the case, it would seem clear that the Indians should have been removed to reservations further west, or, like the Menomonees, to reservations in this State, and required to remain upon those reservations. Instead of this, however, they are allowed to wander at will over the wide region lying between the Wisconsin, Mississippi, and St Croix rivers, portions of which are already well settled, while other portions are being rapidly occupied by the pioneer settlers, who have purchased their lands of government, and rely upon its protection.* (Emphasis added).[20]

... The slightest gatherings of the wandering bands in this State, even where no overt acts of murder or plunder are committed, excite alarm among the unprotected frontier people, and already, last fall, resulted in extensive panics in some quarters, involving the abandonment of the new farms and crops, and hard-earned property of the settlers. I respectfully, but earnestly, urge the immediate attention of your department to this subject ... The State authorities must necessarily await the action of the government—have long waited and will so wait, until an issue may come between the settlers and these wandering bands. When that issue comes—and late developments indicate that it may arise at any moment—*the State must do what it can to protect the lives and property of its people*. (Emphasis added).[21]

It is uncertain if the situation was as serious as stated by the Governor. Nonetheless, it was a basis for Wisconsin seeking the removal of all Indians from the State.

> St. Paul, September 14, 1863. These reports I traced back to a Mr. Reynolds, a son of the one above named, who stated in my presence that the reports and the letter to Governor Salomon, respecting Indian troubles in that vicinity, were gotten up for the purpose of securing, if possible, the presence of a company of soldiers at that place. It was reported that there had been depredations committed at Wolf creek, fifteen miles from St. Croix Falls. I visited that place, and upon making inquiries of parties reported as being sufferers from the Indians, *I was unable to learn that there had been any depredations committed*. I am satisfied that there are but a few roving Chippewas ... J. C. Ramsey. (Emphasis added).[22]

This demand for removal of the Winnebago Tribe continued to fester in the State. In 1872, Governor Washburn proclaimed, once more, the responsibility of the federal government to move them to Nebraska.

> The northwestern part of the state has been long infested with roving bands of Indians, mostly of the Winnebago tribe. They have reservations in Kansas or Nebraska to which they should long since have been removed. Their wanderings and depredations are not confined to any particular locality, but are mostly felt in the counties of Clark, Jackson, Trempealeau, Monroe and La Crosse. The people are justly dissatisfied that they have not been removed, and have practiced great forbearance up to this time. Our State Prison now contains one or two inmates from this tribe. Two years ago, an appropriation was made for their removal, but for some reason the law was never executed. I recommend that Congress be memorialized upon the subject.[23]

In 1873, the settled purpose of the federal government to move the Wisconsin Winnebagoes, numbering 1,000, to the Winnebago Reservation in Nebraska was reported by the Indian Agent in Nebraska.[24]

Nature of Winnebagoes

There was scant evidence of the Winnebagoes posing a threat to the white settlers. In fact, it was repeatedly noticed that they had little trouble with the whites. As a reported Stray Band in 1867 with a Special Agent, what they desired was to stay in their homeland of Wisconsin. They feared and dreaded removal. Yet when removed, they returned once more to what all of us yearn for—our home. A Special Agency for Stray Bands of Winnebago and Pottawatomi Indians of Wisconsin was established, though, with the goal of removal. They "eked" out a bare existence, suffering from cold and starvation.

SPECIAL AGENCY FOR STRAY BANDS, ETC., 1867

I take great pleasure in reporting the fact that since my last annual report there has not been an instance which has come to my knowledge of any difficulty between them and the whites, but they have been uniformly peaceable and quiet. O. H. Lamoneux, Special Agent.[25]

SPECIAL AGENCY FOR STRAY BANDS, ETC., NEW LISBON, Wis., September 23, 1869.

The Winnebagoes range between the Wisconsin and Black Rivers, on the Mississippi, east as far as Buffalo Lake, in Marquette County, and north to Juneau and Adams Counties. *This comprises the original country occupied by these Indians. As a general thing they have but little trouble with the whites*, being well disposed; indeed the whites desire a remunerative trade with them by buying the wild berries, (blueberries and cranberries,) which they gather in large quantities all through this country. They also cultivate small patches of corn and potatoes in isolated spots, but being so scattered, it is impossible to arrive at an accurate estimate of the quantity. They also assist at harvesting and picking hops. They are well off in ponies, and in winter engage in hunting and trapping. Their condition is fully as good if not better than those I have met with on the plains. … *I find them much averse to, and dreading even the mention of removal from this section of country, as the government has tried this before, they returning back almost immediately. I do not think it would be advisable to undertake it again, but if their improvement is to be attempted I would recommend that a tract of land near their old homes be set apart or obtained for them.* … Wandering and scattered about as they now are, it is impossible to improve their condition, and the small stipend that is now given them would then relieve the most pressing wants of the old and helpless. D. A. Griffith, Special Indian Agent. (Emphasis added).[26]

The numerous bands of Indians in this agency, scattered as they are over so large a section of country, and in constant intercourse with the whites, *have been remarkably quiet and inoffensive, giving no cause of complaint from the latter*; on the contrary, the towns and villages where they trade their berries, maple sugar, &c., are deriving considerable benefit from them; a larger number have also been employed in the past year in lumbering, harvesting and hop-picking. A number of lumbermen and mill owners have informed me that the Indians they have employed in their business have been steady, good hands, and are showing a greater desire to work than heretofore.…

Census: I find this will not vary materially from the former estimates, and is as follows: Winnebagoes, 995; Pottawatomies, 720; Chippewas, 208. Total 1,923. In visiting their scattered and isolated camps, I was surprised to find that they were cultivating more acres of corn and potatoes than I had supposed; quite a number of them have become owners of a few acres, while *others again rent a few from the whites*, and nearly all of them are desirous of doing the same. *In all their councils with me they have expressed a great desire and hope that the Great Father at Washington would give them a home and reservation in this country, that was formerly their own, and allow them to remain here. They evince a great repugnance and fear of being removed from the State, and will undoubtedly return as fast as they are taken away, as has been proved in former attempts to remove them.* (Emphasis added).[27]

These Indians, now about 1,312 in number, form a class in themselves. They are the part of the Winnebago tribe who refused to remain in Nebraska when they were placed on the Winnebago Reservation in that State. They are scattered over this State as indicated in previous reports, perhaps half of them have homesteads, mostly of little value, and the remainder have practically nothing. Those who have the homesteads make practically no use of them. It is reported, I think truthfully, that some Indians do not know where their homesteads are; they proved up on them under compulsion and then paid no further attention to them. *The majority of these people eke out a bare existence by means of berry picking, potato digging, and an occasional day's work, in addition to the annual payment of annuity, which amounts to about $20.* .... Many of the old and helpless Indians suffer from hunger and cold every winter. Some of these are so feeble as to be unable to take care of themselves, and some of them are blind. The counties in which they live take the stand that they are wards of the Government, and that they are not proper charges on the county. The Government does not help them for the reason that they are citizens. This makes their lot hard. S.A.M. Young, Superintendent and Special Disbursing Agent. (Emphasis added).[28]

3. The Menominees

Menominee Treaties [Brief summary. This list is not meant to be inclusive. This list does not infer any legality or validity of any of the Treaties listed.]			
1817	Peace Treaty		Restored peace between U. S. and Menominee after War of 1812. Tribe sold no lands.

Menominee Land Cession Treaties [Brief summary. This list is not meant to be inclusive. This list does not infer any legality or validity of any of the Treaties listed.]			
Year	Ceded Land	Compensation	Purpose
1821 Not ratified by Congress.			Provide land (860,000 acres) for three tribes emigrating from New York.
1822 Not ratified by Congress.			6.72 million acres - western shore of Lake Michigan to emigrant tribes.
1825	Prairie du Chien Peace Treaty		Established boundary between Menominee and Ojibwe.
1827 Butte des Morts Treaty	No action taken.		
1831	Senate changed boundaries to give better land to emigrant tribes.	Five farm instructors for ten years, grist and lumber mill, gunsmith, and blacksmith shop; $8,000 in clothing; $1,000 in food; $1,000 in cash, and $6,000 annuity for 12 years.	500,000 acres near Green Bay for the New York Indians.
1832	Third compromise treaty on land for emigrant tribes.	Menominee approved boundaries established by Senate.	$1,000 in gifts, 500 bushels of corn, ten barrels of pork, and ten barrels of flour.

Land Cessions for Wisconsin Settlements [Brief summary. This list is not meant to be inclusive. This list does not infer any legality or validity of any of the Treaties listed.]			
Year		Ceded Land	Compensation
1836 Treaty of the Cedars		Land in N/E Wisconsin and strip along Wis. River. 1831 Treaty provisions ag. instructors, grist and lumber mill, gunsmith, and blacksmith shop. Get $76,000 in stocks with interest payable annually.	$20,000 in cash; $3,000 worth of food; 2,000 lb. of tobacco; 30 barrels of salt; $500 for agricultural supplies, such as plows and cattle every year for 20 years. Paid off $99,710.50 alleged debts with traders.
1848 Treaty of Lake Poygan		Ceded all Wis. land, 600,000 acres in Minn. Able to remain two more years in Wis.	$350,000, utilizing 1/2 for moving and remaining $200,000 in equal cash installments for ten years beginning in 1857.
1850		Refuse to move to Minn. Delegation met with President Fillmore.	
1852			Temporary reservation along Wolf River, 250,000 acres.
1854		$15,000 for manual-labor school, grist mill, and blacksmith shop. $40,000 to be used at discretion of President; $242,686 over 15 years for land ceded in 1848.	Reservation along Wolf River, 250,000 acres, permanent. Gave up all claims to Minnesota lands.
1856		46,000 acres of s/w corner for Stockbridge-Munsee.	Paid six cents an acre.

In James K. Polk's Fourth Annual Message, December 5, 1848, he specifically announced the Treaty of Lake Poygan, proclaiming its importance for ratification.

> A most important treaty with the Menomonies has been recently negotiated by the Commissioner of Indian Affairs in person, by which *all their land in the State of Wisconsin—being about 4,000,000 acres—has been ceded to the United States*. This treaty will be submitted to the Senate for ratification at an early period of your present session. (Emphasis added).[29]

They were allowed to remain for two years in Wisconsin during which time they successfully entreated President Fillmore for a reservation at Wolf Creek.

In an ongoing controversy, the State claimed land as swamp lands, even when many of them were not. Under the Swamp Lands Act, the U.S. granted swamp lands to the various states on condition that they would drain and reclaim them. In this one instance, it turned out the Commissioner of the General Land Office erroneously patented Menominee Indian lands to the State as swamp lands. It came to the attention of Secretary Harlan who wrote to Governor Fairchild, to return the patent.

> A letter has been addressed to the Governor of Wisconsin (copy enclosed herewith) requesting him to return the patent to this department, that the same may be cancelled as far as the tracts embraced therein are within the said Indian reservation. The right of the Indians to land embraced within a tract reserved for their exclusive use should be scrupulously respected, and nothing should be done to disturb their possession or to bring their title in question. Jas. Harlan, Secretary.[30]

Acting Commissioner H. R. Clum argued in 1875 that these swamp lands were some of the choicest lands on reservations used for subsistence purposes by the Indians. The State of Wisconsin acquired title to all swamp-lands in said tracts, wherever located, on the date of its admittance to the Union which was May 29, 1848.

4. The Ojibwe (aka Chippewa)

Under the Treaty of 1837,[31] the Wisconsin Ojibwe lost the northern half of Wisconsin. The Chippewa agreed to sell the land to the U.S., but insisted on preserving their right to hunt, fish, and gather in the ceded territory.

The term of the usufructuary right was ill-defined. "The privilege of hunting, fishing, and gathering the wild rice, upon the lands, the rivers, and the lakes included in the territory ceded, is guarantied [sic] to the Indians, *during the pleasure of the President of the United States*." Under the Treaty in 1842, the Indians stipulated for "the right of hunting on the ceded territory, with the other usual privileges of occupancy, *until required to be removed by the President* of the United States." (Emphasis added).

The Treaty of 1854 (La Pointe Treaty) established four reservations for the Wisconsin Ojibwe. This treaty also involved the Ojibwe bands in Upper Michigan and Minnesota. The 1854 Treaty stands out from preceding treaties because it confined the Indians to reservations.
Settlers and the Territory prized the north woods because of its abundance of pine timber. In 1850, the Chippewa faced removal to Minnesota, which, for the most part, they successfully avoided.

Ojibwe Treaties [This list is not meant to be inclusive. This list does not infer any legality or validity of any of the Treaties listed.]

Year	Peace Treaty or Cession	Compensation	Special Terms
1825 Prairie du Chien	Peace Treaty		Establish boundaries between tribes. Effort to end inter-tribal warfare over land.
1827 Lake Butte des Morts	Peace Treaty	Three tribes receive $15,682 in goods and $3,000 to establish schools to split.	Establish boundaries between Ojibwe, Menominee, and Ho-Chunk.
1837 Near Minneapolis-St. Paul.	Ceded majority of their lands in Wis.	20-year annuity of $9,500 in cash; $19,000 in goods (blankets, rifles, and cooking utensils); $2,000 worth of provisions; $3,000 to establish and maintain three blacksmiths' shops; $500 worth of tobacco; $75,000 to pay alleged debts to traders.	The privilege of hunting, fishing, and gathering the wild rice, upon the lands, the rivers, and the lakes included in the territory ceded, is guarantied [sic] to the Indians, during the pleasure of the President of the United States.
1842 La Pointe on Madeline Island.	Ceded lands in northern Wisconsin and part of Michigan's Upper Peninsula.	$12,500 in cash for 25 years; $10,500 in goods; $2,000 in food and tobacco; $2,000 for two blacksmiths; $1,000 for farmers to teach ag.; $1,200 for two carpenters; $2,000 for schools. $5,000 in an agr. trust fund; $75,000 for alleged debts to traders.	Reserved the right of hunting on the ceded territory, with the other usual privileges of occupancy, until required to be removed by the President of the United States.
1854		20-year annuity of $5,000 in cash, $8,000 in goods, $3,000 in farming equipment, carpenters' tools, and cattle, and $3,000 to support schools. Young men - one-time gift of rifles, traps, ammunition, and clothing. Blacksmith shops to be continued for an additional 20 years.	Established four reservations for Wisconsin Ojibwe.
1887	Dawes Act		

Fishing, Hunting, Gathering Rights Cases [Brief summary. This list is not meant to be inclusive. This list does not infer any legality or validity of any matter listed. It is included to evidence the exhaustive time-consuming and costly and prodigious litigation Indian Nations have to endure to secure their constantly threatened Treaty rights.]

Year	Case	Complaint	Ruling
1901		John Blackbird - Ojibwe man arrested for netting fish on the Bad River Reservation.	$25 fine; in default of payment received a sentence of thirty days imprisonment at hard labor.
1901	In re Blackbird 109 F. 139 (W. D. Wis. 1901), Federal District Court for the Western District of Wisconsin.	Challenged State's right to regulate hunting and fishing on Ojibwe reservations. Set aside Mr. Blackbird's citation and arrest.	Wisconsin did not have right to regulate hunting and fishing on Ojibwe reservations. Mr. Blackbird released.
1908	State v. Morrin 136 Wis. 552 (1908), Wisconsin Supreme Court.	Morrin arrested under state statute for fishing with a gill net in Lake Superior.	Act of Congress admitting Wisconsin as a state abrogated Chippewa treaty rights pertaining to hunting and fishing within borders of state. Morrin arrest upheld. Adverse to Chippewas.

State fines, jail terms, car impoundments, and rifle confiscations became common.

The Lac Courte Oreilles Band of Chippewa were the original plaintiffs; they were joined by the Red Cliff Band of Lake Superior Chippewa Indians, the Sokaogon Community/Mole Lake Band of Wisconsin, the St. Croix Chippewa Indians of Wisconsin, the Bad River Band of the Lake Superior Chippewa Indians, and the Lac Du Flambeau Band of Lake Superior Chippewa Indians. The court found that all plaintiff groups were successors to the Chippewa who signed the treaties of 1837 and 1842. *Lac Courte Oreilles v. State of Wisconsin* (LCO IV), 707 F. Supp. 1034, 1036 (W.D. Wis. 1989). **This information is included to demonstrate the persistence of the Chippewa Bands in a controversy that started with the arrest of John Blackbird in 1901.** The Final Judgement in *Lac Court Oreilles Band of Chippewa Indians v. Lester P. Voigt* was issued in 1991.

A series of "unjust arrests" of Chippewa fishers and hunters by state conservation officials led the Bad River Band Tribal Council to issue the following

> "Declaration of War" on November 10, 1959: When, in the course of human events, it becomes necessary to protect the rights and liberties of certain peoples of this great nation from encroachment by other peoples, it is the duty of the Tribal Council, the governing body of the Bad River Band of the Lake Superior Tribe of Chippewa Indians of Wisconsin, to take measures that will protect the members of said Band from unjust arrests by State Conservation officials.
>
> IT IS HEREBY DECLARED, that a state of cold war exists between the Bad River Band of Chippewa Indians and the officials of the Wisconsin Department of Conservation, and that such state shall exist until such time as the State of Wisconsin shall recognize Federal treaties and statutes affording immunity to the members of this Band from State control over hunting and fishing within the boundaries of this reservation. During this period, State conservation officials shall be denied access to all tribal and restricted lands within the boundaries of this reservation. Nothing in this declaration shall be construed to mean that the Tribal Council condones any un-Christian act, or any act of violence upon any person, or to be taken to sanction any riot, or in any manner disturbing the peace. It is known that any such acts are punishable under State Law, such jurisdiction having been given by this Band under {Public Law280,} the Act of August 15, 1953.[32]

Part 7. Tribes Removed to Wisconsin from Northeastern U.S.

In the early to mid 1800s, three eastern tribes, the Oneida, Stockbridge, and Brothertown, arrived in Wisconsin. Removed from their native lands in the east, these tribes traveled to Wisconsin to find a place to call home.[33]

1. The Oneida

In the 1820s, many Oneidas migrated to Wisconsin and settled on land granted to them by the Menominee. After a series of treaties, the Oneida obtained a reservation west of Green Bay in 1838. Eventually, the Oneida sold off their individual allotments, reducing the reservation to a fraction of its original size.

2. The Stockbridge

The Stockbridge, a Massachusetts tribe, faced many of the same pressures as the Oneida. White settlers forced the Stockbridge off of their native lands in 1785. The Stockbridge first relocated to New York, then to Indiana, and eventually to Wisconsin. In 1856, the Stockbridge were removed to a reservation northwest of Green Bay that was established pursuant to negotiations with the Menominee and the federal government.

3. The Brothertown

The Brothertown tribe consisted of two groups of Indians that banded together in the late 1700s. As many as five Algonquian tribes coalesced to form the Brothertown tribe in New York. This group later joined with a Delaware tribe named the Brothertown. As with the Oneida and the Stockbridge, the federal government pressured the Brothertown into removing to the western United States. After arriving in Wisconsin, the Stockbridge ceded a portion of their land to the Brothertown. In 1832, many tribe members chose to become citizens and allotted tribal lands to individuals. Others joined the Stockbridge on reserved lands near Green Bay, hoping to maintain tribal community and traditions.

Part 8: U.S. Treaty Obligations Ignored

In the majority of cases, the U.S. failed to honor the obligations made under Indian treaties. It was no different with the indigenous tribes of Wisconsin. Once they had the land for white settlement and the exploitation of its extractive resources, the U.S.' failure was proved up by its Indian Agents.

Part 9: Sandy Lake Tragedy and Wisconsin Death March

Annuities Used as Economic Sanctions

Annuities are a fixed sum of money or goods that the U.S. government paid to Indians on a regular basis for the sale of their lands. Treaties specified payments in dollar amounts or goods over a period of years in return for land cessions. They are part of the legal obligations under treaties negotiated between the U.S. and particular Indian Nations as consideration for the cession of Indian lands to the U.S. They are not a gratuity.

Annuities were typically distributed at Indian agencies operated by federally appointed agents. As a stipulation of their treaties, late, absent, or poor-quality goods caused considerable distrust of the federal government. Due to the decline in game, Indians depended on the clothing, blankets, and food distributed. If they were not distributed in time for winter, great suffering could result.

For the government, acquisition, shipping, and accounting for goods provided the opportunity for fraud. Goods were contracted for in bulk from New York vendors. The shipping charges were exorbitant and paid for by the Indians out of the annuity amount. Most Indian agents did not document the goods received or the quality or have a way to handle damages or the receipt of useless goods, other than disposing of them as waste. Agents were also subject to accusations of misappropriating annuity goods and selling them on their own account for personal gain.

Policy of Withholding Annuities to Secure Cession of Lands

As early as 1808, there is written evidence of using annuities as economic sanctions if a particular tribe was not doing what the federal government wanted. A letter to Thomas Jefferson from Meriwether Lewis, December 15, 1808, details the withholding of goods as intimidation to require land cessions:

> ... they were reduced in the course of a few months to a state of perfect submission without bloodshed; this has in my opinion very fairly proven the ***superiority which the policy of withholding merchandize*** from the Indians has over the chastizement of the swoard, when their local situations are such as will enable us to practice it. In this state of humiliation Genl. Clark found them in September (sic) last when he established the post near the Fire Prarie (sic); ***he very properly seized this favourable moment, to enter into a treaty with them*** ... It extinguishes their title to a country nearly equal in extent to the state of Virginia and much more fertile. (Emphasis added).[34]

Chippewa Indians Request Homeland in Wisconsin

> In the late fall of 1848, a contingent of Chippewa Indians including chiefs representing sixteen Lake Superior bands traveled to Washington to meet with governmental officials to avoid their removal to the west.[35]

Chippewa Indians Submit Petition to Congress

Early in 1849, the Chippewa presented a petition to Congress requesting the establishment of a "permanent home" in Wisconsin.

> "Our people," they said, "desire a donation of twenty-four sections of land, covering the graves of our fathers, our sugar orchards, and our rice lakes and rivers, at seven different places now occupied by us as villages. ..."[36]

1850 President Taylor's Executive Order to Remove Ojibwe from Wisconsin and Michigan

Without any prior warning whatsoever, President Zachary Taylor signed an Executive Order on February 6, 1850, to remove the Ojibwe from Wisconsin and Michigan, and to revoke their rights to hunt, fish and gather on ceded land. As unconstitutional as his Order was, no pressure was brought to bear to have it rescinded. President Taylor died five months later on July 9, 1850, shortly after taking office. Millard Fillmore succeeded him and delegated the Ojibwe matter to the Department of the Interior.

Minnesota Clamoring to Have Tribes

Minnesota had been clamoring to have Indians relocated there so the state could benefit from monies Indians would spend from their annuities. They also thought a considerable number of federal patronage positions would be available. Governor Ramsey chose Sandy Lake as a site for a new reservation. It is about 70 miles west of Duluth. Most important, though, was its distance from the Ojibwe homelands in Wisconsin—three to five hundred canoe and portage miles.

Minnesota's Plan for Indian Removal

Minnesota used the 1848 Wisconsin Chippewa annuity payment as an example of Wisconsin's Indian Agency's mismanagement and corruption to support the removal of the Chippewas to Minnesota.

The 1848 payment, like many others, began much later than the announced time. As a result, "thousands of Indians traversed many miles of forest, wasted six weeks' time, and lost the crop of wild rice upon which they depended for their winter's subsistence." Traders, who charged what the Ohio reporter called "exorbitant rates" for "the necessaries of life," claimed their profits were "moderate." Yet, for every pound of pork or flour Indians purchased on credit to feed their families, the traders required them to spend an equivalent amount on "dry goods and gewgaws" as well as other "trash" that "had no value for them." By the time the annuity funds arrived, traders "raked" more than eighty-five percent from the payment table; only a few thousand dollars remained to be divided equally among the Indians, who received about one dollar each. According to the reporter, "it was whispered that ... {the traders} were using all their influence to have the future payments made at some point so far West that competition would not force them to be content with moderate profits." These were the reasons, the reporter observed, "it was necessary to remove the Chippewas further West."[37]

Ojibwe Refuse to Move to Minnesota

Charging the U.S. officials with broken promises made at the 1842 Treaty of La Pointe negotiation, the Lake Superior Ojibwe refused to move from their lands in Wisconsin to Minnesota.

Governor Ramsey's Secret Plan

Governor Ramsey and John Watrous, a sub-agent at La Pointe, conspired to lure the Ojibwes to Minnesota and then make it impossible for them to return. The Ojibwe were told that if they did not remove to Sandy Lake, Minnesota, along with their families, they would not receive their annuities or any services required under the 1837 and 1842 Treaties.

On July 15, 1850, Governor Ramsey wrote to the new Commissioner of Indian Affairs, Luke Lea, that the Ojibwe's annuity payment would be made at Sandy Lake and timed "in such a way as to interpose obstacles to a return to the country they left."[38] Ramsey would delay the payment until so late in the year that the waterways would freeze over. This would prevent the Ojibwe from returning to their homes.

Governor Ramsey urged Commissioner Lea to secure a Congressional appropriation to cover the costs of moving the Ojibwes. On September 30, 1850, $25,000 was appropriated to the Indian Department "for expenses of removal and subsistence of the Chippewas of Lake Superior and Mississippi from the lands ceded under the [1842] Treaty." 9 Stat. 544.

The Ojibwe were told payment of their annuities would be made at Sandy Lake on October 25, 1850. Every man, woman and child had to be present. By November 10, almost 4,000 Chippewa had gathered at Sandy Lake. Winter had set in. Agent Watrous, however, did not arrive until November 24. By then many Ojibwe were suffering and dying from hunger and the cold. Measles and dysentery broke out causing many to die.

Watrous contracted with local traders at high prices to provide the Ojibwe with a small amount of food, but the annuity goods would not be distributed until Dec. 2. *After Watrous' visit to Sandy Lake on December 10, he wrote to Gov. Ramsey that as many as 150 Ojibwe had died.*[39]

With the waterways frozen over, the Ojibwe abandoned their canoes and returned home to Wisconsin on foot. According to estimates of Ojibwe leaders, another 230 died during the long, cold march home.[40]

On December 23, the Minnesota Chronicle and Register reported that 167 Ojibwe had died at Sandy Lake from starvation and disease.

Ojibwes' Opposition to Removal Stiffens

In a January 21, 1851, letter to Governor Ramsey, William Warren, of Ojibwe and French descent, legislator in Territorial government, wrote:

> Not only in their councils, but throughout the whole length of my journey I heard in every lodge and from the mouth of every man and woman a determination expressed not to remove.
>
> Since the order for removal has been promulgated other causes have unhappily arisen which had infinitely strengthened in the minds of the Indians a determination not to remove. I have reference [sic] to their being summoned to Sandy Lake to receive their annuity payment when through unavoidable circumstances, they were detained on short allowance of provisions a long length of time, and during their best hunting season. They were made to suffer severely from the cold for want of their goods, which could not be paid to them till their agent had returned from St. Louis to procure their money annuity. Sickness also made its appearance amongst them and in this totally destitute condition cut off nearly two hundred of their number. All this, together with the non-payment of their money, is looked on by them, but as a foretaste of the consequences of their removal, and of the country to which they believe they are to be removed.[41]

Notwithstanding their opposition to removal, on February 27, 1851, Congress appropriated an additional $25,000 "for expenses of removal and subsistence of the Chippewa of Lake Superior and the Mississippi from the lands ceded under the Treaties of [1837] and [1842]." 9 Stat. 570.

Governor Ramsey Defends His Actions

Anxious to deflect any criticism, Governor Ramsey wrote a long defense of his actions to Commissioner Lea.

> "Far from famine or starvation ensuing from any negligence on the part of Government officers," he claimed, "the Chippewas received all that Government was under treaty obligations to furnish to them, except their money; and this, as every one is aware, who is at all familiar with the thriftless habits of the Indians, and the fatal facility with which they incur debts whenever opportunity presents, is usually all of it due to their traders."[42]

Battle of the Wills

Notwithstanding the immense tragedy at Sandy Lake, Governor Ramsey sought Commissioner Lea's approval to continue the same deadly annuity gambit, making payment only at Sandy Lake. On June 19, 1852, Commissioner Lea wrote to Ramsey that he was authorized to decide whether to implement a policy of paying only those who removed with any appropriate exceptions.[43]

Ramsey told sub-Agent Watrous: "You will therefore announce to all of them, that if they wish in future to participate in the annuities of the tribe they will be expected to remove off the ceded lands, & within the lines of their own country."[44]

Commissioner Lea endorsed this approach in his Annual Report to the Secretary:

> A considerable number of the Chippewas yet remain at their old homes in the country ceded to the United States, but by adhering to the policy of paying them their annuities only in their own territory, it is thought that such of them as it may be desirable to remove will soon be induced quickly to abandon their ceded lands.[45]

It does not appear that anyone in the chain of command received any reprimand for their policies. Those in the chain of command included the President, Congress, Commissioner Lea, Governor Ramsey and sub-Agent Watrous. They all bear responsibility for this brutality.

Despite the DOI's policy, the Ojibwe remained on their lands and continued to hunt, fish, and gather. To compensate for annuities lost because of this decision, Reverend Wheeler told Treat that "more of them than usual have gone a hunting, their furs bringing them the ready cash or its equivalent in something else." In April 1853, a mission employee from La Pointe wrote that the Chippewa were making maple sugar.[46]

Even though, the Lake Superior Ojibwe sent a delegation to Washington City (Washington, D.C.) in 1852 to protest the removal Order, it was not until 1853 that removal efforts ended.

Lake Superior Ojibwe Sign New Treaty at La Pointe

Then, in 1854, the Lake Superior Ojibwe signed a new treaty at La Pointe that promised permanent reservations and on-site annual payments in their homeland.

Part 10: Theft, Theft and More Theft of Indian Timber

In 1860, the Indian Agent for the Chippewas of Lake Superior reported the repeated theft of timber by "whites."

> The lands occupied by these bands are heavily timbered with pine, and the whites have trespassed upon them from time to time, cutting down and removing the most valuable they could reach, to the great annoyance and injury of the Indians. I truly hope that, before another year, the conditions of the treaty touching these reservations will be fulfilled.[47]

Ongoing Theft of Timber on Menominee Reservation

In 1865, Commissioner Cooley reported on the theft of timber occurring on the Menominee Reservation. While he reported that the Agent took steps to prosecute the thieving parties, it is unlikely it had any effect. Territorial courts failed to offer a deterrence to whites, who were willing to risk getting caught and finding a willing court to prosecute a white over theft of an Indian's timber. Usually, the reservations had not been accurately surveyed, if surveyed at all, and whites argued Indians couldn't prove up the theft. The cost of a prosecution and the distance to a territorial court also served as disadvantages to protecting Indian property rights.

> Depredations upon the timbered (pine) lands of the tribe have been made to a large extent by whites, and the agent has taken the necessary steps to prosecute the guilty parties, and recover for the tribe the value of the timber.[48]

Theft of Timber Predicted to Continue

In 1879, Commissioner Hayt averred that the timber on the Chippewa lands in Wisconsin was of no value to them. Their reservation was "covered with a heavy growth of very valuable timber." The objective of the Commissioner, as stated, was to have the Chippewas cede this land, move to a new reservation where the DOI could concentrate them and allot the land in severalty. Their timber land could be opened for sale to whites.

> Large quantities of timber have also been removed in years past by trespassers. There are probably ***600,000,000 feet of merchantable pine timber*** on these reservations, which, under present circumstances, ***is of no value to the Indians***. (Emphasis added).[49]

Mill Owners' Conspiracy to Keep Menominee Timber Price Low

The DOI was fully aware of the theft of timber on Wisconsin Indians' land. In this particular sale the Menominee Indians received $5.71 per 1000 feet. *It was 1896*, decades past with repeated trespasses, cheating on the value paid for ceded lands and timber sold to whites. *The Agent noted a solution – a sawmill could be built for $20,000 on Indian land and let them do the milling*. What a novel idea. The DOI simply could not plead ignorance or an ability to protect this land and its resources. This was an extractive resource which would be forever lost.

> There was evidently a combination among the lumbermen to obtain the logs at a low price.

> The mill men form a combination or trust and keep the price of the logs down by not bidding against each other. *The only way to prevent these combinations is for the Government to erect a large sawmill on the reservation*, in which can be sawed the entire cut of logs banked by the Indians on Wolf River and tributaries, if in the judgment of the Department the logs did not sell for what they were worth. A complete sawmill could be built for $20,000, and it is my opinion that it would break up the combination among the mill men and would more than pay for itself every year if a log was never sawed in it. If such a mill was erected it would give employment to the Indians and the lumber sell for many thousand dollars more than the logs do at present. (Emphasis added).[50]

Agent's Wholesale Permission for Fraudulent Logging

In 1888, Agent Gregory flagrantly defied the Commissioner of Indian Affairs and let whites cut timber under unapproved and fraudulent contracts. The Commissioner even repeated and repeated his instructions to no avail.

> La Pointe Agency. As indicated in the last annual report, full instructions were given Agent Gregory, October 29, 1888, regarding the sale of pine timber on the reservations under his charge, said instructions containing the following clause:
>
> It must be distinctly understood that *no operations can be commenced until you are notified that the contract has been approved by this office*, and that no contracts should be made for the sale of timber upon tracts where the allotments have not been approved by the President.
>
> On the same day Agent Gregory telegraphed those having such contracts as follows: You can go on and complete your last winter contracts.
>
> December 8, 1888, a form of new contract for the sale of pine timber was prepared and forwarded to Agent Gregory, he being again instructed as follows:
>
> Permit no operations to be commenced on any tract until you receive notice of the approval of a contract covering the same. (Emphasis added).[51]

Following an investigation, due to Agent Gregory's failure to follow these instructions, he was terminated. Suit was brought against the contractor to recover the value due for timber cut.

Fraudulent Timber Contracts

> Subsequently (February 14, 1889), the Department authorized an investigation ... This investigation was duly made, and as a result thereof some 211 contracts for the sale of pine timber on the Lac Court d'Oreilles, Bad River, and Lac du Flambeau Reservations were approved by my immediate predecessor in April last. Full settlement has been made under these contracts. ... The amount recovered was $147,131.[52]

Menominees' Unrealized Timber Industry Potential

The Menominee's Agent noted again that the Indian's could log and mill the timber themselves. Instead, it is reported over and over, what great menial labor the Indians made for white timber companies.

> Also, if they were allowed to cut and sell the spruce and poplar pulp wood on the reservation, which is now going to waste, they could earn considerable money, and as the most of the value to pulp wood is the labor preparing it for market, I would recommend that they be allowed to cut and sell it, each Indian to receive the product of his own labor. Or, if a pulp mill were allowed to be built on the reservation, it would give employment to a large number in preparing the wood and working in the mill.[53]

Green Bay Agency – 300,000,000 Feet of Pine Logged

> The logging operations in the past have been confined almost exclusively to pine timber, with the result that over 300,000,000 feet of this class of timber has been marketed, aggregating over $3,000,000.[54]

Timber Trespasses on Stockbridge and Munsee Reservation

> Timber trespasses on the Stockbridge and Munsee Reservation continue to be a source of great annoyance to this office. It seems to be impossible to stop these people from cutting. They are acting under legal advice, assuring them of their right to cut, and they have no trouble in finding a purchaser for their logs. Numerous arrests have been made during the past two years, but with very unsatisfactory results. In the first place, the United States district attorney advised me personally, also Superintendent of Logging Farr, that he would nolle (cease to prosecute) all cases where arrests were made for past trespasses, and that we must confine our arrests to new trespasses. In the next place, the local United States court commissioner has refused to hold for trial in any case where the defendant could prove that be had made an actual clearing within a reasonable time following the cutting.[55]

Menominees Get to Conduct Lumber Operations

As lumber was becoming scarce, several Wisconsin legislators tried to pass legislation which would open the Menominee reservation to timber harvesting by non-Indians. Menominee tribal members refused. They wanted to log and benefit from their own reservation resources. Federal law, however, only allowed the Menominee to harvest dead and down timber for personal use or to harvest standing green timber to clear land for farming.

This situation changed in June 1890, when Congress approved "An act to authorize the sale of timber on certain lands reserved for use by the Menominee tribe of Indians in the State of Wisconsin."

The new Act compelled the Indian agent to hire Menominee people to run the logging operations. In addition, the law allowed the tribe to sell the logs and retain the proceeds for their own benefit. Tribal members considered the 1890 Act as a way to use their collective resources to provide for the tribe. Many Menominee began to view logging as a way to provide the tribe with needed employment and economic resources.[56]

Cornell University's Investment in Wisconsin's 'Virgin White Pine Lands'

Senator Justin Morrill of Vermont advocated for the necessity of establishing public universities to address the practical requirements of agriculture and industry. To him, existing private universities did not address the practical concerns of life, especially agriculture. He argued the public colleges should be funded by federal grants of land. From this came the term, land-grant colleges. The Morrill Act was based on the federal government's ability to sign treaties with, dispossess, and remove Indians from the land.

The first bill was vetoed on February 26, 1859, by President James Buchanan due to fiscal concerns. Based on intense lobbying, the bill was re-introduced, passed, and signed by President Lincoln in 1862.[57] Each state was to receive 30,000 acres of land for each Congressional representative; both senators and members of the House. The income from this land-grant would constitute an endowment for at least one college in the state providing instruction in agriculture and the "mechanic arts."

Eastern states with no available public lands at that time, such as New York, received what was referred to as "land scrip" (paper certificates). Each piece of land scrip entitled the bearer to claim a quarter-section (160 acres) of unappropriated public land to sell, anywhere in the United States. Since the Morrill Act prohibited one state from taking direct ownership of land in another state, the assumption was that eastern states would sell their scrip allocations to individuals and then invest the proceeds in "safe" stocks or bonds yielding a minimum of five percent interest annually.

New York

New York State accepted the Congressional grant provided by the Morrill Act on March 4, 1863. It received nearly one-tenth of the "public land" granted by the Act, due to its population, resulting in a large number of Congressional representatives. On May 5, 1863, the State Legislature authorized the Comptroller to receive 6,187 pieces of land scrip (160 acres each, totaling 989,920 acres) and sell it for the benefit of what at the time was to be determined as the state's land-grant college(s).

Cornell University

Into this context stepped then New York State Assemblyman Ezra Cornell. While in the State Senate, he made the acquaintance of Andrew Dickson White of Syracuse. Through discussions with White, the idea of a university grew in Cornell's mind. When the Legislature met in 1865, White introduced a bill in the Senate "to establish the Cornell University and to appropriate to it the income of the sale of public lands granted to this State."[58]

After much political maneuvering, the bill was passed in the Assembly on April 21, in the Senate on April 22, and was signed by Governor Reuben E. Fenton on April 27. Mr. Cornell endowed the university through an outright gift of $500,000, to which would be added the sum realized by his purchase of the Morrill land scrip from the state.

He decided that rather than have the State sell the scrip outright at a face value of $1.25 per acre, he would buy it from the State and use the scrip to purchase lands, speculating that the value would appreciate. He would locate and manage the land purchased, selling it as "opportunity offered, for the interest of the university."[59]

Cornell concluded that timberlands offered the best chance for high returns and set his sights on the "excellent stands of virgin white pine" in Wisconsin and Minnesota. He purchased almost 500,000 aces in Wisconsin and almost 8,000 acres in Minnesota. The lands were part of the cessions of the Sioux and Chippewa.

In 1881–1882 Weyerhaeuser acquired 100,200,000 feet of timber from fourteen different owners. In 1882, he purchased 109,601 acres from Cornell University, estimated to have 597,931,000 board feet of pine.[60]

These, and his other transactions, resulted in Cornell receiving a windfall from its land scrip—Cornell University generated nearly one-third of the total Morrill Act land-grant revenues received by all the states, $5,047,623.60, equivalent to about $150 million today. It enabled Cornell to weather difficult economic times.

LOCATION OF THE LAND SELECTED AND ENTERED BY EZRA CORNELL WITH MORRILL ACT LAND SCRIP[61]

Location of Land	# of Pieces of Scrip	Acreage
Wisconsin	3,182	499,126.33
Minnesota	50	7,968.27
Kansas	25	3,974.93
TOTAL	3,257	511,069.53

UNRESTRICTED REVENUES ACCRUED TO CORNELL ENDOWMENT FUND FROM MANAGEMENT OF LAND OBTAINED UNDER MORRILL ACT, 1865-1923[62]

INCOME		EXPENSES	
Land	$4,542,563.21	Purchase price of Land Scrip	$309,200
Timber	$2,211,616.59	Land location, surveying, and examination expenses	$205,171.16
Trespass Fees Collected	$20,063.90	Taxes	$648,204.05
Hay	$4,268.14	Interest	$329,039.70
Rent on Farmland	$758.05	Salaries	$146,219.93
Sale of 52 pieces of Land Scrip by W.A. Woodward	$408.00	Commission on sales	$22,513.69
Land Unsold as of June 30, 1923 (160 acres valued at $5/acre)	$800.00	Travel expenses	$7,893.62
TOTAL INCOME	$6,776,209.75	Postage and stationery	$3,037.41
		Legal fees	$30,392.43
		Miscellaneous, contingent, and unclassified expenses	$26,914.16
		TOTAL EXPENSES	$1,728,586.15
NET INCOME	$5,047,623.60		

288   THE IRON TRIANGLE

When title to the Sioux and Chippewa lands was extinguished, and passed over to the United States, the lands were promptly surveyed and open to purchase and settlement. This being the case, Cornell's purchase was lawful. Yet its windfall from the fraudulent dispossession of Indian lands should not go unheeded.

Lumber Barons

The lumber barons, having stripped Wisconsin bare, moved on to the Pacific Northwest leaving Wisconsin to deal with its deforestation.

By far the most difficult part of the forest problem in Wisconsin is the question as to what shall be done with those large tracts now existing which have been denuded of the pine formerly growing on them, and now lie idle, subject to the ravages of the fire. ... It appears that in their present uncared for situation they are liable to a progressive deterioration of the soil. ... There is consequently no prospect that our denuded lands will be put to agricultural uses.[63]

Notes: Wisconsin's Forced Indian Removal

1. Washinawatok, James. Recognizing an American Holocaust http://nahmus.org/TOCscholarlyarticles.html#americanholocaust (accessed online April 23, 2022).
2. Documents from the War Department accompanying the President's Message to Congress, Part II, 1827. http://images.library.wisc.edu/History/EFacs/CommRep/AnnRep2639/reference/history.annrep2639.i0003.pdf (accessed online November 18, 2021).
3. See Current, Richard N. The Civil War Era, 1848–1873: History of Wisconsin, Volume II. United States, Wisconsin Historical Society Press, 2013.
4. https://www.sierraclub.org/wisconsin/issues/mining (accessed online April 25, 2022).
5. Current, Richard Nelson. The History of Wisconsin. State Historical Society of Wisconsin, 1976.
6. "Hoard Reviews Past and Paints Future." Oshkosh Northwestern (5 December 1916); http://www.wisconsinhistory.org/turningpoints/search.asp?id=706 (accessed online April 25, 2022).
7. Journal of the Council, Volume 1, Part 2, Wisconsin. Legislative Assembly. Council, 1838, p. 248.
8. Ibid., p.14.
9. Ibid., p.7.
10. Report of the Commissioner of Indian Affairs to the Secretary of the Interior, Office of Indian Affairs, United States. U.S. Government Printing Office, 1864, p. 372.

11. Miscellaneous Documents: 30th Congress, 1st Session – 49th Congress, 1st Session, Volume 3, United States congressional serial set, United States Congress, House, 1874, Oxford University.
12. Report of the Commissioner of Indian Affairs to the Secretary of the Interior, Office of Indian Affairs, United States. U.S. Government Printing Office, 1887, p. 231.
13. Report of the Commissioner of Indian Affairs to the Secretary of the Interior, Office of Indian Affairs, United States. U.S. Government Printing Office, 1864, p. 374.
14. Ibid., p. 370.
15. See https://digicoll.library.wisc.edu/cgi/f/findaid/findaid-idx?c=wiarchives;cc=wiarchives;view=text;rgn=main;didno=uw-whs-ser00180 (accessed online April 27, 2022).
16. Report of the Commissioner of Indian Affairs to the Secretary of the Interior, United States. Office of Indian Affairs, U.S. Government Printing Office, 1864, p. 372.
17. Ibid., p. 359.
18. Ibid., p. 361.
19. Ibid., p. 363.
20. Ibid., p. 358.
21. Id.
22. Ibid., pp. 356-374.
23. Annual message of C. C. Washburn, Governor of Wisconsin, delivered to the Legislature in joint convention, January 11, 1872.
24. Report of the Commissioner of Indian Affairs to the Secretary of the Interior, United States. Office of Indian Affairs, U.S. Government Printing Office, 1873, pp. 189-191.
25. Report of the Commissioner of Indian Affairs to the Secretary of the Interior, United States. Office of Indian Affairs, *Special Agency for Stray Bands of Winnebago and Pottawatomi Indians of Wisconsin*. U.S. Government Printing Office, 1868, p. 349.
26. Report of the Commissioner of Indian Affairs to the Secretary of the Interior, United States. Office of Indian Affairs, *Special Agency for Stray Bands of Winnebago and Pottawatomi Indians of Wisconsin*. U.S. Government Printing Office, 1870, pp. 447-448.
27. Ibid., pp. 323-324.
28. Report of the Commissioner of Indian Affairs to the Secretary of the Interior, Office of Indian Affairs, United States. U.S. Government Printing Office, 1906, p. 380.
29. https://millercenter.org/the-presidency/presidential-speeches/december-5-1848-fourth-annual-message-congress (accessed online April 27, 2022).

30. Report of the Commissioner of Indian Affairs to the Secretary of the Interior, Office of Indian Affairs, United States. U.S. Government Printing Office, 1866, p. 293.
31. Under the Treaties of 1837: Treaty of St. Peter's, July 29, 1837, art. I, 7 Stat. 536; 1842 Treaty of La Pointe, Oct. 4, 1842, art. I, 7 Stat. 591, 591-92.
32. Act of August 15, 1953. Rosier, Paul C. Native American Issues. Greenwood Publishing Group, 2003, p. 36.
33. The Wisconsin State Legal System and Indian Affairs in the Nineteenth Century: A Lost Chapter in Wisconsin's Legal History, 87 Marq. L. Rev. (2003). http://scholarship.law.marquette.edu/mulr/vol87/iss2/5 (accessed online April 24, 2022).
34. "To Thomas Jefferson from Meriwether Lewis, 15 December 1808," Founders Online, National Archives, https://founders.archives.gov/documents/Jefferson/99-01-02-9323. (accessed on line April 24, 2022).
35. "The Removal Order and the Wisconsin Death," Wisconsin Academy of Sciences, Arts & Letters, pp. 88-89.
36. Id.
37. Apfelbeck, Laura, and Satz, Ronald N. Chippewa Treaty Rights: The Reserved Rights of Wisconsin's Chippewa Indians in Historical Perspective. United States, University of Wisconsin Press, 1996, p. 53.
38. Ramsey to Lea, July 16, 1850. Fish in the Lakes, Wild Rice, and Game in Abundance: Testimony on Behalf of Mille Lacs Ojibwe Hunting and Fishing Rights, Editor James M. McClurken, MSU Press, 2000, p. 187.
39. Watrous to Ramsey, Dec. 10, 1850. Fish in the Lakes, Wild Rice, and Game in Abundance: Testimony on Behalf of Mille Lacs Ojibwe Hunting and Fishing Rights, Editor James M. McClurken, MSU Press, 2000, p. 193.
40. Buffalo et al., to Lea, Nov. 6, 1851. Fish in the Lakes, Wild Rice, and Game in Abundance: Testimony on Behalf of Mille Lacs Ojibwe Hunting and Fishing Rights, Editor James M. McClurken, MSU Press, 2000, p. 39.
41. W. Warren to Ramsey, Jan. 21, 1851. Fish in the Lakes, Wild Rice, and Game in Abundance: Testimony on Behalf of Mille Lacs Ojibwe Hunting and Fishing Rights, Editor James M. McClurken, MSU Press, 2000, p. 196.
42. Report of the Commissioner of Indian Affairs to the Secretary of the Interior, United States. Office of Indian Affairs, U.S. Government Printing Office, 1850, p. 162.
43. Lea to Ramsey, June 19, 1852. Lea was smart enough to leave the decision to Ramsey. Fish in the Lakes, Wild Rice, and Game in Abundance: Testimony on Behalf of Mille Lacs Ojibwe Hunting and Fishing Rights, Editor James M. McClurken, MSU Press, 2000, p. 251.
44. Ramsey to Watrous, Aug. 9, 1852. Fish in the Lakes, Wild Rice, and Game in Abundance: Testimony on Behalf of Mille Lacs Ojibwe Hunting and Fishing Rights, Editor James M. McClurken, MSU Press, 2000, p. 258.

45. Report of the Secretary of the Interior Ex. doc., United States congressional serial set, United States. Department of the Interior, 1850, p. 295.
46. Wheeler to Treat, Nov. 20, 1852. Pulsifer to Treat, April 14, 1853. Fish in the Lakes, Wild Rice, and Game in Abundance: Testimony on Behalf of Mille Lacs Ojibwe Hunting and Fishing Rights, Editor James M. McClurken, MSU Press, 2000, p. ?
47. Report of the Commissioner of Indian Affairs to the Secretary of the Interior, United States. Office of Indian Affairs, U.S. Government Printing Office, 1865, p. 52.
48. Report of the Commissioner of Indian Affairs to the Secretary of the Interior, United States. Office of Indian Affairs, U.S. Government Printing Office, 1879, p. XLII.
49. Report of the Commissioner of Indian Affairs to the Secretary of the Interior, United States. Office of Indian Affairs, U.S. Government Printing Office, 1896, p. 323.
50. The Abridgment ... Containing the Annual Message of the President of the United States to the Two Houses of Congress ... with Reports of Departments and Selections from Accompanying Papers, Secretary of the Interior, U.S. Department of the Interior, U.S. Government Printing Office, 1890, pp. 683-684.
51. Report of the Commissioner of Indian Affairs to the Secretary of the Interior, United States. Office of Indian Affairs, U.S. Government Printing Office, 1889, p. 85.
52. Report of the Commissioner of Indian Affairs to the Secretary of the Interior, United States. Office of Indian Affairs, U.S. Government Printing Office, 1898, p. 308.
53. Report of the Commissioner of Indian Affairs to the Secretary of the Interior, United States. Office of Indian Affairs, U.S. Government Printing Office, 1904, p. 369.
54. Report of the Commissioner of Indian Affairs to the Secretary of the Interior, United States. Office of Indian Affairs, U.S. Government Printing Office, 1906, p. 374.
55. Report of the Commissioner of Indian Affairs to the Secretary of the Interior, Office of Indian Affairs, United States. U.S. Government Printing Office, 1908, p. 1.
56. http://www.mikedockry.net/wp-content/uploads/2012/09/Chapter-3-Menominee-Forest-Management-Histories-1890–1973.pdf (accessed online April 5, 2022)
57. 12 Stat. 503 (1862).
58. I Would Found an Institution, The Ezra Cornell Bicentennial https://rmc.library.cornell.edu/ezra/exhibition/founding/index.html (accessed online June 28, 2022).

59. Waterman Thomas Hewett, "The History of Cornell University in the Twenty-Five Years of Its Existence, 1868–1893" in John H. Selkreg, ed., Landmarks of Tompkins County, New York (Syracuse, NY: D. Mason & Co., 1894.), p. 416.
60. Andreano, Ralph. "Timber and Men: The Weyerhauser Story. By Ralph W. Hidy, Frank Ernest Hill, and Allan Nevins. New York and London: Macmillan Company, 1964, p. 84. https://www.in2013dollars.com/us/inflation/1862?amount=5047623 (accessed online June 28, 2022).
61. Jon Parmenter, "Flipped Scrip, Flipping the Script: The Morrill Act of 1862, Cornell University, and the Legacy of Nineteenth-Century Indigenous Dispossession" https://blogs.cornell.edu/cornelluniversityindigenousdispossession/2020/10/01/flipped-scrip-flipping-the-script-the-morrill-act-of-1862-cornell-university-and-the-legacy-of-nineteenth-century-indigenous-dispossession/ (accessed online June 28, 2022).
62. Id.
63. Report of the Forestry Commission of the State of Wisconsin, Wisconsin, Forestry Commission. Democrat Printing Company, State Printer, 1898, pp. 17-18.

CHAPTER 9: MONTANA:
BIG BUSINESS' CORRUPT POLITICAL CLOUT

Introduction

Even though this Chapter is on the theft of Indian timber in Montana, the web of interlocking mining, lumber and railway companies wielded **tremendous** political and economic power in the U.S.' westward expansion and are, accordingly, addressed. Most importantly, is the need to analyze the continuous failure of the U.S. to protect the sovereignty, lives, land and property of Indians. Congress and the executive branch repeatedly sacrificed its wards to the dominating control of colonial settlers and businesses, actively aligning against Indians. Their deceptive justifications, that removing Indians from their land was for their benefit or ceding valuable lands was in their interest, went unchecked. Many times, the judiciary joined in this grave injustice. It will be up to Indians to admit the horrible, unwarranted abuse of its trustee, before it can decide a path forward. This chapter is part of the proof of that abuse.

Part 1: Lady Liberty Heads West

The westward expansion of the U.S. was guided by the imperialist design of its 'Founding Fathers.' Prior to becoming President at the end of the Revolutionary War, General George Washington referred to Americans as "the sole Lords and Proprietors of a vast Tract of Continent" and believed the success of the Revolutionary struggle was nothing less than the "foundation of our Empire[.]"[1]

In 1801, President Thomas Jefferson predicated his vision of continental expansion on a homogenous population, with a uniform set of social mores defining what was politically, economically and socially acceptable.

> It is impossible not to look forward to distant times, when our rapid multiplication will…cover the whole northern, if not the whole southern continent, with a people speaking the same language, governed in similar forms, and by similar laws; nor can we contemplate with satisfaction either blot or mixture on that surface.[2]

Jefferson did not envision indigenous peoples with varied speech, political organization, economic behavior and culture tolerable – there could be no "blot or mixture" to his unitary system. Different entities (tribes, bands) each existed as an autonomous independent sovereign, with the fundamental attributes of self-governance and self-determination. Most of them modeled their economic system on communal property as, opposed to a capitalist economic system based on individual ownership with the objective of personal profit. The mosaic of different indigenous cultures diverged from the singular White Anglo-Saxon Protestant ethic. Yet, indigenous cultures had a millennial continuity, transmitted to succeeding generations, each as unique as the whorls of a finger print. Jefferson, instead, coined the concept of a homogenous empire, governed by the U.S. Constitution. The fact that tribal sovereignty predated federal recognition, predated the birth of the Republic and predated the U.S. Constitution was foreign to Jefferson.[3]

> ... we should have such an *empire for liberty* as she has never surveyed since the creation: & I am persuaded no constitution was ever before so well calculated as ours for extensive empire & self government... (Emphasis added).[4]
> Each indigenous entity in Jefferson's ideology constituted, an 'imperio in imperium,' a government within a government, that could not exist within the U.S.'s unitary system.

Indian Land Title Questionable

Our sixth President, John Quincy Adams, proudly delivered his position regarding Indian's ownership of the land. His 1839 oration, at the Jubilee of the Constitution, set the stage for westward expansion and the divestment of Indian lands and property by dogmatically asserting that Indian possession was questionable.

> ***The Indian right of possession itself stands, with regard to the greatest part of the country, upon a questionable foundation.*** (Emphasis added).[5]

The United States would dominate the Americas, Adams said, and assert its hemispheric hegemony without challenge. "We have it; we constitute the whole of it."[6]

"Manifest Destiny"

The European colonial settlers espoused this doctrine that they alone were meant to reign over this vast continent. Their dispossession of the indigenous inhabitants, of their rights to sovereignty, life, liberty, and property, was ordained and canonized in the phrase "Manifest Destiny."

In an 1839 article, journalist John O'Sullivan articulated this understanding of American Exceptionalism, outlining the contours of the 'new' nation: "Its floor shall be a hemisphere—its roof the firmament of the star studded heavens, and its congregation an Union of many Republics, comprising hundreds of happy millions, calling, owning no man master, but governed by God's natural and moral law of equality, the law of brotherhood—of 'peace and good will amongst men.'"[7]

In 1845, he gave the 'doctrine of discovery' a uniquely American flavor when he coined the term Manifest Destiny to defend U.S. expansion and claims to new territory:

> ... the right of our manifest destiny to over spread and to possess the whole of the continent which Providence has given us for the development of the great experiment of liberty... is right such as that of the tree to the space of air and the earth suitable for the full expansion of its principle and destiny of growth.[8]

It captured and consolidated longstanding concepts from the Crusades and the papal-sanctioned colonization process such as holy war, divine sanction, chosen people, promised land, terra nullius (if land was not being cultivated or put to good use it could be considered vacant, even if inhabited by indigenous peoples), and the proselytizing and conversion of heathens.

As the emigrants traversed Indian trade routes that crisscrossed the country, their encounter with peoples different from themselves was bound to be brutal. By the Northwest Ordinance of 1787,[9] the federal government set the rules for their settlement, absent any input, whatsoever, from those who ruled the domain they sought for themselves. The rectangular division of the land ignored the countless millennia of the kinship inhabitation of the original peoples with the contiguous, interrelated spheres of earth and sky, the subterranean and the terrestrial.

Part 2: Boots on Ground

Fifty-Four Forty or Fight

The Oregon Country, according to the U.S., encompassed the present states of Oregon, Washington, Idaho, and parts of Montana and Wyoming, along with part of British Columbia. The U.S. claimed this territory based on American sea captain Robert Gray's 'discovery' of the mouth of the Columbia River in 1792. An axiom of the illusory 'doctrine of discovery' held that he who first discovered the mouth of a river earned the right to the drainage basin of the river.

James Polk's campaign battle cry was "Fifty-four forty or fight," which meant the United States would accept nothing less from the British than all of the Oregon Country. Their contested ownership came to the brink of war. To protect its claim, in this scramble for ownership, the U.S. had to put 'boots on the ground.' Colonial settlers had proved over and over again in their march across the U.S. that their possession of the land meant more than a military presence alone. The presence of multitudes of Indian Nations, reported on by Lewis and Clark, was wholly irrelevant to England or the United States. It was about the willingness of the United States to go to war with England to win what are now the states of Washington, Oregon and Idaho, along with parts of Montana and Wyoming. It was about building an empire. The United States and Britain came to agreement over the possession of the Oregon country, setting the international boundary at the 49th parallel.

Without the need to buoy up the U.S.' 'discovery claim,' legislation for western settlement might have addressed Indian land titles. The U.S. might have kept its promise under the Northwest Ordinance of 1787:

> The utmost good faith shall always be observed towards the Indians; their lands and property shall never be taken from them without their consent; and, in their property, rights, and liberty, they shall never be invaded or disturbed, unless in just and lawful wars authorized by Congress; but laws founded in justice and humanity, shall from time to time be made for preventing wrongs being done to them, and for preserving peace and friendship with them.[10]

Instead, colonial settlers traveled in waves over the Oregon Trail and the Bozeman Trail headed to the California and Montana Gold Rushes. They relied on U.S. military forts, posted with Army soldiers, to facilitate their travel and provide for their safety. The government's decision to prioritize protecting its citizenry militated against its role as the trustee for American Indians.

To encourage settlement, Congress passed the Distribution-Preemption Act of 1841, which recognized squatters' rights and allowed settlers to claim 160 acres of land. After residing on the property for 14 months, a claimant could purchase the property at $1.25 an acre.

On September 27, 1850, the Donation Land Claim Act of 1850 offered 320 acres at no charge to qualifying adult U.S. citizens (640 acres to married couples), subject to occupying their claims for four consecutive years. Indians were not U.S. citizens and therefore could not own land under the law, although Section 4 of the Act allowed "American half-breed Indians" of legal age, who were citizens of the United States (or declared to be), to participate.

The Donation Land Claim Act promised "Free land! Gold in the rivers! Settlers and miners streamed into the valley carrying more than baggage. Many brought with them intense prejudice toward the Indians whose land they were invading."[11]

Oregon Trail

The Oregon Trail, used by settlers, farmers, miners, ranchers, and business owners and their families, was a 2,170-mile east–west, large-wheeled wagon route and emigrant trail spanning the country from St. Louis, Missouri to the Willamette Valley in Oregon. It was laid by Indians, fur traders and trappers and was only passable on foot or by horseback. By 1836, when the first migrant wagon train was organized in Independence, Missouri, a wagon trail had been cleared to Fort Hall, Idaho. Major side routes would branch off from the Oregon Trail, including the California, the Mormon and the Bozeman Trails.

The construction of four forts along the Oregon Trail and posting U.S. Army soldiers to provide military protection to the emigrants evidence the importance of encouraging and protecting settlement of the Territory. Fort Laramie (1834), Fort Hall (1834), Fort Boise (1834) and Fort Bridger (1842) served emigrants as post offices and resupply points on the Trail.[12]

Frontier Trading Posts

Montana's trading post at Fort Benton, built in 1846, for buying furs from Indians and for the acquisition of goods would assume a prominent role. Built by the Chouteau brothers, Astor's American Fur Company's western agents, its modest façade belied its importance as the entryway for trade on the Missouri River. During a brief spring window, the snow-melt enabled steamboat traffic 2,600 miles to St. Louis. This unpredictable River transit cost less than wagon freighting for transporting supplies, equipment and people.

Part 3: Coming of Railroads

Railroad Surveys

The U.S. needed reliable, year-round, transportation. To accomplish this, the principal focus was on developing a railroad system. In the early 1850s, Congress funded surveys for viable rail routes. The northernmost of these, directed by Washington Territorial Governor and ex officio Superintendent of Indian Affairs Isaac Stevens, was to find a route along the Missouri River through the northern Rockies, to connect with major settlements in the Oregon and Washington Territories. The result of Stevens' nearly six-month trek was a two-volume book entitled Report of Explorations for a Route for the Pacific Railroad near the 47th and 49th Parallels of North Latitude, from St. Paul, Minnesota, to Puget Sound. It was released in full between 1855 and 1860.

U.S. Army Lt. John Mullan was a tag-along. A recent West Point engineer graduate, Stevens assigned him the task of surveying a pre-existing wagon route which stretched from Fort Benton all the way to Fort Walla Walla in Washington. He and his men spent the winter of 1853–1854 tramping over 1,000 miles through the Rocky Mountains proving up a route for a restored road and railroad route. By March 1854, he had a $30,000 Congressionally-approved budget for a road which would be named after him. Within months of its completion in 1861, miners and travelers started using it. Its success affected Congress' decision to back the railroad construction of the 1880's. Mullan Pass can be traversed by train today.

Railroads' Advantages

Technological advances fast-forwarded settlement of the west. The transcontinental railroad cut travel to the west down from six months to six days. It made it cheaper and safer. It made it possible for Territories to expand their white population exponentially. Train stations along the railroad route provided the impetus for founding towns and cities. The colonial settlers' need for goods and services coincided with the railroads need for profit. It freed up individual time, previously devoted to farming. Urbanization and industrialization would lead to wage-based economies. Minerals and timber resources could be exploited with a transportation network that could connect the east to the west. Trains could carry the heavier-weighted, valuable cargo more reliably than wagon trains or schooners. Money was to be made and invested.

Railroads Cut through Indian Lands

The railroads had to cross Indians lands. Legislation was enacted to extinguish Indian land ownership impeding the railroad. Instead of waiting for Congress to act, powerful businessmen lobbied for the removal of Indians to concentrated areas so that the federal government could better exercise control. They pressured the government and Indians for the cession of Indian lands for cents on the dollar. They campaigned for right-of-way legislation which would grant them not just an easement, but the fee to the right-of-way.

Part 4: Strategies to Divest Indians of Their Lands

Pacify the Indians

It became important to the U.S. to pacify Indians, since war was too costly:

> The increase of the annual overland emigration to the Pacific coast, and the desirableness of increased facilities for its speedy and safe transit, have brought to the notice of the public various projects for the *construction of railroads* from various points on the western frontiers of the States to different points on the Pacific, and the prospect that one or more such railroads may eventually be constructed, renders it peculiarly proper that all hostile Indian tribes or bands along such routes be *permanently pacified*. (Emphasis added).[13]

Enter into Peace Treaties

In 1851, Commissioner Lea and Agent Fitzpatrick had met with more than ten thousand Indians from the Lakota, Cheyenne, Arapaho, Crow, Mandan, Sahnish, Assiniboine, and Gros Ventres (Hidatsa) Nations to negotiate a Peace Treaty. It *was* intended to delineate the boundaries between the tribes, who would agree to respect these boundaries and maintain peace. *In exchange for fifty thousand dollars a year in goods for fifty years*, the signatory Nations would (1) allow the U.S. to construct roads and military posts through their country; (2) maintain peace amongst themselves; (3) abstain from all depredations upon the whites passing through the country; (4) make restitution for any damages or loss that a white man would sustain by the acts of the Indians; and (5) settle up all former complaints on the part of the Indians for the destruction of their buffalo, timber, grass, &c., caused by the passing of the whites through their country, in exchange for gifts presented to them. In return, the U.S. would protect the Indians against the depredations of whites. *"This treaty was ratified by the Senate, with an amendment, changing the fifty years to ten years, which was not agreed to by certain of the tribes, parties thereto, and hence failed of final ratification. Appropriations have been made by Congress, however, in accordance with its stipulations."* (Emphasis added).[14]

In 1851, Superintendent D. D. Mitchell reported to Commissioner Lea the value received for the *$50,000 for ten years* payable in goods:

> laying off of the country into geographical or rather national domains ... will take away a great cause of quarrel among themselves, and at the same time enable the Government to ascertain who are the depredators, should depredations hereafter be committed.[15]

This ***non-ratified document*** was wholly one-sided and entirely for the benefit of the U.S. (1) It was an effort to unilaterally 'pacify' the Indians. (2) It delineated tribal boundaries amongst the participating tribes which would make future negotiations over Indian lands easier, given the resolution of this matter. (3) It allowed for the construction of roads and military posts, through an incredibly vast Indian country. (4) It set the compensation for the destruction of the buffalo, timber and grass in Indian country. The demise of the buffalo alone is considered one of the most adverse capital devaluations to a people to have occurred on this continent. It is uncertain how much of the consideration under this "peace treaty" was allocated for that loss alone. (5) It would enable the Government to ascertain the Indian depredators against whites should depredations thereafter be committed. Though it is not stated, the amount of the depredations would be deducted from amounts due Indians under treaties. It didn't matter whether the damages were occasioned by an Indian person or an Indian tribe – they were deductible as if a tribal action. Also, there was absolutely no accounting for verification or auditing of the claims asserted by colonial settlers for damages occasioned from Indian actions or for debts due traders, with accumulated usurious interest. (6) It was a de minimis amount, given the cost of lives in an outright war. The U.S. **knew** it couldn't win a war against the Indians, so it used other strategies to weaken them; it divided the Indians, pitting them, one against the other; it paid them to betray each other.

In 1868, Commissioner N.G. Taylor calculated the cost of exterminating the Indians as follows:

It would seem that the cost price of Indians slain in the Florida war, in the Sioux war, and in the late Cheyenne war, has been on a fair average about a million of dollars each; and if our Indian troubles are to be ended by exterminating the race, it is evident, *at the present rate of one Indian killed per month, that the achievement will be completed at the end of exactly 25,000 years; and if each dead Indian is to cost the same hereafter as heretofore, the precise sum total we will have to expend is $300,000,000,000 to complete the extermination. But besides the cost to the treasury, it is found by actual comparison, approximating closely the truth, that the slaying of every Indian costs us the lives of 25 whites, so that the extermination process must bring about the slaughter of 7,500,000 of our people.* Extermination by arms is simply an absurdity, unless we could get the Indians under the protection of the flag in large masses, surround and butcher them as at Sand Creek. But admitting, for the argument, they deserve extermination without mercy, and that we might achieve the grand consummation, it seems to me that the glory of the result would bear no proportion to the fearful sum of the cost. (Emphasis added).[16]

While the "Fort Laramie Treaty" bound the U.S. to protect the Indians against the depredations of whites, the U.S. failed, repeatedly, to do so. Year after year, the Commissioners of Indian Affairs informed the Secretary of the Interior and through him the President, in their annual written reports, of the depredations committed by whites against Indians. In 1856, Commissioner Manypenny candidly recounted these abuses in his Annual Report:

It cannot be disguised that a portion of the white population of the Pacific Territories, entertain feelings deeply hostile to the Indian tribes of that region, and are anxious for the extermination of the race. The existing laws for the protection of the persons and property of the Indian wards of the government are sadly defective. ... Trespasses and depredations of every conceivable kind have been committed on the Indians. They have been personally maltreated, their property stolen, their timber destroyed, their possessions encroached upon, and divers other wrongs and injuries done them.[17]

Extinguish Indian Title

The stimulus behind extinguishing Indian title began, in March 1853, with an act of Congress declaring "[t]hat the President of the United States be, and he hereby is, authorized, immediately after the passage of this act, to enter into negotiation with the Indian tribes west of the States of Missouri and Iowa for the purpose of extinguishing the title of said Indians in whole or in part to said lands."[18]

In 1853, Secretary McClelland authorized Commissioner Manypenny to enter into negotiations with tribes, for the extinguishment of their title to their lands:

> Should you deem it expedient and proper, however, to enter into any negotiations with the tribes in question, or either of them, for the extinguishment of their title to the lands now claimed by them, or for securing their assent to their settlement by citizens of the United States, you are fully authorized, in the exercise of a sound discretion, aided by your experience in the management of our Indian relations, to do so.[19]

DOI Rallies for Extinguishing Indian Title in Montana

In 1868, the Indians' trustee, Commissioner N. G. Taylor, advised Secretary Browning, in a common refrain, that it would *benefit Indians* and Montana citizens to:

> extinguish the Indian title to the lands in Montana claimed by some of the tribes, and of the location of all the Indians upon suitable reservations. … The Blackfeet and Crow nations claim much the larger portion of the Territory, and there can be no question but that *it would be for their interest, as well as for the benefit of the citizens of Montana, to yield their title* and be restricted to tracts of country of much less extent yet sufficient for their need. (Emphasis added).[20]

Part 5: "There's Gold in Them Thar Hills"[21]

Grasshopper Creek

In Montana, in July 1862, a prospector named John White and his partner discovered gold at Grasshopper Creek. Panning in the river, they found flecks of gold in a slurry of sediment. "There's Gold in Them Thar Hills" wasn't a secret for long, as the prospectors were required to file notice of their mining claims in the General Land Office District Office.

The Montana Gold Rush was on. Prospectors flooded the Oregon Trail. These miners had small placer operations—mining methods that used water to separate the gold from surrounding sediment. It required simple equipment—a gold pan, pick, shovel, and a water source. Other placer miners added items such as a rocker, which two people operated to sift the gold from the gravel. It was hard manual labor.

Merchants came out, with their families, to "mine the miners." They made their fortunes selling picks, shovels and supplies. The wagon trains headed to Montana numbered over 100 wagons per group. Their leaders were western legends, such as Jim Bridger. Some of them would deviate off the Oregon Trail, trying to find a faster way to the gold fields, only to be disappointed as they found the routes impassable. Reversing, having wasted precious time, at times getting lost, they would head back to the well-trod Oregon Trail.

Grasshopper Creek produced five million dollars in gold dust in its first year. The town of Bannack was founded nearby.

Alder Creek

In May 1863, two prospectors left Bannack to search for gold. Crow Indians accosted them, taking their equipment, and ordered them off their land. On their way back, the men camped along Alder Creek. Undeterred, they panned anyway, discovering gold. Within a few months, hordes flocked to the area around Virginia City.

Last Chance Gulch

On July 14, 1864, a group known as the Four Georgians struck gold at Last Chance Gulch. *Their Last Chance produced nineteen million dollars in gold over the next four years.* The city of Helena grew up around the Gulch.

Bozeman Trail Cuts through Indian Country

In response to the influx of prospectors, explorers kept trying to find a shorter route to Montana's mining mecca. John Bozeman was one of them, who persisted for several years. He finally proved up a 535-mile shorter route in 1863 that would be named after him, the Bozeman Trail. It skirted north of the Bighorn Mountains, ending up in Virginia City. The only problem was that it went straight through Indian country. Desperate prospectors and settlers were willing to take the risk and traveled at night.

Renegades and Thieves

The tremendous wave of people brought on by Montana's gold rushes created a need for law and order. The gold fields were havens for the lawless. Miners' courts lacked the authority, to deal with the violent crime prevailing in the mining districts. Henry Plummer, the sheriff of the Bannack District, led a gang, himself, suspected of robbing gold shipments and killing miners for their gold. In 1863, President Lincoln sent Sidney Edgerton, lawyer and judge, to present-day Montana to become Chief Justice.

Montana Territory Created

Chief Justice Edgerton and businesses and settlers pressed for creating the Montana Territory. On May 26, 1864, Congress agreed. President Lincoln appointed Edgerton as the first Territorial Governor.

Governor's Conflict of Interest

In 1864, Territorial Governor Edgerton expressed the prevailing sentiment regarding Indians:

> "I trust that the Government will, at an early day, take steps for the extinguishment of the Indian title in this territory, in order that our lands may be brought into market."[22]

His statement evidences the conflict of interest he would have as Territorial Governor and ex officio Superintendent of Indian Affairs. His lack of attention to his duties as Superintendent of Indian Affairs was blatant, as reported by the Commissioners of Indian Affairs in 1865 and 1866 in their Annual Reports to the Secretary. Commissioner Dole singled out individuals by name, and he included Edgerton in his remarks describing Montana conditions:

> No annual report from this superintendent has been received. The governor, and ex-officio superintendent, Ho. Sidney Edgerton, has been absent from the Territory a considerable portion of the time, and the general interests of the service have been in the hands of General Meagher, secretary and acting governor, who, at last accounts was about to leave the capital of the Territory to visit the Flathead agency.[23]

Montana Militia

General Meagher tended to have an over-wrought personality and an unfounded fear of Indians. On April 24, 1867, yielding to the false-founded alarms of the settlers regarding Indians, he summoned six hundred volunteers for three months' service in the Gallatin Valley and on the Yellowstone River:

> ... it is calculated that there were not more than eighty men at the end of April. During May there were probably 150, and from that time until the middle of July the number probably was about 250.[24]

Former Agent A. H. Chapman for Montana decried Meagher's actions:

> Acting Governor Meagher's Indian war in Montana is the biggest humbug of the age, got up to advance his political interest, and to enable a lot of bummers who surround and hang on to him to make a big raid on the United States treasury.... Acting Governor Meagher's Indian war in Montana, told those under his command in a general order, that they shall have all the property they capture, such as robes, horses, &c., it would be strange indeed if they did not create unnecessary trouble with the Indians.[25]

Frontier Forts

The U.S. responded to the fear of western settlers, and on their behalf, established Fort Ellis (1867), Fort Keogh (1876) and Fort Custer (1877) and posted soldiers, to protect them from real and imagined Indian threats. Unfortunately, the military presence in this region heightened Indian fears for survival of their peoples and retention of their lands.

Miners' Demand for Timber

The gold mining ushered in a greater demand for lumber. Miners needed everything from sluice boxes, to firewood, to cabins, to stores. Wagons, bridges and other transportation infrastructure required wood. Lack of access to proper tools forced many loggers to improvise tools for logging.

The first commercial lumbering commenced in Montana in the mid-1800s. A hand-powered saw pit built at St. Mary's Mission in 1845 provides an idea of the lack of technology in the start-up period. After the founding of Virginia City, dozens of small steam or water-powered lumber mills were soon operating. They were labor intensive and only produced small quantities of lumber.

Clamor for Railroads

Miners, loggers, merchants, farmers and cattlemen arriving in waves in Montana in the 1860s, clamored for railroads. Territorial legislatures did whatever they could to attract them.

Montana considered railroads vital to its growth. They could carry heavy freight long distances, quickly and inexpensively. Travel by horse-drawn wagons was expensive and time-consuming. By stagecoach, it took about 1 hour to travel 6 miles. The exploitation of the state's gold, copper, iron ore, coal and timber was dependent on cheap and reliable transport, which meant constructing railroads. The U.S. wanted its cut of Montana's extractive resources that would be developed and sold on a wider market, if there were more transcontinental routes across the country. It took prompt action, subrogating Indians' rights to the need for settlement.

Montana's Railroads, A Greater Good

Montana would end up having four railroads. They served as a precursor to exploiting the state's extractive resources. They would connect the state with global markets for copper and timber. They would need to cross Indian lands, which required a national determination as to the 'condemnation' of these lands for what was considered a greater good.

1881: The Utah and Northern connects Butte to the America's first transcontinental railroad, the Union Pacific, at Corinne, Utah.
1883: The Northern Pacific Railroad completes its transcontinental line.
1887: The Great Northern Railway builds across northern Montana, reaching Seattle in 1893.
1907: The Chicago, Milwaukee, St. Paul and Pacific (the Milwaukee Road) enters southeast Montana, completing its transcontinental line in 1909 linking Chicago with Tacoma and Seattle.

Part 6: The Iron Horse

Northern Pacific Railroad Land Grant

On July 2, 1864, Congress passed legislation for a northern transcontinental railroad from Lake Superior to the Pacific Ocean.[26] Montana got its wish; it would traverse the Montana Territory. The right of way across the public domain was granted to the Northern Pacific Railroad Company. Over 2,000 miles of track needed to be installed. Of critical importance, the Act required the U.S. to extinguish Indian title impeding the railroad.

> The United States shall extinguish, as rapidly as may be consistent with public policy and the welfare of the said Indians, the Indian titles to all lands falling under the operation of this act, and acquired in the donation to the [road] named in this bill.²⁷

The Northern Pacific would receive 14,740,000 acres or sixteen per cent of the total land area of Montana.

Subjugate Lawless Indians

William Welsh, the former chairman of the Board of Indian Commissioners, supported the construction of the Northern Pacific Railroad stating in 1872 that it would "bring the lawless Indians of the North into subjection, and thus aid effectively the religious bodies charged with bringing Christian civilization."²⁸

Northern Pacific Railroad Cuts through Indian Lands

To get to Montana, the Northern Pacific Railroad had to cross the lands of the Mandan, Hidatsa and Sahnish (Arikara) ("MHA") Tribes in North Dakota. The DOI extinguished their title for the land for the right-of-way.

The MHA Tribes were parties to the 1851 Fort Laramie Treaty, guaranteeing them 13 million acres of land. In 1864, Chief White Shield reported that "We, the Arikara, have been driven from our country on the other side of the Missouri River by the Sioux."²⁹ They also complained of their dwindling wood supply due to whites cutting timber and selling it to passing steamboats. Before taking action to protect the MHA Tribes, the Secretary of War instigated an investigation of these complaints.

The Navajos, fellow Indians in the southwest, had been warned of the consequences of complaining to the federal government. Many times, on the verge of starvation, they received $5,000 in appropriations for 16,000-17,000 Navajoes, amounting to twenty-five cents per capita. Other tribes, in the same region, received $60 per capita or more. Their federal agent counseled them to "behave better than ever," due to the covetous eyes of those who would take any opportunity to divest them of their lands.

> "But in the face of these shameful facts, these Indians still listen to their agent, when I tell them *they must behave better than ever before, for evidently the plotters and the large majority of the whites and Mexicans residing in the Territories of New Mexico and Arizona desire their 6,000,000 acres of reserved lands*." (Emphasis added).³⁰

The Secretary of War's investigation of the MHA Tribes' complaints would have horrific consequences for the MHA Tribes. In six months, the Indians would lose 4,686,612 acres.

Uncertain if a reservation had been established for the Mandan-Hidatsa-Arikara Tribes, Major General Winfield S. Hancock, commanding Department of Dakota, instructed Captain Wainwright, assigned to Fort Stevenson, "to examine the country about Berthold and to recommend what portion should be set off for them." After examining the land in the area, Captain Wainwright met with the chiefs and ***recommended that specific land which he designated be set aside as a reservation***. (Emphasis added). His September 25, 1869, recommendation was accepted by Major General Winfield S. Hancock; the assistant adjutant-general of the Military Division of the Missouri; and the Adjutant General.

While Captain Wainwright did not have the authority to create a reservation, his recommendation was passed on to his chain of command and then reviewed and approved by Commissioner of Indian Affairs Ely S. Parker. Com'r Parker stated the following in regard to the Treaty of Fort Laramie and recommendation for a MHA reservation:

> "the boundaries of a reservation were *identified* by the Treaty of Fort Laramie, and that other treaties have followed the same outlines of territory." He then goes on to state: *"There are no treaty stipulations with these Indians relative to a reservation for them which have been ratified."* He then *"recommends that an order of the Executive may be invoked, directing the setting apart of a reservation for said Indians as proposed [by Captain Wainwright]"*. (Emphasis added).[31]

MHA Reservation Established by Executive Order

On April 12, 1870, ***President Grant concurred with the Secretary*** and responded to him accordingly:

> Let the lands indicated in the accompanying diagram be set apart as *a reservation* for the Arickaree, Gros Ventre, and Mandan Indians, as recommended in the letter of Secretary of the Interior of the 12th instant. (Emphasis added).[32]

President Grant's 1870 Executive Order confined the Mandan, Hidatsa and Arikara (Sahnish) Tribes to the south side of the Missouri, except for a tiny strip north of the river which included the already existing Indian village of Berthold. ***The Executive Order confiscated 4,686,612 acres*** of the 13 million acres identified as their land under the Fort Laramie Treaty, leaving them 8,313,386 acres.[33]

It wasn't until 1930 that the DOI conceded, when sued by the MHA Tribes, that they were acting upon erroneous information when they said they had no prior reservation. The Court of Claims upheld the Fort Laramie Treaty of 1851 and the 13 million acres allotted under that Treaty to the MHA Tribes.[34] It compensated the Tribes, *not with the return of the land taken*, but with money. *It valued the acreage taken at 50 cents per acre.*

MHA Forced Cession for Northern Pacific Right-of-Way (ROW)

On July 13, 1880, the MHA Tribes ceded 1,674,131 acres for the Northern Pacific Railroad right-of-way:

> *The construction of the Northern Pacific Railroad ... ran through the Indians' reservation as fixed by the Fort Laramie treaty of 1851. Section 2 of the land grant provided for the extinguishment of Indian titles.* .... In July, 1879, the Commissioner of Indian Affairs recommended the withdrawal from the reservation of a large acreage of lands, ceding the Indians lieu lands on the north bank of the Missouri River. On July 13, 1880, by Executive order the recommendations of the commissioner were made effective. (Emphasis added).[35]

Crow Tribe Forced Cession for Northern Pacific ROW

On July 10, 1882, the Crow Tribe ceded 5,084 acres for the Northern Pacific Railroad right-of-way for $25,000, to be spent at the discretion of the Secretary.[36]

Asst. AG McCammon to Negotiate Northern Pacific ROW

Commissioner Hiram Price delegated the task of negotiation for the Northern Pacific Railroad Right-of-Ways with other tribes to Assistant Attorney-General McCammon.

> You will advise the Indians to agree upon a fair and reasonable compensation to be paid by the Government for the quantity of land required by the railroad company, impressing upon them the opinion held by the Department that the *construction of the road will advance their welfare, be beneficial to the Indian service, and subserve a general public interest* in the vicinity through which it will pass. (Emphasis added).[37]

Tribes Bullied by Asst. AG McCammon

Bullied by Assistant Attorney-General McCammon, the Confederated Tribes of the Flathead, Kootenay, and Upper Pend d'Oreille Indians ceded 1,430 acres for $11 an acre. Maj. William H. Jordan, Third Infantry, was present during the negotiations.

> That for the consideration hereinafter mentioned, said confederated tribes of Flathead, Kootenay, and Upper Pend d'Oreille Indians do hereby surrender and relinquish to the United States all the right, title, and interest which they now have under and by virtue of the aforesaid treaty of July sixteenth, eighteen hundred and fifty-five, in and to all that part of the Jocko (or Flathead) reservation situated in the Territory of Montana ...[38]

Even though Chief Michelle and others told McCammon that their previous Treaties did not agree to railroads, but to roads, McCammon insisted a road and railroad were the same thing. Also, he threatened them that the "Great Father" would think they were not "good Indians" if they didn't agree to cede their lands.

> Chief Michelle stated: "When we made the treaty we did not say railroads could pass through our country, only common roads."[39]

Note: Previous Treaties entered into by the Tribes agreed to the construction of *roads*. In that treaty you and your fathers agreed "if necessary for the public convenience *roads* may be run through the said reservation." By another treaty, made the same year ... which treaty was signed by the Flathead Nation and other Indians, it was provided that "for the purpose of establishing traveling thoroughfares through the country the aforesaid nations and tribes do hereby consent and agree that the United States, may ... *construct roads* of every description, establish lines of telegraph," &c. (Emphasis added).[40]

McCammon argued with Chief Michelle:

> *Another kind of road is a railroad*. ... The Great Father will be sorry when he hears that the Indians do not believe in his good faith. Shall I go back and say to the Great Father that these Indians do not believe he is treating them right if He has but one object, and that is your good; and if I go back without your having named a price for the lands, *he will say they are not the good Indians and faithful friends I thought*. (Emphasis added).[41]

Congress Starves Montana Indians

At the same time the U.S. was negotiating with the Montana Indians to cede their lands for the Northern Pacific Railroad, Congress reduced the appropriations for their subsistence—for their food. It is uncertain why they took this action.

The reduction in the appropriations for the Blackfeet, Blood, and Piegan Indians, and the Indians at Fort Peck and Fort Belknap Agencies, in 1883, caused a great deal of suffering. ***Children starved to death. Six to seven hundred Indians died.*** (Emphasis added).[42]

On July 26, 1883, the Indian inspector at the Blackfeet Agency reported to the Commissioner:

> There can be no doubt but many of the young children died from lack of food during last winter and spring. Never before have I been called upon to listen in an Indian council to such tales of suffering. *I cannot believe that Congress was fully aware of the change in the surroundings of these Indians when the annual appropriation was diminished.* (Emphasis added).[43]

On August 14, 1883, the Indian inspector at the Fort Peck Agency reported to the Commissioner that the Indians "returned hungry from a hunt which was unsuccessful. It will require at least 1,000,000 pounds of beef to keep them from suffering."[44]

On August 21, 1883, the Fort Belknap Agent reported to the Commissioner of the Gros Ventres and Assinaboines:

> Game on this reservation is practically exhausted. ... My Indians are already coming in every day complaining of hunger, but *I can feed them very little as the winter will soon be here when they must be fed or they will starve* and commit depredation. (Emphasis added).[45]

Striking Spike

On September 8, 1883, Northern Pacific celebrated completing its route to Montana. Four trains carried dignitaries to Gold Creek, including Former United States President and Civil War Hero, Ulysses S. Grant; Secretary of the Interior Henry M. Teller; Attorney General B.H. Brewster; Carl Schurz, Former Secretary of the Interior; the Governors of all the States and Territories through which the Railroad ran; ex-Secretary of State William Evarts; Captain John Mullan; former President of the Northern Pacific, Frederick Billings; the "Empire Builder," James J. Hill; Joseph Pulitzer, publisher of the New York World and various Crow Indians.

A local magazine chronicled what the railroad meant to Montana:

> The driving of the Golden Spike ... will mark the completion of the conquest of thousands and thousands of square miles of desert and wilderness. ***An empire has been taken from barbarism, from savages and wild beasts, and added to the domain of civilization***. There is no civilizer like the railway; it brings the market nearer ... to the great centers of commerce, of manufacture, of social and literary activity. ... The scream of the locomotive is the triumphant shout of progress. The school house and the church, private wealth and public prosperity, all the intellectual and moral forces that educate and refine and bless mankind, follow in the track of the plodding grader and the patient tracklayer. Without the railway, our present civilization would have been retarded two hundred years. (Emphasis added).[46]

In supporting why Helena should be the state capitol, the following pamphlet was printed:

> In proportion to population Helena has more balls, parties, hops, routs, toots, soirees, receptions, musicales, drive whists, pink teas, conversaziones, high fives and low dresses, drinks more champagne, runs bigger bar bills, keeps later hours, dances longer, kicks higher and practices a larger number and greater variety of bows, scrapes, courtesies, obeisances, genuflections, salaams, salutes and squirms than any other city East or West.[47]

All of this celebration occurred while Montana's Indians starved to death, due to Congress' reduction in appropriations for food.

The Northern Pacific built its branch lines directly to the mines and various smelters. The northern cross-country route was known as the Hi-Line, since it was the northernmost transcontinental route in the U.S. Branch lines would connect to other cities. Huge markets were opening up.

Part 7: Indians Fight Invasion

Settlers Killing Bison, Squatting on Indian Lands

In 1874, Montana Indian Agent, Wm. A. Alderson, warned that Indian hostilities would continue due to the "unrestrained lawlessness of white men in killing their game, destroying and appropriating their timber, and permanently residing on their reservations without their consent":

Indians should also be protected on their reservations in all their rights and privileges, especially against the unrestrained lawlessness of white men in killing their game, destroying and appropriating their timber, and permanently residing on their reservations without their consent. These are sources of almost endless annoyances and provocations, which not unfrequently generate into open hostilities.[48]

Massacre of Piegan Indians

With more forays into Indian country in Montana by the military and white settlers, the Indians engaged in retaliatory strikes. In response, the U.S. Cavalry was ordered to attack the camp of Piegan warrior, Mountain Chief. On January 19, 1870, four cavalry companies under the command of Col. E.M. Baker set out from Fort Benton, Montana. They mistakenly attacked the camp of Heavy Runner, a longtime American ally. It was totally destroyed, and 173 Indians, most of whom were women, children, and men ill with smallpox, were massacred. The furor the Baker Massacre generated prevented the contemplated transfer of the Indian Bureau from the Department of the Interior to the War Department.

Indians Wage War against Railroads

Regardless of the Indians' warnings that they would wage war against any invasions to their lands, the Northern Pacific continued its railroad surveys. In 1871, a war party of Sioux, Northern Cheyenne, and Arapaho with 400 to 1,000 warriors found a survey party's camp and attacked. No fatalities were recorded.

Indian Agent Simmons met with Black Moon at Fort Peck where the leader stated the terms necessary to avoid war: the removal of whites from Sioux lands, abandonment of forts, and the redirection of the Northern Pacific Railroad.[49]

Aware of the consequences, railroad surveyors, under military escort, at first continued their Yellowstone survey. With the threat of Indian attacks, though, the surveyors moved north to the Musselshell River, an optional route for the railroad route. Skirmishes continued in the Indians' hunting grounds. In 1872, Spotted Eagle met with Colonel Stanley, commanding Fort Sully, to warn the Americans that the Sioux [Sans] Arcs would kill the builders and tear up the tracks of the Northern Pacific Railroad. The Railroad was driving off the buffalo and Spotted Eagle would fight, even knowing that he would be beaten.[50]

Part 8: Railroad Spurs

Utah Northern Railroad from Salt Lake to Idaho

The original 75 miles of the Utah Northern Railroad was intended to connect the Mormon communities in the Cache Valley in Idaho to Salt Lake. It was a 3-foot narrow gauge spur off the Union Pacific transcontinental railroad, built by the Mormons. Construction started on August 24, 1871, but was halted in May 1874 due to the financial Panic of 1873. The Utah Northern went bankrupt and was sold in foreclosure in 1878 to the Union Pacific Railroad.

Utah & Northern Railway to Butte, Copper Polestar

Industrialist Jay Gould transformed the bankrupt Utah Northern, changing the name to the Utah & Northern Railway, infusing the railroad with capital. He knew that transporting the copper from the mines near Butte would pay for the railroad. After three years of construction, they completed the rail to Butte, the largest copper producing city in the world. Butte, with its "Copper Kings" and population of 100,000, became the second largest city in the West, with more influence than Salt Lake City, Denver, Sacramento, Seattle, or Portland. Only San Francisco remained larger and more important. Butte, Montana was dubbed the 'Pittsburg of the West.'

Part 9: Montana Gets Third Railway

Great Northern Railway from St. Paul to Washington State

When tycoon, James J. Hill, nicknamed the "Empire Builder" decided to build his own northern 'transcontinental railroad' from St. Paul to the State of Washington, he was entering a saturated market. The Northern Pacific had the benefit of legislation which paid it in land. Hill would have to finance his own railway, under legislation passed in 1875,[51] granting *"the right of way through the public lands of the United States"* to any railroad company. Northern Pacific also had the benefit of the U.S.' obligation to extinguish any Indian title along the route. Hill would have to secure the right to cross the reservations on his route on his own.

Hill planned to break Northern Pacific's hold under an 1880 pooling agreement with Montana Central Railroad, under which they charged exorbitant freight rates.[52] He would generate business by charging lower rates.

In 1884, Hill visited Great Falls, Montana, to assess its potential for coal and hydroelectric development to fuel his railway. In 1886, his agent paid $13,000 for 1,300 acres of coal land. It would enable his exploitation of the huge Sand Coulee coal field.

His steam generating plant [at the mine was] large enough to contain four smoke stacks. Its black rock helped to power locomotives over the Rocky Mountains to the west coast and to smelt and refine Anaconda Copper Mining Company ore in Anaconda and Great Falls, Montana.[53]

The Minnesota Club

Hill was a charter member of the influential Minnesota Club. The James Jerome Hill Room was the main lounge. Through the Club, he would use his contacts to connect with the President, the Secretary of the Interior and Congress.

General Henry Hastings Sibley, Territorial Delegate and thereafter Governor, Director of the First National Bank of St. Paul, and Indian trader, served as President of the Minnesota Club for two decades. An advisor to the Treaty Commission which secured the 1851 Sioux Treaties ceding 35 million acres for white settlement, he was known for creating the military commission which sentenced 307 Sioux men to death. He was the only Minnesota Club member eulogized at his death, with his portrait draped in black for thirty days.

Frank B. Kellogg, Nobel Peace Prize winner, former U.S. Secretary of State, former Senator, with the law firm of Briggs & Morton was featured in The Law Room.

Given Minnesota's Indian history, several members of the Club played an active role in this arena. Henry Mower Rice was an Indian trader, legislator, U.S. Senator and public official. Charles E. Flandrau was an Indian agent, attorney, author, defender in the New Ulm Sioux Uprising in 1862, and justice on the Minnesota Supreme Court.

The Club's standing made an appropriate site for a reception for President Cleveland in 1887.[55]

Hill's Team

From his corporate perch, Hill had access to the most powerful men in the country. He knew, as if running a political bid for office, he needed a home team in Montana and North Dakota, which connected seamlessly to the executive and Congressional milieu of Washington D.C. Montana, itself, was a strong pressure point. Home to the powerful and extremely wealthy Anaconda copper mining company, it pursued policies favorable to business.

Not unlike a general with his cavalry officers, Hill used his point men for intelligence reports, suggestions on tactics, and reactions to overall strategies. Hill provided the power of corporate investment and decision making, while the point men prepared the ground in Montana between 1884 and 1888, the critical years of the Manitoba's extension into the Territory.[54]

For his home team in Montana, Hill appointed [Major] Martin Maginnis, a Montana Territorial Delegate to Congress for his lead. Rep. Maginnis' **numerous and varied** accomplishments listed in Progressive Men of the State of Montana, provided the contacts Hill needed. Major Maginnis was described as a "factor of eminent usefulness in the development of Montana from the early pioneer days ... who has been identified with those productive activities which have advanced the progress and prosperity of the country, who has honorably held positions of high public trust: ..."

"He successfully abolished the Indian reservations which then covered the large portion of the territory." He opened former Flathead Indian Nation lands in the Bitterroot Valley to white settlement; reduced several Crow Indian Nation holdings, including those in the Gallatin Valley; and secured passage of the 1874 Act severing the Blackfeet Indian Nation claim to lands south of the Marias River.

"He procured appropriations from congress and caused to be established and built for the protection of the frontier these army posts: Fort Logan, Fort Keogh, Fort Custer, Fort Maginnis, Fort Assinnaboine and Fort Missoula, the assay office at Helena, and the Unites States penitentiary at Deer Lodge..."

"He procured appropriations for the payment of Indian depredation claims and the Montana militia claims ... [It is important to continually reiterate that there was no accounting for verification or auditing of the claims by the DOI which were asserted by colonial settlers for damages occasioned from Indian actions or debts due traders, with accumulated usurious interest.]

"He was active in the passage of land and timber laws for the benefit of the settlers."

He carried through Congress passage of the "general right of way for railways across the public lands."

He secured a "grant of lands for the university..."

He was intimately involved in Montana's admission to statehood.[55]

Thus, Major Maginnis possessed the necessary expertise pertaining to Indian land reduction and railways, along with the ability to push legislation through Congress.

As part of his financial team, Hill selected Charles A. Broadwater, President of the Montana National Bank of Helena. Broadwater's wealth came from contracts to build and supply military posts in Montana. On a national level, the House of Morgan and J. P. Morgan committed their financial backing to Hill's undertaking.

Rep. Nelson, from Minnesota, would be the lead as stratagem director for Hill's Indian removal and railroad right-of-way bills. Nelson had secured passage of the Indian allotment act pertaining to Minnesota.

More Political Contacts

Rep. Maginnis brought Rep. William Scott, Pennsylvania, onboard as a "personal favor to me and to our friends, for which I will be glad any time to reciprocate." Scott, an extremely wealthy businessman, engaged in shipping, coal mining, iron manufacturing, banking, and railroad construction through various partnerships and the firm of W. L. Scott & Co. He served as president of a number of railroad companies, including the New York, Pennsylvania, and Norfolk Railroad and the Erie and Pittsburgh Railroad. Of Rep. Scott, it was said: "It was his lot to have the fullest confidence and personal friendship of the President and Speaker of the House." The President and Governor were the head pallbearers at his funeral.[56]

Should he need them, Hill had friends of the President aligned with him: William F. Vilas, former Secretary of the Interior, later appointed by President Cleveland as the Postmaster General, and thereafter, elected as a Senator; and William E. Smith, former Assistant Secretary of the Treasury and Governor of Wisconsin, a partner in the wholesale grocery business with Smith, Roundy & Co.[57]

Part 10: Hill's Plan to Get Across Indian Reservations

Subpart A: Remove, Cede, ROW Three-Prong Strategy

Hill pursued a simultaneous three-prong strategy to secure the land needed for his railway across the Dakota and Montana Indian lands. Legally, Indian reservations were not public lands and railroads needed special permission from the federal government in order to secure right-of-way easements. This contrasted with easements across public lands which had been assured by the General Railroad Right of Way Act in 1875.

Hill's three-prong strategy made his lobbying very confusing as he was (1) advocating removal while (2) trying to get Rep. Maginnis on the Northwest Commission which was pursuing a strategy of large cessions; and (3) introducing right-of-way legislation. We will cover each of these prongs which pursue timelines that often overlap. Hill used his political contacts in pursuing each of these game plans. One thing is crystal clear: Hill was up to his neck in trying to get across Fort Berthold Reservation in North Dakota and the reservations in Montana.

First, he would advocate for the removal of the Fort Berthold Indian Nation from North Dakota to the Indian Territory in present-day Oklahoma; he would also advocate for the removal of the Blackfeet Indian Nation from the lands he needed for his railroad.

Second, he would seek a cession of lands from the Indian Nations.

Third, he would seek a right-of-way across the Reservations.

Subpart B: Urge MHA Indian Nations to Move to Indian Territory

The removal of Indian Nations was not unheard of and, in fact, was a favored DOI position. Removal reduced federal costs and brought Indians under tighter federal control. Of prime benefit, it opened the previous Indian lands to white settlement under the Homestead Act.

In 1874, the U.S. *unilaterally* determined that it wanted several tribes removed to the Indian Territory, including the MHA Tribes on Fort Berthold Reservation. The Commissioner of Indian Affairs, Edward P. Smith, urged the MHA to leave Fort Berthold, with its unproductive soil, unfriendly climate, scant supply of wood, poor water, high winds, dust, drought, frost, flood, grasshoppers, and the Sioux. That year a delegation from the Three Tribes went to the Indian Territory (Oklahoma) to investigate the possibilities of moving to that area. Although pleased with the country, they refused, fearing it would be too warm, dreading the long journey, and, most of all, losing their attachment to the place of their birth and homes of their dead.[58]

Remove Tribes Due to Depredations

If federal action is being sought, it is important to give them all the ammunition and not expect them to do much. Hill did just that. In correspondence between March and April 1886, he and Rep. Maginnis laid out the reasoning for removal of the northern tribes:

He contended that United States reservations located near the Canadian border protected renegades and outlaws from both sides of the boundary. Such reservations also encouraged Indian horse theft and other unnamed depredations. Hill cited Canadian complaints of Indian raids and mischief—activities allegedly initiating from bordering reservations in Minnesota (probably the Red Lake Reservation) and the Turtle Mountain Reservation in Dakota Territory. Hill also sent to the Interior Department maps he had secured from the Canadian Government which showed that *every Canadian reservation was located away from the international border*. (Emphasis added).[59]

Hill's Canadian information demonstrates the lengths he went to secure evidence for his position.

> Maginnis, Martin April 6, 1886, Washington, D.C. I have just received from Canadian Govt. their latest map showing the location of their Indian Reservations every one of which are located away from the international boundary line and at points where they can be easily reached by rail. As long as our Government locates the reservations on the international boundary line they will feel compelled to feed Canadian Inds. and will have trouble from renegades and outlaws from both sides. It is more than surprising that the Government has not seen this sooner. Of course the desiring men among the Indian traders have an interest in avoiding the restrictions of the law, and the Indians are advised by them to ask for locations on the boundary. I will soon have a historic statement prepared by the Rev. E.D. Neill to send you.[60]

A letter from James J. Hill to George S. Engle, March 19, 1886, referenced the Canadian Indians location in Canada. Engle was the Attorney General for the Dakota Territory in 1866.

> March 19,1886 Hill to George. S. Engle, Washington, D.C. It was late Friday night when I returned to the hotel and I left early Saturday morning without being able to see you. The President assured me that Sparks' order would be revoked at once, and seemed annoyed that it had not already been done. The Turtle Mountain survey will, I think, speedily follow. I am having prepared for the Department of the Interior some valuable information, with maps showing the location of the Canadian Indians north of the Boundary, and also some information in regard to the Red Lake Treaty of 1863 under which the Chippewas claimed Turtle Mountain. The facts are that this land was at the time occupied by the Sioux and was never Chippewa land in any sense.[61]

The Sparks order stipulated that public timber removed from mineral lands was for individual use and prohibited from sale. It also prohibited the timber's use for smeltering purposes. *Hill's note evidences his direct Presidential contact and influence. The order was withdrawn and Secretary Lamar saved face by stating he didn't know it had been issued.*

Hill wasn't the only one opposed to Sparks' aggressive policies. When Sparks begin indicting major logging companies for illegally cutting timber, it generated a vociferous response. Northern Pacific Vice President Thomas F. Oakes sent Territorial Governor Samuel T. Hauser a *threatening letter*:

> Read this over carefully and let me know if you intend to take this position in reference to our timber interests. If we have no rights in this property you will respect, I shall at once with draw all of our deposits from your bank, put the Wickes Branch [a twenty mile Northern Pacific branch line which served Hauser's mines and smelters near Helena] on a strictly local basis and in *every other respect make things so hot for you, you will think the devil is after you*. The Northern Pacific Company has not spent $70,000,000 to be bull dozed by you or any body else. The Northern Pacific Company has the right to demand of you the fullest support in every reasonable effort to protect its interests. *It has never asked anything of you thus far but has done a great deal for you and your interests thus far with very little return*. (Emphasis added).[62]

On September 17, 1895, Hill wrote to banker W. G. Conrad (who also had holdings in real estate, ranching and mining) continuing his argument against Indian reservations being located near the International Boundary with Canada. Conrad was a Montana banker.

> Hill to W. G. Conrad, Great Falls Unfortunate location of any Indians on a reservation adjoining the International Boundary, affording opportunity for renegades from one side ... to find a home on the other side... Better to keep Indians on small reservations where the agent can travel about and take the census in one or two days.[63]

The presence of "renegades and outlaws" was consistently asserted by Indian Agents on reservations across the country. It reflected poorly on the DOI's oversight and management. Also, the fact that it could not police its areas of responsibility was a constant complaint from the public and Congress.

Reverend E.D. Neill's curriculum vitae would be impressive to Hill's inner circle.

He was a Presbyterian minister who founded multiple churches in Minnesota. He was also state superintendent of education and chancellor of the University of Minnesota from 1858–1861. He then served as a chaplain of the First Minnesota Volunteer Infantry during the Civil War. Later, he would become the private secretary to Presidents Abraham Lincoln and Andrew Johnson. Neill served as president of Macalester College in St. Paul, Minnesota, from 1873–1874, and taught history and literature.[64]

Neill's writings on Indians though did not fit a ministerial image. They were hate-filled diatribes.

> In his "History of Freeborn County," Neill wrote that, "The white race ... came in contact with a race of savages with many of the traits peculiar to a common humanity, yet, with these, exhibiting all, or nearly all, the vices of the most barbarous savage races ... The inferior race must either recede before the superior, or sink into the common mass, and, like the raindrops falling upon the bosom of the ocean, lose all traces of distinction." On the brief Minnesota Sioux War in his 1883 book, "The History of Minnesota: From the Earliest French Explorations to the Present Time" ... Neill wrote that "the fiends of hell could not invent more fearful atrocities than were perpetrated by the savages upon their victims. The bullet, the tomahawk and the scalping-knife spared neither age nor sex, the only prisoners taken being the young and comely women, to minister to the brutal lusts of their captors, and a few children."[65]

Blackfeet Will Be Tough to Move

Hill's point man, Rep. Maginnis expressed which tribes he thought would be willing to move. He opined that even though the Blackfeet belonged in Canada, it would be difficult to get them to move.

> Rep. Maginnis stated: I have no doubt that the Indians at the Fort Peck Agency, (sic) would be more than willing to rejoin their own nation the Sioux at one of the Sioux reservations. They were originally gathered at Fort Peck and cut off from the rest of their people, by parties who were interested in creating new agencies, and new fields for Government expenditure, if not for Government plunder.

> The Assinaboines (sic) and Gros Ventres have natural affiliations with the Crow tribe and this tribe has ample room for them even if their reservation is reduced as it should be.

The Blackfeet will be more difficult to deal with. All their blood and kindred are in British America, where they really belong themselves, and they have been in antagonism to most of the Indians on our side of the line.[66]

Subpart C: Private Meeting with DOI and Congress

In March or April 1886, Hill met with the leading Senate and House Indian Affairs Committee members and the Indian Commissioner, J.D.C. Atkins, for four hours, "to discuss the northern Montana Indian situation."[67]

On June 1, 1886, *Hill ordered Rep. Maginnis to meet secretly with Indian Commissioner Atkins and find the best way to secure a right-of-way.*[68]

Subpart D: Hill Lobbies for Indian Land Cessions

As early as 1881, Hill contacted Senator S.J.R McMillan, who later served as a Minnesota Supreme Court Chief Justice:

> Senator S.J.R McMillan, U.S. Senator Re need for extinguishment of Indian title to land in some counties in northern part of Dakota Territory. Settlers are already going onto these lands.[69]

Reducing reservation lands by a cession from the Indians, surprisingly, was not unusual. An outright cession would mean money to the tribes for the ceded lands. The Commission appointed by the President, was negotiating with the several tribes of Sioux and Cheyenne Indians of the Upper Missouri, and any other tribes in that region to "accomplish some arrangement by which a permanent peace with the people of the United States and with each other may be secured."[70]

Hill considered any negotiations with the MHA Tribes or northern Montana tribes that might occur beneficial, given as most of the treaties the Northwest Commission was negotiating provided for large cessions and railroad right-of-ways. Dennis Smith notes that Rep. Maginnis drafted an amendment to the 1866 Appropriations Act to add the MHA Tribes and northern Montana tribes to the Northwest Commission's agenda.[71]

The Appropriation Act of May 15, 1866 (24. Stat. 29, 44) did add the MHA and Montana Tribes to the Northwest Commission's schedule:

> To enable the Secretary of the Interior to negotiate with the several tribes and bands of Chippewa Indians ... and also to enable said Secretary to negotiate with the various bands or tribes of Indians in northern Montana and at Fort Berthold, in Dakota, for a reduction of their respective reservations, or for removal therefrom to other reservations...[72]

On April 20, 1886, Rep. Maginnis wrote to Hill as follows:

> Martin Maginnis to Hill from Washington, D.C. *Re amendment to the Indian appropriation bill* which he encloses. "*You will see that the money is made available immediately on the passage of the bill*. Then the commission will be appointed. I also enclose you a letter of the Hon. Com. of Indian Affairs. You will see that it concurs in our views." (Emphasis added).[73]

To assure control of the Northwest Commission appointed to negotiate with the North Dakota and Montana tribes, Rep. Maginnis' friends petitioned President Cleveland to nominate Maginnis as a commissioner. Even though Rep. Maginnis wasn't appointed as a Commissioner, the Northwest Commission negotiated and entered into agreements with the Tribes of interest. *In order to be effective, though, they required Congressional ratification*.[74]

> May 10, 1886 Hill to Samuel Thorne The Hon Martin Maginnis has spent six weeks in Washington ... & has succeeded in getting a bill reported to which there is, I understand, no opposition, providing for the removal to existing reservations of the Piegan and Blackfeet Indian and for their support; also, opening the territory lying between the Missouri River and the International boundary line in Montana including the Milk River valley, to settlement. The bill provides for a commission with authority to treat with the Indians, "*Asks Thorne and "our friend Smith Weed" to help by writing the president to appoint Maginnis,* who "represented Montana in Congress for thirteen years, and was the only democrat they could elect. He was the choice of his party for Governor," and the successful opponent; the present governor, has become increasingly unpopular since election." (Emphasis added).[75]

Smith Weed was a New York Congressional Representative involved in businesses including lumber, mines, and railroads. Thorne was President of the Pennsylvania Coal Company at one time. Besides the Central Trust, he was a trustee of the New York Life Insurance and Trust Company, and a director of the Chicago, Burlington, & Quincy Railroad Company, the Colorado and Southern Railway, the Great Northern Railway, the Sixth Avenue Railroad Company, the Northern Securities Company, the New York Dock Company, and the Bank of America.

Allegedly,

> Montana Delegate Martin Maginnis, who received much approbation from his fellow Montanans as a champion of their interests, would not be immune to the siren call of graft; in 1886, he received $3000 from railroad magnate James J. Hill to lobby President Grover Cleveland to grant the railway transit rights through land in Montana.[76]

This would seem suspect, as a bribe, given the minimal amount.

Subpart E: Hill Piggybacks on Northwest Commission's Land Cessions

MHA Agree to Cede 1,600,000 Acres

In what must have been a surprise to Hill, the Northwest Commission was successful in entering into an agreement with the MHA Tribes, on December 14, 1866, for the cession of over 1,600,000 acres of their Reservation for $800,000. Thereafter, in lockstep, it was (1) recommended by Indian Agent Abram. J. Gifford; (2) approved by Commissioner of Indian Affairs J.D.C. Atkins; (3) approved by Acting Secretary of the Interior Muldrow; and (4) forwarded by President Cleveland to Congress. It took only nine days to get the agreement to Congress for enactment.

Commissioner Atkins's January 8, 1887, letter to Secretary Muldrow, adamantly supported its passage:

> By the terms of the agreement the Indians in question *cede to the United States over 1,600,000 acres of their reservation for the sum of $800,000,* payable in ten yearly installments of $80,000 each, which sum is to be expended in the civilization and education of the Indians, and in establishing them in comfortable homes as an agricultural people. It also provides for the survey of their diminished reserve, and for the allotment of lands in severalty, and for the issue of patent therefor, with restrictions as to alienation. (Emphasis added).[77]

On January 11, 1887, in just three days, Secretary Muldrow forwarded his recommendation for approval and the agreement to President Cleveland. On January 17, 1887, President Cleveland transmitted the agreement to Congress:

> *The agreement, together with the recommendations of the Department, is presented for the action of Congress.* (Emphasis added).[78]

Congress took no action until 1890 when it approved the cession.

Blackfeet Agree to Cede 17,500,000 Acres

The President's transmittal of the Secretary of the Interior's recommendation in regard to the Blackfeet Nation stated:

> Briefly stated, the agreement concluded with the various bands or tribes occupying the Great Blackfeet Reservation, in northern Montana, provides for the cession to the United States of by far the greater part of that vast reservation ... the territory ceded to the United States under the agreement embraces an area of about 17,500,000 acres—more than three fifths of the entire reservation.[79]

The compensation agreed to be paid annually for ten years was as follows: Fort Peck Agency, $165,000 per year, Fort Belknap Agency $115,000 per year, and Blackfeet Agency $150,000 per year.

Northwest Tribes Agree to Cede Land

Agreements were also entered into with the Upper and Middle Bands of Spokane Indians; the Coeur d'Alene Indians; the Pend d'Oreilles or Calispel Indians; and the Indians upon the Jocko Reservation in Montana for cession of lands and concentration of reservations.[80]

ROW Provision

The railroad right-of-way provision in the Agreements, concluded December 28 and 31, 1886, and January 21, 1887, with the Indian [sic] of the Gros Ventre, Piegan, Blood, Blackfeet, and River Crow Reservation in Montana, by John V. Wright, Jared W. Daniels, and Charles F. Larrabee, Commissioners, reads as follows:

> ARTICLE VIII. It is further agreed that whenever in the opinion of the President the public interests require the construction of railroads, or other high ways, or telegraph lines, through any portion of either of the separate reservations established and set apart under the provisions of this agreement, right of way shall be, and is hereby, granted for such purposes, under such rules, regulations, limitations, and restrictions as the Secretary of the Interior may prescribe; the compensation to be fixed by said Secretary and by him expended for the benefit of the Indians concerned.[81]

MHA Cession Still on Table in 1888, Not Enacted until 1890

Early in the next Congressional session, Commissioner Atkins reminded the Secretary of the pendency of the MHA Cession:

> January 13, 1888 I concur in the opinion of Agent Gifford [December 12, 1887] that the agreement ought to be ratified with as little delay as possible. ... **Furthermore, by the terms of this agreement a tract of land estimated to contain 1,600,000 acres is made available to white settlement**. ... As I remarked in my letter of January 8, 1887, forwarding the agreement for transmittal to Congress, I regard the agreement as exceedingly favorable alike to the Government and the Indians, as, if faithfully carried out, it will enable the Indians to become self-supporting, and to be entirely independent of the Government at the expiration of the ten years for which the annual installments are to run. (Emphasis added).[82]

On January 14, 1888, Acting Secretary Muldrow forwarded the agreement to the Secretary of the Treasury for transmittal to Congress. On January 19, 1888, Secretary of the Treasury Fairchild transmitted it to Congress. On January 21, 1888, it was referred to the Committee on Indian Affairs. It wasn't passed by Congress and ratified by the President until 1890.

Subpart F: Hill Lobbies for ROW Legislation

Hill kept his home team informed on the progress of the right-of-way effort.

> March 13, 1886–January 13, 1887 Telegrams to C. A. Broadwater Re right of way bill through Indian reservations before Congress. March 13, March 16, June 21 and 22, 1886 and January 11 and 13, 1887.[83]

On April 3, 1886, Rep. Maginnis sent Hill the following note:

> Re getting a bill through Congress providing for right of way across Indian reservations, with comments on attitudes of specific senators and representatives.[84]

On May 8, 1886, Hill forwarded Broadwater a draft of the bill:

> Enclosing draft of a bill for right of way through the Indian reservation in northern Montana recently received from Martin Maginnis.[85]

On July 20, 1886, Hill wrote to William E. Smith, a Rep. from Georgia, interim appointment as Secretary of the Treasury, regarding the bill and mentioned Rep. Nelson from Minnesota was an ardent supporter of the "pineries" and Indian tribal land reduction and reservation concentration.

> Maginnis left for home last evening and wishes if bill passes Senate to have you get Nelson to have it referred to the Indian Committee and held in the House for the present.[86]

On December 7, 1886, Montana Rep. Toole introduced "*H.R. 10056 for a right-of-way through the Indian reservations in Northern Montana and Northwestern Dakota.*" On December 22, 1886, he sought expedited consideration of his bill which was granted. It was approved by the House on that day.

> Mr. TOOLE. Mr. Speaker, I ask unanimous consent that the Committee of the Whole be discharged from the further consideration of the bill (H.R. 10056) granting to the Saint Paul, Minneapolis and Manitoba Railway Company, the right of way through the Indian reservations in Northern Montana and Northwestern Dakota; and that the bill be put upon its passage.
>
> The bill will be read, after which the Chair will ask for objections.
>
> The bill was read, as follows: [It applied to the Fort Berthold and Blackfeet Reservations].

Commissioner J. D. C. Atkins and Secretary L. Q. C. Lamar stated that there was no objection to the bill by the DOI. The House Committee on Indian Affairs was unanimous in its recommendation for approval. Rep. Nelson explained that the land sought was not in excess of what the federal government allowed on public lands, in fact, it was less.

It was signed by the House Speaker and Senate President Pro-Tempore and then headed to the President's desk.[87]

President Cleveland Vetoes Generic ROW Bill

To all observers, President Cleveland's approval seemed assured. On July 1, 1886, certain unnamed friends tipped Hill that officials from the Northern Pacific and the Union Pacific Railroads were secretly pressuring the President to veto the right-of-way bill.

In an unexpected move, Cleveland did just that—vetoing the right-of-way bill on July 7, 1886. As to his reason, he stated in part:

I return without approval Senate bill No. 2281, entitled "An act granting to railroads the right of way through the Indian reservation in northern Montana."

The bill before me ... is a new and wide departure from the general tenor of legislation affecting Indian reservations. It ignores the right of the Indians to be consulted as to the disposition of their lands, opens wide the door to any railroad corporation to do what, under the treaty covering the greater portion of the reservation, is reserved to the United States alone; it gives the right to enter upon Indian lands to a class of corporations carrying with them many individuals not known for any scrupulous regard for the interest or welfare of the Indians; it invites a general invasion of the Indian country, and brings into contact and intercourse with the Indians a class of whites and others who are independent of the orders, regulations, and control of the resident agents.[88]

Hill's Forces Waste No Time to Get Tailored ROW Bill

Hill wrote to William F. Vilas who promptly forwarded his letter to the President citing evidence implicating his Northern Pacific rivals in derailing the right-of-way legislation. Hill's legislative forces wasted no time in drafting a very specific right-of-way bill to counter any effort on President Cleveland's part to veto Hill's bill due to political pressure from his very powerful railroad and mining rivals.

Legislation was introduced and followed the requisite protocol quickly. Hill kept his colleagues informed.

Feb. 7, 1887 Railroad right of way Hill to Broadwater (C.A.) Right-of-way bill passed the Senate today.[89]

Enough of a furor must have been raised as President Cleveland, signed Hill's bill for the Fort Berthold and Blackfeet Reservations Right-of-Way into law on February 15, 1887.[90]

By an act of Congress approved February 15, 1887,[91] a right of way was granted to the Saint Paul, Minneapolis and Manitoba Railway Company, for the extension of its line of road from Minot, Dak., across the Fort Berthold reservation; thence along the Missouri river by the most convenient and practicable route to the valley of the Milk river on the Blackfeet reservation; thence along the valley of the Milk river to Fort Assinniboine, and thence southwesterly to the Great Falls of the Missouri river. The provisions of the act have been fully complied with by the company, tribal compensation fixed, and damages to individual Indians assessed, and paid to the Indians, and the road is now being rapidly constructed on the route defined.

Subpart G: Hill Strikes Spike

Hill celebrated completing the route to Helena on November 21, 1887. He completed his transcontinental Great Northern Railway between St. Paul, Minnesota, and Everett, Washington, in 1893.

Hill Recruits Emigrants to Northwest

Almost immediately upon completion, Hill's company began recruiting emigrants to the Northwest: 750,000 Acres Indian Land Open to Settlers. Railroads were expensive to build and operate. They needed passengers, freight and income, and their publicity staffs worked hard to entice people to travel to the Northwest and settle in cities and on farms—and, of course, rely on the railroads for goods and services. The journey to the promised land that took months by covered wagon in the 1840s could be completed in a week or so by the last decade of the 19th century. Largely as a result of the completion of the transcontinental lines, population in Idaho, Washington and Oregon jumped from about 251,000 in 1880 to 705,000 in 1890.[92]

Glacier National Park Tourism

Louis Hill, Jay Hill's son, arranged to bring ten members of the Blackfoot Nation to New York City to be part of "the scenery" at the Glacier National Park exhibit at the Travel and Vacation Show, held at the Grand Central Palace in 1913. Naturally, they traveled to the east coast in a special car on the Great Northern Railway. The Indians inhabited the exhibition area from March 20 through March 29 and were visited by more than 10,000 people a day. Tipis were erected on the roof of the hotel.[93]

Part 11: Chicago, Milwaukee, St. Paul & Pacific Railroad

In 1907, The Chicago, Milwaukee, St. Paul & Pacific Railroad, "Milwaukee Road," built by John D. Ryan, finished its lines from Livingston to Paradise, via Helena and Mullan Pass and from Logan to Garrison via Butte and Homestake Pass. It would partner with the Anaconda Copper Mining Company. The railroad operated using electrified lines, so electric motors could pull trains over steep grades. Ryan owned Montana power companies, many of which supplied electricity to the train company.

> It advertised for homesteaders and in one pamphlet declared that *"one by one, the Indian reservations are being turned over to the settlers who can till the ground intelligently."* The company published "homeseekers' round-trip fares" to Missoula, Spokane and Coeur d'Alene for the purpose of settling on Indian reservations.[94]

Part 12: King Copper

Anaconda Company

Marcus Daly, one of the "Copper Kings," purchased the Anaconda Mine in 1880. He financed the construction of the Anaconda Smelter and created the Anaconda Mining Company. He mined silver deposits in the Butte area, but the company's real success lay with the Butte copper mines. With discoveries of massive copper deposits on "The Richest Hill on Earth," Daly enlarged the Anaconda smelter. His railroad company, the "Butte, Anaconda and Pacific Railway," hauled ore to the smelter.

In 1899, Daly sold the Anaconda Copper Mining Company to Standard Oil, who then renamed it the Amalgamated Copper Mining Company. His original investment of $30,000 grew to nearly $40,000,000. The expanding use of metal in electrical light filaments required copper, which resulted in the continued rise in copper prices.

> The Anaconda Copper Company, called "the company" by the employees, was a huge political power. The company owned the mines, smelters, and many of the state newspapers, and bribed politicians. Men under the control of the company were said to wear the "copper collar." In 1903, the company shut down, forcing thousands of employees out of work until the legislature passed the legislation it sought. The company also paid men to join the unions and to seek positions of leadership, so eventually they controlled the unions too. Meaderville, McQueen, and East Butte, once thriving Butte neighborhoods, were destroyed so the company could create Berkeley pit.[95]

Copper and Timber Team Up

Around 1900, Marcus Daly owned more than 1.1 million acres of timberland. Soon after organizing his lumbering business in the Bitter Root Valley, he began forming a series of corporations with numerous shareholders: Bitter Root Development Company, Anaconda Mining Company, Anaconda Copper Company, Anaconda Copper Mining Company and Mining Improvement Company. These companies owned timber lands, timber cutting privileges and rights, timber, logs, mills, water rights, and water ditches, flumes, pipe lines, and rights of way. In the next decade, Anaconda cut nearly one-half of the total timber cut in Montana.[96]

The federal government sued Daly's Bitter Root Development Company alleging the willful trespass upon the U.S.'s lands, cutting millions of feet of logs and hauling them to the Bitter Root River and thence to the mill of the defendant, Bitter Root Development Company, where they were converted into lumber and sold to the general public. The U.S. further charged that the proceeds, with a value of two million dollars and upwards, were appropriated in large part by said Marcus Daly and the balance by his associates.[97]

The U.S. "further shows that at the time that these trespasses were committed the territory on which the same took place was but sparsely settled, and was thousands of miles away from the seat of government, and it was impossible with the means that your orator had at hand to properly patrol and protect its domain from the willful trespasses of the defendants, and that the Government of the United States used such care in the protection thereof as it had the means to do."[98]

The problem simply was that the U.S. "was unable to show just when or by whom the cutting had been performed, or the logs manufactured into lumber had been sold, or just when and by whom the proceeds thereof were obtained and when the same were divided."[99]

The federal government argued that this web of corporations was designed so that these companies could evade being charged with the illegal cutting of timber and to confuse any governmental investigation. Regardless of the government's position, there was nothing illegal in forming these corporations and financing them through shareholder investments.

Even though the accounting of these companies and their shareholders was a labyrinth of immense proportion, the court refused to order an accounting by the companies. In essence, the federal government wanted the defendants to admit their wrongdoing and determine how much they owed the government. This the court was unwilling to do. Even though Clark and Daly were acquitted in 1906, the government continued its attempts to indict the large depredators, which were unsuccessful.

Part 13. Timber Operations in Montana

Lumber Baron Andrew Hammond

The lumber requirements in the mining industry, were becoming immense. The Anaconda Copper Mining Company used more than 200,000 board feet of timber every day in its mines. Smelters burned thousands of cords per day in their smelting processes.

In 1881, Andrew Hammond, an early entrepreneur, secured an exclusive contract to supply all of the Northern Pacific Railroad's lumber requirements from Mullan Pass to Thompson Falls, a distance of 175 miles.

> The massive timber requirements included 3,000 cross ties for every mile, plus lumber for tunnels, trestles and bridges, for a total of 21 million bf. In addition, Eddy, Hammond and Co. would supply the railroad with all its provisions: clothing, blankets, everything the railroad needed, save steel. This contract enabled the firm to go from an annual business of $180,000 in 1880 to $450,000 two years later and continue growing by about half a million a year for the next ten years.[100]

To feed that demand, Hammond needed a mill. He bought land on the Blackfoot River for the sawmill and a dam to contain the mill's supply of logs.

Logging Partners: Northern Pacific Railroad, Copper Magnate Daly and Hammond

In 1882, lumber baron Andrew Hammond, Richard Eddy, E.L. Bonner and M.J. Connell joined with copper magnate Marcus Daly and Northern Pacific in the formation of an enterprise christened "The Montana Improvement Company" (MIC). The Northern Pacific Railroad provided most of the capital. Their aggressive practices included cutting timber wherever they could.

Hammond's Vertical and Horizontal Integration Strategies Pay Off

Hammond needed timber to feed his giant sawmill at Bonner. So it was in his interest also to have liberal federal policies in acquiring timber.

In 1887, he completed the Bitterroot Railroad from Missoula to Grantsdale. The valley was now a short train ride from Missoula; farmers could send their wheat to Hammond's flour mills near the city, and ore could be shipped from Hammond's Curlew copper mine. But the primary cargo was timber.

While milling was not profitable, if Hammond bought out smaller mills or mills in financial trouble, he could corner the market. He also pioneered the vertical integration of transportation and marketing as part of the production process. He soon controlled everything from raw materials to retail sales and construction contracts. Furthermore, Hammond engaged in nearly every possible western industry, diversifying his portfolio, including banking, railroads, shipping lines, fishing and canning, livestock, mining, real estate, merchandising, land speculation, and most of all, lumbering.

Scratching Each Other's Backs

In 1887, the federal government brought suit against the Northern Pacific Railroad and the Montana Improvement Company for $1,100,000, for illegally cutting timber. Samuel Hauser, a banker, land speculator, railroad and mining investor, associate of Hammond and Territorial Governor of Montana, used his position to finagle a solution. *He contacted Montana State. Rep. Toole who was ahead of the game and had already contacted Secretary Lamar to have all "suits discontinued against MIC."* (Emphasis added).[101]

MIC and Northern Pacific Indicted

Ignoring Secretary Lamar's insistence that they cease logging until the case was resolved, the MIC continued to expand its operations. MIC controlled almost the entire lumber trade of Western Montana, with a sawmill production capacity of 25 million bf a year, 10 million of which was destined for Daly's Anaconda Mining Company.[102]

It was a good call. Again, the federal government lacked proof that the trees were being cut from its property. The Montana Territorial Court ruled in 1887 that a survey was necessary to show the exact rights of the parties involved in the action before the government could seek compensation for any trees cut illegally. No surveys had been performed. *The Court ruled that the government could not lawfully demand an injunction against the timber operation until it could show specifically that its property had been injured or threatened.* (Emphasis added).[103] When it failed to get any bids for surveying, the government gave up its attempt to indict the two companies.

Not only had MIC taken de facto control of the forests, it had the politicians in its back pocket. With Cleveland, Lamar, and especially Sparks, all out of office, and with Republican Benjamin Harrison in Washington, the government lost its enthusiasm for pursuing timber trespass. The suits against Hammond languished in bureaucratic limbo.

Hammond's Navy

Hammond continued his businesses. For logging, he had no intention of being held hostage over transportation rates.

> With his purchase of the Vance Lumber Company in 1900, he acquired four sailing schooners. Within the year, he sold them in favor of building up a fleet of oil burning steam schooners. The first of these was the Arctic with a lumber capacity of 325,000 bf. Hammond would eventually acquire some seventy-two ships (although not all were owned simultaneously) and the Hammond Navy would be one of the largest and the only non-union lumber shipping line [sic] on the West Coast.
>
> Shortly after purchasing the Arctic, Hammond contracted with Henry Huntington's Newport News shipyard to begin construction on the largest lumber vessel ever built in Newport to date. In an age when most steamers were coal-fired, the Francis H. Leggett would be an oil-burner, taking advantage of California's low oil prices. With a capacity of 1.5 million bf, the ship would also be the largest to enter the Pacific lumber trade at the time.[104]

Gregory Llewellyn Gordon's research and article on Hammond is invaluable.

Part 14. Post-War Depression

The post-war depression hit Montana particularly hard, sending the sta[te] economy into a twenty-year downward spiral. Long before the rest of the nati[on] Montana began to suffer from the combined effects of an overextended econom[y,] low commodity prices, harsh winters, and summer droughts. By the end of 192[?] Herbert McLeod, business partner and friend, informed Hammond—Montana is broke.

Notes: Montana: Big Business' Corrupt Political Clout

1. "From George Washington to The States, 8 June 1783," *Founders Online,* National Archives, https://founders.archives.gov/documents/Washington/99-01-02-11404 (accessed online November 13, 2020).
2. "From Thomas Jefferson to James Monroe, 24 November 1801," *Founders Online*, National Archives, https://founders.archives.gov/documents/Jefferson/01-35-02-0550. [Original source: *The Papers of Thomas Jefferson*, vol. 35, *1 August–30 November 1801*, ed. Barbara B. Oberg. Princeton: Princeton University Press, 2008, pp. 718–722.] (accessed online November 13, 2020).
3. *State of R.I. v. Narragansett Indian Tribe*, 19 F.3d 685, 694 (1st Cir. 1994).
4. "Thomas Jefferson to James Madison, 27 April 1809," *Founders Online*, National Archives, https://founders.archives.gov/documents/Jefferson/03-01-02-0140. [Original source: *The Papers of Thomas Jefferson, Retirement Series*, vol. 1, *4 March 1809 to 15 November 1809*, ed. J. Jefferson Looney. Princeton: Princeton University Press, 2004, pp. 168–170.] (accessed online November 13, 2020).
5. Orations, John Quincy Adams, "The Jubilee of the Constitution, delivered at New York, April 30, 1839, before the New York Historical Society." https://www.gutenberg.org/files/896/896-h/896-h.htm (accessed online December 12, 2020).
6. Adams, John Quincy. *Memoirs of John Quincy Adams: comprising portions of his diary from 1795 to 1848*. JB Lippincott & Company, 1874, 5:176.
7. John L. O'Sullivan, "The Great Nation of Futurity," *The United States Democratic Review*, Volume 6, Issue 23, 1839, pp. 426-430. https://www.mtholyoke.edu/acad/intrel/osulliva.htm (accessed online November 21, 2020).
8. Id.
9. Northwest Ordinance, Act of Aug. 7, 1789, ch. 8, 1 Stat. 50, 52.
10. Northwest Ordinance, Act of Aug. 7, 1789, ch. 8, 1 Stat. 50.
11. https://www.nps.gov/cali/learn/historyculture/upload/No-Land-is-Free-10-11-16.pdf (accessed online November 11, 2020).

ory.com/brochures/scbl/forts-on-the-oregon-trail.pdf ine April 15, 2022).

ations from the Secretary of the Interior and the Commissioner Affairs to the Chairman of the Committee on Indian Affairs of ate, recommending certain appropriations for the Indian service. S. Doc. No. 34, 33d Cong., 1st Sess. (1854), p. 2.

port, Indians at Fort Berthold Agency, in North Dakota, To accompany ill H. R: 664 for the passage of the agreement. House documents, Volume 1; Volume 415, 1891, p. 7.

15. Report of the Commissioner of Indian Affairs to the Secretary of the Interior, Office of Indian Affairs, United States. Gideon & Co., Printers, 1851, pp. 27-28.

16. Report of the Commissioner of Indian Affairs to the Secretary of the Interior, United States. Office of Indian Affairs, U.S. Government Printing Office, 1868, pp. 7-15.

17. Report of the Commissioner of Indian Affairs to the Secretary of the Interior, United States. Office of Indian Affairs. Printer: A.O.P. Nicholson, 1857, p. 21.

18. (10 Stat. 226, 238). Indian tribes west of Missouri and Iowa. Message from the President of the United States, transmitting a report in regard to the extinguishment of the Indian title to lands west of Missouri and Iowa, &c, H.R. Exec. Doc. No. 84, 33d Cong., 1st Sess. (1854).

19. Letter dated August 18, 1853, from Secretary of the Interior McClelland to Commissioner of Indian Affairs Manypenny. Indian tribes west of Missouri and Iowa. Message from the President of the United States, transmitting a report in regard to the extinguishment of the Indian title to lands west of Missouri and Iowa, &c, H.R. Exec. Doc. No. 84, 33d Cong., 1st Sess. (1854), p. 4.

20. Report of the Commissioner of Indian Affairs to the Secretary of the Interior, United States. Office of Indian Affairs. U.S. Government Printing Office, 1868, p. 223.

21. Twain, Mark. The American Claimant. 1901.

22. "Governor Edgerton's First Message", Contributions to the Historical Society of Montana, Vol. III, 1900, p. 344.

23. Report of the Commissioner of Indian Affairs to the Secretary of the Interior, United States. Office of Indian Affairs, 1866, p. 40.

24. Montana Indian War claims. Letter from the Secretary of War, transmitting a report upon the Montana Indian War claims of 1867. H.R. Exec. Doc. No. 98, 41st Cong., 3rd Sess. (1871).

25. Report of the Commissioner of Indian Affairs to the Secretary of the Interior, Montana Superintendency, Office of Indian Affairs, United States. U.S. Government Printing Office, 1868, pp. 259-260.

26. AN ACT to amend an act entitled "An act to aid in the construction of a railroad and telegraph line from the Missouri river to the Pacific ocean, and to secure to the government the use of the same for postal, military, and other purposes,"—approved July first, eighteen hundred and sixty-two.
27. Northern Pacific Land Grant Act, 13 Stat. 365 (1864).
28. Genetin-Pilawa, C. Joseph. Crooked paths to allotment: The fight over federal Indian policy after the Civil War. Univ. of North Carolina Press, 2012, p. 97.
29. Dunn, Adrian R., A History of Fort Berthold, State Historical Society of North Dakota, 1964, p. 55; Serial 1220, 38th Congress, 2. Session, Vol. 5, House Executive Document No. 1, p. 408.
30. Report of the Commissioner of Indian Affairs to the Secretary of the Interior, Office of Indian Affairs, United States. U.S. Government Printing Office, 1882, p. 128.
31. Letter of Commissioner of Indian Affairs Ely S. Parker, April 2, 1870. https://www.ndstudies.gov/gr8/content/unit-iii-waves-development-1861–1920/lesson-1-changing-landscapes/topic-4-reservation-boundaries/section-4-creating-fort-berthold-reservation (accessed online April 18, 2022).
32. See Executive orders, establishing, enlarging, or reducing Indian reservations, also restoring certain Indian reservations to the public domain, from May 14, 1855 to October 29, 1878; Report of the Commissioner of Indian Affairs to the Secretary of the Interior, Office of Indian Affairs, United States. U.S. Government Printing Office, 1878, pp. 244-246.
33. *Indians of Fort Berthold Indian Reservation in the State of North Dakota v. United States*, 71 Ct. Cl. 308 (1930), pp. 308-341.
34. Ibid., p. 337.
35. Ibid., pp. 337-338.
36. An act to accept and ratify an agreement with the Crow Indians, July 10, 1882, for the sale of a portion of their reservation in the Territory of Montana required for the use of the Northern Pacific Railroad, and to make the necessary appropriations for carrying out the same.
37. Message from the President of the United States, transmitting a communication of the 6th instant from the Secretary of the Interior, submitting a draft of a bill "to accept and ratify an agreement with the confederated tribes of the Flathead, Kootenay, and Upper Pend d'Oreilles Indians for the sale of a portion of their reservation in Montana Territory required for the Northern Pacific Railroad." S. Exec. Doc. No. 15, 48th Cong., 1st Sess. (1883).
38. S. Exec. Doc. No. 15, 48th Cong., 1st Sess. (1883).
39. Id.
40. Id.
41. Id.

42. Smith, Jr., Quinn, A Stolen History, Future Claims: The Blackfeet Nation and Glacier National Park, October 14, 2020, The Wellian Magazine.
43. Report of the Commissioner of Indian Affairs to the Secretary of the Interior, Office of Indian Affairs, United States. U.S. Government Printing Office, 1883, pp. LIX-LXI.
44. Report of the Department of the Interior ... [with Accompanying Documents], Volume 2, United States. Dept. of the Interior. U.S. Government Printing Office, 1883, p. 49.
45. Report of the Commissioner of Indian Affairs to the Secretary of the Interior, Office of Indian Affairs, United States. U.S. Government Printing Office, 1883, pp. LIX-LXI.
46. The Northern Pacific Railroad and Helena's Emergence as a Social, Economic, and Political Center, 1883–1894. Cody Lamb Research Seminar: Carroll College Northwest Magazine, September 1887, p. 1.
47. "Ten Reasons Why Helena Should Be The Capital." "Helena's Social Supremacy: Political Sarcasm and the Capital Fight," Montana: The Magazine of Western History 37, no. 4 (Autumn 1987): 72; The Northern Pacific Railroad and Helena's Emergence as a Social, Economic, and Political Center, 1883–1894. Cody Lamb Research Seminar: Carroll College Northwest Magazine, September 1887, p. 19.
48. Report of the Commissioner of Indian Affairs to the Secretary of the Interior, Montana, Milk River Agency, Fort Peck, United States. Office of Indian Affairs, U.S. Government Printing Office, 1874, p. 269.
49. Utley, Robert M. Sitting Bull: The Life and Times of an American Patriot. Holt Paperbacks, 2014, p. 95.
50. Lubetkin, M. John, ed. Before Custer: Surveying the Yellowstone, 1872. Vol. 33. University of Oklahoma Press, 2015, p. 37.
51. General Railroad Right of Way Act, 18 Stat. 482 (1875).
52. Lang, William L., "Corporate Point Men and the Creation of the Montana Central Railroad, 1882–87" (1990). Great Plains Quarterly. 481. https://digitalcommons.unl.edu/greatplainsquarterly/481 (accessed online April 8, 2022).
53. Erickson, George L. History of Sand Coulee, Montana 1880 through 1900. Diss. Montana State University-Bozeman, College of Letters & Science, 2008, pp. ix, 6.
54. Baker, Robert Orr. The Minnesota Club: St. Paul's Enterprising Leaders And Their 'Gentlemen's Social Club.' https://publishing.rchs.com/wp-content/uploads/2015/11/RCHS_19-02_1984_Baker.pdf (accessed online April 19, 2022).
55. Lang, William L., "Corporate Point Men and the Creation of the Montana Central Railroad, 1882–87" (1990). Great Plains Quarterly. 481, p. 154.
56. "Maj. Martin Maginnis": Progressive Men of the State of Montana. Chicago: A.W. Bowen & Co., pp. 300-302.

57. Nelson, S. U. "Nelson's Biographical Dictionary and Historical Reference Book of Erie County." Erie, Pa (1896), pp. 546-548.
58. Wisconsin. Legislature. Legislative Reference Bureau. The State of Wisconsin Blue Book. Legislative Reference Bureau, 1960, p. 124.
59. Report of the Commissioner of Indian Affairs to the Secretary of the Interior, Office of Indian Affairs, United States. U.S. Government Printing Office, 1874, pp. 243-245.
60. Smith, Dennis J., "Procuring a right-of-way: James J. Hill and Indian reservations 1886–1888" (1983). Graduate Student Theses, Dissertations, & Professional Papers. 7981, p. 15.
61. JJH Letter Book, 3/22/86 - 10/22/86, p. 80. http://collections.mnhs.org/hill_index_cards/jj_hill/ma-mining/JJHM00266.pdf (accessed online April 15, 2022).
62. http://collections.mnhs.org/hill_index_cards/jj_hill/ (accessed online April 15, 2022).
63. Butcher, Edward Bernie, "Analysis of timber depredations in Montana to 1900" (1967). Graduate Student Theses, Dissertations, & Professional Papers. 4709, pp. 45-46.
64. JJH Letter Book, 7/9/95 - 9/24/95, p. 433 http://collections.mnhs.org/hill_index_cards/jj_hill/hillier_j/JJHI00111.pdf (accessed online April 15, 2022).
65. Adams, Arthur T., 1872–1955. Portrait of Reverend Edward D. Neill, early minister and state historian of Minnesota. 1920–1929. Hennepin History Museum, collection.mndigital.org/catalog/hchm:1236 (accessed online April 11, 2022).
66. Who Was Edward Duffield Neill? https://themacweekly.com/76882/neill-hall/who-was-edward-duffield-neill/ (accessed online April 11, 2022).
67. Smith, Dennis J., "Procuring a right-of-way: James J. Hill and Indian reservations 1886–1888" (1983). Graduate Student Theses, Dissertations, & Professional Papers. 7981, pp. 16-17.
68. Ibid., p. 18.
69. Ibid., p. 22.
70. St. P.M. & M. Ry. Letter Book 4:573 (10/4/80-4/12/81) http://collections.mnhs.org/hill_index_cards/jj_hill/hillier_j/JJHI00128.pdf (accessed online April 15, 2022).
71. Letter from Secretary James Harlan to Indian Peace Commissioners, dated August 18, 1865.
72. Smith, Dennis J., "Procuring a right-of-way: James J. Hill and Indian reservations 1886–1888" (1983). Graduate Student Theses, Dissertations, & Professional Papers. 7981, p. 19.

73. An act making appropriations for the current and contingent expenses of the Indian Department and for fulfilling treaty stipulations with various Indian tribes, for the year ending June 30, 1887, and for other purposes. (24. Stat. 29, 44).
74. General Correspondence by Date, enclosing J.D.C. Atkins to Sec. of the Interior, April 6, 1886 and copy of a draft of a bill submitted by Wellborn. http://collections.mnhs.org/hill_index_cards/jj_hill/hillier_j/JJHI00138.pdf (accessed online April 15, 2022).
75. Smith, Dennis J., "Procuring a right-of-way: James J. Hill and Indian reservations 1886–1888" (1983). Graduate Student Theses, Dissertations, & Professional Papers. 7981, p. 19.
76. JJH Letter Book, 3/22/86 - 10/22/86, p. 213 http://collections.mnhs.org/hill_index_cards/jj_hill/hillier_j/JJHI00141.pdf (accessed online April 15, 2022).
77. Indians at Fort Berthold Agency, in North Dakota. H.R. Rep. No. 82, 51st Cong., 1st Sess. (1890), p. 6.
78. Id., p. 5.
79. Reduction of Indian reservations. Message from the President of the United States, transmitting a communication from the Secretary of the Interior, with accompanying papers, relating to the reduction of Indian reservations, H.R. Exec. Doc. No. 63, 50th Cong., 1st Sess. (1888), p. 4.
80. Ibid., p. 2.
81. Ibid., p. 17.
82. Report of the Commissioner of Indian Affairs to the Secretary of the Interior, Office of Indian Affairs, United States. U.S. Government Printing Office, 1888, p. 44.
83. March 13–1886–January 13, 1887 Telegrams to C. A. Broadwater Re right of way bill through Indian reservations before Congress. March 13, March 16, June 21 and 22, 1886 and January 11 and 13, 1887. Papers of Montana Central Railway Company http://collections.mnhs.org/hill_index_cards/jj_hill/ma-mining/JJHM00264.pdf (accessed online April 15, 2022).
84. http://collections.mnhs.org/hill_index_cards/jj_hill/hillier_j/JJHI00113.pdf (accessed online April 15, 2022).
85. JJH Letter Book, 3/22/86 - 10/22/86, p. 196 http://collections.mnhs.org/hill_index_cards/jj_hill/hillier_j/JJHI00126.pdf (accessed online April 15, 2022).
86. JJH Letter Book, 3/22/86 - 10/22/86, p. 389 http://collections.mnhs.org/hill_index_cards/jj_hill/hillier_j/JJHI00105.pdf (accessed online April 15, 2022).
87. U.S. Congress, House, A Bill Granting to Saint Paul, Minneapolis and Manitoba Railway Company the right of way through the Indian reservations in Northern Montana and Northwestern Dakota, H.R. 10056, 49th Cong., 2nd sess., 1886, pp. 329-331.

88. https://www.presidency.ucsb.edu/documents/veto-message-264 (accessed online April 8, 2022).
89. Feb.7,1887 Railroad right of way Hill to Broadwater (C.A.) Right-of-way bill passed the Senate today. JJH Letter Book, 11/26/86 - 6/6/87, p. 261 http://collections.mnhs.org/hill_index_cards/jj_hill/hillier_j/JJHI00129.pdf (accessed online April 15, 2022).
90. Act of February 15, 1887, An act granting to the Saint Paul, Minneapolis and Manitoba Railway Company the right of way through the Indian reservations in Northern Montana and Northwestern Dakota. 24 Stat. 402 (February 15, 1887). Blackfeet (Montana) and Fort Berthold (Dakota) reserves.
91. By an act of Congress approved February 15, 1887 (24 Stat. 402).
92. https://www.nwcouncil.org/reports/columbia-river-history/railroads/ (accessed online April 8, 2022).
93. The New York Times, March 19, 1913; https://www.huffpost.com/entry/the-blackfoot-indians-in-_b_847936 (accessed online April 8, 2022).
94. http://www.milwaukeeroadarchives.com/Homesteading/AdvertisingHomesteading.htm (accessed online April 15, 2022); https://www.nwcouncil.org/reports/columbia-river-history/railroads/ (accessed online April 15, 2022).
95. Boom and Bust: The Industries That Settled Montana. European Immigrants. https://dp.la/exhibitions/industries-settled-montana/industry-displaced-people/european-immigrants (accessed online April 13, 2022).
96. Hewitt, "Early History of Montana's Lumber Industry," historical files, Nine Mile Ranger Station, Lolo National Forest, Missoula; Malone and Roeder, Montana, pp. 253-254. http://npshistory.com/publications/usfs/region/1/history/chap3.htm (accessed online July 18, 2022).
97. *United States v. Bitter Root Development Company*, 200 U.S. 457 (1906).
98. Ibid., pp. 457, 461 (1906).
99. Ibid., pp. 457, 474 (1906).
100. Gordon, Gregory Llewellyn, "Money Does Grow on Trees: A. B. Hammond and the Age of the Lumber Baron" (2010). Graduate Student Theses, Dissertations, & Professional Papers. 676, p. 80.
101. Ibid., p. 207.
102. *United States v. Northern Pacific Railroad Company*, 4 Montana Reports 351 (1887).
103. Butcher, Edward Bernie, "Analysis of timber depredations in Montana to 1900" (1967). Graduate Student Theses, Dissertations, & Professional Papers. 4709, pp. 45-46.
104. Gordon, Gregory Llewellyn, "Money Does Grow on Trees: A. B. Hammond and the Age of the Lumber Baron" (2010). Graduate Student Theses, Dissertations, & Professional Papers. 676, p. 365.

CHAPTER 10: OREGON: GOVERNOR CURRY'S PRIVATE WARS OF EXTERMINATION

Part 1: Introduction

Spain, Russia and England claimed ownership of the present-day states of Oregon, Washington and parts of Idaho, Montana and Wyoming. Their disputed claim, based on the 'doctrine of discovery,' gave absolutely no consideration to the numerous indigenous peoples who had lived in the Oregon Territory from time immemorial. A Convention had been agreed to between the England and the U.S. countries in 1818 and 1826 where they retained joint rights.

Polk ran his 1844 Presidential campaign with the slogan 'Fifty-four Forty or Fight!' meaning he supported claiming the Oregon Territory to the 54th parallel for the United States and he was willing to go to war with the British to claim it. In 1846, President Polk directed the Secretary of State to deliver notice to the British Government of the U.S.'s abrogation of the Convention of August 6, 1827. Ending the Convention, instead of renewing it or continuing negotiations, meant the U.S. was ready to assert its sole rights to the Territory.

In the meantime, the United States pushed for 'boots on the ground' to support its claim. There was no basis for entering into treaties with the Indian Nations over this internationally disputed region. Congressman Breese of Illinois, along with others, favored encouraging settlement and terminating the Convention. The U.S. could then

> ... incorporate the country into our Union; protect the emigrant on his way to its fertile plains, and pledge to all who seek them, the honor and faith of the Government that *they shall be made secure in their possessions by perfect grants of land, at the earliest period within the competency of the Government to act*... (Emphasis added).[1]

To win Britain over, the U.S. argued they would provide a means for further English immigration:

The United States and England are the only Powers who lay any claim to that country, the only nations which may and must inhabit it. It is not, fortunately, in the power of either Government to prevent this taking place; but it depends upon them whether they shall unite in promoting the object, or whether they shall bring on both countries the calamities of an useless war, which may retard but not prevent the ultimate result. ... ***The emigrants to Oregon, whether Americans or English, will be united together by the community of language and literature, of the principles of law, and of all the fundamental elements of a similar civilization.***[3] (Emphasis added).[2]

Neither Britain nor the U.S. wanted to fight what would have been the third war in 70 years against the other. England caved in because it lacked the finances necessary for another war. The 1846 Oregon Treaty, resolving the dispute, divided the territory west of the Continental Divide along the 49th parallel to the Georgia Strait in favor of the United States, with all of Vancouver Island remaining under British control. This border today divides British Columbia from neighboring Washington, Idaho and Montana.

In the meantime, America's dispossession of Indian lands and resources in what would become the Oregon Territory was underway. Starting in the 1830's, Protestant missionaries moved into the Willamette Valley. Their testimony of the fertile soil spread rapidly to the East, which set in motion a massive migration of thousands of American families westward along the Oregon Trail. It increased each subsequent year. President van Buren (1837–1841) was more absorbed in avoiding war with Britain and the Panic of 1837 then to give any heed to the protection of Indian land and property rights.

Oregon's history, given the acquiescence of the U.S. to the settlement of Indian lands before extinguishing Indian title, is replete with Indian wars and genocidal massacres. Its Governor, legislature and citizens demanded the outright removal of Indians from the state. If not, they were willing to exterminate them. Having reached the Pacific Ocean, there was no more land left. The settlers' desperation to become part of the landed class was unleashed against the Indian peoples, in an unmitigated fury. They morphed into killing machines to satisfy their covetous hunger. Oregon's government facilitated the ethnic cleansing and extermination of Indians by arming its citizens. The federal government provided the ammunition.

Preemption Act of 1841

To encourage settlement, Congress passed the Preemption Act of 1841,[3] which granted purchasing rights to settlers living on federal land. They could claim 160 acres of land, after residing on the property for 14 months, for $1.25 an acre. It was signed by President John Tyler (1841–1845).

Great Migration of 1843

Christened "The Great Migration of 1843," wagons blanketed the westward trail.[4] Indians would lose valuable property and in a disingenuous policy of protecting them from this onslaught of settlers, they became subject to a disarray of federal and Territorial policies of brigand war, cession of vast tracts of land, forced removals, the reservation system, allotment, assimilation and, in some cases, the termination of tribal governmental status.

The tables had been reversed. Europe wouldn't be establishing colonies in the New World; the United States would be creating colonies for the Indians. Indians would become the "colonial settlers." Tribes would be combined on reservations, without regard to enmity, tribal affiliation, language, culture or background.

Provisional Government of Oregon (1843)

While Great Britain sought to establish its hegemony over the Pacific Northwest in debates with the United States, the new settlers in Oregon formed a Provisional Government in May–July 1843. They postulated their understanding of the right to land as follows:

> We are thus particular to point out the facts showing the exact legal and political status of the country, so that the reader may get a clear idea of the magnitude of the work achieved by the early Oregon pioneers. Oregon was from 1818 down to 1846 practically and substantially in the position of being.
>
> NO MAN'S LAND
> and open to the application of
> "The good old rule, the simple plan,
> That they should take who have the power,
> And they should keep who can."[5]

Presidential Charge: Settle Oregon

In President Polk's First Inaugural Address in 1845, when Britain was still claiming title to the Oregon country, he emphasized the need for settlement by families. Men with their wives and children were building homes, with the intent of permanent settlement. Establishing occupation by the U.S. was so important, notwithstanding that the U.S. didn't have title, resulting in a failure to address Indian title. This would be the basis for hostilities and war between the U.S. and the Indian inhabitants.[6]

Polk's 1845 State of the Union Address underscored the growing emigration to Oregon and the responsibility the federal government would assume to protect settlers, by "cultivat[ing] amicable relations with the Indian tribes." In lauding the frontier settlers, President Polk recognized them as the first tier of expansion of the U.S. claim to frontier regions. They would be the ones to occupy, claim and, most importantly, defend their settlements.

> Our title to the country of the Oregon is "clear and unquestionable," and already are our people preparing to perfect that title by occupying it with their wives and children. ... The increasing emigration to Oregon and the care and protection which is due from the Government to its citizens in that distant region make it our duty, as it is our interest, to cultivate amicable relations with the Indian tribes of that Territory. For this purpose I recommend that provision be made for establishing an Indian agency and such subagencies as may be deemed necessary beyond the Rocky Mountains.
>
> For the protection of emigrants whilst on their way to Oregon against the attacks of the Indian tribes occupying the country through which they pass, I recommend that a suitable number of stockades and blockhouse forts be erected along the usual route between our frontier settlements on the Missouri and the Rocky Mountains, and that an adequate force of mounted riflemen be raised to guard and protect them on their journey.
>
> *It is to the enterprise and perseverance of the hardy pioneers of the West, who penetrate the wilderness with their families, suffer the dangers, the privations, and hardships attending the settlement of a new country, and prepare the way for the body of emigrants who in the course of a few years usually follow them, that we are in a great degree indebted for the rapid extension and aggrandizement of our country.* (Emphasis added.)[7]

In Polk's Special Message on May 29, 1848, Regarding the Oregon Territory, he urged Congress to admit Oregon as a Territory, given its hostilities with Indians. Recognition as a Territory would open the door to the federal coffers.

> They represent that *"the proud and powerful tribes of Indians" residing in their vicinity have recently raised "the war whoop and crimsoned their tomahawks in the blood of their citizens;"* that they apprehend that "many of the powerful tribes inhabiting the upper valley of the Columbia have formed an alliance for the purpose of carrying on hostilities against their settlements;" that the number of the white population is far inferior to that of the savages; that they are deficient in arms and money, and fear that they do not possess strength to repel the "attack of so formidable a foe and protect their families and property from violence and rapine." (Emphasis added).[8]

This war mongering speech by the President employed the artifice of savage stereotypes to incite Congress to action. It succeeded. Shortly thereafter, Oregon was admitted as a Territory under the Oregon Organic Act of 1848. It encompassed the present-day states of Oregon, Washington and Idaho, along with parts of Wyoming and Montana.

Governor George Abernethy's Memorial of the Legislative Assembly of Oregon, on December 7, 1847, highlighted the need for the federal government to compensate Indians for the land taken up by white settlers:

> Our relation with the Indians becomes every year more embarrassing. They see the white man occupying their lands-rapidly filling up the country, and they put in a claim for pay. They have been told that a chief would come out from the United States and treat with them for their lands. They have been told this so often that they begin to doubt the truth of it. At all events, they say, "he will not come until we are all dead, and then what good will blankets do us? We want something now." This leads to trouble between the settler and the Indians about him. Some plan should be devised by which a fund can be raised, and presents made to the Indians of sufficient value to keep them quiet, until an agent arrives from the United States. ... A number of robberies have been committed by the Indians in the upper country on the immigrants, as they were passing through their territory. This should not be allowed to pass.[9]

President Polk: Trifling Amount Will Avoid War

In President Polk's Fourth Annual Message on December 5, 1848, he implored Congress to enact legislation to prevent Indian warfare in Oregon. Congress needed to set aside appropriations to negotiate land cession treaties with the Indians, requiring only a "trifling" amount. The failure to compensate Indians, for the taking of their lands, resulted in their plunder.

> Indeed, the immediate and only cause of the existing hostility of the Indians of Oregon is represented to have been the long delay of the United States in making to them some ***trifling compensation, in such articles as they wanted, for the country now occupied by our emigrants, which the Indians claimed and over which they formerly roamed***. ... The Indians ... ***sought redress by plunder and massacre, which finally led to the present difficulties***. (Emphasis added).[10]

The volunteer armed anti-Indian squads sought compensation. Given their absolute failure to adhere to the customary rules of war, they shouldn't have been compensated in any manner. Unfortunately, President Polk recommended Congress approve their compensation.

> In this Indian war our fellow-citizens of Oregon have been compelled to take the field in their own defense, have performed valuable military services, and been subjected to expenses which have fallen heavily upon them. Justice demands that provision should be made by Congress to compensate them.[11]

Donating Oregon to Colonial Settlers

The Donation Land Claim Act of 1850,[12] permitted ***qualifying adult U.S. citizens 320 federal acres at no charge,*** subject to the claimant residing on the property on or before December 1, 1850, and occupying it for four consecutive years, which could be counted retroactively. The donated land in part in Oregon is described as follows by the DOI's Agent:

> In the northern and eastern portions, a growth of valuable timber covers alike valley and summit; whilst along the coast, and winding to the southward, the timber is displaced by a most luxuriant growth of rich, nutritious grass, forming a region for grazing purposes scarcely surpassed. Stretching along many of the streams are found prairies of the richest alluvial formations, as well as plains of considerable extent, well adapted to the cultivation of grain and vegetables.

> Though this region, for its timber and agricultural productions, may justly be regarded as valuable, yet when its mineral wealth is taken into consideration ... The beach, through the whole extent of the district, is a deposit of the precious metals, and is already dotted with towns and villages of miners; and it has been recently discovered that its mountains abound in placers equal in richness to those of California ... and thousands are now rushing to offer their devotions at this nearer shrine of mammon. J. L. Parrish, Indian Agent, Port Orford District.[13]

Extinguish Indian Title West of Cascade Mountains

The Governor, Sup't and Oregon Territory's first Congressional Delegate, Samuel Thurston, worked in concert to secure Congressional authority and funding to commence negotiations for cession of Indian lands.[14] This occurred without contest and the Department of the Interior's broad brushed mandate "to extinguish the Indian title west of the Cascade Mountains" was acted upon quickly. The archetype employed across the country would be imposed on the Oregonian Indians – Indians would cede massive amounts of land for the benefit of white settlers; Congress would allocate a minimal amount to purchase Indian lands; no account would be made for the valuable extractive resources Indians would be compelled to surrender – in this case the arable lands, the gold discoveries in the Colville area of eastern Washington and mining activity in the Rogue River country of Oregon and the vast standing timber.

Congress' directive to extinguish Indian title, insuring a fair return to the Indians for their ceded lands was absolutely impossible – Congress refused to open its coffers to allocate the full funding for the fair market value of Indian lands to be ceded. The greed, in the swirling interlocking directorates of business and government, was focused only on expansion and money. Indians were a speck on the horizon which would disappear, if the Iron Triangle of business, settlers and government had their way. By the end of the nineteenth century, Manifest Destiny had been fulfilled as the United States expanded from the Atlantic to the Pacific, and historian Frederick Jackson Turner declared that the frontier was dead.

Manifest Destiny

This article on Pioneer Practices in the Daily Alta California newspaper evidenced the brutal and merciless war of annihilation that Indians would face on the Pacific Coast as colonial settlers proceeded to exercise their ordained prescription to usurp the North American continent. The extermination of Indians was part of that divine, natural process.

Pioneer Practices

> From the days of the Plymouth colony on the Atlantic to the present period when the Pacific bounds—for how brief a time let us not attempt to say—the "area of freedom," ***the extermination of the Indian race on the continent has been as gradual and as natural as the growth of an empire***, and the increase of the whites over the hunting grounds once possessed by the dusky tribes of America. ... His path has been downward from the day that disclosed to him the stranger's track upon the Atlantic shore. His destiny, or doom, has been to perish with his native wilds. Slowly he has receded before the paleface, in a line of march towards the setting sun. He has reached the last "vestige of dry land," and even thither he has been followed, until the waters of the Pacific wash alike the feet of the white and the red man.
>
> ... Today we overlook the Pacific wave, and build our homes upon the crumbling ashes of Indian huts and above the mounds of whole tribes that have been swept from before us.
>
> ***This we call "manifest destiny."*** ... The practices and usages of our people, from the days of the pilgrim fathers to the present moment, have involved the annihilation of the Indian race as a necessity and a part of the irresistible impulse of America's destiny. ... We may labor at "policy," and perhaps provide for a few tribes a few years' lengthened period of existence or lingering decay, but we never can save.[15]

The article in the Alta California goes on to glorify pioneer emigration through the "rifle."

> And more than this, the cause of pioneering immigration admits of no mild, humane, pacifying or conciliatory doctrines and practices. When the march of civilizing improvement is seriously impeded or obstructed, peace or war are the only and ready alternatives. ... The axe and the rifle bear out their only ideas of improvement. ... When it becomes necessary to subdue them, the rifle is substituted for the axe ...

The self-proclaiming superiority of the white race as a governing doctrine was unquestionable. It was engrained in the animus of dehumanizing Indians to enable their slaughter as moral.

> The Rogue River Indians are an unalterably vicious and dangerous people. ... they can only be removed by the exterminating encroachments of their superior enemy—by the law of the rifle and the axe, and the code of practice usually "served out" by the pioneer.

This writer was quiescent to the genocide of a people. Murdering Indians had become a respectable more, without protest.

> That extermination is only another name for the warfare already commenced in this country is shown by the following extract from a letter written by one of an expedition at present ranging the Rogue River country. He says:
> *"During this period we have been searching about in the mountains, destroying villages, killing all the males we could find, and capturing women and children. We have killed about 30 altogether, and have 28 prisoners now in camp."*

That settlement and civilization is consummated by the government's willingness to encourage and endorse the "barbarous practices" of the western colonial death squads is here righteously proclaimed as the law of the land.

> *This system of singling out and deliberately destroying "all the males" is on the plan of indiscriminate massacre. We may treat these things with strong disfavor, but by such process, and by this barbarous practice, do our pioneers prepare the way for settlement and civilization.* (Emphasis added).[16]

Shock and Awe

Joseph Lane, the Late Sup't and Isaac I. Stevens, Delegate to the U.S. House of Representatives from Washington Territory, proposed to the House of Representatives and Chas. E. Mix, Acting Com. Ind. Aff., on Feb. 17, 1858, that a group of Indian leaders from Oregon and Washington be taken on a tour of the principal cities to realize that there was no way they could fight the array of forces possessed by the U.S. or the policies imposed by them. 'Shock and awe' is a military tactic used as early as General George Washington's Sullivan Campaign against the Six Nations to destroy the will of the adversary to fight or oppose the policy aims of an opponent.

> We would respectfully recommend that Congress be asked to appropriate thirty thousand dollars to defray the expenses of bringing a delegation of Indian chiefs from the Territories of Oregon and Washington to the States, the object being to take them to the principal cities and on great routes of travel, to the end that they may take back to the Indian tribes accurate information of the strength, resources and friendly disposition of our government and people.[17]

Part 2: Starvation or Plunder

In 1851, President Fillmore blamed the Indian hostilities on the destruction of their subsistence base. He understood that their very survival mandated plunder.

> Along the Mexican frontier and in California and Oregon there have been occasional manifestations of unfriendly feeling and some depredations committed. *I am satisfied, however, that they resulted more from the destitute and starving condition of the Indians than from any settled hostility toward the whites.* As the settlements of our citizens progress toward them, the game, upon which they mainly rely for subsistence, is driven off or destroyed, and the only alternative left to them is starvation or plunder. (Emphasis added).[18]

President Fillmore: Indians in Oregon Are Tenants at Sufferance

Yet, in President Fillmore's 1852 State of the Union Address, he affirmed that whites could freely move Indians off their land in Oregon and California, whenever and wherever they wanted. Indians in Oregon and California had no rights to land, whatsoever. It created the legitimized free-for-all stage for the execution of 'might makes right.'

> In other parts of our territory particular districts of country have been set apart for the exclusive occupation of the Indians, and their right to the lands within those limits has been acknowledged and respected. *But in California and Oregon there has been no recognition by the Government of the exclusive right of the Indians to any part of the country. They are therefore mere tenants at sufferance, and liable to be driven from place to place at the pleasure of the whites.* (Emphasis added).[19]

Part 3: Substituting Robbery for Purchase

Giving the rising militancy and death count, the U.S. Attorney General was noticed by federal Indian agents that white settlers were willfully taking lands possessed by Indians. Not understanding the reality that whites fully believed they had the right to steal Indian lands, he described it as **"*absurd*"** without the possibility of a **"*reasoned reply.*"** *It was robbery and a violent disregard for law.* **Yet, the federal government took no action to protect its wards. Vigilantes controlled the state.**

For the record, we have Attorney General C. Cushing's reply to Sup't Palmer on June 22, 1855, regarding the effect of federal law in Oregon territory, and the claim by many white settlers that it didn't apply:

There is one other idea suggested by the Commissioner of Indian Affairs, and the documents he communicates, as being current in Oregon, namely, that *any white settler may rightfully take possession of any of the lands occupied by the Indians*, and oust them prior to the extinguishment of their occupancy title by the United States. This idea is too absurd to admit of any reasoned reply. Suffice it to say that *a white settler has the same right thus to oust the Indians as he has to oust white men, and no more, that is, the right to substitute robbery for purchase and violence for law.* (Emphasis added).[20]

A solitary voice in the Oregon wilderness, Sup't Palmer tried to argue for the Indians' property rights (Letter of July 30, 1854, to Mr. Perry, Umpqua Valley). The settlers would trample on the Indians rights, regardless of his protective stance. He needed the U.S. to employ its military might for the benefit of the Indians which they refused to do. A continental empire with valuable extractive resources was needed to fund a fledging government.

I am of opinion that although your right to make a claim under the donation act may justify you in holding this tract of land as against any other white man, it can by no means take precedence or be regarded as superior to that of the Indian who had possession, occupied and cultivated the same for several years prior to your removal to it. I am aware the general impression is that an Indian can lay no claim to land, and hold it as against a white man, and that the donation act secures to the latter any tract he may designate although occupied by an Indian. I do not so regard it. The act of Congress on the 14th August 1848 declares *That nothing in this act shall be construed to impair the rights of person or property now pertaining to the Indians in said Territory, so long as such rights shall remain unextinguished by treaty between the United States and such Indians.* This provision clearly acknowledges the rights of Indians, and no act of Congress has subsequently passed repealing this provision, for all subsequent acts have been in accordance and not in contrariety to that act. (Emphasis added).[21]

Following his visit to many of the tribes to discern the reasons for Indian hostilities, on October 9, 1855, Joel Palmer, Sup't, wrote to Com'r Moneypenny. The primary reason for conflict was the settlement of the Oregon Territory without any consideration whatsoever of Indian rights to their land. Euro-American settlers invading Indian lands promptly claimed the best agricultural lands, and mining claims for gold proliferated across Indian occupied land.

To Com'r Manypenny from Joel Palmer, Sup't, Oct 9 1855:

> ***The crisis of the destiny of the Indian race in Oregon and Washington Territories is now upon us***; and the result of the causes now operating, unless speedily arrested, will be disastrous to the whites, destructive to the Indians, and a heavy reproach upon our national character. ***Much of the present difficulty is traceable to the mistaken policy of permitting the settlement of this country prior to the extinguishment of the Indian title and the designation of proper reservations***. (Emphasis added).[22]

Let Colonial Settlers Exterminate Indians

J.W. Nesmith, Superintendent Indian Affairs, Oregon & Washington Territories, reported to Commissioner Denver, on September 1, 1857, that the Indians considered promises for the purpose of conciliating their friendship, "as an extension of a very long catalogue of falsehood already existing…" Also, he noted a grim awareness of a policy of letting the settlers exterminate the Indians. Nesmith further divulged that if extermination of the Indians was the U.S.'s policy it need only continue its course:

> The land laws which permit the occupation and settlement of both Washington and Oregon Territories, regardless of the rights of the Indians, render the intercourse laws, practically, a nullity. The wants of those "untutored wards of the government" should be supplied, and their rights protected, ***unless the government has determined that they should be doomed to extermination at the hands of the whites***. (Emphasis added).[23]

Part 4: Cayuse Indians Fight Invasion of Their Lands

In 1836, missionary couple Marcus and Narcissa Whitman founded the Whitman or Waiilatpu Mission adjacent to Cayuse lands. They were sponsored by the Boston-based American Board of Commissioners for Foreign Missions ("Missionary Board"). Their goal was to convert Indians to Christianity. Initially cordial to the mission couple, the Cayuse were indifferent to converting to Christianity or changing their nomadic lifestyle.

The Mission, though, due to its location, began to serve as a way station along the Oregon Trail. The Whitman's supported the incoming emigrants. When the Missionary Board decided to close their Mission, Whitman traveled to Boston to dissuade them. He argued that the Mission was a strategic rest stop and supply station for travelers to Oregon. The Missionary Board rescinded their order and Whitman returned in the fall of 1843 at the head of a wagon train of more than 800 emigrants.

Marcus wrote to Narcissa's parents of their new focus: "I have no doubt our greatest work is to be to aid the white settlement of this country ... The Indians have in no case obeyed the command to multiply and replenish the earth, and they cannot stand in the way of others doing so."[24]

The Cayuse Indians opposed the emigrants crossing their land. The large wagon trains compacted the soil and their stock freely grazed on the abundant grasses. Narcissa wrote: "The Indians are roused a good deal at seeing so many emigrants."[25] In 1847, a measles epidemic, thought to have spread from the wagon trains to the Cayuse, killed about half of them. The pallor of death hung over their villages. They blamed Marcus, a practicing physician, for not checking the epidemic.

The epidemic, along with the unending trail of emigrants, provoked a band of Cayuse warriors to attack a group of colonial settlers. They also attacked the Whitman Mission on November 29, 1847, killing fourteen settlers and the missionaries. Fifty-three women and children were held captive. Peter Skene Ogden, a Hudson's Bay Company official from Fort Vancouver, ransomed the captives.

Volunteer Regiment of Riflemen

A large armed mob marched through Cayuse territory and demanded the surrender of the warriors responsible for the massacre. The Cayuse refused to turn anyone over. The Provisional Governor George Abernethy demanded "immediate and prompt action" to punish the perpetrators: *I therefore call on the citizens of this territory to furnish five hundred men...* (Emphasis added).[26]

> BILL PASSED BY THE OREGON PROVISIONAL LEGISLATURE ON DECEMBER 7, 1847
>
> SEC. 1. That the Governor of Oregon Territory be and is hereby authorized and required forthwith to issue you his proclamation to the people of said territory to raise a Regiment of riflemen by volunteer enlistment, not to exceed five hundred men, to be subject to the rules and articles of war of the United States Army, and whose term of service shall expire at the end of ten months, unless sooner discharged by the proclamation of the governor.
> SEC. 2. That said Regiment of volunteers shall rendezvous at Oregon City on the twenty fifth day of December, A. D. 1847, and proceed thence with all possible dispatch to the Walla Walla Valley for the purpose of punishing the Indians, to what tribe or tribes soever they may belong, who may have aided or abetted in the massacre of Dr. Marcus Whitman and his wife, and others at Waiilatpu, or be otherwise employed as the Governor may direct.[27]

Volunteers Hunt Indians as Beasts of Prey

In response to the Whitman massacre, an armed volunteer outfit was organized under the leadership of Reverend Cornelius Gilliam to fight the Indians. Gilliam assumed the rank of Colonel. In spreading terror across the region, they hunted Cayuse Indians, burned villages and stole their stock and property. They fought the Cayuse at Sand Hollows but failed to defeat them. In a subsequent battle with seasoned Palouse and Walla Walla warriors, the volunteer outfit retreated. While preparing to camp that night, Colonel Gilliam was drawing a rope from the wagon with which to tether his horse when it caught upon the trigger of a gun lying in the bottom of the wagon, discharging it, the bullet entering his body and causing instant death.[28]

One news editorial demanded that "the barbarian murderers ... be pursued with unrelenting hostility, until their lifeblood has atoned for their infamous deeds; *let them be hunted as beasts of prey*." (Emphasis added).[29]

Cayuse Indian Lands Forfeited

In a July 6, 1848, Proclamation, the Superintendent of Indian Affairs, Oregon ("Sup't") didn't help to conciliate the outbreak by declaring Cayuse Indian lands forfeited. The Cayuse would shoulder all of the blame for the theft of their lands and resources. The Proclamation read in part:

> In consideration of the barbarities and insufferable conduct of the Cayuse indians [sic] tribe as portrayed in the massacre of American families at Waiilatpu, and the subsequent cause of the hostilities against Americans generally, and with a view to inflict upon them a just and proper punishment, as well as to secure and protect our fellow citizens immigrating from the United States to this territory against a course of reckless aggression so long and so uniformly practiced upon them by the said Cayuse indians [sic] I, H.A.G. Lee, Sup't Indian Affairs [Oregon Provisional Government] hereby *declare the territory of said Cayuse indians [sic] forfeited by them, and justly subject to be held by American residents in Oregon*. (Emphasis added).[30]

Oregon's Sup't Indian Affairs didn't have the authority to dispossess the Cayuse Indians of their land, only Congress did.

Causes of Cayuse War

Joseph Lane, the first Governor of the Oregon Territory and by default, the ex officio Sup't, listed the causes of the Cayuse War and the costs in a Letter to the Secretary of State, dated April 9, 1849:

> They [Indians] say the whites have settled their country, killed their game, brought among them sickness, which has caused many deaths, that they are rapidly passing off and will soon all be gone. That the white people have promised them from year to year and from time to time that the United States government would send out a Governor with presents for them, and commissioners to purchase their lands and pay for them. They are anxious to sell.[31]

He estimated the costs of the war at $190,000—the present-day value of the war would be about $7,094,254. It would continue with bloody skirmishes for another seven years.[32]

In 1850, in an effort to end hostilities, five Cayuse warriors were surrendered to the military by the Cayuse for the murder of the Whitman's. They were convicted and hanged on June 3, 1850. Their bodies were not returned to their people. Instead, they were publicly displayed to send a clear message to other Indians who might be considering war against the Americans. It failed to quell the ongoing brutal War.

Part 5: Clamor to Remove Indians

By 1850, a cry for the removal of Oregon's Indians could be heard in Washington, D.C. Joseph Lane, the Late Sup't, pronounced what would become the policy of the federal government: purchase of Indian lands and resettlement of them away from Euro-Americans. It was dressed up as a humane alternative to extermination by the settlers. Indians weren't asked what they wanted; instead, their trustee, acting on their behalf, in a fiduciary capacity, would knowingly deprive them of the incalculable value of their lands.

> Surrounded as many of the tribes and bands now are by the whites, whose arts of civilization, by destroying the resources of the Indians, doom them to poverty, want, and crime, the extinguishment of their title by purchase, and the locating them in a district removed from the settlements, is a measure of the most vital importance to them. Indeed, the cause of humanity calls loudly for their removal from causes and influences so fatal to their existence.[33]

Petition for Rogue River Military Force June 5, 1851

Without considering the impact of their invasion of Indian lands, miners demanded military protection:

> To the Honorable the Governor of the Territory of Oregon
> We, the undersigned, respectfully represent that the Indians on the road through the Rogue River country are at this time very hostile, having recently committed several murders and robberies on the **citizens of Oregon passing to and from the mines**.
> We, the undersigned, respectfully represent that we deem it highly important that some military force should be kept in the country in order to protect those that are passing through. (Emphasis added).[34]

Oregon Governor's Death Squads

Governor Gaines didn't lack in volunteers to chastise the Indians. John Thorp, a wagon train guide, offered to lead the Oregon Rifles mercenary squad:

> Allow me to suggest to your excellency the propriety of ordering (under the auspices of the govt.) a company of mounted volunteers to serve as Rangers, to reconnoiter the southern portion of our Territory ... The good to be obtained by this movement will be to cause the surrender of such of them as may have been engaged in the murder of the unfortunate individuals that was killed on the trail the other side of the Umpqua Valley, and also to demand and obtain the murderers of Mr. Newton in the year '46, ... I tender my services to take charge of the expedition ...[35]

Volunteers desired an "energetic prosecution of the war,"[36] as well as "nativist policies and the removal or even outright genocide of Oregon's indigenous people."[37] In contrast, officers in the U.S. army favored "negotiation and paternalistic (if less deadly) solutions."[38] The conflicting goals of the two groups created confusion about the legitimacy of command and orders for each party. The result was mayhem.

No Judicial Remedy for Indians

While settlers engaged wholeheartedly in the wanton, wholesale slaughter of Indians, the Indians had no judicial remedy. Sup't Anson Dart reported on the law prohibiting Indians from testifying as witnesses against a white person in his Annual Report. Absent protection by the federal government, which was resolutely denied, Indians had no alternative but to engage in retaliatory warfare which would result in their further decimation.

In consequence of a territorial law of Oregon, there is no way by which a white man can be punished for offenses committed against Indians, unless there be some other white person to testify as a witness against him. *The legislature of the provisional government enacted in its day a law in these words: 'A negro, mulatto or Indian shall not be a witness in any court or in any case against a white person,' which law was in full force at the time of the passage by Congress of the act organizing the Territory. Thomas Nelson Chief Justice of the Su. Co. of Oregon.* (Emphasis added). Anson Dart, Annual Report Superintendent of Indian Affairs for Oregon Territory, September 4, 1851.[39]

Brig. Gen. E. A. Hitchcock denounced the settlers for crying wolf, alleging that they were threatened by hostile Indians. Their war mongering was intended to provoke the Indians so they could achieve their agenda – moving the Indians off their rich agricultural, timber, and mineral lands.

Daily Alta California, San Francisco, April 4, 1852.

The writer represents the Coquille and Rogue River Indians as hostile, and would leave the public to infer that the people of the settlement at Port Orford are exposed to massacre in the very presence of the troops placed there for their protection. This account is false. … This talk about Indian hostility at Port Orford is a game perfectly understood. *If the people will let the Indians alone, the Indians will not trouble them. The cry of wolf cannot always succeed*, besides running the risk of failure when really well grounded, which your correspondent would do well to remember. E. A. Hitchcock, Brig. Gen. U.S.A. (Emphasis added).[40]

"Citizens are arming in all directions to march against the Indians and scatter them or exterminate them wherever they can be found."[41]

The ominous letter below warned the Sup't that the Curry County citizens were willing to shoot Indians if they were found in the County. The Chetco Indians considered this region home. The conflict between the Euro-American settlers and the Indians resulted in bloody, mortal skirmishes and the Abbott Indian Massacre.

Port Orford Curry County, Oregon February 15, 1867

To Sup't Huntington from Richard Pendergast, Late Sheriff of Curry County

> As there are quite a number of Indians in Curry County that belongs on the reservation, and as their presence amongst us is creating a hostile feeling towards them, I have been requested by several citizens of the county to write to you and inform you of their presence in our neighborhood. The people heretofore have suffered by these same Indians, and they say that unless they are taken away that they will be dealt harshly with, and *some go as far as to say that they will shoot them.* [W]e wish you would *remove them* back to the reservation. (Emphasis added).[42]

Inflammatory reports from the media didn't help: Idaho's Owyhee Avalanche reported a meeting of citizens who chose twenty-five men to go Indian hunting and offered bounties of $100 for an Indian man's scalp, $50 for a woman's scalp, and $25 for the scalps of children under ten years of age, provided that "each scalp shall have the curl of the head."[43]

The only solution the U.S. would proffer to accomplishing the "Manifest Destiny" of the U.S. was delegating to the lowest level of federal officials the duty to remove Indians from the land they had inhabited from time immemorial. Indian Agents were ordered and empowered to negotiate treaties which would dispossess Indians of their homelands. One example of this authority is set forth in the Special Instructions to Special Agent E. P. Drew from Sup't Palmer, dated Sept. 30, 1854.

> The policy of the government in regard to the Indians in Oregon is to extinguish their title to the country and colonize them on suitable reserves.[44]

Part 6: True Purpose of Indian Removal

The true purpose of removal wasn't about being humane; it was about moving a perceived obstacle out of the way of the westward expansion of settlers. It was about control of the west's immense and valuable natural resources, which would benefit the U.S. Treasury and economy, and the tycoons, the lumber barons, the industrialists of the east and the European investors. They were aware of the value of the land on which the diminishing timber, gold, fertile soil, water and oil abounded. The outright, blatant theft of resources would be facilitated by the government exercising militant control of the Indians. If they were in a limited, prescribed area that control would be easier. Whenever an Indian Nation offered any resistance, the Interior Department transferred its authority to the War Department.

Inexhaustible Mineral and Agricultural Wealth

Indian Agent J. L. Parrish, for the Port Orford District, corroborated the immense value of the Indian lands, on the southern coast alone, to Joel Palmer, Sup't, on July 10, 1854:

Its value to government may be inferred from what I have heretofore said of the *inexhaustible mineral wealth* of its mountain lands, and the adaptation of its plains and valleys to the agricultural pursuits of the white man. (Emphasis added).[45]

Part 7: President Orders Military Protection of Settlers

While Indians in Oregon were marginalized to the status of mere tenants on their own lands, President Franklin Pierce urged Congress, in his second annual address in December 1854, to increase the military forces necessary to protect frontier settlers.

> The experience of the last year furnishes additional reasons, I regret to say, of a painful character, for the recommendation heretofore made to provide for increasing the military force employed in the Territory inhabited by the Indians. *The settlers on the frontier have suffered much from the incursions of predatory bands, and large parties of emigrants to our Pacific possessions have been massacred with impunity*. The recurrence of such scenes can only be prevented by teaching these wild tribes the power of and their responsibility to the United States. (Emphasis added).[46]

Quieting Indian Hostilities in Oregon

In 1855, the President had to declare to the American public that 'hostilities' raged in Oregon. It was assured "efficient measures" were being taken to quiet the Indians.

> Information has recently been received that *the peace of the settlements in the Territories of Oregon and Washington is disturbed by hostilities on the part of the Indians*, with indications of extensive combinations of a hostile character among the tribes in that quarter, the more serious in their possible effect by reason of the undetermined foreign interests existing in those Territories, to which your attention has already been especially invited. *Efficient measures have been taken, which, it is believed, will restore quiet and afford protection to our citizens*. (Emphasis added).[47]

Rogue River Indians – Remove Whites, Not Us

Ben Wright, Spl. Indian Agent, reported to Genl. Joel Palmer, Sup't on March 20, 1855, the Indians astute retort to their removal:

I have always endeavored to convince them [Rogue River Indians] that it would be to their advantage to have a home of their own separate from the whites, and where the whites would not be allowed to intrude on them. Many of them agree with me, but had much rather have the whites removed than to remove themselves. (Emphasis added).[48]

Twenty Percent Mortality Blanketed Rogue River Indians

At the same time the Euro-American settlers were delivering ultimatums for Indian removal, Sup't Joel Palmer reported to Com'r Manypenny, on September 11, 1854, that twenty percent of the Rogue River Indians died during the harsh winter from lack of food and disease. Their seasonal occupation of the coast and rivers for fishing, the prairies for gathering roots and berries, and the mountains for hunting game was precluded, with the very real threat of outright, unjustified murder.

> I found the Indians of the River Valley excited and unsettled. The hostilities of last summer had prevented the storing of the usual quantities of food; the occupation of their best root grounds by the whites greatly abridged that source of subsistence; their scanty supplies and the *unusual severity of the winter had induced disease, and death had swept away nearly one-fifth of those residing on the reserve*. (Emphasis added).[49]

Part 8: Rogue River War Precipitated by Lupton Massacre

Clashes in nearby Northern California in the summer and autumn of 1855, along with agitation by rival politicians, led to an anti-Indian meeting in Jacksonville, Oregon, on October 7. Most of those present expressed approval of a plan put forward by a newly elected Democratic territorial representative, James A. Lupton. His plan was to exterminate Indians living off of the reservation. Early the next morning, seven parties of about 115 men, the self-described "Exterminators," set out to attack Indian camps. In those attacks, Lupton and another white man were mortally wounded, and ten more were injured in the initial assault, by one report; forty Indians were killed in the first attack. One witness said half the dead were women and children. The massacre was confirmed by Indian Agent Ambrose.

> I received a message from Capt. Smith, informing me that the *volunteers* had made a descent upon a small band of Indians. ... We then proceeded to Jake's camp, where we found *twenty-three dead [Indian] bodies, and a boy who escaped said he saw two women floating down the river, and it is quite probable several more were killed whose bodies were not found*. Upon the part of the whites, *James Lupton*, the captain of the company, received a mortal wound ... (Emphasis added).[50]

In a report to Congress, General Charles S. Drew defended the brutality, writing:

> "The attack commenced while it was yet too dark to distinguish one Indian from another, and by this reason it happened so that several squaws and children were killed. None were killed after it became light enough to distinguish the sexes."[51]

Unfriendly Indians Are Our Enemies

The Rogue River Indian outbreak wouldn't have come as a surprise, after the Lupton Massacre. An Indian Agent and military officer would be part of the presumed dead in this accelerating conflict.

> I had sent Lieut. Chandler with the agent [Wright] to bring down to the mouth of the river, all those who were friendly ... [T]hey seemed [to] adhere to their agreement with Genl. Palmer to move on the Reserve this summer ... That the present outbreak is extreme and serious in this quarter there is not the slightest doubt involving all the Indians on Rogue River and some of the coast Indians. ... [T]he number of persons killed or missing at 21 or 22, and the Indians engaged at between two and three hundred. The following is the list of whites missing from the mouth of Rogue River and vicinity. Benj. Wright, Indian agent, Capt. J. M. Poland, and others.[52]

The Governor singlehandedly accelerated the state of panic in the Territory. On October 15, 1855, Governor Curry enlisted two battalions of mounted volunteers from southern and middle Oregon, for the purpose of suppressing Indian hostilities. He made no attempt whatsoever to broker a peace. Instead, he sought an attack in the dead of winter, when the tribes were most vulnerable. The national hysteria he occasioned led to a war without any rules, leading to the indiscriminate mayhem and slaughter of peaceful Indians, including the elderly, women and children.

The U.S. Army was notified of an alleged threat of combined hostile tribes, including the Yakima, Pelouse, Klikatat, Walla-Walla, Cayuse, Deschute, Umatilla in the north, and the Rogue-River, Klamath, Shasta, and other bands in the south, engaging in hostilities against settlers. The extent and number of those hostile tribes wasn't fully known.

Admitting the lack of sufficient information, E. M. Barnum, Adjutant General of Oregon, nonetheless, issued General Order No. 3, on October 15, 1855, that unfriendly Indians were to be treated as enemies. Outnumbered and outgunned by the Army's soldiers and burdened with noncombatant villagers, the Indians were forced to fight.

> For the purpose of effectually chastising those savages who have perpetrated the merciless outrages in their midst, they will treat all Indians as enemies who do not show unmistakable signs of friendship, and deal with them accordingly.[53]

Settler passions were already raging for war and put peace seeking Indians in a dangerously untenable position. There were no criteria for differentiating hostile Indians from friendly ones; and it was unlikely, and was proven so, that the whites would make any effort to discern the nature of the Indians. The Order was grossly inadequate in directing how unfriendly Indians were to be treated. Were they to be killed, taken as prisoners-of-war and if tried for their aggression, would they be considered lawful combatants or hung?

Barnum's Order would backfire within days. On October 20, 1855, he filed a damning report, condemning the "war of extermination" waged by the Governor's volunteers. It wouldn't be the last:

> ... armed parties have taken the field in southern Oregon, with the ***avowed purpose of waging a war of extermination against the Indians*** in that section of the Territory, and have ***slaughtered, without respect to age or sex, a friendly band of Indians upon their reservation***, in despite (sic) of the authority of the Indian agent and the commanding officer of the United States troops stationed there, and contrary to the peace of the Territory. (Emphasis added).[54]

The U.S. Army lacked an understanding of the culture and motivations of the Northwestern settlers and Indians. After this Report, the U.S. Army realized the volunteers would be impossible to control.

Part 9: Rogue River War Chronology

The Rogue River Valley Indians could expect no protection from the U.S. Government. The increase in population, which became harmful to the Indians, resulted in (1) a decline in game, (2) *conflict over land since Indian title hadn't been extinguished* and no surveys had been done, and (3) *depredation to Indian property, due to the open-access land policy permitting free farming, grazing, use of timber and other extractive resources*. The brutal treatment of Indians left them with the only alternative of war.

Rogue River Wars (1855-1856), Southern Oregon			
1850s Governor Stevens of Washington Territory clashed with U.S. Army over Indian policy: Stevens wanted to displace Indians and take their land, but Army opposed land grabs.			
1830's	Skirmishes	CA Gold Rush, Oregon Trail	
1834	American Ewing Young murdered several Indians.		
1835	Indians attack American fur trapping party.		
1837	Willamette Cattle Co. kill Indian boy.	Indians retaliate.	
1846	Southern Route to Willamette Valley open.	90 to 100 wagons and 450 to 500 emigrants used new trail passing through Rogue tribe's homelands.	
1850-1855	White settlers attack Rogue River Indians.		
1850	Terr. Gov. Lane negotiates Treaty with Takelma.	Gov. will protect Indians rights and Indians will grant safe passage for miners and settlers.	
Late 1851	Discovery of gold on Jackson Creek.		
1852	28 Donation Land Act claims recorded in Rogue Valley.		
1853	Oregon voluntary citizen militias form.		
1853	Joseph Lane, territorial delegate to Congress, approves attacks on Indians at Table Rock.		
September 8, 1853	Indian Service Sup't Joel Palmer	Negotiates Treaty of Peace.	New reservation - 100 sq. miles.
September 10, 1853	Indian Service Sup't Joel Palmer	Treaty of Cession and Relinquishment signed.	Indians cede 2000 sq. miles.
Oct. 7, 1855	Anti-Indian meeting in Jacksonville.	Democratic Territorial Rep., James A. Lupton, authorizes extermination of Indian people living off reservation.	115 Volunteers attack Indian camps, Lupton killed.
Oct. 8, 1855	Militia attacks Indians.	Indians attack settlers, burn mining camp.	
Oct. 8, 1855	Captain Smith Commandant of Fort Lane took Indians in for safety.	Mob of settlers burns villages, kill 27 Indians.	Indians kill 27 settlers.
October 31, 1855	Battle of Hungry Hill	Indians held off more than 300 dragoons, militiamen and volunteers.	
February 22, 1856	Ellensburg attacked by Indians and burned.		
Feb. 1856	Table Rock Reservation, Principal Chief Toquahear declines to fight.	Removed under military escort to Grande Ronde Reservation; guarded by troops at Fort Yamhill.	
May 20, 1856	Indians confer with Bvt. Lt. Col. Robert Buchanan, Commander of Regulars, at Oak Flat.	Some Indians agree to surrender.	
May 27, 1856	Captain Smith arranged surrender of Indians.	U.S. soldiers attacked.	
May 27, 1856	Indians attack Capt. Andrew J. Smith at Big Bend, Smith reinforced by Buchanan.		
June 1856	Chief Tecumtum surrenders.	Indians removed under military escort to present-day Siletz Reservation.	

Part 10: "Oregon's Trail of Tears"

After their defeat in June 1856, the Rogue River Indians were removed forcibly to the Grande Ronde Reservation. Their removal is known as "Oregon's Trail of Tears." They were shot at and vilified. One of them was killed, even though under military escort. A 'volunteer' was arrested for the murder but evaded judicial prosecution by leaving the jurisdiction. Settlers petitioned against their settlement on the Grande Ronde Reservation, threatening extermination. During their removal, they suffered from sickness and eight of them died. The dead were hurriedly buried along the way.

Rogue River Indians Threatened with Slaughter

Before they were even removed, settlers were threatening to kill them along the way. They didn't want Indians in their counties. The veracity of this situation is in the DOI's communication, in advance of the removal, and during the thirty-three-day Trail of Tears.

> **To C. M. Walker, Esq., from Joel Palmer, Sup't, Nov. 26, 1855:**
>
> You are hereby designated a special agent to aid in removing the friendly bands of Rogue River and Umpqua Indians from their present encampments to the Grand Ronde ... ***The reported opposition of a portion of the citizens to the removal of the Indians and an avowal to shoot them*** and those who attempt to cause such a movement may render it necessary to have an escort the entire route. (Emphasis added).[55]
>
> **To George Ambrose, Indian Agent, Jackson County, from Nathaniel Ford, Indian Agent, December 18, 1855:**
>
> *Some designing bad men have represented that it was your (Palmer's) design to have them all killed off, that if you sent for them it would only be to get them in a better place to kill them off... (Ambrose to Palmer, Dec. 14, 1855).*
>
> **To George Ambrose, Indian Agent, Jackson County, from Nathaniel Ford, Indian Agent, December 18, 1855**

General Palmer is now on his way to Rogue River with a view of moving the Rogue River Indians ... ***I will not be surprised if every Indian brought in by him is immediately killed*** ... The people of Polk ... are determined the Rogue River Indians shall not settle in our midst nor on our borders. ... ***if they come with General Palmer they come at the risk of being beat off by the citizens of our country.*** (Emphasis added).[56]

Whites Meddling with Removal

To Sup't Palmer from Agt. Ambrose, Jan. 31, 1856:

Circumstances have rendered it impossible for [us] to remove these Indians for the past two months, although they are quite willing to go... ***The military escort asked for is not sufficient to afford them protection*** ... Some meddlesome evil-disposed persons are in the habit of frequenting the encampment, telling the Indians all sort of stories in relation to the contemplated move, warning them of the danger they will be in if they should go, representing to them that they will surely be killed by the way by persons who are laying in wait for that purpose, that at least five hundred persons were preparing to march against them, and their only chance of safety lay in flight to the mountains in the night unknown to the authorities of Fort Lane. Such meddlesome interference keeps them in constant alarm and renders it imperatively necessary that they should be accompanied by a sufficient military force to ward off any threatened danger. (Emphasis added).[57]

Indian Agent George H. Ambrose kept a Journal[58] during the Indians removal to Grande Ronde. In a non-emotional tome, he reveals the difficulty of the terrain and most importantly, that there were several ill, elderly and infirm Indians to transport. The number grew greater during the journey and twice they had to add more teams and wagons to carry them. Deaths are reported, without names. They were buried as quickly as possible alongside the trail, in order to avoid any delay. None of the ceremonial rites of the Indians could be performed. Today, we don't know who these Indians were, their ages, if they left family behind, or where they were buried. It is very common to have the DOI refer to Indians in the abstract and prepare inventories of numbers, not persons. Yet, the Indian Agents and soldiers delegated to this task will be listed by name and rank, with information about them.

Journal of the Removal of the Rogue River Tribe of Indians Commencing on the February 22, 1856, George H. Ambrose

23rd Friday ... Also two additional teams were secured to convey the sick, aged and infirm. Our teams now number eight, which I fear will not be sufficient. Thirty-four Indians are disabled from traveling by reason of sickness aside from the aged & infirm, who will as a matter of course have to be hauled.

28th Thursday ... while about preparing to leave camp some person killed an Indian who had wandered off some distance from camp in search of his horse ... We learned this evening that a party of evil-disposed persons have gone in advance of us as is supposed to annoy us, or kill some friendly Indian. A messenger was immediately dispatched to Capt. Smith at Fort Lane for an additional force to escort us... We also learned that an individual by the name of Timoleon Love was the person who killed the Indian this morning.

29th Friday ... We had another (sic) Indian to die, the first by diseases on the road, although many are very sick. However there are no new cases of sickness occurring.

March 1st Saturday ... we learned that Mr. Love and some others were awaiting us at the house, intending to kill an Indian. Upon going to the house I found it to be a fact, talked with the gentlemen & told them the consequences, went back & requested Capt. Smith to arrest Mr. Love and turn him over to the civil authorities.

5th Wednesday ... An Indian girl died. ... Mr. Love, who still continued to follow us, was arrested & put under guard.

7th Friday ... An Indian woman died this morning & the number of sick increasing it was found necessary to hire or buy another team.

10th Monday. This morning a writ of habeas corpus was served on Lieut. Underwood to show cause why ... he held in custody unlawfully the person of Timoleon Love ... Lieut. Hazen was left ... to turn the prisoner over to the proper officers of the law.

11th I then proceeded to Judge Deady's and caused a writ to be issued for the arrest of Timoleon Love ... Before the service of the warrant Mr. Love had effected his escape.

12th Wednesday ... Two deaths occurred today ... one man & one woman.

13th Thursday ... This morning we had quite a shower of rain, rendering it quite unpleasant traveling. After burying the dead we took up on our line of march...

15th Saturday... One woman died today.

18th Tuesday ... an Indian died, which delayed us a short time to bury.

25th Tuesday ... after a period of thirty-three days, in which time we traveled a distance of two hundred & sixty-three miles. *Started with three hundred and ninety-five Indians. Eight deaths and eight births, leaving the number the same as when started*. (Emphasis added).[59]

On February 12, 1856, General Wool was informed of Governor Curry's 'death squads.' These 'frenzied' volunteers, murdering Indians and stealing their property, were sanctioned by the Governor of Oregon.

> ...that the *friendly Cayuses are every day menaced with death by Governor Curry's volunteers*. ... *Today he says these same volunteers, without discipline and without orders, are not yet satisfied with rapine and injustice*, and wish to take away the small remnant of animals and provisions left. (Emphasis added).[60]

Even after the dangerous journey was complete, the Indians faced the continuing deadly threat of the settlers in the region. They didn't want any Indians in the Willamette Valley. On January 8, 1856, a petition was sent from Oregon citizens to President Pierce opposing the purchase of the land and colonization of the "thousands" of Indians in the Willamette Valley. So strong was the opposition that Joel Palmer was forced to organize civilian protection and request the presence of United States troops. On April 11, 1856, Joel Palmer wrote the Com'r:

> The threatening attitude of the community led me to apprehend a general and combined attack upon the camp of friendly Indians, located the Grand Ronde, and the slaughtering or driving into hostile positions all who might be residing in the valley. I accordingly deemed it necessary to organize a force of armed citizens and place them on the eastern line of the reservation, cutting off all communication between settlements and the Indians. And whilst engaged in this line, to construct a fence from mountain to mountain, as a line of demarcation, across which no one could pass. This I have attempted putting into operation and have good reason to believe will be successful. It will require a force of about sixty men, and to remain until relieved by the promised Company of United States Troops.[61]

The influence of personal prejudices and hatreds toward Indians that existed led to indecisiveness, poor preparation for the Army, and poor support for the DOI.

Grande Ronde Indians Sick and Dying

The Grande Ronde Reservation would include the Umpqua-Cow Creek Band, the Rogue River Indians, the Chasta, the Umpqua and Kalapuya, and the Molalla.

A. G. Henry, M.D., the Resident Physician at the Grand Ronde Agency would report on Jan. 2, 1857, of the Indians sick and dying:

> The number of lung complaints have been increased, and since the snow has gone off quite a number of cases of "bloody flux" have occurred, and it will most certainly *become epidemic* with the opening of spring, unless active sanitary measures are adopted speedily. Eight Deaths. (Emphasis added).[62]
>
> I found that very little preparation had been made for ... the large number of naked, diseased Indians. I found them sick & dying. *We find them most generally destitute of every [omission] necessary, often suffering extremely for want of sufficient covering, and in such cases we could not refrain from loaning them a blanket... [A] large number who apply for medicine are suffering mainly from mental depression.* (Emphasis added).[63]

Part 11: 'Off the Reservation'

Sup't Palmer issued instructions to his agents on how to treat Indians. Male Indians on reservations who are over age 12 were to be confined to the reserve, while *Indians off the reservation were to be treated as outlaws.* Palmer was willing to permit Indians to work for white settlers, if the whites would guarantee good conduct.

> REGULATIONS FOR THE GUIDANCE OF AGENTS IN THE OREGON INDIAN SUPERINTENDENCY PENDING EXISTING HOSTILITIES. Office Supt. Ind. Affairs, Oct. 13th, 1855.
>
> The names of all adult males and boys over 12 years of age shall be enrolled, and the roll called daily
>
> *When anyone shall be absent at roll call, the fact shall be noted, and unless a satisfactory reason be rendered, the absentee shall be regarded as a person dangerous to the peace of the country and dealt with accordingly.*
>
> Any Indian found outside of his designated temporary reservation, without being able to satisfactorily account therefor, *shall be arrested and retained in custody so long as shall be deemed necessary...*

Any Indian who has joined or may hereafter join the hostile bands, give them information, or in any way aid or assist them in making war against the whites shall be regarded as having thereby forfeited all rights under the treaty and excluded from any benefits to be derived therefrom. He will, moreover, be regarded as an enemy, and it will be the duty of all friendly Indians to deliver such up to the agents or civil officers, and in no case to afford them encouragement or protection.

Citizens generally are requested to ... exercise a due degree of forbearance in their dealings with the Indians, but at the same time to keep a vigilant watch over them ... Joel Palmer, Sup't. (Emphasis added).[64]

These Regulations were in accord with the U.S.'s reservation policy. The reservation system was to curtail the movement of Indians and to control their behavior.

In the first announcement made of the reservation system, it was expressly declared that the Indians should be made as comfortable on, and as uncomfortable off, their reservations as it was in the power of the Government to make them; that such of thein as went right should be protected and fed, and such as went wrong should be harassed and scourged without intermission.[65]

Part 12: Congressional and Executive Branches Countenance Massacre of Indians

In 1856, Congress requested a report on the Rogue River Indian War. The blatant massacres, clearly reported by the U.S. Army and Sup't, were white-washed. On April 4, 1856, the settlers submitted a Petition to remove Palmer to President Pierce.[66]

President Pierce: Remove Indian Obstacle

Fully aware of the bloody war going on under his watch, President Pierce gave carte blanche authority to the state and federal governments to chastise the Indians, by whatever means necessary. As the highest government official to protect Indians, he chose to focus, instead, on the agricultural and mining riches on Indian lands. They were being dedicated wholesale to the colonial settlers, by our President.

> Extensive combinations among the hostile Indians of the Territories of Washington and Oregon at one time threatened the devastation of the newly formed settlements of that remote portion of the country. From recent information we are permitted to hope that the ***energetic and successful operations conducted there will prevent such combinations in future and secure to those Territories an opportunity to make steady progress in the development of their agricultural and mineral resources***. (Emphasis added).[67]

Part 13: King Midas Touches Blood

The settlers in various areas continued their requests for removal of Indians. Unfortunately, gold was discovered in the Coquille Valley and the Indians had to go.

> We the undersigned settlers of the Coquille Valley in Coos County O.T. would humbly beg and pray your attention to the ***removal*** of the Coquille Indians from the Coquille River. ... We have had some difficulties with the Upper Coquille Indians and have good and sufficient evidences from reliable Indians that the above Indians have an understanding with the Rogue River Indians to unite and kill all the whites in this valley and all that kept them from accomplishing it was our being on our guard, which we believe to be necessary yet and will be until the Coquille Indians are removed from the valley (Emphasis added).[68]

Sup't Palmer was very clear in his response in support of these settlers. First, the Department would do everything in its power to relieve the Euro-American settlers of the annoyance of the Indians. Second, this annoyance would be assuaged by moving the Indians away from their homelands, not the other way around. Third, the Department's objective was to prioritize this policy and effect their coerced relocation as quickly as possible. No thought was given to the immense task involved of force marching a whole people to a new destination, that they didn't choose. Oregon would have its "Trail of Tears." Fourth, the government was visiting different areas in the state to determine where the Indians would be reserved. It was predestined; Indians would have no say. To resist meant the Departments' abdicating its responsibility over Indians to the military.

> To Settlers from Joel Palmer Sup't, February 18, 1856

Upon the whole I may say that every possible effort will be made by the Indian Department to secure a strict observance to treaty stipulations and rid the settlements from the annoyance of Indians by their *removal*, at the earliest possible moment, to districts designed as Indian reservations. (Emphasis added).[69]

Demonizing Indians

Given the immense value of the coastal lands, removal of the Indians was a foregone conclusion. The methodology was frightening. The war mongering evidences the impact of stereotypical, biased thinking. These Oregonian Euro-Americans' entreat, "under the color of law," volunteers to keep the redskins within "their proper limits and duty." An action by Indians isn't even required; it is enough that the settlers 'know' that the Indians are merely waiting for an opportunity.

If Indians are seen as demons with some form of evil, supernatural powers, they forfeit any sense of humanity, just by an association with Satan. Superhuman force would be considered justifiable in keeping the 'black magic' redskins in-place.

Benton County O.T. March 22, 1856.

To Geo. L. Curry, Gov. of Oregon Territory from Settlers

The undersigned, citizens of the frontier situate along the Coast Range ... beg permission to represent ... that there are many Indians located on the coast ... do pass up and down the coast ... unrestrained. We know these Indians; they are unworthy [of] the confidence of civilized men; *they are mere demons in human form, thirsting for blood; they only wait a favorable opportunity to wreak their hellish vengeance on the unprotected and defenseless frontier pioneers, their wives and their unoffending children.* Now, Gov. Curry, we pray you to deliver us from This Evil, by sending a company of citizen volunteers to patrol the coast and keep these evil redskins within their proper limits and duty. (Emphasis added).[70]

Coast Indians

To Capt. A. F. Hedges from R. B. Metcalfe, Ind. Agent, Dec. 28, 1856

> There is great complaint and much dissatisfaction among the Indians in consequence of promises made them by Gen. Palmer and not complied with. There are many of them in a *destitute* condition. Their wardrobe consists of nothing more than they brought into the world with them, and exposed to this inclement season [it] is enough to drive men with less forbearance than Indians generally possess to desperation, and if the government does not do something for these people there is *nothing more certain than we will have them to fight next spring*. (Emphasis added).[71]

Part 14: "Private War"

By early 1856, it was obvious to the U.S. military that the warfare occurring in Oregon was due to the desire of settlers to rid Oregon of Indians, and not the actual threat imposed by the Indians. As a result, lives were needlessly lost, Indians were deliberately exposed to cruel and barbarous suffering—exposure, starvation and death—while federal dollars were being expended on a private war.

In a deplorable Report from General Wool to Lieutenant Colonel L. Thomas, Assistant Adjutant General, U.S. Army, Benicia Headquarters, Department of the Pacific, dated January 19, 1856, he cited the frightening motives of the white settlers:

> In Oregon, as well as in the northern part of California, *many whites are for exterminating the Indians*. This feeling is engendered by two newspapers that go for extermination, and is more or less possessed by the volunteers as well as others not enrolled under the banners of Governor Curry. *As long as individual war is permitted and paid for by the United States, and which is expected by all the citizens of Oregon, we shall have no peace*, and the war may be prolonged indefinitely, especially as *it is generally asserted that the present war is a God-send to the people*. (Emphasis added).[72]

In a subsequent letter to the Governor of Oregon, General Wool reiterated the "private" war being fought by the citizens.

It is, however, greatly to be regretted that there are too many white inhabitants, both in Oregon and northern California, who go for exterminating the Indians, and, consequently, do not discriminate between friends and foes; the result of which has been the cause of the death of many innocent and worthy citizens, both in southern Oregon and in northern California. ***Could the citizens be restrained from private war, I have no doubt peace and quiet would soon be restored to the people of that region of country***. (Emphasis added).[73]

A letter from Agt. Ambrose to Sup't Palmer, dated February 29, 1856, repeated the wish of certain citizens to prolong the war, which would mean more loss of lives and property.

It is the desire of many persons here to protract the war, men who have no interest in the country and might properly be considered vagrants in any country in the world but this. That our country is infested with such a set of men none will question who are acquainted with the country. (Emphasis added).[74]

A letter from Joel Palmer, Sup't, to Com'r Manypenny, dated April 11, 1856, elucidated the strategy to keep the settlers up in arms, at the cost of Indian lives. Importantly, it highlights the dissension between the governing entities in the War. It is a well-known fact that the easiest way to prevent success in war is the inability to express and act upon a unified plan. No decisive victory was possible due to the splintered approach for war. The political infighting led to the Indians out maneuvering, outflanking, and soundly beating the disunited forces fighting them.

> These outrages and those in Southern Oregon have created a state of feeling among our citizens almost uncontrollable. ... Not a little of this unnecessary excitement, I am forced to believe, grew out of efforts of disappointed politicians who strove ... by circulating the most outrageous, exaggerated and groundless reports in regard to the acts of Indians and the agents in this Department to excite the fears and prejudices of the people. Meetings were held by the citizens simultaneously in different parts of the Territory ... petitions and memorials, resolutions and remonstrances were drawn up by the few present and passed condemnatory of almost every movement made by the Indian Department, tending to inflame the minds of the people (who were ignorant of the facts) and drive them to acts of desperation.

> The ***dissensions between the different functionaries of the government***, civil and military, tends greatly to destroy the efficiency of the service: crimination & recrimination but adds to the flame, and whilst a considerable portion of the energies of the respective parties are exhausted in striving to gain the ascendancy and convince others of the correctness of their policy, the enemy goes unwhipped, their forces continually augmenting, our citizens slaughtered, and our settlers cut off and destroyed. (Emphasis added).[75]

Com'r Manypenny's unheeded report on November 22, 1856, evidences, at the highest level of those entrusted to protect Indians, the threat of extermination and abuses Indians endured:

> It cannot be disguised that a portion of the white population of the Pacific Territories, entertain feelings deeply hostile to the Indian tribes of that region, and are anxious for the extermination of the race. ... The existing laws for the protection of the persons and property of the Indian wards of the government are sadly defective. ... Trespasses and depredations of every conceivable kind have been committed on the Indians. They have been personally maltreated, their property stolen, ***their timber destroyed***, their possessions encroached upon, and divers other wrongs and injuries done them. (Emphasis added).[76]

Part 15: Dividing Up Oregon: Casting Lots

By 1856, more than 7,000 settlers had acquired more than 2.5 million acres in the Willamette, Umpqua, and the Rogue Valleys, home to many indigenous peoples. In the beginning were the farmers, followed by the cattle and sheepmen of eastern Oregon, subsequently by the 'lumberjack,' and thereafter by the railroad sponsored homesteader.

The Oregon & California Railroad had an office in Portland and Boston and later Topeka and Omaha to encourage and direct immigration to the Northwest. Oregon didn't have the legal tangle of Spanish land grants impeding clear land titles that enmeshed California, so for many settlers Oregon was the better choice. They would avoid the lengthy, costly legal wrangles in California courts.

Disposition of the Public Domain in Oregon [In Acres]	
Homestead Act	11,097,982 acres
Railroad Grants	1,588,532
Sales	6,455,551
Grant to State	4,329,445
Miscellaneous	992,921
Donation Claims	2,614,082
Wagon Road Grants	2,490,890
Total	29,569,403

Twenty-nine million acres were transferred from public to private ownership. This is approximately one-half of Oregon, the most immediately important half. It included the western farms, the ranches of eastern Oregon, and 11 million of the choice timbered acres of the 28 million forested acres in Oregon.[77]

Additional Acreage Information			
Oregon & California Railroad (Portland to CA Border)	3,728,000 acres	2,890,000 acres revested	
Wagon-Road Grants	2,490,000 acres	2/3 of all Wagon Road Grants in US	
Private Ownership of Forests	11 million acres	Total in State 28 million acres	
Education	4,035,000 acres	4,329,435 acres (State Lands Total)	1/3 sold during timberland boom 1900-1910

Oregon Population 1850	
1850	92,597
1860	379,994
1850 population is for all of Oregon Territory. 1860 Population is for Oregon state only.[78]	

Part 16: Oregon Admitted as State in 1859

Oregon was admitted as a state in 1859. Washington Territory was enlarged to include the remaining Oregon Territory, not included in the new state.

As to Oregon's Indians, the Com'r warned the reservation system was the "last resort to save the race from extermination; and, if it fails or is abandoned, their doom may then be pronounced."[79]

On May 12, 1866, an editor of the Idaho Statesman likened Indians to animals, referring to their dead bodies as "carcasses." Repeatedly, Indians are referred to as animals to eliminate any residue of immorality in murdering them.

> On July 29, 1867, an editor for the Idaho Statesman was of the opinion: ... that the military should continue killing Indians 'until the last Indian in the Territories was either on his reservation or enriched the sagebrush with his decaying carcass.' ... 'The idea that the Indians have any right to the soil is ridiculous. ...They have no more rights to the soil of the Territories of the United States than wolves or coyotes...'[80]

It wasn't just the government pushing for the Indians' ouster from their lands. The citizens were incited to even greater heights in their opposition, demanding military extermination. Again, using terminology such as "decaying carcass," wolves or coyotes implied that Indians were animals. Once groups formed, they could wantonly exercise violent unrestrained behavior against savages. The government's stubborn refusal to protect Indians only exacerbated the potential for bloodshed.

Posturing for the support of their constituents, many politicians made matters worse. On Sep. 26, 1866, Governor George L. Woods wrote to Secretary of War Edwin Stanton that Indians were overrunning eastern Oregon:

> Hostile Indians are overrunning eastern Oregon. Department Columbia has not troops enough to furnish need. Regiment cannot be raised in time. Immediate protection must be given. ... Shall I appoint officers, or will you. Or shall I call out five hundred volunteers for one year and officer them, and have them mustered into service United States? Give me instructions.[81]

The problem with volunteers was that the civilians didn't have the funding, military discipline and training or equipment needed to conduct sustained offensive operations, which limited their actions to mere raids, rather than coordinated actions that could bring about the circumstances for peace. The hostile and prejudiced actions of civilians led them to the outright murder of men, women and children and massacres of groups of Indians. When faced with large groups of warriors, they lacked the command and control, and tactical proficiency, leading to their embarrassing defeat. Smaller groups of warriors used their superior tactical mobility and guerilla warfare to their advantage.

Part 17: Rogue-Umpqua Rivers Glittering Sands

The Rogue-Umpqua Waterway was spattered with gold. The fifteen waterfalls provided the hydro-power to support gold and timber mining.

The Northern Indian Difficulties. What Is to Be Done with Them? June 24, 1857

> So far as the rivers have been prospected, it has been conclusively shown that, throughout that entire belt of country, there is a field for *placer mining* ... The beach, too, from Rogue River to the Umpqua is *glittering with sands, golden*, in truth, that only call for the exercise of Yankee inventive powers, to bring forth some kind of machinery, to enable them to be worked successfully.... Its agricultural resources are unsurpassed, and its magnificent forests have long ago been fully described in the public prints. Yet, for years, this section of our Pacific possessions has been overrun by these wild tribes, and government has doled out her aid with a stingy hand, to keep them in subjection.

The Midas touch emboldened the settlers to arrogantly demand extermination of the savages.

> Were everyone well acquainted with the locality, there would be no need for us to attempt to portray the great importance of immediate government aid to suppress this outbreak, and *if actually necessary, to exterminate these savages to enable the country to be permanently settled*.

Whether it be the point of the bayonet or the rifle bullet, the settlers didn't care – "final extermination" was warranted, if they went "off the reservation."

> Prompt and decided action is demanded to drive them back to the reservation which has been set apart for them, at the point of the bayonet, if necessary. *The whistle of the rifle bullet is the only mandate that they will obey, and they should be taught this time to keep within their prescribed limits, or pay the forfeit by their final extermination.* (Emphasis added).[82]

Strong inducements continued to be held out to whites to emigrate and settle in the Oregon Territory, even though Indian land hadn't been purchased. The result, according to Com'r Mix's 1858 Report to the Secretary, was Indian depredations and hostilities due to them having been "intruded upon, ousted of their homes and possessions without any compensation, and deprived, in most cases, of their accustomed means of support, without any arrangement having been made to enable them to establish and maintain themselves in other locations."[83]

Com'r Mix presumed Indians would be left to starve or steal. His 1858 Report further relayed this unbelievable message to the Secretary: *either the government must provide for them or exterminate them.*

> We have no longer distant and extensive sections of country which we can assign them, abounding in game, from which they could derive a ready and comfortable support; ... and in consequence of which they must, at times, be subjected to the pangs of hunger, if not actual starvation, or obtain a subsistence by depredations upon our frontier settlements. If it were practicable to prevent such depredations, the alternative to providing for the Indians in the manner indicated, would be to leave them to starve; but as it is impossible, in consequence of the very great extent of our frontier, and our limited military force, to adequately guard against such occurrences, the only alternative, in fact, to making such provision for them, is to exterminate them.[84]

In a December 31, 1862, Letter from Governor Pickering to Senator Trumbull, Pickering fell into line with the time worn petition to the Senate for the extinguishment of Indian title to a vast territory: *all lands from the South Pass of the Rocky Mountains down Snake River Valley, to the Columbia River*, over which the present Emigrant travel road passes. His request for military forts would be granted. He certainly wasn't "sad" at the "fact that full ten millions of gold" had been mined in the present year alone with up to "fifty millions" possible in the future.

> Taking into consideration the fact that full *ten millions of gold has been gathered from the tributaries of the Columbia River during the past season; with upwards of twenty millions of dollars worth being the result of the labors of miners during the next year; and the certain prospects of thirty millions the 2nd year and forty millions the third year and fifty millions* carried away every year from then on, these gold fields will operate as a magnet of attraction. (Emphasis added).[85]

Part 18: Terror Tactics Used to Force Tribes to Cede Lands

Through withholding food and clothing, the U.S. utilized a strong lever. A starving, freezing people were much more likely to surrender or sell their lands. A letter to Thomas Jefferson from Meriwether Lewis, December 15, 1808, details the withholding of goods as intimidation to require land cessions.[86]

To Geo. H. Ambrose, Esq., Ind. Agt. from Joel Palmer, Supt. Ind. Affrs:

> Economic Sanctions: You will be very careful that the goods be delivered to those for whom they are particularly designed. ***Preferences should, however, be made in favor of those residing on the reserve***, while all should be treated kindly and receive your care and protection. It may be proper also to make a judicious discrimination in favor of such as you may thus ***induce to remove*** to and reside upon the reserve. (Emphasis added).[87]

This practice of favoritism in issuing articles furnished by the U.S., even though purchased with the Indian tribes' own trust fund monies, became a common tactic to influence behavior. It also fomented animosities within tribes, thereby preventing unified responses.

> The policy of rewarding the progressive by a generous issue of the articles furnished by the Government and imposing privation upon others who obstinately persist in refusing to adopt civilized habits has been productive of good results. It has brought forcibly to them an object lesson and the realization of the fact that, while the Government is disposed to be kind and generous to them if they will accept the instruction and advice imparted through its representatives, it will not support them in idleness.[88]

Delay in Delivery and Insufficiency of Goods and Monies

Many problems of transporting goods to the remote reservations resulted in not delivering them timely or at all. Goods were purchased in New York, which added a substantial cost, not only to the goods, but the transport of them. Adequate storage space wasn't available which led to waste. The amount of the annuities was many times not worth traveling to the delivery point.

> The promised annuities of goods and provisions often did not reach the reservations in a timely manner or were not in adequate quantity. This caused Oregon's Sup't of Indian Affairs, William Rector, to remark that "to compel even Indians to remain on a reservation without food and clothes, or even the means of obtaining them, is unjust and inhuman."[89]

Sup't W. Nesmith pointed out the fraud to Com'r Dole in a report on Dec. 13, 1861:

> ***Great inconvenience has resulted to the service in Oregon and Washington from the neglect of the Department promptly to remit funds for the current expenses of the service.*** ... by such ***criminal neglect*** of the Department the superintendents and agents have been forced to make purchases *on credit,* at prices varying from 20 to 50 percent above what the same purchases could have been made for in cash.

The practice of purchasing goods in New York ... should be dispensed with; *some person has defrauded the government and the Indians of immense sums of money by such purchases*. (Emphasis added).⁹⁰

Agent A.P. Dennison pointed out to Com'r Greenwood on May 17, 1860, that agents in Oregon could purchase the goods cheaper. Not only did purchasing goods in New York add to their cost and shipping time, many times the goods purchased were worthless or broken during transport or not the type of goods required.

J. W. Perit Huntington, Supt. Ind. Affrs. in Oregon, similarly, reported this situation to then Senator Nesmith:

> In regard to the quality and suitableness of the goods shipped, it has generally been such as could have been anticipated when the purchaser was entirely unacquainted with the country, or the Indians who inhabit it. There has uniformly been an unfavorable discrepancy between the invoices and the articles actually shipped. ...
>
> ... *"Fancy mirrors"* costing $5 per dozen were sent. They proved to be little looking glasses, about two inches in diameter, and worth absolutely nothing to the Indians. Tinware packed in roomy cases until the freight was far in excess of the value. ...
>
> *In short, the entire purchases show either ignorance of the Indians' wants, or design to defraud them.*
>
> 1st. The purchase of goods should invariably be made by a person acquainted with the Indians and their wants, and with the character of the climate and country where they are to be consumed.
> 2nd. That purchases should be made at the wholesale mart nearest to the agency where they are required.
> 3rd. That purchase in New York and Baltimore necessarily involves enormous transportation charges, or else the withholding of the goods from the Indians for a year. (Emphasis added).⁹¹

Appropriations Weapon

Congress acknowledged that from "the beginning, Federal policy toward the Indian was based on the desire to dispossess him of his land."⁹² Decreasing the amount of appropriations to tribes was a way to get them to cede lands. Congress' pattern of this inhuman practice is evident.

On May 29, 1868, Oregon U.S. Senator Geo. H. Williams warned State Congressional Representative Benj. Simpson, Salem, Ore., that Congress was cutting Indian appropriations:

> There is a crazy determination to cut down the Indian appropriations. We are going to have a hard struggle to prevent their total abolition in some cases. There never was such a frenzy to reduce expenses.[93]

Pitting Indian against Indian

The fear of removal and the need to curry favor with the whites resulted in regrettable actions by Indians, pitting Indian against Indian.

> **Men and Matters at Yreka.** Yreka, May 20, 1859.
>
> Editor *Evening Bulletin*: Considerable excitement was created in town today by the appearance of *Lalake, one of the chiefs of the Klamath Lake Indians, having in his possession the heads of three Indians killed by him at or near the Klamath River.* As you have already been informed, there were some five persons murdered lately, at the head of Butte Creek, in Oregon, who were on their way to Klamath Lake to settle there. When found, they were horribly mutilated; their horses, arms and everything valuable gone. Suspicion fell upon the Klamath Lake Indians as having committed the murder, none others being known to have been about that country, and some who were in Jacksonville at the time were arrested. Lalake, their chief, being here, and himself and tribe always having been friendly towards the whites, resolved to find the murderers and if possible bring them to punishment. He started out, and found near the scene of the murder three Indians (a father and two sons) who detailed and confessed to him all the circumstances of the murder, and even had the horses, guns etc. of the murdered men in their possession. *These Indians were a remnant of the Rogue River tribe ...* (Emphasis added).[94]

Part 19: Umatilla Reservation's Wealth Mandates Removal or Reservation Reduction

What was amazing was that a Sup't had the authority to determine where tribes should be located. It required the approval of the Com'r, yet many tribes are where they are today due to the broad authority of a Sup't. On Oct. 31, 1859, Sup't Geary would establish just such a reservation.

> ***The Umatillas should be sent to the Warm Spring Reservation.*** The Cayuses are a very small tribe and not only speak the Nez Perce language but are being rapidly absorbed by that tribe and should be sent to the Nez Perce Res. The Walla Wallas ... should be sent to the Simcoe Res. The Palouses should be sent to the [Nez Perce] reservation. ... This would be satisfactory to them owing to their great decrease within the last four years from war, famine and disease. (Emphasis added).[95]

Sup't Huntington reported to Com'r Cooley on Oct. 26, 1866, the attempts by whites to take over the Umatilla Reservation due to its fertile land, timber, water resources and location. They were willing to encroach on the Umatilla's land, to locate on it, and to incite war.

> The superior quality of the land, and its location on a great thorough fare convenient to the gold mines of Powder River, Boise Basin, Owyhee and other points, of course make it attractive to whites. ***There are constant attempts to encroach upon it, constant attempts under various pretexts to locate upon it, and occasional attempts to exasperate the Indians into the commission of some overt act which will justify—or at least palliate--retaliation and thus give an excuse for plunging the country into another Indian war, the—end of which, they well know, would be the expulsion of the Indians from the coveted tract. This cupidity is the cause of constant trouble to the agent and apprehension to the Indians.*** (Emphasis added).[96]

At the Umatilla Indian Reservation, Oregon Indian Agent Wm. H. Barnhart reported threats of violent removal of the Umatillas by local citizens and the state legislature also requested that Congress remove them.

> The reservation is completely surrounded by white settlements ... So anxious are the white people in the vicinity to possess this land, that threats to remove the Indians by violence are not unfrequently heard. ... At the last session of the legislature of Oregon, a memorial to Congress was passed asking the removal of these Indians ...[97]

By 1877, demands were still unceasing for the 'most productive region of Eastern Oregon' as described in The Report of the Civil and Military Commission to the Nez Percé Indians, Washington Territory and the Northwest:

Its location is in the most productive region of Eastern Oregon, surrounded by thrifty farmers, and embracing from fifteen thousand to twenty-five thousand acres of the best quality of land, valued at not less than ten dollars per acre. Its extensive tracts of timber-land are equally if not more valuable, and would be eagerly purchased if opened to settlement. Besides, there are upon this reservation pasture-lands almost without limit, and water-power furnished by the Umatilla River of great value. (Emphasis added).[98]

Part 20: Treaty Chaos

The Cayuse (1847–1855), Rogue River (1853–1856), Yakama (1855–1858) and Snake (1864–1868) Indian Wars would result in treaties of duress signed between the United States and the tribes. Anson Dart, Sup't, negotiated nineteen treaties ceding 6 million acres of land, none of which were ratified by Congress. Joel Palmer, Sup't for Washington and Oregon, and Isaac Stevens, Governor and Sup't for Washington Territory, were to act on behalf of the Oregon Indians in the treaty councils with the Cayuse, Umatilla, Yakima, Walla Walla and Nez Perce Indians.

In June of 1855 approximately 5,000 Nez Perces, Yakamas, Cayuses, Walla Wallas, Umatillas, and other Columbia River bands attended a council with U.S. representatives at Walla Walla, Washington. Governor Stevens and Indian Agent Joel Palmer, with a military escort, held a series of meetings with Indian representatives.

Stevens asked for their cooperation:

> What shall we do at this council? We want you and ourselves to agree upon tracts of land where you shall live; in those tracts of land we want each man who will work to have his own land, his own horses, his own cattle, and his home for himself and his children. . . Now we want you to agree with us to such a state of things: You to have your tract with all these things; the rest to be the Great Father's for his white children. . . Besides all these things, these shops, these mills and these schools which I have mentioned, we must pay you for the land which you give to the Great Father.[99]

Gov. Stevens assigned leaders or "chiefs" according to his own perceptions, granting them the authority to make decisions for large groups of people. The Indians listened suspiciously, and after much wrangling and coercion signed the treaties. Chief Lawyer signed for all the Nez Perce, although many disagreed. Peopeo-mox-mox signed for the Walla Wallas. The Cayuse, Umatilla, and Walla Wallas received a reservation for the "Confederated Tribes" near the Blue Mountains. Kamiakin of the Yakamas signed the Yakima Treaty reluctantly, becoming head chief of all the tribes and bands of the "Yakama, Palouse, Pisquose, Wenatshapam, Klicatat, Klinquit, Kow-was-say-ee, Li-ay-was, Skin-pah, Wish-ham, Shyiks, Oche-chotes, Kah-milt-pah and Se-ap-cat. They signed away 45,000 square miles (28,800,000 acres).[100]

Sup't Palmer urged the tribes to relinquish their land. He told them that the whites and their railroads were unstoppable. *"Can you prevent the wind from blowing? Can you prevent the rain from falling? Can you prevent the whites from coming? You are answered No!"* he said. (Emphasis added).[101]

The resulting treaties were a travesty. The Indian Nations were granted the most incredibly minuscule payments and undesirable reservations established in exchange for their land cessions. In addition, the U.S. delayed interminably in fulfilling its obligations. Across Oregon, tribes were forced onto reservations with other tribes who spoke different languages and had different customs. Most of the Indians lived in extreme poverty, amidst sickness, hunger, exposure and death.

Com'r Manypenny reported to Secretary of the Interior, Robert McClelland, the Indians were outraged over the one-sided Treaties they entered into, without fully understanding the consequences:

> They say that they made bad bargain in the sales made & they know of no way to get out of those bargains but to fight out. Their hatred and dislike is for those who made the treaties with them… & to get at them they have had to wage an indiscriminate war against all Americans.[102]

Sup't Nesmith of the Oregon and Washington Territories described the sharp techniques of negotiators used to get bargain prices. His Report that the Indians didn't receive "fair compensation" was included in the Congressional debate in 1928 on this topic.

> My own observation in relation to the treaties which have been made in Oregon leads me to the conclusion that in most instances the Indians have not received a fair compensation for the rights which they have relinquished to the government.

> It is too often the case in such negotiations that the agents of the government are over anxious to drive a close bargain ... The Indians ... begin to conclude that they have been defrauded, finally resort to arms ... and the government expends millions in the prosecution of a war.
> A notable instance of this kind is exhibited in the treaty of September 10, 1853, with the Rogue River Indians. ... The country which they ceded embraces nearly the whole of the valuable portion of the Rogue River valley, embracing a country unsurpassed in the fertility of its soil and value of its gold mines; and the compensation which those nine hundred and nine people now living receive ... [amount to] *two dollars and fifty cents per annum to the person*, which is the entire means provided for their clothing and sustenance. (Emphasis added).[103]

As written by Jerry A. O'Callaghan in "The Disposition of the Public Domain in Oregon:"

The record of these cessions is one of war, intrigue, promises broken or delayed in fulfilment. The purchase of Indian title can in no way be envisioned as a free sale where the seller did not have to sell or the buyer did not have to buy. ...

[The] antagonist and [the] protagonist are bound by circumstances and forces which they may not circumvent. There are no felicitous resolutions. It is heightened when the barbaric peoples foredoomed to defeat possess the determination, courage, and skill to fight to a bitter end. ... **There is no justice** in such situations. The sense of justice must reconcile itself to ameliorations. (Emphasis added).[104]

To add to the confusion and complexity, between 1850–1855, *Indian agents signed more than 20 treaties with Oregon Indians, none of which was ratified in the Senate.*

In 1885, former Com'r Manypenny wrote of his disillusionment with the treaty program. He convicted himself of "high crimes."

> When I made those treaties I was confident that good results would follow... Events following the execution of these treaties proved that I had committed a grave error. I had provided for the abrogation of the reservations, the dissolution of the tribal relation, and for lands in severalty and citizenship; thus making the road clear for the rapacity of the white man. ... Had I known then, as I now know, what would result from those treaties, *I would be compelled to admit that I had committed a high crime*. (Emphasis added).[105]

His high crimes were summarized in the Oregon Weekly Times:

> *Its results [treaty negotiations] are summed up in 6,000,000 acres ceded to the United States at a cost of about 3 cents per acre, and 4000 natives put upon reservations and guarded and protected by the government.* (Emphasis added).[106]

I Can't Spend It in Grave

There were tribes willing to sell their lands in exchange for the necessities of life. Also, the Sup't reported individual Indians feared they would die before they would receive a permanent home in which they would be protected. Yet, they had no real understanding of the monetary value of their land or the effect this loss of land would have on their future.

> Their concern was that they might be driven into extinction before its payment. Joseph Lane, first territorial Governor and Superintendent of Indian Affairs, has described how Indians besieged him upon his arrival ... and generally expressed a desire to sell their possessory rights to any portion of their country that our Government should wish to purchase.[107]

Unratified and Ratified Treaties in Oregon

Unratified and Ratified Treaties in Oregon
[This list is not meant to be inclusive. This list does not infer any legality or validity of any of the Treaties listed.]

Treaty	Acres Ceded	Date	Date Ratified by Cong.	Proclamation Date	Consideration (Payment)	Special Circumstances
Rogue River		9/10/1853	4/12/1854	02/05/1855	$60,000 (goods & farm impl.); $15,000 on move to Table Rock	$15,000 withheld for alleged Rogue River War damages.
Umpqua (Cow Creek Band)		9/19/1853	4/12/1854	02/05/1855	$12,000	
Shastas		11/18/1854	3/3/1855	4/10/1855	$36,000	
Umpqua, Calapooia		11/29/1854	3/3/1855	3/30/1855	$40,000; $10,000 for removal costs	
Calapooia & Confederated Bands Will. Valley		1/22/1855	3/3/1855	4/10/1855	$165,000	
Walla Walla, Cayuse, and Umatilla	6.4 million	6/9/1855	3/9/1859	4/11/1859	$100,000	Partly in Washington.
Warm Springs, Wasco and Paiute	10 million					
Nez Perce		6/11/1855	3/9/1859	4/29/1859	$200,000	Large part in Idaho.
Confederated Bands of Middle Oregon	1.9 million	6/25/1855	3/8/1859	4/18/1859	$100,000	
Oregon Coast Tribes		8/11/1855 – 9/8/1855	None			Never ratified.
Molala		12/21/1855	3/8/1859	4/29/1859	$12,0000	To be shared with Umpqua, Calapooia.
Nez Perce, Klamaths Modocs, Two Bands Snakes		6//9/1863	4/7/1867	4/20/1867	$262,500	Ceded land in Wash, Id, Ore.
Klamaths Modocs, Yahooskin Band Snakes		10/14/1864	7/2/1866	2/10/1870	$80,000	Amendmts. 7/2/1866; partly in CA.
Woll-pah-pe Band Snakes		8/12/1865	7/5/1866	7/10/1866	$27,000	Overlaps Klamath cession.

The consideration wasn't turned over to the tribes in cash, but was distributed in annual installments of goods, provisions, and equipment. The consideration is specified in the treaties. The treaties also provided reservations for the tribes. The reservations as established by treaty or Executive Order with their acreages as of 1880 were:

Reservation	Acres
Grande Ronde (Western Oregon)	61, 440
Klamath (Southeastern Oregon)	1,056,000
Malheur (Southeastern Oregon)	1,778,560
Siletz (Oregon Coast)	225, 000
Umatilla (Northeastern Oregon)	268, 800
Warm Springs (Central Oregon)	464,000

President Chester Arthur restored the Malheur Reservation to the public domain in 1882 and 1883. This government fiat is still challenged by Indians today.[108]

Part 21: Concentration Camps

Fort Hall Reservation

In 1868, the Fort Hall Indian Reservation was established, with the Boise and Bruneau Shoshone and Bannock being removed there. It was a failure as a reservation. Annuities were lacking or late in coming. Throughout the 1870s, circumstances deteriorated. They led to a number of Indian wars against the whites (i.e., Bannock War of 1878, Sheepeater War of 1879, and the Nez Perce War of 1877).[109]

Klamath Reservation

As to the Klamath Reservation, Agent Applegate reported its sterility:

> These people have, many of them, been given allotments ... Many of these allotments, I am informed, are on dry or sterile lands where irrigation is impossible and upon which the most industrious and progressive white man could not possibly make a living. O. C. Applegate, Indian Agent.[110]

Siletz Indian's Diet of Frozen, Rotten Potatoes

The DOI cannot claim surprise at the outbreaks in Oregon. The letter below from P. H. Sheridan, 2nd Lt. 4th Inf., to Capt. C. C. Augur clearly evidences the discontent of the Siletz Indians:

> Mr. Metcalfe, has surrounded himself with employees who were engaged in hostilities with them in the lower country and who do not hesitate to *express the most improper and hostile language towards them.*
>
> ***2nd. The suffering from want of food*** during the last winter. (Emphasis added).[111]

Also, the threat of hostilities is in the Letter to Wm. H. Rector, Supt. Indian Affairs from B. R. Biddle, Indian Agent, dated February 1, 1861:

> In view of the ***probable outbreak of the Indians within this agency to which I have referred in former communications, I deem it of the highest importance that the Department be early informed of the threatened danger, so as to be prepared to meet or ward it off in time***. It is through you that I hope to impress upon the military authorities of this district the necessity of immediately reinforcing the post at this agency. I am thoroughly convinced that the Indians intend to make hostile demonstrations early in the spring. This conviction does not arise from any sudden impulse of fear, nor from idle rumors, but from personal observation and unmistakable signs apparent to anyone acquainted with Indian character. (Emphasis added).[112]

The Indians decried the failure of the government to ratify the treaty the Indians signed. They had performed the stipulations binding on them. B. R. Biddle, Indian Agent, in his December 31, 1861, report to Supt. Wm. H. Rector pronounced the Discontent of the Coast Tribes of Indians at Siletz Agency as coming to a head. It was gross negligence on the part of the DOI not to defuse this situation.

Discontent of Coast Tribes of Indians at Siletz Agency

They say they have acted in good faith—entered into a solemn treaty with the government—given up their lands and homes and submitted to the humiliation of being placed on a reserve—and although this treaty was made several years ago, *the "Great Council" at Washington has never ratified it--and the government has never paid them except in small presents and "big" promises.* They say they have made the same complaints annually—and it seems to them instead of doing them any good has a contrary effect—the "pile" of presents grows smaller and smaller while the promises grow larger and larger, so that by and by there will be no annuities or presents at all, but an immense pile of promises. They say they do not like to complain—and that they wish to be at peace with and learn to live like white men—yet their patience is almost exhausted, and *they have very "sick hearts" towards their great Father at Washington*. (Emphasis added).[113]

Agent Biddle further warned of an outbreak in his letter of January 30, 1862

On my arrival at the agency last September to take charge of its management I discovered a general spirit of discontent, and at my *first interview with the chiefs and other influential Indians they told me of their wrongs and the broken promises of the government, that they had sold their country, the contract and terms of sale was put on paper, and they signed their names to it. The white men told them it "was all right," but that was a long time since; many winters have passed, and a great many of their people had died. They said they had performed their part of the contract and have been patiently waiting for their great Father at Washington to fulfill his—but fear he has forgotten them. Taking this reasonable view they said unless the treaty was soon ratified and something done for them more than mere empty promises, they intended to go back to their old homes.* It was thus that I found things, and in view of this state of the Indian mind I have ever since been expecting an outbreak, and have kept an eye on certain influential leaders. (Emphasis added).[114]

Sup't Rector promptly notified Col. A. Cady, Commanding Dist. Oregon, Ft. Vancouver W.T., on February 10, 1862, concerning fears of an Indian outbreak:

> I transmit herewith a copy of a letter received at this office from Benj. R. Biddle, U.S. Indian Agent for the coast tribes of Indians located at Siletz Agency, expressing **strong fears that the Indians under his charge are determined upon an outbreak** with a view of redressing their imaginary wrongs both past and present. This has been anticipated by this office for some time past, and the attention of the Department has been repeatedly called to it both by my predecessor and myself. **The failure on the part of Congress to ratify their treaties, as well as to make appropriations commensurate with the promises made to them from time to time, has undoubtedly produced this dissatisfaction. Unscrupulous and reckless whites**, well aware of these delinquencies on the part of the government, have used it to convince and satisfy the Indians that we have no government, and that they will not receive any further remuneration for their land which they have ceded. (Emphasis added).[115]

Sup't Rector visited the Agency and found the Indians eating rotten and frozen potatoes to survive. He requested the removal of Agent Biddle in a Letter to Com'r Wm. P. Dole, dated June 7, 1862.

> I have just returned from a visit to Siletz Reservation under charge of Agent B. R. Biddle. My object as expressed in my letter to you of the 7th ult. was to inspect the condition of this agency and investigate the official conduct of Agent Biddle. *I regret very much to inform you that the management of said agency is far from being satisfactory to this office. I found a large portion of the Indians subsisting on potatoes which had remained in the ground the entire winter and were frozen, rotten and loathsome.*

> Shortly after Mr. Biddle assumed the duties of his office he requested permission from this office to purchase two mules for the purpose of threshing. ... *These mules were not used on the threshing machine... but were used by Mr. Biddle in packing his own private property, he charging the cost thereof to government at the rate of $80 to 100 per ton, and after the packing was done turning two of the mules over to government, at 50 percent above cost, reserving the third animal as his own private.* (Emphasis added).[116]

Sup't Rector followed this up with a report on Sept. 2, 1862, that Indians had died from starvation and exposure.[117]

Alsea Indian Sub-Agency: Death by Exposure

It wasn't any better at the Siletz Sub-Agency, Alsea, as reported by Linus Brooks, Special Ind. Agt., to Sup't Rector, on April 1, 1862. Indians were dying from the cold and suffering from frostbite.

> These Indians have *suffered severely from cold* during the winter & to the present time for *want of clothing. Many are more or less frostbitten*, yet I have seen none whose lameness will be likely to be permanent. *Some have died*. Some 19 are absent with & without permits. *Universal disappointment and distrust prevail*. (Emphasis added).[118]

Samuel Case, Chief Commissary, Alsea Indn. Sub-Agency reported to Sup't Meacham, on December 17, 1870, that the only food available was *"two hundred bushels of potatoes."* (Emphasis added).[119]

The destitute condition prevailed year after year, unremitted. Special Indian Agent W. C. McCarthy pleaded with the Com'r for funding in his September 11, 1875, report:

> I labored under financial embarrassment the first sixteen months that I was in charge, *without a single dollar salary or funds to purchase supplies*, except a small amount of credit that I obtained, which is still unpaid. (Emphasis added).[120]

Hoping to gain Congressional assistance, Ben Simpson, Indian Agent, reported to Oregon's Senator Mitchell on Sep. 8, 1877, that many of the Siletz Indians were dying from starvation.

> I noticed yesterday in the Corvallis Gazette a letter written over the signature of George Harney—an Indian chief at Siletz Agency ... that ... [many of] the Alsea and Nestucca Indians, that were brought on to the Siletz Reservation two years ago are ... *dying with starvation*... I am satisfied that to some extent this is true. ... I am satisfied that the whole affair is in bad condition—and something should be done immediately to relieve them. (Emphasis added).[121]

Part 22: No More Promises

Reduce the Size of Siletz Reservation

Instead of increasing appropriations to prevent more starvation deaths, Congress responded with a demand to reduce the size of the Reservation. Senator Mitchell, from Oregon, wrote to Secretary Delano arguing that it was necessary to reduce the size of the "Siletz" and "Alsea" Indian reservations. Secretary Delano concurred in this recommendation. Congress passed legislation reducing the reservation and consolidating Alsea and Siletz Indians on one reservation.[122]

The Alsea and Siletz Indians were opposed as well as their federal Agent.[123]

In a Letter to Senator Mitchell from Ben. Simpson, Special Agent, August 26, 1875, Agent Simpson categorized the appointment of Agent Litchfield as a treaty commissioner a mistake as he was opposed to the decision to reduce the reservation and consolidating the Alsea and Siletz Indians on one reservation as it was not in their best interest. He would have nothing to do with it.

> Agent Litchfield would have but little to do with it; in fact, it was a terrible mistake making him one of the commissioners, as *he is opposed to the removal of the Indians. He said he could not say to the Indians that it was best for them to go, when he did not believe it.* (Emphasis added).[124]

Geo. Cameron, a Coos Tribal Member represented the Alsea and Siletz Indians opposition at a June 17, 1875, Council held regarding removal:

> My heart is full & sick with this talk of leaving this country. It seems as though bad white people took us away from our old homes & brought us to this country. Today I do not want to be removed again. How long is [it] to be before we are like the whites, to be improved as we have been promised. We received this country from the Washington Chief a long time ago. The treaty made with Genl. Palmer was never carried out, & that is one trouble with us today. *The whites don't lie to each other when they make a treaty; why do they lie when they make a treaty with Indians. When they owe one another they pay; why don't they pay us. I want to hear no more of their promises, nor do I want to hear any more of our leaving our country.* Our Chief never received any benefits from the treaty; he has been dead several years. I don't want to give up my country any more. I am comfortably fixed now. It would be good for us if the Washington Chief could hear what we have today. (Emphasis added). Proceedings of a council held on the Alsea Indian Reservation, Oregon with the Alseas, Coos, Umpquas and Siuslaw tribes of Indians in regard to their removal to Siletz, Alsea Agency, June 17, 1875.[125]

Geo. P. Litchfield, Special U.S. Indian Agent, cautioned the Indians *"not to give the whites any cause of offense."*[126]

Part 23: Snake Indians Hunted like Wolves

It isn't surprising that the story of Oregon is one of Indian war after Indian war in the mid-to-late 1800s. In a missive from General Alvord to General Wright, he states the only satisfactory response against the Snake Indians is *"a good whipping."* (Emphasis added).[127]

The Army's leadership problems contributed to poor command and control, low morale among soldiers, and enlisting Indian allies not bound by military rules, which led to unacceptable encounters with the Indians, which would stain the legacy of the military. The Army employed the tactic of "divide and conquer" within tribes as well as among them. Also, the U.S. willingly preyed on the animosities between Indian Nations. Sup't Huntington reported a massacre of Snake Indians by other Indians, ordered by General Steele and Lt. Bolton:

> Lieutenant Wm. Bolton, in a speech to the Indians at the time of enlistment, enjoined upon them that *they should take no prisoners, regardless of age or sex.* Under these orders the scouts, under command of Lieutenants McKay and Darragh, surprised a camp of Snakes in a narrow canon, on a small fork of Crooked river, killed all the men, seven in number, and took fourteen women and children prisoners. Their officers directed them to carry out their orders. They remonstrated but, finally, reluctantly killed and scalped all the women and children, they offering no resistance. *I shudder when I recall the fact that this is the first instance on record in which soldiers in the service and wearing the uniform of the United States have, by express orders, butchered in cold blood unresisting women and children.* (Emphasis added). J. W. Perit Huntington, Sup't.[128]

Indian Agent L. Applegate informed Sup't Huntington of the Snake Indians' destitute condition, on August 28, 1868, and their removal to the Klamath Reservation.

> ... Wal-pah-pe Snake Indians ... have all come onto the reservation. ... **They have been reduced to great extremity, having been hunted like wolves until they have eaten their last horses. Not having had any ammunition for many months, they have been able to get but little game, and their fear of the troops has kept them confined to mountain fastnesses where it is impossible to dig roots or gather wocus. They say they have long had a desire to get onto the reservation, but fear of the troops prevented them. Beside their want of provisions they are almost entirely naked, and if possible should be supplied with some blankets and clothing before winter.** (Emphasis added).[129]

Part 24: Butcher Indians

A decade after the extermination of Indians was raised in 1858, it is repeated in this 1867 Commissioner's Report. The colonial settlers bragged about killing the "bucks." Their total disregard for the law caused the Indians to live in a state of chaos and fear.

> I had a conversation with one of the most prominent of this class, and I have used nearly his exact language. ... They evidently think that an Indian "has no rights that a white man is bound to respect;" that *all should be killed off except such as the settlers covet as men servants or maid servants*. This class of settlers are continually creating disturbances among the Indians by selling or giving away liquor among them; by enticing women and children away from the reservation, and not unfrequently by boasting of the number of "buck" Indians they have killed, as if it were an achievement to be proud of. (Emphasis added).[130]

Anson Dart, former Sup't, Oregon and Washington Territory, categorized the action of the military as absurd. The only way the Indians could be exterminated was to "butcher them as at Sand Creek."

> On the Pacific coast ... nearly all our troubles with the Indians there, marring our history with cruel massacres, and in some instances with the extermination of whole bands, had their origin in the presence and unwise action of our military. In evidence of this statement, I refer to the letter of Mr. Anson Dart, [Sup't of Indian Affairs], Oregon and Washington Territory:

But besides the cost to the treasury ... the slaying of every Indian costs us the lives of 25 whites, so that the extermination process must bring about the slaughter of 7,500,000 of our people. Extermination by arms is simply an absurdity, unless we could get the Indians under the protection of the flag in large masses, surround and butcher them as at Sand Creek. But admitting, for the argument, they deserve extermination without mercy, and that we might achieve the grand consummation, it seems to me that the glory of the result would bear no proportion to the fearful sum of the cost.[131]

If might makes right, we are the strong and they the weak; and we would do no wrong to proceed by the cheapest and nearest route to the desired end, and could, therefore, justify ourselves in ignoring the natural as well as the conventional rights of the Indians, if they stand in the way, and, as their lawful masters, assign them their status and their tasks, or put them out of their own way and ours by extermination with the sword, starvation, or by any other method.[132]

Part 25: Modoc War (1872–1873)

The Modocs, Maklaks, meaning the People, lived along the California-Oregon border. In this northeastern, southwestern region of the Pacific Northwest, they fished, hunted and gathered. Their peace was disrupted with the onslaught of colonial settlers – the Oregon Trail cut right through their lands.

The 1849 California Gold Rush's destructive impact still continues today. California's Governor Peter Burnett signed into law the Act for the Government and Protection of Indians, which enabled the enslavement of California Indians and contributed to their genocide. He declared in an 1851 speech "[t]hat a war of extermination will continue to be waged between the races until the Indian race becomes extinct must be expected. While we cannot anticipate the result with but painful regret, the inevitable destiny of the race is beyond the power and wisdom of man to avert."[133]

Settlers demanded that the Modocs be removed from Lost River to the Klamath Reservation. Conditions on the reservation, though, were poor. Unease between the Modocs and Klamaths led Modocs, under the leadership of Captain Jack, to return to Lost River. Com'r F. A. Walker was well-aware of the enmity between the Klamath and Modocs. Yet still the DOI chose to forcibly move the Modocs to the Klamath reservation.

As documented by a January 27, 1872, Letter from Sup't Meachem to Com'r Walker, the DOI failed to protect the Modocs who were forced onto the Reservation of their hereditary enemy:

> ***They were ill treated and abused by the Klamath Indians, and the sub-agent failing to protect them, they vacated. Peace has been disturbed and danger seems imminen***t, and on a strong petition of the white settlers of the Modoc country I have made a requisition on the commander of the Dept. of the Columbia for assistance. ... I should regret bloodshed, but I am powerless to prevent it without I was authorized to locate these people on a new home. They steadily declare their determination to resist any effort to remove them. (Emphasis added).[134]

Sup't Meacham clearly conveyed the message from the Modocs that they would resist removal from their homeland in the Lost River area.

The case now stands that the Modocs, numbering 300 souls, belong by treaty to Klamath, but have not resided within the limits of the reservation except perhaps three months, beginning of '70.[135]

In spite of their petition for a reservation of their own, Sup't Alfred Meachem, convinced Captain Jack to return to the Klamath Reservation late in 1869. After their return, conditions were no better.

Return to Lost River

In April of 1870, Captain Jack, along with 371 other Modocs, left the Reservation and returned to their Lost River homeland. Some Modocs remained on the Reservation.

In a revealing letter of Mr. Applegate, Commissary in Charge to Oregon Sup't Odeneal, he evidences the odious willingness of the DOI to disregard the agreement to allow the Modocs to remain at Lost River.

> Camp Yainax, May 8, 1872
>
> To T. B. Odeneal, Supt. Indn. Affrs. From I. D. Applegate, Commissary in Charge

> [T]he military might be averse to taking any action while they consider the agreement made with Capt. Jack by the late Supt., A. B. Meacham, is still in force. The nature of which agreement was—as you will see by records in your office—that *until the matter of setting apart a separate reservation for them should be adopted or disapproved, and the matter of their permanent location be positively determined by the Dept., they should remain unmolested in the Modoc country*, they, on their part, "doing nothing that would have a tendency to cause a collision between them and the settlers." (Emphasis added).[136]

In a communication addressed to Supt. A. B. Meacham, under date of Feb. 17, 1872, Gen. E. R. S. Canby stated:

> "The commanding officer has been advised that the question of new location has been by you submitted to the Commsr. of Indian Affairs, and that pending the decision of this question force will not be used by the military to compel the return of the Modocs to the reservation." Unless assured that the new-location idea is abandoned, perhaps the military would not give the order to arrest those men.

> If it could be arranged, it is my opinion that the arrest of Capt. Jack, Black Jim, Scar-faced Charley, Boston, and En-choaks—the medicine man—would settle all trouble, and I am satisfied that if properly planned and managed with *great caution* it can be done with no very great risk and with a comparatively small force. *Only for the appearance of being a breach of faith on the part of the Dept., it could have no bad influence on the other Indians.* (Emphasis added).[137]

In *a critical Letter from E. R. S. Canby, to the Adjutant General, dated Feb. 21, 1872,* he explicitly broadcast the message that the DOI had given permission to the Modocs to remain at Lost River, pending a determination of a new location for them, other than the Klamath Reservation. He refused to forcibly remove them. His Letter also enclosed a "petition from citizens of Jackson County, Oregon, asking for a force to compel these Indians to return to the reservation."

First, General Canby precisely sets forth the delay in not ratifying the 1864 Treaty until December 1869, with one-sided changes by the Senate which created suspicion and uncertainty, not just to the changes but to the lengthy time delay. "Captain Jack, the present leader of the troublesome Modocs, protested that it did not represent what they had agreed to." He was countenanced to accept it by other chiefs.

> The treaty with the Klamaths, Modocs and Yahooskin Snakes was made on the 14th of October 1864 and approved by the Senate with certain amendments on the 2nd of July 1866, but not finally ratified until the 10th of December 1869. This long delay made the Indians who were parties to the treaty very suspicious, and I have been informed by the Superintendent that when the treaty as amended by the Senate was interpreted and explained to them, Captain Jack, the present leader of the troublesome Modocs, protested that it did not represent what they had agreed to. He was, however, convinced by the testimony of the other chiefs and finally assented to it. ...

Second, General Canby incontrovertibly sets forth the facts that the Modocs made every effort to make their removal to the Klamath Reservation successful.

> When they were established on the reservation, they went to work with a good deal of interest to build cabins and enclose ground for cultivation...

Third, General Canby undeniably notes the awareness of the DOI of the difficulties between the Klamath and Modoc. The only solution the local Agent offered was to move them three times to try and avoid the conflict.

> [Modocs] but were so much annoyed by the Klamaths that they complained to the local agent, who, instead of protecting them in their rights, endeavored to compromise the difficulty by removing them to another location. At this point the same difficulties recurred and a third selection was made. The Modocs then abandoned the reservation, alleging that the last point selected was a trap to place them in the power of their enemies, the Klamaths.

Fourth, General Canby markedly identifies the lack of communication between the local Agent and the Sup't concerning the conflict. The Sup't wasn't aware of the three relocations of the Modocs on the Klamath Reservation.

> These changes were made without the concurrence of the Superintendent, and I believe did not come to his knowledge until after the Modocs had fled from the reservation.

Fifth, General Canby sets forth the knowledge that the DOI and the U.S. Army possessed that the Modocs had left the Klamath Reservation for Lost River, with no intent to return. No one was ordered to stop them.

> All subsequent attempts to induce them to return have failed.

Sixth, of major import, General Canby unequivocally states that THE MODOCS WERE AUTHORIZED BY THE PEACE COMMISSIONERS TO REMAIN AT LOST RIVER UNTIL THE SUP'T WOULD MEET WITH THEM AND A PERMANENT ARRANGEMENT COULD BE REACHED BY THEM.

> In the summer of last year and in consequence of complaints against these Indians the Superintendent sent commissioners to confer with them (see my reports of September 2nd and November 3rd 1871) who *authorized the Modocs to remain where they then were until the Superintendent would see them. This has been understood as a settlement of the questions until some permanent arrangement could be made for them...*

Seventh, General Canby stated it would be unjust to apply force to remove them without (1) notifying them that a new location had been selected for them; (2) providing for their wants; (3) permitting *a reasonable and definite time to remove their families;* (4) *fully warning them of the determination by the U.S. that they had no choice, but to remove to the reservation;* (5) *informing them of the appointed time;* and (6) *unmistakably conveying to them the U.S. position that refusal or failure to remove to the reservation within the appointed time would be followed by such measures as may be necessary to compel them.*

> *I do not think that the immediate application of force as asked for would be either expedient or just.* They should at least be notified that a new location has been selected for them and provision made for their wants. *They should also be allowed a reasonable and definite time to remove their families and fully warned that their refusal or failure to remove to the reservation within the appointed time would be followed by such measures as may be necessary to compel them.*

Eighth, General Canby lucidly confirms the Modoc's unwillingness to return to the Klamath Reservation and their reasons for it and *allies* with them.

> I am not surprised at the unwillingness of the Modocs to return to any point of the reservation where they would be exposed to the hostilities and annoyances they have heretofore experienced (and without adequate protection) from the Klamaths.

Ninth, General Canby, with certitude, expresses his actual, factual, knowledge of the Superintendent's willingness to endeavor to secure this location for them but they have expressed a desire to be established upon Lost River, where they would be free from this trouble, and the Sup't informed me last summer that he would endeavor to secure such a location for them. (Emphasis added to General Canby's original text).[138]

The warfare initiated by the Oregon Rifles must be acknowledged as genocide and a massacre of the Modoc's, given their right to stay there until otherwise determined. On January 17, 1873, 300 soldiers and volunteer "Oregon Rifles" launched their assault against the Modocs. The Battle of the Stronghold resulted in a Modoc victory. The Oregon Rifles were forced to retreat, leaving behind their dead and armaments.

Peace Commission Doomed to Fail

A Peace Commission was appointed to mediate a peace. It was doomed from the start. In a Feb. 10, 1873, Letter from L. F. Grover, Governor of Oregon, to the commissioners appointed to conclude peace with the Modoc Indians, he vehemently refused to consider a reservation on the Lost River land. He claimed it was Oregon's land.

> As to the land on Lost River, which some have suggested should be surrendered to the Modocs as a peace offering, allow me to say that *these lands lie wholly within the state of Oregon*, and within the jurisdiction of the Superintendent of Indian Affairs for Oregon, that the *Indian title to these lands was extinguished by treaty* fairly made through the Oregon Superintendency between the Modocs and the general government on the 14th day of October 1864. These lands have been extensively taken and are *now occupied by bona fide settlers* under the homestead and preemption laws of the United States. ... For the interests of Southern Oregon and *for the future peace of our southern frontier*, I will express the hope and confidence that the project of a reservation on Lost River will not be entertained by the commission, and that the Modocs will either consent to return to their own reservation or to be assigned to bounds beyond the settlements. (Emphasis added).[139]

Even though they were repeatedly warned that the Modocs planned an ambush by interpreters, Mr. Riddle and his wife, *four times in advance of the meeting*, and by A. B. Meachem (former Sup't), Brigadier General Canby, Dr. Thomas and Meachem *chose to proceed with meeting* with the Modocs on Apr. 16, 1873.

> Before leaving the camp, as chairman of the commission [A. B. Meachem], I again sought to avert the peril, calling to them, and stating again the warnings and proof of danger, and proposing to take with us a force sufficient for protection. Both the General and Doctor objected, saying it would be a "breach of faith." ... They proceeded to the council tent, followed by Commissioner Dyar, interpreters Riddle and wife, and myself. On arrival it was evident that we were entrapped, and would be betrayed. *Eight armed,* instead of six unarmed Modocs, were present: Capt. Jack, Schonchin, Shacknasty Jim, Ellen's Man, Hooka Jim, Boston Charlie, Bogus Charlie and Black Jim. Any attempt to signal for assistance or to retreat would have precipitated the assassination.[140]

A. B. Meacham, Chr. Modoc Peace Comsn., reported of these advance warnings to Secty. Interior. C. Delano, when notifying the Com'r of the death of Canby and Thomas and his own injuries. Capt. Jack would have adversely impacted his military leadership and control if he didn't carry through with his warning—that he did not wish to meet with the Peace Commission:

> On that morning [Friday, 11th] terms were agreed upon for a meeting satisfactory to Dr. Thomas and Gen. Canby, though not to Mr. Dyar, nor myself or the Modoc woman, ***Gen. Canby remarking that they dare not molest us, because his forces commanded the situation***, and Dr. Thomas said that where God called him to go *he would* go, trusting to His care. ***The meeting was held according to time and place agreed upon.*** Canby, Meacham, Thomas and Dyar, and eight armed instead of six unarmed Inds., as was agreed upon. ***The "talk" was short, the Modoc chiefs both saying that unless the soldiers were withdrawn from the country no further talk would be had***. About this time two armed Indians suddenly appeared from the brush in our rear. An explanation was asked, and ***Capt. Jack replied by snapping a pistol at Gen. Canby, saying in Indian "all ready," after which Gen. Canby was dispatched by Cap. Jack with a pistol and knife, Dr. Thomas by a pistol shot in the breast and a gunshot in the head*** by Boston. Meacham attempting to escape toward camp, the former followed by Schonchin John, and the latter by Black Jim and Hooker Jim. Schonchin fired six shots at Meacham, hitting him four times and leaving him for dead. Boston, attempting to scalp him, was deterred by the Modoc woman. Dyar escaped unhurt, although fired at three times by Black Jim, who was only a few feet away, and twice by Hooker Jim, by whom he was pursued. After running about two hundred yards, he turned upon his pursuers with a small pocket derringer, when the Ind. turned and ran back—thus letting Dyar get away. ***We believe that complete subjugation by the military is the only method by which to deal with these Indians***. (Emphasis added).[141]

Modocs to Be Punished

President Grant sanctioned the most severe punishment of the Modocs. The U.S. Army combined its forces against the **60 Modoc warriors**. To support the troops, General Gillem still had the two mountain howitzers and had increased his artillery with the addition of four Coehorn mortars. Either at hand or enroute were four batteries of artillerymen (prepared to fight as infantry), five troops of cavalry, five companies of infantry, and 70 Warm Springs Indians. Col. Mason's total strength was in the neighborhood of 300 officers and men. Major Green's command was somewhat larger. *The total number of officers and men* in Troops F and K, Batteries A, E, K, and M, and Companies E and G, 12th Infantry, *was approximately 375*. (Emphasis added).[142]

Again, using Indians against Indians, captured Modocs [Steamboat Frank, Bogus Charley, Hooker Jim, and Shacknasty Jim] were enlisted as scouts to track down Captain Jack.

> The squadrons learned on May 28 that the Modoc scouts had discovered Captain Jack camped on Willow Creek, a small swift stream that drained the highlands east of Clear Lake. At three-thirty in the morning, May 29, both squadrons rode toward the rising sun ... Hooker Jim guided Captain Hasbrouck; Steamboat Frank guided Captain Jackson; Bogus Charley and Shacknasty Jim accompanied Major Green who chose to ride with Jackson's squadron...[143]
>
> ***It was a sad ending for this man who with less than 70 men had defeated the army repeatedly for seven months***. (Emphasis added).[144]

In the end six Modocs faced the commission: Captain Jack, Schonchin John, Black Jim, Boston Charley, Barncho, and Sloluck. The commission found all six guilty of two charges, each having two specifications:

> Charge 1 — Murder, in violation of the laws of war.
>
> Specification 1 — murder of General Canby.
>
> Specification 2 — murder of Dr. Thomas.
>
> Charge 2 — Assault, with intent to kill, in violation of the laws of war.

Specification 1 — attack on A. B. Meacham.

Specification 2 — attack on Agent Dyar.

The sentence for the six read "to be hanged by the neck until they be dead." President Grant approved the findings on August 22. General Court Martial Orders No. 32, War Dept. On October 3, 1873, Captain Jack, Schonchin John, Black Jim, and Boston Charley were hanged.

> *"The warriors' heads were cut off and shipped in alcohol to the Army Medical Museum for "scientific investigation.""* (Emphasis added).[145] "This is vengeance, indeed," screamed the San Francisco Chronicle. "Captain Jack said that he would like to meet the Great White Chief in Washington face to face. The government evidently intends that his dying wish shall be respected."[146]

President Grant commuted the death convictions of two others, and they were sent to Alcatraz.

U.S. Holds Grudge

Twelve days after the hanging, 163 Modocs were taken in cattle cars, as prisoners of war, to the Quapaw Agency in Oklahoma.[147]

While imprisoned, over one-half died. The Indian Agent Hiram Jones was tried in 1879 for giving the Modocs substandard food, supplies, and medical care. His punishment was to be "relieved of duty."

Part 26: High and Frequent Turnover of Agents Cause of Modoc War

A. B. Meacham's, Chairman Special Com. to Modocs, Report of October 5, 1873, listed the high and frequent turnover of agents and inconsistent federal policies as the reasons for the Modoc War.

> In compliance with your instructions I herewith submit report of the late "Modoc war" ...

First. That Capt. Jack, being a lineal descendant of "Old Modocs," was ambitious to be recognized *"head chief,"*

2nd. Had they been thus protected in their rights as against the insults of the Klamath Indians they would have remained, and no second stampede would have followed, that the failure to keep the promise of protection impaired the confidence of the Modocs in subsequent promises.

3rd. That in 1870 an understanding was had that an effort would be made to obtain a small reservation for them on Lost River, on condition that they kept the peace. No action was taken by the Department on this matter. The Modocs, discouraged by the delay and emboldened thereby, became an unbearable annoyance to the settlers, and removal or location could not be deferred.

4th. *A small reservation, as recommended, would have averted all trouble with these people, and the failure to notify them that no action would be had on the matter was a blunder*.

5th. Had they been fully apprised of the fact in a way to give them confidence that no home would be allowed them on Lost River, and an appeal been properly made by some officer of the Indian Department, they might not have resisted.

6th. Superstitious Indian religion had much to do in causing them to resist.

7th. Want of adaptability of government agents produces confusion, and sometimes war.

Finally, this war was the result of changing agents and policies too often, and the absence of well-defined regulations regarding the relative duties and powers of the Indian and Military Departments, the citizens and Indians. While the "humane policy" is the correct one, it ought to be well defined, and then entrusted to men selected on account of fitness for the work. No branch of public service more imperatively demands observance of this rule, and when it shall have been fully recognized and adhered to by appointing men to the care of our Indian population whose hearts are in the work, and who understand the duties assigned, and whose term of office depends on faithfully achieved success, we may hope to hear of Indian wars *no more*. (Emphasis added).[148]

Maj. Genl J. M. Schofield, also recognized the inadequate size of the military force committed to the Modoc War, in reporting on Dec. 17, 1872, to the Adjutant General:

> It appears evident that a serious mistake was committed in sending a small force to do what, from the defiant attitude of the Indians, would manifestly require a much larger force.[149]

Cost of Modoc War

The cost of the war is estimated at $400,000; equivalent in purchasing power to about $10,087,859 today.[150]

Part 27: Nez Perce 'Thief' War (1877)

In the Treaty of 1855, the Nez Perce ceded 5.5 million acres of their 8-million-acre Reservation, reserving the right to off-reservation hunting, fishing, and gathering. The Senate ratified the Treaty, creating the Nez Perce Reservation. This Treaty was negotiated at the same time the Cayuse War was winding down and the Rogue River Wars were ongoing.

On October 15, 1855, Governor Curry enlisted two battalions of mounted volunteers from southern and middle Oregon, for the purpose of suppressing Indian hostilities. The U.S. Army was notified. Lacking sufficient information, the Army responded to the Governor's warning that combined hostile tribes, comprising the Yakima, Pelouse, Klikatat, Walla-Walla, Cayuse, Deschute, Umatilla, and other tribes on the north, and the Rogue-River, Klamath, Shasta, and other bands in the south, were engaged in hostilities against settlers. The extent and number of those hostile tribes wasn't fully known.

Governor Curry accelerated the state of panic in the Territory. He singlehandedly raised the Militia Volunteers, with the stated purpose of making war on Indians. He made no attempt whatsoever to broker a peace. Instead, he sought an attack in the dead of winter, when the tribes were most vulnerable. The national hysteria he occasioned led to a war without any rules, leading to the indiscriminate mayhem and slaughter of peaceful Indians, including the elderly, women and children.

Gold Discovered

On Oct. 15, 1855, E. M. Barnum, Adjutant General, stated the understanding of the U.S. military:

> The policy of the government in regard to the Indians in Oregon is to extinguish their title to the country and colonize them on suitable reserves.[151]

Unfortunately, the government's promise to them of a permanent home didn't last long. Gold was discovered.

On July 2, 1860, Superintendent of Indian Affairs Geary's reported to Acting Commissioner Charles E. Mix "that in consequence of the rumored discoveries of rich and extensive gold mines within the reservation of the Nez Perce, great excitement had been occasioned by the rush of a crowd of miners into the country of that tribe."[152]

Com'r Mix strongly supported Sup't Geary's decisions to protect the Reservation from invasion.

> The action which you have taken in the premises toward the protection of the Reservation from lawless invasion is approved and you will further instruct the local agents to give public notice to all parties concerned that *the treaties with the Indians are paramount and the Government is determined to exercise its full authority to prevent intrusions upon the Reserves of the Indians*, under all circumstances, as no person except the proper officers of the Department have any right whatever under any pretense to go upon said Reservations. (Emphasis added).[153]

> By the spring of 1861, the lawless invasion of Nez Perce lands had not been stemmed, but instead had worsened. Sup't Geary, alerted Com'r Dole, by letter dated April 23, 1861, of the Indians furor:

> Great excitement prevailed among the Indians on finding that instead of the miners being expelled on the opening of spring, as they had been promised, their number on the Reservation was daily augmented, and that thousands of white men were about to over run the country so recently garanteed [sic] them as an asylum and permanent home by our government.[154]

On March 20, 1862, the Indian Agent, Charles Hutchins informed Com'r Dole of the severity of the continued "licentiousness" of the white settlers and the Indians complaints:

> *It is not necessary that I should now enumerate instances of daily recurrences of overreaching, fraud, plundering, licentiousness, and rascality, that is incessantly practiced by unprincipled white men on the Nez Perce Indians. Sufficient to say that outrages the most base and glaringly mean are daily complained of to me, and I am without any force whatever for arrest or punishment*, and without a dollar of public money to employ special police for prevention or redress of crime. (Emphasis added).[155]

The military refused to act. On June 30, 1862, Nez Perce Indian Agent Chas. Hutchins said in his annual report to Congress:

> My repeated requisitions for troops, made on the military commanders of the adjoining post at Walla-Walla have not been supplied, and my representation of the necessity, of troops being permanently quartered here, made to the several alternate commanders of this district, at Vancouver, Washington Territory, during the past year, has likewise been of no avail.[156]

Brigadier-General, U.S. Volunteers, Benjamin Alvord explained that "wherever these masses of gold miners and emigrants go, it has been my policy to encourage the formation of counties, and the putting in force some civil law and order as quickly as possible." Alvord abhorred the prospect of imposing martial law on the Reservation.[157]

On June 30, 1862, the Indian Agent reported to Congress:

> [T]he funds appropriated for the maintenance of this agency, due on the expiring year, have been withheld, thus leaving this district without military force to compel obedience to the laws, and the agent with no means to employ special police to arrest and commit the most miscreant and infamous violators of the public peace.[158]

No Spirit Will Hinder Me

In a talk with the Nez Perce on Oct. 24, 1862, General Alvord stated the common refrain: "*It is very sad to find that the discovery of gold* and the consequent rush of miners to this country should have brought such a mass of the very worst white men in contact with you ..."

I have come to see you in order to *assure you that the Government desires to do all in its power to protect you*. ... the best the Government can do for you is to provide, as it has, for the making of a new treaty, so as to compensate you as far as possible for the unauthorized occupation of the gold mines by our people. (Emphasis added).[159]

In treaty negotiations in 1863 with Major General O. O. Howard, the Nez Perce were pressured into ceding 1,750,000 acres.

> *After [General] Howard spoke, Nez Perce Chief Toohoolhoolzote became enraged and asked "What person pretends to divide the land, and put me on it?" General Howard had lost his patience, and replied to Toohoolhoolzote, "I am that man. . . . I stand here for the President, and there is no spirit good or bad that will hinder me."* (Emphasis added).[160]

Fifty-one Nez Perce affixed their marks to the 1863 Treaty retaining 750,000 acres. Some of the Bands walked out of the negotiations. The U.S. Senate ratified it in 1867. The 1863 Treaty is still referred to today as the 'Thief Treaty' or 'Steal Treaty.' It created the conditions that would eventually lead to war.

Raging Torrent Unstoppable

On May 14, 1877, General Oliver Otis Howard ordered the non-treaty Nez Perce to report to the Nez Perce Reservation for permanent coerced relocation. Chief Joseph asked for a delay until Fall, when the Snake River would be lower. Howard refused his request. Many of the tribe's leaders agreed with Chief Joseph, including Chief White Bird, Chief Looking Glass, and Chief Toohoolhoolzote. Nonetheless, on or around June 1, 1877, they started the journey for the Reservation and a tumultuous River crossing ensued. It was a raging torrent from the melting snow run off.

Several of the younger Indians, prodding their horses into the swirling current of the Snake, tested it and managed to get across. Gradually, more of the band followed them, making rafts and bullboats out of buffalo robes, and piling children and old people on top of the baggage. Three or four ponies, guided by riders and swimmers, towed each of the tossing craft across the torrent, while the passengers held on fearfully. Around them, the women and younger men clung to the backs of struggling mounts, urging them on toward the opposite shore. When the herds of livestock were driven into the turbulent water, eddies and high waves caught many of the riderless animals and swept them off downstream. For two days the struggle continued. The tumultuous river scattered people, possessions, and animals for thousands of yards along the Idaho bank. The noise of the river, roaring across rapids in the canyon, combined with the cries of the children, the shouts of horsemen and the bawling of cattle. Eventually, all of the people were across safely, but many of their possession had gone whirling off in the current, and a large part of their herd of horses and cattle perished. The Band members rested for a while on the Idaho bank, collecting their goods and letting their animals graze. On June 2, Joseph met with all the non-treaty Nez Perce at Tolo Lake near Grangeville, Idaho.[161] The danger General Howard placed the lives of the Nez Perce lingered on as a bitter memory.

On May 16, 1877, the fragile peace broke, and violence erupted. Angered by the treatment of their people, two young Nez Perce warriors attacked and killed a group of settlers (some of whom had cheated or fought with the tribe). Richard Devine, who "had been guilty of brutal conduct to Indians," was one of the murdered. The uprising continued for at least two more days and with that the "Nez Perce War of 1877" started.[162]

Polishing a Diamond

General Oliver O. Howard gathered together a group of soldiers to capture the Nez Perce and force them onto the reservation. The Nez Perce decided to head for the Crow Reservation, former allies, hoping to be taken in by them.

General Howard employed twenty-two Bannock scouts to assist him in his pursuit and fight against the Nez Perce. The U.S. Army had long pitted Indians against Indians. Colonel George Crook, who had used the Eastern Shoshones in his battles against the Lakota, *described the idea of using Indians against Indians by saying "to polish a diamond there is nothing like its own dust."* (Emphasis added).[163]

Although the Nez Perce tried to evade the pursuing soldiers, they were attacked or forced into battle at White Bird Canyon (Idaho), Clearwater River (Idaho), Big Hole (Montana) and Camas Meadow (Idaho). The battle at White Bird Canyon (Idaho) was a win for the Nez Perce, Clearwater River (Idaho) was a draw. At Camas Meadow, instead of attacking the soldiers, the target was their horses. The Nez Perce broke through the stockade and stole over two hundred horses and mules. This move was a big blow to the army's supplies and transportation. His men exhausted and without transportation, General Howard's strategy at this point was to return to Fort Boise with his exhausted men and let military units in Montana take over. On August 24, Howard telegrammed General Sherman, "I think I may stop near where I am, and in a few days' work my way back to Fort Boise slowly."[164]

General Sherman feared that no other force could get into position to head off the Indians, and instructed Howard to have his army continue on the trail of the Nez Perce to the bitter end. *"That force of yours should pursue the Nez Perce to the death, lead where they may... If you are tired, give the command to some young energetic officer."* (Emphasis added).[165]

Refuge in Canada

Unfortunately, the Crow refused to help the Nez Perce. The Nez Perce then decided to head for Canada to join with Sitting Bull, who had escaped and gone there after the Battle of the Little Big Horn. When the Nez Perce stopped to make camp 40 miles short of Canada, they thought they had eluded General Howard. They didn't know that General Miles was joining forces with Howard. To trick the Nez Perce, Howard slowed his pace, but ordered Miles to force march from the Tongue River Cantonment near Miles City, Montana, and intercept the fleeing Nez Perce.

Charles Erskine Scott Wood transcribed Howard's directive for Colonel Miles as follows:

> Joseph and his band have eluded Sturgis and he is now continuing his retreat toward British Columbia, and we believe is aiming at refuge with Sitting Bull. He is traveling with women and children and wounded at a rate of about twenty-five miles a day; but he regulates his gait by ours. We will lessen our speed to about twelve miles a day and he will also slow down. *Please at once take a diagonal line to head him off with all the force at your command*, and when you have intercepted him send word to me immediately and I will by forced marching unite with you. (Emphasis added).[166]

> *For four months, ten different Army units fought against Chief Joseph's impressive band of around eight hundred Nez Perce Indians. During those four months, some of the toughest battles were fought by the troops under the command of Brigadier General Oliver Otis Howard.* (Emphasis added).[167]

With elements of the 7th and 2nd Cavalries, the 5th Mounted Infantry, and 30 to 40 Cheyenne and non-Indian scouts, Colonel Miles' command totaled 400 men. In the Bear Paw Mountains, the depleted band of 418 Nez Perce, three quarters of them women and children, surrendered after a final five-day battle that took the lives of Looking Glass and twenty-four others.

Surrendering His Rifle

Chief Joseph insisted that General Miles, not General Howard, accept his surrender. On the afternoon of October 5, Chief Joseph, representing many of the remaining Nez Perce, ended the Battle of Bear Paw and the Nez Perce War by handing his rifle to Colonel Miles.[168]

Joseph and the remaining Nez Perce made a deal with Colonel Miles. The tribe would stop fighting and return to the reservation the U.S. government had created.

During the war, the Army failed to decisively defeat the Indians in any of the thirteen battles and engagements fought over a four-month period, along a 1,350-mile trek, prior to the Bear Paw Battle that resulted in the Nez Perce finally surrendering due to exhaustion. (Emphasis added).[169]

In 1877, war with the Nez Perce alone, would tally a heavy cost for the government. In 4 1/2 months of traveling and fighting from Idaho to Montana, the Army counted 123 dead soldiers, 55 dead civilians, and about as many wounded. The government estimated its cost of fighting the war at $931,329, not including destroyed property or stolen stock. The Nez Perce losses were incalculable. They had lost somewhere in the neighborhood of 155 of the 800 people who started on the journey. Another ninety were wounded, and hundreds more died in exile after their surrender. The proud Nez Perce people, who had thrived for so many years, left their homeland rich and powerful before they began their war on 17 June, and they found themselves poverty stricken and demoralized at trail's end on 5 October 1877, their homeland removed, their horses gone, and their freedom lost.[170]

White Bird and Wottolen (spiritual leader) escaped to Canada where they and several other Nez Perce, including Yellow Wolf, Peopeo Tholekt, Black Eagle, and Joseph's daughter, Kapkap Ponmi, received refuge from Sitting Bull at his Sioux village.[171]

The present-day value of $931,329 is about $25,501,029.[172]

On October 5, 1877, Chief Joseph's speech, as he surrendered, immortalized him in American history forever:

> I am tired of fighting. Our chiefs are killed. Looking Glass is dead. Toohoolhoolzote is dead. The old men are all dead. It is the young men who say, 'Yes' or 'No.' He who led the young men [Olikut] is dead. It is cold, and we have no blankets. *The little children are freezing to death. My people, some of them, have run away to the hills, and have no blankets, no food. No one knows where they are—perhaps freezing to death. I want to have time to look for my children, and see how many of them I can find. Maybe I shall find them among the dead.* Hear me, my chiefs! I am tired. My heart is sick and sad. From where the sun now stands I will fight no more forever. (Emphasis added).[173]

Unfortunately, the government broke General Miles' promise that they could return to the Idaho reservation. Chief Joseph and the remaining survivors were force marched and imprisoned at Fort Leavenworth and in the Indian Territory for *eight years*. When released, some went to Lapwai, but Chief Joseph and 150 others were sent to the Colville Reservation in Washington, not to Nez Perce, and certainly not to their home in the Wallowa Valley.

Before the war, General Sherman, said on September 26, 1876: **"These Indians require to be soundly whipped ... and the ringleaders in the present trouble hung, their ponies killed, and such destruction of their property as will make them very poor."** (Emphasis added).[174]

After the war, General Sherman paid tribute to the Nez Perce performance when he said, "Thus terminated one of the most extraordinary Indian wars of which there is any record. The Indians throughout displayed a courage and skill that elicited universal praise." (Emphasis added).[175]

Nez Perce Leaders
Chief Joseph (Elder)
Twisted Hair (Wilewmutnin)
Lawyer (Hallalhotcuut)
Ollocot
Tom Hill (Hustul)
White Bird
Looking Glass
Yellow Wolf (Paxaat Tamkikeechet)
Wottolen
Toohoolhoolzote
Peopeo Tholekt (Bird Alighting, White Swan Alighting)
Wahchumyus (Rainbow): Warrior of many battles, he claimed to have derived his power from the air and the rainbow which gave him might and power. He said that, like the Rainbow, his power could not be seen, nor could it be grasped.
Pahkatos (Five Wounds)
Chief Joseph (younger), (Hin-mah-too-yah-lat-kekt or Thunder Rolling in the Mountains) (1840–1904)

Nez Perce Battles
Whitebird Canyon Battle
Clearwater Battle
Kamiah Crossing Skirmish
Big Hole Battle
Bear Paw Mountain Battle

Nez Perce Leads and Battles[176]

1877 Nez Perce Treaty

Those on the reduced Reservation would be subjected to forced allotment. The surplus lands that were not allotted were opened for non-Indian settlement. Many allottees would sell their land and the Reservation became checkerboarded, with lands owned by Indians and non-Indians intermixed. This reduced the ability of the Nez Perce to exercise their sovereignty throughout the Reservation.

Good Words Do Not Last Long

In 1879, Chief Joseph went to Washington to plead for the return of his incarcerated people to Idaho. He was refused.

His speech is set forth in full. At last I was granted permission to come to Washington and bring my friend Yellow Bull and our interpreter with me. I am glad I came. I have shaken hands with a good many friends, but there are some things I want to know which no one seems able to explain. I cannot understand how the Government sends a man out to fight us, as it did General Miles, and then breaks his word. Such a government has something wrong about it. I cannot understand why so many chiefs are allowed to talk so many different ways, and promise so many different things. I have seen the Great Father Chief [President Hayes]; the Next Great Chief [Secretary of the Interior]; the Commissioner Chief; the Law Chief; and many other law chiefs [Congressmen] and they all say they are my friends, and that I shall have justice, but while all their mouths talk right I do not understand why nothing is done for my people. *I have heard talk and talk but nothing is done. Good words do not last long unless they amount to something. Words do not pay for my dead people. They do not pay for my country now overrun by white men. They do not protect my father's grave. They do not pay for my horses and cattle. Good words do not give me back my children.* Good words will not make good the promise of your war chief, General Miles. Good words will not give my people a home where they can live in peace and take care of themselves. I am tired of talk that comes to nothing. It makes my heart sick when I remember all the good words and all the broken promises. There has been too much talking by men who had no right to talk. Too many misinterpretations have been made; too many misunderstandings have come up between the white men and the Indians. *If the white man wants to live in peace with the Indian he can live in peace. There need be no trouble. Treat all men alike. Give them the same laws. Give them all an even chance to live and grow.* All men were made by the same Great Spirit Chief. They are all brothers. The earth is the mother of all people, and all people should have equal rights upon it. You might as well expect all rivers to run backward as that any man who was born a free man should be contented penned up and denied liberty to go where he pleases. If you tie a horse to a stake, do you expect he will grow fat? If you pen an Indian up on a small spot of earth and compel him to stay there, he will not be contented nor will he grow and prosper. I have asked some of the Great White Chiefs where they get their authority to say to the Indian that he shall stay in one place, while he sees white men going where they please. They cannot tell me.

I only ask of the Government to be treated as all other men are treated. If I cannot go to my own home, let me have a home in a country where my people will not die so fast. I would like to go to Bitter Root Valley. There my people would be happy; where they are now they are dying. Three have died since I left my camp to come to Washington.

When I think of our condition, my heart is heavy. I see men of my own race treated as outlaws and driven from country to country, or shot down like animals.

I know that my race must change. We cannot hold our own with the white men as we are. We only ask an even chance to live as other men live. We ask to be recognized as men. We ask that the same law shall work alike on all men. If an Indian breaks the law, punish him by the law. If a white man breaks the law, punish him also.

Let me be a free man, free to travel, free to stop, free to work, free to trade where I choose, free to choose my own teachers, free to follow the religion of my fathers, free to talk, think and act for myself—and I will obey every law or submit to the penalty.

Whenever the white man treats the Indian as they treat each other then we shall have no more wars. We shall be all alike— brothers of one father and mother, with one sky above us and one country around us and one government for all. Then the Great Spirit Chief who rules above will smile upon this land and send rain to wash out the bloody spots made by brothers' hands upon the face of the earth. For this time the Indian race is waiting and praying. I hope no more groans of wounded men and women will ever go to the ear of the Great Spirit Chief above, and that all people may be one people.

Hin-mah-too-yah-lat-kekht has spoken for his people. (Emphasis added).[177]

On September 21, 1904, Chief Joseph died in exile.

Part 28: Bannock War (1878)

General George Crook warned of the possibility of a Bannock war due to the starvation they were facing:

> It cannot be expected that they will stay on reservations where there is no possible way to get food, and see their wives and children starve and die around them. We have taken their lands, deprived them of every means of living.

> With the Bannocks and Shoshones our Indian policy has resolved itself into a question of war-path or starvation, and being merely human, many of them will always choose the former alternative, where death shall at least be glorious.[178]

Under authority of the Act of March 3, 1855, the 9th Infantry was again organized. Lieutenant-Colonel George Wright, 4th Infantry, was appointed colonel; Captain Silas Casey, 2d Infantry, lieutenant-colonel; and Captains Edward J. Steptoe, 3d Artillery, and Robert S. Garnett, 1st Cavalry, majors. They were posted at Fort Vancouver and Fort Steilacoom, W. T., in January 1856.[179]

In 1878, many Bannocks near starvation, left the Fort Hall Indian Reservation in Idaho Territory and clashed with white farmers and federal troops. A small group of Bannock warriors planned to join forces with Sitting Bull's Sioux. Traveling through Yellowstone National Park, they encountered a survey team and captured their animals and supplies. The U.S. Army, under the command of Col. Nelson Miles, surprised a Bannock camp near Heart Mountain, killing 11 and capturing 31. On September 5, 1878, at Charles' Ford, Wyoming, 20 Bannock lodges were attacked and some 140 Bannock men, women and children were killed. This attack ended in their surrender.

Bannock Indians that surrendered were restricted to Fort Hall Reservation. Others were sent to the Malheur Reservation. While the Paiute had been more peripherally involved, in November 1878, General Howard moved about 543 Bannock and Paiute prisoners from the Malheur Reservation to internment at Yakama Indian Reservation in southeastern Washington Territory. They suffered privation for years. In 1879 the Malheur Reservation was closed, due to pressure from settlers. The Northern Paiute from Idaho and Nevada were eventually released and relocated from Yakama to an expanded Duck Valley Indian Reservation with the Western Shoshone in 1886. The Duck Valley Reservation straddles the border between southern Idaho and northern Nevada.

President Hayes: Lack of Food

In his 1878 State of the Union address, President Hayes pointed to the leading cause of the Bannock War: Congress' abject failure to appropriate monies for their bare subsistence.

> The discontent among the Bannocks, which led first to some acts of violence on the part of some members of the tribe and finally to the outbreak, appears to have been caused by an *insufficiency of food* on the reservation, and this insufficiency to have been *owing to the inadequacy of the appropriations made by Congress* to the wants of the Indians at a time when the Indians were prevented from supplying the deficiency by hunting. (Emphasis added).[185]

Cost of Bannock War

The cost of the war was estimated at $500,000; equivalent in purchasing power to about $14,375,200 today.[180]

Second Bannock War 1895

The alleged Second Bannock War of 1895 started when several Bannock were arrested for elk hunting off-reservation at Jackson Hole. They paid the fine and there was no conflict. *News media, though, on the Eastern Coast exaggerated the encounter and their headlines read – "Jackson Hole Settlers Butchered by Bannocks."* They reported that all the settlers were dead. On July 27, the Cheyenne Daily Sun Leader headline read, "Settlers Massacred: At Least Sixteen Families Butchered in Jackson Hole by the Red Devils."

> Five companies of troops were dispatched from Fort Robinson, Nebraska. When they crossed Teton Pass into Jackson Hole they found no dead settlers, no hostile Indians and no wasteful elk slaughter.[181]

The army general in charge of the Ninth Cavalry, John J. Coppinger, said, "I do not consider the Indians to blame for the Jackson Hole affair. ... They are entirely quiet now and have been. In fact, they will not say 'Boo' to a goose."[182]

> Indeed, Wyoming's U.S. Attorney wrote, "The whole affair was, I believe, a premeditated and prearranged plan to kill some Indians ... and ultimately have the Indians shut out from Jacksons Hole." He called Se-we-a-gat's death "murder." But, he said, "there are no officials in Jacksons Hole—county, State, or national—who would hold any of Manning's posse for trial."[183]

On August 3, 1895, Indian Agent Teter reported as to the Bannock: "Their hearts felt good ... [they were] leaving their grievances to the justice of the white man."[184] Litigation would follow regarding off-reservation hunting rights, continuing into the twenty-first century.

Part 29: President Hayes: Moral Duty

In his 1878 State of the Union address, President Hayes acknowledged the moral duty of the U.S. to the Indians. Unfortunately, he was in the minority. Those that followed would violate his trust.

> It may be impossible to raise them fully up to the level of the white population of the United States; but *we should not forget that they are the aborigines of the country, and called the soil their own on which our people have grown rich, powerful, and happy.* We owe it to them as a moral duty to help them in attaining at least that degree of civilization which they may be able to reach. It is not only our duty, it is also our interest to do so. (Emphasis added).[186]

Part 30: President Garfield: Treaties with Savages Mockery

Thirteen years before he took office as president of the United State, James Garfield, predicted the extinction of the American Indian. As Congressman of Ohio, chairman of the House Military Committee, he introduced H.R. 1482, a bill to restore the Indian Bureau to the War Department as of January 1, 1869. ... This change, Garfield argued, would eliminate expenses for the salaries of many civil officials and prevent corruption, by making Indian authorities subject to courts-martial. It passed the House but not the Senate.[187]

He called it a "mockery... for the representatives of the great Government of the United States to sit down in a wigwam and make treaties with a lot of painted and half naked savages, only to have those treaties trampled under foot ... This whole practice of making treaties with our wards is ridiculous."[188]

In a letter of advice to President-elect James A. Garfield, Interior Secretary Schurz warned Garfield of the corruption of the Department of the Interior.

> The Interior Department is the most dangerous branch of the public service. ... It is a constant fight with the sharks that surround the Indian Bureau, the General Land Office, the Pension Office and the Patent Office, and a ceaseless struggle with perplexing questions and situations, especially in the Indian Service. Unless the head of the Interior Department well understands and performs his full duty, your Administration will be in constant danger of disgrace...[189]

Garfield's Presidency was abruptly terminated six months after his taking office by his assassination.

Part 31: President Arthur: No Sovereigns

In his first message to Congress, in December 1881, President Arthur pointed to historic errors in the conduct of Indian affairs. His opinions of Indians wouldn't be propitious. He (1) opposed recognizing tribes as sovereigns; (2) protested the treaty and reservation policy; (3) disputed any support for pursuing their cultural practices; and (4) assailed the failure of civilizing them.

> "It was natural, at a time when the national territory seemed almost illimitable and contained many millions of acres far outside the bounds of civilized settlements, that a policy should have been initiated which more than aught else has been the fruitful source of our Indian complications," he said. "I refer, of course, to the policy of dealing with the various Indian tribes as separate nationalities, of relegating them by treaty stipulations to the occupancy of immense reservations in the West, and of encouraging them to live a savage life, undisturbed by any earnest and well-directed efforts to bring them under the influences of civilization."[190]

Part 32: President Cleveland: Allotment

During President Cleveland's first term in office, from 1885 to 1889, Congress enacted three measures with devastating effects on Indians. First, the Major Crimes Act[191] instituted federal jurisdiction over serious crimes committed by Indians on their own land. This deprived Indian Nations of this vital aspect of sovereignty, especially since the federal government lacked the manpower and the will to prevent criminal activities. Second, the General Allotment Act[192] authorized the President to divide Indian tribal land into individual allotments, forcing Indians into private property ownership whether they desired it or not. Third, the Indian Appropriations Act of 1889[193] opened "unassigned" lands to white settlers. This would lead, for example, to the Oklahoma Land Run of 1889.

Allotments

The federal government coupled allotment with Indian land dispossession. As soon as lands on a reservation were allotted, the remainder were considered "surplus lands." In most instances, they were sold to white homesteaders. When Indians were permitted to sell their allotments, many who needed the money did so. This left many reservations with a checkerboard pattern of land ownership, between the federal government, states, and non-Indians. It made governing the reservation, as a whole, by tribes, difficult.

The United States used monies resulting from the sale of ceded lands to pay for the attempted assimilation process of Indians, e.g., funds were used for purchasing agricultural implements and machinery. The Indian Agent was instructed to distribute the goods to those pursuing agricultural subsistence. Thus, the Indian Agent was given carte blanche to play favorites and to reward those compliant with the government's policies.

> The essential feature of the Government's great educational program for the Indians is the abolition of the old tribal relations and the treatment of every Indian as an individual. *The basis of this individualization is the breaking up of tribal lands into allotments to the individuals of the tribe*. This step is fundamental to the present Indian policy of the Government. Until their lands are allotted, the Government is merely marking time in dealing with any groups of Indians. (Emphasis added).[194]

Warm Springs Debacle

If allotments were meant to benefit Indians, this wasn't the case on many reservations, such as Warm Springs. It was a pattern of mismanagement across the country.

> About six years ago allotments were made to these Indians in severalty ... but there has been so much trouble over boundary lines, so many unwise selections, allotments wholly unfit for any purpose, or two allotments of good land made to the same person under different names, that they refuse to accept the patents until corrections are made and these matters definitely settled. James E. Kirk, Superintendent and Special Disbursing Agent.[195]

U.S.' Genocidal Indian War (1887)

Attorney, James Washinawatok, Menominee, categorized the General Allotment Act as America's one-sided genocidal war against Indians.

Since the late eighteenth and early nineteenth centuries, non-Indian America, asserted its cultural superiority by both assuming and asserting that Indians either must assimilate or blend into the American "melting-pot" and perish as a distinctive people or must gradually die off as their culture and skills fail to cope with the changes imposed on them by the advance of an allegedly superior white civilization. This asserted cultural superiority manifested into actual governmental policies affecting Native Americans, such as the General Allotment Act (GAA). This article argues that the GAA and its effects constitute genocide.[196]

Part 33: President Harrison: Eradicating Tribal Relations

President Benjamin Harrison was the grandson of the ninth U.S. president William Henry Harrison. In his first message to Congress, in December 1889, Harrison called Indians an "ignorant and helpless people." In his opinion, breaking up tribal relations should have occurred much earlier.

> "It is to be regretted that the policy of breaking up the tribal relation and of dealing with the Indian as an individual did not appear earlier in our legislation," Harrison told Congress. "Large reservations held in common and the maintenance of the authority of the chiefs and headmen have deprived the individual of every incentive to the exercise of thrift, and the annuity has contributed an affirmative impulse toward a state of confirmed pauperism."[197]

Part 34: Death Squads' Atrocities

A few of the atrocities committed by the volunteer Death Squads' were reported by the DOI and the U.S. Army.

Coose County Death Squad's Coquille Massacre

F.M. Smith, Sub-Indian Agent, reported the Coquille Massacre to his superiors:

> On January 28, 1854, forty armed miners organized under the command of George H. Abbott, with A. H. Soap as first lieutenant, and W. H. Packwood as second lieutenant attacked the Nason tribe and in a "most horrid massacre," "an out-and-out barbarous murder" killed sixteen indians and burned the village homes.

> *Thus was committed a massacre too inhuman to be readily believed. I regard the murder of those Indians as one of the most barbarous acts ever perpetrated by civilized men.* But what can be done? The leaders of the party cannot be arrested, though justice loudly demands their punishment. Here we have not even a justice of the peace; and as to the military force garrisoned at Fort Orford, it consists of but four men. If such murderous assaults are to be continued, there will be no end of Indian war in Oregon. *Bold, brave, courageous men! to attack a friendly and defenceless tribe of Indians; to burn, roast, and shoot sixteen of their number.* (Emphasis in original). F. M. Smith, Sub-Indian Agent.[198]

Massacre at Miller's Ferry

> *On February 15, 1854, twenty-three Indians and several squaws were killed by eight or nine miners who then went on a rampage burning lodges and killing other Indians. ... What adds to the atrocity of the deed is that shortly before the massacre the Indians were induced to sell the whites their guns, under the pretext that friendly relations were firmly established.* The rampage resulted from the refusal of the ferry operator to allow the Indians to use it, even though it was built on Indian land. (Emphasis added).[199]

> Miller was subsequently arrested and placed in the custody of the military at Port Orford; but on his examination before a justice of the peace, was set at large on the ground of justification, and want of sufficient evidence to commit. ... Arrests are evidently useless, since no act of a white man against an Indian, however atrocious, can be followed by a conviction.[200]

Sup't Joel Palmer advised Com'r George W. Manypenny on July 14, 1855, of these atrocities:

> The perusal of these communications [from Agent George Ambrose] will show the frequent occurrence of events in that region calculated to disturb the public quiet and endanger the personal safety both of whites and Indians, and the necessity of the constant exercise of prudence and vigilance on the part of the officers in the Indian service in order to prevent actual war. ... where misunderstandings embroiling the whites and Indians constantly arise, and where the slightest offense or mere suspicion often *excites the fury of reckless and unprincipled men*, but little reason would exist for apprehending hostile manifestations on the part of the savages ... nearly all the Indians are now collected upon the reservation. (Emphasis added).[201]

Agent Geo. H. Ambrose, reported on Sept. 19, 1855 to Sup't Joel Palmer, that a mob of volunteers were demanding that he surrender Indians in his care to them. Supt' Palmer approved his refusal to turn them over, which would have been the equivalent of sentencing them to murder.

> I approve [of] your course in not consenting to surrender those Indians into the hands of the "volunteers." The laws of the country clearly indicate a different mode of disposing of such cases. *Besides, some of those suspected may not be guilty, and their delivery into the hands of a mob (and such I apprehend the "volunteers" were in the view of the law) would have been equivalent to shooting them down.* If the perpetrators of the atrocious deed, they deserve death, but an excited and enraged population are illy qualified to discriminate between the innocent and the guilty, and however deserved the punishment, all experience proves that executions without the forms of law are not only without salutary effect, but of [a] positively injurious tendency.
>
> It cannot be too strongly impressed upon the Indians that their only security against violence and wrong from reckless whites is to remain quietly on the reservation, that if they leave it and mingle with the vagabond Indians infesting the region adjacent to the boundary between Oregon and California, or at any time give countenance and protection to any fleeing to the reservation to escape detection and punishment, and that their security, happiness and prosperity as individuals and as a people rests upon their upright and peaceful deportment and prompt surrender of all among them guilty of violence, robbery or theft. (Emphasis added).[202]

Confirming the lawless white hordes roaming Indian country, **Maj. Genl. John E. Wool, Comdr. Pacific Division, United States Army, confirmed Sup't Joel Palmer fears. The General himself was apprehensive about his ability to prevent the slaughter of innocent Indians. His lengthy report corroborates the settlers' war of extermination and is an important document evidencing this violent history:**

> *The existence of a war of extermination by our citizens against all Indians in Southern Oregon* which by recent acts appears to evince a determination to carry it out, in violation of all treaty stipulations and the common usages of civilized nations, has induced me to take steps to remove the friendly bands of Indians now assembled at Fort Lane and upon Umpqua reservation to an encampment on the headwaters of the Yamhill River, distant about sixty miles southwest of Vancouver and adjoining the Coast Reservation.

This plan has been adopted with a view of saving the lives of such of those Indians as have given just and reasonable assurances of friendship.

The tremendous excitement among the miners and settlers in that country, goaded on by reckless and lawless miscreants who slaughter alike innocent and guilty of both sexes, induced those friendly bands to abandon the reservation and claim protection of the United States troops stationed at Fort Lane. Over three hundred of these people are now encamped at that point, and as many more in the Umpqua Valley, but little less menaced. These people are deprived of their usual means of obtaining subsistence and must necessarily be furnished by the government. The enormous expense attending the transportation of supplies at this season of the year will, I think, alone justify their removal.

In my instructions to the Indian agents directing this movement, they were required to call upon the commandant at Fort Lane for such an escort as was deemed requisite to secure a safe passage through the disturbed district. Since these instructions were given, I have received intelligence *that meetings of the citizens of the Willamette Valley,* residing along the route to be traveled by these Indians in reaching the designated encampment, as well as those in the vicinity of the latter, have resolved upon resisting such removal, and *avowing a determination to kill all [Indians] who may be brought among them* as well as those who sought to effect that object. This feeling appears so general among our citizens *I am apprehensive they may attempt carrying it into effect*; to avoid which I have to request that if it be deemed by you practicable, that a command of twenty men be directed to accompany these Indians on their removal, with directions to remain at or near the encampment so long as their presence may be required to insure the safety of the Indians.

Believing, as I do, that the cause of the present difficulty in Southern Oregon is wholly to be attributed to the acts of our own people, I cannot but feel that it is our duty to adopt such measures as will tend to secure the lives of these Indians and maintain guarantees secured them by treaty stipulations. *The future will prove that this war has been forced upon these Indians against their will, and that too, by a set of reckless vagabonds, for pecuniary and political objects, and sanctioned by a numerous population who regard the treasury of the United States a legitimate subject of plunder.*

> *The Indians in that district have been driven to desperation by acts of cruelty against their people; treaties have been violated and acts of barbarity committed by those claiming to be citizens that would disgrace the most barbarous nations of the earth, and if none but those who perpetrated such acts were to be affected by this war, we might look upon it with indifference, but unhappily this is not the case.* (Emphasis added).[203]

In a horrific Report from General Wool to Lieutenant Colonel L. Thomas, Assistant Adjutant General, U.S. Army, Benicia Headquarters, Department of the Pacific, dated January 19, 1856, he documented the mayhem and mutilation of Walla Walla Chief Peo peo mox mox:

Again, when the volunteers marched against the Walla-Wallas, the *chief, Pu-pu-mux-mux met them under a flag of truce, and declared "He was for peace*, and did not wish to fight; that his people did not wish to fight, and if his young men had done wrong, he would make restitution;" and at the same time offered them cattle for food. *He, however, was taken prisoner, and afterwards barbarously murdered, scalped, his ears and hands cut off, and these preserved and sent to the friends of the volunteers in Oregon, all which was reported by volunteers*. (Emphasis added).[204]

His direct descendant states his feet were also cut off; his back was skinned, and strips of his flash were made into souvenir razor straps, and part of his scalp made into buttons.[205]

The cruel, merciless, and unlawful hunting of Indians continued. The U.S. utterly failed to protect these Indians.

> Captain Smith, at Fort Lane, reports, 8th January, that, on the 23d December last, a party of volunteers … made a visit to a camp of friendly Indians. The object of this visit … was to ascertain the strength, position, &c. of the Indian camp; and finding them unarmed, with the exception of a few bows and arrows, marched there on the following night, *surrounded the camp, and killed nineteen men, burned their houses and stores, and left the women and children exposed to the severe cold weather. The squaws and children are now at this post suffering severely from frozen limbs*. … another company of volunteers paid a similar visit to [Old Jake's] camp … and at night surrounded camp and *massacred all the men. The squaws and children from this camp are also here, suffering with frozen limbs*. Captain Smith further reports, the 23d of February, that the day before, four hundred friendly Indians set out for the coast reservation, under a *strong escort to protect them from the whites, who have threatened not only to kill the Indians, but all who might accompany them.* (Emphasis added).[206]

A clash of policy between the Military and Indian departments only made the situation worse:

> **The commander of Ft. Klamath last autumn received orders to execute all Indians found off the reservation without permission, before they have even been ordered onto it**, and he now states that he has received orders to protect settlers in the lake country, *before, as I understand it, any person can rightfully settle there.* (Emphasis added).[207]

A 'Personal' Hanging

Lt. Col. Drew engaged in his own personal hanging of George, an Indian, for no reason other than he was Indian. A dramatic play was written on the incident. I am simply unable to convey in words the total inhumanity demonstrated by the Oregon settlers towards Indians.

In a Letter from J. W. Perit Huntington, Supt. Indian Affairs in Oregon to Amos E. Rogers Esq., U.S. Ind. Sub-Agent, dated November 27, 1863, he emphasized the complete violation of law and principles of right conduct:

> The action of Lieut. Col. Drew in hanging an Indian in time of peace, without trial, without indeed any charge of crime of a capital nature, after having notified the agent that the Indian would be removed to Fort Klamath, and not having given any notice of his intention to do otherwise, is so extraordinary, so gross a violation not only of law but of the principles of right and the dictates of good policy ... You are directed to make immediate inquiry as to the details of the action of Lieut. Col. Drew in the premises and report the same to this office without delay.[208]

> (Private) Dec. 2, 1863
> Letter to J. W. P. Huntington, J. W. Perit Huntington, Supt. Indian Affairs in Oregon from E. L. Applegate

> Since the hanging of Indian "George," the arrest of "Jack" and the shooting of "Skookum John" and the consequent impression made upon the mind of the Indians and sought to be made in regard to the agent and his authority, the case to my mind scarcely admits of a doubt. In fact it seems to me that the proceeding was calculated to impress upon the mind of the Indians that the gravest of the offenses for which he suffered death was that he attempted to recognize that the agent had any authority at all.

The Col. [*Drew*] actually appears to ignore the agent, his authority and that of the whole department and to treat as a usurpation and a crime the mere claim of it in any shape.

There is a dreadful state of affairs here, and some incredible things have transpired which could only be known by a personal interview with the agent. The war made upon him is so bitter, and the spirit manifested so reckless and malicious, there is in my candid opinion no judging to what extreme lengths it might be carried towards him. ... There is no telling, I say again, what might happen to the agent under this most unfortunate train of circumstances.[209]

James T. Glenn only a few moments ago confessed to Rogers, in my presence, that George positively had no trial of any kind whatever. He also stated that he was the man who took down the Indian's testimony, which was published in the *Intelligencer*. [*That issue of the* Intelligencer, *along with George's testimony, is now lost.*][210]

The article below is one of many reporting the hanging of George and the shooting of John. Its accuracy can't be verified but it is one of numerous articles printed. A drama was even written and performed locally.

THE LAST ACT IN THE ROGUE RIVER INDIAN WARS

The soldiers who had gone to round up Jack, finding that he had fled, returned to camp about 2 o'clock that afternoon, and at once preparations were made for the hanging of George, which took place at 3 o'clock. No trial was given George, and he was hung on a military order issued by Colonel Drew. Among the fine old oaks that were on the camp ground was one with a large horizontal limb about fifteen feet from the ground. Over this a rope was passed, one end made fast to the tree and the other end was left hanging with the noose ready for George's neck. A box was placed in a wagon, and upon it George was made to stand. The wagon was then by a team hauled under the limb of the oak, the noose adjusted about George's neck, and then driven on leaving the Indian hanging in the air. His hands had been tied behind his body, but his feet were not tied nor was he blindfolded. As he swung off the box the rebound of his body brought him near the tree and he threw his legs around it. He held this way but a moment when the strangulation on his neck caused his muscles to relax and his legs released the tree and his body swung by the rope, and after a few struggles he was dead.

> Indians condemned to die usually maintain a stolid disdain and make no plea to be spared, but George begged frantically for his life as he was being placed upon the wagon and saw no chance of escape. From the defiant, desperate attitude that he had maintained up to the hour of his execution he broke down entirely and promised to be a good Indian, but Colonel Drew and all the other whites felt that the only good Indian was a dead Indian.[211]

Letter from E. Steele, Late Agt. Ind. Affairs N.W. Cal to Com'r Dole, dated March 2, 1864, confirming the murder of George:

> Col. Drew arrested and caused to be executed an Indian commonly known as George and killed an Indian commonly known as "Skookum John," two very, very vicious and illy disposed chiefs, who were counseling war continuously.[212]

Part 35: Liabilities

The U.S. would be left with a war debt and losses which were completely avoidable:

> **Outstanding Debts**
>
> Upon a careful examination of the books in the office of the Superintendent, at Salem, I have derived the following data: The outstanding liabilities in Oregon up to June 30th 1857, as estimated and reported by the different agents, are $176,511.29. J. Ross Browne, Special Agent of the Treasury Department.[213]
>
> **Spoliation Claims**
>
> Schedule of spoliation claims against hostile Indians in Oregon Territory filed in the office of the Superintendent and forwarded to the Commissioner Ind. Affrs. November 15, 1857. $63,116.24.[214]
>
> **War Costs**
>
> I have learned since that he [Gov. Stevens] called for two regiments, one for Washington Territory and the other for southern Oregon, both mounted, and which required about two thousand horses. ... The expense of all which, together with the enormous prices paid for everything the volunteers have received, will amount to more than two millions-some say three millions; and ***General Adair, collector of customs at Astoria, says it will amount to four millions***. (Emphasis added).[215]

Part 36: Back-Biting

The DOI burned through Superintendents during the period of Oregon's Indian conflict. Their correspondence is filled with 'he-said, she-said' and 'when am I getting paid.' The jealousy and pettiness between players are unbelievable. Fortunately, it is evidenced in their correspondence. Some of their letters are incredibly long. When you add in the U.S. Army, it is who can be blamed for this. They point a very pointy figure at the DOI.

Democratic Members of the Oregon Council and House of Representatives, petitioned President Pierce on Jan. 8, 1856, to remove Sup't Palmer:

> We, the undersigned Democratic members of the Council and House of Representatives of the Territory of Oregon, would most respectfully but earnestly pray your excellency to remove the present incumbent, Joel Palmer, from the office of Sup't of Indian Affairs of this Territory.[216]

Sup't Wm. H. Rector, removed B. R. Biddle, Ind. Agt., for malfeasance, who then filed a grievance on April 26, 1862:

> Your favor enclosing a copy of certain charges preferred against me has been received, and ... you must furnish me with the names and the affidavits of the parties preferring the charges. You say that I stand "*charged with malfeasance in office* &c." and go on to state what those charges are but *do not mention the name of the person or persons making the same. This I demand as a right, so that I may be enabled to meet my enemies on equal terms.* (Emphasis added).[217]

DOI: "Damnedest Humbug"

Col. Drew considered the DOI the "Damnedest Humbug:"

Col. Drew said! "When I get established here, I shall muster the Indians every day for roll call and make every one answer to his name! No Indian shall leave here either, without a *pass* from *me*. **I shall plow up a piece of ground next spring, and by G-d they have got to put it in too—if it has to be done at the point of the bayonet!** I will show Uncle Sam that there is a way to get along with Indians without having a set of whining Indian-sympathizing agents about to make promises to Indians never to be fulfilled." ... If I cannot show the damnedest state of things in this Dept. that ever existed in any Dept. of any country, then I will ask no pay for my trouble! *The Ind. Dept. is decidedly the damnedest humbug* ... the *Ind. Dept. is directly and indirectly responsible for the murder of every white man by Indians on this coast.* (Emphasis added).[218]

You're Fired

On February 19, 1870, the *Democratic News,* in Jacksonville, reported the removal of an Indian Agent as his being "Decapitated:"

> DECAPITATED. The telegraph announces, among other removals, that of Capt. Knapp, Indian agent at Ft. Klamath. His successor has not been named.[219]

Sup't A. B. Meacham, on Sep. 21, 1870, in his Second Annual Report of the Condition of Indian Affairs in Oregon to Com'r Parker stated that the suspension of civilian agents was embarrassing. These agents would be replaced by military officers, which was disconcerting to the Indians. Most significantly, he noted the "degraded whites" and the "hordes of spectators" waiting to line their pockets at the expense of the Indians.

> The changes made, suspending civilians and appointing military agents at the commencement of the current year, created some embarrassment, which for a time seemed [to] retard prosperity and to dishearten the Indians.

> One great obstacle in the way of the successful management of Indians is the ***bad influence exerted over them by degraded whites who hover like wolves and vultures*** around the borders of the reservation, constantly poisoning and inflaming the Indian mind. They degrade and prostitute the Indian women, and in every way use their greatest endeavors to create disaffection, are ever inciting the Indians to disobey the counsels and orders of their agents. Through the actions of these men, the Indians, instead of forming an exalted opinion of the white man, are led to regard him with doubt, distrust, fear and hatred, and too often men are employed both as agents and agency employees who are more or less dissipated and dishonest, who take less interest in their duties than in the accumulation of money and in the gratification of their baser passions. Such I know is not the intention of the government, but that such is the case often, we are compelled to confess with shame and sorrow. Too often, men are chosen for such places as a reward for some political assistance they may be able to render, and not for their knowledge or merit. In fact there is all to discourage, and little to encourage, honest, conscientious men to labor in this cause. ***The Department is surrounded by hordes of speculators and petty politicians who stand ready to defeat every honest effort at improvement, unless their pockets are lined with the patronage of the Dept.*** (Emphasis added).[220]

Whose Side Are You On Anyway?

Supt. Nesmith reported to Com'r J. W. Denver on January 25, 1859, of the savage barbarism of the Indians in Oregon:

> When we contemplate that two hundred and seventy-three persons of the small population of Oregon alone have fallen victims to the treachery and barbarity of the Indians in so short a period we are impressed with the conviction that the sufferings of our citizens have been without parallel in frontier life. [Excluding citizens who have fallen in battle].[221]

So that there would be no denial or delay of the westward expansion, the highest levels, within the Interior Department, continued to denounce any defiance by Indians. Com'r Francis A. Walker decreed that Indians that resisted removal would be "relentlessly crushed." Indian Nations and peoples didn't stand a chance. Their guardian pronounced providence on its side; their God's patronage aided the prompt incarceration of Indians on barren, isolated lands.

SUBMISSION THE ONLY HOPE OF THE INDIANS. If they stand up against the progress of civilization and industry, they must be relentlessly crushed. The westward course of population is neither to be denied nor delayed for the sake of all the Indians that ever called this country their home. They must yield or perish; and there is something that savors of providential mercy in the rapidity with which their fate advances upon them, leaving them scarcely the chance to resist before they shall be surrounded and disarmed. (Emphasis added).²²²

Part 37: Shout of 'Timber' – Green Gold

The impetus for the removal of Indian tribes in the Oregon Territory: millions of acres containing immensely valuable standing timber – Green Gold.

In the Commissioner's Report of the General Land Office to the Secretary of Interior in 1913, Oregon's more than twenty million acres containing standing timber with 225 billion board feet is reported. This is after logging for fifty years. ²²³

Privately Owned Standing Timber in Oregon	Holders	3 Major Holders	Acquisition Method
238 billion feet or nearly 11% of privately owned timber.	48% held by 195 holders. Small holders "blocked" in or "controlled by" larger holders.	Northern Pacific Railway, Southern Pacific Company and Weyerhaeuser Timber Company - Own 20% of timber in Pacific Northwest. (11% of timber in U.S.)	Northern Pacific –Gov't Grants in WI, MINN, ND, MT, WY, ID, OR, WASH; Southern Pacific – Gov't Grants from OR to CA; Weyerhaeuser 80% purchased from No. Pacific grant (77 billion feet in WA, 18.7 billion ft. in OR, small % in CA).

Oregon's Railroads (1866 Grant to State, 1870–1880 Completed)

Federal railroad land grants in the Pacific Northwest consisted of two large land grants, one the western portion of a grant to the Northern Pacific for a railway from Lake Superior to the Puget Sound and the other for a railway from Portland to the California-Oregon border. Under these grants (as amended through subsequent legislative acts), the Northern Pacific received almost forty-million acres stretching from Wisconsin to Washington, and the Oregon & California received over three-million acres in Oregon along the Willamette Valley. The Northern Pacific was completed to Portland in 1883. James J. Hill built his Great Northern to Puget Sound in 1893.

The Oregon & California prepared a list of lands for approval for the General Land Office and received patents. The patents were recorded in the various counties in which the lands were located; the Company further established its ownership by paying taxes on the lands.

If a party was occupying its land, agents were sent to investigate and determine the rights, if any, of the party. If the person was a trespasser, the Company asserted its ownership and demanded that the party either take a lease on the land or vacate it. If the party refused, the company would file an ejectment suit to force them from the land. The company also patrolled its land to prevent depredations, destruction, waste or theft of timber.

In a lawsuit for theft of its timber, the Oregon & California sought redress not just for the value of the timber taken but also for being deprived its right of exclusion. They sought to make it unprofitable for people to cut their timber without authority. *Its ownership entitled it not just to the market value of commodities on the land, but also to decide how and when they were to be extracted and to determine who would receive the benefits from such use.*

Railroad land grant recipients played a key role in bringing "open access" to an end. Their pecuniary interest in protecting their lands from trespasses and theft and their active policing of their massive land holdings, challenged the frontier custom of treating all public resources as free for the taking. These powerful railroad corporations enforced their "right of exclusion," a right attending ownership. The General Land Office was unable to do this, due to understaffing and lack of money for this function.

Corporate Logging Empires

Turning the western forests into green gold gave rise to the lumber barons and the railroad tycoons. While Indians struggled to survive the extermination nightmares of the settlers and the government, Andrew Hammond's dream of a Montana lumber empire morphed into an Oregon Territory lumber empire.[224] Hammond had the capital from his contract with the Northern Pacific Railroad to log the timber and supply it with goods. He relied on trusted family members as managers and served as the General, incorporating new technologies to increase productivity. Weyerhaeuser and Hancock Forest Management controlled large timber tracts for speculation.

Midstream Businesses – Sawmills

Hammond used vertical and horizontal integration to grow his business, increase his profit margins, and avoid logjams in delivering his services under his dream contract. Vertical integration meant strategic ownership of the businesses responsible for the stages of the production process, rather than relying on external contractors or suppliers. The advantages were greater efficiencies, reduced costs and economies of scale.

His first step was building sawmills, buying out small sawmill businesses and driving smaller operators out of business by controlling pricing. He knew too many sawmills wouldn't be profitable due to the slim profit margins. He priced them out of business until the midstream industry drifted into the control of the Hammond Lumber Company (HLC). Horizontal integration helped HLC to grow in size and revenue, expand into new markets, diversify product offerings and reduce competition. Survival of the fittest was his game.

Downstream Businesses – Lumber Yards

Integrating vertically, HLC built sash and door factories next to its mill supplying the high demand for settlers building lumber homes. It opened lumber yards, increasing ownership until it would be categorized as a "line company," a company owning many lumber yards.

Hammond ruled his empire as a "lumber baron:" (1) consolidating timberlands, (2) using railroads to gain better access to timber stands, (3) modernizing sawmills, (4) implementing factory assembly line strategies for sash and door and furniture manufacturing, (5) owning shipping lines (the 'Hammond Navy' would be one of the largest and the only non-union lumber shipping line on the West Coast), and (6) wholesale and (6) retail lumber yards and, lastly (7) expanding into construction contracts.

Scratching Each Other's Backs

Political, social and financial elements were intertwined. Lumbermen, financiers, industrialists, and politicians not only shared office buildings but lived in the same neighborhood and moved in the same social circles. Their offices, too, were all clustered. Their industry Associations hadn't yet come under the anti-trust laws, and they could reach agreements on production ceilings and prices—cartels of their time.

Denuding Lands in which Indians Have Beneficial Interest

The Umatilla Indians reported the deforestation of their ceded lands which were to be sold for their benefit:

> [Ceded lands were] not so sold and are now being squatted on by whites, who are denuding those lands of the timber in a most reckless manner.[225]

Indians' Lost Opportunities

Given the Indians' forced focus on survival, they never even had a chance to retain their vast timber resources.

Notes: Oregon: Governor Curry's Private War of Extermination

1. Speech of Hon. S. Breese, of Illinois, on the Oregon question. Delivered in the Senate of the United States, Monday, March 2, 1846.
2. Gallatin, Albert, The Oregon Question. New York: Bartlett & Welford, 1846. Number V: 27.
3. 5 Stat. 453 (1841) (repealed 1891).
4. https://en.wikipedia.org/wiki/Oregon_Trail (accessed online May 8, 2022).
5. Gaston, Joseph. The centennial history of Oregon, 1811–1912. Vol. 1. SJ Clarke Publishing Company, 1912, p. 219.
6. http://www.let.rug.nl/usa/presidents/james-knox-polk/first-inaugural-address-1845.php (accessed online April 28, 2022).
7. Id.
8. https://millercenter.org/the-presidency/presidential-speeches/may-29-1848-message-regarding-oregon-territory (accessed online April 27, 2022).
9. Memorial of the Legislative Assembly of Oregon Territory, Relative to Their Present Situation and Wants. August 10, 1848, Tippin & Streeper, 1848, p. 9.
10. http://www.let.rug.nl/usa/presidents/james-knox-polk/state-of-the-union-1848.php territory (accessed online April 27, 2022).
11. Id.
12. Donation Land Claim Act of 1850, ch. 76, 9 Stat. 496 (1850).
13. Report of the Commissioner of Indian Affairs to the Secretary of the Interior, Office of Indian Affairs, United States. Printer: A.O.P. Nicholson, 1855, p. 289.
14. Act of June 5, 1850, ch. 16, 9 Stat. 437.
15. *Daily Alta California,* San Francisco, August 15, 1851, p. 2.
16. Id.

17. *NARA Series M234 Letters Received by the Office of Indian Affairs 1824–1881, Reel 611 Oregon Superintendency, 1858–1859.* Original on NARA Series M234 Letters Received by the Office of Indian Affairs 1824–1881, Reel 611 Oregon Superintendency, 1858–1859, frames 193-194.
18. http://www.let.rug.nl/usa/presidents/millard-fillmore/state-of-the-union-1851.php (accessed online April 28, 2022).
19. Id.
20. *NARA Series M234, Letters Received by the Office of Indian Affairs, Reel 608 Oregon Superintendency 1853–1855,* frames 820-837.
21. *NARA Series M2, Microcopy of Records of the Oregon Superintendency of Indian Affairs 1848–1873, Reel 4; Letter Books C:10.*
22. *NARA Series M234, Letters Received by the Office of Indian Affairs Reel 608 Oregon Superintendency 1853–1855,* frames 1237-1247.
23. Report of the Commissioner of Indian Affairs to the Secretary of the Interior, Oregon and Washington Superintendency, Office of Indian Affairs, United States. William A. Harris, Printer, 1858, pp. 217-218.
24. Narcissa Whitman, The Letters of Narcissa Whitman, 1836–1847, May 16, 1844 (Fairfield, Washington: Ye Galleon Press, 1986).
25. Id.
26. Proclamation by Geo Abernethy, Governor of Oregon Territory, December 25, 1847.
27. THE OFFICIAL HISTORY OF THE WASHINGTON NATIONAL GUARD VOLUME 1 HERITAGE OF THE WASHINGTON TERRITORIAL MILITIA HEADQUARTERS MILITARY DEPARTMENT STATE OF WASHINGTON OFFICE OF THE ADJUTANT GENERAL CAMP MURRAY, TACOMA 33, WASHINGTON, p. 23. https://mil.wa.gov/asset/5ba41fe17f150 (accessed online May 8, 2022).
28. Ibid., p. 25.
29. "The Massacre at Waiilatpu," Oregon Spectator, January 20, 1848, p. 1.
30. O'Callaghan, Jerry A. The Disposition of the Public Domain in Oregon. U.S. Government Printing Office, 1960, p. 24.
31. *NARA Series M234, Letters Received by the Office of Indian Affairs, Reel 607 Oregon Superintendency 1842–1852,* frames 629-634.
32. https://www.officialdata.org/us/inflation/1782?amount=400000 (accessed online May 7, 2022).
33. Report of the Commissioner of Indian Affairs to the Secretary of the Interior, Office of Indian Affairs, United States. 1850, p. 135.
34. *NARA Series M234, Letters Received by the Office of Indian Affairs, Reel 607 Oregon Superintendency 1842–1852,* frames 1092-1095.
35. *NARA Series M234, Letters Received by the Office of Indian Affairs Reel 607 Oregon Superintendency 1842–1852,* frames 1092-1095.
36. Bernarr, Cresap, "Captain O.C. Ord in the Rogue River Indian War," Oregon Historical Quarterly, 54:2 (June 1953), 84.

37. Tveskov, Mark A. "A 'Most Disastrous' Affair: The Battle of Hungry Hill, Historical Memory, and the Rogue River War." *Oregon Historical Quarterly*, 118:1 (Spring 2017), p. 53.
38. Id.
39. *NARA Series M234, Letters Received by the Office of Indian Affairs, Reel 607 Oregon Superintendency 1842–1852, frames 924-948. A copy can be found on NARA Series M2, Microcopy of Records of the Oregon Superintendency of Indian Affairs, Reel 11, Instructions and Reports 1850–1855, pages 23-44.*
40. *Daily Alta California,* San Francisco, April 4, 1852, p. 2.
41. *Daily Alta California,* San Francisco, August 21, 1853, p. 2.
42. *NARA Series M2, Microcopy of Records of the Oregon Superintendency of Indian Affairs 1848–1873, Reel 23; Letters Received, 1866–1867, No. 165.*
43. Snodgrass, Mary Ellen. The Civil War Era and Reconstruction: An Encyclopedia of Social, Political, Cultural and Economic History, Routledge, 2015, p. 25.
44. *Microcopy of Records of the Oregon Superintendency of Indian Affairs, Reel 11, Instructions and Reports 1854–1855, pages 179-181. A copy can be found on NARA Series M234, Letters Received by the Office of Indian Affairs, Reel 608 Oregon Superintendency 1853–1855, frames 713-715.*
45. Report of the Commissioner of Indian Affairs to the Secretary of the Interior, Office of Indian Affairs, United States. A.O.P. Nicholson, Printer, 1855, p. 291.
46. http://www.let.rug.nl/usa/presidents/franklin-pierce/state-of-the-union-1854.php (accessed online February 26, 2022).
47. Id.
48. *NARA Series M2, Microcopy of Records of the Oregon Superintendency of Indian Affairs 1848–1872, Reel 5; Letter Book D, pages 238-239.*
49. Report of the Commissioner of Indian Affairs to the Secretary of the Interior, Office of Indian Affairs, United States. A.O.P. Nicholson, Printer, 1855, p. 255.
50. Letter from Indian Agent Ambrose, Rogue River Valley, to Genl. Joel Palmer, Sup't. *NARA Series M2, Microcopy of Records of the Oregon Superintendency of Indian Affairs 1848–1873, Reel 13; Letters Received, 1855, No. 93. A transcription can be found in NARA Series M2, Microcopy of Records of the Oregon Superintendency of Indian Affairs 1848–1872.*
51. U.S. Senate, Charles S. Drew, Communication from C.S. Drew: Late Adjutant of the Second Regiment of Oregon Mounted Volunteers, Giving an Account of the Origin and Early Prosecution of the Indian Wars in Oregon. 36th Cong. 1st Sess. (May 9, 1860).
52. *NARA M2, Microcopy of Records of the Oregon Superintendency of Indian Affairs 1848–1873, Reel 14; Letters Received, 1856, enclosure to No. 89.*

53. Indian hostilities in Oregon and Washington Message from the President of the United States, communicating information relative to Indian hostilities in the Territories of Oregon and Washington. H.R. Rep. No. 93, 34th Cong., 1st Sess. (1856), p. 4.
54. Ibid., pp. 6-7.
55. *A transcription can be found in NARA Series M2, Microcopy of Records of the Oregon Superintendency of Indian Affairs 1848–1872, Reel 5; Letter Book D, pages 391-392.*
56. *NARA Series M2, Microcopy of Records of the Oregon Superintendency of Indian Affairs 1848–1873, Reel 14; Letters Received, 1856, enclosure to No. 5.*
57. *NARA Series M2, Microcopy of Records of the Oregon Superintendency of Indian Affairs 1848–1873, Reel 14.*
58. *NARA Series M2, Microcopy of Records of the Oregon Superintendency of Indian Affairs 1848–1873, Reel 14; Letters Received, 1856, No. 165.*
59. Id.
60. Indian hostilities in Oregon and Washington. Message from the President of the United States, communicating information relative to Indian hostilities in the Territories of Oregon and Washington. H.R. Rep. No. 93, 34th Cong., 1st Sess. (1856), p. 38.
61. *NARA Series M234, Letters Received by the Office of Indian Affairs, Reel 609 Oregon Superintendency 1856, frames 647-662.*
62. *NARA Series M2, Microcopy of Records of the Oregon Superintendency of Indian Affairs 1848–1873, Reel 15; Letters Received, 1857, No. 35.*
63. *NARA Series M234, Letters Received by the Office of Indian Affairs, Reel 610 Oregon Superintendency 1857, frames 267-288.*
64. *NARA Series M234, Letters Received by the Office of Indian Affairs, Reel 608 Oregon Superintendency 1853–1855, frame 1197. A copy is also on NARA Series M234 Letters Received by the Office of Indian Affairs 1824–1881, Reel 611 Oregon Superintendency, 1858–1859, frame 559. Interpreter John Flett's copy is at the Beinecke Library, WA MSS 370.*
65. Report of the Commissioner of Indian Affairs to the Secretary of the Interior, Office of Indian Affairs, United States. 1872, pp. 5-6.
66. United States Congressional Serial Set, Volume 858, United States. Congress, U.S. Government Printing Office, 1856, House Ex. Doc. No. 93, p. 134.
67. http://www.let.rug.nl/usa/presidents/franklin-pierce/state-of-the-union-1856.php (accessed online April 27, 2022).
68. *NARA Series M2, Microcopy of Records of the Oregon Superintendency of Indian Affairs 1848–1873, Reel 14; Letters Received, 1856, No. 10.*
69. *NARA Series M2, Microcopy of Records of the Oregon Superintendency of Indian Affairs 1848–1873, Reel 6; Letter Books E:10, pages 43-44.*
70. *NARA Series M2, Microcopy of Records of the Oregon Superintendency of Indian Affairs 1848–1873, Reel 14; Letters Received, 1856, No. 111.*

71. *NARA Series M2, Microcopy of Records of the Oregon Superintendency of Indian Affairs 1848–1873, Reel 15; Letters Received, 1857, No. 9.*
72. Senate Documents, Otherwise Publ. as Public Documents and Executive Documents: 14th Congress, 1st Session-48th Congress, 2nd Session and Special Session, Volume 10, 1856, p. 50. But see Communication from C. S. Drew, late Adjutant of the Second Regiment of Oregon Mounted Volunteers, giving an account of the origin and early prosecution of the Indian War in Oregon. S. Misc. Doc. No. 59, 36th Cong., 1st Sess. (1860). Letter to California Governor J. N. Johnson, from Major Gen. John E. Wool, Jan. 21, 1856.
73. Indian hostilities in Oregon and Washington. Message from the President of the United States, communicating information relative to Indian hostilities in the Territories of Oregon and Washington. H.R. Rep. No. 93, 34th Cong., 1st Sess. (1856), pp. 35-36; Ex. Doc. 76, 34th Congress, 3rd session, 1857, pp. 103-104.
74. *NARA Series M2, Microcopy of Records of the Oregon Superintendency of Indian Affairs 1848–1873, Reel 14; Letters Received, 1856, No. 95.*
75. *NARA Series M234, Letters Received by the Office of Indian Affairs, Reel 609 Oregon Superintendency 1856, frames 647-662.* To James Clugage Esq. Grand Ronde *NARA Series M2, Microcopy of Records of the Oregon Superintendency of Indian Affairs 1848–1873, Reel 6; Letter Books E:10, pages 184-185.*
76. Report of the Commissioner of Indian Affairs to the Secretary of the Interior, Office of Indian Affairs, United States. A.O.P. Nicholson, Printer, 1857, p. 18.
77. O'Callaghan, Jerry A. The Disposition of the Public Domain in Oregon. U.S. Government Printing Office, 1960, p. 2.
78. https://www.washington.edu/uwired/outreach/cspn/Website/Classroom%20Materials/Pacific%20Northwest%20History/Lessons/Lesson%209/Census%20Data.html (accessed online February 25, 2022).
79. The Abridgment ... Containing the Annual Message of the President of the United States to the Two Houses of Congress ... with Reports of Departments and Selections from Accompanying Papers, Vol. 1, George W. Bowman, Printer, 1860, p. 159.
80. Madsen, Brigham D. The Northern Shoshoni. Caxton Press, 1980, p. 51.
81. *NARA Series M2, Microcopy of Records of the Oregon Superintendency of Indian Affairs 1848–1873, Reel 23; Letters Received, 1866–1867, no number.*
82. *Daily Alta California,* San Francisco, June 24, 1857.
83. Report of the Commissioner of Indian Affairs to the Secretary of the Interior, Office of Indian Affairs, United States. William A. Harris, Printer, 1858, p. 7.
84. Ibid., p. 9.

85. THE OFFICIAL HISTORY OF THE WASHINGTON NATIONAL GUARD VOLUME 3 WASHINGTON TERRITORIAL MILITIA IN THE CIVIL WAR HEADQUARTERS MILITARY DEPARTMENT STATE OF WASHINGTON OFFICE OF THE ADJUTANT GENERAL CAMP MURRAY, TACOMA 33, WASHINGTON, p. 37. https://mil.wa.gov/asset/5ba41fe280330 (accessed online May 8, 2022).
86. "To Thomas Jefferson from Meriwether Lewis, 15 December 1808," *Founders Online*, National Archives, https://founders.archives.gov/documents/Jefferson/99-01-02-9323 (accessed online November 5, 2020).
87. *NARA Series M2, Microcopy of Records of the Oregon Superintendency of Indian Affairs 1848–1872, Reel 5; Letter Book D, pages 132-133.*
88. Annual Report of the Secretary of the Interior, Report of the Commissioner of Indian Affairs, Part 1, Reports Concerning Indians in New Mexico, Office of Indian Affairs, United States. U.S. Government Printing Office, 1905, p. 251.
89. U.S. Department of the Interior. Bureau of Indian Affairs. Certified Copy of the Original Minutes of the Official Proceedings at the Council in Walla Walla Valley, Which Culminated in the Stevens Treaty of 1855. Portland, Oregon: Bureau of Indian Affairs, 1953.
90. *NARA Series M234 Letters Received by the Office of Indian Affairs 1824–1881, Reel 613 Oregon Superintendency, 1862–1863, frames 213-218.*
91. United States. Congress. Joint Special Committee to Inquire into the Condition of the Indian Tribes. U.S. Government Printing Office, 1867, p. A014.
92. First Annual Report to the Congress of the United States from the National Advisory Council on Indian Education, U.S. Government Printing Office, 1974, p. 142.
93. *NARA Series M2, Microcopy of Records of the Oregon Superintendency of Indian Affairs 1848–1873, Reel 30; Miscellaneous Loose Papers 1850–1873.*
94. *San Francisco Bulletin*, June 3, 1859, p. 3.
95. Letter from Edward R. Geary, Sup't of Indian Affairs, Portland, Oregon (Oct. 31, 1859) to Commissioner of Indian Affairs, Department of the Interior (on file with the U.S. National Archives).
96. *NARA Series M2, Microcopy of Records of the Oregon Superintendency of Indian Affairs 1848–1873, Reel 10; Letter Books I:10, pages 51-63.*
97. Report of the Commissioner of Indian Affairs to the Secretary of the Interior, Office of Indian Affairs, U.S. Government Printing Office, 1868, p. 83.
98. Commissioners D. H. Jerome, O. O. Howard, Wm. Stickney, A. C. Barstow. "Report of the Commissioner of Indian Affairs," pp. 397-728. In U.S. House. 45th Congress, 2d Session. Report of the Secretary of the Interior, 1877 (H. Ex. Doc. 1, Pt. 5, Vol. 1). Washington: Government Printing Office, 1878. (Serial Set 1800); Report of the Commissioner of Indian Affairs to the Secretary of the Interior, Vol. 1, United States, Office of Indian Affairs, U.S. Government Printing Office, 1877, p. 611.

99. U.S. Department of the Interior. Bureau of Indian Affairs. Certified Copy of the Original Minutes of the Official Proceedings at the Council in Walla Walla Valley, Which Culminated in the Stevens Treaty of 1855. Portland, Oregon: Bureau of Indian Affairs, 1953.
100. Ibid., p. 32.
101. Id.
102. Gilmore Hays, *Joseph Lane Papers, OHS Mss 1146, Oregon Historical Society Research Library. Undated.*
103. Report of the Commissioner of Indian Affairs to the Secretary of the Interior, Office of Indian Affairs, United States. William A. Harris, Printer, 1858, pp. 321-323. Claims of California Indians: Hearings, Seventieth Congress, First Session, United States. Congress. House Committee on Indian Affairs. U.S. Government Printing Office, 1928.
104. O'Callaghan, Jerry A. The Disposition of the Public Domain in Oregon. U.S. Government Printing Office, 1960, p. 21.
105. Ruby, Robert H., Brown, John Arthur. The Cayuse Indians: Imperial Tribesmen of Old Oregon, Volume 120 of Civilization of the American, p. XVIIII.
106. *Oregon Weekly Times,* Portland, October 9, 1852, p. 2.
107. Report of the Commissioner of Indian Affairs to the Secretary of the Interior, United States. Government Printing Office, 1850, p. 125.
108. Thomas Donaldson, "The Public Domain, Its History with Statistics" (Washington, 1881), p. 247.
109. Madsen, Brigham D. The Northern Shoshoni. Caxton Press, 1980, pp. 83-88.
110. Annual Report of the Department of the Interior, Office of Indian Affairs, Part 1, Report of the Commissioner of Indian Affairs to the Secretary of the Interior, Reports Concerning Indians in Oregon, U.S. Government Printing Office, 1902, p. 344.
111. *NARA Series M2, Microcopy of Records of the Oregon Superintendency of Indian Affairs 1848–1873, Reel 15; Letters Received, 1857, second enclosure to No. 197.*
112. *NARA Series M2, Microcopy of Records of the Oregon Superintendency of Indian Affairs 1848–1873, Reel 20; Letters Received, 1862, No. 22.*
113. *NARA Series M2, Microcopy of Records of the Oregon Superintendency of Indian Affairs 1848–1873, Reel 20, Letters Received. 1862. No. 17.*
114. *NARA Series M2, Microcopy of Records of the Oregon Superintendency of Indian Affairs 1848–1873, Reel 20; Letters Received, 1862, No. 21.*
115. *NARA Series M2, Microcopy of Records of the Oregon Superintendency of Indian Affairs 1848–1873, Reel 9; Letter Books H:10, pages 100-101.*

116. *NARA Series M2, Microcopy of Records of the Oregon Superintendency of Indian Affairs 1848–1873, Reel 9; Letter Books H:10, pages 142-144. Original on NARA Series M234 Letters Received by the Office of Indian Affairs 1824–1881, Reel 613 Oregon Superintendency, 1862–1863, frames 378-382.*
117. *NARA Series M2, Microcopy of Records of the Oregon Superintendency of Indian Affairs 1848–1873, Reel 9; Letter Books H:10, pages 197-212.*
118. *NARA Series M2, Microcopy of Records of the Oregon Superintendency of Indian Affairs 1848–1873, Reel 20; Letters Received, 1862, No. 52.*
119. *NARA Series M2, Microcopy of Records of the Oregon Superintendency of Indian Affairs 1848–1873, Reel 27; Unregistered Letters Received, 1870-73.*
120. Report of the Commissioner of Indian Affairs to the Secretary of the Interior, United States. Government Printing Office, 1875, pp. 344-345.
121. Conditions of the Alsea Indians and the Salmon River Encampment 1876–1878, https://ndnhistoryresearch.com/2018/04/07/conditions-of-the-alsea-indians-and-the-salmon-river-encampment-1876-1878/ (accessed online July 11, 2022).
122. Letter dated Nov. 11, 1875, to Hon. Ben Simpson, Special Indian Agent from J. H. Fairchild, U.S. Indian Agt. at Siletz. *NARA Series M234 Letters Received by the Office of Indian Affairs 1824–1881, Reel 621 Oregon Superintendency, 1875.*
123. Id.
124. *NARA Series M234 Letters Received by the Office of Indian Affairs 1824–1881, Reel 621 Oregon Superintendency, 1875.*
125. Proceedings of a council held on the Alsea Indian Reservation, Oregon with the Alseas, Coos, Umpquas and Siuslaw tribes of Indians in regard to their removal to Siletz, Alsea Agency, June 17, 1875. *NARA Series M234 Letters Received by the Office of Indian Affairs 1824–1881, Reel 621 Oregon Superintendency, 1875.*
126. Id.
127. THE OFFICIAL HISTORY OF THE WASHINGTON NATIONAL GUARD VOLUME 3 WASHINGTON TERRITORIAL MILITIA IN THE CIVIL WAR HEADQUARTERS MILITARY DEPARTMENT STATE OF WASHINGTON OFFICE OF THE ADJUTANT GENERAL CAMP MURRAY, TACOMA 33, WASHINGTON, p. 34. https://mil.wa.gov/asset/5ba41fe280330 (accessed online May 8, 2022).
128. J. W. Perit Huntington, Sup't. Report of the Acting Commissioner of Indian Affairs to the Secretary of the Interior, U.S. Government Printing Office, 1868, p. 70.
129. *NARA Series M2, Microcopy of Records of the Oregon Superintendency of Indian Affairs 1848–1873, Reel 25; Letters Received, 1868–1870, No. 111.*
130. Report of the Acting Commissioner of Indian Affairs to the Secretary of the Interior, U.S. Government Printing Office, 1868, p. 104.

131. Ibid., p. 470.
132. Ibid., p. 16.
133. https://governors.library.ca.gov/addresses/s_01-Burnett2. html#:~:text=That%20a%20war%20of%20extermination,wisdom%20 of%20man%20to%20avert (accessed online May 1, 2022).
134. *NARA Series M2, Microcopy of Records of the Oregon Superintendency of Indian Affairs 18*
135. *NARA Series M2, Microcopy of Records of the Oregon Superintendency of Indian Affairs 1848-1873, Reel 10; Letter Books I:10, page 657. Original on NARA Series M234 Letters Received by the Office of Indian Affairs 1824-81, Reel 617 Oregon Superintendency, 1872, frames 435-437. A copy is on NARA Series M234 Letters Received by the Office of Indian Affairs 1824-81, Reel 617 Oregon Superintendency, 1872, frames 709-710.*
136. *48-1873, Reel 10; Letter Books I:10, page 657. Original on NARA Series M234 Letters Received by the Office of Indian Affairs 1824–1881, Reel 617 Oregon Superintendency, 1872, frames 435-437. A copy is on NARA Series M234 Letters Received by the Office of Indian Affairs 1824–1881, Reel 617 Oregon Superintendency, 1872, frames 709-710.*
137. Id.
138. *NARA Series M234 Letters Received by the Office of Indian Affairs 1824–1881, Reel 617 Oregon Superintendency, 1872, frames 544-549.*
139. Letter from the Acting Secretary of the Interior, accompanying information called for by the Senate resolution of January 8, 1873, relative to the Modoc and other Indian tribes in Northern California. S. Exec. Doc. No. 29, 42nd Cong., 3rd Sess. (1873), p. 5.
140. House Documents, Otherwise Publ. as Executive Documents: 13th Congress, 2d Session-49th Congress, 1st Session, Volume 9, United States Congress. House. 1874, pp. 214-215.
141. Ibid., p. 263.
142. Report of the Commissioner of Indian Affairs to the Secretary of the Interior, Office of Indian Affairs, U.S. Government Printing Office, 1874, p. 77.
143. *NARA Series M234 Letters Received by the Office of Indian Affairs 1824–1881. Reel 618, Oregon Superintendency, 1873, frames 297-302.*
144. Thompson, Erwin N. Modoc War; Its Military History & Topography. Argus Books, 1971, p. 69.
145. Ibid., p. 110.
146. Ibid., p. 115.
147. Ft. Klamath, Post Medical History, p. 142, Record for October, 1873.
148. California's 'Forgotten War' Virtually Destroyed a 10,000-Year-Old Culture, Cecilia Rasmussen, Dec. 22, 2002. https://www.latimes.com/archives/la-xpm-2002-dec-22-me-then22-story.html (accessed online May 6, 2022).

149. Modoc Homeland https://www.nps.gov/labe/learn/historyculture/modochomeland.htm (accessed online July 11, 2022).
150. Report of the Commissioner of Indian Affairs to the Secretary of the Interior, Office of Indian Affairs, U.S. Government Printing Office, 1874, pp. 81-82.
151. House Documents, Otherwise Publ. as Executive Documents: 13th Congress, 2d Session-49th Congress, 1st Session, Volume 9, United States Congress. House. 1874, p. 33.
152. https://www.officialdata.org/us/inflation/1782?amount=400000 (accessed online May 7, 2022).
153. *NARA Series M2, Microcopy of Records of the Oregon Superintendency of Indian Affairs, Reel 11, Instructions and Reports 1854–1855, pages 179-181. A copy can be found on NARA Series M234, Letters Received by the Office of Indian Affairs, Reel 608 Oregon Superintendency 1853–1855, frames 713-715.*
154. Letter from Charles E. Mix, Acting Commissioner of Indian Affairs, Department of the Interior, to Edward R. Geary, Sup't of Indian Affairs, Portland, Oregon (July 2, 1860) (on file with the U.S. National Archives. https://archives.yvl.org/bitstream/handle/20.500.11867/6818/TRA-042-03-003.pdf?sequence=1&isAllowed=y (accessed online July 12, 2022).
155. Id.
156. Letter from Edward R. Geary, Superintendent of Indian Affairs, to W.P. Dole, Comm'r of Indian Affairs (Apr. 23, 1861).
157. Letter from Charles Hutchins, Indian Agent, Washington Territory, to W.P. Dole, Commissioner of Indian Affairs, Washington D.C. (Mar. 20, 1862) (on file with the U.S. National Archives).
158. Report of the Commissioner of Indian Affairs to the Secretary of the Interior, United States. Office of Indian Affairs. U.S. Government Printing Office, 1863, p. 422.
159. Letter from Benjamin Alvord, Brigadier-General, U.S. Volunteers, to W.P. Dole, Commissioner of Indian Affairs, Washington D.C. (Sept. 8, 1863) (on file with the U.S. National Archives).
160. Report of the Commissioner of Indian Affairs to the Secretary of the Interior, United States. Office of Indian Affairs. U.S. Government Printing Office, 1863, p. 423.
161. TALK OF BRIGADIER GENERAL ALVORD TO THE CHIEFS OF THE NEZ PERCE INDIANS ASSEMBLED AT THE LAPWAI AGENCY, WASH. TERR., ON THE 24TH OF OCTOBER, 1862.
162. Williams, Mathyn D. Indian Wars: Failings of the United States Army to Achieve Decisive Victory During the Nez Perce War of 1877. ARMY COMMAND AND GENERAL STAFF COLL FORT LEAVENWORTH KS, 2005, p. 94.

163. Josephy, Alvin M. The Nez Perce Indians and the opening of the Northwest. Houghton Mifflin Harcourt 1997, p. 498.

164. Ibid., p. 514.

165. Williams, Mathyn D. Indian Wars: Failings of the United States Army to Achieve Decisive Victory During the Nez Perce War of 1877. ARMY COMMAND AND GENERAL STAFF COLL FORT LEAVENWORTH KS, 2005, p. 66.

166. Ibid., p. 83.

167. Ibid., pp. 83-84.

168. Ibid., p. 96.

169. Ibid., p. 90.

170. Ibid., p. 39.

171. Ibid., p. 8.

172. Ibid., p. 19.

173. Ibid., p. 120.

174. https://www.officialdata.org/us/inflation/1782?amount=400000 (accessed online May 7, 2022).

175. https://www.history.com/this-day-in-history/chief-joseph-surrenders (accessed online May 1, 2022).

176. Williams, Mathyn D. Indian Wars: Failings of the United States Army to Achieve Decisive Victory During the Nez Perce War of 1877. ARMY COMMAND AND GENERAL STAFF COLL FORT LEAVENWORTH KS, 2005, p. 65.

177. Chester Anders Fee, Chief Joseph: The Biography of a Great Indian, Wilson-Erickson, 1936.

178. Williams, Mathyn D. Indian Wars: Failings of the United States Army to Achieve Decisive Victory During the Nez Perce War of 1877. ARMY COMMAND AND GENERAL STAFF COLL FORT LEAVENWORTH KS, 2005.

179. Chief Joseph Speaks Selected Statements and Speeches by the Nez Percé Chief https://www.pbs.org/kenburns/the-west/chief-joseph-speaks (accessed online July 11, 2022).

180. George Crook, in J.F. Santee, "Egan of the Piutes," Washington Historical Quarterly 26, 1 (January, 1935), 18-19. Report of the Secretary of War, Executive Documents, Vol. II, 90.

181. https://history.army.mil/books/r&h/r&h-9in.htm (accessed online May 22, 2022).
182. https://www.officialdata.org/us/inflation/1782?amount=400000 (accessed online May 7, 2022).
183. https://www.jhnewsandguide.com/opinion/columnists/common_ground/why-a-general-wrote-in-1895-i-do-not-consider-the-indians-to-blame-for/article_6e8a9b91-9471-548f-87d8-7f8412d124f3.html (accessed online May 6, 2022).
184. John Clayton. When White People Stopped Indigenous Elk Hunts In Jackson Hole FRONTIER RACISM AND INJUSTICE PROMPTED LEGAL ACTION THAT STILL RIPPLES ACROSS AMERICA, INVOLVING NATIVE HUNTING AND FISHING RIGHTS. RED LODGE WRITER JOHN CLAYTON TAKES A DEEP DIVE. https://mountainjournal.org/jackson-hole-was-flashpoint-for-battle-over-indigenous-hunting-rights (accessed online July 11, 2022).
185. Who gets to hunt Wyoming's elk? Tribal Hunting Rights, U.S. Law and the Bannock 'War' of 1895. https://wyohistory42.rssing.com/chan-61458836/latest.php (accessed online May 8, 2022).
186. Report of the Commissioner of Indian Affairs to the Secretary of the Interior. Office of Indian Affairs. United States. U.S. Government Printing Office, 1895, p. 65.
187. http://www.let.rug.nl/usa/presidents/rutherford-birchard-hayes/state-of-the-union-1878.php (accessed online April 28, 2022).
188. Id.
189. Waltmann, Henry George, "The Interior Department, War Department and Indian Policy, 1865–1887" (1962). Dissertations, Theses, & Student Research, Department of History. 74. p. 178. http://digitalcommons.unl.edu/historydiss/74 (accessed online July 11, 2022).
190. The works of James Abram Garfield. Volume 1, James A. Garfield, Best Books, 1882, p. 367.
191. Carl Schurz, Speeches. Correspondence and Political Papers. (New York, 1913 (8I-B2I).
192. Indian Policy Reform Extract from President Chester Arthur's First Annual Message to Congress, https://www.presidency.ucsb.edu/documents/first-annual-message-13 (accessed online February 21, 2022).
193. (18 U.S.C.S. §1153).
194. (25 U.S.C.S. §§331 et seq.).
195. (c. 412, 25 Stat. 980).
196. Report of the Commissioner of Indian Affairs to the Secretary of the Interior, Office of Indian Affairs, United States. U.S. Government Printing Office, 1910, p. 28.

197. Annual Report of the Department of the Interior, Office of Indian Affairs, Part 1, Report of the Commissioner of Indian Affairs to the Secretary of the Interior, Reports Concerning Indians in Oregon, U.S. Government Printing Office, 1902, p. 357.
198. www.nahmus.org (accessed online February 22, 2022).
199. http://www.let.rug.nl/usa/presidents/benjamin-harrison/state-of-the-union-1889.php (accessed online July 11, 2022).
200. Report of the Commissioner of Indian Affairs to the Secretary of the Interior, Office of Indian Affairs, United States. A.O.P. Nicholson, Printer, 1855, pp. 268-271.
201. Ibid., p. 258.
202. Ibid., p. 259.
203. *NARA Series M2, Microcopy of Records of the Oregon Superintendency of Indian Affairs 1848–1872, Reel 5; Letter Book D, pages 247-248. The original is on NARA Series M234, Letters Received by the Office of Indian Affairs, Reel 608 Oregon Superintendency 1853–1855, frames 1106-1109.*
204. Id.
205. *NARA Series M2, Microcopy of Records of the Oregon Superintendency of Indian Affairs 1848–1872, Reel 5; Letter Book D, pages 289-292.*
206. Message of the President of the United States, in compliance with a resolution of the Senate, of the 11th instant, calling for copies of correspondence relative to the Indian disturbances in California. S. Exec. Doc. No. 26, 34th Cong., 1st Sess. (1856), p. 49.
207. The Story of Walla Walla Chief Peo peo mox mox. https://www.youtube.com/watch?v=OuoQHqlt-NU] (accessed online May 6, 2022).
208. Indian hostilities in Oregon and Washington. Message from the President of the United States, communicating information relative to Indian hostilities in the Territories of Oregon and Washington. H.R. Rep. No. 93, 34th Cong., 1st Sess. (1856), p. 45.
209. *NARA Series M2, Microcopy of Records of the Oregon Superintendency of Indian Affairs 1848–1873, Reel 24; Letters Received, 1867–1868, No. 28.*
210. Microcopy of Records of the Oregon Superintendency of Indian Affairs 1848–1873, Reel 9; Letter Books H:10, pages 441-443.
211. *NARA Series M2, Microcopy of Records of the Oregon Superintendency of Indian Affairs 1848–1873, Reel 9; Letter Books H:10, pages 455-456.*
212. *NARA Series M2, Microcopy of Records of the Oregon Superintendency of Indian Affairs 1848–1873, Reel 21; Letters Received, 1863–1865, no number.*
213. https://truwe.sohs.org/files/tyeegeorge.html (accessed online July 6, 2022).
214. https://truwe.sohs.org/files/tyeegeorge.html (accessed online July 6, 2022).
215. *NARA Series M234 Letters Received by the Office of Indian Affairs 1824–1881, Reel 614 Oregon Superintendency, 1864–1865, frames 589-592.*
216. *NARA Series M234, Letters Received by the Office of Indian Affairs, Reel 610 Oregon Superintendency 1857, frames 34-150.*

217. *NARA Series M2, Microcopy of Records of the Oregon Superintendency of Indian Affairs 1848–1873, Reel 7; Letter Books F:10, pages 114-115.*
218. *NARA Series M234, Letters Received by the Office of Indian Affairs, Reel 609 Oregon Superintendency 1856, frames 486-490.*
219. *NARA Series M2, Microcopy of Records of the Oregon Superintendency of Indian Affairs 1848–1873, Reel 20; Letters Received, 1862, No. 65. An original can be found on NARA Series M234 Letters Received by the Office of Indian Affairs 1824-81.*
220. *NARA Series M2, Microcopy of Records of the Oregon Superintendency of Indian Affairs 1848–1873, Reel 21; Letters Received 1863–1865, no number.*
221. The Democratic News, February 19, 1870, page 3.
222. *NARA Series M2, Microcopy of Records of the Oregon Superintendency of Indian Affairs 1848–1873, Reel 26; Letters Received, 1870, no number.*
223. *NARA Series M2, Microcopy of Records of the Oregon Superintendency of Indian Affairs 1848–1873, Reel 7; Letter Books F:10, page 332.*
224. Report of the Commissioner of Indian Affairs to the Secretary of the Interior, Office of Indian Affairs, United States. 1872, p. 9.
225. Conant, Luther, and Joseph Edward Davies. *The Lumber Industry: Standing timber*. U.S. Government Printing Office, 1913, p. XVIII.
226. See seminal article on Andrew Hammond: Gordon, Greg. When Money Grew on Trees: AB Hammond and the Age of the Timber Baron. University of Oklahoma Press, 2014.
227. Report of the Commissioner of Indian Affairs to the Secretary of the Interior, Office of Indian Affairs, United States. 1898, p. 262.

CHAPTER 11: WASHINGTON: GOVERNOR STEVENS' PRIVATE WARS OF EXTERMINATION

Part 1: Washington Territory's Governor's Private Wars

What is so tragic about the history of Washington Indians is the skirmish after skirmish, battle after battle, war after war engaged in between the mobster Volunteers, the U.S. Army and Indian Nation after Indian Nation, when Governor Stevens could have engaged in legitimate diplomacy and avoided war. U.S. Army Major General Wool was convinced that Governor Stevens of Washington and Governor Curry of Oregon were engaged in a private war, bent upon exterminating the Indians. The wars were considered a "God-send;" a subterfuge to dispossess Indians of their land and resources.

Major Mathyn D. Williams in his book, *Indian Wars: Failings of the United States Army to Achieve Decisive Victory During the Nez Perce War of 1877*, provides insight into the failures of the U.S. to avoid unnecessary wars with the Indians. His analysis of the Nez Perce War is equally applicable to the Indian wars in Washington. These wars decimated the populations of the Indian Nations. The avaricious, predatory colonial settlers, bent on the outright theft of prime Indian land, triumphed over a pre-occupied, distant, financially strapped federal government which categorically failed to protect its 'alleged' wards. A moral vacuum was created in which Indian leaders and individuals could be murdered at the will of armed, blood thirsty citizens.

Part 2: Prized Indian Forests

Early explorers who met many indigenous peoples living along the Pacific Coast and the Puget Sound were amazed at the forests. The coastal temperate climate of the Pacific Northwest supports the dense growth of the conifers which serve as towering, massive, spire-shaped trees, natural canopies over forest floors rich in moss and lichen and invertebrate, amphibious and bird life. The heavy cloud cover and fog, common year-round, provide the precipitation for Douglas-fir, red cedar and western hemlock. Sitka spruce thrive in the sea spray. From time immemorial, native peoples fished for the sacred salmon and hunted the marine mammals in their hand-carved canoes.

Lewis and Clark Reported "Great Quantities of Excellent Timber"

Arriving at the mouth of the Columbia River in 1805, Meriwether Lewis and William Clark, after completing their two-year trans-American trek (1804–1806), wrote in their journal:

> "The whole neighborhood of the coast is supplied with **great quantities of excellent timber**. [The species of fir] grows to an immense size, and is very commonly twenty-seven feet in circumference, six feet above the earth's surface: they rise to the height of two hundred and twenty of that height without limb. We have often found them thirty-six feet in circumference." (Emphasis added).[1]

Hudson's Bay Company Proclaim Fortuitous Large Timber Profits

From the earliest British colonial settlements, the certitude of the value of the timber on the Northwest coast was unquestionable. Logging and milling were broadcast as being certain of yielding "large profits." The forests were commodified resources to colonial settlers from the start.

In 1827, Hudson's Bay Company founded the first mill in the Pacific Northwest at Fort Vancouver. Six years later, they began lumbering at their second post, Fort Nisqually, 100 miles north of Fort Vancouver.

> Governor George Simpson to Captain Aemelius Simpson of the Cadboro
>
> [No date on the letter; probably written in October 1828]
>
> Now that our Saw Mill is in operation we can supply timber of various kinds in such quantity as to meet all demands either in the Sandwhich Islands [now called the Hawaiian Islands], or at the Spanish Missions, and if the prices as so high as they have been represented to us, *the Timber Trade as a distinct branch of business would yield us large profits* in proportion to the Tonnage employed therein—at the lowest quotations given us say 60 Dollars per M [M is the roman numeral for 1,000] feet we can furnish 200,000 feet annually by the shipping employed in our Coasting Fur Trade, & *realize handsome profits* & even at 40 Dollars per M it will be an object worthy of our attention, but if 200 Dollars the highest quotation can be had, we shall undertake to supply any quantity required for a term of Years. (Emphasis added).[2]

The commodification of the timber is evident in this 1829 letter from Governor George Simpson to John McLoughlin, Chief Factor of Fort Vancouver. Coupled with the logging was the need for seafaring vessels to accommodate trade. Logging and milling would complement the lucrative fur trade.

> The timber trade promises to become a valuable branch of the business combined with the Fur Trade of the Coast as the latter cannot afford employment all the Year round. . . . [Simpson directed McLoughlin to build two vessels of 200 tons each for the timber trade.] The Saw Mill will require Eight Men and should be kept constantly at Work, as I expect that fully as much advantage will be derived from the Timber as from the Coasting Fur Trade. (Emphasis added).[3]

British Captain Vancouver Described Entry to Puget Sound as "Continuous Forest"

Aboard the *Discovery*, British Captain George Vancouver traveled along the southern shore of the Strait of Juan de Fuca in 1792 and described the landscape as "luxurious." "The whole had the appearance of a continued forest extending as far north as the eye could reach," he wrote, "which made me very solicitous to find a port in the vicinity of a country presenting so delightful a prospect of fertility." Vancouver described other parts of the Puget Sound region as "impenetrable wilderness of lofty trees, rendered nearly impassable by the underwood, which uniformly incumbers the surface."[4]

U.S. Naval Officer Wilkes Astonished at Magnificent Forests

In 1838, Congress authorized an expedition to explore the shores of the Pacific Ocean from Antarctica to Alaska. U.S. naval officer Charles Wilkes was chosen to lead the mission, which lasted nearly four years. The expedition traveled through the Pacific Northwest in 1841. His journal entries document his impressions of the region's vast forests, along with the profitability of the HBC operations. While he lost a ship at the mouth of the Columbia River, it only served to highlight the safety and quality of the harbors in Puget Sound. The commercial possibilities and advantageous location solidified the U.S. resolve to acquire the Puget Sound area.

> May 3rd [1841]. This day I made the survey of this Harbour [Port Discovery] employing 12 boats & officers, the wind blew fresh which prevented all the soundings from being carried through. The weather has been variable and the wind changeable. This harbour is surrounded by Hills **wooded to the waters edge**. . . .

6 May. Mount Baker shows over Hudson Point. A large fleet might anchor and maneuver here, there is a Bluff that joins the beach abreast the ships, the top of which slopes to the water and is a beautiful lawn here and *there with groups of trees and to the N[orth] and W[est] a fine copse of pine trees upwards of 1000 acres all ready for the plough*. The soil is a light sandy loam but seems exceedingly productive....

19th [May]. The Nisqually overflows its banks in the spring and autumn together with all the Rivers which take their rise in the Cascade Mountains— Our route lay through most beautiful park scenery with the prairies here and there breaking through the magnificent pines.... *About 7 miles of our route lay through the gigantic fine cedar forest and although they are called sapplings, [the cedars] were 6-1/2 feet in diameter and upwards of 200 feet in height. I could not control my astonishment*....

21st [May]. Our route lay through alternate prairies & *the magnificent forest of tall pines and cedar* passing by fords several fine streams of water. [Wilkes and his party traveled from Cowlitz Farm to Fort Vancouver, the regional headquarters of the Hudson's Bay Company.]
June 1st, 1841. These prairies are indeed beautiful *covered with fine pines of gigantic heights, some whose branches are nearly touching the green sward, with oaks, maples, fir, & cedar*, with intervening spaces of prairie. (Emphasis added).[5]

Part 3: Promoting Washington's Lumber Industry

During this early period, three Peninsula logging companies emerged as leading firms: Pope & Talbot based in Port Gamble, Polson Brothers Logging Company in the Gray's Harbor area, and Simpson Logging Company located in Shelton.

> Timber milling rapidly became a part of the Puget Sound economy. Some tribal members were enlisted as labor for various frontier mills that served the agricultural communities of the region:

"With the advent of the white man, about 1850, [traditional subsistence practices were] violently upset by new ideas and new conditions. First in importance was an unsuspected value given to timber. The establishing of mills throughout the country, the development and exploitation of the Indian as a labor supply, and of his property as a reservoir of material, laid the foundation for several fortunes of present West Coast residents, and for the utter discomfiture of the Indians.

Politicians and businessmen seeking to increase the population growth in Washington, necessary for statehood, appealed to prospective emigrants by touting the region's expanding lumber industry and the increasing markets for timber. Asa Mercer, a Seattle settler, who served in the upper house of the territorial legislature, published a Washington Territory promotional guide in 1865. "Here is now a great trade in lumber," he remarked, "and every year will see it increase."[6]

His position as President of the Territorial University added credibility to his press.

> Puget Sound is emphatically a lumber district. We manufacture annually a hundred and thirty million feet of lumber, twenty-two and a half million laths [strips of wood], twenty and a half million shingles, a hundred thousand feet of piles, and about two thousand spars, also a large number of ship knees. The supply of logs for lumber will only be exhausted when the mountains and the valley surrounding the Sound are destroyed by some great calamity of nature. For when this generation shall have perished, the forests by them laid low will have begun anew to assume proportions that do honor to the former growth. Thus nearly as rapidly as is the axe laid at the root of the tree will others grow into place, so quickly does the fir tree grow in Puget Sound climate. It is fair to presume that, as we now manufacture over a hundred million [board] feet per annum, with so small a population, when the coast generally, and our own Territory in particular, multiplies its people by a hundred, the production will increase in like proportion.[7]

Similarly, Ezra Meeker, another early settler in Washington Territory, described the region's infinite timber resources, noting, "We need have no fear that [the supply] will ever be exhausted."

> The value of any commodity lies in its demand as well as in its availability, yet it is often the case that the facility for obtaining it cheaply increases the consumption far beyond what it would be were the article scarce and costly. Such is the case with our lumber products. Although the imperative demand is great, yet we find increased sale in consequence of being able to furnish [timber] at so low a price. Already the lumber product of the [Puget] Sound region alone amounts to fully one hundred and eighty million feet per annum [year], which can be increased from year to year as the wants of the commerce demand.

Already the foreign trade is great, supplying all quarters of this coast, the islands of the Pacific, Japan and China, and even European countries. Ships now come to us principally in ballast [empty of cargo], but with the North Pacific Railroad completed, this will not continue long [because] they will bear the freight of commerce for the great interior [of the U.S.], as well as that [cargo] in transit to the Atlantic sea board and to Europe.

Although water power is abundant, yet steam is the power commonly used ... Hence, nine-tenths of the lumber is manufactured by steam power, and *many vacant harbors await the action of capitalists and the demands of trade upon which to found large manufacturing establishments and thriving villages;* and many such [lumber mills] are yearly being added to the number already here. (Emphasis added).[8]

University of Washington Professor Edmund Meany directed Washington's publicity at the Chicago World's Fair of 1893. The exhibit focused on commercial opportunities to attract settlers and investors to the state. Many of Meany's press releases emphasized the potential of Washington's growing lumber industry.[9]

As logging operations developed around the outer fringes of the Peninsula and more and more readily accessible timber was taken from tidewater rivers and coastal areas, logging companies began looking inland for a continuing supply of trees. In 1878, Eugene Ellicott observed, "The upper part of Puget Sound ... has all been logged over; you see everywhere the remnants of logging roads. The mill companies have taken all the good timber near the shore."[10]

The late 1880s and 1890s initiated years of interior exploration and survey work. Numerous written accounts of the State's vast interior timber reserves were reported in popular literature and government documents alike.

Part 4: Puget Sound Mills

In the mid 1840s, mill machinery was purchased from Hudson's Bay Company by a small group of U.S. settlers and in the winter of 1846–1847 the first power mill on Puget Sound was set up near the present site of Olympia, Washington.[11]

On the Strait of Juan de Fuca, the Port Discovery Bay mill, established inside Discovery Bay in the early 1860s, was a large consumer of logs for many years. Between 1860 and 1890, major logging operations were initiated at Port Angeles, Crescent Bay and Gettysburg on the north Peninsula shoreline. On the Pacific Coast the first commercial logging operations began in the early 1880s at Gray's Harbor. In 1885 in an official report by the Governor of Washington Territory, lumbering was listed as one of the principal industries of all of the Olympic Peninsula counties.[12]

> The Port Blakely Mill Company was a giant forest products firm dating from the 1860s. Captain William Renton and Daniel S. Howard established their mill on Puget Sound in 1864, and its initial capacity of 50,000 board feet a day had expanded to 200,000 by 1881. Renton and Howard acquired their own ships to distribute the growing output of the enterprise.

> Another giant lumbering operation, ... was the Tacoma Mill Company established by Charles Hanson on Commencement Bay on Puget Sound. The 40,000-board-feet-capacity mill began operation in 1869; by 1883 capacity was 225,000 board feet. Like his giant competitors, Hanson shipped lumber to markets along the Pacific Coast when profitable and exploited foreign markets (Central America and Australia) to guarantee sale of the large output necessary to keep his investments remunerative.[13]

Part 5: Lumber Kings of Pacific Coast

The first known residents of Port Gamble were Nooksclime, Clallam, or S'Klallam peoples who fished and gathered food along Hood Canal. Colonial businessmen would follow, including Andrew J. Pope, Charles Foster, and Captain Josiah P. Keller who all belonged to families that had logged and built ships in Maine since the American Revolution. They came west with funding from their eastern relatives to analyze the lumber mill business, which they quickly did.

Given the rough and choppy waters of the Washington coast, there were no suitable locations for a port. So, William Talbot investigated the Puget Sound as a possible location for a mill. There, he spotted a sand spit at the mouth of the bay that offered a perfect location for a lumber mill. The spit sheltered sailing ships from the prevailing winds and timber grew right up to the coast, providing the lumber needed for a milling operation.

Trading Land for Christmas Presents

S'Klallam and other indigenous peoples already lived on the spit and on the bluff above. Talbot's partner, Josiah Keller, induced the natives to move across the bay to Point Julia in exchange for free lumber, firewood, and Christmas gifts. The S'Klallams called the site Teekalet, "brightness of the noonday sun," because of the way the sun reflected off the water and sand. Sunlight was a most welcome presence in the precipitous, cloud covered environment. Talbot borrowed that name for the mill, which was later changed to Port Gamble.

Port Gamble S'Klallam elder Sammy Charles, born in 1869, described their agreement to move to the other side of the bay. They may not have considered the long-term consequences of relinquishing their homeland. Their new location provided no respite from the winds and flooding. Many of them died.

> Boston [white people] are located just about on the edge of what was once the Nooksclime's [S.Klallam] grounds.... It just happened that the Nooksclime were camped and fishing on the Gamble spit when the Bostons came. There was talk, talk, talk. The Bostons said that they wanted to put a sawmill there, and would the Indians please move to the other side. There were inducements. There would be lumber, free lumber, and all that the Nooksclime needed to build big houses. They could have the trimmings for firewood, fine firewood, and all they wanted. The clincher was the Christmas treat.. The Nooksclime didn't know what Christmas was, but it sounded good.[14]

Martha John, who was born in 1891, also spoke of the move:

> The Klallams used to live in Port Gamble, where the general store is now, and all around where the Cemetery is located. The Mill people came along and sent the Indian (sic) over across the Bay, on the Spit. They promised to always have jobs for the men and also gave them enough lumber to build a small house for each family. Every winter the spit would be flooded. A lot of the people died.[15]

The S'Klallam people never lost interest in building their new homeland at Point Julia (Little Boston) by acquiring additional land.

On December 8, 1886, Charley Jones, John Solomon, and Cookhouse Charley each bought eleven acres fronting the bay near Point Julia. In 1891, Joseph Anderson received the final certificate on his eighty-acre parcel under the Indian Homestead Act. Other Port Gamble S'Klallam who purchased land were George Dan Howell in 1887, Jacob Jones in 1903, and Ed Purser in 1921. More S'Klallam members obtained land through purchase or gift from other S'Klallam. The process of purchasing land and ensuring that it remained with S'Klallam families demonstrates the importance the S'Klallam placed on maintaining residence near Point Julia. Unfortunately, much of this land was lost to county tax foreclosures in the 1930s.[16]

With the help of their Maine-based partner, Charles Foster, Pope, Talbot, and Keller recruited experienced mill workers from East Machias, Maine, to come west. The company took care of virtually every need, from childbirth to a mortuary and burial services. Port Gamble was a replica of East Macias.

By September 1853, the mill at Teekalet was cutting logs into lumber.

Helen Hunt Jackson provides a vivid description of milling operations as they developed at Port Gamble:

Our next stop was at Port Gamble. ... The air was resonant with shrill saw-mill noises. Lurid smoke, like that from smelting works, poured up from the fires. The mill itself was a deafening, blinding, terrifying storm of machinery: saws by dozens, upright, horizontal, circular, whirring and whizzing on all sides; great logs, sixty, a hundred feet long, being hauled up, dripping, out of the water, three at a time, by fierce clunking chains, slid into grooves, turned, hung, drawn, and quartered, driven from one end of the building to the other.

... the mills on Puget Sound, when all at work, have a cutting capacity of three hundred millions of feet a year, three of them cutting over a hundred thousand feet a day each, and a fourth being put into condition to cut two hundred thousand. Americans are often reproached, and justly, for their lack of reverence for the past; there seems even a greater dishonor in there lack of sense of responsibility for the future.

Now and then, a weird shape glided past, with warning cries: a steamboat, or a big log boom drawn by a tug. These log booms are ... sometimes fifteen hundred feet long and sixty wide, and contain a million feet of lumber.[18] See Notes for more history.[17]

Treaty of Point No Point Ceded Land around Port Gamble

On January 26, 1854, the Treaty of Point No Point ceded the land around Port Gamble to the United States and relegated the S'Klallams to a reservation with the Skokomish at the bend of Hood Canal. The S'Klallams chose not to share a small reservation with another tribe, so they continued to reside at Point Julia.

Legally, land wasn't available for non-Indian settlement until March 8, 1859, when Congress ratified the Treaty of Point No Point, which was signed January 26, 1855, by representatives of the United States and the Chemakum, S'Klallam and Skokomish Nations. By that time, the S'Klallam were entrenched at Point Julia, where they chose to stay.

There was no legal basis for the Talbot agreement, which was negotiated between the Indians and settlers, with no official intermediary. The consideration of firewood, wood for houses and "Christmas presents" is suspect and fails the litmus test of fair market value. Nonetheless, Governor Stevens negotiated away their rights.[18]

Pope & Talbot

Pope & Talbot adopted a modern organizational structure with many specialized subsidiaries for its diverse operations. It also instituted modern accounting procedures well before any other firm in the industry. It weathered intermittent depressions in the economy because of its owners' policy of borrowing money only from family members and by engaging in the various phases of logging, milling, manufacturing, wholesaling, retailing and shipping.

> While California remained the primary market, it could not absorb all that the Puget Sound mills produced, and before long the Puget Mill Company was exporting lumber to Hawaii, Australia, and South America. Employing "a ruthless approach to competitors," the firm dominated the export trade. Headquartered in San Francisco, Pope & Talbot ran door and window factories as well as lumberyards, dabbled in real estate, and were considered the "lumber kings of the Pacific Coast."[19]

The vessels included towboats to maneuver boats by pushing or pulling them out of the Puget Sound. Companies such as Pope & Talbot set up separate affiliates (e.g., Puget Lumber Co., Puget Shipping Co., Puget Trading Co., Puget Mercantile Co., and Puget Commercial Co.) which facilitated international travel and reduced liability and lowered taxes for the parent company.[20]

Lumber would become a global commodity as worldwide shipping became technologically possible.

> 10 December 1888 [To Cyrus Walker, Manager of the Puget Mill Company and the leading lumberman in Washington:]
> The foreign business is gradually increasing for our timber, and if our ventures in the London market are a success, there will be no limit to what they will take.[21]

The stories of the ship enterprises were fantastical in themselves.

> "We make so much lumber we must have vessels. Early on, it became evident that efficient operations required the continually loading," Pope pointed out. With shipping constantly available, costs could be reduced to a minimum and profits obtained from rum cargoes on the return voyages to the mills. By owning the Vessels, Pope observed, "we make the thing pay all round." By 1861,the Puget Mill Company controlled a fleet of eleven vessels and the other mills operated a smaller number of ships. With the coming of the great lumber firms, the Strait of Juan de Fuca was filled with the sails of ships departing for and arriving from San Francisco.[22]

To further the profitability of the timber companies, they entered the downstream wholesale and retail marketing on vast scales.

> ...men associated with the firm of Pope & Talbot bought interests in *a string of lumberyards that stretched from Sacramento through the San Joaquin Valley to Los Angeles and beyond to San Diego*. (Emphasis added).[23]

Part 6: Extinguish Indian Title West of Missouri

Helen Hunt Jackson, a writer and Indian rights advocate, in an article for the Atlantic Monthly, expressed her profound concern about how continued migration and economic growth would impact native peoples and betray the promises of an Indian Territory west of the Mississippi.

In the United States government's earlier treaties with the Indians, the country "west of the Mississippi" is again and again spoken of as beyond the probable reach of white settlement. ...And as late as 1812, one Mr. Mitchell, a superintendent of Indian affairs, said in a report, "If we draw a line running north and south, so as to cross the Missouri about the mouth of the Vermillion River, we shall designate the limits beyond which civilized men are never likely to settle." At this point the Creator seems to have said to the tides of emigration that are annually rolling toward the west, "Thus far shalt thou go, and no farther." To read such records as these today is half-comic, half-sad.

In the north, across Montana and Idaho ... immigrants by the thousand are steadily pouring into Oregon and Washington Territory. Two railroads are racing, straining muscles of men and sinews of money, to be first ready to carry this great tide.[24]

Part 7: Washington Territory Established (1853)

As in Oregon, colonial settlement in Washington preceded extinguishing Indian title. The Washington Territory was carved out of the Oregon Territory in 1853, during the closing days of Millard Fillmore's administration. The appointment of the territorial governor then fell to the newly elected Democratic President Franklin Pierce. He chose Isaac I. Stevens, a military officer, veteran of the Mexican War, and a political supporter. Stevens was given a triple charge as Territorial Governor, ex officio Superintendent of Indian Affairs, and chief surveyor for a possible route for a transcontinental railroad. It fell to Stevens to negotiate the treaties with the Indians in the Territory, persuading them to transfer their lands to the federal government and move onto reservations. By the time he left office in August 1857 to represent the territory in Congress, Stevens had negotiated ten treaties providing for the quieting of Indian title to some hundred thousand square miles of land.

Isaac Stevens, Surveyor of Northern Transcontinental Railroad Route, Governor and ex officio Superintendent of Indian Affairs for the Washington Territory

After his appointment on March 17, 1853, Steven's preference of first leading the survey of a northern transcontinental route became paramount. Ambitious territorial governors, such as Stevens, wanted statehood and that required a population of 60,000. Railroads would advance settlement and, more importantly, fuel commerce.

Surveillance of Indians in Washington Territory

By Letter, dated, May 9, 1853, Com'r Manypenny requested Gov. Stevens to report specific information regarding the tribes in the Washington Territory which would serve as a basis for Congressional legislation. The information detailed below provided (1) military intelligence; (2) data for use in negotiating for cessions of Indian lands; and/or (3) unilaterally determining areas for reservations.

Request for information regarding Indians in Washington Territory in contemplation of Congressional legislation pertaining thereto.

FIND OUT:

1st. The number and names of the several tribes, and their particular and general locality.

2d. The number of each separate tribe or band, and the probable number of warriors in each.

3d. Their general character and disposition, whether warlike and unfriendly or the reverse.

4th. Their present relations with the white inhabitants and the Hudson's Bay Company.

5th. Whether any conventional arrangements, and, if so, of what character, exist between them and our citizens which should be respected and conformed to by the government, and in what manner this should be effected.

6th. What number of agents and sub-agents will be indispensably necessary for the proper management of our relations and intercourse with them.

7th. The points at which agencies and sub-agencies should be established.

8th. The tribe or tribes which should be embraced within each agency or sub-agency; the latter in no case to be embraced within the former.

9th. The number of interpreters and other employes, if any, that will be necessary.

10th. The amount that will probably be required for the erection of the necessary agency buildings and fixtures, of a plain and cheap, yet substantial, character.

11th. The amount that will, in all probability, be required per annum for contingent expenses; to include fuel, stationery, travelling expenses of superintendent, agents, &c.

12th. ***The amount required to provide annually such small presents as it may be expedient to make to the Indians, to conciliate them.***

13th. The amount that will probably be necessary to expend annually in provisions, to be given to Indians visiting the superintendent or agents on business.

14th. What alterations, if any, it may be requisite and proper to make in the present law regulating trade and intercourse with our Indian tribes, so as better to adapt it to the condition and circumstances of our white and Indian population there. (Emphasis added).[25]

Indian Land Title Obstructing State's Growth

As Governor Steven's noted in his first address to the territorial legislature on February 28, 1854, Indian land title stood as an obstacle to territorial growth:

> The Indian title has not been extinguished, nor even a law passed to provide for its extinguishment east of the Cascade Mountains. Under the land law of Congress it is impossible to secure titles to the land, and thus the growth of towns and villages is obstructed, as well as the development of the resources of the Territory.[26]

It is obvious that of his triple duties, his role as trustee for the Indians would rank last. Railroad construction would further the growth and development of cities and towns, along with development of the Territory's resources. As Governor and ex officio Superintendent, his only concern with Indians was extinguishment of their land title which was impeding his ambition for statehood and possibly a future congressional seat.

Part 8: Secretary of Interior Authorizes Treaty Negotiations with Tribes

The solicitation of surveillance information on the Washington Territory tribes was followed up with Secretary McClelland's authorization to Commissioner Manypenny, on Aug. 18, 1853, to enter into negotiations with said tribes, for the extinguishment of their title to their lands and settlement thereof by white settlers:

> Should you deem it expedient and proper, however, to enter into any negotiations with the tribes in question, or either of them, for the extinguishment of their title to the lands now claimed by them, or for securing their assent to their settlement by citizens of the United States, you are fully authorized, in the exercise of a sound discretion, aided by your experience in the management of our Indian relations, to do so.[27]

Stevens to Conduct Treaty Negotiations

Acting Commissioner Charles E. Mix authorized Stevens to conduct the treaty negotiations with the Pacific Northwest Indians. He provided him with policy guidelines and with several recently concluded treaties to use as models but left much to his discretion and experience.

> It is the expectation of the Department that the sum appropriated, will prove sufficient to defray all expenses incurred in and incidental to making conventional arrangements *designed to be permanent*, with all the Tribes and fragments of Tribes within your Superintendency, by which the United States will extinguish their claim of title to all the lands within the Territory, excepting such limited districts as it may be necessary to assign them for their occupancy in future ... In concluding articles of agreement and convention with the Indian Tribes in Washington Territory, you will endeavor to *unite the numerous bands and fragments of tribes into tribes and provide for the concentration of one or more of such tribes upon the reservations which may be set apart for their future homes*. The formation of distinct relations with each of the forty or fifty separate bands of Indians in Washington Territory would not be as likely to promote the best interests of the white settlers or of the Indians as if the latter could be concentrated on a limited number of reservations, or on contiguous reservations, in a limited number of districts of country, apart from the settlement of the whites. (Emphasis added).[28]

Superintendent of Indian Affairs Stevens was to consolidate the forty or fifty separate bands of Indians into as few as possible tribes. It didn't matter whether they were related to each other or wanted to be joined together or not. The government-assigned lands were to be permanent.

> It is ... proposed, if practicable to remove all the Indians on the East side of the sound as far as the Snohomish; as also the S'Klallam to Hood's Canal, and generally to admit as few Reservations as possible, with a view of *finally concentrating them in one*. (Emphasis added).[29]

Com'r Mix specifically counseled Stevens that the Pacific Northwest Indian lands were of less value and that he should be certain to address all issues:

> [1] [their] claims of title [were] based on occupancy alone, and [2] that occupancy of a nature not fixed, and well defined as to boundaries, and [3] the lands which they claim are far removed from the portions of the Country which have been long settled, & [4] highly improved and [5] cultivated. ... and you will take care, in all treaties made, to leave no question open, out of which difficulties may hereafter arise, or by means of which the Treasury of the United States may be approached.[30]

As seen earlier, San Franciscan capitalists engaged in the Washington timber industry, were well aware of the incalculable value of the timber in the Pacific Northwest forests. Not only that, but they were also aware of how that value would increase with more railroad segments and export to larger domestic and foreign markets. The Department of the Interior completely failed to factor in the timber value in the consideration which would be set by the Department for the ceded lands. It also failed to recognize the boundaries of the seasonal use of lands for subsistence through fishing, hunting and gathering.

Consolidation and Concentration of Indian Tribes

According to Kent Richards, Steven's biographer, the treaty commissioners adopted and adhered to nine guiding principles in their negotiations:

1. Tribes would be concentrated together if possible and practical.
2. Agriculture and other "civilized" habits were to be encouraged.
3. Indian lands were to be purchased with annuities—payments of goods—rather than cash.
4. The government was to provide teachers, doctors, farmers, blacksmiths, and carpenters to care for and train the Indians.
5. Intertribal warfare was to be prohibited.
6. Indian slaveholding was to be abolished.
7. The liquor trade was to be eliminated.
8. Indians were to be allowed to hunt, fish, and gather other traditional foods until they had been fully "civilized."
9. The eventual division of reservation lands into individual allotments had to be provided for in the treaty language.[31]

A tenth principle, overlooked by Richards, was that each treaty needed to include a provision that unilaterally allowed the President of the United States to relocate the Indians to another reservation within the territory and decree their consolidation.

With the Indians of western Washington, Stevens also encountered another dilemma: Few of the tribes had a formal political organization with a leader who had the clear authority to negotiate and cede lands to the government. Stevens resolved this by appointing his own chiefs that were amenable to ceding lands:

> In making the reservations it seems desirable to adopt the policy of uniting small bands under a single head. The Indians are never so disposed to mischief as when scattered, and therefore beyond control.[32]

Part 9: Stevens' Treaties

The first Treaty concluded by Stevens, on December 26, 1854, was with the chiefs, headmen, and delegates of the Nisqually, Puyallup, Steilacoom, Squawksin, S'Homamish, Steh-chass, T'Peek-sin, Squiaitl and Sa-heh-wamish tribes and bands of Indians, occupying the lands lying round the head of Puget's sound and the adjacent inlets.

By the terms of the treaty, referred to as the Medicine Creek Treaty, the Indians ceded their title to the lands, except certain parts to be held as reservations. Under the terms, the Nisqually, a people who lived on fish and the local vegetation, were required to relocate away from the river and its basin to a heavily forested area in the hills. As compensation for the land cession the government would pay annual installments aggregating the sum of $32,500 and an additional sum of $3,250 to prepare the reservations for occupancy. The rights of the Indians to fish and hunt at the usual places were protected. *If occasion should arise, the President of the United States might remove the Indians to other reservations.* The treaty was ratified by the Senate and proclaimed by President Franklin Pierce on April 10, 1855.

During that same winter, three other treaties were made with the western Washington Indians, all similar in their provisions to the Medicine Creek Treaty. They were concluded in rapid succession whereby the United States extinguished Indian title to most of the land in Washington Territory west of the Cascade Mountains.

Neah Bay Treaty

On January 31, 1855, about 600 Makah gathered to hear Stevens explain the treaty:

The Great Father has sent me to see you, and give you his mind. The whites are crowding in upon you. The Great Father wishes to give you your homes, to buy your land, and give a fair price for it, leaving you land enough to live on and raise potatoes. He knows what whalers you are, how far you go to sea to take whales. He will send you barrels in which to put your oil, kettles to try it out, lines and implements to fish with. The Great Father wants your children to go to school, and learn trades.[33]

Then, "the treaty was ... read and interpreted in Chinook and explained, clause by clause." *The treaty contained provisions that allowed the Makah to continue fishing, sealing and whaling "at usual and accustomed grounds or stations," and permitted hunting and gathering on "open and unclaimed lands."* It required that they "acknowledge their dependence on the Government of the United States." The "Neah Bay Treaty" allowed the President of the United States to relocate other tribes onto the Makah reserve or, at his discretion, remove the Makah to another location. ... Observers recalled that Stevens asked the Makah leaders if they were satisfied with the treaty or if they had any objections. In reply the Indians presented white flags to Stevens, and Kalchote responded by saying "What you have said is good, and what you have written is good."[34]

Medicine Creek Treaty, Stevens' Treaty with Nisqually Indian Nation

The conflict began after the Treaty of Medicine Creek was negotiated in 1854 with the Nisqually, Puyallup, Steilacoom, Squawskin, S'Homamish, Stehchass, T'Peeksin, Squi-aitl, and Sa-heh-wamish tribes and bands of Indians, occupying the lands lying round the head of Puget's Sound and the adjacent inlet, which set aside reservations for the tribes. Three reservations were granted to the Indians in the Medicine Creek Treaty's second article: Squaxon Island, situated opposite the mouths of Hammersley and Tottens inlets, and separated from Hartstene Island by Peale Passage, containing about *two sections of land*, or 1280 acres, a square tract of *two sections* near and south of the mouth of McAllister's Creek, and another equal tract on the south side of Commencement Bay, now covered by the city of Tacoma. Six sections (3,840 acres) were thus set aside as reservations in return for the cession of 2.5 million acres, with the reservation of certain rights, including "The right of taking fish, at all usual and accustomed grounds and stations, is further secured to said Indians in common with all citizens of the Territory." The consideration for the land cession was the sum of $32,500 payable in installments over thirteen years in goods.[35]

Gov. Stevens wrote to Com'r Manypenny that Article 6 allowed the President to move or consolidate reservation sites whenever it suited the U.S. Government, and he planned to move the Medicine Creek Treaty tribes onto a single, consolidated reservation, perhaps as early as the summer of 1855. Also, consensual allotment was permissible.

> The President may hereafter, when in his opinion the interests of the Territory may require, and the welfare of the said Indians be promoted, remove them from either or all of said reservations to such other suitable place or places within said Territory as he may deem fit, on remunerating them for their improvements and the expenses of their removal, or may consolidate them with other friendly tribes or bands. And he may further, at his discretion, cause the whole or any portion of the lands hereby reserved, or of such other land as may be selected in lieu thereof, to be surveyed into lots, and assign the same to such individuals or families as are willing to avail themselves of the privilege ...[36]

On March 3, 1855, the Medicine Creek Treaty was ratified by the United States Senate. President Franklin Pierce proclaimed it into law on April 10, 1855.

The lands ceded were described as fertile, but densely timbered.

> Surveyor General Tilton, in his last annual report [1859] to the Commissioner of the General Land Office, writes as follows: "Fine bodies of rich land have been explored in the vallies of the Chehalis river, which falls into the Pacific at Gray's Harbor." *The bottom lands of the Nesqually, the Puyallup, the Snohomish, White and Green rivers, the waters of all which disembogue in Puget Sound, are broad, rich, and of the most fertile quality, but densely timbered*. "East of the Cascades, and upon the Columbia river, and its northern tributaries, are also *large bodies of excellent lands*." The Cowlitz river, running southwardly and falling into the Columbia, also drains *fertile lands*, and has many of the oldest settlers in the territory among its prosperous farmers. "All cereal grains, except Indian corn, flourish admirably here, the wheat being of excellent quality and abundant in quantity." If a permanent peace should be made with them (several powerful tribes of Indians east of the Cascade mountains) it will throw open a large extent of excellent country. That there are *valuable gold mines* in the interior, requiring only protection to our people to the growing up of a hardy, mining community, is no longer a matter of doubt. (Emphasis added).[37]

For the Nisqually tribe, their new reservation was situated on rocky high ground which was unsuitable for farming and cut them off from access to the river that provided the mainstay of their livelihood, salmon.

White Men Beat and Abuse Indians – Indians Need to Move

A treaty council was scheduled for February 1855 on the Chehalis River at which Stevens expected to purchase Indian title to the rest of western Washington. For one week, from February 24 – March 2, 1855, Governor Stevens and his treaty commission met with representatives of various Indian tribes living along the Pacific coast and in the southwestern part of Washington Territory. At the Chehalis River, Stevens met the first concerted Indian resistance to his treaty negotiations in Washington Territory. For the first time, he was not able to reach an agreement.

At the Chehalis River treaty council there were representatives from the Quinault and Queets, from the north side of Gray's Harbor, from the Satsop, from the Lower Chehalis, Upper Chehalis, Shoalwater Bay, Chinook, and Cowlitz.[38]

> Stevens opened the Council explaining his purpose: to negotiate a treaty whereby the Indians would relinquish their lands in return for *"a tract of land on the Coast of the Pacific between Gray's Harbor and Cape Flattery."* (Emphasis added).[39]
>
> The specific reservation Stevens was negotiating for was undetermined, other than it would lay on the coast between Gray's Harbor and Cape Flattery. The amount of acreage was not set.

ART. II. provided as follows:

> There shall however be reserved for the use and occupation of the said Tribes and Bands a tract of land on the Coast of the Pacific between Gray's Harbor and Cape Flattery, sufficient for their wants, to be selected by the President.

ART. VI. articulated the President's ability to remove them to another location; consolidate them with other friendly tribes; and/or allot land to them. It stated:

> *The President may* hereafter, when in his opinion the interests of the Territory shall require, and the welfare of the said Indians be thereby promoted, *remove them from said reservation to such other suitable place or places within said Territory as he may deem fit* on remunerating them for their improvements and the expenses of their removal, or may *consolidate them with other friendly tribes and bands*. And he may further at his discretion cause the whole or any portion of the lands to be reserved, or of such other land as may be selected in lieu thereof, to be surveyed into lots, and assign the same to such individuals or families as are willing to avail themselves of the privilege, and will locate on the same as a permanent home… (Emphasis added).[40]

Steven's tone throughout the negotiations was belligerent. He specifically stated he knew the whites beat and ill-treated them. His solution, however, did not address any accountability by them for their criminal actions. Again, the Indians would 'allegedly' be removed out of harm's way. Stevens knew the amount to be offered to them, but not what the exchange lands were.

Gov. Stevens: What is your state now though? Do you now own all your old burying grounds and potato patches—have you not been told by the Whites "Let us have these places, and the Great Father will pay you for them?" The Whites now have these lands, but you have not got your pay. And now the Great Father has sent me here and know what he should pay you for them. *And the bad white men as you know are the ones who beat and ill treat you*.. Now I have put my mind on a paper, which will be read to you. He knows all about you and in the paper which will be read to you has done what he thinks will be for your good. (Emphasis added).[41]

Aside from the Quinault Indians, the remaining tribes were opposed. Their response was as stated by Yowannus: "He does not want to sign till he knows where he is going to. He wants to stay in his own country and not be moved elsewhere." This included:

Yowannus. Head Chief of the Upper Chihalis;

Ta-Ho-La, Head Chief of the Kwinai-Utl;

Tu-Leh-Uk, Head Chief of the Lower Chihalis;

Kish-Kok, Head Chief of the Cowlitz and Ow-Hye, a Cowlitz Delegate;

Nah-Kot-Ti and Moos-Moos – Chinooks;

Chah-Lat, a Sub Chief from the North Side of Gray's Harbor; and

Tee-Whit of Satsop and Squatsen.

Stevens threatened the delegates at the Chehalis Council to force them to sign his treaty.

He said that if they did not agree to his terms, their lands would be taken any way and they would be placed on reservations. He said that they would not be offered another treaty.

> I want them to leave it to the Great Father to say where their home should be.
>
> This paper has to go to the Great Father and it will be a long time before it will get back. I cannot give a paper showing where their land is till it does. The Great Father wanted another thing. When they got on their permanent home that each should take a small field and improve it as his own, as the whites did.
>
> There was a saw mill and two settlers on that creek and two settlers on the prairie. They had cut a road which he could not take away. ... The Great Father was constantly sending settlers here. The Boston country was full and he had to send them away.
>
> What will you do then? Will you leave it to the President by Treaty, when the paper promises you a good place, or is he to select it himself without? for it comes to that finally.
>
> One of the reasons why the former treaties were rejected was that they gave the same sort of little reserves as they now wanted.
>
> Mr. Shaw and Judge Ford joined in: But that the Whites were constantly increasing and pushing them off of one piece and another of land and that unless some arrangement was made they would be driven away from those grounds altogether.
>
> We have now been here a week. I have heard you all. There will then be no treaty, no promises but you will be in the hands of the Great Father to do as we please. (Emphasis added).42

During these treaty negotiations, no protection, other than removal to an unknown location, was offered.

In July, Stevens sent a member of the Treaty Commission to the Quinault River to negotiate a separate treaty with the Quinault. Stevens signed that treaty at his office in Olympia in January 1856. It is known as the Treaty of Olympia.

> Indian Agent W. B. Gosnell reported in 1861 that whites had taken up and fenced almost all of the Chehalis lands, leaving them with only an acre or two. The U.S. took no protective action on behalf of the Chehalis.43

Stevens' Treaty Statistics

On April 30, 1857, Governor Stevens sent to George W. Manypenny, Commissioner of Indian Affairs, a map showing the distribution of the Indians of Washington Territory. On the map are marginal notes giving statistics. One of these in the Governor's handwriting is as follows:

Total number of Indians west of the Cascade Mountains 9,712

Total number of Indians east of the Cascade Mountains 12,000

Total number of Indians, Territory of Washington 21,712

Treaties have been made with 17,497

Treaties remain to be made with 4,215

Treaties entered into with 75% of Indians.[44]

Location	No. of Indians	Reservations
East of Cascade Mt.	12,000	3 Reservations
West of Cascade Mt.	9,712	15 Reservations
Territory of Washington	21,712	18 Reservations

Made	To Be Made
No. of Indians	No. of Indians
17, 497	4,215

Part 10: Reservations in Washington

Reservations in Washington			
Name	Acreage**	Tribe	Industries
[This list is not meant to be inclusive. This list does not infer any legality or validity of any of the Reservations listed.]			
Chehalis Reservation	2,076.06	Chehalis	Timber
Columbia Reservation	25,172	Moses's Band (Sinkiuse)	
Colville Reservation	1,059,199.08	Confederated Tribes	Timber
Hoh River Reservation	443.00	Hoh	Timber
Jamestown Klallam		Klallam	
Kalispel Reservation	4,557.41	Kalispel	Timber
Lower Elwha Reservation	427.48	Clallam	Timber
Lummi Reservation	7,678.13	Lummi & Nooksack	Timber
Makah Reservation	27,243.37	Makah	Timber
Muckleshoot Reservation	1,274.99	Muckleshoot	Timber
Nisqually Reservation	925.00	Nisqually	Timber
Nooksack Reservation	.97		
Ozette Reservation	719.00	Ozette	
Port Gamble Reservation	1,303.00	Clallam	Timber
Port Madison Reservation	2,871.46	Suquamish	
Puyallup Reservation	101.37	Puyallup	
Quileute Reservation	814.07	Quileute	Timber
Quinault Reservation	129,307.54	Quinault	Timber
Sauk-Suiattle Reservation (State)	23.21		
Shoalwater Reservation	335.00	Quinault, Chinook, Chehalis	Timber
Skokomish Reservation	2,984.51	Skokomish	
Spokane Reservation	133,237.27	Spokane	Timber
Squaxin Island	883.37	Squaxin Island	Timber
Stillaguamish			
Swinomish Reservation	3,601.76	Swinomish	Timber
Tulalip Reservation	10,667.48	Snohomish	Timber
Upper Skagit Reservation	74.17		Upper Skagit Wood Products Co.
Yakama Reservation	1,130,014.64	14 Confederated Tribes	Timber, Mt. Adams Furniture

Unratified and Ratified Treaties in Washington		
[This list is not meant to be inclusive. This list does not infer any legality or validity of any of the Treaties listed.]		
Treaty	Date	Tribes or Bands
Treaty of Medicine Creek 10 Stat. 1132	Dec. 26, 1854	Nisqually
Treaty of Point Elliott, 12 Stat. 927	Jan. 22, 1855	Dwamish, Suquamish Lummi and the Skagit
Treaty of Point No Point, 12 Stat. 933	Jan. 26, 1855	S'Klallam
Treaty of Neah Bay, 12 Stat. 939	Jan. 31, 1855	Makah Tribe
Treaty with the Yakama, 12 Stat. 951	June 9, 1855	
Quinault Treaty, 12 Stat. 971 (Olympia)	Jan. 25, 1856	Quinault, Queets, Quileute, and Ho
Treaty with Walla Walla 12 Stat. 945	June 9, 1855	Walla Walla, Cayuse, Umatilla
Spokane Treaty Council	Dec. 5, 1855	
Chehalis River Treaty Council	Feb. 24-27, 1855	Quinault, Queets, Satsop, Lower Chehalis, Upper Chehalis, Cowlitz, and Chinook Indians

The consideration wasn't turned over to the tribes in cash, but was distributed in annual installments of goods, provisions, and equipment. The consideration is specified in the treaties.

A horrific occurrence after the treaty making period in Washington was that the Executive Orders creating reservations did not contain rights to *continue fishing "at usual and accustomed grounds or stations," and hunting and gathering on "open and unclaimed lands."* This is still a contested issue today.

Part 11: Rumblings of War

Numerous skirmishes were fought throughout the Puget Sound and the Plateau regions. Many of them occurred when U.S. troops and volunteers accidentally encountered Indians encamped and others were deliberately planned. There is an overlap of times and tribes involved, as it was a very haphazard, reactionary response by the U.S. Army and volunteers.

Military Records Short on Substance

Military records of this period are not very detailed. With the information gleaned from the existent reports, many inconclusive engagements occurred. Also, it is difficult to label battles as specifically aligned with specific tribes. Different tribes united to fight east and west of the Cascades and soldiers responded accordingly. Also, the Puget Sound and the Yakama were ongoing at the same time and the Spokane/Coeur d'Alene Wars would erupt later. The military was simply not prepared for war on three fronts.

They reflect the Indians' advantages that the volunteers didn't give the Indians credit for, including (1) knowledge of the land, (2) excelling in hit-and-run and guerrilla tactics, (3) marksmanship and training in war horse combat, (5) ability to live off the land, and (6) mobility. Nonetheless, they would experience hunger, suffering, death, injury, grief and total exhaustion.

1st Washington Territory Volunteers

The Washington Territorial volunteers were authorized by the Legislative Assembly Jan. 26, 1855. Acting Governor Charles H. Mason then issued a proclamation for Volunteer companies to make up the 1st Washington Territory Volunteers. They were mustered into U.S. Army service on Oct. 14, 1855. The Volunteer companies were mustered out in December 1855. They would continue to be used in the fighting.

This was a citizen army, composed of individuals who stood to gain from eradicating Indians to secure their land and resources. This amounted to essentially arming a hate-mongering mob and pitting them against the Indians. As critiqued by Major Williams:

> [T]he caliber of soldier that fought the Indians was often less than stellar due to cultural issues, low morale related to pay problems, a lack of civilian education, poor military training, and the hardships associated with soldiering in the Frontier Army.[45]

The volunteers would have to play catch-up. They didn't have a headquarters, other than their gathering destination in a town or village or, if fortunate, a fort. Their armaments were mixed. Volunteers would crisscross from east to west of the Cascades to react to Indian attacks, tripping over each other, unsure of their exact destination, getting lost, arriving too late; in other words, not having zones of operation. Without an interest or method for inquiring into the status of the Indians, a wholesale slaughter would occur, whether the Indians were hostile or not.

Reason for Indian Hostilities

On Nov. 3, 1855, Major General John E. Wool explained to Lieut. Col. L. Thomas, Asst. Adjt. Gen., Army Headquarters, New York, that the outbreaks of the Indians in Oregon and Washington were due to the invasion of the settlers and miners and what that would mean for the Army:

> The Yakimas, Walla-Wallas, Klititats, Des Chutes, and Cayuses, are doubtless in arms. They have been excited by fears at seeing their country rapidly filling up with settlers and miners, least their fate shall be like that of the California Indians, and hope to exterminate the whites at a blow.[46]

Gold Discovered

Capt. George McClelland exploring for a possible railroad route discovered gold in 1853 in the Yakima River valley. By 1855, prospectors were active in the Colville district although the first discoveries were not made until 1883. The pattern of trespass on Indian lands, theft of horses and property and mistreatment, with no accountability, ensued. The federal government failed to initiate any punitive or protective action on behalf of the Yakamas. Prospectors mobbed the area. In retaliation, miners were killed. When some of the Yakama warriors retaliated by killing miners in random incidents, Andrew J. Bolon, the Indian sub-agent, was sent to investigate. When he too was killed, troops were sent into the Yakama Valley, starting the Yakama War in October 1855.

Routing of Major Haller's Volunteer Forces

Major Granville O. Haller was ordered to head to Yakama territory from Fort Dalles. On October 6, 1855, Haller's force was met and routed at the edge of Yakama territory by a large group of Yakama warriors. The 600 Yakama and Palouse Indians were led by Yakama Chief Kamiakin and Palouse Chief Owhi.

By letter from J. Cain, Actg. Supt. of Indian Affairs to Actg. Gov. Mason, W.T., October 9, 1855, Major Haller's circumstances were relayed to Gov. Mason:

> ... *Major Haller and his command being surrounded by Indians and cut off from wood and water ... all the force that can be sent in the field is absolutely necessary for his preservation.* ... The Yakima's number are evidently largely swollen by acquisition from tribes on the south side of the Columbia. The Pelouses have all gone over and should Major Haller be defeated there is much apprehension in that the Walla Wallas, Cayuses and Des Chutes will at once unite in the War. (Emphasis added).[47]

In a frantic letter, dated October 9, 1855, Major Rains, Volunteer, W.T., advised his command that "*He [Major Haller] was surrounded, and in that position, has called for reinforcement.* All the disposable force in the district will at once take the field, and I have the honor to make a requisition upon you for two companies of volunteers to take the field the earliest possible moment." (Emphasis added).[48]

Reinforcements would have to be called up, armed, and mobilized to Yakama Territory. It was even uncertain, due to the delay in communication, where the Yakamas would be. The telegraph and railroads had not yet reached the Pacific Northwest, so horseback delivery or steamboat was used.

> In the dense forests and swamps the savages lurked at the very doors of the settlements, and no man ventured out, for fear of ambush by the wily and omnipresent foe.[49]

Fragmented State Leadership

While Gov. Stevens was off negotiating treaties, Acting Governor George Mason was his stand-in. This fragmented state leadership resulted in difficulties for Indians seeking peace.

On October 14, 1855, Acting Governor George Mason ordered two companies of volunteer militiamen under territorial jurisdiction to be drafted, one for Olympia and the other for Ft. Vancouver. He further requested the U.S. Army to supply the volunteers with transportation and subsistence.[50] The volunteers need to procure, transport and distribute supplies from a distant logistical base worked to the advantage of the Indians.

On October 16, 1855, Lt. James McAlister, a member of the Eaton Rangers, whose friendship with Chief Leschi had become strained over the Medicine Creek Treaty, wrote to Sup't Palmer that he should stop Chief Leschi from preparing for war:

> From the most reliable Indians that we have in this country, we have information and are satisfied that Leschi, a sub-chief and half Clickitat is and has been doing all that he could possibly do to unite the Indians of this country to raise against the Whites in a hostile manner and has had some join in with him already. I am of the opinion that he [Leschi] should be attended to as soon as convenient for fear that he might do something bad.[51]

Acting Gov. Mason invited Chief Leschi to meet in his office October 22, 1855, where Leschi again expressed his desire for peace and a reservation on the river.[52]

Acting Gov. Mason responded, on October 22, 1855, by calling for four additional companies of Volunteers.

> EXECUTIVE OFFICE, OLYMPIA, WASH TERR PROCLAMATION Whereas, by proclamation bearing date of October 14, 1855, a call was made upon the people of the Territory of Washington for two companies of Volunteers to **augment the force operating against the Yakima Tribe of Indians**. Now therefore, in order more fully, to secure the lives and property of our inhabitants from any incursions or outbreak on the part of the Indians, and to be prepared for any emergency, I make this proclamation calling upon the people of Washington Territory for **four additional companies of volunteers** ... (Emphasis added).[53]

The Eaton Rangers, led by a local citizen, Charles Eaton, and James McAllister as a citizen-lieutenant proceeded to apprehend Leschi and his brother, Quiemuth. They would be interred at Olympia, given the rumors of Leschi's leadership in agitating for active hostilities against the settlements. Leschi and Quiemuth fled from their village. Captain Eaton divided his forces and dispatched Lt. McAllister, with a small party, to conduct reconnaissance in the vicinity of White River. McAllister and a local mining claimant, Michael Connell, were killed in an ambush on October 27.[54]

Volunteer Citizen Group

A volunteer citizen group was formed west of the Cascades, to counter Indians who would "butcher their white neighbors:"

> PREAMBLE AND RESOLUTIONS PASSED AT A PUBLIC MEETING OF THE CITIZENS OF GRAND MOUND AND ITS VICINITY, OCTOBER 23rd, 1855:
>
> WHEREAS War exists between the United States and various Indian tribes east of the Cascade Mountains, the issues of which are at present uncertain; and believing that some of the band of Indians on this side of the mountains would not hesitate to butcher their white neighbors if a favorable opportunity occurred, believe it to be our duty to provide for the safety of our families should danger become imminent. ...
> RESOLVED 2ND – That we enroll ourselves into a Volunteer Company, and place ourselves at the disposal of the Acting Governor of this Territory, requesting that we may be immediately armed and equipped for service, and employed where duty calls for the defense of the country.[55]

White River Assault

The Indian's restraint over the invasion of their land, as settlers continued to move into the area, at last exceeded the boundaries of their endurance. Disturbed by the continuing disregard for their lands, the White River Indians, including the Muckleshoot and Klickitat tribes, attacked several settlers in the area on October 28, 1855. Three families—nine people, in all—were killed, igniting a simmering war.

John Nugen, 2d Lieut. 4th Infantry, Fort Steilacoom, reported to Acting Governor Mason that war had broken out with the Indians on White River:

> I have just received an express from Captain Sterrett, Commanding "Decatur" informing me that the Indians on White River have broken-out and that seven Whites and two Indians have been murdered. On the 28th, *fifty-five men* under the command of Volunteer Captain C. C. Hewitt left for the White River country. (Emphasis added).[56]

A wave of hysteria hit the settlers. Acting Governor Mason ordered the emergency construction of blockhouses. Settlers would be moved into these structures when necessary for safety which led to this period being known as the era of the blockhouses.

Part 12: War

Military Rendezvous Fails

On Oct. 28, 1855, Major Rains and his men left Fort Steilacoom to rendezvous with Capt. Maurice Maloney in Yakama country. After starting out, he received information that Capt. Maloney would be delayed. This failure of communication could have had drastic consequences as Major Rains reported there were two to three thousand Indians in his front.

> On the 24th, I commenced my march for the Yakima Country expecting to find you in the field. ... I received ... information that you will not be on your march for from one to two weeks. I have also got information that ***there are from two to three thousand Indians well armed, and determined to fight in my front***, and, after considering the matter over, have concluded that ***it is my duty to return to Steilacoom***. My reasons are as follows, Viz; first, ***my forces are not sufficiently strong to fight them...***[57]

Volunteers Mustered into Service

On Nov. 2, 1855, the volunteers were mustered into service with the U.S. Army. This would permit furnishing supplies, armaments and soldiers.

James Tilton, Adjutant General, Olympia, W. T., issued the following Order on Nov. 2, 1855:

> GENERAL ORDERS: NO. 1
>
> 1st. The Company "D", Captain Wallace, raised and organized at Steilacoom, is accepted and mustered into service, and will cooperate with the garrison at Fort Steilacoom until an expedition against the enemy is made.
>
> 2nd. The Company of Mounted Rangers of Mound Prairie, Captain Henness, is accepted, and will be mustered in upon rendition of their muster and descriptive rolls.
>
> 3rd. Captain Hewitt's Company of Seattle, being upon an expedition against the enemy, will be placed upon the rolls of this office in the service, upon rendition of their muster and descriptive rolls.[58]

Washington and Oregon Volunteers' Yakama Stalemate

In November 1855, Volunteer Major Gabriel J. Rains led an expedition of 370 men, including Oregon and Washington volunteers, to the Yakama Valley *"to punish the Indians for the defeat of Major Haller the previous month*." He encountered Chief Kamiakin leading a force of Yakama warriors. The Army bombarded the Indians, in their guarded hilltop position, with cannon fire for several hours. Realizing they had to take the hill, Major Rains ordered Captain Ferdinand Augur to charge it. It was each volunteer for himself. Augur was able to disperse the Indians and they scattered. Major Rains and his troops did not pursue them.[59]

This impasse would merely serve to fuel the two-sides hatred, desire for retaliation and further hostilities, without forging a path forward for peace. Given the inability to communicate with one another, or build a rapport or trust, there was no room for diplomacy. A lop-sided fight would continue, with only one goal for the volunteers, obliteration of the enemy. The motivation of the Indians hardened their determination; they were fighting for their land and lives.

Death of Volunteer Moses in Aborted Action

In the meantime, troops from the U.S. Army based at Fort Steilacoom (west of the Cascades) had marched eastward to help those on the other side. *When that action was aborted*, the captain sent a dispatch back to Fort Steilacoom to inform those still there of the return. One of those in the dispatch party was a volunteer named A. Benton Moses. On the journey, he and another (Joseph Miles) were killed. Report of John Nugen, 2d Lieut. 4th Infantry to Major Rains, Volunteer, W.T., Nov. 2, 1855.[60] It was alleged that Nisqually Chief Leschi was responsible for the death of Moses.

Ruin of Industrial Community

Commercial activity was, allegedly, endangered even more than the lives of settlers.

> If the natives were not promptly and soundly defeated, Governor Isaac Stevens informed the territorial legislature, "the whole industrial community [of Puget Sound] would be ruined."[61]

Over half the adult white males in the territory joined the volunteers summoned to fight Indians, forcing a sharp curtailment of lumber production.

> In November 1855, Josiah Keller, a prominent Pope & Talbot partner reported:

"The mills above I learn have all stopped, & we may have to stop ours by & by to assist our friends above."[62]

With so much at stake, lumbermen became vigorous supporters of the war effort. The Puget Mill Company was the leading supplier of provisions for the volunteers and the regular army contingents, accepting government scrip in payment. By the spring of 1856, the company had made at least $30,000 from the war. "We are obliged to furnish supplies liberally," Keller explained, "in order to secure ourselves as much as possible in carrying on our business."[63]

Part 13: Puget Sound War

At the same time the U.S. Army and volunteers were facing war with the Yakama, war broke out in the Puget Sound region with the Puyallup, Nisqually, and Squaxon Indian Nations. A Command 238 strong was organized in the Puget Sound but their march up the White River was aborted due to the deep snow. Acting Gov. Mason ordered Captain Maloney to dispatch to the Yakima country.[64]

As Maloney's force retreated, about 150 warriors of the Puyallup, Nisqually, and Squaxon tribes pursued and attacked them on November 7, 1855. "After a day-long fight, the Indians retreated, pursued by the soldiers. The action continued for another day or two until the Indians halted their assault. The Indians had about 30 casualties and in Captain Maloney's group, 22 were killed and three wounded".[65]

Battle of Brennan's Prairie, Dec. 4, 1855

In another haphazard collision, Lt. William A. Slaughter and his troops of about 40 soldiers were encamped on Brennan's Prairie, just east of present-day Auburn, Washington. On November 3, 1885, they were attacked in a hit-and-run engagement by Nisqually Indians. Later that month, on November 24, they lost about 40 horses in an Indian night raid.

On December 3, Lt. Slaughter was reinforced by Cap. Gilmore Hays detachment of volunteers. They were surprised by a night-time attack by warriors from the Puyallup, Nisqually, and Klickitat tribes, led by Klickitat Chief Kanaskat. Lt. Slaughter and three other soldiers were killed before the Indians warriors withdrew, under the protective cover of darkness.[66]

Battle of Seattle, Jan. 26, 1856

The Battle of Seattle was fought on Jan. 26, 1856, between the U.S. Navy and warriors of various tribes. Congress' failure to ratify the treaties of 1854–1855, left a vacuum as to who owned what.

On the early morning of January 26, 1856, after months of raids and clashes with federal troops in southern King County and in Thurston County, Washington, Indians attacked Seattle. The Indians were driven off by artillery fire from the U.S. Navy sloop-of-war Decatur, which was anchored in Elliott Bay. Volunteers under Volunteer Captain Christopher C. Hewitt also fired upon the attackers, but it was primarily the Decatur's guns that dispersed the Indians.[67]

Two settlers and an unknown number of Indians perished in the all-day Battle of Seattle. The psychological impact was great. A few days before, Governor Stevens had visited and reassured Seattle, "I believe the cities of New York and San Francisco would as soon be attacked as Seattle."[68]

Battle of Muckleshoot Prairie, March 1, 1856

In late February 1856, Captain Erasmus D. Keyes and his troops captured Klickitat Chief Kanaskat, who had led the attack on Lt. Slaughter and his men on December 4, 1855, at Brennan's Prairie. While apprehending him, the Chief struggled furiously, and soldiers shot him in the back. When he continued to struggle, Corporal O'Shaughnessy shot him in the head.[69]

In retaliation, on March 1, 1856, about 200 warriors of various Puget Sound tribes struck the White River encampment of Lt. August V. Kautz and his troops. Lt. Kautz sent for help, and Captain Keyes and his troops responded. Together, the two forces stormed the Indians defensive position on a hilltop, scattering the Indians. Two soldiers were killed in the fight and eight were wounded, including Lt. Kautz.

Gov. Stevens would report to Sec. of War Jefferson Davis, on March 9, 1856, the signal defeat of the Indians at Muckleshoot:

In the movement of the regular troops upon the *Muckleshoot*, a decisive battle was fought with the *Indians*, in which the latter were *signally defeated*. (Emphasis added).[70]

Battle at Connell's Prairie, March 10, 1856

In March 1856, about 100 men under Volunteer Major Gilmore Hays, approached the White River crossing at Connell's Prairie on March 10, 1856. They encountered a force of about 150 Nisqually, Klickitat, and Yakama warriors. Four volunteers were wounded.

Mashel Massacre, March 31, 1856

The Mashel Massacre, on March 31, 1856, was the last episode of the Puget Sound War that had begun in 1855. Governor Isaac Stevens ordered the Washington Mounted Rifles, led by Captain Hamilton J. G. Maxon, to move from the Columbia River to patrol the Nisqually River vicinity in late March 1856. They killed any Indians they encountered. When Maxon and his troops came upon several Indians who were encamped where Ohop Creek and the Mashel River join with the Nisqually River, the soldiers attacked, killing everyone. Those encamped were not warriors, but mostly women, children, and elderly men. One witness counted only two men in the camp. The number killed was unknown but, estimated to have been as many as 30.[71]

Gov. Stevens reported to Sec. of War Jefferson Davis on May 24, 1856, on the successful conclusion of the Indian War west of the Cascades:

> THE WAR IN THE TERRITORY OF WASHINGTON, WEST OF THE CASCADES The war has been prosecuted with exceeding vigor, energy and success. The Indians have been defeated in two battles, one by the regulars at the crossing of White River, the other by the volunteers at Connell's Prairie. The Indians have been repeatedly struck since by the regulars, by the volunteers, and by the Indian auxiliaries. The country has been thoroughly and repeatedly scouted in every direction, and is now firmly held by blockhouses and roads. Two hundred Indians have been got back of Seattle by the volunteers, and those believed to have been engaged in the war, are now being tried by a military commission ordered by me at Seattle.[72]

Puget Sound War, Washington Territory (Nisqually, Muckleshoot, Puyallup, and Klickitat Tribes)		
Date	Location	Comments
Dec. 4, 1855	Battle of Brennan's Prairie	
January 26, 1856	Battle of Seattle	
March 1, 1856	Battle of Muckleshoot Prairie	
March 10, 1856	Battle at Connell's Prairie	
March 31, 1856	Mashel Massacre	
On December 10, 2004, the Wash. Supreme Court (a special historical court) exonerated Chief Leschi of the charge of murder, because he and Moses were both legal combatants in a war.		

Part 14: Indian War on Plateau

Gov. Stevens', May 24, 1856, Report to Sec. of War Jefferson Davis informed him that the war east of the Cascades on the Washington plateau was ongoing. "Twelve to fifteen hundred warriors [were] determined to fight."

> THE WAR EAST OF THE CASCADES It is not to be disguised that the tribes east of the mountains thus far consider themselves the victors. When Colonel Wright commenced his march into the Yakima country early this month, they practically held the whole country for which they had been fighting. Not a white man now is to be found from the Dalles to the Walla Walla; not a house stands, and Colonel Wright, at the last advices, was on the Nachess in presence of twelve to fifteen hundred warriors, determined to fight. All the confederated bands are there.[73]

Battle of Union Gap, Nov. 9-10, 1855

Volunteer Major Gabriel J. Rains, U.S. Army soldiers, and Oregon and Washington volunteers accidentally encountered a group of Yakamas returning home from the Battle at White River. A two-day battle ensued. One volunteer was killed, and the Yakamas were forced to retreat.

Cascades Rapids Battle, March 26, 1856

Angered over broken treaties and in an attempt to repel white settlers from their lands, warriors of the Yakima and Cascade tribes attacked settlers living near the Cascades Rapids on the Columbia River on March 26, 1856. The Indians killed 14 settlers and three soldiers in the attacks. It was the costliest event in terms of white casualties during the Yakima War. However, it would ultimately be costly for the Indians as well.

Philip Sheridan, then a second lieutenant, left Vancouver with a detachment of forty dragoons to rescue the settlers held hostage in a blockhouse at the Cascades. Under Sheridan, the troops successfully freed the settlers. Sheridan arrested thirteen Indians, and despite questionable culpability, 9th Infantry commander, Colonel Wright, ordered ten of them hanged.

> ... I have given them a lesson which they will long remember. Ten of these Indians, including their chief, have been hung by sentence of a military commission. The residue, some forty men, and seventy or eighty children have been placed on an island without any means of leaving it, and are under the observation of troops.[74]

Battle of Second Walla Walla Council, Sep. 1856

In September, Colonel Edward Steptoe repelled an attack led by Qualchan and Quit-ten-e-nock, who attacked Gov. Stevens party following an unsuccessful treaty council. Major General Wool closed the territory beyond The Dalles to white migrants and ordered Colonel Steptoe to keep settlers from returning to the Walla Walla Valley.

Yakama War (1853-1858), Washington Territory [This list is not meant to be inclusive].		
Walla Walla, Umatilla, Cayuse, Yakama Treaty with U. S. Ceding 6,000,000 Acres for $200,000 – Reservation Negotiated by Gov. Isaac Stevens and Joel Palmer		
Gold discovered in Colville area and Fraser River area of British Columbia Trespasses and depredations against Indians by whites results in war.		
October 6-8, 1855	Battle of Toppenish Creek	Indians defeat volunteers.
November 9 -10, 1855	Battle of Union Gap	Major Gabriel J. Rains, Volunteer, W.T., U.S. Army soldiers, and Oregon and Washington volunteers fail to suppress Indian War. Accidently come upon Yakamas after Battle at White River.
September 8-18, 1856	Second Walla Walla Council	Gov. Stevens tries to end war. Parley unsuccessful.
September 1856	Battle of Second Walla Walla Council	Led by Qualchan and Quit-ten-e-nock, warriors attacked Stevens' party. Colonel Edward Steptoe repelled attack.
	St. Joseph's Mission burned by Oregon militia.	

Part 15: Deadly Miscalculations

Governor Stevens and Acting Governor Mason's serious leadership problems directly affected the conduct of the war. Gov. Stevens' direction to exterminate the Indians was impossible when he was encountered by determined Indian leaders and warriors on three fronts: the Puget Sound, the Southern Plateau and later the northern Plateau. Stevens, and thus Mason, failed to effectively coordinate volunteer and U.S. Army forces. Stevens' despotic approach to the hostilities where he interfered by taking over field operations and tactics, rather than relying on the U.S. Army, contributed to poor command and control and weak performance during encounters with the unconventional Indians warriors. His vengeful approach led to the Indians forming several different alliances which were unexpected. At the end of the wars, the Indians received the concessions they had sought prior to the war.

Gov. Stevens: Strike Indians Now (Dec. 22, 1855)

Gov. Stevens response in his Dec. 22, 1855, letter to Com'r Manypenny demands the immediate continuation of war:

The country is good for a winter campaign. The Indians can and should be struck and punished now. My plan is to make no treaty whatever with the tribes now in arms; to do away entirely with the reservations guaranteed to them; to make a summary example of all the leading spirits, and to place as a conquered people, under the surveillance of troops, the remains of those tribes on reservations selected by the President, and *on such terms as the Government in its justice and mercy now vouchsafe to me*. (Emphasis added).[75]

Underestimating Your Opponent

A November 12, 1855, letter from Lt. John Withers to Adj. Gen. Col. S. Cooper evinces the miscalculation of the Army in the alliances the Indians were capable of forming:

> *As you will already have learned, the Indian war has become general, and a combination, for purposes of hostility to the whites, been formed on a scale which those most intimately acquainted with Indian character have heretofore believed impossible.* ... The total number of warriors in the field is variously estimated at from three to four thousand. (Emphasis added).[76]

Lack of Coordination between U.S. Army and Volunteers

Major General John E. Wool's Letter of Nov. 24, 1855, to Colonel J. W. Nesmith, Volunteer, W.T., reiterates the common refrain of the lack of coordination between forces and preparation for war.

> I have no authority either to employ or to receive volunteers in the service of the United States. ... Hitherto, *the operations against the Indians have been made in too much of a hurry, unable to act efficiently, and without supplies to keep the field.* Unless prepared to keep the field, it would be worse than folly to attempt to encounter the Indians with any expectation of success. (Emphasis added).[77]

Lack of Preparation

Captain E. D. Keyes wrote to Major E. D. Townsend, Assistant Adjutant General, on Nov. 27, 1855, that his forces were cut off from the rest of the world in the winter:

> To reduce the force here much lower would be imprudent, as we are threatened by the near approach of the Indians, and if the stores and ammunition at this station should be lost, we should have no other reliance. There being no steam communication between this part of the Territory and California, ***the people along Puget sound must be considered, so far as supplies and succor are concerned, as nearly cut off from all connexion during the winter months with the rest of the world***. As our pack animals are small in number and nearly broken down by hard work, and as there is a lack of feed in the places where the troops have to operate, we may be reduced shortly to the necessity of acting entirely on the defensive, and must wait for the summer and a larger force before we can subdue the Indians. The Indians are principally located in a densely wooded country, admirably adapted to ambuscades, and full of trails crossing each other in every direction. ***We have no guides that know the country, and must pursue the enemy at random***. It rains nearly the whole time, and will continue to rain or snow for three or four months to come. (Emphasis added).[78]

Lack of Discipline and Command: Scalping Redskins

The prejudices and hatreds toward Indians, which were exacerbated by military action through untrained and undisciplined settlers, acting as soldiers, is evident in Lt. Nugen's letter to Act. Gov. Mason, documenting the resolve of the volunteers to "scalp" every "Redskin" in their path.

> John Nugen, 2d Lieut. 4th Infantry, Fort Steilacoom, reported to Acting Governor C.H. Mason, W.T., on Oct. 23, 1855, that *"the men [are] in fine spirits and apparently with a determination of taking the Scalp of every Redskin who may be so unfortunate as to fall in their way."* (Emphasis added).[79]

Military Force "Totally Inadequate"

Isaac Sterrett, Commander of the U.S.S. Decatur, berthed in Seattle, wrote to Secretary of the Navy Dobbin on December 5, 1855:

> The valor and prowess of the Indians has been greatly underrated... ***The whole military resources of the Territory are totally inadequate to conduct war with success, even to afford protection to the settlers***... it is the opinion of well informed men here, that it will require regiments instead of companies, and years instead of months, to conquer these tribes. (Emphasis added).[80]

Captain E.D. Keyes, by letter dated Dec. 7, 1855, advised Acting Gov. Mason that he couldn't continue on the White, Green or Puyallup Rivers in the winter: To continue such a course will break down all our men and *effect no harm to the Indians*. Our pack animals are broken down... (Emphasis added).[81]

Acting Governor Mason's, Sept. 26, 1855, requisition for troops for Major Rains, Volunteer, W.T., was "to effect *permanent results*." (Emphasis added).[82] Lt. Slaughter's engagements certainly had no permanent effect.

Command Center Six Thousand Miles Distant

On Dec.13, 1855, Major General Wool requested the authority to receive and authorize the raising of more volunteers. He explained the need to Lt. Col. L. Thomas, Assistant Adjutant General, New York, given the extreme distance between the command center and the field of operations:

[Occupying their territory] ... cannot be accomplished as soon as I could wish, owing to the want of a sufficient number of troops, the means of transportation, and the want of clothing for the 4th infantry. It may not be improper here to remark, that I have, in no instance, received or authorized the raising of volunteers in the Pacific department. I have adhered to this rule, because I applied to the Secretary of War for the authority, which was not granted. *This authority, it appears to me, should be granted, being six thousand miles distant from the seat of government, whilst it takes two months and a half before a response can be had to communications*. An Indian war, extending from northern California through Oregon and Washington territories, has suddenly sprung upon us without the slightest warning, at the same time threatened with a war with the Indians on the Colorado, and yet I have no authority to call for volunteers, no matter how great the necessity may be. (Emphasis added).[83]

Part 16: Nisquallies Seek Peace

On Jan. 5, 1856, Leschi met with John Swan, the white warden on Fox Island. Chief Leschi asked Swan to convey his message that his people were not fighters by nature and had taken up arms only because they had been misled at Medicine Creek into accepting a hellish reservation; they wanted no more than enough space to live as they were accustomed ...they would gladly talk peace and reconciliation with any Indian agent but Simmons for whom he harbored a "deadly hatred."[84] Swan sent a messenger to Ft. Steilacoom with Leschi's peace proposal, but Captain Erasmus Keyes tried instead to capture Leschi.[85]

Shortly after the Battle of Seattle (Jan. 26, 1856), Leschi again made an offer of peace through John McLeod, a white settler who had remained near Muck Creek.[86]

Part 17: "Nothing but Death Is Mete Punishment" (Jan. 25, 1856)

Stevens addressed a packed session of the Washington Territorial Legislature, whose members he told – to "deafening cheers," according to the account in the Pioneer and Democrat newspapers – that "the war shall be prosecuted until the last hostile Indian is exterminated."

> "Let the blow be struck where it is deserved," and promised that "*nothing but death is a mete punishment for their perfidy* – their lives only shall pay the forfeit...The guilty ones shall suffer, and the remainder placed on reservations under the eye of the military." (Emphasis added).[87]

The governor then issued a call for six new companies of militiamen to replace those whose terms were expiring – the new recruits would enlist for six months.

As demonstrated in the tenor of the reports on Indians that had been captured, many officers were influenced by the virulent opinion of Gov. Stevens on how they should fight and treat Indians.

War Chief Tenaskut Murdered in Cold Blood

War Chief Tenaskut, Okanogan, was murdered in cold blood by Stevens' Volunteers on March 2, 1856. To Gov. I. I. Stevens from Gilmore Hays, Maj., Comdg, Volunteer, W.T., Camp Puyallup, March 2, 1856:

> I am able this morning to communicate the gratifying intelligence of the death of the celebrated War Chief "Te-nas-kut". He was shot this morning at the break of daylight by Private Kehl of Company D, Ninth US Infantry. Two companies of US soldiers encamped on the evening of the 28th instant a half a mile east of our camp. At the break of day an Indian was seen at a distance of one hundred yards by the sentinel approaching the camp in the most stealthy manner, occasionally beckoning to others in his rear to advance. When he drew within forty yards, the sentinel fired his ball taking effect in the shoulder and ranging to the hip. He was then brought into camp. He told them, he was ***"Tenaskut"—that he wanted them to kill him—that his voice was for war and that the voice of his people was for war that his Tillicum's were men and would avenge his death***. He urged those that accompanied him to come to his relief and fight to the last. The Indian guide recognized him as "Tenaskut", also Mr. Brannan and others of the Volunteers. Of the death of "Tenaskut" there is not doubt. Colonel Casey of the Ninth Infantry ordered that he be hanged immediately. A rope was placed about his neck, and while looking for a tree on which to suspend him, the appearance of Indians in the vicinity changed the purpose and the savage murderer ***"Tenaskut" was shot through the brain***. His gun was a fine rifle with fifty rounds of powder and ball. He had on his person a butcher knife and a spear. The same party have doubtless been hanging about our camp every night since our arrival, but for some reason have not approached so near our sentinels. (Emphasis added).[88]

Stevens Orders Chief Leschi's Hanging by Executioner

By letter dated June 18, 1856, Gov. Stevens ordered Col. Wright to render up murderers and instigators of war for punishment – "Leschi, Nelson, Kitsap and Quiemuth and to suggest no arrangement be made which shall save their necks from the Executioner."[89]

Col. Wright refused. Gov. Stevens denounced his refusal by letter dated October 4, 1856:

> I have received your letter of this date, in answer to my requisition for the delivery of Leschi, Nelson, Qui-e- muth, Kitsap and Stehi, to be sent to the Sound to be tried by the civil authority. ... ***These men are notorious murderers, and committed their acts of atrocity under circumstances of treachery and blood-thirstiness almost beyond example***. All belong to bands with whom treaties have been made ... I am of opinion that men guilty of such acts should be at least tried, and if convicted, punished ... Gov. Stevens (Emphasis added).[90]

Major Gen. Wool backed Col. Wright. In a letter to Lt. Col Casey, he said, "His removal from office of governor alone can prevent it [a return to war]." Major Gen. Wool expressed regret over Stevens' vindictive spirit. He said, "Do not fail to give protection... to Leschi and all Indians peaceably inclined to the whites...if Stevens' militia return to the fray arrest them."[91]

Stevens placed a reward of $500, or fifty blankets for an Indian, for whoever would bring in Leschi. Leschi was captured by his nephew, Sluggia, for a reward. Sluggia was later killed by Leschi Lieutenant Wa He Lut.

On November 3, 1856, Stevens summoned a grand jury to consider a charge against Leschi for the ambush murder one year earlier of Abram Moses. Leschi was initially indicted and tried in Pierce County, Washington. However, the judge declared a mistrial when the jury could not reach a unanimous verdict.

Leschi was then tried a second time and found guilty in Thurston County, Washington, (home of Olympia, the territorial capitol) and sentenced to death by hanging. The Thurston County court also denied various post-trial motions. The conviction was then affirmed by the territorial supreme court. (Emphasis added).[92]

The military at Ft. Steilacoom refused to hang Leschi so the Washington state authorities built a scaffold a mile east of the fort and hanged him February 19, 1858.[93]

Part 18: Political Infighting

Governor Stevens was involved in ugly political fighting regarding the Indian wars with (1) Major General John Wool, the U.S. Army Pacific Coast Commander; (2) the Commissioner of Indian Affairs; (3) settlers; (4) the state judiciary; and (5) President Pierce.

Dissension Between Governor Stevens and Major General John Wool

Major General John Wool, the U.S. Army Pacific Coast Commander, strongly disapproved of the civilian militia, considering them little better than vigilantes, generally ill-trained and poorly disciplined. He considered them a greater threat to the peace given their license to kill, plunder and profiteer. Volunteer Major Rains complained to the Governor when Major General Wool ordered him to cease and desist from any further action.

To Gov. Stevens from Major Rains, Volunteer, W.T., Jan. 18, 1856:

...I beg leave to state in reply that from the instructions received from Major General Wool, commanding Department of the Pacific, and his policy pursued, I am left no discretion nor judgment in the matters requiring the action you consider necessary. *The General has thought proper to put a stop upon my course of action* in the Campaign against the hostile Indians, and it only remains for me to carry out his views entirely... (Emphasis added).[94]

Major General John Wool Pronounces Stevens' Barbarous Determination to Exterminate Indians a Deterrent to Peace

Major General Wool wrote to Gov. Stevens on Feb. 12, 1856, that the war could be brought to a close within a few months "provided the extermination of the Indians, which I do not approve of, is not determined on, and private war prevented, and the volunteers withdrawn from the Walla Walla country."[95]

> The crux of the controversy was Wool's conviction that Governor Stevens and Oregon Governor Curry were bent upon exterminating the Indians.[96]

Governor Stevens Rudely Complains to Major Gen. Wool and Appeals to Secretary of War

By letter dated March 20, 1856, Stevens complained to, and insulted, Major Gen. Wool:

> I warn you, sir, that unless your course is changed, you will have difficulties [with the Territories of Washington and Oregon] whose services you have ignored, whose people you have calumniated, and *whose respect you have long since ceased to possess*. You have erred in your judgment as to volunteers being needed at all here... (Emphasis added).[97]

He also sent a stinging rebuke of Major Gen. Wool to Sec. of War Jefferson.

October 22, 1856

> Is, sir, the army sent here to protect our people, and to punish Indian tribes who, without cause, and in cold blood, and in spite of solemn treaties, murder our people, burn our houses and wipe out our entire settlements?
>
> *Is it the duty of Gen. Wool and his officers to refuse to cooperate with me in my appropriate duties as Supt. of Indian Affairs, and thus practically to assume these duties to themselves.*

Is it the duty of Gen. Wool, in his scheme to pacifying the Indians, to trample down the laws of Congress—to issue edicts prohibiting settlers returning to their claims, and thus for at least one county, Walla Walla, make himself dictator of the country? (Emphasis added).[98]

Dissension between Gov. Stevens and Commissioner of Indian Affairs

Stevens was unmoved by advice from Commissioner Manypenny urging him to "avoid indictive and unnecessary bloodshed" and to bear in mind that Indians "who were criminal may be treated with magnanimity after laying down arms."[99]

In Stevens' March 9, 1856, letter to Com'r Manypenny, he stated that surrendering Indians would be treated in a "spirit of humanity and kindness."

> The Indians were on the rampage ... threatening "entirely unprotected" settlements, targeting supply trains, inciting hostility among friendlies by "wiles and falsehoods" – all requiring that the white community be saved from "the treacherous and ferocious Indians who have barbarously murdered men, women and children and laid waste nearly two entire counties...and whilst they shall be made to unconditionally surrender and their leaders to be made to suffer death, the Indians generally shall be dealt with in a spirit of humanity and kindness."[100]

All Indians Are Enemies to Governor Stevens

> At the same time, Stevens spurred his volunteers to a new level of death by issuing his unit commanders a license that all Indians not in internment camps were legitimate targets: "All Indians found in your field of operations...are to be considered as enemies."[101]

Dissension between Gov. Stevens and Settlers: Compulsory Military Service

> Stevens pointed out that while some white farmers remained on their claims unmolested, others were in blockhouses. "There is no thing in my humble opinion as neutrality in an Indian war, and whoever can remain on his claim unmolested is an ally of the enemy and must be dealt with."[102]

On March 9, 1856, Isaac W. Smith, acting Secretary of the Territory, by order of Gov. Stevens, compelled L. A. Smith, John McLeod, Charles Wren and others in their vicinity, to leave their claims and reside either at Olympia, Nisqually or Steilacoom.

> A dozen Muck Creek white farmers were taken into custody.[103] Five of them, including John McLeod, returned to their farms only to be recaptured, labeled prisoners of war, and told they would be tried for treason—a capital crime—not by a civil court but by a five-man military tribunal chosen by Stevens. The Muck Creek Five hired a lawyer who got a judge to order the release of the prisoners.[104]

Dissension between Gov. Stevens and Judiciary: Stevens Declares Martial Law

> To keep the Muck Creek Five from being freed, the next day, April 14, 1856, Stevens decreed martial law in Pierce County, suspending all functions of civil government, including courts and called the prisoners "evil-disposed persons."[105]

Judge Lander, Chief Justice of Washington's Supreme Court, held firm that he would hold court and rule on the Muck Creek Five's request. The Judge wrote that Stevens' decree "shows no necessity whatever for taking the law into his own hands."

Gov. Stevens sent Frank Shaw to stop the court so martial law could not be challenged. Judge Lander ordered every able-bodied male over sixteen in the county to attend court as posse comitatus to protect civil law. Thirty citizens, many of them lawyers, defended the court and civil rule over martial law, among them George Gibbs.

> Shaw said he would arrest the Judge and take him to the fort. ***Judge Lander submitted at gunpoint to Shaw and the militia.*** Steilacoom, in shock over the thuggish tactic that shut down the court, held a torchlight parade and street rally.[106]

The lawyers of the county met to protest the arrest of Judge Lander and documented in writing the Proceedings of a meeting of the bar, third Judicial district, Washington Territory, on the arrest of the honorable Edward Lander, chief justice of said Territory, and John M. Chapman, clerk of the district court, by an armed force, under orders of Governor Isaac Stevens together with the proceedings of a mass meeting of citizens of Pierce County, Washington Territory:

This day marks an era in territorial history. For the first time in the annals of our country does the exhibition present itself of an armed force marching into a court of justice, and while the presiding judge thereof is in the exercise of judicial authority, the court is overawed, its judge taken from the bench, its clerk arrested, the records seized, and they removed by an armed force out of the county in which by law the court was to be held.[107]

Resolved, That we look upon the act this day perpetrated by an armed force, under the authority of Governor I. I. Stevens, in arresting the judge and clerk of this judicial district, as an outrage, which, if tamely submitted to, would be entirely subversive of our liberties.[108]

Gibbs drew up a petition to President Pierce, attacking Gov. Stevens for his "flagrant usurpation of power" and his despotic conduct. The citizens drew up a petition as well: Resolved, That the tyrannical and despotic acts of the executive of this Territory are such usurpations of law and authority as require the interposition of the supreme authority of the United States…[109]

On May 10, 1856, Gov. Stevens submitted to President Pierce a lengthy document entitled: "Vindication of Governor Stevens for proclaiming and enforcing martial law in Pierce County, Washington Territory."[110]

Judge Lander was released after a few days in custody and was able to open court in Thurston County. **On May 14, 1856, Gov. Stevens declared martial law there as well.** According to Richard Kluger, the Judge issued a bench warrant to Gov. Stevens. The U.S. Territorial Marshall assigned to serve the summons on the Governor found the door to his office barred by as many as a dozen of his bulkiest loyalists among them militiamen, including Adjutant General James Tilton and Tony Rabbeson. When the Territorial Marshall forced the issue, a fistfight broke out, with Gov. Stevens himself reportedly part of the scuffle, and the summons went unserved.[111]

The militiamen then marched to the house that served as Judge Lander's court and, finding that the Judge had barricaded himself in his clerk's room, broke down the door and for the second time in eight days hauled away the Chief Justice of the Territory. The Chief Justice's defiance landed him in the territorial jail at Camp Montgomery, the militia headquarters, in a cell alongside the Muck Creek Five.

The following week, Judge Chenowith, his health restored, returned to his courtroom in Steilacoom and denounced Gov. Stevens for his continuing usurpation of executive power. Judge Chenowith issued a fresh habeas corpus writ ordering Shaw to produce the prisoners in his courtroom. Gov. **Stevens then ordered Maxon to send thirty volunteers and arrest the Judge if he reopened court on May 24, 1856**. Judge Chenowith called on the law-abiding citizenry to protect his courtroom, asking the Pierce County Sheriff to round up enough power to form a defense posse.

The Judge further enlisted the help of Colonel Casey of Fort Steilacoom. Between fifty and sixty citizens had mustered in front of the courthouse when a force of thirty volunteer militia approached. In the end, the prisoners were brought to the county courthouse and the charges were dropped.

On May 28, 1856, Gov. Stevens ended his protracted tantrum by rescinding the martial law decree.

In July 1856, Judge Lander issued a warrant for Gov. Stevens' arrest on a contempt-of-court charge for having refused to accept the summons and explain why he had ignored Judge Chenowith's original habeas corpus writ. Gov. Stevens momentarily submitted and appeared before Judge Lander, but when the Judge found him guilty and fined him a token fifty dollars to establish the principle that no official, not even a governor, could flout the law with impunity, Gov. Stevens invoked the powers of his office to pardon himself temporarily until President Pierce had an opportunity to review the entire matter.

Dissension between Gov. Stevens and President Pierce: No Justification for Martial Law

> A Sep. 12, 1856, letter to Gov. Stevens from Secretary of State Marcy advised him of President Pierce's opinion: "After a full consideration of them [the facts relating to the declaration of martial law], the President has not been able to find in the case you have presented a justification for that extreme measure."[112]

Part 19: Post-War

> Gov. Stevens went to Fox Island to end the war and grant the expanded reservations. Com'r Manypenny *laid the blame* for the need for the decision to expand the reservations due to the fact that they were initially of insufficient size *clearly on Gov. Stevens*. Secretary McClelland recommended the President approve the changes, which he did.[113]

The Puyallups were given an additional 36 square miles. The Nisqually's new reservation was 7.5 square miles of fertile bottomland and adjacent prairie for about four miles from where Muck Creek joined into a point close to the estuary.

Indian Internment Camps

Michael T. Simmons, an Indian agent appointed by Gov. Stevens, had interned Indians along the Pacific Coast during the Indian wars. A decision would have to be made regarding their return to their homelands.

Indian Internment Camps		
Name of Camp	No. Interred	Tribal Affiliations
Bellingham Bay	847	
Holmes Harbor	1400	
Olympic Peninsula	1522	
Penn's Cove	1300	
Ft. Kitsap	942	
Squaxin Island	460	
Fox Island	1200	
Fort Steilacoom	1200	Shattmahmish, Shamahmish, Puyallup and Nisqually
Squaxin Island	460	Squaxin, Nisquallies, and Sahawamish

Fox Island had quartered hostile Indians. Many of them died. Sixty Indians were shot and hanged.[114]

Stevens Elected to Congress

In 1857, Stevens campaigned for Washington Territory's lone delegate to Congress. He won and left for Washington, DC. Fayette McMullin replaced him as Governor. While in Congress, Stevens pursued a claim for $6 million dollars owed to Oregon and Washington as a result of the Indian wars. Speech to Congress, May 31, 1858.[115]

Seattle Removes Indians

On February 7, 1865, the Seattle Board of Trustees passed Ordinance No. 5, calling for the removal of Indians from the town. Also, a proposed reservation along the Duwamish River for the Duwamish Tribe, near Seattle, was blocked by non-Native residents in 1866.

Part 20: Puget Sound – Business as Usual

In *Time, Tide and Timber, A Century of Pope & Talbot* by Edwin Coman & Helen Gibbs, the impact of the Indian Puget of Sound War on Pope & Talbot's business is noted as *"of very minor import."* A great deal of property had been destroyed, but few people had lost their lives. … ***While history, was being made, the Puget Mill Company continued to manufacture lumber and to prepare to manufacture more lumber***. (Emphasis added).[116]

Pope & Talbot Partner Advocated Indiscriminately Hanging Indians

Even though Indian warfare ceased, an underlying brutal hostility still existed among the colonial settlers. The lumber mogul, Josiah Keller, a Pope & Talbot partner, advocated indiscriminately shooting and hanging Indians.

> The final battle occurred across the bay from Port Gamble. All that remained was to devise a permanent solution to the Indian problem, a solution that was both clear and bloody to Josiah Keller. "I had hoped that the necessity of destroying these miserable creatures with powder & ball would never occur here," he had written at the beginning of the war. By the end of the fighting, though, he was sure of what must be done: ***"My doctrine & I think it would be my example ... would be to shoot & hang without regard to treaty or treaties." Moreover, the "bad white men in the Territory," defined as those who had befriended Indians, "should be killed with them."*** Amounting to a campaign of genocide in the service of commerce, Keller's proposal was too extreme for most Indian-haters, who were satisfied with the surrender and execution of native leaders and the confinement of the tribes on reservations.[117]

Keller would write "I shall ever feel, that we, the P. Mill Co. have done but a duty they owed to themselves & their business, & the inhabitants of the Territory generally in furnishing supplies & necessaries for the Vol. force."[118]

Part 21: Coeur d'Alene/Spokane War

Battle of Pine Creek (May 15, 1858)

Under pressure from local miners, Col. Steptoe responded to a petition for military troops by preparing an ill-equipped march from Fort Walla Walla to the Colville country. The Coeur d'Alene Indians didn't understand why the soldiers were traveling through their country, when a more direct route was available outside of their country.

Ultimately, Steptoe concluded that his troops were outnumbered and decided to retreat. The full retreat began on May 17. Battles broke out during the retreat and several casualties resulted on both sides. As the sun set, Steptoe's troops found themselves surrounded and nearly out of ammunition. Under cover of night, the troops managed to slip past their enemies and made a run for the Snake River crossing.

> Col. Steptoe was criticized for this embarrassing defeat. He was ill after the battle and was unable to participate in any subsequent action. He resigned his commission in 1861 and died four years later, at the age of forty-nine.[119]

Battle of Four Lakes (Sep. 1, 1858)

> In a punitive military expedition after Col. Steptoe's defeat, 500 of Col. George Wright's troops defeated the Spokane, Coeur d'Alene, Yakama and their allies after a seven-hour battle at Four Lakes on September 1, 1858. Colonel Wright attributed his military success at the Battle of Four Lakes to the long-range rifles which fired newly developed minié balls.[120]

> His troops captured and hanged or shot twenty-four principal Indian leaders, along Latah Creek which was later called Hangman Creek. They shot 900 Indian ponies. Yakama Chief Kamiakin fled to Canada.[121]

Battle of Spokane Plains (Sep. 5, 1858)

In a last stand by the Indians, U.S. Army soldiers under Colonel George Wright defeated them at the Battle of Spokane Plains. The soldiers and the warriors fought over a distance of 14 miles and one soldier was wounded.[122]

Spokane/Coeur d'Alene War (Coeur d'Alene, Kalispell, Spokane, Palouse and Northern Paiute) [This list is not meant to be inclusive].		
Event	Date	Result
Battle of Pine Creek	May 15, 1858	Col. Steptoe forced to retreat.
Battle of Four Lakes	September 1, 1858	Yakama Chief Kamiakin, fled to Canada, 24 other chiefs were captured and then hanged or shot.
Battle of Spokane Plains	September 5, 1858	Final stand – U.S. long range artillery, able to fight at distance.

Part 22: Pacific Northwest Ruled by Timber Speculation

The name of the timber game in the Pacific Northwest was speculation. Industry titans, such as Friedrich Weyerhaeuser, focused on acquiring and concentrating as much timberland as possible.

With the rise in timber prices, came speculation.

> The undeveloped markets of the Pacific Northwest ... offered timber speculators a chance to buy hundreds-of-thousands of acres of forestland at bargain prices. After purchasing their land all they had to do was wait for the lumber market to improve and they could unload the land at a significant profit, all without the cost of building mills and establishing logging operations. Speculation, the availably of forestland, and the relative ease with which speculators could acquire that land would, in a short time, create an entirely new geography of landholding in the Northwest's forests.
>
> The strangers arrived in the Northwest at a peculiar moment in the history of forest management and regulation, when American control had been established but propriety law was unenforceable. Although the federal government and railroads had laid claim to what, for centuries, had been Native lands, the earliest laws regulating timberland ownership were quite loose since the state hadn't yet established a regulatory structure. This meant, in practice, that *throughout the mid- to late-nineteenth century, the trees belonged to anyone willing to take them*. (Emphasis added).[123]

Part 23: Timber Companies Grow by Violating/Evading Laws

Pope & Talbot Partner Indicted and Found Guilty of Theft of Timber

Arriving on Puget Sound in the summer of 1861, the new United States attorney, John McGilvra, discovered that "there is now and has been for years past great and continued trespass upon the government lands, in the cutting and removing of timber by Mill Companies and those who supply said Companies with logs."

He quickly secured the indictment of Josiah Keller, Marshall Blinn, and several other lumbermen for theft of timber. Returning from court, Pope & Talbot partner, Keller informed his partners in the Puget Mill Company that he had been "Indicted for $10,000, which if we are eventually convicted for, the fine will be three times the amt. ... [if] in the end we are obliged to pay $30,000 or $40,000 & costs, you will probably find it out."[124]

U.S. Attorney McGilvra's ambition for advancement, wealth and political office resulted in his retreat from an aggressive prosecution of the timber laws. He yielded to public opinion that "vigorous prosecution" would force sawmills to go out of business.

In a surviving letter, though, Cyrus Walker notes that "Mr. McGilvery is evidently in the market and I think he puts to high a price on his services," suggesting a corrupt relationship between the federal prosecutor and the industry.

Those indicted for trespass in 1861 received only modest fines. Edwin G. Ames of the Puget Mill Company later described the court proceedings, as recounted to him by Walker. "At a time agreed upon," Ames wrote, "they appeared in court, plead guilty to the charge of stealing Government timber, were fined a nominal fine, and sentenced to one day in jail, and *I have heard that after the sentence was passed that with the judge and the sheriff, and a box of cigars, they went into jail, turned the key, lighted their cigars, staid a few minutes, and then went out, having satisfied the law.*" (Emphasis added).[125]

U.S. Attorney McGilvra decided that the government should just assess a charge for timber illegally removed from its lands. While a fee of fifty cents per thousand feet was ordered to be assessed, McGilvra reduced it to fifteen cents.

Fraud under Timber and Stone Act of 1878

Robert Ficken in *The Forested Land* further describes the fraudulent methods used by Puget Sound mill companies to get around the limitations in the Timber and Stone Act.

To the everlasting fortune of the Puget Sound mill firms, the provisions of the Timber and Stone Act were easily circumvented. ...[126] To disguise the identity of the ultimate purchasers, deeds were passed from entrymen to the mill companies through third parties. Land titles were transferred from the mills to individuals or to new companies especially created for the purpose of owning land. Urging speedy action on these matters, William H. Talbot, the president of Pope & Talbot since 1881, noted that "it is a very serious question & we must act as soon as possible & get things into shape."[127]

Bribery of Indian Agents

Outright bribery, though, was the principal weapon wielded by lumbermen. In the summer of 1883, for example, Interior Department agent T. H. Cavanaugh was sent to Puget Sound to investigate fraudulent entries. William Renton informed Cyrus Walker that the agent was a close friend of Seattle attorney H. G. Struve and that several of the mills had paid Struve "to have him use his influence to present the matter in as favorable a light as possible to the Agent whom he (Struve) thinks can be fixed." Subsequently, a Renton assistant wrote that Cavanaugh had "been entertained by Gamble and us and we know him to be all right."[128]

Will Talbot, for one, wished to "forever put to rest the thieving of Government agents in blackmailing large timber claim owners."[129]

Improper Influence of Secretary of Interior Planned

The most complex of such schemes involved an effort to persuade William F. Vilas, secretary of the interior in the Cleveland Administration, to revoke the suspension of Timber and Stone entries and approve contested land patents ...[130] [The] Puget Mill Company contributed $1,500 to a lumbermen's fund for this purpose.[131]

Talbot Circumvents State Land Limits

In February 1888, the Legislature for the Territory of Washington passed a law providing that a corporation could not own more than 5,000 acres of land, unless the land had been acquired before 1886. ... The Puget Mill Company which owned considerably more than 150,000 acres, had acquired some 3,100 acres between 1886 and 1888. C.F.A. Talbot, as president of the Puget Mill Company, wrote Cyrus Walker on March 3, 1888, to transfer the 3,100 acres to the Puget Sound Commercial Company. ... If the company acquired more timberlands, their ownership could be registered to affiliated companies.[132]

Part 24: Washington Admitted as State in 1889

With Washington's population growth fanned by its commercial success, it was admitted as a state in 1889. Seattle was the largest city and the chief supply point for the gold rush to the Yukon territory in Alaska.

Further Reconnaissance of Pacific Northwest: 1890 Gilman and O'Neil Expeditions

Further exploration expeditions documented the natural resources of the Pacific Northwest. Two expedition teams, that of C. A. and S. C. Gilman and of Lieutenant Joseph P. O'Neil, were instructed to "make a reconnaissance and find out, if practicable, what the country was, its character and its resources in case of military emergency." They prepared a complete and detailed description of the topography, vegetation, wildlife and geology of the country they explored.[133]

Mineralogist, Nelson Linsley, while the trip was in progress, wrote: "Curse this country! I have prospected all the mountains of the United States and I never saw one to equal this in difficulty of progression and at the same time in lack of any valuable minerals."[134]

Part 25: Timber Industry Surges

With the Indians forced on reserves, the unimpeded timber industry grew as railroad transport became available and new technologies developed in logging and milling.

Railroads spurred timber production in several ways. As reported by the Center for the Study of the Pacific Northwest, University of Washington:

> First, they were enormous consumers of wood products themselves, using 20-25 percent of the annual timber production between the 1870s and 1900 for railroad ties, bridges, stations, fences, and fuel. Second, railways enabled loggers to penetrate deeper into the forests by providing access to many more trees than before. Third, they imported to the Pacific Northwest more machinery and more people than ever before and put them to work in the timber industry. ... Fifth, they lowered the cost of transporting logs out of the forests to mills, and from mills to the eastern states. In short, railroads were machines that revolutionized the timber industry.[135]

In 1881, the Northern Pacific Railway reached Spokane. In 1883, James J. Hills' Great Northern Railway reached Lowell.

Weyerhaeuser's Bold Arrival on Scene (1900)

On January 3, 1900, the timber industry in Washington underwent one of the biggest changes in its history. Frederick Weyerhaeuser purchased 900,000 acres of land from the Northern Pacific railroad. On that day, Midwestern lumber magnate in the largest private land transaction in American history to that point in time. He paid $6 an acre. "It would seem as though these parties," observed William H. Talbot, the president of Pope & Talbot, "were intent upon capturing a great amount of timber land, and it may be their idea to eventually control the business."[136]

The company was the foremost participant in the migration of Great Lakes lumbermen to the Northwest following the completion of transcontinental railroad lines to Puget Sound. Its incorporation dramatized the growing concentration of timberland in the hands of large holders, transforming the focus of the industry from sawmills and manufacturing to land and speculation in timber.[137]

Other investors, including such important figures as William E. Boeing, Congressman Joseph Fordney of Michigan, and R. D. Merrill, became familiar sights on Puget Sound and Grays Harbor, buying up timber claims from small holders. Agents for John D. Rockefeller, E. H. Harriman, and English syndicates supposedly were at work across the region. "All the choice timber lands are being taken up by capitalists who are able to hold for a higher rate of stumpage," observed Cyrus Walker, manager of the Puget Mill Company and the leading lumberman in Washington. George H. Emerson, the most important operator on Grays Harbor, noted that there were "millions of dollars in the air ready to light on any tracts of timber that can be had at reasonable prices."[138]

Weyerhaeuser's focus on holding timber land, and not immediately harvesting it recognizes the economic significance of the potential future income to be derived from the resource itself. By deferring present income, Weyerhaeuser gambled that more income could be had from controlling access to the resource. Timber could be released into the market based on prices of the commodity. Weyerhaeuser played to the scarcity of the resource itself. By managing the resource, he was establishing the foundation for the long-term sustainability, profitability, growth and vitality of his business.

Weyerhaeuser operated on the principle that "the only times he ever lost money on timberlands were the times when he didn't buy…"[139]

In Ficken's study of the Pacific Northwest Timber Industry, he writes:

The arrival of Weyerhaeuser signaled the beginning of the era when control of timber, not ownership of sawmills, was the key to success in the Northwest forest industry. ... Henceforth, those companies that had failed to take advantage of the once cheap prices of timber to acquire extensive holdings were doomed to extinction ...[140]

Weyerhaeuser knew profit was derived from a diminishing timber supply. With the growth of the country, the demand for more timber and its further concentration and control was tied to timberland ownership.

Weyerhaeuser's company brought economies of scale that modernized the industry. Part of the company's deal with Northern Pacific included low shipping rates to the eastern markets. At the same time, the formerly thriving lumber industries in Wisconsin and Minnesota were in decline, due to deforestation. Thus, the national prominence of the Pacific Northwest timber industry was ensured.
Eventually, the Weyerhaeuser interests would accumulate some two million acres and possess a legion of mills in Oregon, Washington, and Idaho.

Washington 1st in Timber Production in 1905

By 1905, the state ranked first in timber production, and it continued to lead the nation for every year but one until the 1930s.

Part 26: Forest Conservation

Many Indian Nations have been concerned that forest conservation occurred at their expense, negatively impacting their land and resources.

Olympic National Park (1897, 1909, 1938)

Eight federally recognized tribes (the Port Gamble S'Klallam Tribe, Skokomish Indian Tribe, Jamestown S'Klallam Tribe, Lower Elwha Klallam Tribe, Makah Tribe, Quileute Nation, Hoh Tribe, and Quinault Indian Nation) have, since time immemorial, sustained ties to the Olympic Peninsula. Hundreds of archeological and ethnographic sites attest to more than 12,000 years of continuous use and connection.[141] Under the federal stimulus for forest conservation, the tribes ceded Olympic Peninsula lands in three separate treaties. Tribal lands were incorporated first in the 1897 Olympic Forest Reserve, then the smaller 1909 Mount Olympus National Monument and finally the expanded 1938 Olympic National Park. In exchange for most of their land, the Indians received three reservations, money and schools as well as other aid for a period of twenty years.[141]

To understand what was forfeited by the tribes, the Olympic National Park description follows:

> Encompassing nearly a million acres, the park protects a vast wilderness, thousands of years of human history, and several distinctly different ecosystems, including glacier-capped mountains, old-growth temperate rain forests, and over 70 miles of wild coastline.
>
> Olympic National Park contains the finest remaining stands of old-growth temperate coniferous forest in the contiguous United States, including one of the finest remaining examples of temperate rain forest in the United States. These extensive forests of ancient and immense trees provide important habitat for complex communities of plants and animals, including a number of imperiled species.
>
> The Olympic rocky intertidal community is considered to be one of the most complex and diverse shoreline communities in the United States. Olympic National Park includes about 1,400 square miles of intertidal, island, and shoreline habitat and contributes to a large, protected landscape of coastal and ocean habitats, including approximately 64 miles of coastline, 52 of which are along designated or potential wilderness.[142]

USGS Timber Survey of Olympic Forest Reserve (1897–1900)

> The surveying team of Arthur Dodwell and Theodore F. Rixon, under the direction of geographer Henry Gannett of the U.S. Geological Survey, surveyed 3,483 square miles of the newly created Olympic Forest Reserve between 1897 and 1900. They reported on "the timbered, burned, cut and nontimbered areas; the depth of humus and forest litter; the total stand of timber and the principle species recognized by the lumber trade; the average height, diameter and clear length; and the percentage of dead and diseased trees." Ninety-seven townships, or partial townships, were surveyed in all. Based on field notes taken by the Dodwell-Rixon team, only sixteen square miles had been logged; nearly sixty-one billion board feet of timber remained undisturbed.[143]

Dodwell and Rixon noted that, although very little of the reserve had been logged to date because major rivers were unsuitable for driving logs, railroads could be easily built up almost any of the rivers, particularly those on the west side of the reserve. They reported, "Taken as a whole, there is very little timber on the west slope of the reserve that can not easily be reached, and when the time comes when that quality of timber is marketable there are few reserves, if any, that can be logged so easily and thoroughly as the western slope of the Olympic Forest Reserve." According to Dodwell and Rixon, only in the higher parts of the mountains, where the quality of the timber was poor, would railroad construction be difficult and expensive. They observed, "it will probably be many generations before the timber in these regions will be needed."[144]

Clear-Cutting – "I Hope The Son-Of-A-Bitch Who Logged That Is Roasting In Hell"

When President Franklin Roosevelt toured Washington's Olympic Peninsula in 1937, he passed miles of raw and ugly clear-cuts of timber. According to historian Murray Morgan (1916-2000), then a young reporter on the peninsula, Roosevelt said to two Washington Congressmen, Representatives Monrad Wallgren and Martin Smith on the tour with him, "I hope the son-of-a-bitch who logged that is roasting in hell."[145]

Notes: Washington: Governor Stevens' Private Wars of Extermination

1. http://www.lewis-and-clark-expedition.org/lewis-clark-journals/lewis-clark-journals-trees.htm (accessed online May 21, 2022).
2. George Simpson Describes the Importance of the Timber Trade for the HBC, 1828–1829 Frederick Merk, ed., Fur Trade and Empire: George Simpson's Journal, rev. ed. (Cambridge, Mass.: Harvard University Press, 1968), pp. 298, 309-10. https://www.washington.edu/uwired/outreach/cspn/Website/Classroom%20Materials/Curriculum%20Packets/Evergreen%20State/Documents/document%201.html (accessed online May 27, 2022).
3. Id.
4. https://www.washington.edu/uwired/outreach/cspn/Website/Classroom%20Materials/Curriculum%20Packets/Evergreen%20State/Section%20II.html (accessed online July 15, 2022).
5. Edmond S. Meany, ed., "Diary of Wilkes in the Northwest," Washington Historical Quarterly 16 (1925): 56-58, 140-45, 297-98.

6. Asa Mercer, Washington Territory: The Great Northwest, Her Material Resources and Claims to Emigration (Utica, N.Y.: L. C. Childs, 1865), pp. 8, 17-18, 22-23.
7. Id.
8. Ezra Meeker, Washington Territory West of the Cascade Mountains: Containing a Description of Puget Sound, and Rivers Emptying into It, the Lower Columbia, Shoalwater Bay, Gray's Harbor; Timber, Lands, Climate, Fisheries, Ship Building, Coal Mines, Market Reports, Trade, Labor, Population, Wealth and Resources (Olympia: Washington State Transcript Office, 1870), pp. 18-19.
9. Edmund S. Meany, selected press releases, 1891–1893, compiled under the title "Washington World's Fair Commission," Special Collections, University of Washington Libraries, Seattle.
10. Eugene Ellicott. Puget Sound Nomenclature and General Description: An Interview and Notes. Olympia, Wash. United States, n.p, 1878, p. 9.
11. Olympic Historic Resource Study III. SKID ROADS AND SLUICE BOXES: COMMERCIAL DEVELOPMENT AND INDUSTRIAL DEVELOPMENT https://www.nps.gov/parkhistory/online_books/olym/hrs/chap3.htm#:~:text=In%20the%20mid%201840s%20mill,59%2C%2097%2D98) (accessed online May 21, 2022).
12. Id.
13. Whitten, David O., and Bessie Emrick Whitten. The Birth of Big Business in the United States, 1860–1914: Commercial, Extractive, and Industrial Enterprise. Greenwood Publishing Group, 200, p. 102.
14. The Port Gamble S'Klallam Cultural History https://www.pgst.nsn.us/content/pdfs/Cultural-history.pdf (accessed online July 14, 2022).
15. Id.
16. Olympic Peninsula Intertribal Cultural Advisory Committee. Native peoples of the Olympic Peninsula: who we are. University of Oklahoma Press, 2003, p. 55.
17. H. H. [Helen Hunt Jackson], "Puget Sound," Atlantic Monthly 51 (February 1883): pp. 218-31. Note: Under the Indian Reorganization Act of 1934, the U.S. Government bought 1,234 acres from Puget Mill Co. for the tribe.
18. Port Gamble S'Klallam Tribe Treaty of Point No Point https://www.pgst.nsn.us/land-and-people-and-lifestyle/treaty-of-point-no-point (accessed online July 14, 2022).
19. Gordon, Greg. When Money Grew on Trees: AB Hammond and the Age of the Timber Baron. University of Oklahoma Press, 2014, p. 63.

20. Washington Public Documents, Volume 2. Washington (State), 1898, p. 114, https://books.google.com/books?id=fvZDAQAAMAAJ&pg=RA1-PA114&lpg=RA1-PA114&dq=Puget+Shipping+Co.,+Puget+Trading+Co.,+Puget+Mercantile+Co.,+and+Puget+Commercial+Co&source=bl&ots=xnBZIOGi9D&sig=ACfU3U3oGDdssAT8_bWb20yi50MQj24xEw&hl=en&sa=X&ved=2ahUKEwjzqLm3o_v4AhXaAzQIHWfICKsQ6AF6BAgqEAM#v=onepage&q=Puget%20Shipping%20Co.%2C%20Puget%20Trading%20Co.%2C%20Puget%20Mercantile%20Co.%2C%20and%20Puget%20Commercial%20Co&f=false (accessed online July 15, 2022).
21. http://www.washington.edu/uwired/outreach/cspn/Website/Classroom%20Materials/Curriculum%20Packets/Evergreen%20State/Documents/document%2012.html (accessed online July 14, 2022).
22. Ficken, Robert E. The Forested Land: A History of Lumbering in Western Washington. University of Washington Press, 2012, p. 33.
23. Thomas R. Cox, Mills and Markets: A History of the Pacific Coast Lumber Industry 1900, Emil and Kathleen Sick Lecture-Book Series in Western History and Biography (Seattle: University of Washington Press, 1974), pp. 116-21.
24. H. H. [Helen Hunt Jackson], "Puget Sound," Atlantic Monthly 51 (February 1883): pp. 218-219.
25. Report of the Commissioner of Indian Affairs to the Secretary of the Interior, Office of Indian Affairs, United States. 1853, Robert Armstrong, Printer, pp. 214-215.
26. Gates, Charles Marvin. "Messages of the Governors of the Territory of Washington to the Legislative Assembly, 1854–1889." (1940), p. 4.
27. Letter dated August 18, 1853, from Secretary of the Interior McClelland to Commissioner of Indian Affairs Manypenny. Indian tribes west of Missouri and Iowa. Message from the President of the United States, transmitting a report in regard to the extinguishment of the Indian title to lands west of Missouri and Iowa, &c, H.R. Exec. Doc. No. 84, 33d Cong., 1st Sess. (1854), p. 4.
28. Letter dated August 30, 1854. https://www.washingtonhistory.org/wp-content/uploads/2020/04/chehalisCouncil-1.pdf (accessed online April 13, 2022).
29. Treaty Minutes: Transcription of Commission Journal and Negotiations with the Klallam, Skokomish, Twana, and Chemakum; George Gibbs; 1855. See Stevens' Handwritten note at https://mtsgreenway.org/wp-content/uploads/bsk-pdf-manager/2020/01/JHovenkotter_1-16-20.pdf. (accessed online April 13, 2022).

30. Charles E. Mix, Acting Commissioner His Excellency Isaac I. Stevens Governor of Washington Territory Present https://www.washingtonhistory.org/wp-content/uploads/2020/04/chehalisCouncil-1.pdf (accessed online April 13, 2022).
31. Richards, Kent D. Isaac I. Stevens: Young Man in a Hurry. Brigham Young University Press, 1979.
32. A History of Treaty Making and Reservations on the Olympic Peninsula Center for the Study of the Pacific Northwest https://www.washington.edu/uwired/outreach/cspn/Website/Classroom%20Materials/Curriculum%20Packets/Treaties%20&%20Reservations/III.html (accessed online April 13, 2022).
33. Id.
34. Id.
35. The Medicine Creek Treaty of 1854. https://www.smithsonianmag.com/blogs/national-museum-american-indian/2017/03/23/medicine-creek-treaty-1854/ (accessed online July 15, 2022).
36. The Treaty of Medicine Creek. https://goia.wa.gov/tribal-government/treaty-medicine-creek-1854 (accessed online July 15, 2022).
37. Governor Isaac I. Stevens to the Fourth Annual Session of the Legislative Assembly, December 3, 1856. Messages of the Governors of the Territory of Washington to the Legislative Assembly, 1854–1889, 12 U. WASH. PUBL'NS IN THE SOC. SCI. 1, 7 (Charles M. Gates ed., 1940), p. 45.
38. Text of Proceedings of Chehalis Council https://www.washingtonhistory.org/wp-content/uploads/2020/04/chehalisCouncil-1.pdf (accessed online May 21, 2022). https://www.washingtonhistory.org/wp-content/uploads/2020/04/chehalisCouncil-1.pdf (accessed online May 21, 2022).
39. Id.
40. Id.
41. Id.
42. Id.
43. Report of the Commissioner of Indian Affairs to the Secretary of the Interior, United States. Office of Indian Affairs, U.S. Government Printing Office, 1861, p. 188.
44. Stevens, Hazard. The Life of Isaac Ingalls Stevens. Vol. II. Boston: Houghton, Mifflin, 1900, p. 504.
45. Williams, Mathyn D. Indian Wars: Failings of the United States Army to Achieve Decisive Victory During the Nez Perce War of 1877. ARMY COMMAND AND GENERAL STAFF COLL FORT LEAVENWORTH KS, 2005, p. 5.

46. Message of the President of the United States, in compliance with a resolution of the Senate, of the 11th instant, calling for copies of correspondence relative to the Indian disturbances in California. S. Exec. Doc. No. 26, 34th Cong., 1st Sess. (1856), p. 67.
47. THE OFFICIAL HISTORY OF THE WASHINGTON NATIONAL GUARD VOLUME 2 WASHINGTON TERRITORIAL MILITIA IN THE INDIAN WARS OF 1855–1856 HEADQUARTERS MILITARY DEPARTMENT STATE OF WASHINGTON OFFICE OF THE ADJUTANT GENERAL CAMP MURRAY, TACOMA 33, WASHINGTON, p. 2. https://mil.wa.gov/asset/5ba41fele3bel (accessed online May 8, 2022).
48. Ibid., p. 3.
49. Stevens, Hazard. The Life of Isaac Ingalls Stevens. Vol. II. Boston: Houghton, Mifflin, 1900, p. 159.
50. THE OFFICIAL HISTORY OF THE WASHINGTON NATIONAL GUARD VOLUME 2 WASHINGTON TERRITORIAL MILITIA IN THE INDIAN WARS OF 1855–1856 HEADQUARTERS MILITARY DEPARTMENT STATE OF WASHINGTON OFFICE OF THE ADJUTANT GENERAL CAMP MURRAY, TACOMA 33, WASHINGTON, p. 4. https://mil.wa.gov/asset/5ba41fele3bel (accessed online May 8, 2022).
51. Id.
52. https://www.historylink.org/file/21193 (accessed online May 27, 2022).
53. THE OFFICIAL HISTORY OF THE WASHINGTON NATIONAL GUARD VOLUME 2 WASHINGTON TERRITORIAL MILITIA IN THE INDIAN WARS OF 1855–1856 HEADQUARTERS MILITARY DEPARTMENT STATE OF WASHINGTON OFFICE OF THE ADJUTANT GENERAL CAMP MURRAY, TACOMA 33, WASHINGTON, p. 5. https://mil.wa.gov/asset/5ba41fele3bel (accessed online May 8, 2022).
54. Ibid., p. 6.
55. Id.
56. Ibid., p. 7.
57. Ibid., p. 9.
58. https://www.sos.wa.gov/archives/timeline/detail.aspx?id=262 (accessed online May 26, 2022).
59. THE OFFICIAL HISTORY OF THE WASHINGTON NATIONAL GUARD VOLUME 2 WASHINGTON TERRITORIAL MILITIA IN THE INDIAN WARS OF 1855–1856 HEADQUARTERS MILITARY DEPARTMENT STATE OF WASHINGTON OFFICE OF THE ADJUTANT GENERAL CAMP MURRAY, TACOMA 33, WASHINGTON, p. 8. https://mil.wa.gov/asset/5ba41fele3bel (accessed online May 8, 2022).

60. Kunsch, Kelly (2006) "The Trials of Leschi, Nisqually Chief," Seattle Journal for Social Justice: Vol. 5 : Iss. 1 , Article 14. Available at: https://digitalcommons.law.seattleu.edu/sjsj/vol5/iss1/14 262 (accessed online May 26, 2022).
61. Gates, Charles Marvin. Messages of the Governors of the Territory of Washington to the Legislative Assembly, 1854–1889. (Seattle, 1940), pp. 26-27.
62. Letter from Keller to Foster, Nov. 11, Dec. 31, 1855; March 17 and May 9, 1856 - Keller Papers; Pope to Pope & Sons, March 4, 1856. Pope Papers.
63. Letter from Keller to Foster, March 17, May 9, June 5, 1856, Keller Papers.
64. Stevens, Isaac Ingalls. Message of the Governor of Washington Territory: Also, the Correspondence with the Secretary of War, Major Gen. Wool, the Officers of the Regular Army, and of the Volunteer Service of Washington Territory. Edward Furste, 1857, pp. 180-181.
65. White River/Payallup River Battle, Washington https://www.legendsofamerica.com/white-river-battle-washington/ (accessed online July 14, 2022).
66. https://www.legendsofamerica.com/battle-brennans-prairie-washington/ (accessed online July 14, 2022).
67. Native Americans attack Seattle on January 26, 1856. Walt Crowley and David Wilma https://www.historylink.org/file/5208 (accessed online July 14, 2022).
68. Id.
69. Meeker, Ezra. Pioneer Reminiscences of Puget Sound: The Tragedy of Leschi... Lowman & Hanford Stationary and Print. Company, 1905, p. 334; Puget Sound Courrier, February 8, 1856.
70. Messages of the Governors of the Territory of Washington to the Legislative Assembly, 1854–1889, 12 U. WASH. PUBL'NS IN THE SOC. SCI. 1, 7 (Charles M. Gates ed., 1940), p. 69.
71. Wonacott, Abbi. Where the Mashel meets the Nisqually: the Mashel massacre of 1856. Bellus Uccello Pub., 2008; Emerson, Stephen B. Mashel (sometimes Maxon) Massacre, (March 1856) https://www.historylink.org/File/8941 (accessed online May 28, 2022).
72. Messages of the Governors of the Territory of Washington to the Legislative Assembly, 1854–1889, 12 U. WASH. PUBL'NS IN THE SOC. SCI. 1, 7 (Charles M. Gates ed., 1940), p. 77.
73. Ibid., p. 79.
74. Ibid., p. 166.

75. Indian disturbances in Oregon and Washington. Message from the President of the United States, transmitting a communication from the Secretary of the Interior, in relation to Indian disturbances in the Territories of Oregon and Washington. H.R. Exec. Doc. No. 48, 34th Cong., 1st Sess. (1856), pp. 5-6.
76. Ibid., p.11.
77. Ibid., p. 33.
78. Ibid., p. 34.
79. THE OFFICIAL HISTORY OF THE WASHINGTON NATIONAL GUARD VOLUME 2 WASHINGTON TERRITORIAL MILITIA IN THE INDIAN WARS OF 1855–1856 HEADQUARTERS MILITARY DEPARTMENT STATE OF WASHINGTON OFFICE OF THE ADJUTANT GENERAL CAMP MURRAY, TACOMA 33, WASHINGTON, p. 7. https://mil.wa.gov/asset/5ba41fele3bel (accessed online May 8, 2022).
80. Message of the President of the United States, in compliance with a resolution of the Senate, of the 11th instant, calling for copies of correspondence relative to the Indian disturbances in California. S. Exec. Doc. No. 26, 34th Cong., 1st Sess. (1856), p. 67.
81. Messages of the Governors of the Territory of Washington to the Legislative Assembly, 1854–1889, 12 U. WASH. PUBL'NS IN THE SOC. SCI. 1, 7 (Charles M. Gates ed., 1940), p. 191.
82. THE OFFICIAL HISTORY OF THE WASHINGTON NATIONAL GUARD VOLUME 2 WASHINGTON TERRITORIAL MILITIA IN THE INDIAN WARS OF 1855–1856 HEADQUARTERS MILITARY DEPARTMENT STATE OF WASHINGTON OFFICE OF THE ADJUTANT GENERAL CAMP MURRAY, TACOMA 33, WASHINGTON, p. 2. https://mil.wa.gov/asset/5ba41fele3bel (accessed online May 8, 2022).
83. Message of the President of the United States, in compliance with a resolution of the Senate, of the 11th instant, calling for copies of correspondence relative to the Indian disturbances in California. S. Exec. Doc. No. 26, 34th Cong., 1st Sess. (1856), p. 30.
84. Kluger, Richard, The Bitter Waters of Medicine Creek: A Tragic Clash between White and Native America (New York: Random House, 2011), p. 148.
85. Meeker, Ezra. Pioneer Reminiscences of Puget Sound: The Tragedy of Leschi... Lowman & Hanford Stationary and Print. Company, 1905, Puget Sound Courrier, February 8, 1856, pp. 149-150.
86. Leschi (1808–1858), Part 2, John Caldbick https://www.historylink.org/file/21195 (accessed online July 14, 2022).

87. Kluger, Richard, The Bitter Waters of Medicine Creek: A Tragic Clash between White and Native America (New York: Random House, 2011), pp. 150-151.
88. THE OFFICIAL HISTORY OF THE WASHINGTON NATIONAL GUARD VOLUME 2 WASHINGTON TERRITORIAL MILITIA IN THE INDIAN WARS OF 1855–1856 HEADQUARTERS MILITARY DEPARTMENT STATE OF WASHINGTON OFFICE OF THE ADJUTANT GENERAL CAMP MURRAY, TACOMA 33, WASHINGTON, p. 25. https://mil.wa.gov/asset/5ba41fele3bel (accessed online May 8, 2022).
89. House Documents, Otherwise Publ. as Executive Documents: 13th Congress, 2d Session-49th Congress, 1st Session, Volume 5, United States congressional serial set, United States. Congress. 1857.
90. Messages of the Governors of the Territory of Washington to the Legislative Assembly, 1854–1889, 12 U. WASH. PUBL'NS IN THE SOC. SCI. 1, 7 (Charles M. Gates ed., 1940), p. 171.
91. Kluger, Richard, The Bitter Waters of Medicine Creek: A Tragic Clash between White and Native America (New York: Random House, 2011), p. 193.
92. The LESCHI Murder Trial as Transcribed from the Official Court Ledger, 2nd Judicial District, Wash. Terr., 1856–1858. https://digital.lib.washington.edu/researchworks/bitstream/handle/1773/36941/LESCHI%20Murder%20Trial%20-%20Transcribed%20from%20Ledger%20-1857.pdf?sequence=1&isAllowed=y (accessed online May 23, 2022).
93. Id.
94. Berland, Sidney. Strategy Strife on the Indian War Front, Columbia The Magazine of Northwest History, Vol. 2, No. 1, 1988. p. 5.
95. Messages of the Governors of the Territory of Washington to the Legislative Assembly, 1854–1889, 12 U. WASH. PUBL'NS IN THE SOC. SCI. 1, 7 (Charles M. Gates ed., 1940), p. 69.
96. Ibid., p. 148.
97. Stevens, Hazard. The Life of Isaac Ingalls Stevens. Vol. II. Boston: Houghton, Mifflin, 1900, p. 148.
98. THE OFFICIAL HISTORY OF THE WASHINGTON NATIONAL GUARD VOLUME 2 WASHINGTON TERRITORIAL MILITIA IN THE INDIAN WARS OF 1855–1856 HEADQUARTERS MILITARY DEPARTMENT STATE OF WASHINGTON OFFICE OF THE ADJUTANT GENERAL CAMP MURRAY, TACOMA 33, WASHINGTON, p. 77. https://mil.wa.gov/asset/5ba41fele3bel (accessed online May 8, 2022).
99. Ibid., p. 12.

100. Kluger, Richard, The Bitter Waters of Medicine Creek: A Tragic Clash between White and Native America (New York: Random House, 2011), p. 160.
101. Messages of the Governors of the Territory of Washington to the Legislative Assembly, 1854–1889, 12 U. WASH. PUBL'NS IN THE SOC. SCI. 1, 7 (Charles M. Gates ed., 1940), p. 293.
102. Stevens, Isaac Ingalls. Message of the Governor of Washington Territory: Also, the Correspondence with the Secretary of War, Major Gen. Wool, the Officers of the Regular Army, and of the Volunteer Service of Washington Territory. Edward Furste, 1857, p. 5.
103. Kluger, Richard, The Bitter Waters of Medicine Creek: A Tragic Clash between White and Native America (New York: Random House, 2011), p. 168.
104. Id.
105. Ibid., p. 169.
106. Ibid., p. 170.
107. Message from the President of the United States, communicating, in further compliance with a resolution of the Senate of the 30th ultimo, information respecting the proclamation of martial law in the Territory of Washington, &c., S. Exec. Doc. No. 47, 34th Cong., 3rd Sess. (1857), p. 6.
108. Ibid., p. 9.
109. Ibid., p. 8.
110. Ibid., p. 9.
111. Kluger, Richard. The bitter waters of Medicine Creek: A tragic clash between white and native America. Vintage, 2012, p. 173.
112. Ibid., p. 175.
113. George Manypenny, Commissioner of Indian Affairs, letter to Robert McClelland, Secretary of the Interior, January 19, 1857, UW Digital Archives, http://digitalcollections.lib.washington.edu/cdm/compoundobject/collection/lctext/id/733/rec/1 (accessed online May 27, 2022).
114. Carpenter, Cecelia Svinth. Tears of Internment: The Indian History of Fox Island and the Puget Sound Indian War. Tahoma Research Service, 1996.
115. https://www.sos.wa.gov/legacy/images/newspapers/sl_dir_olympiapiondemo/pdf/sl_dir_olympiapiondemo_08061858.pdf (accessed online April 13, 2022).
116. Palais, Hyman. "Time, Tide and Timber: A Century of Pope & Talbot, by Edwin T. Coman, Jr. and Helen M. Gibbs." (1950).
117. Letter from Keller to Foster, Nov. 11, 1855, and July 6, 1856, Keller Papers.
118. Letter from Keller to Foster, July 6, 1856, and April 14, 1857, Keller Papers.

119. Scott, Lea Anne. The Steptoe Defeat, 1858. https://spokanehistorical.org/items/show/235 (accessed online May 28, 2022).

120. Wilma, David. U.S. Army defeats Native Americans at Battle of Four Lakes on September 1, 1858. https://www.historylink.org/File/5143 (accessed online May 28, 2022).
121. Lieutenant William E. Birkhimer, "The Third United States Artillery" Journal of the Military Service Institution 14 (Sept./Oct. 1904), 473-474; George Wright, Appendix, "Official Reports of Colonel Wright," in Lawrence Kip, Army Life on the Pacific (New York: Redfield, 1859; reprint, Ye Galleon Press), pp. 133, 138.
122. Wilma, David. Battle of Spokane Plains occurs on September 5, 1858. https://www.historylink.org/File/5144 (accessed online May 28, 2022).
123. Beda, Steven Christopher. Landscapes of Solidarity: Timber Workers and the Making of Place in the Pacific Northwest, 1900–1964. Diss. 2014, p. 55.
124. Ficken, Robert E. The Forested Land: A History of Lumbering in Western Washington. University of Washington Press, 2012, p. 43.
125. Id.
126. Ibid., p. 49.
127. Ibid., p. 50.
128. Id.
129. Id.
130. Id.
131. Id.

132. Walker to W. Talbot, Oct. 26, Nov. 1, 21, 1899, CW. Pacific Lumber Trade Journal, Vol. 5 (November 1899), 16; W. Talbot to Walker, Nov. 6, 1899, Pope & Talbot Records, Ames Collection, University of Washington Libraries.
133. FOREST CONDITIONS IN OLYMPIC FOREST RESERVE, WASHINGTON. Geological Survey Professional Paper No. 7, United States Geological Survey https://www.nps.gov/parkhistory/online_books/geology/publications/pp/7/sec1.htm; https://www.nps.gov/parkhistory/online_books/olym/hrs/chap1.htm (accessed online June 6, 2022).
134. Olympic Historic Resource Study III. SKID ROADS AND SLUICE BOXES: COMMERCIAL DEVELOPMENT AND INDUSTRIAL DEVELOPMENT https://www.nps.gov/parkhistory/online_books/olym/hrs/chap3.htm#:~:text=In%20the%20mid%201840s%20mill,59%2C%2097%2D98) (accessed online May 21, 2022).

135. Industrialization, Technology, and Environment in Washington https://www.washington.edu/uwired/outreach/cspn/Website/Classroom%20Materials/Pacific%20Northwest%20History/Lessons/Lesson%2014/14.html (accessed online July 14, 2022).
136. Ficken, Robert E. "Weyerhaeuser and the Pacific Northwest timber industry, 1899–1903." The Pacific Northwest Quarterly 70.4 (1979). 1985 "The Social Context of Forestry: The Pacific Northwest in the Twentieth Century." Western Historical Quarterly, Vol. XVI, No. 4, pp. 413-427.
137. Id.
138. Ibid., p. 140.
139. Ibid., p. 144.
140. Ibid., p. 150.
141. Foundation Document Overview, Olympic National Park, Washington http://npshistory.com/publications/foundation-documents/olym-fd-overview.pdf (accessed online June 7, 2022).
142. https://www.nps.gov/olym/index.htm?page=4 (accessed online July 15, 2022).
143. FOREST CONDITIONS IN OLYMPIC FOREST RESERVE, WASHINGTON. Geological Survey Professional Paper No. 7, United States Geological Survey https://www.nps.gov/parkhistory/online_books/geology/publications/pp/7/sec1.htm; https://www.nps.gov/parkhistory/online_books/olym/hrs/chap1.htm (accessed online June 6, 2022).
144. Id.
145. Kit Oldham. President Franklin Roosevelt tours the Olympic Peninsula on October 1, 1937. https://www.historylink.org/File/5434 (accessed online June 6, 2022).

CHAPTER 12: TIMBER IS THE CRY

What was true as to the plunder of Indian timber resources in the Great Lakes and Pacific Northwest, occurred in other states/territories. These states/territories experienced the familiar lack of protection, as well. First, the executive branch, including the military, failed to protect Indian timber lands from encroachment, which they knew was occurring. Second, the Congressional branch failed to enact legislation preventing Indian lands from being stripped of timber, even when the DOI repeatedly warned them, for decades, of the spoilation. Third, neither the federal nor the state courts provided a forum for addressing Indian grievances.

The state/territories discussed below include in alphabetical order: Arizona, Colorado, the Dakota Territory, Indian Territory, Kansas, Nebraska, Nevada, North Carolina and Oklahoma.

Part 1: Arizona Papago Reservation

In the 1870 and 1880's, the Papagos in Southern Arizona continually experienced the theft of valuable timber from their reservation, which was being supplied to Tucson. Indian Agent, Charles Hudson, reported the loss.

> The *timber on the reserve, which is yearly becoming more valuable, is being cut and hauled off, by persons so engaged, as a business, supplying Tucson and vicinity with wood; and all this without any compensation to the Indians*. (Emphasis added).[1]

Indian Agent, Roswell G. Wheeler, reported this continuing theft a decade later. The authorities refused to take action on the pretext that it would stir up strife between the Indians and the whites.

> The lands used by the Indians at Gila Bend have been continually encroached upon by the whites. Water has been appropriated, stock molested, and personal violence threatened, until the Indians have been compelled to seek subsistence elsewhere, and are scattered throughout the Papago country. The matter has been fully reported to the Department, and the removal of the intruders has been repeatedly urged. *The reason given for not acting in the matter is a dislike on the part of the authorities to stir up strife between*

the Indians and the whites. It is a noticeable fact, however, that the white settlers on this reservation have no hesitancy in stirring up strife with the Indians whenever opportunity offers. (Emphasis added).²

Commissioner Atkins, recognizing the importance of this matter, reported this theft *directly* to the *Secretary of the Interior, with no remedy proffered.*

The difficulty experienced during the last few years in preventing the occupation of the Papago Reservation in Southern Arizona by white settlers and *the unlawful cutting and removal of timber therefrom renders it important that more effective measures be adopted than are now being employed,* or that are possible under the present system. (Emphasis added).³

Part 2: Colorado Utes

In Colorado, in a serious oversight, the Utes' Indian Agent reported that the U.S. had not paid for a timber reserve it confiscated.

In 1880 the Uncompahgre, White River, and Southern Utes made a treaty by which ... they ceded about 8,000,000 acres. ... So far as I can ascertain there has never been any settlement of this claim nor any statement as to the amount of money collected for this land. ... I believe the *Government has appropriated from this Colorado land a large timber reserve,* for which, it seems to me, the Indians are justly entitled to pay. (Emphasis added).⁴

Part 3: Dakota Territory

Black Hills

In 1866, the Northwest Commission declared the Black Hills' considerable timber and coal could be readily exploited, advancing "the development of the northwest prairies."⁵ With no shame, they negotiated an annuity of "three to six dollars' worth of clothing and food ... enough to protect them from starvation..."⁶ On top of this, they disclosed the "more mortifying evidence of negligence by former agents, and most probably *stupendous frauds* and outrages in the administration of Indian affairs..." (Emphasis added).⁷

In 1874, during an economic depression, the U.S. sent General George Custer, with his 7th Cavalry, on an Expedition of the Black Hills to choose a location for a new fort and to investigate the area's natural resources. The Expedition included 1,000 soldiers, 110 wagons, 70 Indian scouts, four reporters, and two gold miners. On August 2, Custer reported the discovery of gold which quickly became public. In a further analysis, it was measured as a gold field of eight hundred square miles. In addition, an area of three thousand miles of timber, grazing, and arable land was delineated.[8]

Henry Newton, the author of the geological Report, judged it unfortunate that gold had been discovered "for if it were not for its discovery, this beautifully timbered and grassed region would afford them [Sioux] an excellent retreat."[9]

Newton further noted: *"The Black Hills are a well-wooded country.... nearly eight hundred square miles, equal to 500,000 acres, is covered by timber of merchantable quality."* (Emphasis added).[10]

Commissioner Smith knew that the Black Hills were "best adapted to their [Sioux] immediate and paramount necessities. I doubt whether any land now remaining in the possession of the General Government offers equal advantages."[11] Yet, he took no action, as their trustee, to protect their property rights.

Commissioner Smith reported that since the Sioux were dependent on the U.S. for rations, and would starve if they were withheld, that provided a basis to negotiate with them for the Black Hills. Again, the U.S. would use the upper-hand it had in assuring that the Sioux wouldn't be reduced to starvation. The Sioux were doomed to lose the Black Hills from the very beginning. The unspoken threat of starvation would be weaponized to deliberately undervalue the Black Hills, which the Sioux have not accepted to this day.

> They are not now capable of self-support; they are absolute pensioners of the Government in the sum of a million and a quarter of dollars annually above all amounts specified in treaty-stipulations. *A failure to receive Government rations for a single season would reduce them to starvation*. They cannot, therefore, demand to be left alone, and the Government, granting the large help which the Sioux are obliged to ask, is entitled to ask something of them in return. On this basis of mutual benefit the purchase of the Black Hills should proceed. (Emphasis added).[12]

In a desultory repetition of what previously occurred, the claim of Manifest Destiny would rule. Commissioner Smith reported to Secretary of the Interior that miners had already staked out claims, expecting the Government to protect them or they would do it themselves.[13]

In 1875, a commission chaired by Senator Allison was appointed to negotiate with the Sioux for the cession of the Black Hills.[14]

Fort Berthold Reservation

The cession by the Arikarees, Mandans, and Gros Ventres was noted to contain coal and timber valuable to the region, which was sure to be settled by whites.

> There is a good showing of coal on this land, the quality of which seems very uncertain, but if at all capable of being made available as fuel, will be of great value to commerce in a country where wood is extremely scarce. There is also ... considerable timber ... The soil, coal or lignite, and *timber, united with the exorbitant prices paid for everything in that region, will probably invite settlements* ... (Emphasis added).[15]

South Dakota Lower Brule Reservation

In 1881, Indian Agent W. H. Parkhurst reported the plundering of timber on the Lower Brule Reservation. This was especially detrimental given the scant supply of wood and the almost wholesale pillaging of what was left.

> The "Missouri bottoms," that a few years since were so thickly studded with oak, ash, elm, and cottonwood timber, have been ruthlessly stripped. In this connection permit me respectfully to call the attention of the department to the wanton and reckless manner in which the timber lands set apart for Indians have been and are now *mercilessly plundered of valuable standing timber* and wood, valuable cedar, oak, and elm, cut and converted into cordwood by steamboat woodcutters, squatters, and others, without any benefit being derived from the same. (Emphasis added).[16]

Part 4: Indian Territory

Shawnee and Wyandot Reserve

Shawnee and Wyandot Indian Agent, Robert C. Miller, reported in 1854 that even though he posted notices and published in the press that cutting timber on Indians lands was prohibited, it was of no effect. "*The most valuable portions of the timbered lands are being entirely stripped. Having no force at my disposal, I have been unable to prevent this.*" (Emphasis added).[17]

Four years later, Indian Agent Benjamin J. Newsom, reported the continuing theft and "various trespasses, including one where wood was cut and sold to persons on boats running on the Missouri River."[18]

Osage and Miami Reserves

M. McCaslin, Osage River Indian Agent, notified the Superintendent that "white settlers ... were wantonly encroaching on Osage and other Indian lands." Acting on the Superintendent's alert, Commissioner Manypenny's requested military reinforcements, but met with no success.

> The lands thus occupied are amongst the best in this part of the Territory. They are generally selected along the streams and watercourses, and consequently embrace the finest timber, which is regarded as a valuable item in this country.[19]

After three years at his post, Agent McCaslin, stated his predicament eloquently:

> ***Timber is the cry, and timber they will have***; if not by fair play, they do not hesitate to employ the opposite means. Something should be done to abate the evils which are daily growing out of this state of things, and to obviate the numerous complaints made against the government by both Indians and white people. (Emphasis added).[20]

Agent McCaslin, continued in his 1857 Report that the Miami Reservation was also being overrun by white settlers who were stealing timber. Given the gravity of this situation, he had sent a letter previously on June 16, 1857, to report it. At the same time this theft was occurring, the Miamies were complaining that the saw-mill they wanted purchased out of their funds to build homes was still in abeyance.

> The Miami reservation contains over thirty six thousand acres, and it is now ***overrun with settlers, many of them cutting and selling timber***, while outsiders are stealing all they can, as has been reported by me to the Indian office at Washington, by letter dated June 16, 1857. ... Another complaint made by the Miamies is, for want of building material; many of them are building, or trying to build, but cannot get along without lumber. They want a saw-mill ... (Emphasis added).[21]

The recommended solution for the Miamis' complaints to the theft of timber on their lands was the sale of their lands:

The continued trespass, by the destruction of timber on the head rights, and thefts perpetrated, continue to be a source of much annoyance. *The sale of these lands will relieve the Indians from many cares, in the use of means to protect their lands*; and the proceeds arising from the sales, if properly taken care of and applied, will be of far more practical utility to the Indians than the land. (Emphasis added).[22]

Delaware and Osage Agencies

The same helplessness was reported by Delaware and Osage Indian Agent, B. F. Robinson. Even though he couldn't protect the Indians in his charge, by putting it in writing, we have another piece of evidence of the government's abject failure to fulfill its trust responsibilities.

> I have experienced a good deal of difficulty in protecting the people of this agency. Numerous wrongs have been perpetrated; in many parts of the reserve the *white man has wasted their most valuable timber* with an unsparing hand; the trust lands, also, have been greatly injured in consequence of the settlements made thereon. The Indians have complained, but to no purpose; I have found it useless to forewarn and threaten legal proceedings. The destruction of timber is still persisted in; and, unless remedies of a preventive character are entrusted in the hands of the agent, whereby he may be enabled to expel trespassers who may be found on reserved lands committing waste, large annual appropriations of money will be required in instituting and prosecuting lawsuits; for, in good faith, the government is bound to protect these people. (Emphasis added).[23]

In 1860, Thos. B. Sykes, Indian Agent for the Delawares, asked if any legal action could be taken to protect against timber thieves. The answer was no.

> Their greatest complaints have been against [white] persons who reside on their borders for cutting timber from their reserve, and stealing their horses and cattle. This has been carried to an almost unlimited extent with nearly perfect impunity. A large portion of the very finest walnut, oak, and hickory timber has been cut and removed from their reserve. On examination of the existing intercourse laws I could find no provision against such acts. I submitted the question to some of the United States judges for the Territory, and they advised me *there was no law providing for the punishment of persons for cutting timber from Indian reservations*. (Emphasis added).[24]

Part 5: Kansas Territory

In the Kansas Territory, in 1856, Commissioner Manypenny, highlighted the severity of the lawlessness in his Secretarial Report: personal maltreatment, property stolen, timber destroyed, possessions encroached upon and diverse other injuries.

> The general disorder so long prevailing in Kansas Territory, and the consequent unsettled state of civil affairs there, have been very injurious to the interests of many of the Indian tribes in that Territory. ....[25]

Commissioner Dooley Warns Secretary of Timber Theft

In his 1866 Report to the Secretary, Commissioner D. N. Cooley denounced the continuing timber theft.

> Among these settlers (Kansas) are too many who are unscrupulous as to the rights of the Indians; ***their timber, scarce in Kansas at the best, is cut down***, and their stock run off in many instances, and the hope of redress is very small. (Emphasis added).[26]

Osage River Agency

The breadth of Indian Agent Seth Clover's investigation, in 1858, on the Osage River Agency in the Kansas Territory, is reported at length due to its value to this subject:

> ***The destruction of valuable timber has been immense***. The timber taken is principally first class, such as is usually appropriated for building and fencing purposes. The trespass has been committed, not only upon the lands selected as head rights and occupied by Indians, but upon head rights, occupied and unoccupied, of widows and orphans, and of those who are deaf, blind, afflicted, and helpless. No respect appears to have been shown to any condition of life. Trespasses have been committed on the Wea sections, as well as on the Miami national reserves.

The trespassers are numerous, and embrace nearly every grade of character; are generally men accustomed to a frontier life, bold and reckless in disposition, seizing every favorable opportunity to accomplish their own individual purposes. These trespassers are generally squatters who reside in the vicinity of the reserve, on land purchased by the government from the Miami Indians, under the treaty of 1854, and have disregarded all notices served by Agent McCaslin and frequent warnings given by others, and in several instances have threatened the lives of persons, who might inform on them or attempt to institute proceedings against them. ... There is a class of intruders, numbering about seventy-five families, who for the last two or three years past have occupied and are now occupying large tracts of land on the Miami Indian national reservation. They have during this time cut timber, built houses, made rails, fenced and farmed large bodies of land. The timber in many instances is manufactured into rails, plank, boards, shingles, and square timbers for building purposes, and sold to people in the State of Missouri, by which it is said they are not only making comfortable livings, but are accumulating money by the operation. They claim to hold these lands under the pre-emption laws, as squatters, and that there is no Miami Indian national reserve in this Territory, and a large majority of them allege that they have assurances from leading and distinguished men in the State of Missouri that they have a clear and indisputable right to occupy, buy, and sell these squatter claims and improvements, without let or hindrance, and in defiance of the government or its agents. ...

There is a class of co-operating intruders and trespassers residing in the State of Missouri, who consider themselves beyond the limits of territorial laws, and come on the Miami reservation and stake off such claims as suit their purposes; cut, destroy, sell, and haul away large quantities of valuable timber, and often sell claims and improvements to innocent and unsuspecting persons, at prices ranging from two hundred to one thousand dollars a claim, thus realizing large profits from small investments. ...

A number of persons living on the reserve are equally and like censurable for a similar course of reprehensible conduct. Considering the relationship of the deceiver and the deluded, it is not surprising that the notices served by my predecessor on these intruders have passed unnoticed and unhonored. No punishment is too severe for the intriguing, designing, and avaricious deceiver, while the execution of justice without mercy would seem too severe for the deluded. (Emphasis added).[27]

Sac and Foxes of Missouri in Kansas

Labeled as "blanket Indians" and ridiculed for wanting to be "let alone" in their "ignorance and superstition," the Sac and Foxes of Missouri had been removed to Kansas. They would face more hardship by the U.S.' decision to sell their timbered and resource laden lands. Some chose to remain on what was left of their Reserve, others moved to Iowa and others moved to Indian Territory.

> I cannot close without an allusion to the lands of the *Sacs and Foxes of Missouri*, to be sold for the joint benefit of the two tribes. ... *It is well-timbered and has many indications of coal; is watered by numerous tributaries of the Great Nemaha, and has water-power unsurpassed in Kansas or Nebraska. In addition to a natural road-bed up the Great Nemaha valley for a railroad westwardly to Fort Kearney from St. Joseph, abounding in timber and stone, in point of soil, climate, and location, this reservation is unequalled by any in the hands of government for disposal.* (Emphasis added).[28]

Agent John A. Burbank didn't even protest the decision to sell the productive lands of the Sac and Foxes. In fact, he advocated for their rapid disposal. *It is important to know why the federal government would eagerly dispossess the Sacs and Foxes of these land*s.

> They were well-timbered. Timber was essential for building homes for emigrating settlers.
>
> They were coal bearing. Coal was in high demand, as oil was not yet serving the purpose of powering steam engines for trains, mills, machinery and heating.
>
> They were well-watered which was critical to agriculture, in an area that was intermittently subject to drought.
>
> The rivers were capable of providing hydro-power as an energy source.
>
> They abounded in stone, useful in construction.
>
> They possessed good soil.
>
> The climate was positive which made it an attractive area for settlement.
>
> Location, location, location.

Transportation was key to growth and connectivity with other areas. Accessibility was a key component of value. The Sac and Fox lands had an existing road.

It was a prime station stop for a railroad from Fort Kearney to St. Joseph. Railroads precipitated the transformation of a regional agrarian society to an industrial one. Railroads opened broader markets for agricultural products and industrial products such as lumber and coal. They were highly prized fostering growth, commerce and profit-making.

Prairie Band of Pottawatomie Reserve

The federal judiciary was again signaled out as a culprit. In Kansas, the legal system was closed to Indian plaintiffs.

> The idea seems to prevail among the white settlers that that particular reserve [Prairie Band of Pottawatomies], with its ***valuable timber, pure water, and rich prairie soil***, containing over seventy five thousand acres, within an hour's ride from the dome of our State capitol, could never have been intended as a home for the Indian, the land to remain, to a great extent, uncultivated, and forever free from taxation. They enter upon these lands stealthily and take away timber, or make a contract with some worthless Indian for such timber as they want, (the land being held in common they can buy of the same Indian in one part of the reserve as well as another,) and under this contract they go on defiantly cutting and destroying. While the contract furnishes a sort of pretext, they very well know it confers no right; but they at the same time know that the United States district court for the district of Kansas never did, and probably never will, convict a white man for depredating upon Indian lands. (Emphasis added).[29]

Indian Agent L. R. Palmer, for the Prairie Band of Pottawatomies, recommended "prevailing upon white men to be honest and just toward the Indian" or removing the Prairie Band to Indian Territory, leaving behind the "valuable timber, pure water, and rich prairie soil."[30]

Part 6: Nebraska

What is astounding is that even in states where timber was not the leading industry engine, theft abounded. White settlers, similar to pirates of the past, plundered Indian lands with no regard whatsoever for their rights. Congress failed to enact legislation to protect Indians from this illegal pillage. The vigilance required to prevent this theft wasn't a priority at all. Many times, the solution was a sale, not just of the timber, but the Indians' lands, as well.

Otoes and Missourias

Even with forty-seven per cent (47%) of Otoe and Missouria lands confiscated for white settlement, settlers still continued to steal timber from the reservation. Again, the answer to the problem for the U.S. was to sell tribal land, which was just another form of theft.

> The confederated tribes of Otoes and Missourias, have a reservation on the southern boundary of Nebraska, containing 162,854 acres of excellent land for both tillage and grazing, with a growth of timber along the streams. From this 77,174 acres have been surveyed to be sold in trust for these Indians. ***The continued depredations of the whites are rapidly stripping the reservation of its timber***. (Emphasis added).[31]

> The destruction of timber on the [Otoe] reservation by white men continues. Its destruction is an injury to the country, a heavy loss to the tribe, and an exhibition of a low moral condition in many of the surrounding settlers who have disregarded the provisions of law and the rights of others. Some efforts have been made by the judiciary of the district to prevent it, but they have not been effectual.[32]

Iowa Reserve

Given Congress' unwillingness, over decades, to enact preventative legislation, the theft of timber on the Iowa Reserve at the Great Nemaha Agency can only be tagged as sanctioned.

> ***A large quantity of timber has been stolen from this reservation [Iowas] during the year by lawless white men***. There are no laws by which they can be protected from being plundered by their white neighbors in Nebraska, who act on the theory that an Indian has no title a white man is bound to respect. (Emphasis added).[33]

Part 7: Nevada Truckee Reservation

O. J. Reed, Josiah Hayes, and others filed a false claim, through their attorney, Andrew Reed, to have the right to, and possession of, a certain portion of the timber on the Truckee Reservation. It was determined to be inadmissible.

> ***These parties went upon the land and cut a large amount of timber***, which now lies upon the ground gradually decaying. (Emphasis added).[34]

Part 8: North Carolina Eastern Cherokees

Deciding they were better off getting some money, rather than none from the repeated theft of timber and land, the Eastern Cherokee agreed, in 1904, to sell part of their lands.

> Another source of trouble and contention is *their timber and unoccupied lands, which are subject to continual trespass and the schemes of unprincipled white men*, in addition to being a burden on account of the tax thereon. It is the desire of the band to sell these lands, which, in my judgment, should be done under the proper approval and supervision of the Secretary of the Interior, and the proceeds held in trust for a period of years. (Emphasis added).[35]

Part 9: Oklahoma Muskogee Reserve

John Q. Tufts, Indian Agent, Muskogee Reserve, was stymied by the continued theft of timber by white settlers, even when the Army removed intruders at his request, because the settlers wantonly returned.

> When my last report was made, there were about 6,000 intruders in this agency, who have no rights in the country. Most of them were in the Choctaw and Chickasaw country ... Again it has been decided by the United States court that the laws for the protection of timber on Indian reservations do not apply to this agency, hence it is not unlawful to steal timber from these people, though they have the same title that the parties that do the stealing have to their homes in the States. *The inhabitants of adjoining States are fast destroying the finest timber and the government is almost powerless to prevent.* On several occasions the military have been called upon to remove intruders, and the troops were promptly furnished. Several hundred intruders were removed by Lieutenant Shoemaker, Fourth Cavalry. (Emphasis added).[36]

Four years later, admitting defeat, he sought funding for Indian police to control the "uncontrollable" intruders:

> Along the border the intruders steal timber and coal and use the Indian grass without compunction. ... This plan [of employing Indian Police] is practical and will enable an element to be controlled which has not been controlled heretofore, and which has been a source of many serious difficulties and crimes.[37]

In 1899, in an act from the theater of the absurd, the white farmer, assigned to the eleven allotment districts, was assigned the duty of "prosecuting" timber thieves and trespassers on allotments.[38]

Notes: Timber Is the Cry

1. Report of the Commissioner of Indian Affairs to the Secretary of the Interior, Reports of Agents in Arizona, Pima Agency, Indian Agent, Charles Hudson, United States. Office of Indian Affairs, U.S. Government Printing Office, 1876, pp. 8-9.
2. Report of the Commissioner of Indian Affairs to the Secretary of the Interior, Reports of Agents in Arizona, Pima Agency, Indian Agent, Roswell G. Wheeler, United States, Office of Indian Affairs. U.S. Government Printing Office, 1885, p. 4.
3. Ibid., pp. XLVII-XLVIII.
4. Report of the Commissioner of Indian Affairs to the Secretary of the Interior, United States. Office of Indian Affairs, U.S. Government Printing Office, 1898, p. 294.
5. Report of the Commissioner of Indian Affairs to the Secretary of the Interior, United States. Office of Indian Affairs, U.S. Government Printing Office, 1866, p. 173.
6. Ibid., p. 174.
7. Ibid., pp. 168-174.
8. Report of the Commissioner of Indian Affairs to the Secretary of the Interior, United States. Office of Indian Affairs, U.S. Government Printing Office, 1874, p. 731.
9. U. S. Department of the Interior, Geographical and Geological Survey of the Rocky Mountain Region; Report on the geology and resources of the Black Hills of Dakota: with atlas, Newton, Henry, Jenney, Walter Proctor, Washington: Govt. Print. Off., 1880, p. 5.
10. Ibid., p. 323.
11. Report of the Commissioner of Indian Affairs to the Secretary of the Interior, United States. Office of Indian Affairs. U.S. Government Printing Office, 1875, p. 8.
12. Id.
13. Ibid., p. 7.
14. Id.
15. Report of the Secretary of the Interior Ex. Doc., United States congressional serial set, United States. Department of the Interior, Dakota Superintendency, 1866, p. 172.

16. Report of the Commissioner of Indian Affairs to the Secretary of the Interior, Reports of Agents in Dakota, United States. Office of Indian Affairs, U.S. Government Printing Office, 1881, p. 39.
17. Report of the Commissioner of Indian Affairs to the Secretary of the Interior, United States. Office of Indian Affairs, U.S. Government Printing Office, 1854, p. 414.
18. Report of the Commissioner of Indian Affairs to the Secretary of the Interior, United States. Office of Indian Affairs, Wm. A. Harris, Printer, 1858, p. 112.
19. Report of the Commissioner of Indian Affairs to the Secretary of the Interior, United States. Office of Indian Affairs, Printer: A.O.P. Nicholson, 1856, p. 109.
20. Report of the Commissioner of Indian Affairs to the Secretary of the Interior, Office of Indian Affairs, United States. William A. Harris, Printer, 1858, p. 188.
21. Ibid., pp. 189-190.
22. Report of the Commissioner of Indian Affairs to the Secretary of the Interior, Osage River Agency, United States. Office of Indian Affairs, U.S. Government Printing Office, 1860, p. 115.
23. Report of the Commissioner of Indian Affairs to the Secretary of the Interior, United States. Office of Indian Affairs, A.O.P. Nicholson, Printer, 1856, p. 92; Report of the Commissioner of Indian Affairs to the Secretary of the Interior, Office of Indian Affairs, United States. A.O.P. Nicholson, Printer, 1857, p. 125.
24. Report of the Secretary of the Interior Ex. doc., United States congressional serial set, United States. Department of the Interior, 1860, p. 103.
25. Report of the Commissioner of Indian Affairs to the Secretary of the Interior, United States. Office of Indian Affairs, U.S. Government Printing Office, 1856, p. 21.
26. Report of the Commissioner of Indian Affairs to the Secretary of the Interior, Osage River Agency, United States. Office of Indian Affairs, U.S. Government Printing Office, 1866, p. 49.
27. Report of the Commissioner of Indian Affairs to the Secretary of the Interior, Osage River Agency, United States. Office of Indian Affairs, William A. Harris, Printer, 1858, pp. 123-124.
28. Report of the Commissioner of Indian Affairs to the Secretary of the Interior, Central Superintendency, Great Nemaha Agency, Nebraska, United States. Office of Indian Affairs, U.S. Government Printing Office, 1864, pp. 264-265.
29. Report of the Commissioner of Indian Affairs to the Secretary of the Interior, Central Superintendency, Pottawatomie Agency, United States. Office of Indian Affairs. U.S. Government Printing Office, 1870, p. 373.
30. Ibid., p. 374.

31. Report of the Commissioner of Indian Affairs to the Secretary of the Interior, Information, With Historical And Statistical Statements, Relative To The Different Tribes And Their Agencies, United States. Office of Indian Affairs, U.S. Government Printing Office, 1874, p. 34.
32. Report of the Commissioner of Indian Affairs to the Secretary of the Interior, Reports of Agents in Nebraska, Otoe Agency, United States. Office of Indian Affairs, U.S. Government Printing Office, 1876, p. 99.
33. Report of the Commissioner of Indian Affairs to the Secretary of the Interior, Information, With Historical And Statistical Statements, Relative To The Different Tribes And Their Agencies, United States. Office of Indian Affairs, U.S. Government Printing Office, 1874, p. 32.
34. Report of the Secretary of the Interior Ex. Doc., United States congressional serial set, United States. Department of the Interior, 1865, p. 140.
35. Report of the Commissioner of Indian Affairs to the Secretary of the Interior, Office of Indian Affairs, United States. U.S. Government Printing Office, 1905, p. 266.
36. Report of the Commissioner of Indian Affairs to the Secretary of the Interior, United States. Office of Indian Affairs, U.S. Government Printing Office, 1881, p. 104.
37. Report of the Commissioner of Indian Affairs to the Secretary of the Interior, United States. Office of Indian Affairs, U.S. Government Printing Office, 1885, p. 106.
38. Report of the Commissioner of Indian Affairs to the Secretary of the Interior, Reports Concerning Indians in Oklahoma, United States. Office of Indian Affairs, U.S. Government Printing Office, 1899, pp. 282, 284.

CHAPTER 13:
PATTERNS OF DISPOSSESSING INDIANS
OF THEIR LAND AND RESOURCES

Part 1: Common Trajectory

Congress acknowledged that from "the beginning, Federal policy toward the Indian was based on the desire to dispossess him of his land."[1] Dispossessing Indians of their land and resources followed a common trajectory. It started with the legal fiction that Indians didn't own their land, but were mere tenants at sufferance, permitting their ouster from their land. If they were tenants, they didn't own the natural resources on their lands.

The common trajectory to accomplish this dispossession included lying, stealing, cheating, harassing, trespassing, fraud, mispresenting and undervaluing the value of Indian land and resources, removal, extermination, massacres, private wars funded by the federal government, war crimes, massive cession of lands, concentration and consolidation of Indians on reservations, allotment of tribal land to individuals to break up the tribal mass, and alienability of allotments. Repudiating the sovereignty of Indian Nations and assimilating Indians into the body politic wasn't questioned. These practices were endorsed by the President, the executive branch, the military, Congress and the judiciary. With this impetus, states selected their own method for securing for their citizens the *inexhaustible mineral, agricultural and natural resources within their dominion. Big business used its political and economic clout to assure its imperial control of the country's natural wealth. Settlers were the boots-on-the-ground.*

> The policy of the Government for many years past has been to destroy the tribal relations as fast as possible, and to use every endeavor to bring the Indians under the influence of law. To do this the agents have been accustomed to punish for minor offenses, by imprisonment in the guardhouse and by withholding rations ...[2]

To destroy the solidarity of Indian Nations, members were paid and used by the military and federal government to fight one another. To weaken and destroy the tribal relationship, Congress authorized Indian Police to inform on and prohibit participation in traditional dances and feasts, polygamy, reciprocal gift giving, medicine men and funeral practices, and intoxication or sale of liquor. Punishment was meted out by Indian judges appointed to the Court of Indian Offenses. Annuities were used to reward conforming behavior and punish disobedience – not only of individuals, but of entire families.

Indian Agents were in charge of assimilating Indians into the common body politic and exercising the tyrannical power to accomplish that aim:

Executive Conflict of Interest

The President's conflict of interest between the trust responsibilities to Indians and the obligations to the citizenry started early on. By 1821, their policies of removal, cession of lands, and allotment of tribal land to individuals to break up the tribal mass were voiced well in advance of any legislation.

President John Adams: Indian Trust Responsibilities Are Subordinate to Obligations to U.S. Citizenry

President John Adams (1797-1801) captured the essence well of the executive responsibility to its "white children" in this 1878 letter to the Cherokee Nation objecting to the invasion of squatters:

> His "stronger obligations" were to "hear the complaints, and relieve, as far as in my power, the distresses of my white children, citizens of the United States."[3]

President Thomas Jefferson (1801–1805)

Thomas Jefferson (1801–1805) would become the (1) architect of the U.S.' Indian removal policy, well before the Indian Removal Act of 1830; and (2) the "Manifest Destiny" of the U.S. to expropriate Indian lands:

From Thomas Jefferson to John Breckinridge (U.S. Attorney General), 12 August 1803, regarding the Louisiana Purchase:

> ... the best use we can make of the country for some time will be to give establishments in it to the Indians on the East side of the Mispi in exchange for their present country, and open land offices in the last, & thus make this acquisition the means of filling up the Eastern side instead of drawing off it's population. *when we shall be full on this side, we may lay off a range of states on the Western bank from the head to the mouth, & so range after range, advancing compactly as we multiply*. (Emphasis added).[4]

His ideology of expansionism was voiced in 1780 when he coined the phrase "Empire of Liberty," while the American Revolution was still being fought. In his instructions to George Rogers Clark to take Fort Detroit he envisioned a future of commerce and expansion:

> We shall divert through our own Country a branch of commerce which the European States have thought worthy of the most important struggles and sacrifices and ... shall form to the American union a barrier against the dangerous extension of the British Province of Canada and add to the Empire of Liberty an extensive and fertile Country ...[5]

President James Madison (1809–1817), Policy Is Precursor to Allotment

Our fourth President, James Madison, planned to complete the work of transitioning the Indians from the "habits of the savage to the arts and comforts of social life" and divide up their land in a terrifying precursor to future allotment. By the political administration of Indians in reduced areas, land expropriation and exploitation would be easier.

> [T]he facility is increasing for *extending that divided and individual ownership, which exists now in movable property only, to the soil itself,* and of thus establishing in the culture and improvement of it the true foundation for a transit from the habits of the savage to the arts and comforts of social life. (Emphasis added.)[6]

President James Monroe: Extinguishment of Indian Title Inevitable; Removal of Indians Paramount; Assimilation Policy Defunct

Our fifth President, James Monroe, in his Second Annual Message to Congress in 1821 (1) discredited the U.S. recognition of Indian tribes as Nations; (2) disclaimed their sovereignty over their territorial lands; (3) relegated to them the right for a 'reasonable equivalent" to the lands they ceded; and (4) secured to each individual the right to a "competent" portion of land. Neither what was a "reasonable equivalent" nor a "competent" parcel were defined. His policies would essentially destroy Indian Nations as sovereigns with the fundamental right to govern their peoples and exercise control of their lands.

The care of the Indian tribes ... has not been executed in a manner to accomplish all the objects intended by it. *We have treated them as independent nations, without their having any substantial pretensions to that rank*. The distinction has flattered their pride, retarded their improvement, and in many instances paved the way to their destruction. The progress of our settlements westward, supported as they are by a dense population, has constantly driven them back, with almost the *total sacrifice of the lands which they have been compelled to abandon. Their sovereignty over vast territories should cease, in lieu of which the right of soil should be secured to each individual and his posterity in competent portions*. They have claims on the magnanimity and, I may add, on the justice of this nation which we must all feel. We should become their real benefactors; we should perform the office of their Great Father, the endearing title which they emphatically give to the Chief Magistrate of our Union. Their sovereignty over vast territories should cease, in lieu of which the right of soil should be secured to each individual and his posterity in competent portions; and for the territory thus ceded by each tribe some reasonable equivalent should be granted, to be vested in permanent funds for the support of civil government over them and for the education of their children, for their instruction in the arts of husbandry, and to provide sustenance for them until they could provide it for themselves. My earnest hope is that Congress will digest some plan, founded on these principles, with such improvements as their wisdom may suggest, and carry it into effect as soon as it may be practicable. (Emphasis added).[7]

Stereotypical View of the Indian Expressed at Highest Levels of Government

Congress

Congressional representatives employed the artifice of dehumanizing stereotypes to justify legislation that assured the protection of the colonial authority. In their debates on the floor of the House, Indians were demeaned as having contributed nothing to promote civilization. They were caricatured as part horse and human. It was urged that they be pushed off into the ocean.[8]

Legislation in time would be enacted in line with President Monroe's policies.

U.S. Supreme Court Chief Justice Epithet of Indians Savagery, 1823

The usual practice of assimilating conquered people as citizens of the conquering government was not possible with 'fierce savages,' according to the U.S. Supreme Court Chief Justice John Marshall in his decision in *Johnson v. M'Intosh*, 21 U.S. 543, 590 (1823):

> "But the tribes of Indians inhabiting this country were fierce savages, whose occupation was war, and whose subsistence was drawn chiefly from the forest. To leave them in possession of their country was to leave the country a wilderness; to govern them as a distinct people was impossible, because they were as brave and as high spirited as they were fierce, and were ready to repel by arms every attempt on their independence."

Commissioner of Indian Affairs Stereotypical View

John N. Oberly, Commissioner of Indian Affairs, in his Annual Report to the Secretary of the Interior in 1888, inscribed the stereotypical view of Indians that dominated federal and state policy-making in the nineteenth century:

The Indian has indeed begun to change with the changing times. He is commencing to appreciate the fact that he must become civilized—must, as he expresses it, "learn the white man's way"—or perish from the face of the earth. He can not sweep back with a broom the flowing tide. The forests into which he ran whooping from the door of "William and Mary" [Indian School in Virginia] have been felled. The game on which he lived has disappeared. The war-path has been obliterated. He is hemmed in on all sides by white population. The railroad refuses to be excluded from his reservation-that hot-bed of barbarism, in which many noxious social and political weeds grow rankly. The Christian missionary is persistently entreating him to abandon paganism. Gradually the paternal hand of the Government is being withdrawn from his support. His environments no longer compel him, or afford to him opportunities, to display the nobler traits of his character. On the warpath and in the chase he was heroic: all activity; patient of hunger; patient of fatigue; cool-headed-a creature of exalted fortitude. "But, says a writer, sketching his character, "when the chase was over, when the war was done, and the peace-pipes smoked out, he abandoned himself to debauchery and idleness. To sleep all day in a wigwam of painted skins, filthy and blackened with smoke, adorned with scalps, and hung with tomahawks and arrows, to dance in the shine of the new moon to music made from the skin of snakes, to tell stories of witches and evil spirits, to gamble, to sing, to jest, to boast of his achievements in war, and to sit with a solemn gravity at the councils of his chiefs constituted his most serious employment. His squaw was his slave. With no more affection than a coyote feels for its mate, he brought her to his wigwam that she might gratify the basest of his passions and minister to his wants. It was Starlight or Cooing Dove that brought the wood for his fire and the water for his drink, that plowed the field and sowed the maize."[9]

These stereotypes became embedded in the consciousness of whites and are still expressed today.

DOI Labeled Indians as Colonizers of Reservations

The Department of the Interior, in fact, switched the status of Indians to 'colonizers' versus indigenous sovereigns when Commissioner Manypenny in 1856 expounded on the need to "colonize" Indians on reservations of land to prevent their extermination due to the expanding western population, the growth of cities and the incursion of railroads.

> As sure as these great physical changes are impending, so sure will these poor denizens of the forest be ***blotted out of existence***, and ***their dust be trampled under the foot of rapidly advancing civilization***, unless our great nation shall generously determine that the necessary provision shall at once be made, and appropriate steps be taken to designate suitable tracts or ***reservations of land***, in proper localities, for permanent homes for, and provide the means to ***colonize, them thereon***. (Emphasis added).[10]

Commissioner Morgan in 1890 would explicitly state that the success of the U.S. Indian policy to "destroy tribal relations" could be measured by the "reduction of reservations and allotment of lands."

> ***It has become the settled policy of the Government to break up reservations, destroy tribal relations, settle Indians upon their own homesteads, incorporate them into the national life, and deal with them not as nations or tribes or bands, but as individual citizens.*** The American Indian is to become the Indian American. How far this process has advanced during the past year will be shown under the head of the reduction of reservations and allotment of lands. (Emphasis added).[11]

States Maneuver for Removal of Indians

Indian Nations faced numerous states thirsting for their removal, including the following States/Territories that went as far as passing state legislation petitioning for Presidential extinguishment of Indian title in their States/Territories: Georgia, Illinois, Indiana, Kentucky, Michigan Territory, Mississippi, Missouri, New York, North Carolina, Ohio, South Carolina, Tennessee and Wisconsin.[12]

In 1864, Sidney Edgerton was appointed as ***Montana's first territorial governor and ex-officio superintendent of Indian Affairs***. With regard to his Indian policy, he said:

> "I trust that the Government will, at an early day, take steps for the extinguishment of the Indian title in this territory, in order that our lands may be brought into market."[13]

States with Timber Resources Pursued Removal or Extermination

States with timber resources were allowed to pursue their goals to remove or destroy Indian inhabitants to access their extractive resources.

For Michigan, it was the massive cession of Indian lands and consolidation and concentration of Indians on small reserves.

For Minnesota, it was monumental fraudulent legislation enabling massive acquisition of Indian allotted fee-patented lands.

For Wisconsin, it was the vast removal of all Indians. It didn't matter where, just outside of our state.

For Montana, it was using big-business' corrupt political clout to secure Indian lands.

For Oregon and Washington, it was private wars of extermination.

Indians Left Destitute

Washington, Tulalip Reservation, Destitute

In the State of Washington, Indians would be relegated to menial laborers as technology and capitalization, due to the scale of the fishing and lumbering industries, passed them by.

> The two great industries of the State are fishing and lumbering, and their tremendous development, capitalization, and the application of all modern improvements, have left the Indian (dependent upon these industries for his livelihood) with his primitive methods well-nigh stranded and well-nigh destitute, and may give rise to an Indian problem where none has hitherto existed.[14]

> Hop picking begins in September and keeps a large number of children out of school until well into October. This not only occasions a serious loss of time from school but, what is of more importance, the free and easy manners attending these gatherings have very bad effect on children of all ages and especially on the older girls. After the first of December the boarding school is well filled, the average attendance after that time being about 230.[15]

On Grand Ronde Reservation in Oregon, Income Below Poverty Line and Employment Menial

On the Grand Ronde Reservation in Oregon, income was below the poverty line and employment could only be considered as menial.

It is estimated that these Indians obtain from the sale of basket, a chitem bark, hay, wood, and other articles about $4,000 per annum. All of them are employed in the hop yards during September, making from $1 to $2 per day; most all of them have a garden; all own some stock, principally cattle, horses, and hogs.[16]

New York – Common Laborers

In New York, where most of the *valuable timber on the reservation had been cut off and sold, the men worked for the whites as common laborers.*

A large part of the male Indians on the Allegany reservations support themselves principally by working out among the whites. *Many of them find employment in the lumber woods, cutting timber and pealing bark.* Others are track hands on the various railroads which run through the reservation. They are good workers usually, and are *growing in favor among the whites as common laborers. Most of the valuable timber on the reservation has been cut off and sold.* There are some good farmers on the reservation, and on the whole the Indian residents are making fair progress. (Emphasis added).[17]

Crow Indians in Montana – Scant Opportunity for Employment

For the Crow Indians in Montana, there was scant opportunity for employment, much less at a reasonable wage.

Outside work. The chances for obtaining work outside for the Indians is very meager, as it is from 30 to 75 miles to white settlements. We have, however, obtained work on a large irrigation canal in the northern part of Rosebud County, and will send from 50 to 60 teams from the Black Lodge district, as they can be spared from this district on account of failure of crops. We have arranged with the contractor to pay the Indian and team 40 cents per hour, and he can work eight or ten hours a day.[18]

Failure to Protect Indians

The extract below is from the Report of a commission of citizens appointed by the President under the act of Congress of April 10, 1869, to cooperate with the administration in the management of Indian affairs. The commissioners included: Felix R. Brunot, Chairman. Robert Campbell. H. S. Lane. W. E. Dodge. Nathan Bishop. John V. Farwell. Vincent Colyer. George H. Stuart. Edward S. Tobey.

While it cannot be denied that the government of the United States, in the general terms and temper of its legislation, has evinced a desire to deal generously with the Indians, it must be admitted that the actual treatment they have received has been unjust and iniquitous beyond the power of words to express. Taught by the government that they had rights entitled to respect; when those rights have been assailed by the rapacity of the white man, the arm which should have been raised to protect them has been ever ready to sustain the aggressor. The history of the government connections with the Indians is a shameful record of broken treaties and unfulfilled promises. The history of the border white man's connection with the Indians is a sickening record of murder, outrage, robbery, and wrongs committed by the former as the rule, and occasional savage outbreaks and unspeakably barbarous deeds of retaliation by the latter as the exception.

In addition to the class of robbers and outlaws who find impunity in their nefarious pursuits upon the frontiers, there is a large class of professedly reputable men who use every means in their power to bring on Indian wars, for the sake of the profit to be realized from the presence of troops and the expenditure of government funds in their midst. They proclaim death to the Indians at all times, in words and publications, making no distinction between the innocent and the guilty. They incite the lowest class of men to the perpetration of the darkest deeds against their victims, and, as judges and jurymen, shield them from the justice due to their crimes. Every crime committed by a white man against an Indian is concealed or palliated ...[19]

In his 1890 Report, Commissioner T.J. Morgan expressed the continued flaws in the agency system:

> The entire system of dealing with them [Indians] is vicious, involving, as it does, the installing of agents, with semi-despotic power over ignorant, superstitious, and helpless subjects; the keeping of thousands of them on reservations practically as prisoners, isolated from civilized life and dominated by fear and force; the issue of rations and annuities, which inevitably tends to breed pauperism; the disbursement of millions of dollars worth of supplies by contract, which invites fraud; the maintenance of a system of licensed trade, which stimulates cupidity and extortion, etc.[20]

In 1879, Commissioner E. A. Hayt expressed the only option available to protect Indian land rights: allotment. The federal government lacked the will to curtail encroachment on and theft of Indian lands by colonial settlers. Its obeisance to its voting constituents and big businesses to confiscate valuable timber, mineral and agricultural Indian lands left Indian Nations destitute. With Indian policy a premeditated creature of fluctuating, shifting, divisive and partisan politics, Indian Nations were and are deliberately left mired in uncertainty and fear as to when their obliteration will be exacted in the U.S.' relentless pursuit of its "Manifest Destiny."

> In the last annual report of this office a brief reference was made to the importance of giving to the various Indian tribes of the United States a several, uniform, perfect, and indefeasible title to the lands occupied by them. The insecurity attaching to their settlement upon the various portions of the public domain assigned for their use has, year by year, become more observable, until it appears that *all former methods are entirely inadequate to protect the Indians against the encroachments of the whites upon their reservations, or from the acts of the government itself, whenever an active demand is made that the treaty stipulations under which the Indians hold their lands should be abrogated to open the way for white settlements* or the active contentious which often arise for the possession of the mineral or timber interests which may exist on their reservations. *The experience of the Indian Department for the past fifty years goes to show that the government is impotent to protect the Indians on their reservations, especially when held in common, from the encroachments of its own people, whenever a discovery has been made rendering the possession of their lands desirable by the whites.* (Emphasis added). January 24, 1879. DOI Bill to Allot Indian Land, H.R. Rep. No. 165, 45th Cong., 3rd Sess. (1879), p. 2.

Notes: Patterns of Dispossessing Indians of Their Land and Resources

1. First Annual Report to the Congress of the United States from the National Advisory Council on Indian Education, U.S. Government Printing Office, 1974, p. 142.
2. Report of the Commissioner of Indian Affairs, Vol. 2, Department of the Interior, United States. Office of Indian Affairs, U.S. Government Printing Office, 1885, p. XXI.
3. "From John Adams to Cherokee Nation, 27 August 1798," *Founders Online*, National Archives, https://founders.archives.gov/documents/Adams/99-02-02-2892 (accessed online November 13, 2020).

4. "From Thomas Jefferson to John Breckinridge, 12 August 1803," *Founders Online,* National Archives, https://founders.archives.gov/documents/Jefferson/01-41-02-0139. [Original source: *The Papers of Thomas Jefferson,* vol. 41, *11 July–15 November 1803,* ed. Barbara B. Oberg. Princeton: Princeton University Press, 2014, pp. 184–186.] (accessed online November 13, 2020).
5. "From Thomas Jefferson to George Rogers Clark, 25 December 1780," *Founders Online,* National Archives, https://founders.archives.gov/documents/Jefferson/01-04-02-0295. [Original source: *The Papers of Thomas Jefferson,* vol. 4, *1 October 1780–24 February 1781,* ed. Julian P. Boyd. Princeton: Princeton University Press, 1951, pp. 233–238.] (accessed online November 13, 2020).
6. "From James Madison to United States Congress, 3 December 1816," *Founders Online,* National Archives, https://founders.archives.gov/documents/Madison/99-01-02-5598 (accessed online November 4, 2020).
7. Second Inaugural Address of James Monroe, March 5, 1821 https://avalon.law.yale.edu/19th_century/monroe2.asp (accessed online November 14, 2020).
8. H.R. Rep. No. 183, 48th Cong., 1st Sess. (1884), p. 4991.
9. Report of the Commissioner of Indian Affairs to the Secretary of the Interior, Office of Indian Affairs. U.S. Government Printing Office, 1888, p. lxxxviii.
10. Report of the Commissioner of Indian Affairs to the Secretary of the Interior, Office of Indian Affairs, United States. A.O.P. Nicholson, Printer, 1857, p. 23.
11. Report of the Commissioner of Indian Affairs to the Secretary of the Interior, Office of Indian Affairs, United States. U.S. Government Printing Office, 1890, p. CLXVIII.
12.

GEORGIA
To James Madison from Georgia Legislature, 2 December 1816," *Founders Online,* National Archives, https://founders.archives.gov/documents/Madison/99-01-02-5597 (accessed online November 18, 2020).

ILLINOIS
"To James Madison from Thomas Worthington and Others, 18 March 1814," *Founders Online,* National Archives, https://founders.archives.gov/documents/Madison/03-07-02-0328. [Original source: *The Papers of James Madison,* Presidential Series, vol. 7, *25 October 1813–30 June 1814,* ed. Angela Kreider, J. C. A. Stagg, Mary Parke Johnson, Anne Mandeville Colony, and Katherine E. Harbury. Charlottesville: University of Virginia Press, 2012, pp. 375–378.] (accessed online November 18, 2020).

INDIANA
"To James Madison from Benjamin Lenover and Others, [ca. December 1815]," *Founders Online,* National Archives, https://founders.archives.gov/documents/Madison/03-10-02-0055. [Original source: *The Papers of James Madison,* Presidential Series, vol. 10, *13 October 1815–30 April 1816,* ed. Angela Kreider, J. C. A. Stagg, Mary Parke Johnson, Katharine E. Harbury, and Anne Mandeville Colony. Charlottesville: University of Virginia Press, 2019, pp. 62–63.] (accessed online November 18, 2020).

KENTUCKY
"To James Madison from Matthew Lyon and Others, 20 February 1811 (Abstract)," *Founders Online,* National Archives, https://founders.archives.gov/documents/Madison/03-03-02-0232. [Original source: *The Papers of James Madison,* Presidential Series, vol. 3, *3 November 1810–4 November 1811,* ed. J. C. A. Stagg, Jeanne Kerr Cross, and Susan Holbrook Perdue. Charlottesville: University Press of Virginia, 1996, pp. 175–176.] (accessed online November 18, 2020).

MICHIGAN TERRITORY
"To Thomas Jefferson from Elijah Brush, 11 December 1805," *Founders Online,* National Archives, https://founders.archives.gov/documents/Jefferson/99-01-02-2799 (accessed online November 18, 2020).

MISSISSIPPI
"To James Madison from the Mississippi Territorial Legislature, 22 November 1809 (Abstract)," *Founders Online,* National Archives, https://founders.archives.gov/documents/Madison/03-02-02-0101. [Original source: *The Papers of James Madison,* Presidential Series, vol. 2, *1 October 1809–2 November 1810,* ed. J. C. A. Stagg, Jeanne Kerr Cross, and Susan Holbrook Perdue. Charlottesville: University Press of Virginia, 1992, p. 78.] (accessed online November 18, 2020).

MISSOURI
"To James Madison from Edward Hempstead, 31 March 1814," *Founders Online,* National Archives, https://founders.archives.gov/documents/Madison/03-07-02-0357. [Original source: *The Papers of James Madison,* Presidential Series, vol. 7, *25 October 1813–30 June 1814,* ed. Angela Kreider, J. C. A. Stagg, Mary Parke Johnson, Anne Mandeville Colony, and Katherine E. Harbury. Charlottesville: University of Virginia Press, 2012, pp. 402–403.] (accessed online November 18, 2020).

NEW YORK
"From James Madison to Alexander J. Dallas, 31 July 1815," *Founders Online,* National Archives, https://founders.archives.gov/documents/Madison/03-09-02-0483. [Original source: *The Papers of James Madison,* Presidential Series, vol. 9, *19 February 1815–12 October 1815,* ed. Angela Kreider, J. C. A. Stagg, Mary Parke Johnson, and Anne Mandeville Colony. Charlottesville: University of Virginia Press, 2018, p. 496.] (accessed online November 18, 2020).

NORTH CAROLINA
"To Thomas Jefferson from Joseph Anderson and William Cocke, 5 March 1801," *Founders Online,* National Archives, https://founders.archives.gov/documents/Jefferson/01-33-02-0136. [Original source: *The Papers of Thomas Jefferson*, vol. 33, *17 February–30 April 1801*, ed. Barbara B. Oberg. Princeton: Princeton University Press, 2006, pp. 174–175.] (accessed online November 18, 2020).

OHIO
"To James Madison from the Ohio Congressional Delegation, 3 February 1816," *Founders Online,* National Archives, https://founders.archives.gov/documents/Madison/03-10-02-0213. [Original source: *The Papers of James Madison*, Presidential Series, vol. 10, *13 October 1815–30 April 1816*, ed. Angela Kreider, J. C. A. Stagg, Mary Parke Johnson, Katharine E. Harbury, and Anne Mandeville Colony. Charlottesville: University of Virginia Press, 2019, pp. 207–208.] (accessed online November 18, 2020).

SOUTH CAROLINA
"To James Madison from Henry Middleton, 31 December 1810," *Founders Online,* National Archives, https://founders.archives.gov/documents/Madison/03-03-02-0105. [Original source: *The Papers of James Madison*, Presidential Series, vol. 3, *3 November 1810–4 November 1811*, ed. J. C. A. Stagg, Jeanne Kerr Cross, and Susan Holbrook Perdue. Charlottesville: University Press of Virginia, 1996, pp. 88–89.] (accessed online November 18, 2020).

TENNESSEE
"To James Madison from the Tennessee Congressional Delegation, 17 April 1816," *Founders Online,* National Archives, https://founders.archives.gov/documents/Madison/03-10-02-0401. [Original source: *The Papers of James Madison*, Presidential Series, vol. 10, *13 October 1815–30 April 1816*, ed. Angela Kreider, J. C. A. Stagg, Mary Parke Johnson, Katharine E. Harbury, and Anne Mandeville Colony. Charlottesville: University of Virginia Press, 2019, pp. 397–398.] (accessed online November 18, 2020).

WISCONSIN Miscellaneous Documents: 30th Congress, 1st Session – 49th Congress, 1st Session, Volume 3, United States congressional serial set, United States Congress, House, 1874, Oxford University.

13. Governor Edgerton's Message, Montana Historical Society Contributions, Vol. III, p. 344.
14. Reports Concerning Indians in Washington, Report of Superintendent of Tulalip Reservation, Office of Indian Affairs, United States. U.S. Government Printing Office, 1906, p. 382.
15. Annual Reports of the Department of Interior, Part 1, Report of the Commissioner of Indian Affairs to the Secretary of the Interior, Reports of Agencies in Washington, Report of School Superintendent in Charge of Puyallup Consolidated Agency, Office of Indian Affairs, United States. U.S. Government Printing Office, 1899, p. 358.

16. Annual Report of the Department of Interior, Part 1, Report of the Commissioner of Indian Affairs to the Secretary of the Interior, Reports Concerning Indians in Oregon, Report of School Superintendent in Charge of Grand Ronde Agency, Office of Indian Affairs, United States. U.S. Government Printing Office, 1902, p. 341.
17. Annual Report of the Department of Interior, Part 1, Report of the Commissioner of Indian Affairs to the Secretary of the Interior, Reports Concerning Indians in New York, Report of Agent for New York Agency, Office of Indian Affairs, United States. U.S. Government Printing Office, 1902, p. 285.
18. Annual Report of the Department of Interior, Part 1, Report of the Commissioner of Indian Affairs to the Secretary of the Interior, Reports Concerning Indians in Montana, Report of Agent for Crow Agency, Office of Indian Affairs, United States. U.S. Government Printing Office, 1904, p. 192.
19. Annual Report of the Board of Indian Commissioners (Washington, 1869), 5-11.
20. Report of the Commissioner of Indian Affairs to the Secretary of the Interior, United States. Office of Indian Affairs, U.S. Government Printing Office, 1890, p. V.

CHAPTER 14: EPILOGUE

Michigan

In the summer of 1831, Alexis de Tocqueville, exploring America's wilderness traveled from Detroit to Saginaw, with two Indian guides. "A mile out of town," he wrote, "the road goes into forest and never comes out of it." Yet he knew the westward movement was already started. Saginaw was settled with thirty people.

> "In a few years these impenetrable forests will have fallen; the sons of civilization and industry will break the silence of the Saginaw; its echoes will cease.... So strong is the impetus that urges the white man to the entire conquest of the New World."[1]

Michigan was deforested by 1910.

This deforestation resulted in significant values to logging companies. Usually, extractive values are not fully reported to state or federal governments so these amounts may underrepresent the actual values received by lumber companies.

Michigan Lumber Industry[2]	
Year	Value of Product
1850	2,464,329
1860	7,040,190
1870	31,946,396
1880	52,449,928
1890	83,121,969
1900	54,290,520

Minnesota

As I stood upon the brow of Embarrass Hill...one of the grandest sights I ever looked upon was in view, a veritable ocean of pine. One could see for miles and miles in nearly every direction over the tops of the tall waving forests of virgin pine and a variety of other trees. I will never forget that sight or the impression it left upon my mind, as I stood there gazing upon this wonderful forest...inexhaustible, enough to last for ages as I thought at that time, yet within the course of a very few years not to exceed fifteen, this great forest was laid bare, leaving only a few scattering stands of pine in patches here and there." — Richard Louis Griffin, reminiscing in 1930 about seeing northern Minnesota's pine forests for the first time in the winter of 1890–1891.[3]

Minnesota was deforested by 1905. By the 1920s, the prime pine stands were exhausted and there wasn't enough lumber-quality timber in the woods to justify the expense of maintaining railroads. The large-scale sawmilling industry virtually vanished by 1929.[4]

Again, millions of dollars had been made by lumber companies.

Minnesota Lumber Industry[5]	
Year	Value of Product
1850	57,800
1860	1,234,203
1870	4,299,162
1880	7,366,038
1890	25,075,132
1900	43,585,161

Wisconsin

Timber of No Value to Chippewas of Wisconsin

In 1879, Com'r E.A. Hayt repeated a common refrain within the DOI and elsewhere, that natural resources had no value to Indians, in this case the timber to the Chippewa Indians in Wisconsin.

The Chippewas in Wisconsin "occupy three reservations, embracing a territory largely in excess of their actual wants, covered with a heavy growth of very valuable pine timber, which is deteriorating in value every year of being destroyed by forest fires. Large quantities of timber have also been removed in years past by trespassers. ***There are probably 600,000,000 feet of merchantable pine timber on these reservations, which, under present circumstances, is of no value to the Indians***. ... Com'r Hayt went on to advise consolidating the Indians by removing them to two reservations containing the "best agricultural lands."[6]

While the massive amount of timber was considered without value to the Chippewas, much of this land would be ceded and opened to white settlement. From 1899–1905, Wisconsin led nation in lumber production. Logging peaked in Wisconsin 1892 with over 4 billion board feet. Millions of dollars would be made by lumber companies.

According to the 1890 U.S. census, more than 23,000 men worked in Wisconsin's logging industry and another 32,000 worked at the sawmills that turned timber into boards. Each winter, the lumberjacks occupied nearly 450 logging camps. In the spring, they drove their timber downstream to more than 1,000 mills. Logging and lumbering employed a quarter of all Wisconsinites working in the 1890s.[7]

Wisconsin's forests were depleted by 1920.

Once more, millions of dollars had been made by lumber companies. Yet logging is only the beginning of a supply chain that provides raw material for many products used within the U.S. and exported worldwide for housing, construction, energy, furniture, and consumer paper products.

Wisconsin Lumber Industry[8]	
Year	Value of Product
1850	1,218,516
1860	4,377,880
1870	15,130,719
1880	17,952,347
1890	60,966,444
1900	57,634,856

Pacific Northwest

In the Northwest, logging of native forests began in earnest in the mid–1800s with extensive white settlement. Yet, by 1900 Washington had lost only about 1.6 percent of its forest and even less of Oregon's forests had been logged. The pace of deforestation quickened in the early 20th century and by 1946 about 66 percent of the original forest had been cut. Insect epidemics, root disease, dwarf mistletoe, and other symptoms of mismanagement are rampant. Decades of restoration will be necessary to restore these ecosystems back to health.[9]

Montana

| Montana Lumber Industry[11] ||
Year	Value of Product
1850	1,479,524
1860	3,074,225
1870	6,363,112
1880	5,285,617
1890	8,259,225
1900	11,177,529

Oregon

Sup't Nesmith of the Oregon and Washington Territories declared that in entering treaties Indians were not aware of the land value they were sacrificing:

> [W]hen an aggregate amount is mentioned, it appears large, without taking into consideration that the Indians, in the sale and surrender of their country, are surrendering all their means of obtaining a living; and when the small annuities come to be divided throughout the tribe, it exhibits but a pitiful and meager sum for the supply of their individual wants.[12]

Timber interests had a strong and sometimes illegal hand in state politics which is illustrated by the Oregon Land Fraud Scandal. Early 1900s timber speculators and corrupt public officials illegally transferred thousands of acres of public forest land to private companies. This led to thousands of indictments, including nearly all of Oregon's U.S. congressional delegation.

Yet the logging companies made millions off of timber, part of which was on ceded Indian lands. The high-grade mining of timber, in part, led to the Oregon's eastern forests "state of collapse."

Oregon Lumber Industry[13]	
Year	Value of Product
1850	1,355,500
1860	
1870	1,014,211
1880	2,030,163
1890	6,530,787
1900	10,352,167

Washington

As in other timber areas, the logging companies made millions off of timber.

Washington Lumber Industry[14]	
Year	Value of Product
1860	1,172,520
1870	1,307,585
1880	1,734,742
1890	17,450,301
1900	30,286,280

Forestry Management on Indian Lands

In 1910, Com'r Robert G. Valentine instituted a forestry management program on Indian lands:

> The timber holdings of the Indians are of great value, having been estimated at thirty-six and one-half billion feet (board measure), with a value of $73,000,000. Approximately five and one-half billion feet of the timber, valued at $12,000,000, are on allotted lands, and thirty-one billion feet, valued at $61,000,000, on unallotted lands. The service means to protect and develop these holdings by modern methods and in line with the best thought and experience in forestry, and at the same time so to instruct the Indians in the practical use of their timbered lands that they may receive from them the greatest benefit possible. Under the plan of organization, a forestry section has been established in the Indian Office for the purpose of segregating all timber matters in one unit. ... Patrol districts have been arranged for forest guards, and during the dry period of the past year 109 forest guards were employed on 42 reservations in 15 different States.
>
> The act of June 25, 1910 (36 Stat.,855), so amended the penal laws of the United States that it became a serious offense to unlawfully cut or wantonly injure timber on Indian reservations, as well as to set a fire on Indian reservation forests without exercising due care to extinguish the same. This act also authorizes the Secretary of the Interior under such regulations as he may prescribe to sell the mature living timber, as well as dead and down timber, on the unallotted lands of any Indian reservation, except those within the States of Minnesota and Wisconsin, and upon allotments of Indians held under trust or other patents containing restrictions upon alienation. ... Under the new law the forest work on Indian reservations can ultimately be made self-supporting and ample funds obtained to develop the forests to their greatest productivity.[15]

This activity came after the major deforestation of the Great Lakes and the Pacific Northwest. Lumber barons had made billions of dollars.

Notes Epilogue

1. Extract from the Memoir, Letter, and Remarks of Alexis De Tocqueville. Specifically, "A Fortnight in the Wilderness." Written on board the Steamboat Superior, August of 1831.
2. Pamphlets on the Lumber Industry, Volume 2, 1902. https://books.google.com/books?id=bR9SAQAAMAAJ&dq=1900+30,286,280+washington+lumber+industry&source=gbs_navlinks_s (accessed online July 18, 2022).
3. https://www.mnhs.org/foresthistory/learn/logging (accessed online July 17, 2022).
4. https://www.mnhs.org/foresthistory/learn/logging#:~:text=Harvesting%20dropped%20rapidly%20after%201905,industry%20virtually%20vanished%20by%201929 (accessed online July 17, 2022).
5. Pamphlets on the Lumber Industry, Volume 2, 1902. https://books.google.com/books?id=bR9SAQAAMAAJ&dq=1900+30,286,280+washington+lumber+industry&source=gbs_navlinks_s (accessed online July 18, 2022).
6. Report of the Commissioner of Indian Affairs to the Secretary of the Interior, Vol. 1, United States. Office of Indian Affairs, U.S. Government Printing Office, 1879, p. 102.
7. Edmonds, Michael. Out of the Northwoods: The Many Lives of Paul Bunyan, With More Than 100 Logging Camp Tales. Wisconsin Historical Society, 2010, p. 25.
8. Pamphlets on the Lumber Industry, Volume 2, 1902. https://books.google.com/books?id=bR9SAQAAMAAJ&dq=1900+30,286,280+washington+lumber+industry&source=gbs_navlinks_s (accessed online July 18, 2022).
9. Old Growth Forests: Hearing Before the Subcommittee on National Parks and Public Lands of the Committee on Interior and Insular Affairs, House of Representatives, One Hundred Second Congress, First Session, on H.R. 842, Ancient Forest Protection Act of 1991; H.R. 1590, Ancient Forest Act of 1991; Hearing Held in Washington, DC, April 25, 1991, Volume 4, U.S. Government Printing Office, 1992; U.S Department of Agriculture, Forestry Division, Bulletin No. 6.

10. Pamphlets on the Lumber Industry, Volume 2, 1902. https://books.google.com/books?id=bR9SAQAAMAAJ&dq=1900+30,286,280+washington+lumber+industry&source=gbs_navlinks_s (accessed online July 18, 2022).
11. Report of the Commissioner of Indian Affairs to the Secretary of the Interior, United States. Office of Indian Affairs, Oregon and Washington Superintendency, U.S. Government Printing Office, 1857, p. 321.
12. Pamphlets on the Lumber Industry, Volume 2, 1902. https://books.google.com/books?id=bR9SAQAAMAAJ&dq=1900+30,286,280+washington+lumber+industry&source=gbs_navlinks_s (accessed online July 18, 2022).
13. Pamphlets on the Lumber Industry, Volume 2, 1902. https://books.google.com/books?id=bR9SAQAAMAAJ&dq=1900+30,286,280+washington+lumber+industry&source=gbs_navlinks_s (accessed online July 18, 2022).
14. Report of the Commissioner of Indian Affairs to the Secretary of the Interior, United States. Office of Indian Affairs, U.S. Government Printing Office, 1911, pp. 24-26.
15. Report of the Commissioner of Indian Affairs o the Secretary of the Interior, United States Office of Indian Affairs, U. S. Government Printing Office, 1909, p. 26.

www.ingramcontent.com/pod-product-compliance
Lightning Source LLC
Chambersburg PA
CBHW010832230426
43668CB00019BA/2412